Barrister

The Orator

A Compendium of English Eloquence, Containing Selections from the Most Celebrated Speeches of the Past & Present. Second Edition

Barrister

The Orator
A Compendium of English Eloquence, Containing Selections from the Most Celebrated Speeches of the Past & Present. Second Edition

ISBN/EAN: 9783337279059

Printed in Europe, USA, Canada, Australia, Japan

Cover: Foto ©Thomas Meinert / pixelio.de

More available books at **www.hansebooks.com**

THE ORATOR:

A

COMPENDIUM OF ENGLISH ELOQUENCE,

CONTAINING SELECTIONS FROM

The most Celebrated Speeches of the Past & Present.

EDITED,

WITH SHORT EXPLANATORY NOTES AND REFERENCES,

BY

A BARRISTER.

"Though the public speaker should die, yet the immortal fire shall outlive the organ which conveyed it, and the breath of liberty, like the word of the holy man, will not die with the prophet, but survive him."—GRATTAN.

Second Edition.

LONDON:
ALFRED THOMAS CROCKER, 303 & 304, STRAND.
1868.

PREFACE.

IN bringing this work before the public in its present complete form, the Editor believes that he is justified in saying that it will be found to contain within its pages a wider variety of English eloquence than has hitherto been offered in any other book of a similar character.

The periodical shape in which the "ORATOR" originally appeared, and the popular purpose with which it was composed, have prevented any attempt at chronological arrangement, which might, perhaps, in the opinion of many, have added to the artistic interest of the work; but the carefully prepared Index which now accompanies the speeches will, it is hoped, in no small measure facilitate reference, and so remedy any defect which may have arisen from the miscellaneous nature of the contents.

In conclusion, the Editor has to acknowledge his obligations to the many valuable collections of oratory which have preceded the present attempt in the same field, and of which he has made free and frequent use. Of these he may especially mention Hazlitt's "Eloquence of the British Senate," a work now comparatively rare, but containing much good matter; Dr. Gooderich's "Select British Eloquence," an American volume, admirably selected and arranged; Frank Moore's "American Eloquence," from which two or three of the best specimens of the Transatlantic speakers have been culled; Browne's "British Cicero," and the various standard editions of our older orators. For the many contemporary speeches which form so prominent a feature in this volume, the Editor has to tender his most cordial thanks to several of the leading statesmen and speakers of the present time, who have kindly accorded him full permission to reprint from their published addresses, and in some instances have themselves corrected the proofs of these pages.

THE TEMPLE, APRIL, 1865.

CONTENTS.

	PAGE
ALBERT (PRINCE).	
The Exhibition of 1851	1
Character of Sir R. Peel	94
BRIGHT, JOHN. b.1810	
On the American War	12
BROUGHAM, LORD. 1778	
How to become an Orator	2
Defence of Queen Caroline	24
Salutary Innovation	40
BULWER LYTTON, SIR EDWARD b.1805	
Against the Second Reading of Foreign Enlistment Bill, 1854	245
BURKE, EDMUND. 1730 - 1797	
Election Speeches at Bristol	3, 4
Conciliation with the American Colonies	7
Duty of Representatives	141
Speech on the Nabob of Arcot's Debts	167
Tremendousness of War	210
People and Parliament	225
Marie Antoinette	232
CALHOUN, JOHN CALDWELL.	
On Increase of the Army	252
CANNING, GEORGE. 1770 - 1827	
Speech on the Relations subsisting between Great Britain and Portugal in 1826	121
CARLYLE, THOMAS.	
The Conqueror	30
CHATHAM, LORD. 1708 - 1778	
Protest against the American War	69
COBBETT, WILLIAM. 1762 - 1835	
Address to the Industrious Classes	132
COBDEN, RICHARD. 1800	
Speech at Exeter Hall, 30th October, 1849	148
COLERIDGE, SAMUEL TAYLOR.	
The Promulgation of Truth	119
CROMWELL, OLIVER.	
On Dissolution of the Second Protectorate Parliament	23
The Little Parliament	185
CROSBY (LORD MAYOR).	
At the Bar of the House of Commons on a Charge of Contumacy	152
CURRAN, JOHN PHILPOT. 1750 - 1817	
Employment of Informers by Government	60
Defence of Hamilton Rowan	153
DERBY, EARL OF. Stanly 1799 -	
Estimate of Prince Consort's Character	110
Speech on Disturbances (Ireland) Bill	268

	PAGE
DICKENS, CHARLES.	
Speech at Manchester Athenæum	20
DISRAELI, BENJAMIN. 1805	
Character of the Prince Consort	109
DRUMMOND, HENRY. 1786 - 1860	
Marriage Law Amendment	68
ELIOT, SIR JOHN.	
Speech in the House of Commons, 1628	242
EMMET, ROBERT.	
Speech on his Trial	85
ERSKINE, LORD. 1748 - 1823	
Speech on Trial of Lord George Gordon	94
EVERETT, EDWARD.	
The Character of La Fayette	10
FOX, CHARLES JAMES. 1749 - 1806	
Eulogy on the Duke of Bedford	33
On the Russian Armament	188
FOX, WILLIAM JOHNSON.	
Anniversary of Battle of Waterloo	103
GARIBALDI, GIUSEPPE.	
The Cause of Freedom in 1864	119
GLADSTONE, WILLIAM EWART. 1809 -	
Extension of the Suffrage	52
GOUGH, JOHN B.	
The Cause of Temperance	184
GRATTAN, HENRY. 1750 - 1820	
Character of the First Earl of Chatham	33
The Downfall of Buonaparte	136
HENRY, PATRICK.	
On the Expediency of Adopting the Federal Constitution	226
JEFFERSON, THOMAS.	
Extract from Inaugural Address	118
JEFFREY, LORD.	
Dependence of Kings	207
JUNIUS.	
The Royal Pardon	143
Other short Extracts from	152, 207, 210, 225
KOSSUTH, LOUIS.	
Eloquence of Garibaldi	9
Speech to the Ladies of New York	38
European Freedom	183
LYNDHURST, LORD. 1772 - 1863	
A Review of the Session 1839	203

CONTENTS.

MACAULAY, LORD. 1800 - 1859
   Historical Review of the University of Glasgow 61

MACKINTOSH, SIR JAMES. 1766 - 1832
   Speech in Defence of M. Peltier 44
   Early Eminence 73

MAZZINI, JOSEPH.
   To the Memory of the Martyrs of Cosenza ... 208

MILTON, JOHN.
   Rights and Responsibilities of the Press 24
   Eulogy on Cromwell 115

O'CONNELL, DANIEL. 1775 - 1847
   Repeal of the Union 112
   On the Corn Laws 278

PALMERSTON, LORD. 1784
   In Defence of his Foreign Policy, 1848 98
   On British Liberty 268

PEEL, SIR ROBERT. 1788 - 1850
   Speech at Merchant Tailors' Hall 89

PHILLIPS, WENDELL.
   Public Opinion on the Abolition Question ... 141

PITT, WILLIAM. 1759 - 1806
   The Slave Trade 53
   The First Consul of the French Republic ... 74
   Speech on the Russian Armament 201

PLUNKET, LORD. 1764 - 1854
   Speech on Trial of Robert Emmet 80

PYM, JOHN.
   Charge against Duke of Buckingham 88

ROBERTSON, FREDERICK W.
   True Democracy Defined 120

RUSSELL, EARL. 1792 -
   Propositions for Reform, 1822 62

SAINT AUBIN, SIR JOHN.
   On the Triennial Bill 284

SHEIL, RICHARD LALOR. 1791 - 1851
   Defence of Mr. John O'Connell 211

SHERIDAN, RICHARD BRINSLEY. b.1751 - 1816
   The Perfect Speaker 2
   Speech on Mr. Pitt's Bill for the New Assessed Taxes, 1797 41
   Filial Piety 62
   On Burke 163
   On the Confiscation of Treasures of the Begum Princesses of Oude 250

STANLEY, LORD. 1826
   Speech at King's Lynn, 19th October, 1864 . 159

STRAFFORD, LORD.
   Defence before the House of Lords 164

THURLOW, LORD.
   Speech in Reply to the Duke of Grafton 152

WALPOLE, SIR ROBERT.
   On the Triennial Bill 286

WASHINGTON, GEORGE.
   Address to his Troops before the Battle of Long Island 44

WEBSTER, DANIEL.
   On the Centenary Celebration of Birth of Washington 36
   Character of True Eloquence 135

WELLINGTON, DUKE OF.
   Respect to be paid by Soldiers to Religious Ceremonies 268
   On O'Connell 283

WILBERFORCE, WILLIAM. 1759 - 1833
   Horrors of the Middle Passage 30

WILKES, JOHN.
   The Middlesex Elections 221

WINDHAM, WILLIAM.
   On Moving the Thanks of the House to Sir John Stuart after the Battle of Maida ... 229

WISEMAN, CARDINAL.
   Poetry for the Poor 257

THE ORATOR.

THE LATE PRINCE CONSORT.
Born 1819. *Died* 1861.

[It has been deemed advisable to admit several speeches of the late Prince Consort into this collection; for though His Royal Highness was not to be ranked amongst the greatest orators, yet as a practised and accomplished speaker, considering all the circumstances in which he was placed, he has perhaps never been surpassed. The chief characteristics of his style may be pronounced to have been earnestness, clearness, and exhaustiveness —a desire to aim at great principles of action, and to preach first and foremost the true beauty of usefulness, seemed ever uppermost in his mind. Moreover, his large and generous sympathies with the wants and wishes of the labouring classes of his adopted country, and his hearty co-operation and support in all schemes for the amelioration of their condition, will, it is hoped, cause his words to find always a cherished place in the recollections of Englishmen, though, to estimate his speeches with fairness, the position in which he spoke them must also be remembered. In the language of one who has paid the most graceful tribute to his memory, "It may be said of the Prince's speeches as of much of his life, that the movement of them was graceful, noble, and dignified; but yet it was like the movements of a man in chain armour, which, even with the strongest and most agile person, must ever have been a movement somewhat fettered by restraint. The principal elements that go to compose a great oration had often to be modified largely in the speeches of the Prince. Wit was not to be jubilant, passion not predominant, dialectic skill not triumphant. There remained then nothing as the secure staple of the speech but supreme common sense. Looked at in this way, it is wonderful that the Prince contrived to introduce into his speeches so much that was new and interesting." (See Introduction to "Prince Consort's Speeches and Addresses," published by Mr. Murray.) The specimen given below is fairly representative of his style; and as having been delivered at the time of the opening of that great Palace of Art with which his name and genius are so inseparably associated, it has been deemed the most appropriate first extract for this collection.]

THE EXHIBITION OF 1851.

GENTLEMEN,—I conceive it to be the duty of every educated person closely to watch and study the time in which he lives, and, as far as in him lies, to add his humble mite of individual exertion to further the accomplishment of what he believes Providence to have ordained.

Nobody, however, who has paid any attention to the peculiar features of our present era, will doubt for a moment that we are living at a period of most wonderful transition, which tends rapidly to accomplish that great end to which, indeed, all history points—the realization of the unity of mankind. Not a unity which breaks down the limits and levels the peculiar characteristics of the different nations of the earth, but rather a unity, the result and product of those very national varieties and antagonistic qualities.

The distances which separated the different nations and parts of the globe are rapidly vanishing before the achievements of modern invention, and we can traverse them with incredible ease; the languages of all nations are known, and their acquirement placed within the reach of everybody; thought is communicated with the rapidity, and even by the power, of lightning. On the other hand, the great principle of division of labour, which may be called the moving power of civilization, is being extended to all branches of science, industry, and art.

Whilst formerly the greatest mental energies strove at universal knowledge, and that knowledge was confined to the few, now they are directed on specialities, and in these, again, even to the minutest points; but the knowledge acquired becomes at once the property of the community at large; for, whilst formerly discovery was wrapped in secrecy, the publicity of the present day causes that no sooner is a discovery or invention made than it is already improved upon and surpassed by competing efforts. The products of all quarters of the globe are placed at our disposal, and we have only to choose which is the best and the cheapest for our purposes, and the powers of production are entrusted to the stimulus of competition and capital.

So man is approaching a more complete fulfilment of that great and sacred mission which he has to perform in this world. His reason being created after the image of God, he has to use it to discover the laws by which the Almighty governs His creation, and, by making these laws his standard of action, to conquer nature to his use; himself a divine instrument.

Science discovers these laws of power, motion, and transformation; industry applies them to the raw matter, which the earth yields us in abundance, but which becomes valuable only by knowledge. Art teaches us the immutable laws of beauty and symmetry, and gives to our productions forms in accordance to them.

LORD BROUGHAM AND VAUX.

Born 1778.

[THE next selection, though not, in strictness, itself a specimen of oratory, may, it is deemed, both from the nature of its subject and the high oratorical claims of its now aged author, worthily find a place in this collection. It may be here remarked by way of explanation, that the letter was addressed many years ago by Lord Brougham to Mr. Zachary Macaulay, the father of the great Thomas Babington Macaulay, whose History and Essays are amongst the noblest monuments that genius has bequeathed to us in the present age. As may be gathered from the early part of the letter itself, the future historian and poet was at the time of receiving this excellent advice from his father's friend, a student at Trinity College, Cambridge, and had already greatly distinguished himself by the early brilliance of his eloquence, displayed in the "Union," that Debating Society of the University in which so many of our greatest statesmen and speakers have first tried their powers, and prepared themselves for the larger arena of Parliamentary life. Cotemporary with Macaulay, W. M. Praed, known best to us now as one of the most graceful of modern poets, the present Sir E. B. Lytton, and many others, were then associated in honourable rivalry at Cambridge, and we may well imagine that the wise words and fruitful suggestions of Lord Brougham's letter would not be lost upon them. This letter was, we believe, first printed by Professor Selwyn, of Cambridge, but it is now difficult to obtain. The advice and recommendations which it contains, are, however, with some slight qualifications still applicable to all who make a study of public speaking; and to render it as far as possible of practical use to our readers, we shall attempt to reproduce, in this volume, almost all of the chief speeches referred to in this letter as models for the young orator, those of the classical authors being only omitted from such a collection as the present, elsewhere several examples of Lord Brougham's oratory will also be found.]

HOW TO BECOME AN ORATOR.

I SPEAK on this subject with the authority both of experience and observation. I have made it very much my study in theory; have written a great deal upon it, which may never see the light, and something which has been published; have meditated much and conversed much on it with famous men; have had some little practical experience in it, but have prepared for much more than I ever tried, by a variety of laborious methods, reading, writing, much translation, composing in foreign languages, &c.; and I have lived in times when there were great orators among us; therefore I reckon my opinion worth listening to, and the rather, because I have the utmost confidence in it myself, and should have saved a world of trouble and much time had I started with a conviction of its truth.

1. The first point is this :—the beginning of the art is to acquire a habit of easy speaking; and, in whatever way this can be had (which individual inclination or accident will generally direct, and may safely be allowed to do so) it must be had. Now, I differ from all other doctors of rhetoric in this,—I say, let him first of all learn to speak easily and fluently, as well and sensibly as he can, no doubt; but, at any rate, let him learn to speak. This is to eloquence, or public speaking, what the being able to talk in a child is to correct grammatical speech. It is the requisite foundation, and on it you must build. Moreover, it can only be acquired young; therefore let it by all means, and at any sacrifice, be gotten hold of forthwith. But in acquiring it every sort of slovenly error will also be acquired. It must be got by a habit of easy writing (which, as Wyndham said, proved hard reading); by a custom of talking much in company; by speaking in debating societies, with little attention to rule, and mere love of saying something at any rate, than of saying anything well. I can even suppose that more attention is paid to the matter in such discussions than in the manner of saying it; yet still to say it easily, *ad libitum*, to be able to say what you choose, and what you have to say,—this is the first requisite, to acquire which everything else must for the present be sacrificed.

2. The next step is the grand one—to convert this style of easy speaking into chaste eloquence. And here there is but one rule. I do earnestly entreat your son to set daily and nightly before him the Greek models. First of all, he may look to the best modern speeches (as he probably has already); Burke's best compositions, as *The Thoughts on the Cause of the present Discontents*; speech "On the American Conciliation," and "On the Nabob of Arcot's Debt;" Fox's "Speech on the Westminster Scrutiny" (the first part of which he should pore over till he has it by heart); "On the Russian Armament," and "On the War," 1803, with one or two of Wyndham's best, and very few, or rather none, of Sheridan's; but he must by no means stop here. If he would be a great orator, he must go at once to the fountain head, and be familiar with every one of the great orations of Demosthenes.

SHERIDAN.

Born 1751. *Died* 1816.

THE PERFECT SPEAKER.

IMAGINE to yourselves a Demosthenes addressing the most illustrious assembly in the world, upon a point whereon the fate of the most illustrious of nations depended. How awful such a meeting ! how vast the subject ! Is man possessed of talents adequate to the great occasion ? Adequate—yes, superior. By the power of his eloquence, the augustness of the assembly is lost in the dignity of the orator; and the importance of the subject, for a while, superseded, by the admiration of his talents.—With what strength of argument, with what powers of the fancy, with what emotions of the heart, does he assault and subjugate the whole man, and, at once, captivate his reason, his imagination, and his passions! To effect this, must be the utmost effort of the most improved state of human nature. Not a faculty that he possesses, is here unemployed: not a faculty that he possesses, but is here exerted to its highest pitch. All his internal powers are at work: all his external, testify their energies. Within, the memory, the fancy, the judgment, the passions, are all busy; without, every muscle, every nerve, is exerted; not a feature, nor a limb, but speaks. The organs of the body, attuned to the exertions of the mind, through the kindred organs of the hearers, instantaneously, and as it were with an electrical spirit, vibrate those energies from soul to soul. Notwithstanding the diversity of minds in such a multitude, by the lightning of eloquence they are melted into one mass—the whole assembly, actuated in one and the same way, become as it were, but one man, and have but one voice. The universal cry is—"Let us march against Philip—let us fight for our liberties—let us conquer—or die!"

EDMUND BURKE.

Born 1730. *Died* 1797.

[THE two speeches which follow were delivered on the occasion of Burke's election for Bristol in 1774; the first on his arrival in the city, and the second at the conclusion of the poll. Burke had a few days before been elected for Malton, but, on the earnest solicitation of his friends, was induced to accept the nomination at Bristol, for which place he was returned on the 3rd November, 1774, with Mr. Cruger, a wealthy merchant in that city. Though not specimens of Burke's highest eloquence,—some of which will be given later in this volume—these speeches have been deemed well worthy of reproduction, as showing Burke's high and constantly repeated view of the relations which should exist between a representative and his constituents, and also as to how far the former should be bound by the instructions of the latter. For noble and disinterested sincerity, these speeches would bear favourable comparison with much of the pretentious oratory which is too often heard on the hustings, but forgotten or unfulfilled in the House of Commons.]

ELECTION SPEECH AT BRISTOL, OCT. 13, 1774.

GENTLEMEN,—I am come hither to solicit in person that favour which my friends have hitherto endeavoured to procure for me, by the most obliging, and to me the most honourable, exertions.

I have so high an opinion of the great trust which you have to confer on this occasion; and, by long experience, so just a diffidence in my abilities to fill it in a manner adequate even to my own ideas, that I should never have ventured of myself to intrude into that awful situation. But since I am called upon by the desire of several respectable fellow-subjects, as I have done at other times, I give up my fears to their wishes. Whatever my other deficiencies may be, I do not know what it is to be wanting to my friends.

I am not fond of attempting to raise public expectations by great promises. At this time, there is much cause to consider, and very little to presume. We seem to be approaching to a great crisis in our affairs, which calls for the whole wisdom of the wisest among us, without being able to assure ourselves, that any wisdom can preserve us from many and great inconveniences. You know I speak of our unhappy contest with America. I confess, it is a matter on which I look down as from a precipice. It is difficult in itself, and it is rendered more intricate by a great variety of plans of conduct. I do not mean to enter into them. I will not suspect a want of good intention in framing them. But however pure the intentions of their authors may have been, we all know that the event has been unfortunate. The means of recovering our affairs are not obvious. So many great questions of commerce, of finance, of constitution, and of policy, are involved in this American deliberation, that I dare engage for nothing, but that I shall give it, without any predilection to former opinions, or any sinister bias whatsoever, the most honest and impartial consideration of which I am capable. The public has a full right to it; and this great city, a main pillar in the commercial interest of Great Britain, must totter on its base by the slightest mistake with regard to our American measures.

Thus much, however, I think it not amiss to lay before you: that I am not, I hope, apt to take up or lay down my opinions lightly. I have held, and ever shall maintain, to the best of my power, unimpaired and undiminished, the just, wise, and necessary constitutional superiority of Great Britain. This is necessary for America as well as for us. I never mean to depart from it. Whatever may be lost by it, I avow it. The forfeiture even of your favour, if by such a declaration I could forfeit it, though the first object of my ambition, never will make me disguise my sentiments on this subject.

But—I have ever had a clear opinion, and have ever held a constant correspondent conduct, that this superiority is consistent with all the liberties a sober and spirited American ought to desire. I never mean to put any colonist, or any human creature, in a situation not becoming a free man. To reconcile British superiority with American liberty shall be my great object, as far as my little faculties extend. I am far from thinking that both, even yet, may not be preserved.

When I first devoted myself to the public service, I considered how I should render myself fit for it; and this I did by endeavouring to discover what it was that gave this country the rank it holds in the world. I found that our prosperity and dignity arose principally, if not solely, from two sources—our constitution and commerce. Both these I have spared no study to understand, and no endeavour to support.

The distinguishing part of our constitution is its liberty. To preserve that liberty inviolate, seems the particular duty and proper trust of a member of the House of Commons. But the liberty, the only liberty I mean, is a liberty connected with order; that not only exists along with order and virtue, but which cannot exist at all without them. It inheres in good and steady government, as in its substance and vital principle.

The other source of our power is commerce, of which you are so large a part, and which cannot exist, no more than your liberty, without a connexion with many virtues. It has ever been a very particular and a very favourite object of my study, in its principles, and in its details. I think many here are acquainted with the truth of what I say. This I know, that I have ever had my house open, and my poor services ready, for traders and manufacturers of every denomination. My favourite ambition is to have those services acknowledged. I now appear before you to make trial, whether my earnest endeavours have been so wholly oppressed by the weakness of my abilities, as to be rendered insignificant in the eyes of a great trading city; or whether you choose to give a weight to humble abilities, for the sake of the honest exertions with which they are accompanied. This is my trial to-day. My industry is not on trial: Of my industry I am sure, as far as my constitution of mind and body admitted.

When I was invited by many respectable merchants, freeholders, and freemen of this city, to offer them my services, I had just received the honour of an election at another place, at a very great distance from this. I immediately opened the matter to those of my worthy constituents who were with me, and they unanimously advised me not to decline it. They told me, that they had elected me with a view to the public service; and as great questions relative to our commerce and colonies were imminent, that in such matters I might derive authority and support from the representation of this great commercial city: they desired me therefore to set off without delay, very well persuaded that I never could forget my obligations to them, or to my friends, for the choice they had made of me. From that time to this instant I have not slept; and if I should have the honour of being freely chosen by you, I hope I shall be as far from slumbering or sleeping when your service requires me to be awake, as I have been in coming to offer myself a candidate for your favour.

SPEECH AFTER ELECTION, NOVEMBER 3, 1774.

GENTLEMEN,—I cannot avoid sympathizing strongly with the feelings of the gentleman who has received the same honour that you have conferred on me. If he (Cruger) who was bred and passed his whole life amongst you; if he, who through the easy gradations of acquaintance, friendship, and esteem, has obtained the honour, which seems of itself, naturally and almost insensibly, to meet with those, who, by the even tenor of pleasing manners and social virtues, slide into the love and confidence of their fellow-citizens;—if he cannot speak but with great emotion on this subject, surrounded as he is on all sides with his old friends; you will have the goodness to excuse me, if my real, unaffected embarrassment prevents me from expressing my gratitude to you as I ought.

I was brought hither under the disadvantage of being unknown, even by sight, to any of you. No previous canvass was made for me. I was put in nomination after the poll was opened. I did not appear until it was far advanced. If, under all these accumulated disadvantages, your good opinion has carried me to this happy point of success; you will pardon me, if I can only say to you collectively, as I said to you individually, simply and plainly, I thank you—I am obliged to you—I am not insensible of your kindness.

This is all that I am able to say for the inestimable favour you have conferred upon me. But I cannot be satisfied, without saying a little more in defence of the right you have to confer such a favour. The person that appeared here as counsel for the candidate who so long and so earnestly solicited your votes, thinks proper to deny that a very great part of you have any votes to give. He fixes a standard period of time in his own imagination, not what the law defines, but merely what the convenience of his client suggests, by which he would cut off, at one stroke, all those freedoms which are the dearest privileges of your corporation; which the common law authorizes; which your magistrates are compelled to grant; which come duly authenticated into this court; and are saved in the clearest words, and with the most religious care and tenderness, in that very Act of Parliament, which was made to regulate the elections by freemen, and to prevent all possible abuses in making them.

I do not intend to argue the matter here. My learned counsel has supported your cause with his usual ability; the worthy sheriffs have acted with their usual equity, and I have no doubt that the same equity, which dictates the return, will guide the final determination. I had the honour, in conjunction with many far wiser men, to contribute a very small assistance, but however some assistance, to the forming the judicature which is to try such questions. It would be unnatural in me to doubt the justice of that court, in the trial of my own cause, to which I have been so active to give jurisdiction over every other.

I assure the worthy freemen and this corporation, that, if the gentleman perseveres in the intentions which his present warmth dictates to him, I will attend their cause with diligence, and I hope with effect. For, if I know anything of myself, it is not my own interest in it, but my full conviction, that induces me to tell you—*I think there is not a shadow of doubt in the case.*

I do not imagine that you find me rash in declaring myself, or very forward in troubling you. From the beginning to the end of the election, I have kept silence in all matters of discussion. I have never asked a question of a voter on the other side, or supported a doubtful vote on my own. I respected the abilities of my managers; I relied on the candour of the court. I think the worthy sheriffs will bear me witness, that I have never once made an attempt to impose upon their reason, to surprise their justice, or to ruffle their temper. I stood on the hustings (except when I gave my thanks to those who favoured me with their votes) less like a candidate, than an unconcerned spectator of a public proceeding. But here the face of things is altered. Here is an attempt for a general *massacre* of suffrages; an attempt, by a promiscuous carnage of *friends* and *foes*, to exterminate above two thousand votes, including *seven hundred polled for the gentleman himself, who now complains,* and who would destroy the friends whom he has obtained, only because he cannot obtain as many of them as he wishes.

How he will be permitted, in another place, to stultify and disable himself, and to plead against his own acts, is another question. The law will decide it. I shall only speak of it as it concerns the propriety of public conduct in this city. I do not pretend to lay down rules of decorum for other gentlemen. They are best judges of the mode of proceeding that will recommend them to the favour of their fellow-citizens. But I confess I should look rather awkward, if I had been the *very first to produce the new copies of freedom;* if I had persisted in producing them to the last; if I had ransacked, with the most unremitting industry and the most penetrating research, the remotest corners of the kingdom to discover them; if I were then, all at once, to turn short, and declare, that I had been sporting all this while with the right of election; and that I had been drawing out a poll, upon no sort of rational grounds, which disturbed the peace of my fellow-citizens for a month together—I really, for my part, should appear awkward under such circumstances.

It would be still more awkward in me if I were gravely to look the sheriffs in the face, and to tell them, they were not to determine my cause on my own principles; nor to make the return upon those votes upon which I had rested my election. Such would be my appearance to the court and magistrates.

But how should I appear to the *voters* themselves if I had gone round to the citizens entitled to freedom, and squeezed them by the hand—" Sir, I humbly beg your vote—I shall be eternally thankful—may I hope for the honour of your support?—Well!—come—we shall see you at the council-house;"—if I were then to deliver them to my managers, pack them into tallies, vote them off in court, and: when I heard from the bar—" Such a one only! and such a one for ever!—he's my man!"—"Thank you, good sir—Hah! my worthy friend! thank you kindly—that's an honest fellow—how is your good family?"—whilst these words are hardly out of my mouth, if I should have wheeled round at once, and told them—" Get you gone, you pack of worthless fellows! you have no votes—you are usurpers! you are intruders on the rights of real freemen! I will have nothing to do with you! you ought never to have been produced at this election, and the sheriffs ought not to have admitted you to poll!"?

Gentlemen, I should make a strange figure if my conduct had been of this sort. I am not so old an acquaintance of yours as the worthy gentleman. Indeed, I could not have ventured on such kind of freedoms with you. But I am bound, and I will endeavour, to have justice done to the rights of freemen, even though I should, at the same time, be obliged to vindicate the former* part of my antagonist's conduct against his own present inclinations.

I owe myself, in all things, to *all* the freemen of this city. My particular friends have a demand on me that I should not deceive their expectations. Never was cause or man supported with more constancy, more activity, more spirit. I have been supported with a zeal indeed and heartiness in my friends, which (if their object had been at all proportioned to their endeavours) could never be sufficiently commended. They supported me upon the most liberal principles. They wished that the members for Bristol should be chosen for the city, and for their country at large, and not for themselves.

---

* Mr. Brickdale opened his poll, it seems, with a tally of those very kind of freemen, and polled many hundreds of them.

So far they are not disappointed. If I possess nothing else, I am sure I possess the temper that is fit for your service. I know nothing of Bristol, but by the favours I have received, and the virtues I have seen exerted in it.

I shall ever retain, what I now feel, the most perfect and grateful attachment to my friends—and I have no enmities—no resentment. I never can consider fidelity to engagements, and constancy in friendships, but with the highest approbation; even when those noble qualities are employed against my own pretensions. The gentleman who is not so fortunate as I have been in this contest, enjoys, in this respect, a consolation full of honour both to himself and to his friends. They have certainly left nothing undone for his service.

As for the trifling petulance, which the rage of party stirs up in little minds, though it should show itself in this court, it has not made the slightest impression on me. The highest flight of such clamorous birds is winged in an inferior region of the air. We hear them, and we look upon them, just as you, gentlemen, when you enjoy the serene air on your lofty rocks, look down upon the gulls that skim the mud of your river, when it is exhausted of its tide.

I am sorry I cannot conclude without saying a word on a topic touched upon by my worthy colleague. I wish that topic had been passed by at a time when I have so little leisure to discuss it. But since he has thought proper to throw it out, I owe you a clear explanation of my poor sentiments on that subject.

He tells you, that "the topic of instructions has occasioned much altercation and uneasiness in this city;" and he expresses himself (if I understand him rightly) in favour of the coercive authority of such instructions.

Certainly, gentlemen, it ought to be the happiness and glory of a representative to live in the strictest union, the closest correspondence, and the most unreserved communication with his constituents. Their wishes ought to have great weight with him; their opinion high respect; their business unremitted attention. It is his duty to sacrifice his repose, his pleasures, his satisfactions, to theirs; and above all, ever, and in all cases, to prefer their interest to his own. But his unbiassed opinion, his mature judgment, his enlightened conscience, he ought not to sacrifice to you—to any man, or to any set of men living. These he does not derive from your pleasure—no, nor from the law and the constitution. They are a trust from Providence, for the abuse of which he is deeply answerable. Your representative owes you, not his industry only, but his judgment; and he betrays, instead of serving you, if he sacrifices it to your opinion.

My worthy colleague says, his will ought to be subservient to yours. If that be all, the thing is innocent. If government were a matter of will upon any side, yours, without question, ought to be superior. But government and legislation are matters of reason and judgment, and not of inclination; and what sort of reason is that, in which the determination precedes the discussion; in which one set of men deliberate and another decide; and where those who form the conclusion are perhaps three hundred miles distant from those who hear the arguments?

To deliver an opinion is the right of all men; that of constituents is a weighty and respectable opinion, which a representative ought always to rejoice to hear, and which he ought always most seriously to consider. But *authoritative* instructions—*mandates* issued, which the member is bound blindly and implicitly to obey, to vote, and to argue for, though contrary to the clearest conviction of his judgment and conscience,—these are things utterly unknown to the laws of this land, and which arise from a fundamental mistake of the whole order and tenour of our constitution.

Parliament is not a *congress* of ambassadors from different and hostile interests, which interests each must maintain, as an agent and advocate, against other agents and advocates; but Parliament is a *deliberative* assembly of *one* nation, with *one* interest, that of the whole; where, not local purposes, not local prejudices ought to guide, but the general good, resulting from the general reason of the whole. You choose a member, indeed; but when you have chosen him, he is not member of Bristol, but he is a member of *Parliament*. If the local constituent should have an interest, or should form a hasty opinion, evidently opposite to the real good of the rest of the community, the member for that place ought to be as far, as any other, from any endeavour to give it effect. I beg pardon for saying so much on this subject. I have been unwillingly drawn into it; but I shall ever use a respectful frankness of communication with you. Your faithful friend, your devoted servant, I shall be to the end of my life: a flatterer you do not wish for. On this point of instructions, however, I think it scarcely possible we ever can have any sort of difference. Perhaps I may give you too much, rather than too little trouble.

From the first hour I was encouraged to court your favour, to this happy day of obtaining it, I have never promised you anything but humble and persevering endeavours to do my duty. The weight of that duty, I confess, makes me tremble; and whoever well considers what it is, of all things in the world, will fly from what has the least likeness to a positive and precipitate engagement. To be a good member of Parliament, is, let me tell you, no easy task; especially at this time, when there is so strong a disposition to run into the perilous extremes of servile compliance or wild popularity. To unite circumspection with vigour, is absolutely necessary; but it is extremely difficult. We are now members for a rich commercial *city*; this city, however, is but a part of a rich commercial *nation*, the interests of which are various, multiform, and intricate. We are members for that great nation, which however is itself but part of a great *empire*, extended by our virtue and our fortune to the farthest limits of the east and of the west. All these wide-spread interests must be considered; must be compared; must be reconciled if possible. We are members for a *free* country; and surely we all know, that the machine of a free constitution is no simple thing; but as intricate and as delicate as it is valuable. We are members in a great and ancient *monarchy*; and we must preserve religiously the true legal rights of the sovereign, which form the keystone that binds together the noble and well-constructed arch of our empire and our constitution. A constitution made up of balanced powers must ever be a critical thing. As such, I mean to touch that part of it which comes within my reach. I know my inability, and I wish for support from every quarter. In particular I shall aim at the friendship, and shall cultivate the best correspondence, of the worthy colleague you have given me.

I trouble you no farther than once more to thank you all; you, gentlemen, for your favours; the candidates, for their temperate and polite behaviour; and the sheriffs, for a conduct which may give a model for all who are in public stations.

EDMUND BURKE.

[THE passages here chosen form part of the opening portion of one of Burke's greatest speeches, in which he laid before the House of Commons his thirteen resolutions for reconciliement with America. In the language of Mr. Peter Burke, whose short but admirable Life of his great namesake is well worthy of perusal, it may be observed that in this speech, the great orator, waiving the discussion of right, confined himself to the question of expediency. He proceeded upon a principle admitted by the wisest legislators, that Government must be adapted to the nature and situation of the people for whose benefit it is exercised. Instead of recurring to abstract ideas, he considered the circumstances, modes of marking dispositions, and principles of action of the people in particular, whose treatment was the subject of deliberation. It would, however, be impossible, within the limits of this publication, to give even an outline of the general scope and bearing of this great speech. An extract has therefore been made from the exordium, concluding with the magnificent picture of the greatness of the British colonies in America, which will, it is hoped, induce many of our readers to refer to the speech itself, which may be found in its entirety in the third volume of Burke's complete Works, published in 1826. It is needless to add that these eloquent warnings had no effect on the Ministry.]

CONCILIATION WITH THE AMERICAN COLONIES.

I HOPE, sir, that, notwithstanding the austerity of the Chair, your good-nature will incline you to some degree of indulgence towards human frailty. You will not think it unnatural, that those who have an object depending, which strongly engages their hopes and fears, should be somewhat inclined to superstition. As I came into the House full of anxiety about the event of my motion, I found, to my infinite surprise, that the grand penal Bill, by which we had passed sentence on the trade and sustenance of America, is to be returned to us from the other House.* I do confess, I could not help looking on this event as a fortunate omen. I look upon it as a sort of providential favour; by which we are put once more in possession of our deliberative capacity, upon a business so very questionable in its nature, so very uncertain in its issue. By the return of this Bill, which seemed to have taken its flight for ever, we are at this very instant nearly as free to choose a plan for our American government as we were on the first day of the session. If, sir, we incline to the side of conciliation, we are not at all embarrassed (unless we please to make ourselves so) by any incongruous mixture of coercion and restraint. We are therefore called upon, as it were by a superior warning voice, again to attend to America; to attend to the whole of it together; and to review the subject with an unusual degree of care and calmness.

Surely it is an awful subject; or there is none so on this side of the grave. When I first had the honour of a seat in this House, the affairs of that continent pressed themselves upon us, as the most important and most delicate object of parliamentary attention. My little share in this great deliberation oppressed me. I found myself a partaker in a very high trust; and having no sort of reason to rely on the strength of my natural abilities for the proper execution of that trust, I was obliged to take more than common pains to instruct myself in everything which relates to our colonies. I was not less under the necessity of forming some fixed ideas concerning the general policy of the British empire. Something of this sort seemed to be indispensable; in order, amidst so vast a fluctuation of passions and opinions, to concentre my thoughts; to ballast my conduct; to preserve me from being blown

* The Act to restrain the trade and commerce of the provinces of Massachusetts Bay and New Hampshire, and colonies of Connecticut and Rhode Island, and Providence Plantation, in North America, to Great Britain, Ireland, and the British Islands in the West Indies; and to prohibit such provinces and colonies from carrying on any fishery on the banks of Newfoundland, and other places therein mentioned, under certain conditions and limitations.

about by every wind of fashionable doctrine. I really did not think it safe, or manly, to have fresh principles to seek upon every fresh mail which should arrive from America.

At that period I had the fortune to find myself in perfect concurrence with a large majority in this House. Bowing under that high authority, and penetrated with the sharpness and strength of that early impression, I have continued ever since, without the least deviation, in my original sentiments. Whether this be owing to an obstinate perseverance in error, or to a religious adherence to what appears to me truth and reason, it is in your equity to judge.

Sir, Parliament having an enlarged view of objects, made, during this interval, more frequent changes in their sentiments and their conduct, than could be justified in a particular person upon the contracted scale of private information. But though I do not hazard anything approaching to a censure on the motives of former Parliaments to all those alterations, one fact is undoubted,—that under them the state of America has been kept in continual agitation. Everything administered as remedy to the public complaint, if it did not produce, was at least followed by, a heightening of the distemper; until, by a variety of experiments, that important country has been brought into her present situation;—a situation which I will not miscall; which I dare not name; which I scarcely know how to comprehend in the terms of any description.

* * *

The capital leading questions on which you must this day decide are these two: First, whether you ought to concede; and secondly, what your concession ought to be. On the first of these questions we have gained some ground. But I am sensible that a good deal more is still to be done. Indeed, sir, to enable us to determine both on the one and the other of these great questions with a firm and precise judgment, I think it may be necessary to consider distinctly the true nature and the peculiar circumstances of the object which we have before us. Because, after all our struggle, whether we will or not, we must govern America according to that nature, and to those circumstances, and not according to our own imagination; not according to abstract ideas of right; by no means according to mere general theories of government, the resort to which appears to me, in our present situation, no better than arrant trifling. I shall therefore endeavour, with your leave, to lay before you some of the most material of these circumstances in as full and as clear a manner as I am able to state them.

The first thing that we have to consider with regard to the nature of the object is—the number of people in the colonies. I have taken for some years a good deal of pains on that point. I can by no calculation justify myself in placing the number below two millions of inhabitants of our own European blood and colour; besides at least 500,000 others, who form no inconsiderable part of the strength and opulence of the whole. This, sir, is, I believe, about the true number. There is no occasion to exaggerate, where plain truth is of so much weight and importance. But whether I put the present numbers too high or too low, is a matter of little moment. Such is the strength with which population shoots in that part of the world, that state the numbers as high as we will, whilst the dispute continues, the exaggeration ends. Whilst we are discussing any given magnitude, they are grown to it. Whilst we spend our time in deliberating on the mode of governing two millions, we shall find we have millions more to manage. Your children do not grow faster from infancy to manhood, than they spread from families to communities, and from villages to nations.

I put this consideration of the present and the growing numbers in the front of our deliberation, because, sir, this consideration will make it evident to a blunter discernment than yours, that no partial, narrow, contracted, pinched, occasional system will be at all suitable to such an object. It will show you, that it is not to be considered as one of those *minima* which are out of the eye and consideration of the law; not a paltry excrescence of the State; not a mean dependent, who may be neglected with little damage, and provoked with little danger. It will prove that some degree of care and caution is required in the handling such an object; it will show that you ought not, in reason, to trifle with so large a mass of the interests and feelings of the human race. You could at no time do so without guilt; and be assured you will not be able to do it long with impunity.

But the population of this country, the great and growing population, though a very important consideration, will lose much of its weight, if not combined with other circumstances. The commerce of your colonies is out of all proportion beyond the numbers of the people. This ground of their commerce, indeed, has been trod some days ago, and with great ability, by a distinguished person,* at your bar. This gentleman, after thirty-five years—it is so long since he first appeared at the same place to plead for the commerce of Great Britain,—has come again before you to plead the same cause, without any other effect of time, than, that to the fire of imagination and extent of erudition, which even then marked him as one of the

---

* Mr. Glover.

first literary characters of his age, he has added a consummate knowledge in the commercial interest of his country, formed by a long course of enlightened and discriminating experience.

Then, after reviewing our commercial relations with America, Mr. Burke proceeded:—

The trade with America alone is now within less than £500,000 of being equal to what this great commercial nation, England, carried on at the beginning of this century with the whole world! If I had taken the largest year of those on your table, it would rather have exceeded. But, it will be said, is not this American trade an unnatural protuberance, that has drawn the juices from the rest of the body? The reverse. It is the very food that has nourished every other part into its present magnitude. Our general trade has been greatly augmented, and augmented more or less in almost every part to which it ever extended; but with this material difference,—that of the six millions which in the beginning of the century constituted the whole mass of our export commerce, the colony trade was but one-twelfth part; it is now (as a part of sixteen millions) considerably more than a third of the whole. This is the relative proportion of the importance of the colonies at these two periods; and all reasoning concerning our mode of treating them must have this proportion as its basis, or it is a reasoning, weak, rotten, and sophistical.

Mr. Speaker, I cannot prevail on myself to hurry over this great consideration. It is good for us to be here. We stand where we have an immense view of what is, and what is past. Clouds, indeed, and darkness, rest upon the future. Let us, however, before we descend from this noble eminence, reflect that this growth of our national prosperity has happened within the short period of the life of man. It has happened within sixty-eight years. There are those alive whose memory might touch the two extremities. For instance, my Lord Bathurst might remember all the stages of the progress. He was in 1704 of an age at least to be made to comprehend such things. He was then old enough, *acta parentum jam legere, et quæ sit poterit cognoscere virtus*—suppose, sir, that the angel of this auspicious youth, foreseeing the many virtues which made him one of the most amiable, as he is one of the most fortunate men of his age, had opened to him in vision, that, when, in the fourth generation, the third prince of the house of Brunswick had sat twelve years on the throne of that nation, which (by the happy issue of moderate and healing councils) was to be made Great Britain, he should see his son, Lord Chancellor of England, turn back the current of hereditary dignity to its fountain, and raise him to a higher rank of peerage, whilst he enriched the family with a new one—

if amidst these bright and happy scenes of domestic honour and prosperity, that angel should have drawn up the curtain, and unfolded the rising glories of his country, and whilst he was gazing with admiration on the then commercial grandeur of England, the genius should point out to him a little speck, scarce visible in the mass of the national interest, a small seminal principle rather than a formed body, and should tell him—" Young man, there is America—which at this day serves for little more than to amuse you with stories of savage men, and uncouth manners; yet shall, before you taste of death, show itself equal to the whole of that commerce which now attracts the envy of the world. Whatever England has been growing to by a progressive increase of improvement, brought in by varieties of people, by succession of civilizing conquests and civilizing settlements in a series of seventeen hundred years, you shall see as much added to her by America in the course of a single life!" If this state of his country had been foretold to him, would it not require all the sanguine credulity of youth, and all the fervid glow of enthusiasm, to make him believe it? Fortunate man, he has lived to see it! Fortunate indeed, if he lives to see nothing that shall vary the prospect, and cloud the setting of his day!

KOSSUTH.

[KOSSUTH, in his speech to the New York Militia, December 16th, 1851, pays the following graceful tribute to the eloquence of Garibaldi.]

ELOQUENCE OF GARIBALDI.

DO you know, gentlemen, what is the finest speech I ever heard or read? It is the address of Garibaldi to his Roman soldiers in the last war, when he told them:—"Soldiers, what I have to offer you is fatigue, danger, struggling, and death—the chill of the cold night, the open air, and the burning sun—no lodgings, no munitions, no provisions,—but forced marches, dangerous watchposts, and continued struggling with bayonets against batteries. Let those who love freedom and their country, follow me." That is the most glorious speech I ever heard in my life.

EDWARD EVERETT.

Born 1794. Living.

[THE name of Mr. Everett is not unknown or unhonoured in this country. As a statesman and orator, he has been associated with the political history of America for more than thirty years past, and as a Minister of the United States for some time resident in England, is well and familiarly known to the great leaders of opinion amongst us. His "Mount Vernon Papers," a collection of sketches, relating, as their name would suggest, to Washington and other great American themes, were published in this country a few years since, and met with no small success. Otherwise, his writings and speeches are probably not very generally known to the mass of the reading community, and therefore it has been thought desirable to offer several specimens of his eloquence throughout the course of the present work; and, as examples of a lofty and impassioned type of oratory, they will well bear very careful study and imitation. The following extract is from an oration on one of the brightest and purest names in American history—the memory of the good and brave La Fayette being amongst the richest heritages of the great Republic.]

The Character of La Fayette.

THERE have been those who have denied to La Fayette the name of *a great man*. What is greatness? Does goodness belong to greatness and make an essential part of it? Is there yet enough of virtue left in the world, to echo the sentiment, that

"'Tis phrase absurd to call a villain great?"

If there is, who, I would ask, of all the prominent names in history, has run through such a career, with so little reproach, justly or unjustly, bestowed? Are military courage and conduct the measure of greatness? La Fayette was intrusted by Washington with all kinds of service;—the laborious and complicated, which required skill and patience; the perilous, that demanded nerve;—and we see him keeping up a pursuit, effecting a retreat, out-manœuvering a wary adversary with a superior force, harmonizing the action of French regular troops and American militia, commanding an assault at the point of the bayonet; and all with entire success and brilliant reputation. Is the readiness to meet vast responsibility a proof of greatness? The memoirs of Mr. Jefferson show us, that there was a moment in 1789, when La Fayette took upon himself, as the head of the military force, the entire responsibility of laying down the basis of the revolution. Is the cool and brave administration of gigantic power a mark of greatness? In all the whirlwind of the revolution, and when, as commander-in-chief of the National Guard, an organized force of three millions of men, who, for any popular purpose, needed but a word, a look, to put them in motion,—and he their idol,— we behold him ever calm, collected, disinterested, as free from affectation as selfishness, clothed not less with humility than with power. Is the fortitude required to resist the multitude pressing onward their leader to glorious crime, a part of greatness? Behold him the fugitive and the victim, when he might have been the chief of the revolution. Is the solitary and unaided opposition of a good citizen to the pretensions of an absolute ruler, whose power was as boundless as his ambition, an effort of greatness? Read the letter of La Fayette to Napoleon Bonaparte, refusing to vote for him as consul for life. Is the voluntary return, in advancing years, to the direction of affairs, at a moment like that, when in 1815 the ponderous machinery of the French empire was flying asunder,—stunning, rending, crushing thousands on every side,—a mark of greatness? Contemplate La Fayette at the tribune, in Paris, when allied Europe was thundering at its gates, and Napoleon yet stood in his desperation and at bay. Are dignity, propriety, cheerfulness, unerring discretion in new and conspicuous stations of extraordinary delicacy, a sign of greatness? Watch his progress in this country, in 1824 and 1825; hear him say the right word at the right time, in a series of interviews, public and private, crowding on each other every day, for a twelvemonth, throughout the Union, with every description of persons, without ever wounding for a moment the self-love of others, or forgetting the dignity of his own position. Lastly, is it any proof of greatness to be able, at the age of seventy-three, to take the lead in a successful and bloodless revolution;—to change the dynasty,—to organize, exercise, and abdicate a military command of three and a half millions of men;—to take up, to perform, and lay down the most momentous, delicate, and perilous duties, without passion, without hurry, without selfishness? Is it great to disregard the bribes of title, office, money;— to live, to labour, and suffer for great public ends alone;—to adhere to principle under all circumstances;—to stand before Europe and America conspicuous for sixty years, in the most responsible stations, the acknowledged admiration of all good men?

I think I understand the proposition, that La Fayette was not a great man. It comes from the same school which also denies greatness to Washington, and which accords it to Alexander and Cæsar, to Napoleon and to his conqueror. When I analyze the greatness of these distinguished men, as contrasted with that of La Fayette and Washington, I find either one idea omitted, which is essential to true greatness, or one included as essential, which belongs only to the lowest conception of greatness. The moral, disinterested, and purely patriotic qualities are wholly wanting in the greatness of Cæsar and Napoleon; and, on the other hand, it is a certain splendour of success, a brilliancy of result, which, with the majority of mankind, marks them out as the great men of our race. But not only are a high morality and a true patriotism essential to greatness;— but they must first be renounced, before a ruthless career of selfish conquest can begin. I profess to be no judge of military combinations; but, with the best reflection I have been able to give the subject, I perceive no reason to doubt, that, had La Fayette, like Napoleon, been by principle capable of hovering on the edges of ultra-revolutionism; never halting enough to be denounced; never plunging too far to retreat;—but with a cold and well-balanced selfishness, sustaining himself at the head of affairs, under each new phase of the revolution, by the compliances sufficient to satisfy its demands,—had his principles allowed him to play this game, he might have anticipated the career of Napoleon. At three different periods, he had it in his power, without usurpation, to take the government into his own hands. He was invited—urged to do so. Had he done it, and made use of the military means at his command, to maintain and perpetuate his power,—he would then, at the sacrifice of all his just claims to the name of great and good, have reached that which vulgar admiration alone worships,—the greatness of high station and brilliant success.

But it was of the greatness of La Fayette, that he looked down on greatness of the false kind. He learned his lesson in the school of Washington, and took his first practice in victories over himself. Let it be questioned by the venal apologists of time-honoured abuses,—let it be sneered at by national prejudice and party detraction; let it be denied by the admirers of war and conquest;—by the idolaters of success;—but let it be gratefully acknowledged by good men; by Americans,—by every man, who has sense to distinguish character from events; who has a heart to beat in concert with the pure enthusiasm of virtue.

But it is more than time, fellow-citizens, that I commit this great and good man to your unprompted contemplation. On his arrival among you, ten years ago,—when your civil fathers, your military, your children, your whole population poured itself out, as one throng, to salute him,—when your cannons proclaimed his advent with joyous salvos,—and your acclamations were responded from steeple to steeple, by the voice of festal bells,—with what delight did you not listen to his cordial and affectionate words;—" I beg of you all, beloved citizens of Boston, to accept the respectful and warm thanks of a heart, which has for nearly half a century been devoted to your illustrious city!" That noble heart,—to which, if any object on earth was dear, that object was the country of his early choice,—of his adoption, and his more than regal triumph,—that noble heart will beat no more for your welfare. Cold and motionless, it is already mingling with the dust. While he lived, you thronged with delight to his presence,—you gazed with admiration on his placid features and venerable form, not wholly unshaken by the rude storms of his career; and now that he is departed, you have assembled in this cradle of the liberties, for which, with your fathers, he risked his life, to pay the last honours to his memory. You have thrown open these consecrated portals to admit the lengthened train which has come to discharge the last public offices of respect to his name. You have hung these venerable arches, for the second time since their erection, with the sable badges of sorrow. You have thus associated the memory of La Fayette in those distinguished honours, which but a few years since you paid to your Adams and Jefferson; and could your wishes and mine have prevailed, my lips would this day have been mute, and the same illustrious voice, which gave utterance to your filial emotions over their honoured graves, would have spoken also, for you, over him who shared their earthly labours, enjoyed their friendship, and has now gone to share their last repose, and their imperishable remembrance.

There is not, throughout the world, a friend of liberty, who has not dropped his head when he has heard that La Fayette is no more. Poland, Italy, Greece, Spain, Ireland, the South American republics,—every country where man is struggling to recover his birthright,—has lost a benefactor—a patron—in La Fayette. But you, young men, at whose command I speak, for you a bright and particular loadstar is henceforward fixed in the front of heaven. What young man that reflects on the history of La Fayette,—that sees him in the morning of his days the associate of sages,—the friend of Washington, —but will start with new vigour on the path of duty and renown?

And what was it, fellow-citizens, which gave to our La Fayette his spotless fame? The love of liberty. What has consecrated his memory in hearts of good men? The love of liberty. What nerved his youthful arm with strength, and inspired him in the morning of his days with sagacity and counsel? The living love of liberty. To what did he sacrifice power, and rank, and country, and freedom itself? To the horror of licentiousness;—to the sanctity of plighted faith;—to the love of liberty protected by law. Thus the great principle of your revolutionary fathers, of your pilgrim sires, the great principle of the age, was the rule of his life:— *The love of liberty protected by law.*

You have now assembled within these renowned walls, to perform the last duties of respect and love, on the birth-day of your benefactor, beneath that roof which has resounded of old with the master-voices of American renown. The spirit of the departed is in high communion with the spirit of the place,—the temple worthy of the new name, which we now behold inscribed on its walls. Listen, Americans, to the lesson, which seems borne to us on the very air we breathe, while we perform these dutiful rites. Ye Winds, that wafted the pilgrims to the land of promise, fan, in their children's hearts, the love of freedom; Blood, which our fathers shed, cry from the ground; Echoing Arches of this renowned hall, whisper back the voices of other days; Glorious Washington, break the long silence of that votive canvass;—Speak, speak, marble lips: teach us "THE LOVE OF LIBERTY PROTECTED BY LAW!"

JOHN BRIGHT.
Born 1810.

[THE following extracts are from a speech of Mr. Bright, delivered in the Town Hall, Birmingham, on December 18, 1862. As will be seen from allusions in the speech itself, Mr. Bright had occasion to differ very materially from Mr. Scholefield, his colleague, on several topics then under discussion; but the general bearing of his discourse seems to have been received by his constituents with enthusiastic applause. The robust and manly eloquence of Mr. Bright has seldom been exhibited to better advantage than at the close of this speech—his righteous indignation at that slavery system which has been declared to be "the corner-stone of the Confederacy," being thoroughly in keeping with all his former utterances on the same subject. Much of the speech, in which he supports his views by statistical and other minute argument, has been necessarily omitted to bring our quotations within the compass of the present work.]

THE COTTON SUPPLY AND AMERICAN WAR.

GENTLEMEN,—I am afraid that there was a little excitement during a part of my honourable colleague's speech, which was hardly favourable to that impartial consideration of great questions to which he appealed. He began by referring to a question—or, I might say, to two questions, for it was one great question in two parts—which at this moment occupies the mind, and, I think, must affect the heart, of every thoughtful man in this country—the calamity which has fallen upon the county from which I come, and the strife which is astonishing the world, on the other side of the Atlantic. I shall not enter into details with regard to that calamity, because you have had already, I believe, meetings in this town, many details have been published, contributions of a generous character have been made, and you are doing—and especially, if I am rightly informed, are your artizans doing—their duty with regard to the unfortunate condition of the population amongst which I live. But this I may state in a sentence, that the greatest, probably the most prosperous, manufacturing industry that this country or the world has ever seen, has been suddenly and unexpectedly stricken down, but by a blow which has not been unforeseen or unforetold. Nearly 500,000 persons—men, women, and children—at this moment are saved from the utmost extremes of famine, not a few of them from death, by the contributions which they are receiving from all parts of the country. I will not attempt here an elaborate eulogy of the generosity of the givers, nor will I endeavour to paint the patience and the gratitude of those who suffer and receive; but I believe the conduct of the country, with regard to this great misfortune, is an honour to all classes and to every section of this people. Some have remarked that there is perfect order where there has been so much anxiety and suffering; I believe there is scarcely a thoughtful man in Lancashire who will not admit that one great cause of the patience and good conduct of the people, besides the fact that they know so much is being done for them, is to be found in the extensive information they possess, and which of late years, and now more than ever, has been communicated to them through the instrumentality of an untaxed press. Noble lords who have recently spoken, official men, and public men, have taken upon them to tell the people of Lancashire that nobody is to blame, and that in point of fact, if it had not been for a family quarrel in that dreadful Republic, everything would have gone on perfectly smoothly, and not a word could have been said against anybody. Now, if you will allow me, I should like to examine for a few minutes whether this be true. If you read the papers with regard to this question you will find that, barring whatever chance there may be of our again soon receiving a supply of cotton from America, the hopes of the whole country are directed to India. . . . In 1847 I was in the House of Commons, and I brought forward a proposition for a select committee to inquire into this whole question; for in that year Lancashire was on the verge of the calamity that has now overtaken it, cotton was very scarce, for hundreds of the mills were working short time, and many were closed altogether. That committee reported that, in all the districts of Bombay and Madras, where cotton was cultivated, and generally over those agricultural regions, the people were in a condition of the most abject and degraded pauperism; and I will ask you whether it is possible for a people in that condition to produce anything great, or anything good, or anything constant, which the world requires? It is not to be wondered at that the quality of the cotton should be bad, so bad that it is illustrated by an anecdote which a very excellent man of the Methodist body told me the other day. He said that at a prayer meeting, not more than a dozen miles from where I live, one of the ministers was deep in supplication to the Supreme; he detailed, no doubt, a great many things which he thought they were in want of, and amongst the rest, a supply of cotton for the famishing people in that district. When he prayed for cotton,—some man with a keen sense of what he had suffered—in response, exclaimed, "O Lord! but not Surat." Now, my argument is this, and my assertion is this, that the growth of cotton in India, the growth of an article which was native and common in India before America was discovered by Europeans, that the growth of that article has been systematically injured, strangled, and destroyed by the stupid and wicked policy of the Indian Government. I saw, the other day, a letter from a gentleman as well acquainted with Indian affairs, perhaps, as any man in India—a letter written to a member of the Madras Government—in which he stated his firm opinion, that if it had not been for the Bombay Committee in 1846, and for my committee in 1848, there would not have been any cotton sent from India at this moment to be worked up in Lancashire. Now, in 1846, the quantity of cotton coming from India had fallen to 94,000 bales. How has it increased since then? In 1859 it had reached 509,000 bales; in 1860, 562,000 bales; and last year, owing to the extraordinarily high price, it had reached 986,000 bales; and I suppose this year will be about the same as last year.

I think, in justification of myself, and of some of those with whom I have acted, I am entitled to ask your time for a few moments, to show you what has been, not so much done as attempted to be done, to improve this state of things; and what has been the systematic opposition that we have had to contend with. In the year 1847, I moved for that committee, in a speech from which I shall read one short extract. I said that "We ought not to forget that the whole of the cotton grown in America is produced by slave labour, and this, I think, all will admit—that no matter as to the period in which slavery may have existed, abolished it will ultimately be, either by peaceable means or by violent means. Whether it comes to an end by peaceable means or otherwise, there will in all probability be an interruption to the production of cotton, and the calamity which must in consequence fall upon a part of the American Union will be felt throughout the manufacturing districts of this country." The committee was not refused—Governments do not always refuse committees, they don't much fear them on matters of this kind; they put as many men on as the mover of the committee does, and sometimes more, and they often consider a committee, as my hon. colleague will tell you, rather a convenient way of burying an unpleasant question at least for another Session. The committee sat during the Session of 1848, and it made a report, from which I shall quote not an extract, but the sense of an extract. The evidence was very extensive, very complete, and entirely condemnatory of the whole system of the Indian Government with regard to the land and agricultural produce, and one might have hoped that something would have arisen from it, and probably something has arisen from it, but so slowly that you have no fruit, nothing on which you can calculate, even up to this hour. Well, in 1850, as nothing more was done, I thought it time to take another step, and I gave notice of a motion for the appointment of a Royal Commission to go to India for the express purpose of ascertaining the truth of this matter:—I moved, "That a Royal Commission proceed to India to inquire into the obstacles which prevent the increased growth of cotton in India, and to report upon any circumstance which may injuriously affect the economical and industrial condition of the native population, being cultivators of the soil, within the Presidencies of Madras and Bombay." Now I shall read you one extract from my speech on that occasion, which refers to this question of peril in America: I said, "But there is another point, that whilst the production of cotton in the United States results from slave labour, whether we approve of any particular mode of abolishing slavery in any country or not, we are all convinced that it will be impossible in any country, and most of all in America, to keep between two and three millions of the population permanently in a state of bondage. By whatever means that system is to be abolished, whether by insurrection, —which I would deplore—or by some great measure of justice from the Government, one thing is certain, that the production of cotton must be interfered with for a considerable time, after such an event has taken place, and it may happen that the greatest measure of freedom that has ever been conceded may be a measure, the consequence of which will inflict mischief upon the greatest industrial pursuit that engages the labour of the operative population of this country." Now, it was not likely the Government could pay much attention to this, for at that precise moment the Foreign Office—then presided over by Lord Palmerston —was engaged with an English fleet in the waters of Greece, in collecting a bad debt for one Don Pacifico, a Jew, who made a fraudulent demand on the Greek Government for injuries said to have been committed upon him in Greece. Notwithstanding this I called upon Lord John Russell, who was then the Prime Minister, and asked him whether he would grant the commission I was going to move for. I will say this for him, he appeared to agree with me that it was a reasonable thing. I believe he saw the peril, and that my proposition was a proper one, but he said he wished he could communicate with Lord Dalhousie. But it was in the month of June, and he could not do that, and hear from him again before the close of the Session. He told me that Sir John Hobhouse, then President of the India Board, was very much against it, and I answered, "Doubtless he is, because he speaks as the mouthpiece of the East India Company, against whom I am bringing this inquiry." Well, my proposition came before the House, and, as some of you may recollect, it was opposed by the President of the India Board, and the Commission was consequently not granted. I had seen Sir Robert Peel—this was only ten days before his death—I had seen Sir Robert Peel, acquainted as he was with Lancashire interests, and had endeavoured to enlist him in my support. He cordially and entirely approved of my motion, and he remained in the House during the whole of the time I was speaking; but when Sir John Hobhouse rose to resist the motion, and he found the Government would not consent to it, he then left his seat, and left the House. The night after, or two nights after, he met me in the lobby; and he said he thought it was but right he should explain why he left the House after the conversation he had held with me on this question before. He said he had hoped the Government would agree to the motion, but when he found they would not, his position was so delicate with regard to them and his own old party, that he was most anxious that nothing should induce him, unless under the pressure of some great extremity, to appear, even, to oppose them on any matter before the House. Therefore, from a very delicate sense of honour, he did not say what I am sure he would have been glad to have said, and the proposition did not receive from him that help which, if it had received it, would have surmounted all obstacles. To show the sort of men who are made ministers—Sir John Hobhouse had on these occasions always a speech of the same sort. He said this, "With respect to the peculiar urgency of the time, he could not say the honourable gentleman had made out his case; for he found that the importation of cotton from all countries showed an immense increase during the last three years." Why, we know that the importation of cotton has shown an "immense increase" almost every three years for the last fifty years. But it was because that increase was entirely, or nearly so, from one source, and that source one of extreme peril, that I asked for the inquiry for which I moved. He said he had a letter—and he shook it at me in his hand—from the Secretary of the Commercial Association of Manchester, in which the directors of that body declared by special resolution that my proposition was not necessary, that an inquiry might do harm, and that they were abundantly satisfied with everything that these Lords of Leadenhall Street were doing. He said, "Such was the letter of the Secretary of the Association, and it was a complete answer to the honourable gentleman who had brought forward this motion." At this moment one of these gentlemen to whom I have referred, then President of the Board of Control, Governor of India, author, as he told a committee on which I sat, of the Affghan war, is now decorated with a Norman title,—for our masters, even after a lapse of 800 years, ape the Norman style,—sits in the House of Peers, and legislates for you, having neglected in regard to India every great duty which appertained to his high office; and, to show that it is not only Cabinets and Monarchs who thus distribute honours and rewards, the President of that Commercial Association, through whose instigation that letter was written, is now one of the representatives of Manchester, the great centre of that manufacture whose very foundation is now crumbling into ruin.

* * * *

But I have been asked twenty, fifty times during the last twelve months, "Why don't you come out and say something? Why can't you tell us something in this time of our great need?" Well, I reply, "I told you something when telling was of use; all I can say now is this, or nearly all, that a hundred years of crime against the negro in America, and a hundred years of crime against the docile natives of our Indian Empire, are not to be washed away by the penitence and the suffering of an hour." But what is our position? for you who are subscribing your money here have a right to know. I believe the quantity of cotton in the United States is at this moment much less than many people here believe, and that it is in no condition to be forwarded and exported. And I suspect that it is far more probable than otherwise, notwithstanding some of the, I should say, strange theories of my honourable colleague, that there never will again be in America a crop of cotton grown by slave labour. You will understand—I hope so at least—that I am not undertaking the office of prophet, I am not predicting; I know that everything which is not absolutely impossible may happen; and therefore things may happen wholly different to the course which appears to me likely. But, I say, taking the facts as they are before us—with that most limited vision which is given to mortals,—the high probability is, that there will never be another crop considerable or of avail in our manufactories from slave labour in the United States. We read the American papers or the quotations from them in our own papers, but I believe we can form no adequate conception of the disorganization and chaos that now prevail throughout a great portion of the Southern States; it is natural to a state of war under the circumstances of society in that region. But then we may be asked, what are our sources of supply, putting aside India? There is the colony of Queensland, where enthusiastic persons tell you cotton can be grown worth 3s. a pound. True enough; but where labour is very probably 10s. a day, I am not sure you are likely to get any large supply of that material we so much want, at a rate so cheap that we shall be likely to use it. Africa is pointed to by a very zealous friend of mine, but Africa is a land of savages mostly, and with its climate so much against European constitutions, I should not encourage the hope that any great relief at any early period can be had from that continent. Egypt will send us 30,000 or 40,000 more bales than last year; in all probability Syria and Brazil, with these high prices, will increase their production to some considerable extent; but I hold that there is no country at present from which you can derive any very large supply, except you can get it from your own dependencies in India. Now if there be no more cotton to be grown for two, or three, or four years in America, for our supply, we shall require, considering the smallness of the bales and the loss in working up the cotton—we shall require nearly 6,000,000 of additional bales to be supplied from some source. Now, I want to put to you one question. It has taken the United States 20 years, from 1840 to 1860, to increase their growth of cotton from 2,000,000 of bales to 4,000,000. How long will it take any other country with comparatively little capital, with a thousand disadvantages which America did not suffer from—how long will it take any other country, or all other countries, to give us 5,000,000 or 6,000,000 additional bales of cotton? There is one stimulus, the only one that I know of, and although I have not recommended it to the Government, and I know not precisely what sacrifice it would entail, yet I shall mention it, and I do it on the authority of a gentleman to whom I have before referred, who is thoroughly acquainted with Indian agriculture, and who —himself and his father—have been landowners and cultivators in India for sixty years. He says there is only one mode by which you can rapidly stimulate the growth of cotton in India, except that stimulus coming from the high prices for the time being—he says that if the Government would make a public declaration that for five years they would exempt from land-tax all land which during that time shall grow cotton, there would be the most extraordinary increase in the growth of that article which has ever been seen in regard to any branch of agriculture in the world. I do not know how far that would act, but I believe the stimulus would be enormous; the loss to the Government in revenue would be something, but the deliverance to the industry of Lancashire, if it succeeded as my friend thinks, would, of course, be speedy and perhaps complete. Short of this, I look upon the restoration of the prosperity of Lancashire as distant —most remote. I believe this misfortune will entail ruin upon the whole working population, and that it will gradually engulf the smaller traders and those possessing the least capital.

I do not say it will, becau what is not impossible ma may for years make the who of Lancashire almost entirely this is a very dismal look-ou persons in this country; but said—it comes from that u opportunities and our dutie guished the Government of I

Now, sir, before I sit dow to listen to me for a few mo branch of this great questi that sad tragedy which is eyes in the United States of not, in consequence of an heard from my hon. friend, any of the opinions which I proposed to lay before you if Having given to him, not diversity of opinion, a fair a I presume that I shall recei from those who may differ fr known that my hon. friend an elaborate speech on thi two things I should have don have prepared myself entirely I should have decided not t where there could by any po have been anything like d many—his friends and m room. Since I have been ma ham Mr. Scholefield has tr kindness of a brother. Not be more generous and mor every way than his conduct these several years, and there rather—far rather—that I lo tunity like this of speaking than I would have come he be at variance with him. I say that this great question upon the opinion of any ma or in England, or anywhere fore I could—anxious always duty requires, to avoid eve difference—I could with a cle abstained from coming to an meeting. But I observe th endeavoured to avoid comu what is called a sympathy He takes a political view of —is disposed to deal with would have dealt with the Spain or Portugal, revolting or Greece revolting from I like to state here what I eminent American. He ask give him an idea of the cours in this country from the m the secession of the Cotton deavoured to trace it in th you to say whether it is a fa tion. I said—and my hon. friend has admitted that—that when the revolt or secession was first announced, people here were generally against the South. Nobody thought then that the South had any cause for breaking up the integrity of that great nation. Their opinion was, and what people said, according to their different politics in this country was, "they have a Government which is mild, and not in any degree oppressive; they have not what some people love very much, and what some people dislike,—they have not a costly monarchy, and an aristocracy, creating and living on patronage. They have not an expensive foreign policy; a great army; a great navy; and they have no suffering millions to be discontented and endeavouring to overthrow their Government;—all of which things have been said against Governments in this country and in Europe a hundred times within our own hearing"—and therefore they said, "Why should these men revolt?" But for a moment the Washington Government appeared paralysed. It had no army and navy; everybody was traitor to it. It was paralyzed and apparently helpless; and in the hour when the Government was transferred from President Buchanan to President Lincoln many people—such was the unprepared state of the North—such was the apparent paralysis of everything there—thought there would be no war; and men shook hands with each other pleasantly, and congratulated themselves that the disaster of a great strife, and the mischief to our own trade, might be avoided. That was the opinion at that moment, so far as I can recollect, and could gather at the time, with my opportunities of gathering such opinion. They thought the North would acquiesce in the rending of the Republic, and that there would be no war. Well, but there was another reason. They were told by certain public writers in this country that the contest was entirely hopeless, as they have been told lately by the Chancellor of the Exchequer. I am very happy that though the Chancellor of the Exchequer is able to decide to a penny what shall be the amount of taxes to meet public expenditure in England, he cannot decide what shall be the fate of a whole continent. It was said that the contest was hopeless, and why should the North continue a contest at so much loss of blood and treasure, and so great a loss to the commerce of the whole world? If a man thought—if a man believed in his heart that the contest was absolutely hopeless,—no man in this country had probably any right to form a positive opinion one way or the other— but if he had formed that opinion, he might think, "Well, the North can never be successful; it would be much better that they should not carry on the war at all; and, therefore, I am rather glad that the South should have

success, for, by that, the war will be the sooner put an end to." I think that was a feeling that was abroad. Now, I am of opinion that, if we judge a foreign nation in the circumstances in which we find America, we ought to apply it to our own principles. My honourable friend has referred, I think, to the question of the *Trent*. I was not here last year, but I heard of a meeting—I read in the papers of a meeting held in reference to that affair in this very Hall, and that there was a great diversity of opinion. But the majority were supposed to endorse the policy of the Government in making a great demonstration of force. And I think I read that at least one minister of religion took that view from this platform. I am not complaining of it. But I say that if you thought when the American captain, even if he had acted under the commands of his Government, which he had not, had taken two men most injurious and hostile to his country from the deck of an English ship—if you thought that on that ground you were justified in going to war with the Republic of North America; then I say you ought not to be very nice in judging what America should do in circumstances much more onerous than those in which you were placed. Now, take as an illustration the Rock of Gibraltar. Many of you have been there, I dare say. I have; and among the things that interested me were the monkeys on the top of it, and a good many people at the bottom, who were living on English taxes. Well, the Rock of Gibraltar was taken and retained by this country when we were not at war with Spain, and it was retained contrary to every moral and honourable code. But I will let this pass, and I will assume that it came into the possession of England in the most honourable way, which is, I suppose, by regular and acknowledged national warfare. Suppose, at this moment, you heard, or the English Government heard, that Spain was equipping expeditions, by land and sea, for the purpose of re-taking that fortress and rock —now, although it is not of the slightest advantage to any Englishman living, excepting to those who have pensions and occupations upon it; although every Government knows it, and although more than one Government has been anxious to give it up, and I hope this Government will send my friend, Mr. Cobden, to Madrid, with an offer that Gibraltar shall be ceded to Spain, as being of no use to this country, and only embittering, as statesmen have admitted, the relations between Spain and England (if he were to go to Madrid, with an offer of the Rock of Gibraltar, I believe he might have a commercial treaty with Spain, that would admit every English manufacture, and every article of English produce into that country at a duty of not more than ten per cent.)—I say, don't you think that if you heard

Spain was about to retake that useless rock, mustering her legions and her fleets, that the English Government would combine all the power of this country to resist it? If that be so, then I think—seeing that there was a fair election two years ago, and that President Lincoln was fairly and honestly elected—that when the Southern leaders met at Montgomery, in Alabama, on the 6th of March, and authorized the raising of a hundred thousand men, and when, on the 15th of April, they attacked Fort Sumter—not a fort of South Carolina, but a fort of the Union — then, upon all the principles that Englishmen and English Governments have ever acted upon, President Lincoln was justified in calling out seventy-five thousand men—which was his first call—for the purpose of maintaining the integrity of that nation, which was the main purpose of the oath which he had taken at his election.

Now I shall not go into a long argument upon this question, for the reason that a year ago I said what I thought it necessary to say upon it, and because I believe the question is in the hand, not of my honourable friend, or in that of Lord Palmerston, or in that even of President Lincoln, but it is in the hand of the Supreme Ruler, who is bringing about one of those great transactions in history which men often will not regard when it is passing before them, but which they look back upon with awe and astonishment some years after they are past. So I shall content myself with asking one or two questions. I shall not discuss the question whether the North is making war for the Constitution, or making war for the abolition of slavery. If you come to a matter of sympathy with the South, or recognition of the South, or mediation or intervention for the benefit of the South, you should consider what are the ends of the South. Surely the United States Government is a Government at amity with this country. Its minister is in London—a man honourable by family, as you know, in America, his father and his grandfather having held the office of President of the Republic. You have your own minister just returned to Washington. Is this hypocrisy? Are you, because you can cavil at certain things which the North, the United States Government, has done, or has not done—are you eagerly to throw the influence of your opinion into a movement which is to dismember the great Republic? Is there a man here that doubts for a moment that the object of the war on the part of the South—they began the war—that the object of the war on the part of the South is to maintain the bondage of four millions of human beings? That is only a small part of it. The further object is to perpetuate for ever the bondage of all the posterity of those four millions of slaves. You will hear that I am not in a condition to contest vigorously anything that may be opposed, for I am suffering, as nearly everybody is, from the state of the weather, and a hoarseness that somewhat hinders me in speaking. I could quote their own documents till twelve o'clock in proof of what I say; and, if I found a man who denied, upon the evidence that had been offered, I would not offend him, or trouble myself by trying further to convince him. The object is that a handful of white men on that continent shall lord it over countless millions of blacks, made black by the very hand that made us white. The object is that they should have the power to breed negroes, to work negroes, to lash negroes, to chain negroes, to buy and sell negroes, to deny them the commonest ties of family, or to break their hearts by rending them at their pleasure, to close their mental eye to but a glimpse of that knowledge which separates us from the brute—for in their laws it is criminal and penal to teach the negro to read—to seal from their hearts the book of our religion, and to make chattels and things of men and women and children. Now, I want to ask whether this is to be the foundation, as it is proposed, of a new slave empire, and whether it is intended that on this audacious and infernal basis England's new ally is to be built up. It has been said that Greece was recognised, and that other countries had been recognised. Why, Greece was not recognised till after they had fought Turkey for six years—and the Republics of South America, some of them, till they had fought the mother country for a score of years. France did not recognise the United States of America till some, I think six years, five certainly, after the beginning of the War of Independence, and even then, it was received as a declaration of war by the English Government. I want to know who they are who speak eagerly in favour of England becoming the ally and friend of this great conspiracy against human nature? Now I should have no kind of objection to recognise a country because it was a country that held slaves; to recognise the United States or to be in amity with it. The question of slavery there, and in Cuba, and in Brazil, is, as far as respects the present generation, an accident, and it would be monstrous that we should object to trade with, and have political relations with a country merely because it happened to have within its borders the institution of slavery, hateful as that institution is. But in this case it is a new state intending to set itself up on the sole basis of slavery. Slavery is blasphemously set up to be its chief corner-stone. I have heard that there are ministers of state who are in favour of the South; that there are members of the aristocracy who are terrified at the shadow of the Great Republic; that there are rich men on our commercial exchanges, depraved, it may be, with their riches, and thriving unwholesomely within the atmosphere of a privileged class; that there are conductors of the public press who would barter the rights of millions of their fellow-creatures that they might bask in the smiles of the great. But I know that there are ministers of state who do not wish that this insurrection should break up the American nation; that there are members of our aristocracy who are not afraid of the shadow of the Republic; that there are rich men, many, who are not depraved by their riches; and that there are public writers of eminence and honour, who will not barter human rights for the patronage of the great. But most of all, and before all, I believe—I am sure it is true in Lancashire, where the working men have seen themselves coming down from prosperity to ruin, from independence to a subsistence on charity—I say that I believe that the unenfranchised, but not hopeless millions of this country, will never sympathise with a revolt which is intended to destroy the liberty of a continent, and to build on its ruins a mighty fabric of human bondage.

When I speak to gentlemen in private upon this matter, and hear their own candid opinion —I mean those who differ from me on this matter—they generally end by saying that the Republic is too great and too powerful, and that it is better for us—not " us," meaning you, but the governing classes, and the governing policy of England—that it should be broken up. But we will suppose that we are in New York or Boston, and are discussing England; and if any one there were to say that England has grown too big—not in the thirty-one millions that it has in its own island, but in the one hundred and fifty millions it has in Asia, and nobody knows how many millions in every other part of the globe—and surely an American might fairly say that he has not covered the ocean with fleets of force, or left the bones of his citizens to blanch on a hundred European battle-fields—he could say, and a thousand times more fairly say, that England was large and powerful, and that it would be perilous for the world that she should be so great. But, bear in mind, that every declaration of this kind, whether from an Englishman who professes to be strictly English, or from an American strictly American, or from a Frenchman strictly French, whether he talks in a proud and arrogant strain, and says that Britannia rules the waves, or whether, as an American, he speaks of manifest destiny, and of all creation adoring the stars and stripes, or a Frenchman who thinks that the eagles of that nation having once over-run Europe, may possibly have a right to repeat the experiment,—I say all these ideas and all that language are to be condemned. It is not truly patriotic; it is not rational; it is not moral. Then, I say, if any man wishes that Republic to be severed on that ground, in my opinion he is only doing what tends to keep alive jealousies which in his hand will never die; and if they do not die, for anything I see, wars must be eternal. But then, I shall be told that the North do not like us at all. In fact, we have heard it to-night. It is not at all necessary that they should like us. If an American be in this room to-night, will he think he likes my hon. friend? But if the North does not like England, does anybody believe the South does? It does not appear to me to be a question of liking or disliking. Everybody knows that when the South was in power—and it has been in power for the last fifty years—everybody knows that hostility to this country, wherever it existed in America, was cherished and stimulated to the utmost degree by some of those very men who are now leaders of this very insurrection. My hon. friend read a passage about the Alabama. I undertake to say that he is not acquainted with the facts about the Alabama. That he will admit, I think. The Government of this country have admitted that the building of the Alabama, and her sailing from the Mersey, was a violation of international law. In America they say, and they say here, that the Alabama is a ship of war; that she was built in the Mersey—that she was built, it is said, and I have reason to believe it, by a member of the British Parliament—that she is furnished with guns of English manufacture and produce— that she is sailed almost entirely by Englishmen —and that these facts were represented, as I know they were represented, to the Collector of Customs in Liverpool, who pooh-poohed them, and said there was nothing in them. He was requested to send the facts up to London to the Customs authorities, and their solicitor, not a very wise man, or probably in favour of breaking up the Republic, did not think them of much consequence, but afterwards the opinion of an eminent counsel, Mr. Collier, the member for Plymouth, was taken, and he stated distinctly that what was being done in Liverpool was a direct infringement of the Foreign Enlistment Act, and that the Customs authorities of Liverpool would be responsible for anything that happened in consequence. When this opinion was taken to the Foreign Office the Foreign Office was a little astonished and a little troubled; and after they had consulted their own law officers, whose opinions agreed with that of Mr. Collier, they did what Government officers generally do, and as promptly—a telegraphic message went down to Liverpool to order that this vessel should be arrested, and she happened to sail an hour or two before the message arrived. She has never been into a Confederate port; they have not got any ports; she hoists the English flag when she wants to come alongside a ship; she sets a ship on fire in the night, and when, seeing fire, another ship bears down to lend help, she seizes it, and pillages and burns it. I think that if we were citizens of New York, it would require a little more calmness than is shown in this country to look at all this as if it was a matter with which we had no concern. And, therefore, I do not so much blame the words that have been said in America, in reference to that question. But they do not know in America so much as we know—the whole truth about public opinion here. There are Ministers in our Cabinet as resolved to be no traitors to freedom—on this question, as I am; and there are members of the English aristocracy, and in the very highest rank, as I know for a certainty, who hold the same opinion. They do not know in America—at least there has been no indication of it until the advices that have come to hand within the last two days—what is the opinion of the great body of the working classes in England. There has been every effort that money and malice could use to stimulate in Lancashire, amongst the suffering population, an expression of opinion in favour of the Slave States. They have not been able to get it. And I honour that population for their fidelity to principles and to freedom, and I say that the course they have taken ought to atone in the minds of the people of the United States for miles of leading articles, written by the London press—by men who would barter every human right, that they might serve the party with which they are associated.

But now I shall ask you one other question before I sit down,—how comes it that on the Continent there is not a liberal newspaper, nor a liberal politician that durst say, or ever thought of saying a word in favour of this portentous and monstrous shape which now asks to be received into the family of nations? Take the great Italian minister, Count Cavour. You read some time ago in the papers part of a despatch which he wrote on the question of America—he had no difficulty in deciding. Ask Garibaldi. Is there in Europe a more disinterested and generous friend of freedom than Garibaldi? Ask that illustrious Hungarian, to whose marvellous eloquence you once listened in this Hall. Will he tell you that slavery had nothing to do with it, and that the slaveholders of the South would liberate the negroes sooner than the North through the instrumentality of the war? Ask Victor Hugo, the poet of freedom —the exponent, may I not call him, of the yearnings of all mankind for a better time. Ask any man in Europe who opens his lips for freedom—who dips his pen in ink that he may indite a sentence for freedom—whoever has a sympathy for freedom warm in his own heart; ask him—he will have no difficulty in telling you on which side your sympathies should lie. Only a few days ago a German merchant in Manchester was speaking to a friend of mine, and said he had recently travelled all through Germany, He said, " I am so surprised; I don't find one man in favour of the South." That is not true of Germany only, it is true of all the world except this island, famed for freedom, in which we dwell. I will tell you what is the reason. Our London press is mainly in the hands of certain ruling West End classes; it acts and writes in favour of those classes. I will tell you what they mean. One of the most eminent statesmen in this country—one who has rendered the greatest services to the country —though, I must say not in an official capacity, in which men very seldom confer such great advantages upon the country—he told me twice at an interval of several months, " I had no idea how much influence the example of that Republic was having upon opinion here, until I discovered the universal congratulation that the Republic was likely to be broken up." But, sir, the Free States are the home of the working man. Now, I speak to working men particularly at this moment. Do you know that in fifteen years 2,500,000 persons, men, women, and children, have left the United Kingdom to find a home in the Free States of America? That is a population equal to eight great cities of the size of Birmingham. What would you think of eight Birminghams being transplanted from this country and set down in the United States? Speaking generally, every man of these two-and-a-half millions is in a position of much higher comfort and prosperity than he would have been if he had remained in this country. I say it is the home of the working man; as one of her poets has recently said:

"For her free latch-string never was drawn in
Against the poorest child of Adam's kin."

And there, there are no six millions of grown men—I speak of the Free States—excluded from the constitution of their country and their electoral franchise—there, there is a free Church — a free school, free land, a free vote, and a free career for the child of the humblest-born in the land. My countrymen, who work for your living, remember this; there will be one wild shriek of freedom to startle all mankind, if that American Republic should be overthrown. Now, for one moment let us lift ourselves, if we can, above the narrow circle in which we are all too apt to live and think; let us put ourselves on an historical eminence, and judge this matter fairly. Slavery has been, as we all know, the huge, foul blot upon the fame of the American Republic; it is a hideous outrage against human right and against Divine law; but the pride, the passion of man will not permit its peaceable extinction; the slave-owners of our colonies, if they had been strong enough, would have revolted too. I believe there was no mode short of a miracle more stupendous than any recorded in Holy Writ that could in our time, or in a century, have brought about the abolition of slavery in America, but the suicide which the South has committed and the war which they have commenced. Sir, it is a measureless calamity—this war. I said the Russian war was a measureless calamity, and yet many of your leaders and friends told you that was a just war to maintain the integrity of Turkey, some thousands of miles off. Surely the integrity of your own country at your own doors must be worth as much as the integrity of Turkey. Is not this war the penalty which inexorable justice exacts from America, North and South, for the enormous guilt of cherishing that frightful iniquity of slavery for the last eighty years? I do not blame any man here who thinks the cause of the North hopeless, and the restoration of the Union impossible. It may be hopeless; the restoration may be impossible. You have the authority of the Chancellor of the Exchequer on that point. The Chancellor, as a speaker, is not surpassed by any man in England; but unfortunately he made use of expressions in the North of England—now, I suppose, nearly three months ago —and he seems to have been engaged during the whole succeeding three months in trying to make people understand what he meant. But this is obvious—that he believes the cause of the North to be hopeless; that their enterprise cannot succeed. Well, he is quite welcome to that opinion, and so is anybody else. I do not hold the opinion, but the facts are before us all, and as far as we can discard passion and sympathy, we are all equally at liberty to form our own opinion. But what I do blame is this. I blame men who are eager to admit into the family of nations, a State which offers itself to you as based upon a principle, I will undertake to say more odious and more blasphemous than was ever heretofore dreamt of in Christian or Pagan, in civilized or in savage times. The leaders of this revolt propose this monstrous thing—that over a territory forty times as large as England, the blight and curse of slavery shall be for ever perpetuated. I cannot believe, myself, in such a fate befalling that fair land, stricken as it now is with the ravages of war. I cannot believe that civilization in its journey with the sun will sink into endless night to gratify the ambition of the leaders of this revolt, who seek to—

" Wade through slaughter to a throne,
And shut the gates of mercy on mankind."

I have a far other and far brighter vision before my gaze. It may be but a vision, but I will cherish it. I see one vast Confederation stretching from the frozen North in unbroken line to the glowing South, and from the wild billows of the Atlantic, westward to the calmer waters of the Pacific main—and I see one people, and one law, and one language, and one faith, over all that wide continent, the home of freedom, and a refuge for the oppressed of every race and of every clime.

CHARLES DICKENS.
Born 1812.

[THE name of Charles Dickens is not perhaps often associated with oratory. The inclination of Mr. Dickens has apparently been rather to withdraw himself from the burdensome activities of public life, and he has, in accordance with such inclination, (on more than one occasion, it is believed,) declined the offer of parliamentary honours. The few speeches, however, which he has from time to time delivered in public, have been characterized by many marks of true eloquence; and upon all subjects connected with the advancement, education, and general welfare of the great masses of his fellow-countrymen, he has always spoken as a true and consistent champion of the noblest principles of toleration and sympathy. Above all things, that large-hearted charity and genial common sense, which are among the chief and best attributes of his world-famous writings, are found also to pervade and animate his oratory. The speech which has been here selected as a specimen of Mr. Dickens's genius in this comparatively uncultivated field of his powers, was delivered in the year 1843 at the opening of the Athenæum at Manchester. The address abounds with sterling thought, bright humour, and the soundest common sense.]

MECHANICS' INSTITUTES.

LADIES AND GENTLEMEN—I am sure I need scarcely tell you that I am very proud and happy, and that I take it as a great distinction, to be asked to come amongst you on an occasion such as this, when even with the brilliant and beautiful spectacle which I see before me, I can hail it as the most brilliant and beautiful circumstance of all, that we assemble together here, even here, upon neutral ground, where we have no more knowledge of party differences, or public animosities between side and side, or between man and man, than if we were a public meeting in the commonwealth of Utopia. Ladies and gentlemen, upon this and upon a hundred other grounds, this assembly is not less interesting to me, believe me, although personally almost a stranger here, than it is interesting to you; and I take it, that it is not of greater importance to all of us than it is to every man who has learned to know that he has an interest in the moral and social elevation, the harmless relaxation, the peace, happiness, and improvement, of the community at large. Not even those who saw the first foundation of your Athenæum laid, and watched its progress, as I know they did, almost as tenderly as if it were the progress of a living creature, until it reared its beautiful front an honour to the town, —not even they, nor even you, who within its walls have tasted its usefulness and put it to the proof, have greater reason, I am persuaded, to exult in its establishment, or to hope that it may thrive and prosper, than scores of thousands at a distance, who — whether consciously or unconsciously matters not—have, in the principle of its success and bright example, a deep and personal concern. It well becomes, particularly well becomes, this enterprising town, this little world of labour, that she should stand out foremost in the foremost rank in such a cause. It well becomes her, that among her numerous and noble public institutions, she should have a splendid temple sacred to the education and improvement of a large class of those who, in their various useful stations, assist in the production of our wealth, and in rendering her name famous through the world. I think it is grand to know, that while her factories re-echo with the clanking of stupendous engines and the whirl and rattle of machinery, the immortal mechanism of God's own hand, the mind, is not forgotten in the din and uproar, but is lodged and tended in a palace of its own. Ladies and gentlemen, that it is a structure deeply fixed and rooted in the public spirit of this place, and built to last, I have no more doubt, judging from the spectacle I see before me, and from what I know of its brief history, than I have of the reality of these walls that hem us in, and the pillars that spring up about us. You are perfectly well aware, I have no doubt, that the Athenæum was projected at a time when commerce was in a vigorous and flourishing condition, and when those classes of society to which it particularly addresses itself were fully employed, and in the receipt of regular incomes. A season of depression almost without a parallel ensued, and large numbers of young men employed in warehouses and offices suddenly found their occupation gone, and themselves reduced to very straitened and penurious circumstances. This altered state of things led, as I am told, to the compulsory withdrawal of many of the members, to a proportionate decrease in the expected funds, and to the incurrence of a debt of £3,000. By the very great zeal and energy of all concerned, and by the liberality of those to whom they applied for help, that debt is now in rapid course of being discharged. A little more of the same indefatigable exertion on the one hand, and a little more of the same community of feeling upon the other, and there will be no such thing; the figures will be blotted out for good and all, and from that time the Athenæum may be said to belong to you and to your heirs for ever. But, ladies and gentlemen, at all times now, in its most thriving, and in its least flourishing condition—here, with its cheerful rooms; its pleasant and instructive lectures; its improving library of 6,000 volumes; its classes for the study of the foreign languages, elocution, music; its opportunities of discussion and debate, of healthful bodily exercise; and, though last, not least,—for by this I set great store as a very novel and excellent provision,—its opportunities of blameless, rational enjoyment;—here it is, open to every youth and man in this great town, accessible to every bee in this vast hive, who, for all these benefits, and the inestimable ends to which they lead, can set aside one sixpence weekly. I do look upon the reduction of the subscription to that amount, and upon the fact that the number of members has considerably more than doubled within the last twelve months, as strides in the path of the very best civilization, and chapters of rich promise in the history of mankind. I don't know whether, at this time of day, and with such a prospect before us, we need trouble ourselves very much to rake up the ashes of the dead-and-gone objections that were wont to be urged by men of all parties against institutions such as this, whose interests we are met to promote; but their philosophy was always to be summed up in the unmeaning application of one short sentence. How often have we heard, from a large class of men, wise in their generation, who would really seem to be born and bred for no other purpose than to pass into currency counterfeit and mischievous scraps of wisdom, as it is the sole pursuit of some other criminals to utter base coin,—how often have we heard from them, as an all-convincing argument, that "a little learning is a dangerous thing"! Why, a little hanging was considered a very dangerous thing, according to the same authorities, with this difference, that, because a little hanging was dangerous, we had a great deal of it; and because a little learning was dangerous, we were to have none at all.—Why, when I hear such cruel absurdities gravely reiterated, I do sometimes begin to doubt whether the parrots of society are not more pernicious to its interests than its birds of prey. I should be glad to hear such people's estimate of the comparative danger of "a little learning," and a vast amount of ignorance; I should be glad to know which they consider the most prolific parent of misery and crime. Descending a little lower in the social scale, I should be glad to assist them in their calculations, by carrying them into certain gaols and nightly refuges I know of, where my own heart dies within me, when I see thousands of immortal creatures, condemned, without alternative or choice, to tread, not what our great poet calls—

"The primrose path to the everlasting bonfire,"

but one of jagged flints and stones, laid down by brutal ignorance, and held together like the solid rocks by years of this most wicked axiom. Would we know, from any honourable body of merchants, upright in deed and thought, whether they would rather have ignorant or enlightened persons in their own employment? Why, we

er in this building; we have
; we have it emphatically
ent generosity of your own
iester, of all sects and kinds,
hment was first proposed.
lemen, are the advantages
ople from institutions such
negative character?—If a
a innocent thing, has it no
, and immediate influence
The old doggrel rhyme, so
e beginning of books, says

l lands are gone and spent,
s most excellent;"

ngly disposed to reform the
—
nd lands be never got,
ve what they can *not*."

iat the first unpurchasable
every man who makes an
nself in such a place as the
spect—an inward dignity of
ice acquired and righteously
g — no, not the hardest
direst poverty — can van-
should find it hard for a
the wolf, hunger, from his
ace have chased the dragon,
hearth, and self-respect and
-You could no more deprive
lining qualities by loss or
worldly goods, than you
out his eyes, take from him
isness of the bright glory of
who lives from day to day
e, in his sphere, of hands or
improve himself in such a
æum, acquires for himself
ul which has in all times
men of every degree, but
pecially and always. He
that faithful companion
s ever lent the light of its
of rank and eminence who
has ever shed its brightest
i of low estate and almost
t took its patient seat beside
in his dungeon study in the
head upon the block with
ot disdain to watch the stars
shepherd's boy; it walked
i attire with Crabbe; it was
) in Lancashire with Ark-
tallow-chandler's son with
ked at shoemaking with
irret; it followed the plough
igh above the noise of loom
ispers courage even at this
ild name in Sheffield and
The more the man who

improves his leisure in such a place learns, the better, gentler, kinder man he must become. When he knows how much great minds have suffered for the truth in every age and time, and to what dismal persecutions opinion has been exposed, he will become more tolerant of other men's belief in all matters, and will incline more leniently to their sentiments when they chance to differ from his own. Understanding that the relations between himself and his employers involve a mutual duty and responsibility, he will discharge his part of the implied contract cheerfully, satisfactorily, and honourably; for the history of every useful life warns him to shape his course in that direction. The benefits he acquires in such a place are not of a selfish kind, but extend themselves to his home, and to those whom it contains. Something of what he hears or reads within such walls can scarcely fail to become at times a topic of discourse by his own fireside, nor can it ever fail to lead to larger sympathies with man, and to a higher veneration for the great Creator of all the wonders of this universe. It appeals to his home and his homely feeling in other ways; for at certain times he carries there his wife and daughter, or his sister, or, possibly, some bright-eyed acquaintance of a more tender description. Judging from what I see before me, I think it is very likely; I am sure I would if I could. He takes her there to enjoy a pleasant evening, to be gay and happy. Sometimes it may possibly happen that he dates his tenderness from the Athenæum. I think that is a very excellent thing, too, and not the least among the advantages of the institution. In any case, I am sure the number of bright eyes and beaming faces which grace this meeting to-night by their presence will never be among the least of its excellences in my recollection. Ladies and gentlemen, I shall not easily forget this scene, the pleasing task your favour has devolved upon me, or the strong and inspiring confirmation I have to-night, of all the hopes and reliances I have ever placed upon institutions of this nature. In the latter point of view,— in their bearing upon this latter point,—I regard them as of great importance, deeming that the more intelligent and reflective society in the mass becomes, and the more readers there are, the more distinctly writers of all kinds will be able to throw themselves upon the truthful feeling of the people, and the more honoured and the more useful literature must be. At the same time I must confess, that, if there had been an Athenæum, and if the people had been readers years ago, some leaves of dedication in your library, of praise of patrons, which was very cheaply bought, very dearly sold, and very marketably haggled for by the great, would be blank leaves, and posterity might probably have lacked the information that certain monsters of virtue ever had existence. But it is upon a much better and wider scale, let me say it once again, that it is in the effect of such institutions upon the great social system, and the peace and happiness of mankind, that I delight to contemplate them; and, in my heart I am quite certain, that long after your institution, and others of the same nature, have crumbled into dust, the noble harvest of the seed sown in them will shine out brightly in the wisdom, the mercy, and the forbearance of another race.

OLIVER CROMWELL.
Born 1599. *Died* 1658.

DISSOLUTION OF THE SECOND PROTECTORATE PARLIAMENT, FEB. 4TH, 1657-8.

I HAD very comfortable expectations that God would make the meeting of this Parliament a blessing; and the Lord be my witness I desired the carrying-on the affairs of the nation to these ends. The blessing which I mean, and which we ever climbed at, was mercy, truth, righteousness, and peace; and which I desire may be improved.

That which brought me into the capacity I now stand in, was the petition and advice given me by you; who, in reference to the ancient constitution, did draw me to accept of the place of Protector. There is not a man living can say I sought it; no, not a man nor woman treading upon English ground; but contemplating the sad condition of these nations, relieved from an intestine war, into a six or seven years' peace, I did think the nation happy therein. But to be petitioned thereunto, and advised by you to undertake such a government, a burden too heavy for any creature, and this to be done by the House that then had the legislative capacity; I did look that the same men that made the frame, should make it good unto me. I can say, in the presence of God, in comparison with whom we are but like poor creeping ants upon the earth, I would have been glad to have lived under my wood side, to have kept a flock of sheep, rather than undertook such a government as this is; but, undertaking it by the advice and petition of you, I did look that you that had offered it unto me, should make it good.

I did tell you, at a conference concerning it, that I would not undertake it, unless there might be some other persons that might interpose between me and the House of Commons, who then had the power to prevent tumultuary and popular spirits, and it was granted I should name another House. I named it of men that shall meet you wheresoever you go, and shake hands with you, and tell you it is not titles, nor lords, nor party, that they value, but a Christian and an English interest; me[n] and quality, who will not onl[y obey] you, but to themselves, while[ ] and religion.

Having proceeded upon [this,] finding such a spirit as is too [rare,] everything being too high [for] virtue, honesty, piety, and j[ustice,] I thought I had been doing [my] duty, and thought it would [do,] but if everything must be t[o] you are not to be satisfied.

Again, I would not hav[e under]government, unless I knew [there was] just accord between the gov[ernment and the] verned; unless they would t[ake in] good what the Parliament's [advice] advised me unto; upon that [account] they took another oath upon [being] able to mine; and did not ev[er know] what condition they swore? [I took] it upon the conditions expre[ssed in the Instru]ment, and I did think we [had a good] foundation, and upon a botto[m ...] I thought myself bound to [act as I was] advised by the two Houses o[f Parliament,] we standing unsettled till [then; and] that, the consequences woul[d have] been confusion, if that had [not been done.] Yet there are not constitute[d, in these nations,] nor hereditary kings; the pow[er lies between the] two Houses and myself. I d[o not know] the meaning of your oath [unless you] were to go against my own [judgment or] upon another man's conscienc[e, which is] between me and you. If the[re had been] any intention of settlement, [it would have been] settled upon this basis, and [upon this] judgment and opinion.

God is my witness, I speak [before] all the world, and all people[; my] business hath been seeking in [all] this actual settlement made b[y law. I] do not speak to these ge[ntlemen —] (*pointing to his right hand*) [I] will call them. I speak not [so much] to you; you advised me to r[efuse] to be in a capacity by your [advice] of owning a thing taken for g[ranted I] have I know not what; and [you have] disjointed yourselves, but [that] which is in likelihood of r[aising] confusion, in these fifteen o[r sixteen days] you have sat, than it hath be[en the work] of the last session to this [present; the] intention of devising a com[monwealth,] that some of the people mig[ht] might rule all; and they ar[e ready to] engage the army to carry that [on; but] that man hath been true to this n[ation shall] be, especially that hath take[n an oath not to] prevaricate? These designs the army to break and divide us. I speak this in the presence of some of the army, that these things have not been according to God, nor according to truth, pretend what you will. These things tend to nothing else but the playing the king of Scots' game, if I may so call him; and I think myself bound, before God, to do what I can to prevent it.

That which I told you in the Banqueting House was true; that there were preparations of force to invade us; God is my witness, it has been confirmed to me since, within a day, that the king of Scots hath an army at the water side, ready to be shipped for England. I have it from those who have been eye-witnesses of it; and while it is doing, there are endeavours from some, who are not far from this place, to stir up the people of this town into a tumulting. What if I had said into a rebellion? And I hope I shall make it appear to be no better, if God assist me. It hath been not only your endeavour to pervert the army, while you have been sitting, and to draw them to state the question about the commonwealth; but some of you have been listing of persons, by commission of Charles Stuart, to join with any insurrection that may be made. And what is like to come upon this, the enemy being ready to invade us, but even present blood and confusion? And if this be so, I do assign to this cause your not assenting to what you did invite me to by the petition and advice, as that which might be the settlement of the nation; and if this be the end of your sitting, and this be your carriage, I think it high time that an end be put unto your sitting, and I do dissolve this Parliament. And let God judge between me and you.

JOHN MILTON.

Born 1608. *Died* 1674.

RIGHTS AND RESPONSIBILITIES OF THE PRESS.

I DENY not, but that it is of greatest concernment in the church and commonwealth, to have a vigilant eye how books demean themselves as well as men; and thereafter to confine, imprison, and do sharpest justice on them as malefactors; for books are not absolutely dead things, but do contain a progeny of life in them to be as active as that soul was whose progeny they are; nay, they do preserve as in a vial the purest efficacy and extraction of that living intellect that bred them. I know they are as lively, and as vigorously productive, as those fabulous dragon's teeth; and being sown up and down, may chance to spring up armed men. And yet, on the other hand, unless wariness be used, as good almost kill a man as kill a good book; who kills a man kills a reasonable creature, God's image; but he who destroys a good book, kills reason itself, kills the image of God, as it were, in the eye. Many a man lives a burden to the earth; but a good book is the precious life-blood of a master-spirit, embalmed and treasured up on purpose to a life beyond life. It is true, no age can restore a life, whereof, perhaps, there is no great loss; and revolutions of ages do not oft recover the loss of a rejected truth, for the want of which whole nations fare the worse. We should be wary, therefore, what persecutions we raise against the living labours of public men, how we spill that seasoned life of man, preserved and stored up in books; since we see a kind of homicide may be thus committed, sometimes a martyrdom; and if it extend to the whole impression, a kind of massacre, whereof the execution ends not in the slaying of an elemental life, but strikes at the ethereal and fifth essence, the breath of reason itself; and slays an immortality rather than a life.

LORD BROUGHAM.

Born 1778.

[SPEECH of Mr. Brougham, in defence of Queen Caroline, the Consort of King George the Fourth, on the 3rd and 4th October, 1820, at her trial before the House of Lords, for adultery with Bergami, an Italian in her service.

The proceedings instituted by George the Fourth against his unfortunate and injured wife, for the purpose of degrading her and dissolving the marriage, have become a matter of history, and there is no reason to enter here into the details of that disgraceful inquiry. The exhibition of a sovereign, himself the most unfaithful of husbands, suborning a host of unscrupulous Italians to perjure themselves for the sake of freeing him from a wife whom he did not fancy, might well be suffered to pass unnoticed by us, if it were not for the necessary slight thereby to some of the noblest oratorical efforts of English lawyers.

Though the proceedings ended in the withdrawal of the Bill of Degradation and Divorce, the persecution of the Queen still continued. Her name was not inserted in the Liturgy, and her coronation was refused. The effect of her sorrows upon her mind and body may be traced in the inscription she desired to have placed upon her coffin: "Caroline of Brunswick, the murdered Queen of England."]

DEFENCE OF QUEEN CAROLINE.

MY LORDS, the Princess Caroline of Brunswick arrived in this country in the year 1795—the niece of our sovereign, the intended consort of his heir-apparent, and herself not a very remote heir to the crown of these realms. But I now go back to that period only for the purpose of passing over all the interval which elapsed between her arrival then and her departure in 1814. I rejoice that, for the present at least, the most faithful discharge of my duty permits me to draw this veil; but I cannot do so without pausing for an instant, to guard myself against a misrepresentation to which I know this cause may not unnaturally be exposed, and to assure your lordships most solemnly, that if I did not think that the cause of the Queen, as attempted to be established by the evidence against her, not only does not require recrimination at present,—not only imposes no duty of even uttering one whisper, whether by way of attack or by way of insinuation, against the conduct of her illustrious husband; but that it rather prescribes to me, for the present, silence upon this great and painful head of the case,—I solemnly assure your lordships, that but for this conviction, my lips on that branch would NOT be closed; for, in discretionally abandoning the exercise of the power which I feel I have, in postponing for the present the statement of that case of which I am possessed, I feel confident that I am waiving a right which I possess, and abstaining from the use of materials which are mine. And let it not be thought, my lords, that if either now I did conceive, or if hereafter I should so far be disappointed in my expectation that the case against me will fail, as to feel it necessary to exercise that right,—let no man vainly suppose that not only I, but that any, the youngest member of the profession, would hesitate one moment in the fearless discharge of his paramount duty. I once before took leave to remind your lordships,—which was unnecessary, but there are many whom it may be necessary to remind,—that an advocate, by the sacred duty which he owes his client, knows, in the discharge of that office, but one person in the world,—THAT CLIENT, AND NONE OTHER. To save that client by all expedient means,—to protect that client at all hazards and costs to all others, and among others to himself,—is the highest and most unquestioned of his duties; and he must not regard the alarm—the suffering—the torment—the destruction—which he may bring upon any other. Nay, separating even the duties of a patriot from those of an advocate, and casting them, if need be, to the wind, he must go on reckless of the consequences, if his fate it should unhappily be, to involve his country in confusion for his client's protection!*

* * * *

See, my lords, the unhappy fate of this illustrious woman! It has been her lot always to lose her surest stay, her best protector, when the dangers most thickened around her; and, by a coincidence almost miraculous, there has hardly been one of her defenders withdrawn from her, that his loss has not been the signal for an attack upon her existence. Mr. Pitt was her earliest defender and friend in this country. He died in 1806; and, but a few weeks afterwards, the first inquiry into the conduct of Her Royal Highness began. He left her a legacy to Mr. Perceval, her firm, dauntless, most able advocate. And, no sooner had the hand of an assassin laid Mr. Perceval low, than she felt the calamity of his death, in the renewal of the attacks, which his gallantry, his skill, and his invariable constancy had discomfited. Mr. Whitbread then undertook her defence; and, when that catastrophe happened, which all good men lament without any distinction of party or sect, again commenced the distant growling of the storm; for it then, happily, was never allowed to approach her, because her daughter stood her friend, and some there were who worshipped the rising sun. But, when she lost that amiable and beloved child, all which might have been expected by her—all which might have been dreaded by her if she had not been innocent—all she did dread—because who, innocent or guilty, loves persecution? who delights in trial, even when character and honour are safe?—all was at once allowed to burst upon her head; and the operations began with the Milan Commission. And, as if there were no possibility of the Queen losing a protector without some most important scene against her being played in this too real drama, the day which saw the venerable remains of our revered sovereign consigned to the tomb—of that sovereign who, from the first outset of the Princess in English life, had been her constant and steady defender—that same sun ushered the ringleader of the band of perjured witnesses into the palace of his illustrious successor! Why do I mention these things? Not for the sake of making so trite a remark, as that trading politicians are selfish—that spite is twin-brother to ingratitude—that nothing will bind base natures—that favours conferred, and the duty of gratitude neglected, only make those natures the more spiteful and malignant. My lords, the topic would be trite and general, and I should be ashamed to trouble you with it; but I say this, in order to express once more my deep sense of the unworthiness with which I now succeed such powerful defenders, and my alarm lest my exertions should fail to do what theirs must have accomplished had they survived.

* * * *

But, my lords, I wish I could stop here. There are features of peculiar enormity in the other parts of this case; and in proportion as these disgusting scenes are of a nature to annoy every one, however unconcerned in the cause, who hears them; to disgust and almost contaminate the mind of every one who is condemned to listen to them; in that proportion is especial care taken that they shall not be done in a corner. The place for them is not chosen in the hidden recesses of those receptacles of abomination with which the continent abounds,

---

* Recrimination implied, if it did not include, the Roman Catholic marriage, and forfeiture of the crown.

under the debased and vilified name of palaces; the place is not chosen in the hidden haunts which lust has degraded to its own purposes, some island where vice concealed itself from the public eye of ancient times; it is not in those palaces, in those Capreas of old, that the parties choose to commit such abominations; but they do it before witnesses, in the light of open day, when the sun is at the meridian. And that is not enough: the doing those deeds of. unnatural sin in the public highways is not enough; but they must have a courier of their own to witness them, without the veil of any one part of the furniture of a carriage, or of their own dress, to conceal from his eye their disgraceful situation! My lords, I ask your lordships whether vice was ever known before so unwary; whether folly was ever known so extravagant; whether unthinking passion, even in the most youthful period, when the passions swell high, and the blood boils in the veins, was ever known to act so thoughtlessly, so recklessly, so madly, as this case compels me to fancy, as these shameless witnesses pretend to represent? And when you have put the facts to your minds, let this consideration dwell there, and let it operate as a check, when you come to examine the evidence by which the case is supported.

But all this is nothing. Their kindness to the enemy—their faithfulness to the plot against themselves—their determination to work their own ruin—would be left short indeed, if it had gone no farther than this; for it would then depend upon the good fortune of their adversary in getting hold of the witnesses; at least it might be questionable, whether the greater part of their precautions for their own destruction might not have been thrown away. Therefore, every one of these witnesses, without any exception, is either dismissed without a cause, for I say the causes are mere flimsiness personified, or is refused to be taken back, upon his earnest and humble solicitations, when there was every human inducement to restore them to favour. Even this is not all. Knowing what she had done; recollecting her own contrivances; aware of all these cunning and elaborate devices towards her own undoing; having before her eyes the picture of all those schemes to render detection inevitable and concealment impossible; reflecting that she had given the last finishing stroke to this conspiracy of her own, by turning off these witnesses causelessly, and putting them into the power of her enemy; knowing that that enemy had taken advantage of her; knowing the witnesses were here to destroy her, and told, that if she faced them she was undone; and desired, and counselled, and implored, again and again, to bethink her well before she ran so enormous a risk: the Queen comes to England, and is here, on this spot, and confronts those witnesses whom she had herself enabled to undo her. Menaced with degradation and divorce—knowing it was not an empty threat that was held out—and seeing the denunciation was about to be accomplished—up to this hour she refuses all endeavours towards a compromise of her honour and her rights; she refuses a magnificent retreat and the opportunity of an unrestrained indulgence in all her criminal propensities, and even a safeguard and protection from the court of England, and a vindication of her honour from the two Houses of Parliament! If, my lords, this is the conduct of guilt; if these are the lineaments by which vice is to be traced in the human frame; if these are the symptoms of that worst of all states, dereliction of principle carried to excess, when it almost becomes a mental disease; then I have misread human nature; then I have weakly and groundlessly come to my conclusion; for I have always understood that guilt was wary, and innocence alone improvident.

* * * *

My lords, I would remind you of an argument which is used in the present case, and which I was rather surprised to hear that some persons had been so very regardless of the details, as to allow to influence their otherwise acute and ingenious minds. They say, that if this is a plot—if the witnesses are speaking what is untrue—they have not sworn enough; that they ought to have proved it home, as it were; that they ought to have convinced all mankind, of acts having been unequivocally done which nothing but guilt could account for, acts which were utterly inconsistent with the supposition of innocence. My lords, can those who argue thus, have forgotten two things which every man knows, one common to all cases, and the other happening in every stage of this,—namely, that the most effectual way, because the safest, of laying a plot, is not to swear too hard, is not to swear too much, or to come too directly to the point; but to lay the foundation in existing facts and real circumstances,—to knit the false with the true,—to interlace reality with fiction,—to build the fanciful fabric upon that which exists in nature —and to escape detection by taking most especial care, as they have done here, never to have two witnesses to the same facts, and also to make the facts as moderate, and as little offensive as possible. The architects of this structure have been well aware of these principles, and have followed these known rules of fabrication throughout. At Naples, why were not other people called? Why were there never two witnesses to the same fact? Because it is dangerous; because, when you are inventing a plot, you should have one witness to a fact, and another to a confirmation; have some things true, which unimpeachable evidence can prove; other things fabricated, without which the true would be of no avail,—but avoid calling two witnesses to the same thing at the same time, because the cross-examination is extremely likely to make them contradict each other.

* * * *

But again, my lords—am I to be told by those who have attended to this evidence, that there has been any very great short-coming in the swearing of some of the witnesses,—that they have not sworn unequivocally,—that they have not proved the facts? Why, what more convincing proof of adultery would you have, than you have had in this case, if you believe the witnesses, and they are uncontradicted? I should not indeed say, if they are uncontradicted; for I contend that your lordships ought not to compel me to contradict such witnesses; but if you believe the witnesses, you have a case of adultery as plainly substantiated in proof as ever gained verdict in Westminster Hall, or ever procured Divorce Bill to pass through your lordships' house. All that Demont tells,—all that Majocchi tells,—every tittle of what Sacchi tells at the end of his evidence,—is proof positive of the crime of adultery. If you believe Sacchi, adultery is the least of her crimes—she is as bad as Messalina—she is worse, or as bad as the Jacobins of Paris covered even themselves with eternal infamy by endeavouring to prove Marie Antoinette to have been.

My lords, I have another remark to make, before I leave this case. I have heard it said, by some acute sifters of evidence, "Oh! you have damaged the witnesses, but only by proving falsehoods, by proving perjury indeed, in unimportant particulars." I need but remind your lordships, that this is an observation which can only come from the lay part of the community. Any lawyer at once will see how ridiculous, if I may so speak, such an objection must always be. It springs from an entire confusion of ideas; a heedless confounding together of different things. If I am to confirm the testimony of an accomplice—if I am to set up an informer—no doubt my confirmation ought to extend to matters connected with the crime—no doubt it must be an important particular, else it will avail me nothing to prove it by way of confirmation. But it is quite the reverse in respect to pulling down a perjured witness, or a witness suspected of swearing falsely. It is quite enough if he perjure himself in any part, to take away all credit from the whole of his testimony. Can it be said that you are to pick and choose; that you are to believe part, and reject the rest as false? You may, indeed, be convinced that a part is true, notwithstanding other parts are false—provided those parts are not falsely and wilfully sworn to by the witness, but parts which he may have been ignorant of, or may have forgotten, or may have mistaken. In this sense, you may choose—culling the part you believe, and separating the part you think contradicted. But if one part is not only not true—is not only not consistent with the fact, but is falsely and wilfully sworn to on his part—if you are satisfied that one part of his story is an invention—to use the plain word, a lie, and that he is a forsworn man—good God! my lords, what safety is there for human kind against the malice of their enemies—what chance of innocence escaping from the toils of the perjured and unprincipled conspirator, if you are to believe part of a tale, even though ten witnesses swear to it, all of whom you convict of lying and perjury in some other part of the story? I only pray your lordships to consider what it is that forms the safeguard of each and every one of you against the arts of the mercenary or the spiteful conspirator. Suppose any one man,—and let each of your lordships lay this to his mind before you dismiss the mighty topic,—suppose any one of your lordships were to meet with a misfortune, the greatest that can befall a human being, and the greater in proportion as he is of an honourable mind, whose soul is alien even to any idea or glance of suspicion of such a case being possible to himself, whose feelings shudder at the bare thought of his name even being accidentally coupled with a charge at which his nature revolts—suppose that mischance, which has happened to the best and purest of men, which may happen to any of you to-morrow, and which if it does happen must succeed against you to-morrow, if you adopt the principle I am struggling against—suppose any one of your lordships charged by a mercenary scoundrel with the perpetration of a crime at which we show in this country our infinite horror, by almost, and with singular injustice, considering the bare charge to stand in the place of proof—suppose this plot laid to defame the fairest reputation in England—I say, that reputation must be saved, if escape it may, only by one means. No perjury can be expected to be exposed in the main, the principal part of the fabric—that can be easily defended from any attack against it; all the arts of the defendant's counsel, and all his experience, will be exhausted in vain: the plotter knows full well (as these conspirators have here done) how to take care that only one person shall swear to a fact,—to lay no others present, to choose the time and select the place when contradiction cannot be given, by knowing the time and the place where any one of your lordships, whom he marks for his prey, may have chanced to be alone at any moment of time. Contradiction is not here to be expected,—refutation is impossible. Prevarication of the witness upon the principal part of his case, beyond all doubt, by every calculation of chances, there will not be. But you will be defended by counsel; and the court before whom you are tried will assuredly have you acquitted, if the villain, who has immovably told a consistent, firm tale,—though not contradicted,—though not touched—upon the story itself,—tells the least falsehood upon the most unimportant particulars on which your advocate shall examine him. My lords, I ask for the Queen no other justice than this upon which you all rely, and must needs rely, for your own escape from the charge of unnatural crimes! I desire she may have no other safety than that which forms the only safety to any one of your lordships in such cases, before any court that deserved the name of a court of justice, where it might be your lot to be dragged and tried!

I am told that the sphere of life in which Bergami, afterwards promoted to be the Queen's chamberlain, originally moved, compared with the fortune which has since attended him in her service, is of itself matter of suspicion. I should be sorry, my lords, to have lived to see the day, when nothing more was required to ruin any exalted character in this free country than the having shown favour to a meritorious servant, by promoting him above his rank in society, the rank of his birth. It is a lot which has happened to many a great man—which has been that of those who have become the ornaments of their country. God forbid we should ever see the time, when all ranks, all stations in this community, except the highest, were not open to all men; and that we should ever reckon of itself a circumstance even of suspicion in any person—for neither sex can be exempt from an inference of such a nature if it is once made general and absolute, —that he has promoted an inferior to be his equal! Let me, however, remind your lordships, that the rapidity of the promotion of Bergami has been greatly overstated; and the manner in which it took place is a convincing proof, that the story of love having been the cause of it, is inconsistent with the fact.

* * * *

I do not dwell on this, my lords, as of any importance to the case; for whether I shall think it necessary to prove what I have just stated or not, I consider that I have already disposed of the case in the comments which I have made upon the evidence, and in the appeal which I have made to the general principles of criminal justice. But, as the conduct of her Majesty has been so unsparingly scrutinized, and as it is important to show that even impropriety existed not, where I utterly defy guilt to be proved, I thought it requisite to dwell on this prominent feature in the cause. If the Queen had frequented companies below her station—if she had lowered her dignity—if she had followed courses which, though not guilty ones, might be deemed improper in themselves and inconsistent with her high station—if she had been proved guilty of any such unworthiness—I could have trodden upon high ground still. But I have no occasion to occupy it. I say, guilt there is none—levity there is none —unworthiness there is none. But if there had been any of the latter, while I dared her accusers to the proof of guilt, admitting levity and even indecorum, I might still have appealed to that which always supports virtue in jeopardy,—the course of her former life at home, among her own relations, before she was frowned upon here—while she had protection among you—while she had the most powerful of all protection, that of our late venerable monarch. I hold in my hand a testimonial— which cannot be read, and which I am sure will not be weighed, without the deepest sense of its importance; above all, without a feeling of sorrow, when we reflect upon the reign that has passed, and compare it with the rule we live under. It is a melancholy proof—more melancholy, because we no longer have him who furnishes it amongst us—but it is a proof how that illustrious sovereign viewed her, whom he knew better than all others—whom he loved more than all the rest of her family did—even than those upon whose affections she had a greater claim—nay, whom he loved better than he did almost any child of his own. The plainness, the honesty, the intelligible and manly sense of this letter are such, that I cannot refrain from the gratification of reading it. It was written in 1804:—

"WINDSOR CASTLE, *Nov.* 13, 1804.

"MY DEAREST DAUGHTER-IN-LAW AND NIECE.— Yesterday, I and the rest of my family had an interview with the Prince of Wales at Kew. Care was taken on all sides to avoid all subjects of altercation or explanation, consequently the conversation was neither instructive nor entertaining; but it leaves the Prince of Wales in a situation to show whether his desire to return to his family is only verbal or real"—(a difference which George III. never know, except in others) —"which time alone can show. I am not idle in my endeavours to make inquiries that may enable me to communicate some plan for the advantage of the dear child you and me with so much reason must interest ourselves in; and its effecting my having the happiness of living more with you is no small incentive to my forming some ideas on the subject; but you may depend on their being not decided upon without your thorough and cordial concurrence, for your authority as mother it is my object to support.

"Believe me, at all times, my dearest daughter-in-law and niece, your most affectionate father-in-law and uncle,

"GEORGE R."

Such, my lords, was the opinion which this good man, not ignorant of human affairs, no ill judge of human character, had formed of this near and cherished relation; and upon which, in the most delicate particulars, the care of his grand-daughter and the heir of his crown, he honestly, really, and not in mere words, always acted.

I might now read to your lordships a letter from his illustrious successor, not written in the same tone of affection—not indicative of the same feelings of regard—but by no means indicative of any want of confidence, or at least of any desire harshly to trammel his Royal Consort's conduct. I allude to a letter which has been so often before your lordships in other shapes, that I may not think it necessary to repeat it here. It is a permission to live apart, and a desire never to come together again; the expression of an opinion that their happiness was better consulted, and pursued asunder; and a very plain indication, that her Majesty's conduct should at least not be watched with all the scrupulousness, all the rigour, all the scrutinizing agency, which has resulted in bringing the present Bill of Pains and Penalties before your lordships. [Cries of "Read, read." Mr. Brougham accordingly read the letter, as follows:]—

"MADAM,—As Lord Cholmondely informs me that you wish I would define in writing the terms upon which we are to live, I shall endeavour to explain myself upon that head with as much clearness and with as much propriety as the nature of the subject will admit. Our inclinations are not in our power, nor should either of us be held answerable to the other because nature has not made us suitable to each other. Tranquil and comfortable society is, however, in our power; let our intercourse, therefore, be restricted to that, and I will distinctly subscribe to the condition which you required,* through Lady Cholmondely, that even in the event of any accident happening to my daughter, which I trust Providence in its mercy will avert, I shall not infringe the terms of the restriction, by proposing at any period, a connexion of a more particular nature. I shall now finally close this disagreeable correspondence, trusting, that as we have completely explained ourselves to each other, the rest of our lives will be passed in uninterrupted tranquillity. I am, Madam, with great truth, very sincerely yours,
"GEORGE P.
"WINDSOR CASTLE,
April 30th, 1796."

My lords, I do not call this, as it has been termed, a Letter of Licence; such was the term applied to it, on the former occasion, by those who are now, unhappily for the Queen, no more,—those who were the colleagues and the coadjutors of the present ministers,—but I think it such an epistle as would make it matter of natural wonderment to the person who received it, that her conduct should ever after —and especially the more rigorously the older the parties were growing—become the subject of the most unceasing and unscrupulous watching, prying, spying, and investigation.

Such then, my lords, is this Case. And again let me call on you, even at the risk of repetition, never to dismi[ss] your minds, the two grea[t] rest my attack upon the the accusers have not p[roduced] good witnesses who wer[e] whom they had no shad[ow of] calling;—and secondly, whom they have ventured of them, irreparably dan[ger] How, I again ask, is a covered, except by the principles? Nay, there [are] plots have been discovered of the second principle, happened to fail. Whe[n] have been seen brought f[orth] above all suspicion have season to impure plans— the guiltless seemed open to remain—they have escaped from the snare [by] two principles; by the ev[idence] where it was not expect[ed] weak point being found, from the attack being made to support it. Yo[u] that great passage—I poetically just and eloqu[ently] inspired—in the Sacred Elders had joined thems[elves] had appeared to have suc[h] the Book says, "they had and had turned away t[hat they] might not look at Heaven do the purposes of unju[st] they, though giving a clo[se] tradicted story, were dis[credited] victim was rescued from trifling circumstance of a tamarisk tree. Let not n[o] dictions of those falseho[od] nesses swear to from n[o] falsehood, such as Sacchi his name—or such as De[r] —such as Majocchi abou[t] or such as all the othe[r] falsehoods not going to [the] case, but to the main bod[y] witnesses—let not men ra[ise] these things accidents. than merciful dispensatio[n] which wills not that the g[uilty] and which favourably prot[ects]

Such, my lords, is the [Case?] Such is the evidence in su[pport] —evidence inadequate to tent to deprive a civil convict of the lowest of brought forward to suppo[rt] highest nature which the l[aw?] to ruin the honour, to [the] English Queen! What [a]

---

* The Queen to her last hour positively denied ever having required any such condition, or having ever made any allusion to the subject of it.

this is the proof by which an act of judicial legislation, a parliamentary sentence, an *ex post facto* law, is sought to be passed against this defenceless woman? My lords, I pray you to pause. I do earnestly beseech you to take heed! You are standing upon the brink of a precipice—then beware! It will go forth your judgment, if sentence shall go against the Queen. But it will be the only judgment you ever pronounced, which, instead of reaching its object, will return and bound back upon those who give it. Save the country, my lords, from the horrors of this catastrophe—save yourselves from this peril—rescue that country, of which you are the ornaments, but in which you can flourish no longer, when severed from the people, than the blossom when cut off from the roots and the stem of the tree. Save that country, that you may continue to adorn it—save the Crown, which is in jeopardy—the Aristocracy, which is shaken—save the Altar, which must stagger with the blow that rends its kindred Throne! You have said, my lords, you have willed—the Church and the King have willed—that the Queen should be deprived of its solemn service. She has, instead of that solemnity, the heartfelt prayers of the people. She wants no prayers of mine. But I do here pour forth my humble supplications at the Throne of Mercy, that that mercy may be poured down upon the people, in a larger measure than the merits of their rulers may deserve, and that your hearts may be turned to justice!

THOMAS CARLYLE.
Born 1795.

THE CONQUEROR.

TRULY it is a mortifying thing for your conqueror to reflect how perishable is the metal which he hammers with such violence; how the kind earth will soon shroud up his bloody foot-prints; and all that he achieved and skilfully piled together will be like his own canvass city of a camp,—this evening loud with life—to-morrow all struck and vanished, a few earth-pits and heaps of straw! for here it always continues true that the deepest force is the stillest; that as in the fable, the mild shining of the sun shall silently accomplish what the fierce blustering of the tempest had in vain essayed. Above all, it is ever to be kept in mind that not by material, but by moral power, are men and their actions governed. How noiseless is thought! No rolling of drums, no tramp of squadrons, or immeasurable tumult of baggage waggons, attends its movements. In what obscure and sequestered place may the head be meditating, which is one day to be crowned with more than imperial authority; for kings and emperors will be amongst its ministering servants; it will rule not over, but in, all heads, and with these its solitary combinations of ideas, as with magic formulas, bend the world to its will. The time may come when Napoleon himself will be better known for his laws than for his battles; and the victory of Waterloo prove less momentous than the opening of the first mechanics' institute.

WILBERFORCE.
Born 1759. *Died* 1833.

[It is well known, almost too well known, perhaps, to make it necessary to mention it here, that to Mr. Wilberforce is due the everlasting honour of having introduced the subject of the abolition of the Slave Trade into Parliament; and that it was principally owing to his unwearying zeal and persevering industry in the cause, that this country was freed from as great a national crime as it is possible to conceive.

It is not perhaps as well known—it is hardly possible to realize now—what great obstacles he had to surmount, and how great was the industry and zeal required before his endeavours were crowned with success, and it would be too long to detail them here.

Early in 1787 he announced his intention of bringing forward a motion relative to the Slave Trade, but was prevented from ill-health till 1789, when the House refused to come to a decision upon the propositions he submitted.

No further notice was taken of the subject till the year 1791, when Mr. Wilberforce's motion for the Abolition was lost by a majority of *seventy-five votes*.

Fox, Pitt, and Burke were, however, in the minority; and in the succeeding session their eloquence and zeal were exerted with powerful effect, and the proposition was adopted, "That it shall not be lawful to import any African negroes into any British Colonies, in ships owned or navigated by British subjects, at any time after the 1st day of January, 1796."

Nevertheless, the absolute prohibition of the trade did not take place till 1807, or twenty years after Mr. Wilberforce made his first notice of a motion on the subject.

The speech from which the following extract is taken was delivered on the 2nd April, 1792.]

HORRORS OF THE MIDDLE PASSAGE.

I THINK, sir, I have already laid enough to the charge of this detested traffic; yet, believe me, if I were so disposed, I could add much more of a similar nature; but I will pass it over, just only suggesting one new topic on which I might enlarge, that, I mean, of our staining the commercial honour of Great Britain, by descending to every petty fraud in our dealings with the natives.

But, not to take up any more of your time on this part of the subject, I must pass on to another, which originally struck my mind as being more horrid than all the rest, and which, I think, still retains its superiority; I mean the situation of the slaves on board ship, or what is commonly called the *middle passage*. I will spare the committee, however, the detail of all those perfections in cruelty which it exhibits:

but two or three instances I must mention, because they are of a recent date, and still more because they will tend to convince those who are inclined rather to regulate than abolish the slave trade, that so long as it is suffered to exist, the evils of the middle passage must exist also, though in respect of them, more than any other class, regulation might have been deemed effectual. We were told, I remember, in an early stage of our inquiry, that formerly, indeed, the negroes were but ill accommodated during their conveyance, and, perhaps, there was now and then a considerable mortality; but such had been the improvements of late years, that they were now quite comfortable and happy. Yet it was no longer ago than in the year 1788, that Mr. Isaac Wilson, whose intelligent and candid manner of giving his evidence could not but impress the committee with a high opinion of him, was doomed to witness scenes as deeply distressing as almost ever occurred in the annals of the slave trade. I will not condemn the committee to listen to the particulars of his dreadful tale, but for the present will content myself with pointing your attention to the mortality. His ship was a vessel of 370 tons, and she had on board 602 slaves, a number greater than we at present allow, but rather less, I think, than what was asserted by the slave merchants to be necessary in order to carry on their trade to any tolerable profit. Out of these 602 she lost 155. I will mention the mortality also of three or four more vessels which were in company with her, and belonged to the same owner. One of them bought 450, and buried 200; another bought 466, and buried 73; another bought 546, and buried 158; besides 155 from his own ship, his number being 602; and from the whole four after the landing of their cargoes there died 220. He fell in with another vessel which lost 362; the number she had bought was not specified. To these actual deaths during and immediately after the voyage, add the subsequent loss in what is called the seasoning, and consider that this loss would be greater than ordinary in cargoes landed in so sickly a state. Why, sir, were such a mortality general, it would, in a few months, depopulate the earth. We asked the surgeon the causes of these excessive losses, particularly on board his own ship, where he had it in his power to ascertain them. The substance of his reply was, that most of the slaves appeared to labour under a fixed dejection and melancholy, interrupted now and then by lamentations and plaintive songs, expressive of their concern for the loss of their relations and friends, and native country. So powerfully did this operate, that many attempted various ways of destroying themselves; some endeavoured to drown themselves, and three actually effected it; others obstinately refused to take sustenance, and when the whip and other violent means were used to compel them to eat, they looked up in the face of the officer who unwillingly executed this painful task, and said in their own language, "presently we shall be no more." Their state of mind produced a general languor and debility, which were increased, in many instances, by an unconquerable abstinence from food, arising partly from sickness, partly, to use the language of slave captains, from "sulkiness." These causes naturally produced the dysentery; the contagion spread, numbers were daily carried off, and the disorder, aided by so many powerful auxiliaries, resisted all the force of medicine. And it is worth while to remark, that these grievous sufferings appear to have been in no degree owing either to want of care on the part of the owner, or to any negligence or harshness of the captain. When Mr. Wilson was questioned if the ship was well fitted; as well, says he, as most vessels are, and the crew and slaves as well treated as in most ships; and he afterwards speaks of his captain in still stronger terms, as being a man of tenderness and humanity.

The ship in which Mr. Claxton, the surgeon, sailed, since the regulating Act, afforded a repetition of all the same horrid circumstances I have before alluded to. Suicide, in various ways, was attempted and effected, and the same barbarous expedients were resorted to, in order to compel them to continue an existence too painful to be endured; the mortality also was as great. And yet, here also, it appears to have been in no degree the fault of the captain, who is represented as having felt for the slaves in their wretched situation. If such were the state of things under captains who had still the feelings of their nature, what must it be under those of a contrary description? It would be a curious speculation to consider what would be the conduct towards his cargo of such a man as one of the six I lately spoke of.* It would be curious to trace such a one, in idea, through all the opportunities the middle passage would afford him of displaying the predominant features of his character.

Unhappily, sir, it is not left for us here to form our own conjectures! Of the conduct of one of them at least, I have heard incidents which surpass all my imagination could have conceived. One of them I would relate, if it were not almost too shocking for description; and yet I feel it my duty, in the situation in which I stand, not to suffer myself to pay too much attention to what has been well called squeam-

* Captain Phillips, of the *Thomas;* Capt. Hutchinson, of the *Wasp;* and Capt. Kimber, of the *Recovery,* all of Bristol: Capt. Houston, of the *Martha;* Capt. Doyle, of the *Betsey;* and Capt. Lee, of the *Amachree,* all of Liverpool.

ishness on the part of the committee. If it be too bad for me to recite, or for you to hear, it was not thought too bad for one of those unhappy creatures to suffer, of whom I have this night the honour to be the advocate. There was a poor girl on board, about fifteen years of age, who had unfortunately contracted a disorder, which produced effects that rendered her a peculiar object of commiseration. In this situation, being quite naked, she bent down in a stooping posture, wishing out of modesty to conceal her infirmity: the captain ordered her to walk upright, and when she could not, or would not obey, he hoisted her up, naked as she was, by the wrists, with her feet a little distance from the deck; and whilst she there hung, a spectacle to the whole crew, he flogged her with a whip with his own hands. He then hung her up in a similar way by both legs, and lastly by one leg; till at length having thus exhausted the efforts of his savage invention, he released her from her torments. The poor unhappy young woman never again recovered. What with the pain, and what with the shame she suffered, she fell into convulsions, and died within three days. The person who related this fact to me is a professional man, who is ready to declare it upon his oath. He has related to me other acts of barbarity, nearly as atrocious; and you will be little surprised to hear that the cruelties of this wretch were not confined to slaves alone, but that the sailors came in for their share.* Think only that these things passed but a few months ago, and here too, as I have before had occasion to remark, you will observe that this was at the very moment of our inquiry and discussion; and yet, even then they could not, though but for a short interval, suspend their work of cruelty, but pursued it more daringly and desperately than ever. And so will it ever be whilst you employ such agents as the slave trade either finds or makes: you will in vain endeavour to prevent the effects of those ferocious dispositions which this savage traffic too commonly creates; till your regulations can counteract the force of habit, and change the nature of the human mind, they will here be of no avail.

Nor, as you must have already collected, can they have all that effect which has sometimes been supposed even in preventing the mortality. I do not, indeed, deny that the Regulating act has lessened this mortality, but not in the degree in which it is generally imagined; and even in the last year I know the deaths on shipboard will be found to have been between ten and eleven per cent. on the whole number that was exported. In truth, you cannot reach the cause of this mortality by all your regulations. Until you can cure a broken heart, until you can legislate for the affections, and bind by your statutes the passions and feelings of the mind, you will in vain sit here devising rules and orders: your labour will be nugatory: you cannot make these poor creatures live against their will: in spite of all you can do they will elude your regulations; they will mock your ordinances and triumph, as they have already done, in *escaping* out of your hands.

O, sir, are not these things too bad to be any longer endured? I cannot but persuade myself that whatever difference of opinion there may have been, we shall this night be at length unanimous. I cannot believe that a British House of Commons will give its sanction to the continuance of this infernal traffic. We were for awhile ignorant of its real nature; but it has now been completely developed, and laid open to your view in all its horrors. Never was there, indeed, a system so big with wickedness and cruelty: to whatever part of it you direct your view, whether to Africa, the middle passage, or the West Indies, the eye finds no comfort, no satisfaction, no relief. It is the gracious ordinance of Providence, both in the natural and moral world, that good should often arise out of evil. Hurricanes clear the air, and the propagation of truth is promoted by persecution: pride, vanity, profusion, in their remoter consequences contribute often to the happiness of mankind; in common what is in itself evil and vicious, is permitted to carry along with it some circumstances of palliation; even those descriptions of men that may seem most noxious have often some virtues belonging to their order. The Arab is hospitable. The robber is brave. We do not necessarily find cruelty associated with fraud, or meanness with injustice. But here the case is far otherwise. It is the prerogative of this detested traffic to separate from evil its concomitant good, and reconcile discordant mischiefs; it robs war of its generosity; it deprives peace of its security. You have the vices of polished society without its knowledge or its comforts; and the evils of barbarism without its simplicity. Nor are its ravages restricted, as those of other evils, to certain limits either of extent or continuance; in the latter it is constant and unintermitted; in the former it is universal and indiscriminate. No age, no sex, no rank, no condition is exempt from the fatal influence of this wide wasting calamity! Thus, it attains to the fullest measure of pure, unmixed, unsophisticated wickedness; and scorning all competition or comparison, it stands without a rival in the secure, undisputed possession of its detestable pre-eminence.

---

* Mr. Wilberforce being called upon for the name of the captain, said "Captain Kimber is the man who performed these feats."

HENRY GRATTAN.

Born 1750. *Died* 1820.

[The following noble estimate of the great Lord Chatham is a fine specimen of the splendid style and philosophical insight of Grattan.]

CHARACTER OF THE FIRST EARL OF CHATHAM.

THE secretary stood alone; modern degeneracy had not reached him. Original and unaccommodating, the features of his character had the hardihood of antiquity; his august mind over-awed majesty; and one of his sovereigns thought royalty so impaired in his presence, that he conspired to remove him, in order to be relieved from his superiority. No state chicanery, no narrow system of vicious politics, no idle contest for ministerial victories, sunk him to the vulgar level of the great; but, overbearing, persuasive, and impracticable, his subject was England, his ambition was fame. Without dividing, he destroyed party; without corrupting, he made a venal age unanimous. France sunk beneath him. With one hand he smote the house of Bourbon, and wielded in the other the democracy of England. The sight of his mind was infinite; and his schemes were to affect,—not England, not the present age only,—but Europe and posterity. Wonderful were the means by which these schemes were accomplished; always seasonable; always adequate; the suggestions of an understanding animated by ardour and enlightened by prophecy.

The ordinary feelings, which make life amiable and indolent,—those sensations which soften, and allure, and vulgarize,—were unknown to him. No domestic difficulties, no domestic weakness, reached him; but, aloof from the sordid occurrences of life, and unsullied by its intercourse, he came occasionally into our system, to counsel and to decide.

A character, so exalted, so strenuous, so various, so authoritative, astonished a corrupt age, and the Treasury trembled at the name of PITT, through all her classes of venality. Corruption imagined, indeed, that she had found defects in this statesman, and talked much of the inconsistency of his glory, and much of the ruin of his victories; but the history of his country, and the calamities of the enemy, answered and refuted her.

Nor were his political abilities his only talents: his eloquence was an era in the senate, peculiar and spontaneous; familiarly expressing gigantic sentiments and instinctive wisdom: not like the torrent of Demosthenes, or the splendid conflagration of Tully, it resembled sometimes the thunder, and sometimes the music, of the spheres. Like Murray, he did not conduct the understanding through the painful subtlety of argumentation; nor was he, like Townshend, for ever on the rack of exertion; but rather lightened upon the subject, and reached the point by the flashings of his mind; which, like those of his eye, were felt, but could not be followed.

Upon the whole, there was, in this man, something that could create, subvert, or reform; an understanding, a spirit, and an eloquence, to summon mankind to society, or to break the bonds of slavery asunder, and to rule the wilderness of free minds with unbounded authority; —something that could establish or overwhelm empire, and strike a blow in the world that should resound through its universe.

CHARLES JAMES FOX.

Born 1749. *Died* 1806.

[SPEECH in eulogium of the Duke of Bedford, surnamed the Great, on the occasion of moving for a writ for a new election for the borough of Tavistock, vacated by the elevation of his successor at the Duke's death in March, 1802.

The Duke of Bedford, whose memory is so eloquently preserved in the following speech, was the grandson of the duke who was minister to the Court of France in 1762, and signed the preliminaries of peace with France and Spain at Fontainebleau; was the great-uncle of the present duke, and the uncle of Lord John, now Earl Russell. His early death was viewed at the time as a national calamity, on account of his high senatorial influence, the purity of his character, and the great services which he rendered to the promotion of agriculture.]

EULOGY OF THE DUKE OF BEDFORD.

MR. CHAIRMAN,—If the sad event which has recently occurred were only a private misfortune, however heavy, I should feel the impropriety of obtruding upon the House the feelings of private friendship, and would have sought some other opportunity of expressing those sentiments of gratitude and affection which must be ever due from me to the memory of the excellent person whose loss gives occasion to the sort of motion of course which I am about to make to the House. It is because I consider the death of the Duke of Bedford as a great public calamity—because the public itself seems so to consider it; because, not in this town only, but in every part of the kingdom, the impression made by it seems to be the strongest and most universal that ever appeared upon the loss of a subject; it is for these reasons that I presume to hope for the indulgence of the House, if I deviate in some degree from the common course, and introduce my motion in a manner which I must confess to be unusual on similar occasions. At the same time, I trust, sir, that I shall not be suspected of any intention to abuse the indulgence which I ask, by dwelling, with the fondness of friendship, upon the various excellences of the character to which I have alluded, much less by entering into a history of the several events of his life, which might serve to illustrate it. There was something in that character so peculiar and striking, and the just admiration which his virtues commanded was such, that to expatiate upon them in any detail is unnecessary, as upon this occasion it would be improper. That he has been much lamented and generally, cannot be wondered at, for surely there never was a more just occasion of public sorrow. To lose such a man!—at such a time! so unexpectedly! The particular stage of his life too in which we lost him, must add to every feeling of regret, and make the disappointment more severe and poignant to all thinking minds. Had he fallen at an earlier period, the public to whom he could then, comparatively speaking at least, be but little known, would rather have compassionated and condoled with the feelings of his friends and relations, than have been themselves very severely afflicted by the loss. It would have been suggested, and even we who were the most partial must have admitted, that the expectations raised by the dawn are not always realized in the meridian of life. If the fatal event had been postponed, the calamity might have been alleviated by the consideration that mankind could not have looked for any length of time to the exercise of his virtues and talents. But he was snatched away at a moment when society might have reasonably hoped, that after having accomplished all the good of which it was capable, he would have descended not immaturely into the tomb. He had, on the one hand, lived long enough to have his character fully confirmed and established, while on the other, what remained of life seemed, according to all human expectations, to afford ample space and scope for the exercise of the virtues of which that character was composed. The tree was old enough to enable us to ascertain the quality of the fruit which it would bear, and, at the same time, young enough to promise many years of produce. The high rank and splendid fortune of the great man of whom I am speaking, though not circumstances which in themselves either can or ought to conciliate the regard and esteem of rational minds, are yet so far considerable, as an elevated situation, by making him who is placed in it more powerful and conspicuous, causes his virtues or vices to be more useful or injurious to society. In this case the rank and wealth of the person are to be attended to in another and a very different point of view. To appreciate his merits justly, we must consider, not only the advantages, but the disadvantages, connected with such circumstances. The dangers attending prosperity in general, and high situation in particular, the corrupt influence of flattery, to which men in such situations are more peculiarly exposed, have been the theme of moralists in all ages and in all nations: but how are these dangers increased with respect to him who succeeds in his childhood to the first rank and fortune in a kingdom such as this, and who having lost his parents, is never approached by any being who is not represented to him as in some degree his inferior! Unless blessed with a heart uncommonly susceptible and disposed to virtue, how should he who has scarcely ever seen an equal, have a common feeling, and a just sympathy, for the rest of mankind, who seemed to have been formed rather *for* him, and as instruments of his gratification, than together *with* him for the general purposes of nature? Justly has the Roman satirist remarked,

"Rarus enim fermè sensus communis in illâ Fortunâ ———"

This was precisely the case of the Duke of Bedford; nor do I know that his education was perfectly exempt from defects usually belonging to such situations; but virtue found her own way, and on the very side where the danger was the greatest was her triumph most complete. From the blame of selfishness no man was ever so eminently free. No man put his own gratification so low, that of others so high in his estimation. To contribute to the welfare of his fellow citizens was the constant, unremitted pursuit of his life, by his example and his beneficence to render better, wiser, and happier. He truly loved the public, but not only the public, according to the usual acceptance of the word; not merely the body corporate, if I may so express myself, which bears that name, but man in his individual capacity; all who came within his notice and deserved his protection, were objects of his generous concern. From his station the sphere of his acquaintance was larger than that of most other men; yet in his extended circle, few, very few, could be counted to whom he had not found some occasion to be serviceable. To be useful, whether to the public at large, whether to his relations and nearer friends, or even to an individual of his species, was the ruling passion of his life.

He died, it is true, in a state of celibacy; but if they may be called a man's children whose concerns are as dear to him as his own; to protect whom from evil is the daily object of his care; to promote whose welfare he exerts every faculty of which he is possessed: if such, I say, are to be esteemed our children, no man had ever a more numerous family than the Duke of Bedford.

Private friendships are not, I own, a fit topic for this House, or any public assembly; but it is difficult for any one who had the honour and happiness to be his friend, not to advert, when speaking of such a man, to his conduct and behaviour in that interesting character. In his friendship, not only he was disinterested and sincere, but in him were to be found all the characteristic excellences which have ever distinguished the men most renowned for that most amiable of all virtues. Some are warm, but volatile and inconstant; he was warm too, but steady and unchangeable. Never once was he known to violate any of the duties of that sacred relation. Where his attachment was placed, there it remained, or rather there it grew: for it may be more truly said of this man, than of any other that ever existed, that if he loved you at the beginning of the year, and you did nothing to forfeit his esteem, he would love you still more at the end of it. Such was the uniformly progressive state of his affections, no less than of his virtue and wisdom.

It has happened to many, and he was certainly one of the number, to grow wiser as they advanced in years. Some have even improved in virtue; but it has generally been in that class of virtue only which consists in resisting the allurements of vice, and too often have these advantages been counterbalanced by the loss, or at least the diminution, of that openness of heart, that warmth of feeling, that readiness of sympathy, that generosity of spirit, which have been reckoned among the characteristic attributes of youth. In this case it was far otherwise. Endued by nature with an unexampled firmness of character, he could bring his mind to a more complete state of discipline than any man I ever knew; but he had, at the same time, such a comprehensive and just view of all the moral questions, that he well knew to distinguish between those inclinations, which, if indulged, must be pernicious, and the feelings, which, if cultivated, might prove beneficial to mankind. All bad propensities, therefore, if any such he had, he completely conquered and suppressed, while, on the other hand, no man ever studied the trade by which he was to get his bread—the profession by which he hoped to rise in wealth and honour—nor even the higher arts of poetry or eloquence, in pursuit of a fancied immortality, with more zeal and ardour than this excellent person cultivated the noble art of doing good to his fellow creatures. In this pursuit, above all others, diligence is sure of success, and accordingly it would be difficult to find an example of any other man to whom so many individuals are indebted for happiness or comfort, or to whom the public at large owe more essential obligation.

So far was he from slackening or growing cold in these generous pursuits, that the only danger was, lest, notwithstanding his admirable good sense and that remarkable soberness of character which distinguished him, his munificence might, if he had lived, have engaged him in expenses to which even his princely fortune would have been found inadequate. Thus the only circumstance like a failing in this great character was, that while indulging his darling passion for making himself useful to others, he might be too regardless of future consequences to himself and family. The love of utility was indeed his ruling passion. Even in his recreations (and he was by no means naturally averse to such as were suitable to his station of life), no less than in his graver hours, he so much loved to keep this grand object in view, that he seemed by degrees to grow weary of every amusement which was not in some degree connected with it. Agriculture he judged rightly to be the most useful of all sciences, and more particularly in the present state of affairs, he conceived it to be the department in which his services to his country might be most beneficial. To agriculture, therefore, he principally applied himself, nor can it be doubted but with his capacity, activity, and energy, he must have attained his object, and made himself eminently useful in that most important branch of political economy. Of the particular degree of his merit in this respect, how much the public is already indebted to him, how much benefit it may still expect to derive from the effects of his unwearied diligence and splendid example, is a question upon which many members of this House can form a much more accurate judgment than I can pretend to do. But of his motives to these exertions I am competent to judge, and can affirm without a doubt, that it was the same which actuated him throughout—an ardent desire to employ his faculties in the way, whatever it might be, in which he could most contribute to the good of his country, and the general interest of mankind.

With regard to his politics, I feel a great unwillingness to be wholly silent on the subject, and at the same time much difficulty in treating it with propriety, when I consider to whom I am addressing myself. I am sensible that those principles upon which in any other place I should not hesitate to pronounce an unqualified eulogium, may be thought by some, perhaps by the majority of this House, rather to stand in need of apology and exculpation, than to form a proper subject for panegyric. But even in this view I may be allowed to offer a few words in favour of my departed friend. I believe few, if any of us, are so infatuated with the extreme notions of philosophy as not to feel a partial veneration for the principles, some leaning even to the prejudices of the ancestors, especially if they were of any note, from whom we are respectively descended. Such biases are always, as I suspect, favourable to the cause of patriotism and public virtue; I am sure, at least, that in Athens and Rome they were so considered. No man had ever less of family pride, in the bad sense, than the Duke of Bedford; but he had a great and just respect for his ancestors. Now if, upon the principle to which I have alluded, it was in Rome thought excusable in one of the Claudii to have, in conformity with the general manners of their race, something too much of an aristocratical pride and haughtiness, surely in this country it is not unpardonable in a Russell to be zealously attached to the rights of the subject, and peculiarly tenacious of the popular parts of our constitution. It is excusable, at least, in one who numbers among his ancestors the great Earl of Bedford, the patron of Pym and the friend of Hampden, to be an enthusiastic lover of liberty: nor is it to be wondered at if a descendant of Lord Russell should feel more than common horror for arbitrary power, and a quick, perhaps even a jealous discernment of any approach or tendency in the system of government to that dreaded evil. But whatever may be our differences in regard to principles, I trust there is no member of this House who is not liberal enough to do justice to upright conduct even in a political adversary. Whatever, therefore, may be thought of those principles to which I have alluded, the political conduct of my much lamented friend must be allowed by all to have been manly, consistent, and sincere.

It now remains for me to touch upon the last melancholy scene in which this excellent man was to be exhibited, and to all those who admire his character, let it be some consolation that his exit was in every respect conformable to his past life. I have already noticed that prosperity could not corrupt him. He had now to undergo a trial of an obstinate nature. But in every instance he was alike true to his character, and in moments of extreme bodily pain and approaching dissolution, when it might be expected that a man's very feeling would be concentrated in his personal sufferings—his very thoughts occupied by the awful event impending—even in these moments he put by all selfish considerations; kindness to his friends was the sentiment still uppermost in his mind, and he employed himself, to the last hour of his life, in making the most considerate arrangements for the happiness and comfort of those who were to survive him. While in the enjoyment of prosperity he had learned and practised all those milder virtues which adversity alone is supposed capable of teaching; and in the hour of pain and approaching death, he had that calmness and serenity which are thought to belong exclusively to health of body and a mind at ease.

If I have taken an unusual, and possibly an irregular course, upon this extraordinary occasion, I am confident the House will pardon me. They will forgive something, no doubt, to the warmth of private friendship, to sentiments of gratitude which I must feel, and, whenever I have an opportunity, must express, to the latest hour of my life. But the consideration of the public utility, to which I have so much adverted as the ruling principle in the mind of my friend, will weigh far more with them. They will in their wisdom acknowledge, that to celebrate and to perpetuate the memory of great and meritorious individuals, is in effect an essential service to the community. It was not, therefore, for the purpose of performing the pious office of friendship by fondly strewing flowers upon his tomb, that I have drawn your attention to the character of the Duke of Bedford. The motive that actuates me, is one more suitable to what were his views. It is that this great character may be strongly impressed upon the minds of all who hear me; that they may see it; that they may feel it; that they may discourse of it in their domestic circles; that they may speak of it to their children, and hold it up to the imitation of posterity. If he could now be sensible to what passes here below, I am sure that nothing could give him so much satisfaction as to find that we are endeavouring to make his memory and example, as he took care his life should be, useful to mankind.

I will conclude with applying to the present occasion a beautiful passage from the speech of a very young orator.* It may be thought perhaps to savour too much of the sanguine views of youth to stand the test of a rigid philosophical inquiry; but it is at least cheering and consolatory, and that in this instance it may be exemplified, is, I am confident, the sincere wish of every man who hears me:—"Crime," says he, "is a curse only to the period in which it is successful; but virtue, whether fortunate or otherwise, blesses not only its own age, but the remotest posterity, and is as beneficial by its example as by its immediate effect."

DANIEL WEBSTER.
Born 1782. *Died* 1852.

[THE following extract is from a speech by Webster, one of the greatest American orators, in memory of the greatest of American statesmen; and was delivered on the 22nd Feb., 1832, being the hundredth anniversary of the birth of Washington. The speech is well worthy both of its author and its theme.]

CENTENARY CELEBRATION OF WASHINGTON.

I RISE, gentlemen, to propose to you the name of that great man, in commemoration of whose birth, and in honour of whose character and services, we have here assembled.

I am sure that I express a sentiment common to every one present when I say, that there is something more than ordinarily solemn and affecting on this occasion.

We are met to testify our regard for him, whose name is intimately blended with whatever belongs most essentially to the prosperity, the liberty, the free institutions, and the renown of our country. That name was of power to rally a nation, in the hour of thick-thronging public disasters and calamities; that name shone, amid

---

* The Hon. William Lamb.

the storm of war, a beacon light, to cheer and guide the country's friends; its flame, too, like a meteor, to repel her foes. That name, in the days of peace, was a loadstone, attracting to itself a whole people's confidence, a whole people's love, and the whole world's respect; that name, descending with all time, spread over the whole earth, and uttered in all the languages belonging to the tribes and races of men, will for ever be pronounced with affectionate gratitude by every one in whose breast there shall arise an aspiration for human rights and human liberty.

We perform this grateful duty, gentlemen, at the expiration of a hundred years from his birth, near the place so cherished and beloved by him, where his dust now reposes, and in the capital which bears his own immortal name.

All experience evinces, that human sentiments are strongly affected by associations. The recurrence of anniversaries, or of longer periods of time, naturally freshens the recollection, and deepens the impression of events with which they are historically connected. Renowned places, also, have a power to awaken feeling, which all acknowledge. No American can pass by the fields of Bunker Hill, Monmouth, or Camden, as if they were ordinary spots on the earth's surface. Whoever visits them feels the sentiment of love of country kindling anew, as if the spirit that belonged to the transactions which have rendered these places distinguished still hovered round with power to move and excite all who in future time may approach them.

But neither of these sources of emotion equals the power with which great moral examples affect the mind. When sublime virtues cease to be abstractions, when they become embodied in human character, and exemplified in human conduct, we should be false to our own nature, if we did not indulge in the spontaneous effusions of our gratitude and our admiration. A true lover of the virtue of patriotism delights to contemplate its purest models; and that love of country may be well suspected which affects to soar so high into the regions of sentiment as to be lost and absorbed in the abstract feeling, and becomes too elevated, or too refined, to glow either with power in the commendation or the love of individual benefactors. All this is immaterial. It is as if one should be so enthusiastic a lover of poetry as to care nothing for Homer or Milton; so passionately attached to eloquence as to be indifferent to Tully and Chatham; or such a devotee to the arts, in such an ecstasy with the elements of beauty, proportion, and expression, as to regard the masterpieces of Raphael and Michael Angelo with coldness or contempt. We may be assured, gentlemen, that he who really loves the thing itself, loves its finest exhibitions. A true friend of his country loves her friends and benefactors, and thinks it no degradation to commend and commemorate them. The voluntary out-pouring of public feeling made to-day, from the north to the south, and from the east to the west, proves this sentiment to be both just and natural. In the cities and in the villages, in the public temples and in the family circles, among all ages and sexes, gladdened voices to-day bespeak grateful hearts, and a freshened recollection of the virtues of the father of his country. And it will be so, in all time to come, so long as public virtue is itself an object of regard. The ingenuous youth of America will hold up to themselves the bright model of Washington's example, and study to be what they behold; they will contemplate his character till all its virtues spread out and display themselves to their delighted vision, as the earliest astronomers, the shepherds on the plains of Babylon, gazed at the stars till they saw them form into clusters and constellations, overpowering at length the eyes of the beholders with the united blaze of a thousand lights.

Gentlemen, we are at the point of a century from the birth of Washington; and what a century it has been! During its course the human mind has seemed to proceed with a sort of geometric velocity, accomplishing more than had been done in fives or tens of centuries preceding. Washington stands at the commencement of a new era, as well as at the head of the new world. A century from the birth of Washington has changed the world. The country of Washington has been the theatre on which a great part of that change has been wrought; and Washington himself a principal agent by which it has been accomplished. His age and his country are equally full of wonders, and of both he is the chief.

If the prediction of the poet, uttered a few years before his birth, be true; if indeed it be designed by Providence that the proudest exhibition of human character and human affairs shall be made on this theatre of the western world; if it be true that

"The first four acts already past,
A fifth shall close the drama with the day;
Time's noblest offspring is the last;"

how could this imposing, swelling, final scene be appropriately opened; how could its intense interest be adequately sustained, but by the introduction of just such a character as our Washington?

Washington had attained his manhood when that spark of liberty was struck out in his own country, which has since kindled into a flame, and shot its beams over the earth. In the flow of a century from his birth, the world has changed in science, in arts, in the extent of commerce, in the improvement of navigation, and in all that relates to the civilization of man. But it is the spirit of human freedom, the new elevation of individual man, in his moral, social, and political character, leading the whole long train of other improvements, which has most remarkably distinguished the era. Society, in this century, has not made its progress, like Chinese skill, by a greater acuteness of ingenuity in trifles; it has not merely lashed itself to an increased speed round the old circles of thought and action, but it has assumed a new character, it has raised itself from *beneath* governments, to a participation *in* governments; it has mixed moral and political objects with the daily pursuits of individual men, and, with a freedom and strength before altogether unknown, it has applied to these objects the whole power of the human understanding. It has been the era, in short, when the social principle has triumphed over the feudal principle; when society has maintained its rights against military power, and established, on foundations never hereafter to be shaken, its competency to govern itself.

LOUIS KOSSUTH.
Born 1802. *Living.*

[The following is one of the splendid series of speeches made by the great Hungarian reformer during his tour of agitation in America in 1851-2, after his liberation from imprisonment at Kutahia, in Asia Minor.]

SPEECH TO THE LADIES OF NEW YORK ON DEC. 21, 1851.

LADIES, worn out as I am, still I am very glad that the ladies of New York condescend to listen to my farewell. When, in the midst of a busy day, the watchful care of a guardian angel throws some flowers of joy in the thorny way of man, he gathers them up with thanks: a cheerful thrill quivers through his heart, like the melody of an Æolian harp; but the earnest duties of life soon claim his attention and his cares. The melodious thrill dies away, and on he must go; on he goes, joyless, cheerless, and cold, every fibre of his heart bent to the earnest duties of the day. But when the hard work of the day is done, and the stress of mind for a moment subsides, then the heart again claims its right, and the tender fingers of our memory gather up again the violets of joy which the guardian angel threw in our way, and we look at them with delight; while we cherish them as the favourite gifts of life—we are as glad as the child on Christmas eve. These are the happiest moments of man's life. But when we are not noisy, not eloquent, we are silent, almost mute, like nature in a midsummer's night, reposing from the burning heat of the day. Ladies, that is my condition now. It is a hard day's work which I have had to do here. I am delivering my farewell address; and every compassionate smile, every warm grasp of the hand, every token of kindness which I have received (and I have received so many), every flower of consolation which the ladies of New York have thrown on my thorny way rushes with double force to my memory. I feel happy in this memory—there is a solemn tranquillity about my mind; but in such a moment I would rather be silent than speak. You know, ladies, that it is not the deepest feelings which are the loudest.

And besides, I have to say farewell to New York! This is a sorrowful word. What immense hopes are linked in my memory with its name!—hopes of resurrection for my fatherland —hopes of liberation for the European continent! Will the expectations which the mighty outburst of New York's heart foreshadowed, be realized? or will the ray of consolation pass away like an electric flash? Oh, could I cast one single glance into the book of futurity! No, God forgive me this impious wish. It is He who hid the future from man, and what He does is well done. It were not good for man to know his destiny. The sense of duty would falter or be unstrung if we were assured of the failure or success of our aims. It is because we do not know the future, that we retain our energy of duty. So on will I go in my work, with the full energy of my humble abilities, without despair, but with hope.

It is Eastern blood which runs in my veins. If I have somewhat of Eastern fatalism, it is the fatalism of a Christian who trusts with unwavering faith in the boundless goodness of a Divine Providence. But among all these different feelings and thoughts that come upon me in the hour of my farewell, one thing is almost indispensable to me, and that is, the assurance that the sympathy I have met with here will not pass away like the cheers which a warbling girl receives on the stage—that it will be preserved as a principle, and that when the emotion subsides, the calmness of reflection will but strengthen it. This consolation I wanted, and this consolation I have, because, ladies, I place it in your hands. I bestow on your motherly and sisterly cares the hopes of Europe's oppressed nations,—the hopes of civil, political, social, and religious liberty. Oh, let me entreat you, with the brief and stammering words of a warm heart, overwhelmed with emotions and with sorrowful cares—let me entreat you, ladies, to be watchful of the sympathy of your people, like the mother over the cradle of her beloved child. It is worthy of your watchful care, because it is the cradle of regenerated humanity.

Especially in regard to my poor fatherland, I have particular claims on the fairer and better half of humanity, which you are. The *first* of these claims is, that there is not, perhaps, on the face of the earth a nation which in its institutions has shown more chivalric regard for ladies than the Hungarian. It is a praiseworthy trait of the Oriental character. You know that it was the Moorish race in Spain who were the founders of the chivalric era in Europe, so full of personal virtue, so full of noble deeds, so devoted to the service of ladies, to heroism, and to the protection of the oppressed. You are told that the ladies of the East are degraded to less almost than a human condition, being secluded from all social life, and pent up within the harem's walls. And so it is. But you must not judge the East by the measure of European civilization. They have their own civilization, quite different from ours in views, inclinations, affections, and thoughts. We in Hungary have gained from the West the advantages of civilization for our women, but we have preserved for them the regard and reverence of our Oriental character. Nay, more than that, we carried these views into our institutions and into our laws. With us, the widow remains the head of the family, as the father was. As long as she lives, she is the mistress of the property of her deceased husband. The chivalrous spirit of the nation supposes she will provide, with motherly care, for the wants of her children; and she remains in possession so long as she bears her deceased husband's name. Under the old constitution of Hungary (which we reformed upon a democratic basis—it having been aristocratic) the widow of a lord had the right to send her representative to the parliament, and in the county elections of public functionaries widows had a right to vote alike with the men. Perhaps this chivalric character of my nation, so full of regard towards the fair sex, may somewhat commend my mission to the ladies of America.

Our *second* particular claim is, that the source of all the misfortune which now weighs so heavily upon my bleeding fatherland, is in two ladies—Catharine of Russia, and Sophia of Hapsburg, the ambitious mother of this second Nero, Francis-Joseph. You know that one hundred and fifty years ago, Charles the Twelfth of Sweden, the bravest of the brave, foreseeing the growth of Russia, and fearing that it would oppress and overwhelm civilization, ventured with a handful of men to attack its rising power. After immortal deeds, and almost fabulous victories, one loss made him a refugee upon Turkish soil, like myself. But, happier than myself, he succeeded in persuading Turkey of the necessity of checking Russia in her overweening ambition, and curtailing her growth. On went Mehemet Baltadji with his Turks, and met Peter the Czar, and pent him up in a corner, where there was no possibility of escape. There Mehemet held him with iron grasp till hunger came to his aid. Nature claimed her rights, and in a council of war it was decided to surrender to Mehemet. Then Catharine, who was present in the camp, appeared in person before the Grand Vizier to sue for mercy. She was fair, and she was rich with jewels of nameless value. She went to the Grand Vizier's tent. She came back without her jewels, but she brought mercy, and Russia was saved. From that celebrated day dates the downfall of Turkey, and the growth of Russia. Out of this source flowed the stream of Russian preponderance over the European continent. The depression of liberty, and the nameless sufferings of Poland and of my poor native land, are the dreadful fruits of Catharine's success on that day, cursed in the records of the human race.

The second lady who will be cursed through all posterity in her memory, is Sophia, the mother of the present usurper of Hungary—she who had the ambitious dream to raise the power of a child upon the ruins of liberty, and on the neck of prostrate nations. It was her ambition—the evil genius of the house of Hapsburg in the present day—which brought desolation upon us. I need only mention one fact to characterize what kind of a heart was in that woman. On the anniversary of the day of Arad, where our martyrs bled, she came to the court with a bracelet of rubies set in so many roses as was the number of heads of the brave Hungarians who fell there, declaring that she joyfully exhibited it to the company as a memento which she wears on her very arm, to cherish in eternal memory the pleasure she derived from the killing of those heroes at Arad. This very fact may give you a true knowledge of the character of that woman, and this is the *second* claim to the ladies' sympathy for oppressed humanity and for my poor fatherland.

Our *third* particular claim is the behaviour of our ladies during the last war. It is no arbitrary praise—it is a fact—that, in the struggle for our rights and freedom, we had no more powerful auxiliaries, and no more faithful executors of the will of the nation, than the women of Hungary. You know that in ancient Rome, after the battle of Cannæ, which was won by Hannibal, the Senate called on the people spontaneously to sacrifice all their wealth on the altar of their fatherland. Every jewel, every ornament was brought forth, but still the tribune judged it necessary to pass a law prohibiting the ladies of Rome to wear more than half an ounce of gold, or particoloured splendid dresses. Now, we wanted in Hungary no such law. The women of Hungary brought all that they had. You would have been astonished to see how, in the most wealthy houses of Hungary, if you were invited to dinner, you would be forced to eat soup with iron spoons. When the wounded and the sick —and many of them we had, because we fought hard—when the wounded and the sick were not so well provided as it would have been our duty and our pleasure to do, I ordered the respective public functionaries to take care of them. But the poor wounded went on suffering, and the proper officers were but slow in providing for them. When I saw this, one single word was spoken to the ladies of Hungary, and in a short time there was provision made for hundreds of thousands of sick. And I never met a single mother who would have withheld her son from sharing in the battle; but I have met many who ordered and commanded their children to fight for their fatherland. I saw many and many brides who urged on the bridegrooms to delay their day of happiness till they should come back victorious from the battles of their fatherland. Thus acted the ladies of Hungary. A country deserves to live; a country deserves to have a future, when the women, as much as the men, love and cherish it.

But I have a stronger motive than all these to claim your protecting sympathy for my country's cause. It is her nameless woe, nameless sufferings. In the name of that ocean of bloody tears which the impious hand of the tyrant wrung from the eyes of the childless mothers, of the brides who beheld the executioner's sword between them and their wedding day—in the name of all those mothers, wives, brides, daughters, and sisters, who, by thousands of thousands, weep over the graves of Magyars so dear to their hearts,—who weep the bloody tears of a patriot (as they all are) over the face of their beloved native land—in the name of all those torturing stripes with which the flogging hand of Austrian tyrants dared to outrage human nature in the womankind of my native land—in the name of that daily curse against Austria with which even the prayers of our women are mixed—in the name of the nameless sufferings of my own dear wife [*here the whole audience rose and cheered vehemently*]—the faithful companion of my life—of her, who for months and for months was hunted by my country's tyrants, with no hope, no support, no protection but at the humble threshold of the hard-working people, as noble and generous as they are poor—in the name of my poor little children, who when so young as to be scarcely conscious of life, had already to learn what an Austrian prison is—in the name of all this, and what is still worse, in the name of liberty trodden down, I claim, ladies of New York, your protecting sympathy for my country's cause. Nobody can do more for it than you. The heart of man is as soft wax in your tender hands. Mould it, ladies; mould it into the form of generous compassion for my country's wrongs; inspire it with the noble feelings of your own hearts; inspire it with the consciousness of your country's power, dignity, and might. You are the framers of man's character. Whatever be the fate of man, one stamp he always bears on his brow—that which the mother's hand impressed upon the soul of the child. The smile of your lips can make a hero out of the coward, and a generous man out of the egotist; one word from you inspires the youth to noble resolutions; the lustre of your eyes is the fairest reward for the toils of life. You can kindle energy even in the breast of broken age, that once more it may blaze up in a noble generous deed before it dies. All this power you have. Use it, ladies, in behalf of your country's glory, and for the benefit of oppressed humanity, and when you meet a cold calculator, who thinks by arithmetic when he is called to feel the wrongs of oppressed nations, convert him, ladies. Your smiles are commands, and the truth which pours forth instinctively from your hearts, is mightier than the logic articulated by any scholar. The Peri excluded from Paradise, brought many generous gifts to heaven in order to regain it. She brought the dying sigh of a patriot; the kiss of a faithful girl imprinted upon the lips of her bridegroom, when they were distorted by the venom of the plague. She brought many other fair gifts; but the doors of Paradise opened before her only when she brought with her the first prayer of a man converted to charity and brotherly love for his oppressed brethren and humanity.

Remember the power which you have, and which I have endeavoured to point out in a few brief words. Remember this, and form associations; establish ladies' committees to raise substantial aid for Hungary. Now I have done. One word only remains to be said—a word of deep sorrow, the word, "Farewell, New York!" New York! that word will for ever make every string of my heart thrill. I am like a wandering bird. I am worse than a wandering bird. He may return to his summer home; I have no home on earth! Here I felt almost at home. But "Forward" is my call, and I must part. I part with the hope that the sympathy which I have met here in a short transitory home will bring me yet back to my own beloved home, so that my ashes may yet mix with the dust of my native soil. Ladies, remember Hungary, and—farewell!

LORD BROUGHAM.
Born 1778.
SALUTARY INNOVATION.

THE great stream of time is perpetually flowing on; all things around us are in ceaseless motion; and we vainly imagine to preserve our relative position among them by getting out of the current and standing stock still on the margin. The stately vessel we belong to glides down; our bark is attached to it; we might " pursue the triumph and partake the gale;" but, worse than the fool who stares expecting the current to flow down and run out, we exclaim, "Stop the boat!"—and would tear it away to strand it, for the sake of preserving its connection with the vessel. All the changes that are hourly and gently going on in spite of us, and all those which we ought to make, that violent severances of settled relations may not be effected, far from exciting murmurs of discontent, ought to be gladly hailed as dispensations of a bountiful Providence, instead of filling us with a thoughtless and preposterous alarm.

RICHARD B. SHERIDAN.
Born 1751. *Died* 1816.

[THE following is an extract from one of the few speeches of Sheridan that have been tolerably reported. Even this, though in its present state abounding with wit, must have lost greatly in the clumsy process of reporting then in vogue. Sheridan's speeches have, perhaps, suffered more than those of any other orator of equal celebrity, partially owing, no doubt, to the more sparkling and evanescent character of his eloquence, as different from that of Mr. Pitt or Mr. Burke, as champagne is from port wine. It effervesced; the reporters could not or would not catch its magic sparkle, and the magnificent speech which so disturbed the senators of England, that they found it impossible to continue their deliberations with befitting equability and unbiassed judgment, may now be read without causing an emotion to the orator's most enthusiastic admirer.

The following extract is a fair example of his power of apt and quick reply, and is taken from a speech delivered against the second reading of Mr. Pitt's bill for the New Assessed Taxes presented to the House of Commons in 1797. The bill, in spite of the opposition of Fox and Sheridan, was finally carried, and England received her first lesson in the income tax.]

A WISE MAN, sir, it is said, should doubt of everything. It was this maxim, probably, that dictated the amiable diffidence of the learned gentleman,* who addressed himself to the chair in these remarkable words—" I rise, Mr. Speaker, *if I have risen.*" Now, to remove all doubts, I can assure the learned gentleman † that he *actually did rise;* and not only rose, but pronounced an able, long, and elaborate discourse, a considerable portion of which was employed in an erudite dissertation on the histories of Rome and Carthage. He further informed the House, upon the authority of Scipio, that we could never conquer the enemy until we were first conquered ourselves. It was when Hannibal was at the gates of Rome, that Scipio had thought the proper moment for the invasion of Carthage,—what a pity it is that the learned gentleman does not go with this consolation and the authority of Scipio to the lord mayor and aldermen of the city of London. Let him say, " Rejoice, my friends! Buonaparte is encamped at Blackheath! What happy tidings!" For here Scipio tells us, you may every moment expect to hear of Lord Hawkesbury making his triumphal entry into Paris.* It would be whimsical to observe how they would receive such joyful news. I should like to see such faces as they would make on that occasion. Though I doubt not of the erudition of the learned gentleman, he seems to me to have somehow confounded the stories of Hanno and Hannibal, of Scipio and the Romans. He told us that Carthage was lost by the parsimony or envy of Hanno, in preventing the necessary supplies for the war being sent to Hannibal: but he neglected to go a little further, and to relate that Hanno accused the latter of having been ambitious—

" Juvenem furentem cupidine regni ;"

and assured the senate that Hannibal, though at the gates of Rome, was no less dangerous to Hanno. Be this, however, as it may, is there any Hanno in the British senate? If there is, nothing can be more certain than that all the efforts and remonstrances of the British Hanno could not prevent a single man, or a single guinea, being sent for the supply of any Hannibal our ministers might choose. The learned gentleman added, after the defeat of Hannibal, Hanno laughed at the senate; but he did not tell us what he laughed at. The advice of Hannibal has all the appearance of being a good one—

" Carthaginis mœnia Romæ munerata."

If they did not follow his advice, they had themselves to blame for it.

From the strain of declamation in which the learned gentleman launched out, it seems as if he came to this House as executor to a man whose genius was scarcely equalled by the eccentricities he sometimes indulged. He appears to come as executor, and in the House of Commons, to administer to Mr. Burke's fury without any of his fire. It is, however, in vain for him to attempt any imitation of those declamatory harangues and writings of the transcendent author, which, towards the latter part of his life, were, as I think, unfortunately too much applauded. When not embellished with those ornaments which Mr. Burke was so capable of adding to all he either spoke or wrote, the subject of such declamations could only claim the admiration of a school-boy. The circumstance of a great extensive and victorious re-

---

* Dr. Lawrence.
† Mr. Perceval, afterwards Chancellor of the Exchequer, and in 1809, Prime Minister. He was assassinated in the lobby of the House of Commons, May 11, 1812, by a man named Bellingham.

* Alludes to a boast of his lordship, at an early period of the war against France.

public, breathing nothing but war in the long exercise of its most successful operations, surrounded with triumphs, and panting for fresh laurels, to be compared, much less represented as inferior, to the military power of England, is childish and ridiculous. What similitude is there between us and the great Roman republic in the height of its fame and glory? Did you, sir, ever hear it stated, that the Roman bulwark was a naval force? And if not, what comparison can there be drawn between their efforts and power? This kind of rhodomontade declamation is finely described in the language of one of the Roman poets—

"I, demens, curre per Alpes,
Ut pueris placeas, et DECLAMATIO fias."*
Go, fight, to please school-boy statesmen, and furnish a DECLAMATION for a Doctor, learned in the law.

* * * *

The proper ground, sir, upon which this bill should be opposed, I conceive to be neither the uncertainty of the criterion, nor the injustice of the retrospect, though they would be sufficient. The tax itself will be found to defeat its own purposes. The amount which an individual paid to the assessed taxes last year can be no rule for what he shall pay in future. All the articles by which the gradations rose must be laid aside, and never resumed again. Circumstanced as the country is, there can be no hope, no chance whatever, that, if the tax succeeds, it ever will be repealed. Each individual, therefore, instead of putting down this article or that, will make a final and general retrenchment; so that the minister cannot get at him in the same way again, by any outward sign which might be used as a criterion of his wealth. These retrenchments cannot fail of depriving thousands of their bread; and it is vain to hold out the delusion of modification or indemnity to the lower orders. Every burthen imposed upon the rich in the articles which give the poor employment, affects them not the less for affecting them circuitously. A coach-maker, for instance, would willingly compromise with the minister, to give him a hundred guineas not to lay the tax upon coaches; for though the hundred guineas would be much more than his proportion of the new tax, yet it would be much better for him to pay the larger contribution, than, by the laying down of coaches, be deprived of those orders by which he got his bread. The same is the case with watchmakers, which I had lately an opportunity of witnessing, who, by the tax imposed last year, are reduced to a state of ruin, starvation, and misery; yet, in proposing that tax, the minister alleged, that the poor journeymen could not be affected, as the tax would only operate on the gentlemen by whom the watches were worn. It is as much cant, therefore, to say, that by bearing heavily on the rich, we are saving the lower orders, as it is folly to suppose we can come at real income by arbitrary assessment, or by symptoms of opulence. There are three ways of raising large sums of money in a State: First, by voluntary contributions; secondly, by a great addition of new taxes; and thirdly, by forced contributions, which is the worst of all, and which I aver the present plan to be. I am at present so partial to the first mode that I recommend the further consideration of this measure to be postponed for a month, in order to make an experiment of what might be effected by it. For this purpose let a bill be brought in, authorizing the proper persons to receive voluntary contributions; and I should not care if it were read a third time to-night. I confess, however, that there are many powerful reasons which forbid us to be too sanguine in the success even of this measure. To awaken a spirit in the nation, the example should come from the first authority, and the higher departments of the State. It is, indeed, seriously to be lamented, that whatever may be the burthens or distresses of the people, the Government has hitherto never shown a disposition to contribute anything; and this conduct must hold out a poor encouragement to others. Heretofore all the public contributions were made for the benefit and profit of the contributors, in a manner inconceivable to more simple nations. If a native inhabitant of Bengal or China were to be informed, that in the west of Europe there was a small island, which in the course of one hundred years contributed four hundred and fifty millions to the exigencies of the State, and that every individual, on the making of a demand, vied with his neighbour in alacrity to subscribe, he would immediately exclaim, "Magnanimous nation! you must surely be invincible." But far different would be his sentiments, if informed of the tricks and jobs attending these transactions, where even loyalty was seen cringing for its *bonus!* If the first example were given from the highest authority, there would at least be some hopes of its being followed by other great men, who received large revenues from the Government. I would instance particularly the tellor of the exchequer, and another person of high rank, who receive from their offices 13,000*l.* a year more in war than they do in peace. The last noble lord * had openly declared for perpetual war, and could not bring his mind to think of anything like a peace with the French. Without meaning any personal disrespect, it was the nature of the human mind to receive a bias from such circumstances. So much was this acknowledged in the rules of this House, that any person receiving a pension or high employment from

---

* Juvenal, Sat. x. 166.   * Lord Grenville.

his Majesty, thereby vacated his seat. It was not, therefore, unreasonable to expect that the noble lord would contribute his proportion, and that a considerable one, to carry on the war, in order to show the world his freedom from such a bias. In respect to a near relative of that noble lord, I mean the noble marquis,* there could be no doubt of his coming forward liberally. I remember, when I was secretary to the Treasury, the noble marquis sent a letter there, requesting that his office might, in point of fees and emoluments, be put under the same economical regulations as the others. The reason he assigned for it was, "the emoluments were so much greater in time of war than peace, that his conscience would be hurt by feeling that he received them from the distresses of his country." No retrenchment, however, took place in that office. If, therefore, the marquis thought proper to bring the arrears since that time also from his conscience, the public would be at least 40,000l. the better for it. By a calculation I have made, which I believe cannot be controverted, it appears, from the vast increase of our burthens during the war, that if peace were to be concluded to-morrow, we should have to provide taxes annually to the amount of 28,000,000l. To this is further to be added, the expense of that system, by which Ireland is not governed, but ground, insulted, and oppressed. To find a remedy for all these incumbrances, the first thing to be done is, to restore the credit of the Bank, which has failed, as well in credit as in honour. Let it no longer, in the minister's hands, remain the slave of political circumstances. It must continue insolvent till the connection is broken off. I remember, in consequence of expressions made use of in this House, upon former discussions, when it was thought the minister would relinquish that unnatural and ruinous alliance, the newspapers sported a good deal with the idea that the House of Commons had *forbid the banns* between him and the *old lady.*† Her friends had interfered, it was said, to prevent the *union*, as it was well known that it was her *dower* he sought, and not her *person* nor the *charms of her society*. The old lady herself, however, when wooed, was quickly won, and nothing could be more indelicate than to observe her soon afterwards ogling her swain, and wantonly courting that violence she at first complained of. In the first instance it might be no more than a case of seduction; but from her subsequent conduct, it became arrant prostitution.

"I swear I could not see the dear betrayer
Kneel at my feet, and sigh to be forgiven;
But my relenting heart would pardon all,
And quite forget 'twas he that had undone me."

* Marquis of Buckingham.
† Old lady of Threadneedle Street.

It is, sir, highly offensive to the decency and sense of a commercial people, to observe the juggle between the minister and the Bank. The latter vauntingly boasted itself ready and able to pay; but that the minister kindly prevented, and put a *lock and key* upon it. There is a liberality in the British nation which always makes allowance for inability of payment. Commerce requires enterprise, and enterprise is subject to losses. But I believe no indulgence was ever shown to a creditor, saying, "I can, but will not pay you." Such was the real condition of the Bank, together with its accounts, when they were laid before the House of Commons; and the chairman* reported from the committee, stating its prosperity, and the great increase of its cash and bullion. The minister, however, took care to verify the old saying, "Brag is a good dog, but Hold-fast is better." —"Ah!" said he, "my worthy chairman, this is excellent news, but I will take care to secure it." He kept his word, took the money, gave exchequer bills for it, which were no security, and there was then an end to all our public credit. It is singular enough, sir, that the report upon this bill stated that it was meant to secure our public credit from the avowed intentions of the French to make war upon it. This was done most effectually. Let the French come when they please, they cannot touch our public credit at least. The minister has wisely provided against it, for he has previously destroyed it. The only consolation besides that remains to us, is *his* assurance that all will return again to its former state at the conclusion of the war. Thus we are to hope, that though the Bank now presents a *meagre spectre*, as soon as peace is restored the *golden bust* will make its reappearance. This, however, is far from being the way to inspirit the nation or intimidate the enemy. Ministers have long taught the people of the inferior order, that they can expect nothing from them but by coercion, and nothing from the great but by corruption. The highest encouragement to the French will be to observe the public supineness. Can they have any apprehension of national energy or spirit in a people whose minister is eternally oppressing them?

Though, sir, I have opposed the present tax, I am still conscious that our existing situation requires great sacrifices to be made, and that a foreign enemy must at all events be resisted. I behold in the measures of the minister nothing except the most glaring incapacity, and the most determined hostility to our liberties; but we must be content, if necessary for preserving our independence from foreign attack, to *strip to the skin.* "It is an established maxim," we are told, that men must give up a part for the preservation of the remainder. I do not dispute

* Mr. Bragge.

the justice of the maxim. But this is the constant language of the gentleman opposite to me. We have already given up part after part, nearly till the whole is swallowed up. If I had a pound, and a person asked me for a shilling, to preserve the rest I should willingly comply, and think myself obliged to him. But if he repeated that demand till he came to my *twentieth shilling*, I should ask him,—" Where is the *remainder?* Where is my *pound* now? Why, my friend, that is no *joke* at all." Upon the whole, sir, I see no salvation for the country but in the conclusion of a peace, and the removal of the present ministers.

GEORGE WASHINGTON.
Born 1732. *Died* 1799.
ADDRESS TO HIS TROOPS BEFORE THE BATTLE OF LONG ISLAND, 1776.

THE time is now near at hand, which must probably determine whether Americans are to be freemen or slaves; whether they are to have any property they can call their own; whether their houses and farms are to be pillaged and destroyed, and themselves consigned to a state of wretchedness, from which no human efforts will deliver them. The fate of unborn millions will now depend, under God, on the courage and conduct of this army. Our cruel and unrelenting enemy leaves us only the choice of a brave resistance, or the most abject submission. We have, therefore, to resolve to conquer or to die.

Our own, our country's honour, calls upon us for a vigorous and manly exertion; and if we now shamefully fail, we shall become infamous to the whole world. Let us, then, rely on the goodness of our cause, and the aid of the Supreme Being, in whose hands victory is, to animate and encourage us to great and noble actions. The eyes of all our countrymen are now upon us, and we shall have their blessings and praises, if happily we are the instruments of saving them from the tyranny meditated against them. Let us therefore animate and encourage each other, and show the whole world, that a freeman contending for liberty on his own ground, is superior to any slavish mercenary on earth.

Liberty, property, life, and honour are all at stake; upon your courage and conduct rest the hopes of our bleeding and insulted country; our wives, children, and parents expect safety from us only; and they have every reason to believe that Heaven will crown with success so just a cause.

The enemy will endeavour to intimidate by show and appearance; but remember, they have been repulsed on various occasions by a few brave Americans. Their cause is bad—their men are conscious of it; and, if opposed with firmness and coolness on their first onset, with our advantage of works and knowledge of the ground, the victory is most assuredly ours. Every good soldier will be silent and attentive—wait for orders—and reserve his fire until he is sure of doing execution.

SIR JAMES MACKINTOSH.
Born 1766. *Died* 1832.

[THE following speech was delivered by Sir James (then Mr.) Mackintosh, in defence of M. Peltier, a royalist refugee, on the 21st of Feb., 1803, at his trial at the Court of King's Bench, for libelling Napoleon Buonaparte, then First Consul of the French Republic, in a weekly paper called *L'Ambigu*. It was during the temporary cessation of hostilities procured by the short-lived truce of Amiens, that the English Government allowed this trial to take place, and the verdict, notwithstanding the fine speech of Mackintosh, was unfavourable to his client. Before, however, M. Peltier was called up to receive the judgment of the Court, war broke out again between the two countries, which stopped all further proceedings.]

SPEECH IN DEFENCE OF M. PELTIER.

THE time is now come for me to address you on behalf of the unfortunate gentleman who is the defendant on this record.

* * * *

I cannot but feel, gentlemen, how much I stand in need of your favourable attention and indulgence. The charge which I have to defend is surrounded with the most invidious topics of discussion; but they are not of my seeking. The case and the topics which are inseparable from it, are brought here by the prosecutor. Here I find them, and here it is my duty to deal with them, as the interests of M. Peltier seem to me to require. He, by his choice and confidence, has cast on me a very arduous duty, which I could not decline, and which I can still less betray. He has a right to expect from me a faithful, a zealous, and a fearless defence; and this his just expectation, according to the measure of my humble abilities, shall be fulfilled. I have said a fearless defence. Perhaps that word was unnecessary in the place where I now stand. Intrepidity in the discharge of professional duty is so common a quality at the English bar, that it has, thank God, long ceased to be a matter of boast or praise. If it had been otherwise, gentlemen, if the bar could have been silenced or overawed by power, I may presume to say, that an English jury would not this day have been met to administer justice. Perhaps I need scarce say that my defence *shall* be fearless, in a place where fear never entered any heart but that of a criminal. But you will pardon me for having said so much, when you consider who the real parties before you are.

Gentlemen, the real prosecutor is the master of the greatest empire the civilized world ever saw. The defendant is a defenceless proscribed exile. He is a French royalist, who fled from his country in the autumn of 1792, at the period of that memorable and awful emigration, when all the proprietors and magistrates of the greatest civilized country of Europe were driven from their homes by the daggers of assassins; when our shores were covered, as with the wreck of a great tempest, with old men and women and children and ministers of religion, who fled from the ferocity of their countrymen as before an army of invading barbarians.

The greatest part of these unfortunate exiles, of those I mean who have been spared by the sword, who have survived the effect of pestilential climates or broken hearts, have been since permitted to revisit their country. Though despoiled of their all, they have eagerly embraced even the sad privilege of being suffered to die in their native land.

Even this miserable indulgence was to be purchased by compliances, by declarations of allegiance to the new Government, which some of these suffering royalists deemed incompatible with their consciences, with their dearest attachments, and their most sacred duties. Among these last is M. Peltier. I do not presume to blame those who submitted, and I trust you will not judge harshly of those who refused. You will not think unfavourably of a man who stands before you as the voluntary victim of his loyalty and honour. If a revolution (which God avert) were to drive us into exile, and to cast us on a foreign shore, we should expect, at least, to be pardoned by generous men, for stubborn loyalty, and unseasonable fidelity to the laws and government of our fathers.

This unfortunate gentleman had devoted a great part of his life to literature. It was the amusement and ornament of his better days. Since his own ruin, and the desolation of his country, he has been compelled to employ it as a means of support. For the last ten years he has been engaged in a variety of publications of considerable importance; but, since the peace, he has desisted from serious political discussion, and confined himself to the obscure journal * which is now before you; the least calculated, surely, of any publication that ever issued from the press, to rouse the alarms of the most jealous Government; which will not be read in England, because it is not written in our language; which cannot be read in France, because its entry into that country is prohibited by a power whose mandates are not very supinely enforced, nor often evaded with impunity; which can have no other object than that of amusing the companions of the author's principles and misfortunes, by pleasantries and sarcasms on their victorious enemies. There is, indeed, gentlemen, one remarkable circumstance in this unfortunate publication; it is the only, or almost the only, journal which still dares to espouse the cause of that royal and illustrious family, which but fourteen years ago was flattered by every press, and guarded by every tribunal in Europe. Even the court in which we are met affords an example of the vicissitudes of their fortune. My learned friend has reminded you, that the last prosecution tried in this place, at the instance of a French Government, was for a libel on that magnanimous princess * who has since been butchered in sight of her palace.

I do not make these observations with any purpose of questioning the general principles which have been laid down by my learned friend. I must admit his right to bring before you those who libel any Government recognized by his Majesty, and at peace with the British empire. I admit that whether such a Government be of yesterday, or a thousand years old, whether it be a crude and bloody usurpation, or the most ancient, just, and paternal authority upon earth, we are here equally bound by his Majesty's recognition to protect it against libellous attacks. I admit that if, during our usurpation, Lord Clarendon had published his history at Paris, or the Marquis of Montrose his verses on the murder of his sovereign, or Mr. Cowley his discourse on Cromwell's government, and if the English ambassador had complained, the President de Moli, or any other of the great magistrates who then adorned the parliament of Paris, however reluctantly, painfully, and indignantly, might have been compelled to have condemned these illustrious men to the punishment of libellers. I say this only for the sake of bespeaking a favourable attention from your generosity and compassion to what will be feebly urged in behalf of my unfortunate client, who has sacrificed his fortune, his hopes, his connections, his country, to his conscience; who seems marked out for destruction in this his last asylum.

That he still enjoys the security of this asylum, that he has not been sacrificed to the resentment of his powerful enemies, is perhaps owing to the firmness of the king's Government. If that be the fact, gentlemen; if his Majesty's ministers have resisted applications to expel this unfortunate gentleman from England, I should publicly thank them for their firmness, if it were not unseemly and improper to suppose that they could have acted otherwise—to thank an English Government for not violating the most sacred duties

---

* *L'Ambigu.*

* Marie Antoinette.

of hospitality; for not bringing indelible disgrace on their country.

But be that as it may, gentlemen, he now comes before you, perfectly satisfied that an English jury is the most refreshing prospect that the eye of accused innocence ever met in a human tribunal; and he feels with me the most fervent gratitude to the Protector of empires, that, surrounded as we are with the ruins of principalities and powers, we still continue to meet together, after the manner of our fathers, to administer justice in this her ancient sanctuary.

There is another point of view in which this case seems to me to merit your most serious attention. I consider it as the first of a long series of conflicts between the greatest power in the world, and the only free press remaining in Europe. .... Gentlemen, this distinction of the English press is new; it is a proud and melancholy distinction. Before the great earthquake of the French revolution had swallowed up all the asylums of free discussion on the Continent, we enjoyed that privilege, indeed, more fully than others; but we did not enjoy it exclusively. In great monarchies the press has always been considered as too formidable an engine to be entrusted to unlicensed individuals. But in other continental countries, either by the laws of the State, or by long habits of liberality and toleration in magistrates, a liberty of discussion has been enjoyed, perhaps sufficient for most useful purposes. It existed, in fact, where it was not protected by law; and the wise and generous connivance of Governments was daily more and more secured by the growing civilization of their subjects. In Holland, in Switzerland, in the imperial towns of Germany, the press was either legally or practically free. Holland and Switzerland are no more; and since the commencement of this prosecution, fifty imperial towns have been erased from the list of independent states, by one dash of the pen. Three or four still preserve a precarious and trembling existence. I will not say by what compliances they must purchase its continuance. I will not insult the feebleness of states whose unmerited fall I do most bitterly deplore.

These Governments were in many respects one of the most interesting parts of the ancient system of Europe.

* * * *

The perfect security of such inconsiderable and feeble states, their undisturbed tranquillity, amidst the wars and conquests that surrounded them, attested beyond any other part of the European system, the moderation, the justice, the civilization to which Christian Europe had reached in modern times. Their weakness was protected only by the habitual reverence for justice which, during a long series of ages, had grown up in Christendom. This was the only fortification which defended them against those mighty monarchs to whom they offered so easy a prey. And till the French revolution this was sufficient. Consider, for instance, the situation of the republic of Geneva. Think of her defenceless position in the very jaws of France; but think also of her undisturbed security, of her profound quiet, of the brilliant success with which she applied to industry and literature, while Louis XIV. was pouring his myriads into Italy before her gates. Call to mind, if ages crowded into years have not effaced them from your memory, that happy period when we scarcely dreamt more of the subjugation of the feeblest republic of Europe, than of the conquest of her mightiest empire, and tell me if you can imagine a spectacle more beautiful to the moral eye, or a more striking proof of progress in the noblest principles of true civilization.

These feeble states, these monuments of the justice of Europe, the asylum of peace, of industry, and of literature, the organs of public reason, the refuge of oppressed innocence and persecuted truth, have perished with those ancient principles which were their sole guardians and protectors. They have been swallowed up by that fearful convulsion which has shaken the uttermost corners of the earth. They are destroyed and gone for ever.

One asylum of free discussion is still inviolate. There is still one spot in Europe where man can freely exercise his reason on the most important concerns of society, where he can boldly publish his judgment on the acts of the proudest and most powerful tyrants. The press of England is still free. It is guarded by the free constitution of our forefathers. It is guarded by the hearts and arms of Englishmen, and I trust I may venture to say, that if it be to fall, it will fall only under the ruins of the British empire.

It is an awful consideration, gentlemen. Every other monument of European liberty has perished. That ancient fabric which has been gradually reared by the wisdom and virtue of our fathers still stands—it stands, thanks be to God! solid and entire—but it stands alone, and it stands amidst ruins.

* * * *

The principles of the law of England on the subject of political libel are few and simple, and they are necessarily so broad, that, without a habitually mild administration of justice, they might encroach materially on the liberty of political discussion. Every publication which is intended to vilify either our own Government, or the Government of any foreign State in amity with this kingdom, is, by the law of England, a libel.

* * * *

In all other cases the most severe execution of law can only spread terror among the guilty; but in political libels it inspires even the innocent with fear. This striking peculiarity arises from the same circumstances which make it impossible to define the limits of libel and innocent discussion; which make it impossible for a man of the purest and most honourable mind to be always perfectly certain whether he be within the territory of fair argument and honest narrative, or whether he may not have unwittingly overstepped the faint and varying line which bounds them. But, gentlemen, I will go further. This is the only offence where severe and frequent punishments not only intimidate the innocent, but deter men from the most meritorious acts, and from rendering the most important services to their country. They indispose and disqualify men for the discharge of the most sacred duties which they owe to mankind. To inform the public on the conduct of those who administer public affairs, requires courage and conscious security. It is always an invidious and obnoxious office; but it is often the most necessary of all public duties. If it is not done boldly, it cannot be done effectually, and it is not from writers trembling under the uplifted scourge, that we are to hope for it.

There are other matters, gentlemen, to which I am desirous of particularly calling your attention. These are the circumstances in the condition of this country, which have induced our ancestors, at all times, to handle, with more than ordinary tenderness, that branch of the liberty of discussion which is applied to the conduct of foreign States.

* * * *

Our ancestors never thought it their policy to avert the resentment of foreign tyrants by enjoining English writers to contain and repress their just abhorrence of the criminal enterprises of ambition. This great and gallant nation, which has fought in the front of every battle against the oppressors of Europe, has sometimes inspired fear, but, thank God, she has never felt it. We know that they are our real, and must soon become our declared, foes. We know that there can be no cordial amity between the natural enemies and the independence of nations. We have never adopted the cowardly and short-sighted policy of silencing our press, of breaking the spirit and palsying the hearts of our people, for the sake of a hollow and precarious truce. We have never been base enough to purchase a short respite from hostilities, by sacrificing the first means of defence; the means of rousing the public spirit of the people, and directing it against the enemies of their country and of Europe.

* * * *

Gentlemen, the French revolution—I must pause, after I have uttered words which present such an overwhelming idea.—But I have not now to engage in an enterprise so far beyond my force as that of examining and judging that tremendous revolution. I have only to consider the character of the factions which it must have left behind it.

The French revolution began with great and fatal errors. These errors produced atrocious crimes. A mild and feeble monarchy was succeeded by bloody anarchy, which very shortly gave birth to military despotism. France, in a few years, described the whole circle of human society.

All this was in the order of nature. When every principle of authority and civil discipline, when every principle which enables some men to command and disposes others to obey was extirpated from the mind by atrocious theories, and still more atrocious examples; when every old institution was trampled down with contumely, and every new institution covered in its cradle with blood; when the principle of property itself, the sheet-anchor of society, was annihilated; when in the persons of the new possessors, whom the poverty of language obliges us to call proprietors, it was contaminated in its source by robbery and murder, and it became separated from that education and those manners, from that general presumption of superior knowledge and more scrupulous probity which form its only liberal titles to respect; when the people were taught to despise everything old, and compelled to detest everything new; there remained only one principle strong enough to hold society together, a principle utterly incompatible, indeed, with liberty, and unfriendly to civilization itself, a tyrannical and barbarous principle; but, in that miserable condition of human affairs, a refuge from still more intolerable evils. I mean the principle of military power, which gains strength from that confusion and bloodshed in which all the other elements of society are dissolved, and which, in these terrible extremities, is the cement that preserves it from total destruction.

Under such circumstances, Buonaparte usurped the supreme power in France. I say *usurped*, because an illegal assumption of power is a usurpation. But usurpation in its strongest moral sense, is scarcely applicable to a period of lawless and savage anarchy. The guilt of military usurpation, in truth, belongs to the author of those confusions which sooner or later give birth to such a usurpation.

Thus, to use the words of the historian; " by recent as well as all ancient example, it became evident that illegal violence, with whatever pretences it may be covered, and whatever object it may pursue, must inevitably end at last in the arbitrary and despotic government of a single person." But though the government of

Buonaparte has silenced the revolutionary factions, it has not and it cannot have extinguished them. No human power could reimpress upon the minds of men all those sentiments and opinions which the sophistry and anarchy of fourteen years had obliterated. A faction must exist, which breathes the spirit of the ode now before you.

It is, I know, not the spirit of the quiet and submissive majority of the French people. They have always rather suffered than acted in the revolution. Completely exhausted by the calamities through which they have passed, they yield to any power which gives them repose. There is, indeed, a degree of oppression which rouses men to resistance; but there is another and a greater which wholly subdues and unmans them. It is remarkable that Robespierre himself was safe till he attacked his own accomplices. The spirit of men of virtue was broken and there was no vigour of character left to destroy him, but in those daring ruffians who were the sharers of his tyranny.

As for the wretched populace who were made the blind and senseless instrument of so many crimes, whose frenzy can now be reviewed by a good mind with scarce any moral sentiment but that of compassion; that miserable multitude of beings, scarcely human, have already fallen into a brutish forgetfulness of the very atrocities which they themselves perpetrated. They have already forgotten all the acts of their drunken fury. If you ask one of them, who destroyed that magnificent monument of religion and art, or who perpetrated that massacre, they stupidly answer, the Jacobins! though he who gives the answer was probably one of these Jacobins himself; so that a traveller, ignorant of French history, might suppose the Jacobins to be the name of some Tartar horde, who, after laying waste France for ten years, were at last expelled by the native inhabitants. They have passed from senseless rage to stupid quiet. Their delirium is followed by lethargy.

* * * *

Some of them, indeed, the basest of the race, the sophists, the rhetors, the poet-laureats of murder, who were cruel only from cowardice and calculating selfishness, are perfectly willing to transfer their venal pens to any Government that does not disdain their infamous support. These men, republicans from servility, who published rhetorical panegyrics on massacre, and who reduced plunder to a system of ethics, are as ready to preach slavery as anarchy. But the more daring, I had almost said, the more respectable ruffians cannot so easily bend their heads under the yoke. These fierce spirits have not lost "the unconquerable will, the study of revenge, immortal hate." They leave the luxuries of servitude to the mean and dastardly hypocrites, to the Belials and Mammons of the infernal faction. They pursue their old end of tyranny under their old pretext of liberty. The recollection of their unbounded power renders every inferior condition irksome and vapid, and their former atrocities form, if I may so speak, a sort of moral destiny which irresistibly impels them to the perpetration of new crimes. They have no place left for penitence on earth. They labour under the most awful proscription of opinion that ever was pronounced against human beings. They have cut down every bridge by which they could retreat into the society of men. Awakened from their dreams of democracy, the noise subsided that deafened their ears to the voice of humanity; the film fallen from their eyes, which hid from them the blackness of their own deeds; haunted by the memory of their inexpiable guilt; condemned daily to look on the faces of those whom their hands made widows and orphans, they are goaded and scourged by these real furies, and hurried into the tumult of new crimes, which will drown the cries of remorse, or if they be too depraved for remorse, will silence the curses of mankind. Tyrannical power is their only refuge from the just vengeance of their fellow creatures. Murder is their only means of usurping power. They have no taste, no occupation, no pursuit but power and blood. If their hands are tied, they must at least have the luxury of murderous projects. They have drunk too deeply of human blood ever to relinquish their cannibal appetite.

* * * *

It is no part of my case that M. Peltier has spoken with some unpoliteness, with some flippancy, with more severity than my learned friend may approve, of factions and of administrations in France. M. Peltier cannot love the revolution, or any government that has grown out of it and maintains it. The revolutionists have destroyed his family, they have seized his inheritance, they have beggared, exiled, and proscribed himself. If he did not detest them he would be unworthy of living, and he would be a base hypocrite if he were to conceal his sentiments. But I must again remind you, that this is not an information for not sufficiently honouring the French revolution,—for not showing sufficient reverence for the consular Government. These are no crimes among us; England is not yet reduced to such an ignominious dependence. Our hearts and consciences are not yet in the bonds of so wretched a slavery. This is an information for a libel on Buonaparte, and if you believe the principal intention of M. Peltier to have been to republish the writings, or to satirize the character of other individuals, you must acquit him of a libel on the first consul.

Here, gentlemen, I think I might stop, if I had only to consider the defence of M. Peltier. I trust that you are already convinced of his innocence. I fear I have exhausted your patience, as I am sure I have very nearly exhausted my own strength. But so much seems to me to depend on your verdict, that I cannot forbear from laying before you some considerations of a more general nature.

Believing as I do that we are on the eve of a great struggle; that this is only the first battle between reason and power; that you have now in your hands, committed to your trust, the only remains of free discussion in Europe, now confined to this kingdom: addressing you, therefore, as the guardians of the most important interests of mankind; convinced that the unfettered exercise of reason depends more on your present verdict than on any other that was ever delivered by a jury, I cannot conclude without bringing before you the sentiments and examples of our ancestors in some of those awful and perilous situations by which Divine Providence has in former ages tried the virtue of the English nation. We are fallen upon times in which it behoves us to strengthen our spirits by the contemplation of great examples of constancy. Let us seek for them in the annals of our forefathers.

The reign of Queen Elizabeth may be considered as the opening of the modern history of England, especially in its connection with the modern system of Europe, which began about that time to assume the form that it preserved till the French revolution. It was a very memorable period, of which the maxims ought to be engraven on the head and heart of every Englishman. Philip II., at the head of the greatest empire then in the world, was openly aiming at universal domination, and his project was so far from being thought chimerical by the wisest of his contemporaries, that in the opinion of the great Duc de Sully he must have been successful, "if, by a most singular combination of circumstances, he had not at the same time been resisted by two such strong heads as those of Henry IV. and Queen Elizabeth." To the most extensive and opulent dominions, the most numerous and disciplined armies, the most renowned captains, the greatest revenue, he added also the most formidable power over opinion. He was the chief of a religious faction, animated by the most atrocious fanaticism, prepared to second his ambition by rebellion, anarchy, and regicide, in every Protestant State. Elizabeth was among the first objects of his hostility. That wise and magnanimous princess placed herself in the front of the battle for the liberties of Europe. Though she had to contend at home with his fanatical faction, which almost occupied Ireland, which divided Scotland, and was not of contemptible strength in England, she aided the oppressed inhabitants of the Netherlands in their just and glorious resistance to his tyranny; she aided Henry the Great in suppressing the abominable rebellion which anarchical principles had excited, and Spanish arms had supported, in France, and after a long reign of various fortune, in which she preserved her unconquered spirit through great calamities and still greater dangers, she at length broke the strength of the enemy, and reduced his power within such limits as to be compatible with the safety of England and of all Europe. Her only effectual ally was the spirit of her people, and her policy flowed from that magnanimous nature which in the hour of peril teaches better lessons than those of cold reason. Her great heart inspired her with a higher and a nobler wisdom—which disdained to appeal to the low and sordid passions of her people even for the protection of their low and sordid interests, because she knew, or rather she felt, that these are effeminate, creeping, cowardly, short-sighted passions, which shrink from conflict even in defence of their own mean objects. In a righteous cause she roused those generous affections of her people which alone teach boldness, constancy, and foresight, and which are therefore the only safe guardians of the lowest as well as the highest interests of a nation. In her memorable address to her army, when the invasion of the kingdom was threatened by Spain, this woman of heroic spirit disdained to speak to them of their ease and their commerce, and their wealth and their safety. No! She touched another chord—she spoke of their national honour, of their dignity as Englishmen, of "the foul scorn that Parma or Spain *should dare* to invade the borders of her realms." She breathed into them those grand and powerful sentiments which exalt vulgar men into heroes, which led them into the battle of their country, armed with holy and irresistible enthusiasm; which even cover with their shield all the ignoble interests that base calculation and cowardly selfishness tremble to hazard, but shrink from defending. A sort of prophetic instinct, if I may so speak, seems to have revealed to her the importance of that great instrument for rousing and guiding the minds of men, of the effects of which she had no experience; which, since her time, has changed the condition of the world, but which few modern statesmen have thoroughly understood or wisely employed; which is no doubt connected with many ridiculous and degrading details; which has produced, and which may again produce, terrible mischiefs; but of which the influence must, after all, be considered as the most certain effect and the most efficacious cause of civilization, and which, whether it be a blessing or a curse, is the most powerful engine that a politician can move—I mean the press. It is a curious fact, that in the year of the Armada, Queen Elizabeth caused to be printed the first gazettes that ever appeared in England; and I own, when I consider that this mode of rousing a national spirit was then absolutely unexampled, that she could have no assurance of its efficacy from the precedents of former times, I am disposed to regard her having recourse to it as one of the most sagacious experiments, one of the greatest discoveries of political genius, one of the most striking anticipations of future experience, that we find in history. I mention it to you to justify the opinion that I have ventured to state, of the close connection of our national spirit with our press, even our periodical press.

* * * *

I am aware, gentlemen, that I have already abused your indulgence, but I must entreat you to bear with me for a short time longer, to allow me to suppose a case which might have occurred, in which you will see the horrible consequences of enforcing rigorously principles of law, which I cannot counteract, against political writers. We might have been at peace with France during the whole of that terrible period which elapsed between August, 1792, and 1794, which has been usually called the reign of Robespierre ; the only series of crimes, perhaps, in history, which, in spite of the common disposition to exaggerate extraordinary facts, has been beyond measure underrated in public opinion. I say this, gentlemen, after an investigation which I think entitles me to affirm it with confidence. Men's minds were oppressed by atrocity and the multitude of crimes; their humanity and their indolence took refuge in scepticism from such an overwhelming mass of guilt; and the consequence was, that all these unparalleled enormities, though proved not only with the fullest historical, but with the strictest judicial evidence, were at the time only half believed, and are now scarcely half remembered. When these atrocities were daily perpetrating, of which the greatest part are as little known to the public in general as the campaigns of Genghis Khan, but are still protected from the scrutiny of men by the immensity of those voluminous records of guilt in which they are related, and under the mass of which they will be buried, till some historian be found with patience and courage enough to drag them forth into light, for the shame indeed, but for the instruction of mankind :— when these crimes were perpetrating, which had the peculiar malignity, from the pretexts with which they were covered, of making the noblest objects of human pursuit seem odious and detestable; which has almost made the names of liberty, reformation, and humanity, synonymous with anarchy, robbery, and murder; which thus threatened not only to extinguish every principle of improvement, to arrest the progress of civilized society, and to disinherit future generations of that rich succession which they were entitled to expect from the knowledge and wisdom of the present, but to destroy the civilization of Europe, which never gave such a proof of its vigour and robustness as in being able to resist their destructive power : when all these horrors were acting in the greatest empire of the continent, I will ask my learned friend, if we had then been at peace with France, how English writers were to relate them so as to escape the charge of libelling a friendly government?

When Robespierre, in the debates in the National Convention on the mode of murdering their blameless sovereign, objected to the formal and tedious mode of murder called a trial, and proposed to put him immediately to death, " on the principles of insurrection," because to doubt the guilt of the King would be to doubt of the innocence of the Convention; and if the King were not a traitor, the Convention must be rebels; would my learned friend have had an English writer state all this with "decorum and moderation?" Would he have had an English writer state, that though this reasoning was not perfectly agreeable to our national laws, or perhaps to our national prejudices, yet it was not for him to make any observations on the judicial proceedings of foreign States?

When Marat, in the same Convention, called for two hundred and seventy thousand heads, must our English writers have said that the remedy did, indeed, seem to their weak judgment rather severe, but that it was not for them to judge the conduct of so illustrious an assembly as the National Convention, or the suggestions of so enlightened a statesman as M. Marat?

When that Convention resounded with applause at the news of several hundred aged priests being thrown into the Loire and particularly at the exclamation of Carrier, who communicated the intelligence, "What a revolutionary torrent is the Loire!" when these suggestions and narrations of murder, which had hitherto been only hinted and whispered in the most secret cabals, in the darkest caverns of banditti, were triumphantly uttered, patiently endured, and even loudly applauded by an assembly of seven hundred men, acting in the sight of all Europe, would my learned friend have wished that there had been found in England a single writer so base as to deliberate upon the most safe, decorous, and polite manner of relating all these things to his countrymen?

When Carrier ordered five hundred children under fourteen years of age to be shot, the greater part of whom escaped the fire from their size; when the poor victims ran for protection to the soldiers, and were bayoneted clinging round their knees! would my friend——but I cannot pursue the strain of interrogation. It is too much. It would be a violence which I cannot practise on my own feelings. It would be an outrage to my friend. It would be an insult to humanity. No! Better, ten thousand times better, would it be that every press in the world were burnt, that the very use of letters were abolished, that we were returned to the honest ignorance of the rudest times, than that the results of civilization should be made subservient to the purposes of barbarism, than that literature should be employed to teach a toleration for cruelty, to weaken moral hatred for guilt, to deprave and brutalize the human mind. I know that I speak my friend's feelings as well as my own when I say, God forbid that the dread of any punishment should ever make any Englishman an accomplice in so corrupting his countrymen—a public teacher of depravity and barbarity!

Mortifying and horrible as the idea is, I must remind you, gentlemen, that even at that time, even under the reign of Robespierre, my learned friend, if he had then been Attorney-General, might have been compelled, by some most deplorable necessity, to have come into this court to ask your verdict against the libellers of Barrere and Collot d'Herbois. M. Peltier then employed his talents against the enemies of the human race, as he has uniformly and bravely done. I do not believe that any peace, any political considerations, any fear of punishment, would have silenced him. He has shown too much honour, and constancy, and intrepidity, to be shaken by such circumstances as these.

My learned friend might then have been compelled to have filed a criminal information against M. Peltier, for "wickedly and maliciously intending to vilify and degrade Maximilian Robespierre, President of the Committee of Public Safety of the French Republic!" He might have been reduced to the sad necessity of appearing before you to belie his own better feelings; to prosecute M. Peltier for publishing those sentiments which my friend himself had a thousand times felt, and a thousand times expressed. He might have been obliged even to call for punishment upon M. Peltier for language which he and all mankind would for ever despise M. Peltier if he were not to employ. Then indeed, gentlemen, we should have seen the last humiliation fall on England; the tribunals, the spotless and venerable tribunals of this free country, reduced to be the ministers of the vengeance of Robespierre! What could have rescued us from this last disgrace? The honesty and courage of a jury. They would have delivered the judges of this country from the dire necessity of inflicting punishment on a brave and virtuous man, because he spoke truth of a monster. They would have despised the threats of a foreign tyrant, as their ancestors braved the power of oppression at home.

In the court where we are now met, Cromwell twice sent a satirist on his tyranny to be convicted and punished as a libeller, and in this court, almost in sight of the scaffold streaming with the blood of his sovereign, within hearing of the clash of his bayonets, which drove out Parliament with contumely, two successive juries rescued the intrepid satirist* from his fangs, and sent out with defeat and disgrace the usurper's attorney-general from what he had the insolence to call *his* court! Even then, gentlemen, when all law and liberty were trampled under the feet of a military banditti; when those great crimes were perpetrated on a high place and with a high hand against those who were the objects of public veneration, which more than anything else break their spirits and confound their moral sentiments, obliterate the distinctions between right and wrong in their understanding, and teach the multitude to feel no longer any reverence for that justice which they thus see triumphantly dragged at the chariot wheels of a tyrant; even then, when this unhappy country, triumphant indeed abroad, but enslaved at home, had no prospect but that of a long succession of tyrants wading through slaughter to a throne —even then, I say, when all seemed lost, the unconquerable spirit of English liberty survived in the hearts of English jurors. That spirit is, I trust in God, not extinct; and if any modern tyrant were, in the drunkenness of his insolence, to hope to overawe an English jury, I trust and I believe that they would tell him, "Our ancestors braved the bayonets of Cromwell; we bid defiance to yours. *Contempsi Catalinæ gladios—non pertimescam tuos?*"

What could be such a tyrant's means of overawing a jury? As long as their country exists they are girt round with impenetrable armour. Till the destruction of their country no danger can fall upon them for the performance of their duty, and I do trust that there is no Englishman so unworthy of life as to desire to outlive England. But if any of us are condemned to the cruel punishment of surviving our country — if, in the inscrutable counsels of Providence, this favoured seat of justice and liberty—this noblest work of human wisdom and virtue—be destined to destruction, which I shall not be charged with national prejudice for saying would be the most dangerous wound ever inflicted on civilization; at least let us carry with us into our sad exile the consolation that we ourselves have not violated the rights of hospitality to exiles—that we have not torn from the altar the suppliant who claimed protection as the voluntary victim of loyalty and conscience!

---

* Lilburne.

W. E. GLADSTONE.
Born 1809.

[THE following speech, printed by permission of the Chancellor of the Exchequer, from the speech as corrected and published by him, is too fresh in the memory of our readers to need comment; but, for the satisfaction of those who we trust will read THE ORATOR in days to come, we give the following information.

This speech was delivered by the Right Honourable W. E. Gladstone, when Chancellor of the Exchequer, on May 11th, 1864, in the debate on Mr. Baines' proposed Bill for the Extension of the Suffrage in Towns, and created considerable sensation, as it was thought to express more *advanced* principles on the subject of reform than those hitherto ascribed to Mr. Gladstone.]

EXTENSION OF THE SUFFRAGE.

I MUST begin, Sir, by observing, that the speech of the honourable gentleman opposite (Mr. Cave), in my opinion, went far beyond the scope of the motion which he has submitted to the House. For it was really a speech against all extension of the franchise in the direction of the working classes, and it did not refer merely to the subject of that particular franchise, which we have to adopt or reject in connection with the present Bill. However, it may be said with truth, that it is not the speech in question, but the motion of my hon. friend on the one side, and the amendment of the hon. member opposite on the other, with which we have principally to deal. Let us, then, consider what is the practical issue raised for our present decision.

There are two points bearing upon this question, the one a matter of fact, and the other a matter of judgment, upon which it may be reasonably supposed there will be a general concurrence of opinion. With regard to the matter of fact, there is no doubt that those who sit on the other side may be said to be unanimous in deprecating at the present time —and certainly, as far as the argument of the honourable gentlemen, and the reception of that argument, afforded an indication, at any time —the extension of the franchise. I do not attempt to conceal or deny, on the other hand, that the other great party in the country is not unanimous on the subject. No small number of those who profess liberal opinions are indifferent, some may be even averse, to any change such as is proposed by the Bill, from a ten pound to a six pound franchise in towns. The second point, upon which I think all parties are agreed, is this: that at the present period, and in a state of opinion such as now subsists, it would not be advisable, I might even say it would not be justifiable, for the Government of the Queen, however it might be composed, to submit a measure on this subject to Parliament. Under these circumstances, and with these admissions freely made, the question we have before us for to-day is this: What course ought we to take on the motion of my honourable friend, having regard to the amendment which has been moved in favour of postponement? My honourable friend, without communication with the Government, and acting, as far as I am aware, entirely in the exercise of his own discretion, has brought his proposal before us as a subject for discussion. I treat this, without praise or censure, merely as a fact. And now I admit it may be said that the motion of the honourable gentleman opposite, which is a motion for time, does, in fact, no more than embody the admissions I have myself made, namely, that this is not a period for a Government to deal with this question, and that even the party which represents the liberal opinions of the country is not unanimous on the subject. Why, then, do I vote against the honourable gentleman's motion? It is because, even when taken apart from his speech, although much more if taken in connection with the speech, it appears to me to support, to justify, and to confirm a state of facts and opinions which I deeply deprecate and deplore. Admitting the existence of those opinions within the limits I have described—and it is useless to shut our eyes to their existence—I must say that I deeply deplore them. I will not go the whole length of my hon. friend in respect to the precise terms he used as to the broken pledges of Governments and parties; but I will not scruple to admit that, at least as it appears to me, so much of our Parliamentary history during the last thirteen years—I mean during the years since the vote on Mr. Locke King's Bill in 1851—as touches Parliamentary Reform, is a most unsatisfactory chapter in that history, and has added nothing to the honour of Parliament, or to the safety and well-being of the country. Now I cannot expect any sudden change for the better as likely to arise from any debate or decision on the present Bill. Yet I am convinced that the discussion of the question in the House of Commons must, through the gentle process by which Parliamentary debates act on the public mind, gradually help to bring home the conviction that we have not been so keenly alive to our duties in this matter as we ought to have been; that it is for the interests of the country that this matter should be entertained; and that it ought, if we are wise, to be brought to an early settlement. The conditions requisite for dealing with it can only be supplied by a favourable state of the public mind; but the public mind is itself guided, and opinion modified, in no small degree, by the debates of Parliament.

One especial advantage attends to-day the discussion of this question, that, at present, at all events, it is not to be held strictly a party question. I am afraid, indeed, if I take as a criterion the cheers with which the speech of the hon. gentleman opposite was received, and the quarter from which they proceeded, that the time may come when this may, and will, once more become a party question. For the present, however, we may discuss it without exclusive reference to party associations; and I may take the opportunity of saying that for this reason I am glad—though for others I am not so—that my honourable friend the member for Salisbury * has stepped into the arena on this occasion; because the circumstance enables us the more easily to find our way into the discussion of the question without the apprehension that we are irritating and exciting those passions and party sentiments, which necessarily enter into our debates when party interests are concerned, and which might help to obscure the true merits of the case. I will address myself, then, to the question actually before us, admitting again that if I deeply deplore the state of opinion opposite, I am far from being satisfied with the state of opinion on this side of the House.

My honourable friend the member for Salisbury appears to think that he has made out his case when he has advanced three propositions: one of them, that nobody desires, nobody petitions for, the Bill; the next, that to propose the extension of the franchise downwards is to propose also the encouragement of bribery; and the third, that the working classes have their interests well attended to by the House of Commons as it is at present constituted. Now, sir, I decline altogether to follow my honourable friend into an argument upon the question whether or not the extension of the franchise downwards would really lead to the encouragement of bribery. I would simply record my emphatic dissent from that statement. Again, with respect to the allegation that the working classes have their interests well cared for by this House, far be it from me to deny that this House has a strong feeling of sympathy with the working classes; but permit me to say that that sympathy is not the least strongly felt, and that its practical exhibition has certainly not been least remarkable, among those also who are the immediate promoters and supporters of this Bill. And next I come to the assertion that nobody desires a measure of this sort. But before otherwise dealing with this assertion, I want to know where, in a discussion such as is now before us, lies the burden of proof? Is the *onus probandi* upon those who maintain that the present state of the representation ought not to be touched, or upon those who say it ought to be amended? The honourable member for Shoreham † says the case of the British constitution, after a Bill of this sort, will be like the case of the man over whom was written the epitaph, "I was well;

* Mr. Marsh. † Mr. Cave.

I would be better; here I am;" and he told us again that to venture on a change such as is presented in this Bill was to enter on a "domestic revolution." Sir, I entirely deprecate the application of language of such a kind to the present Bill. I will not now enter into the question whether the precise form of franchise, and the precise figure, which my hon. friend has indicated, may or may not be that which, upon full deliberation, we ought to choose; I will not now inquire whether the franchise should be founded on rate-paying or on occupation; neither will I consider whether or not there should be a lodger's franchise; I put aside every question except the very simple one which I take to be at issue, and on this I will endeavour not to be misunderstood. I apprehend my honourable friend's Bill to mean (and if such be the meaning I give my cordial concurrence to the proposition), that there ought to be, not a wholesale, nor an excessive, but a sensible and considerable addition to that portion of the working classes—at present almost infinitesimal—which is in possession of the franchise.

Now, sir, if I am asked what I mean by a "sensible and considerable addition," I reply that I mean such an addition as I think, and as we at the time contended in argument,* would have been made by the Bill which the present Government submitted to the House in 1860. Does then the *onus* of proof that there is a necessity for such a measure lie with us? Has the honourable member wholly forgotten, or does he set wholly at nought, all the formal and solemn declarations of the years from 1851 to 1860? What, again, is the present state of the constituency, any departure from which the hon. gentleman deprecates and stigmatises as a "domestic revolution?" At present we have, speaking generally, a constituency of which between one-tenth and one-twentieth—certainly less than one-tenth—consists of working men. And what proportion does that fraction of the working classes, who are in possession of the franchise, bear to the whole body of the working classes? I apprehend I am correct in saying that those who possess the franchise are less than one-fiftieth

* "You have got already a borough constituency of 450,000: you are going to add 150,000, or at the most extravagant estimate 200,000. . . . . The labouring classes might be 200,000 in a borough constituency of 650,000: that is, they would be less than one-third of the whole borough constituency, and only in about one-half of the boroughs, or one-third part of the seats, returning members for England and Wales, would thus amount to such numbers as to act with any sensible or appreciable force. Now, sir, is that the lion's share? and does that justify the appeals which have been made, and the lecture we have received to-night on American institutions?"—Speech of the Chancellor of the Exchequer on the Bill for Amending the Representation of the People, May 3, 1860.

of the whole number of the working classes. Is that a state of things which we cannot venture to touch or modify? Is there no choice between excluding forty-nine out of every fifty working men on the one hand, and on the other "a domestic revolution?" I contend, then, that it is on the honourable gentleman that the burden of proof must be held principally to lie; that it is on those who say it is necessary to exclude forty-nine-fiftieths that the burden of proof rests; that it is for them to show the unworthiness, the incapacity, and the misconduct of the working classes, in order to make good their argument that no larger portion of them than this should be admitted to the suffrage. (Oh, oh!) I am sorry to find that it is anywhere thought necessary to treat this question by what, perhaps, to use a mild phrase, I may call "inarticulate reasoning;" and I will endeavour not to provoke more of it from a certain quarter of the House than I can help. But it is an opinion which I entertain that if forty-nine-fiftieths of the working classes are to be excluded from the franchise, it is certainly with those who maintain that exclusion that it rests to show its necessity. On the other hand, my hon. friend indicates that kind of extension of the suffrage which would make the working classes a sensible fraction of the borough constituency; an important fraction, but still a decided minority as compared with the other portion of it. That is the proposition which we have before us for our present consideration.

We are told that the working classes do not agitate for an extension of the franchise; but is it desirable that we should wait until they do agitate? In my opinion, agitation by the working classes, upon any political subject whatever, is a thing not to be waited for, not to be made a condition previous to any Parliamentary movement; but, on the contrary, it is a thing to be deprecated, and, if possible, anticipated and prevented by wise and provident measures. An agitation by the working classes is not like an agitation by the classes above them, the classes possessed of leisure. The agitation of the classes having leisure is easily conducted. It is not with them that every hour of time has a money value; their wives and children are not dependent on the strictly reckoned results of those hours of labour. When a working man finds himself in such a condition that he must abandon that daily labour on which he is strictly dependent for his daily bread, when he gives up the profitable application of his time, it is then that, in railway language, "the danger signal is turned on;" for he does it only because he feels a strong necessity for action, and a distrust in the rulers who, as he thinks, have driven him to that necessity. The present state of things, I rejoice to say, does not indicate that distrust; but if we admit this as matter of fact, we must not along with the admission allege the absence of agitation on the part of the working classes as a sufficient reason why the Parliament of England, and the public mind of England, should be indisposed to entertain the discussion of this question.

I may presume, sir, to mention that I happen to have had a recent opportunity of obtaining some information respecting the views of the working classes on this subject. It arose incidentally; but I thought it worth attention at the time, and I still think it may be worth the attention of the House. It was in connection with the discussions on the Government Annuities Bill, when a deputation, representing the most extensive among all the existing combinations of the working classes of Liverpool, came to me, and expressed their own sentiments and those of their fellows with respect to that Bill.

Mr. HORSFALL.—It was not a deputation from Liverpool, but from London.

The CHANCELLOR OF THE EXCHEQUER.—I am not aware of having said Liverpool. (Yes, yes.) I beg pardon, then, I meant London; and I thank my honourable friend for the correction he has supplied, as it enables me to report the views of a body of men perhaps some six or eight times larger than any corresponding body in Liverpool. After disavowing opposition to that measure, they proceeded to hold language such as this:—"If there has been any suspicion or disinclination to this Bill on the part of the working classes, it is owing in a great measure to their dissatisfaction with the conduct of Parliament during recent years in reference to the extension of the suffrage." Part of my answer to them was, "If you complain of the conduct of Parliament, depend upon it the conduct of Parliament has been connected in no small degree with the apparent inaction, and alleged indifference, of the working classes themselves with respect to the suffrage." The reply which they then returned was one which made a deep impression on my mind. They used language to the following effect:—"It is true that, since the abolition of the corn-laws, we have given up political agitation; we have begun from that time to feel that we might place confidence in Parliament; that we might look to Parliament to pass beneficial measures without agitation. We were told then to abandon those habits of political action which had so much interfered with the ordinary occupations of our lives; and we have endeavoured to substitute for them the employment of our evenings in the improvement of our minds." I do not hesitate to confess that I was greatly struck by that answer. And, after hearing it, I for one am more than ever unable to turn round on the working classes, and say that it is plain they do not care for the extension of the franchise, because they do not agitate in order to obtain it.

The objection made by the honourable gentleman opposite and by many others is, that the working classes, if admitted even in limited numbers, or at all events so as to form any considerable proportion of a constituency, will go together as a class, and wholly separate themselves from other classes. I do not wish to use harsh language, and therefore I will not say that that is a libel; but I believe it to be a statement altogether unjustified by reference to facts. It is not a fact, as I believe, that the working men, who are now invested with the franchise, act together as a class; and there is not the slightest reason to suppose that they would so act together if there were a moderate and fair extension of the suffrage. If, indeed, we were to adopt a sudden and sweeping measure, a measure which might deserve the epithet of revolutionary; if we were to do anything which would give a monopoly of power to the working classes; if, for example, instead of adopting a measure which would raise the proportion of working men in the town constituencies to one-third, you gave the franchise to two-thirds, there would be some colour for the anticipation, and some justification for the language so lightly used; there might then be some temptation to set up class interests on the part of those who might thus have the means of obtaining, or at least a temptation to grasp at, a monopoly of power, and it would, under these circumstances, be for us to show, if we could, that no danger would arise. But I appeal to the evidence of all who know anything of the facts, to say whether we have not seen the working classes, in places where they possessed the franchise, instead of being disposed to go together as a class, rather inclined, us a general rule, and under all ordinary circumstances, to follow their superiors, to confide in them, to trust them, and to hold them in high esteem. Their landlords in the country, their employers in the town, their neighbours, and those whose personal characters they respect—these are the men whom the working classes commonly elect to follow; and, for my part, I believe, if there is anything which will induce them to alter their conduct, and to make it their rule to band together as a class, it will be resentment at exclusion, and a sense of injustice. Whatever tends to denote them as persons open to the influence of bribery—as persons whose admission within the pale of the constitution constitutes "a domestic revolution,"—whatever tends to mark them as unworthy of confidence and respect, is calculated to drive them back to the use of their natural means of self-defence, and might, possibly, in times and circumstances which we can conceive, become the motive cause of an union among the working classes, which would be adverse to other classes of the community.

It would, sir, be worse than idle, after the able and luminous speech of my honourable friend (Mr. Baines) to detain the House with the statistics of the question. But I take my stand, in the first place, on a great legislative fact: on the Reform Bill of 1832. Before 1832 —the epoch of the Reform Act—although the working classes were not supposed to be represented in this House, yet we had among the constituencies some of an important character which were in an entirely preponderating proportion working-class constituencies. I myself was elected by a scot and lot borough, the borough of Newark. At the time that I was first returned for that borough, in December, 1832, the constituency was close upon 1,600. That same constituency is now a little more than 700; nor has it yet, I believe, reached its minimum; in fact, it is in progress of regular decay, until it reaches the limit fixed by the number of ten pound houses. That borough was enfranchised in the time of Charles II., when the Crown did not fear to issue writs calling for the return, in certain cases, of members by constituencies that consisted of all inhabitants who paid scot and lot. But, since the Act of 1832, there has been a large deduction made from the number of working men in the possession of the franchise by the changes which have taken place in the condition of the boroughs called pot-walloping boroughs, scot and lot boroughs, and by other denominations. I greatly doubt whether, even after making fair allowance for the bettered circumstances of working men, as large a proportion of the entire body hold the suffrage now as held it in December, 1832. If that is so, is it fair and proper that, in the thirty-two years which have since elapsed, a reduction should have taken place in the proportion which they bear to the rest of the constituency? Have their condition and character retrograded in a manner to justify this retrogression of numbers? Have they no claims to an extension of the suffrage? I think the facts are clear, and I think my honourable friend has shown that a great portion of the facts are reducible to figures, and are capable of being represented in a form and with a force almost mathematical, with reference to education and to the state of the press. Let me, then, refer to one or two points which are not reducible to figures. We are told, for instance, that the working classes are given to the practice of strikes. I believe it is the experience of the employers of labour that these strikes are more and more losing the character of violence and compulsory interference with the free will of their own comrades and fellow-workmen, and are assuming that legal and, under certain circumstances, legitimate character, which they possess as the only means by which, in the last resort, labour can fairly assert itself against capital in the peaceful strife of the labour market. Let us take, too, that which in former times I believe to have been the besetting sin of labour,—the disposition of the majority not to recognize the right of 'the minority, and, indeed, of every single individual, to sell his labour for what he thinks fit. On behalf of the labouring classes I must, in passing, say that this doctrine is much harder for them to practise than for us to preach. In our condition of life and feeling, we have nothing analogous to that which the working man cannot but feel when he sees his labour being, as he thinks, undersold. Yet still it is our duty to assert in the most rigid terms; and to carry high the doctrine of the right of every labouring man, whether with or against the approval of his class, to sell his labour as high or as low as he pleases. But with respect to this point, which has certainly been in other times, and which I fear still is in certain cases, a point of weakness, I appeal to those who have experience of the working classes, whether there is not reason to believe that the progress of knowledge, and the experience of good government, and the designs of philanthropy and religion, have borne their fruit? Has not the time come when large portions, at the least, of working men admit the right of freedom of labour, as fully as it could possibly be asserted in this House?

Again, sir, let us look for a few moments at the altered, the happily altered, relations of the working classes to the government, the laws, the institutions, and, above all, to the throne of this country. Let us go back—it is no long period in the history of a nation—to an epoch not very many years before the passing of the Reform Bill, and consider what was the state of things at a time when many of us were unborn, and when most of us were children—I mean, to the years which immediately succeeded the peace of 1815. We all know the history of those times; most of us recollect the atmosphere and the ideas under the influence of which we were brought up. They were not ideas which belonged to the old current of English history; nor were they in conformity with the liberal sentiments which pervaded, at its best periods, the politics of the country, and which harmonised with the spirit of the old British Constitution. They were, on the contrary, ideas referable to those lamentable excesses of the first French Revolution, which produced here a terrible reaction, and went far to establish the doctrine that the masses of every community were in permanent antagonism with the laws under which they lived, and were disposed to regard those laws, and the persons by whom the laws were made and administered, as their natural enemies. Unhappily, there are but too many indications to prove that this is no vague or imaginary description. The time to which I now refer was a time when deficiencies in the harvest were followed by riots, and when rioters did not hold sacred even the person of Majesty itself. In 1817, when the Prince Regent came down to open Parliament, his carriage was assailed by the populace of London: and what was the remedy provided for this state of things? Why, the remedy was sought in the suspension of the *Habeas Corpus* Act; or in the limitation of the action of the press, already restricted; or in the employment of spies, and the deliberate defence of their employment, who, for the supposed security of the Government, were sent throughout the country to dog the course of private life, and to arrest persons, or to check them, in the formation of conspiracies real or supposed. And what, let me ask, is the state of things now? With truth, sir, it may be said that the epoch I have named, removed from us, in mere chronological reckoning, by less than half a century, is in the political sphere separated from us by a distance almost immeasurable. For now it may be fearlessly asserted that the fixed traditional sentiment of the working man has begun to be confidence in the law, in Parliament, and even in the executive Government. Of this gratifying state of things it fell to my lot to receive a single, indeed, but a significant proof no later than yesterday. (Cries of "No, no," and laughter.) The quick-witted character of hon. gentlemen opposite outstrips, I am afraid, the tardy movement of my observations. Let them only have a very little patience, and they will, I believe, see cause for listening to what I shall say.* I was about to proceed to say, in illustration of my argument, that only yesterday I had the satisfaction of receiving a deputation of working men from the Society of Amalgamated Engineers. That society consists of very large numbers of highly-skilled workmen, and has two hundred and sixty branches; it is a society representing the very class in which we should most be inclined to look for a spirit of even jealous independence of all direct relations with the Government. But the deputation came to state to me that the society had large balances of money open for investment, and that many of its members could not feel satisfied unless they were allowed to place their funds in the hands of the Government, by means of a modification in the rules of the Post-office Savings-banks. Now,

* The interruption was understood to refer to another deputation received on the same day, with reference to the subject of the departure of General Garibaldi.

that, I think I may say, without being liable to any expression of adverse feeling on the part of honourable gentlemen opposite, was a very small but yet significant indication, among thousands of others, of the altered temper to which I have referred. Instead, however, of uttering on the point my own opinions, I should like to use the words of the working classes themselves. In an address which, in company with my right honourable friend the member for Staffordshire, I heard read at a meeting which was held in the Potteries last autumn, they say, of their own spontaneous motion, uninfluenced by the action of their employers, in relation to the legislation of late years :—

"The great measures that have been passed during the last twenty years by the British Legislature have conferred incalculable blessings on the whole community, and particularly on the working classes, by unfettering the trade and commerce of the country, cheapening the essentials of our daily sustenance, placing a large proportion of the comforts and luxuries of life within our reach, and rendering the obtainment of knowledge comparatively easy among the great mass of the sons of toil."

And this is the mode in which they then proceed to describe their view of the conduct of the upper classes towards them :—

"Pardon us for alluding to the kindly conduct now so commonly evinced by the wealthier portions of the community to assist in the physical and moral improvement of the working classes. The well-being of the toiling mass is now generally admitted to be an essential to the national weal. This forms a pleasing contrast to the opinions cherished half a century ago. The humbler classes also are duly mindful of the happy change, and, without any abatement of manly independence, fully appreciate the benefits resulting therefrom, contentedly fostering a hopeful expectation of the future. May Heaven favour and promote this happy mutuality! as we feel confident that all such kindly interchange materially contributes to the general good."

Now, such language does, in my opinion, the greatest credit to the parties from whom it proceeds. This is a point on which no difference of opinion can prevail. I think I may go a step further, and consider these statements as indicating not only the sentiments of a particular body at the particular place from which they proceeded, but the general sentiments of the best-conducted and most enlightened working men of the country. It may, however, be said that such statements prove the existing state of things to be satisfactory. But surely this is no sufficient answer. Is it right, I ask, that in the face of such dispositions, the present law of almost entire exclusion should continue to prevail? Again I call upon the adversary to show cause. And I venture to say that every man who is not presumably incapacitated by some consideration of personal unfitness or of political danger is morally entitled to come within the pale of the Constitution. Of course, in giving utterance to such a proposition, I do not recede from the protest I have previously made against sudden, or violent, or excessive, or intoxicating change; but I apply it with confidence to this effect, that fitness for the franchise, when it is shown to exist—as I say it is shown to exist in the case of a select portion of the working class—is not repelled on sufficient grounds from the portals of the Constitution by the allegation that things are well as they are. I contend, moreover, that persons who have prompted the expression of such sentiments as those to which I have referred, and whom I know to have been members of the working class, are to be presumed worthy and fit to discharge the duties of citizenship, and that to admission to the discharge of those duties they are well and justly entitled.

The present franchise, I may add, on the whole—subject, of course, to some exceptions—draws the line between the lower middle class and the upper order of the working class. As a general rule, the lower stratum of the middle class is admitted to the exercise of the franchise, while the upper stratum of the working class is excluded. That I believe to be a fair general description of the present formation of the constituencies in boroughs and towns. Is it a state of things, I would ask, recommended by clear principles of reason? Is the upper portion of the working classes inferior to the lowest portion of the middle? That is a question I should wish to be considered on both sides of the House. For my own part, it appears to me that the negative of the proposition may be held with the greatest confidence. Whenever this question comes to be discussed, with the view to an immediate issue, the conduct of the general body of the operatives of Lancashire cannot be forgotten. What are the qualities which fit a man for the exercise of a privilege such as the franchise? Self-command, self-control, respect for order, patience under suffering, confidence in the law, regard for superiors; and when, I should like to ask, were all those great qualities exhibited in a manner more signal, I would even say more illustrious, than under the profound affliction of the winter of 1862? I admit the danger of dealing with enormous masses of men; but I am now speaking only of a limited portion of the working class, and I for one cannot admit that there is that special virtue in the nature of the middle class which ought to lead to our drawing a marked distinction, a distinction almost purporting to be one of principle, between them and a select portion of the working classes, so far as relates to the exercise of the franchise.

But, sir, this question has received a very remarkable illustration from the experience of the last few years. So far as Lancashire is concerned, we have the most extraordinary evidence—evidence amounting almost to mathematical demonstration—of the competency of the working man to discharge those duties of retail trade and the distribution of commodities, which are commonly intrusted to the lower part of the middle class. I allude to the evidence afforded by the marvellous success in that particular county (and I hope the example of that county may not be too eagerly followed elsewhere) of the co-operative system. For my own part, I am not ashamed to say that, if twenty or ten years ago anybody had prophesied to me the success of that system, as it has recently been exhibited in Rochdale and other towns in the north—if I had been told that labouring men would so associate together with mutual advantage, to the exclusion of the retail dealer, who comes between the producer and the consumer of commodities, I should have regarded the prediction as absurd. There is, in my opinion, no greater social marvel at the present day than the manner in which these societies flourish in Lancashire, combined with a consideration of the apparent soundness of the financial basis on which they are built; for the bodies of men who have had recourse to the co-operative system have been, as it would appear, those who have stood out with the most manly resolution against the storms of adversity, who have been the last to throw themselves on the charity of their neighbours, and who have proved themselves to be best qualified for the discharge of the duties of independent citizens. And when we have before us considerable numbers of men answering to this description, it is, I think, well worth our while to consider what is the title which they advance to the generous notice of Parliament in regard to their appeal to be admitted, in such measure as may upon consideration seem fit, to the exercise of the franchise. I, for myself, confess that I think the investigation will be far better conducted if we approach the question at an early date, in a calm frame of mind, and without having our doors besieged by crowds, or our table loaded with petitions, rather than if we postpone entering upon it until a great agitation has arisen.

And now, sir, one word in conclusion. I believe that it has been given to us of this generation to witness, advancing as it were under our very eyes from day to day, the most blessed of all social processes; I mean the process which unites together not the interests only but the feelings of all the several classes of the community, and which throws back into the shadows of oblivion those discords by which they were kept apart from one another. I know of nothing which can contribute, in any degree comparable to that union, to the welfare of the commonwealth. It is well, sir, that we should be suitably provided with armies, and fleets, and fortifications; it is well too that all these should rest upon and be sustained, as they ought to be, by a sound system of finance, and out of a revenue not wasted by a careless Parliament, or by a profligate Administration. But that which is better and more weighty still is that hearts should be bound together by a reasonable extension, at fitting times, and among selected portions of the people, of every benefit and every privilege that can justly be conferred upon them; and, for one, I am prepared to give my support to the motion now made by my honourable friend (Mr. Baines), because I believe and am persuaded that it will powerfully tend to that binding and blending and knitting of hearts together, and thus to the infusion of new vigour into the old, but in the best sense still young, and flourishing and undecaying British Constitution.

WILLIAM PITT.
Born 1759. *Died* 1806.

THE SLAVE TRADE.

SIR,—I lament that my efforts on this subject have hitherto not been successful, but I am consoled with the thought that the House has come to a resolution declarative of the infamy of this trade: that all parties have concurred in reprobating it: that even its advocates have been compelled to acknowledge its infamy. The question now is only the continuance of this abominable traffic, which even its friends think so intolerable that it ought to be crushed. Jamaica has imported 150,000 negroes in the course of twenty years, and this is admitted to be only one-tenth of the trade. Was there ever, can there be, anything beyond the enormity of this infamous traffic? The very thought of it is beyond human endurance. It is allowed, however, that the trade is infamous, but the abolition of it is resolvable to a question of expediency; and then, when the trade is argued as a commercial case, its advocates, in order to continue it, desert even the principles of commerce. So that a traffic in the liberty, the blood, the life, of human beings, is not to have even the advantages of the common rules of arithmetic which govern all other commercial dealings!

The point now in dispute is only one year, as I understand; for the amendment proposes the year 1795 for the abolition, while the year 1796 is only contended for on the other side. As to those who are concerned in the trade, a year would not make much difference; but does it make no alteration to the unhappy slaves? It is true, that, in the course of commercial concerns in general, it is said sometimes to be beneath the magnanimity of a man of honour to insist on a scrupulous exactness in his own favour upon a disputed item in accounts; but does it make any part of our magnanimity to be exact in our own favour in the traffic of human blood? When a man gives up £500 or £1,000 against himself, upon a complicated reckoning, he is called generous; and when he insists on it in his own favour, he is deemed niggardly: the common course, when parties disagree, is what the vulgar phrase calls, "to split the difference." If I could feel that I am to calculate upon the subject in this way, the side on which I should determine it would be in favour of the unhappy sufferers, not of those who oppress them. But this one year is only to show the planters that Parliament is willing to be liberal to them. Sir, I do not understand complimenting away the lives of so many human beings. I do not understand the principle on which a few individuals are to be complimented, and their minds set at rest, at the expense and total sacrifice of the interest, the security, the happiness, of a whole quarter of the world, which, from our foul practices, has for a vast length of time been a scene of misery and horror. I say, because I feel, that every hour you continue this trade you are guilty of an offence beyond your power to atone for; and, by your indulgence to the planters, thousands of human beings are to be miserable for ever. Notwithstanding the bill passed for regulating the middle passage, even now the loss of the trade is no less than ten per cent.; such is still the mortality of this deleterious traffic! Every year in which you continue this abominable trade, you add thousands to the catalogue of miserable beings, which, if you could behold in a single instance, you would revolt with horror from the scene; but the size of the misery prevents you from beholding it. Five hundred out of one thousand that are taken in this traffic perish in this scene of horror; are miserable victims brought to their graves: this is the effect of this system of slavery. The remaining part of this miserable group are tainted both in body and in mind, covered with disease and infection, infecting the very earth on which they tread, and the air in which they breathe, carrying with them the seeds of pestilence and insurrection to your island. Let me, then, ask, if I am improperly pressing upon the House a question, whether they can derive any advantage from these doubtful effects of a calculation on the continuance of the traffic; and whether they think that two will not be better than three years, for its continuance? I feel the infamy of the trade so heavily, the impolicy of it so clearly, that I am ashamed I have not been able to persuade the House to abandon it altogether at an instant, to pronounce with one voice its immediate and total abolition. There is no excuse for us, seeing this infernal traffic as we do. It is the very death of justice to utter a syllable in support of it. Sir, I know I state this subject with warmth: I feel it is impossible for me not to do so; or, if it were, I should detest myself for the exercise of moderation. I cannot, without suffering every feeling and every passion that ought to rise in the cause of humanity to sleep within me, speak coolly on such a subject. Did they feel as I think they ought, I am sure the decision of the House would be with us, for a total and immediate abolition of this abominable traffic.

Why ought the slave trade to be abolished? Because it is incurable injustice. How much stronger, then, is the argument for immediate than gradual abolition? By allowing it to continue even for one hour, do not my right honourable friends weaken—do not they desert their own argument of its injustice? If, on the ground of injustice, it ought to be abolished at last, why ought it not now? Why is injustice to be suffered to remain for a single hour? From what I hear without doors, it is evident that there is a general conviction entertained of its being far from just; and from that very conviction of its injustice, some men have been led, I fear, to the supposition, that the slave trade never could have been permitted to begin, but from some strong and irresistible necessity: a necessity, however, which, if it was fancied to exist at first, I have shown cannot be thought by any man whatever to exist now. This plea of necessity, thus presumed—and presumed, as I suspect, from the circumstance of injustice itself—has caused a sort of acquiescence in the continuance of this evil. Men have been led to place it among the rank of those necessary evils which are supposed to be the lot of human creatures, and to be permitted to fall upon some countries or individuals rather than upon others, by that Being whose ways are inscrutable to us, and whose dispensations, it is conceived, we ought not to look into. The origin of evil is indeed a subject beyond the reach of human understanding, and the permission of it by the Supreme Being is a subject into which it belongs not to us to inquire. But where the evil in question is a moral evil, which a man can scrutinize, and where that evil has its origin with ourselves, let us not imagine that we can clear our consciences by this general, not to say irreligious and impious, way of laying aside the question. If we reflect at all on this subject, we must see that every necessary evil supposes that some other and greater evil would be incurred were it removed: I, therefore, desire to ask, what can be a greater evil which can be stated to overbalance the one in question? I know of no evil that ever has existed, nor can imagine any evil to exist, worse than the tearing of seventy or eighty thousand persons annually from their native land, by a combination of the most civilized nations, inhabiting the most enlightened part of the globe; but, more especially, under the sanction of the laws of that nation which calls herself the most free and the most happy of them all.

Reflect on these eighty thousand persons thus annually taken off! There is something in the horror of it that surpasses all the bounds of imagination. Admitting that there exists in Africa something like to courts of justice, yet, what an office of humiliation and meanness it is in us, to take upon ourselves to carry into execution the partial, the cruel, iniquitous sentences of such courts, as if we also were strangers to all religion and to the first principles of justice! But that country, it is said, has been in some degree civilized, and civilized by us. It is said, they have gained some knowledge of the principles of justice. What, sir! Have they gained principles of justice from us? Their civilization brought about by us! Yes; we give them enough of our intercourse to convey to them the means, and to imitate them in the study, of mutual destruction. We give them just enough of the forms of justice to enable them to add the pretext of legal trials to their other modes of perpetrating the most atrocious iniquity. We give them just enough of European improvements to enable them the more effectually to turn Africa into a ravaged wilderness. Some evidences say, that the Africans are addicted to the practice of gambling; that they even sell their wives and children, and, ultimately, themselves. Are these, then, the legitimate source of slavery? Shall we pretend, that we can thus acquire an honest right to exact the labour of these people? Can we pretend, that we have a right to carry them away to distant regions, men of whom we know nothing by authentic inquiry, and of whom there is every reasonable presumption to think that those who sell them to us have no right to do so? But the evil does not stop here. I feel that there is not time for me to make all the remarks which the subject deserves, and I refrain from attempting to enumerate half the dreadful consequences of this system.

CURRAN.
Born 1750. *Died* 1817.

EMPLOYMENT OF INFORMERS BY THE GOVERNMENT.

THE learned gentleman is farther pleased to say, that the traverser has charged the Government with the encouragement of informers. This, gentlemen, is another small fact that you are to deny at the hazard of your souls, and on the solemnity of your oaths. You are, upon your oaths, to say to the sister kingdom, that the government of Ireland uses no such abominable instruments of destruction as informers. Let me ask you honestly, what do you feel, when in my hearing, when in the face of this audience, you are called upon to give a verdict that every man of us, and every man of you, knows by the testimony of his own eyes, to be utterly and absolutely false? I speak not now of the public proclamations of informers, with a promise of secrecy and of extravagant reward: I speak not of the fate of those horrid wretches who have been so often transferred from the table to the dock, and from the dock to the pillory;—I speak of what your own eyes have seen day after day during the course of this commission, from the box where you are now sitting; the number of horrid miscreants' who avowed, upon their oaths, that they had come from the very seat of Government—from the castle, where they had been worked upon by the fears of death, and the hopes of compensation, to give evidence against their fellows, that the mild and wholesome councils of this government are holden over these catacombs of living death, where the wretch that is buried a man, lies till his heart has time to fester and dissolve, and is then dug up a witness.

Is this fancy, or is it fact? Have you not seen him after his resurrection from that tomb —after having been dug out of the region of death and corruption, make his appearance upon the table, the living image of life and of death, and the supreme arbiter of both? Have you not marked when he entered, how the stormy wave of the multitude retired at his approach? Have you not marked how the human heart bowed to the supremacy of his power, in the undissembled homage of deferential horror? How his glance, like the lightning of heaven, seemed to rive the body of the accused, and mark it for the grave, while his voice warned the devoted wretch of woe and death: a death which no innocence can escape, no art elude, no force resist, no antidote prevent. There was an antidote—a juror's oath— but even that adamantine chain that bound the integrity of man to the throne of eternal justice, is solved and melted in the breath that issues from the informer's mouth; conscience swings from her moorings, and the appalled and affrighted juror consults his own safety in the surrender of the victim.

Innocence shall make false accusation
Blush, and tyranny tremble at patience.

LORD MACAULAY.

Born 1800. *Died* 1859.

[EXTRACT from his Inaugural Address to the Students of the University of Glasgow, on his election as Lord Rector, 21st March, 1849.]

HISTORICAL REVIEW OF THE UNIVERSITY OF GLASGOW.

LOOK at the world a hundred years after the seal of Pope Nicholas the Fifth had been affixed to the instrument which called your College into existence. We find Europe, we find Scotland especially, in the agonies of that revolution which we emphatically call the Reformation. The liberal patronage which Nicholas, and men like Nicholas, had given to learning, and of which the establishment of this seat of learning is not the least remarkable instance, had produced an effect which they had never contemplated. Ignorance was the talisman on which their power depended, and that talisman they had themselves broken. They had called in knowledge as a handmaid to decorate superstition, and their error produced its natural effect. I need not tell you what a part the votaries of classical learning, and especially the votaries of Greek learning, the Humanists, as they were then called, bore in the great movement against spiritual tyranny. They formed, in fact, the vanguard of that movement. Every one of the chief Reformers —I do not at this moment remember a single exception—was a Humanist. Almost every eminent Humanist in the north of Europe was, according to the measure of his uprightness and courage, a Reformer. In a Scottish University I need hardly mention the names of Knox, of Buchanan, of Melville, of Secretary Maitland. In truth, minds daily nourished with the best literature of Greece and Rome necessarily grew too strong to be trammelled by the cobwebs of the scholastic divinity; and the influence of such minds was now rapidly felt by the whole community; for the invention of printing had brought books within the reach of yeomen and of artisans. From the Mediterranean to the Frozen Sea, therefore, the public mind was everywhere in a ferment; and nowhere was the ferment greater than in Scotland. It was in the midst of martyrdoms and proscriptions, in the midst of a war between power and truth, that the first century of the existence of your University closed.

Pass another hundred years, and we are in the midst of another revolution. The war between Popery and Protestantism had, in this island, been terminated by the victory of Protestantism. But from that war another war had sprung, the war between Prelacy and Puritanism. The hostile religious sects were allied, intermingled, confounded with hostile political parties. The monarchical element of the constitution was an object of almost exclusive devotion to the Prelatist. The popular element of the constitution was especially dear to the Puritan. At length an appeal was made to the sword. Puritanism triumphed; but Puritanism was already divided against itself. Independency and Republicanism were on one side, Presbyterianism and limited Monarchy on the other. It was in the very darkest part of that dark time; it was in the midst of battles, sieges, and executions; it was when the whole world was still aghast at the awful spectacle of a British king standing before a judgment-seat, and laying his neck on a block; it was when the mangled remains of the Duke of Hamilton had just been laid in the tomb of his house; it was when the head of the Marquis of Montrose had just been fixed on the Tolbooth of Edinburgh, that your University completed her second century.

A hundred years more, and we have at length reached the beginning of a happier period. Our civil and religious liberties had, indeed, been bought with a fearful price. But they had been bought. The price had been paid. The last battle had been fought on British ground. The last black scaffold had been set up on Tower Hill. The evil days were over. A bright and tranquil century, a century of religious toleration, of domestic peace, of temperate freedom, of equal justice, was beginning. That century is now closing. When we compare it with any equally long period in the history of any other great society, we shall find abundant cause for thankfulness to the Giver of all good. Nor is there any place in the whole kingdom better fitted to excite this feeling than the place where we are now assembled. For in the whole kingdom we shall find no district in which the progress of trade, of manufactures, of wealth, and of the arts of life, has been more rapid than in Clydesdale. Your University has partaken largely of the prosperity of this city and of the surrounding region. The security, the tranquillity, the liberty, which have been propitious to the industry of the merchant, and of the manufacturer, have been also propitious to the industry of the scholar. To the last century belong most of the names of which you justly boast. The time would fail me if I attempted to do justice to the memory of all the illustrious men who, during that period, taught or learned wisdom within these ancient walls; geometricians, anatomists, jurists, philologists, metaphysicians, poets; Simpson and Hunter, Millar and Young, Reid and Stewart; Campbell, whose coffin was lately borne to a grave in that renowned transept which contains the dust of Chaucer, of Spenser, and of Dryden; Black, whose discoveries form an era in the history of chemical science; Adam Smith, the greatest of all the masters of political science; James Watt, who perhaps did more than any single man has done, since the New Atlantis of Bacon was written, to accomplish that glorious prophecy. We now speak the language of humility when we say that the University of Glasgow need not fear a comparison with the University of Bologna.

Another secular period is now about to commence. There is no lack of alarmists, who will tell you that it is about to commence under evil auspices. But from me you must expect no such gloomy prognostications. I have heard them too long and too constantly to be scared by them. Ever since I began to make observations on the state of my country, I have seen nothing but growth, and heard of nothing but decay. The more I contemplate our noble institutions, the more convinced I am that they are sound at heart, that they have nothing of age but its dignity, and that their strength is still the strength of youth. The hurricane which has recently overthrown so much that was great, and that seemed durable, has only proved their solidity. They still stand, august and immovable, while dynasties and churches are lying in heaps of ruin all around us. I see no reason to doubt that, by the blessing of God on a wise and temperate policy, on a policy of which the principle is to preserve what is good by reforming in time what is evil, our civil institutions may be preserved unimpaired to a late posterity, and that under the shade of our civil institutions our academical institutions may long continue to flourish.

RICHARD B. SHERIDAN.
Born 1751. *Died* 1816.
FILIAL PIETY.

FILIAL PIETY!—It is the primeval bond of society—it is that instinctive principle which, panting for its proper good, soothes unbidden each sense and sensibility of man! It now quivers on every lip! it now beams from every eye! It is an emanation of that gratitude which, softening under the sense of recollected good, is eager to own the vast, countless debt it never, alas! can pay, for so many long years of unceasing solicitudes, honourable self-denials, life-preserving cares! It is that part of our practice where duty drops its awe! where reverence refines into love!—it asks no aid of memory!—it needs not the deductions of reason!—pre-existing, paramount over all, whether law or human rule, few arguments can increase and none can diminish it! it is the sacrament of our nature! not only the duty, but the indulgence of man—it is his first great privilege—it is amongst his last most endearing delights! it causes the bosom to glow with reverberated love! it requites the visitations of nature, and retains the blessings that have been received!—it fires emotion into vital principle—it renders habituated instinct into a master passion—sways all the sweetest energies of man—hangs over each vicissitude of all that must pass away—aids the melancholy virtues, in their last sad tasks of life, to cheer the languors of decrepitude and age — explores the thought, elucidates the aching eye—and breathes sweet consolation even in the awful moment of dissolution!

EARL RUSSELL.
Born 1792.

[THE name of Lord John Russell will always be associated with the reform of the representation of this country. He served an early and long apprenticeship to the cause, and met with many a failure before his ultimate success in 1832. On the 14th of December, 1819, his lordship made his first motion on this subject. On the 19th of May, 1820, he brought in his bill for the disfranchising of Grampound; in February, 1821, he proposed to transfer the forfeited franchise to Leeds, but a majority of the House being in favour of giving it to York, it was transferred to that county; later in the same year his proposition for further reforms was negatived by a small majority.

In 1822, in consequence of the depressed state of agriculture, numerous meetings were held to petition Parliament for its relief. Reform being the expedient which seemed to many of these meetings the most promising, petitions for reform were sent up from all parts of the country. Upon the strength of these petitions, especially those from Devonshire and Bedfordshire, Lord John Russell moved, on April 5th, 1822—forty-two years ago—"That the state of the representation required the serious attention of the House," and from his long and elaborate speech on that occasion the following extract is taken. The motion was, however, negatived by a majority of 105.]

PROPOSITIONS FOR REFORM.

LORD JOHN RUSSELL, after stating at some length the evils of the then existing state of the representation, continued:—

Now, in proposing reform, I propose a measure which must be for the advantage of a wise and good administration; nay, it ought to be wished for even by the present ministers. For my own part, I will confess that I have never seen in them any dark or dangerous designs of destroying the liberty of their country; all that I have been able to observe in them is little inclination to do anything, either good or evil, so long as they were permitted to retain unmolested the advantages they derive from power, place, and profit. I believe that in most cases it is perfectly indifferent to them whether the measures they carry are those which they themselves originally proposed, or those which have been altered, framed, and dictated by the indignant sense of the country. I wish them, therefore, to find at once in Parliament an echo of the public voice; to have it in their power to avoid the odium and disgrace of carrying in this assembly measures which they afterwards abandon; to be able, without the delusive support of a majority not acknowledged by the country, to feel at once in this House the pulse of the people of England. Such a reform, I am convinced, would be at once an advantage to the Crown, a blessing to the people, and the safety of the balance of the constitution.

In these conclusions I am happy to think that I am supported by great weight of authority. Lord Clarendon, it is well known, speaking of Cromwell's Parliament, in which the number of members for counties was greatly increased, and the smaller boroughs totally omitted, says it was generally thought "a warrantable alteration, and fit to be made in better times." Mr. Locke complains of the representation of decayed boroughs, and particularly of Old Sarum. Without entering more into detail, I may say, that Mr. Justice Blackstone, Lord Chatham, Mr. Fox, and Mr. Pitt, all concur in recommending a temperate and rational reform.

Thus you have the sanction of Lord Clarendon, the most venerable of Tory statesmen; of Locke, the most liberal of Whig philosophers; of Blackstone, the most cautious of constitutional writers; of Chatham, the boldest of practical ministers; of Mr. Pitt, the theme of eulogy to one great party in this country; of Mr. Fox, the object of affectionate admiration to another. Such an union of the great authorities of men, however different in temper, however opposed in politics, of men forming their judgment upon the most different grounds, living in different times, and agreeing in their conclusions upon hardly any other topic, strikes me as presenting a moral combination in favour of my proposition that is in itself almost irresistible. The opinions of the men whom I have named are blended in our minds with all that is venerable in our constitution and our laws; their united suffrage in favour of any new measure gives to the mind much of that confidence which in general is only obtained by following the lessons of experience; it takes away from reform all the ruggedness of innovation, and constitutes, as it were, a species of precedent in favour of the course which I am urging you to pursue.—Against these authorities I know of no equal names which can be adduced on the other side. There are, it is true, Mr. Burke and Mr. Windham, but they were both, perhaps, men who displayed more fancy than deep reflection in the view which they took of this question, and who have certainly left on record no confutation of the powerful arguments of the great statesmen, who thought differently from them on the subject.

Having now had the honour of stating to the House the unprecedented advance of the country of late times in wealth and knowledge; having stated the great increase of corruption which has crept into the elections, and how much confined the popular force has become in influencing the various modes by which members obtain seats in this House; having also stated the practical injury which has ensued in the wide distinctions prevailing on some great public questions, between the opinions of the people of England and of the members of this House, I now come to the consideration of a plan which I think calculated to remedy a great part of the existing evil. In considering what that plan should be, I have naturally directed my attention to the remedial measures which have been heretofore suggested by persons of weight and authority on this subject. The proposition of Lord Chatham was to add 100 to the number of knights of the shire sitting in this House. Mr. Pitt, likewise following the footsteps of his father, at first proposed an addition of 100 to the number of county members. Mr. Flood, in the year 1790, proposed the same numerical accession of strength to the representation, to be elected by householders throughout the country; and Mr. Fox at the time remarked, that the plan of Mr. Flood was the best he had ever seen submitted to the consideration of Parliament. Feeling, therefore, the weight and influence of such great authorities, I shall adopt their number in my present proposition.

My plan will then be, that a hundred new members shall be admitted into this House; and, as far as I have formed any settled opinion about the distribution of that number, the leaning of my mind is, that 60 members should be added for the counties, and the remaining 40 of the 100 should be for the great towns and commercial interests of the country. However, as to the manner of distribution and the mode of election, that is a branch of the subject which ought to be reserved for the gravest and most deliberate consideration, after the present motion shall have been carried.

It may, however, be said, that since the time when Chatham, Pitt, Fox, and Flood called for an addition to the number of members in this House, their proposed number of 100 has, in point of fact, been added by the Irish Union, which it is known has given that numerical addition to our body. Nor is there any reform more generally unpalatable than that which proposes to add to the numbers of this House, already rather too large than otherwise. In order to get out of this difficulty, I should say, that a number to the same amount as that given for the representation of Ireland might be struck out of the present list, with great benefit to the country; for instance, let the hundred be taken away from the hundred smallest boroughs, which return each two members to sit in Parliament. Let these boroughs return but one member each, and then the present number of the House will be retained.

In proposing this plan, I cannot but recall to the recollection of the House, that it was not long ago since I hoped that much of the real advantages of reform might have been obtained by the detection of prevailing corruption at the borough elections, and the filling up of vacancies so detected by a more popular form. By these means it was possible that a great popular representation might have been introduced, to the exclusion of a wide-spreading corruption. In the hope of accomplishing such a change, I moved for a committee last year to consider of the means of legally convicting boroughs of notorious corruption; and I am not sure that, if the matter had been then taken in a spirit of sincerity, it would not have effected, in a silent and gradual manner, an adequate reform in Parliament. But to be efficacious, it requires the whole co-operation of this House; and such an aid, I am sorry to declare, I have not been so fortunate as to obtain. I am sorry that the House did not, on the occasion to which I allude, evince the sincere wish I had hoped for, to put down corruption. They agreed, it is true, to punish any specific act of corruption, whenever the particular case was brought under the consideration of Parliament; but they would not agree to enact the only measures which were calculated practically to put down the evil they professed so anxious a desire to correct. In that respect their conduct resembled that of a police magistrate, who should declare his readiness to convict any notorious thief who might be brought before him, but who at the same time should proclaim that though he knew there were bands of thieves nightly prowling through the streets, he would not send out a single officer of police to apprehend and detect them.

The indifference of the House to the measures I then proposed has compelled me to look for others more calculated to insure the co-operation of the country at large, and to obtain from the House, in the gross, that reform which they were unwilling to effect by gradual and unpretending means. I therefore press for your consideration the plan which I have now opened; I think it the best and safest proposition which can be suggested for the remedy of a notorious and growing evil.

There are, obviously, many minor details, into which it is unnecessary for me now to enter, and which can only be conveniently considered in a future stage of this proceeding: such, for instance, is the discussion whether copyholders ought to be permitted to vote in the counties; but these matters, I repeat, had better remain over until after the introduction of a bill defining the outline of my plan. The first step must be to ascertain whether the House will consider at all the question of Parliamentary reform. If they once admit the necessity of the principle for which I contend, then I have no doubt they may hereafter, with little difficulty, become reconciled to the measures for its practical application. I think, under such circumstances, the modification of details might easily be accomplished. Leaving, therefore, all these details for future consideration, I will shortly state the answers that strike me as applicable to some of the objections which I have heard from time to time made to the expediency, if not to the principle, of Parliamentary reform.

The first and most plausible objection against any alteration in the present constitution of the small boroughs is, that they constantly furnish the means of bringing into Parliament men of great talents. This is an advantage which I am not in any way disposed to undervalue; but it is one which I submit would remain after my plan is adopted. I have no objection that a number of these boroughs should remain as they now stand; but what I object to respecting them is, that the small boroughs are so numerous, according to the present system, as not only to have their proper weight in the scale of representation, but to have, in addition, the means of commanding a preponderating majority in Parliament. They thus give the sanction of a general Parliamentary assent to measures which have in the main received only the concurrence of a number of individual borough-proprietors. We are thus, for the sake of obtaining a few men of talent, sacrificing the great end of Parliamentary representation, the expression of the feelings and interests of the people. In order to preserve the show, we are giving up the substance of a legitimate House of Commons:—

"Thus, if you dine with my Lord May'r,
Roast beef and venison are your fare;
But tulip leaves and lemon-peel
Serve only to adorn the meal;
And he would be an idle dreamer,
Who left the pie and gnaw'd the streamer."

The next objection to which I shall advert is founded on that inveterate adherence to ancient forms, however unsuitable; to old practices, however abusive, which influences so greatly the decisions of the English Parliament. As this objection has its strength more in the feelings and affections than in any logical argument upon which it is grounded—as it rests on superstition rather than on reason, I know not how to meet it better than by referring to an example in ancient story. The instance I allude to occurs in the history of Rome; and here I must entreat the attention of the honourable member for Corfe Castle, who may be styled the Tory commentator, as Machiavel may be styled the Whig commentator on Roman history. About 370 years after the foundation of Rome, there arose a contest, not very unlike the question we are now debating, whether the two consuls should continue to be chosen from the patricians, or whether one should be chosen invariably from the plebeians. Appius Claudius, who was the prime advocate of aristocracy and existing institutions in that day, argued that the greatest evils would follow if any change was made in the ancient forms. He contended, particularly, that none but a patrician could take the auguries—that if any alteration were made the chickens would not eat—that in vain they would be required to leave their coops. The language given to him by Livy is: "*Quid enim est, si pulli non pascentur? Si ex caveâ tardius exierint? Si occinuerit avis? Parva sunt hæc: sed parva ista non contemnendo majores nostri maximam hanc rem fecerunt.*" Such was the reasoning of the Roman senator: reasoning, be it observed, not very different from that which is used to show that our whole constitution will be subverted, if any invasion is made on the privileges of Old Sarum. But what was the result? After a successful war against a foreign enemy, Camillus the dictator had to encounter the most dangerous seditions at Rome, raised on this subject of the consulship. What did he and the Senate do? It will be imagined that they passed restrictive laws; that they prohibited public meetings of more than fifty persons in the open air; that they punished the seditious orators, and restrained the liberty of speech for the future. No such thing. They assented to the petitions of the people. "*Viu dum perfunctum eum bello atrocior domi seditio excepit; et per ingentia certamina dictator senatusque victus, ut rogationes tribuniciæ acciperentur; et comitia consulum adversâ nobilitate habita quibus L. Sextius de plebe primus consul factus.*" And what was the consequence? Discord and calamity? Quite the reverse. After some further contest, the whole dispute terminated in favour of the people; and the Senate, to celebrate the return of concord between the two orders, commanded that the great games, the *ludi maximi*, should be solemnized, and that an additional holiday should be observed. Rome increased in power and glory; she defeated the Samnites; she resisted Pyrrhus; she conquered Carthage; nor in the whole of her famous history is any complaint to be found on record that the chickens declined to eat, or that they refused to leave their coops on account of the plebeian consul. The honourable member for Corfe Castle, in relating this circumstance, attributes the concession of

NO. IX.

Camillus to two reasons: first, that he thought it prudent to grant what could not long be refused; and, secondly, that he was weary of bearing popular odium. Now, I beseech the honourable member to follow the example of Camillus: let him grant what we cannot much longer refuse, without danger to ourselves and ruin to our country. Let him rest satisfied with the odium we have already acquired, and consent to change a course which has made us so obnoxious to the people of England.

Another objection which I have heard made to reform is, that the people, if not numerically, are at least virtually represented; and as the clearest proof of their agreement in the judgment of Parliament, it is stated, that when that judgment is once pronounced, they acquiesce in it without resistance, and the agitations upon that subject immediately cease throughout the country. This is to my mind anything but a test of popular confidence in the wisdom of Parliament. The acquiescence thus spoken of is what, in fact, has constantly appeared in the conduct of the people under every government throughout the world. For it is one thing for the people to complain, pending the agitation of any question, and another and very different matter to incur the risk of criminality, by declaring any violent dissent from the final adjudication of the constitutional authorities under which they live. The practice of the people is, to express their opinions while a great question is undecided; but when the decision of the supreme magistrate once takes place, they have only to choose between bowing to his authority, or acting in rebellion to his power. The people of England, who are distinguished above all other nations for their respect to law, whose characteristic is a submission to what has been adjudged to be legal, know very well that a decision of the King and his ministers may be altered, but that, once confirmed by Parliament, the act is complete and final: therefore, while a measure is ministerial, they complain; when it becomes parliamentary, they are silent. But nothing is more irrational than under such circumstances to infer the approbation of the people from that silence. When the Parliament decided upon the propriety of omitting her late Majesty's name from the Liturgy, did the people, because they then petitioned no more, acquiesce in the justice of that decision? Were they, when they abstained from remonstrating against the continuance of two postmasters-general, to be supposed as adopting the decision of this House, that two were necessary? All that ought to be inferred from the people's silence, when so situated, is, that a sufficient case for actual resistance had not yet occurred, and that it was useless for them to protest against the decision of Parliament. I think the people

F

judge wisely, because, in the times in which we live, the abuses they endure, though flagrant, do not amount to a justifiable ground for actual resistance. But let not anything be inferred from their obedience, even if pushed still farther. The people, under the very worst species of tyranny, are often found sullen and silent victims. Does the House not know the perfect obedience which was paid to the acts of James II.? Was that tyrant not surrounded in his worst hour of misgovernment by adulatory lawyers, by subservient addressers, by servile surrenderers of corporate rights — in short, by every being who was ready to prostrate the liberties of his country? Did not James enjoy the full measure of this sort of obedience until the evils of his misrule at length compelled him to abandon his throne? Was not the Russian Emperor Paul, notoriously tyrannical as he was, obeyed by the vast population of his empire during years of oppression, and up to the moment when the bowstring put an end to his despotic career? Was not Ferdinand of Spain obeyed when he signed with his own hand the death-warrants of his best subjects, until at last the flame of popular discontent, which remained so long smothered, burst forth in the blaze of rebellion, and consumed all the bulwarks of his arbitrary rule? No doubt that, in the day of these tyrannic acts, the inflictors of them thought, as some men are disposed to think here, that the people were in willing and satisfied obedience because they abstained from open resistance; and there were bad advisers to press for the continuance of fatal and desperate measures, until at length they became intolerable, and recoiled upon the heads of the abettors of them with ruin and destruction. The same fate will befall England, if similar measures are pursued to a desperate extremity. Suppose a war arose, not of the people's own seeking, though the minister were to secure for it the approbation of Parliament—suppose it led to bankruptcy and general confusion, in that melancholy hour, what answer would the uniform opposers of reform have for those whose advice, if timely attended to, would have saved the institutions of their country? What security would you have then that the reform which has not been made from within, may not come with a vengeance from without?

And now, lastly, I come to an objection, which in the failure of all other argument, after the defeat of every specific and tangible objection, is always brought forward as a complete bar to every proposition of reform. This consideration, which addresses itself rather to the nerves than to the understanding of those on whom it is meant to operate, is the example of the civil wars of England and the French Revolution. I likewise beseech your attention to the civil wars of England and the French Revolution; but I beg of you that it may be a sober attention, worthy of men and of Englishmen. And first let me ask, will any man say that it would have been right to permit Charles I. to abolish parliamentary government, to levy money by his own authority, and supersede the ancient liberties of England by the doctrine of divine right?—that it was not lawful and praiseworthy to resist a system of despotism, not intended, not projected, but actually established in England in the early years of that reign? Or will any man say that the mean debauchery of Louis XV. was a fit employment for the resources of a great nation like the French? that the abuses of the French government did not require reform? If there be any man who will say this, let him enjoy his opinion if he will, but let him not presume to think himself worthy to enjoy the benefits of the British constitution; and, above all, let him not venture to think his counsels can be listened to in a British Parliament.

I assume, then—and let us now confine our attention to one of the two countries—I assume that Lord Clarendon, and Lord Strafford, and Lord Falkland were right in their early opposition to the misgovernment of Charles I. But why not stop, it will be said, like Lord Clarendon and Lord Falkland? Alas! sir, who shall say that the policy of Lord Clarendon and Lord Falkland would have procured for us a system of liberty? Who will venture to lay his finger upon that point in the History of Charles I., when it would have been possible to save the monarchy without losing the constitution? Who shall presume himself to possess more learning than Selden, more sagacity than Pym, more patriotism than Hampden?

The question, in fact, was involved in inextricable difficulty. From all I have read, and all I have thought upon this subject, I take the cause of that difficulty to be this: The aristocracy were divided; they were divided between a larger party, who were satisfied to bear arbitrary power for the sake of property and tranquillity; and a smaller party, who were ready to sacrifice property, and even life, for the sake of destroying arbitrary power. But this last party, being the minority, were obliged to call to their aid the assistance of the people. Now the history of the world shows, that to accomplish great changes in government by the active agency of the people, is a task of great hazard and uncertainty. The people, in a state of agitation, are, in times like those I speak of, naturally suspicious: they awake from a dream of confidence, and find that their facility has been abused by those rulers in whom they had implicitly trusted. In this wreck of all their established reliances. in this anxious desire for the benefits of freedom, in this tremorous apprehension of falling back into slavery, what wonder is it that their fears should be continually roused, that they should listen to accusations even against their best friends, and that, with a mixture of zeal and timidity, they should destroy the beautiful temple at the same time that they tear down the foul idol that it contains? What matter of surprise is it that, unable to know exactly the truth, they should rase the very foundations of a society under which they have greatly suffered?

But how are these evils to be avoided? How are these natural and usual calamities, attendant on popular revolutions, to be averted? By a united aristocracy. History here, too, tells us, that if great changes accomplished by the people are dangerous, although sometimes salutary, great changes accomplished by an aristocracy, at the desire of the people, are at once salutary and safe. When such revolutions are made, the people are always ready to leave in the hands of the aristocracy that guidance which tends to preserve the balance of the government and the tranquillity of the State. Such a change was the expulsion of the Tarquins from Rome; of James II. from England. These were revolutions accomplished without bloodshed and confusion, by the influence of an united aristocracy. I call upon the aristocracy of England, therefore, now to unite to make that change safe, which, if they do not unite, may be dangerous, but which will not be the less inevitable. I call upon the Tories to stay the progress of abuses which must end in the convulsion of the State. I appeal still more confidently to the Whigs to unite for a similar object. If I know anything of Whiggism, the spirit of Whiggism is, to require for the people as much liberty as their hands can safely grasp at the time when it is required: and I am so far from agreeing to the flimsy accusations sometimes made against the Whigs, that I think, looking at their conduct from the beginning, their chief fault has been a fault of policy, in asking for more freedom and more securities for freedom than the people wished or could retain. The Exclusion Bill and the whole life of Mr. Fox are instances of this observation. When at the revolution, however, the government of this country was settled, the Whigs retained in their own hands the boroughs which they were able to influence. I really believe that to this measure the settlement of the House of Hanover is mainly owing. During the reigns of the two first kings of the house of Brunswick, the county members consisted almost entirely of the most determined Tories: and had they prevailed, we should probably have seen upon the throne the descendants of James II., granting, perhaps, more securities for our religion, but not more guarantees for our liberty than James himself. I think, therefore, the Whigs were fully justified in retaining a certain quantity of borough influence, which they could not otherwise have justly held. But now, when the people are enlightened, and fully capable of understanding their own interests, the Whigs will act wisely if they yield to the increased intelligence of the country a due share in the return of their representatives. As they formerly retained the boroughs to secure liberty, let them now, for the same noble object, consent to part with them. Let them show to the country that if reform is impeded, the Whig aristocracy stands free from the charge of hindering its progress from any personal and selfish interest of their own. In so doing, they will give energy and effect to their opposition in Parliament; for I do not wish to conceal it, the possession of these boroughs has lessened the energy of their efforts in support of the liberties of the country. They have been able to state, with less firmness and frankness than they might otherwise have done, the causes of the misgovernment of the country; and the people, on the other hand, seem to feel that the Whig aristocracy retain something which properly belongs to themselves. Hence the union between the party of the people within and without the walls of Parliament has been less cordial than it would be if the Whigs were content to yield something to the popular desire for reform. I beseech them to do so; but not them only; all the aristocracy of the land. Sir William Temple, a wise and amiable man, but whom no one will accuse of being too great an enthusiast for liberty, has said, that this great nation never can be ruined but by itself; and that, even in the greatest changes, if the weight and number rolled one way, yet England would be safe. I beseech you that the weight and number may roll one way; I beseech the possessors of great property to consider how nearly it concerns them to retain the affections of the great mass of the people. I beseech you, that, throwing aside all feminine fears, all pedantic prejudices, and all private advantages, you will consider only your duty as men, the wants of the age in which we live, and that permanent and pervading interest which we all have in the maintenance of the English constitution. May you remember that the liberty which was acquired for you by your ancestors will be required of you by your descendants: then will you agree to a temperate and timely reform, reconcile the different classes of society, and prevent a convulsion which may involve all in one common ruin. Then may that proud constitution, which has now subsisted in maturity little more than one hundred years, continue to maintain the spirit of its freedom, and extend the sphere of its salutary influence, until its existence vies with that of the most durable institutions that were ever reared for the happiness of mankind in any age, or in any country.—I now move, "That the present state of the representation of the people in Parliament requires the most serious consideration of this House."

HENRY DRUMMOND.
Born 1786. Died 1860.

[WE here present our readers with a specimen of the oratory of one who was a real old Tory, and who gloried in his principles. Much of the power of his speeches, which were always worth hearing, and which often produced a profound impression in the House, is lost. As Lord Lovaine, his friend, and the editor of a collection of his speeches, well says, "They are the practical, powerful exposition, in terse and cogent terms, of the ideas of the speaker; but they cannot convey to the reader the effect they produced on the listeners. The boldness which challenged opposition—the ready wit which confounded the interrupter—the cutting irony which pierced through every conventionality, and laid bare every hypocrisy—seem dull and lifeless on the printed page."
The short speech which follows is one of the best in the collection, and the fine and happy stroke of satire with which it ends will always be remembered in connection with the speaker's name.
It was delivered on March 13th, 1855, on the question, "That leave be given to bring in a bill to amend the law as to marriage with a deceased wife's sister, or a deceased wife's niece."]

MARRIAGE LAW AMENDMENT.

THE object of the honourable member who has just sat down (Mr. Spooner) was, as I heard him, to inculcate and promote private morality; but he began his task by advising the House to set the law of God at defiance. The honourable gentleman went on to say that there was a vast majority of the people in favour of his views; so that the question of settling an important principle is to be decided by counting noses. This is not an argument usually employed; for every single sect, however small, is in the habit of saying to itself, "Fear not, little flock; it is your Father's good pleasure to give you the kingdom;" and, except from the honourable gentleman, I have never heard that the multitude of those who agree to it is to be taken as the test of a theological proposition. But it is not to answer the arguments of the honourable member for Warwickshire that I rose. The honourable member who opened the discussion stated the true history of this question. There never was a doubt on the mind of the Church as to the true meaning of those passages upon the subject which have been quoted from Scripture. It is very true that from the third to the fifth century for the first time the question of dispensations began to be raised, and the Pope prohibited as much as he could. In so doing the Pope acted most wisely, for the more he prohibited, the more grist was brought to his mill in the shape of money for dispensations. "But," said an honourable and learned gentleman (Mr. Bowyer), who ought to know better, "the Church," by which he meant the Papacy, "never dared to say a word against that which it believed to be the word of God." The honourable and learned gentleman must, however, know that the law of his Church, as described by a great authority, was *Papa potest legem Dei mutare*. The honourable and learned gentleman should also recollect that there is another passage from the same authority, in which it is clearly stated that the Pope can make *vitia* those things which other people suppose to be *virtutes*, and *virtutes* what other people suppose to be *vitia*. It is notorious that the prohibition against these marriages has been set aside in every direction. Have you never read the history of Spain? Have you never read of Kings of Spain marrying their own nieces? Why almost the whole of their history, especially after the arrival of the Bourbons in the country, has been one continual history of incest, for which they have paid enormous sums to procure dispensations. The reason the permission was given to the Jew to marry his brother's wife was, that under the Mosaic economy the land was divided into twelve portions, and no person who belonged to one tribe could acquire land that belonged to another tribe. They were obliged to keep the land in the possession of the tribe to which it pertained; and it was to preserve the succession in that tribe that a man was bound to marry his deceased brother's wife. The honourable member who last addressed the House, instead of arguing as he did, had better get rid of the prohibited degrees altogether, *and marry his grandmother like a man*—or his niece, for perhaps his niece would be much better worth marrying than his grandmother; that is, if you mean to set aside the word of God as a thing that is utterly unworthy and contemptible in your new code of morality. Then let him act like a man, and not stand snivelling there between the canting Methodist on the one hand, and the honest old infidel on the other.

[Mr. J. Ball begged to remind Mr. Drummond that the quotation he had made in support of the power of the Pope came from that eminent writer, Cardinal Bellarmine, and that when it was sought to canonize that individual, the very text which the honourable member quoted was produced against him as erroneous doctrine, and on the ground of that text the canonization was refused.]

Mr. Drummond answered,—

That is all perfectly true, and the very next year it was altered in this way—*Papa non potest legem Dei mutare nisi cum causa.*

LORD CHATHAM.
Born 1708. Died 1778.

[THE following speech was delivered in the House of Lords, on the Address to the Throne, at the opening of Parliament, on the 18th of November, 1777, and is from beginning to end a splendid protest against the proposed continuance of the already hopeless struggle with America. This speech was among the last efforts of this distinguished statesman, and though made in the lingering season of decrepit age, and under the severest pangs of disease, displays undiminished the excellences of Chatham's eloquence. It would, indeed, be difficult to find, in the whole range of parliamentary history, a more splendid blaze of oratorical genius, at once rapid, vigorous, and exalted. Death soon afterwards terminated his glorious career.]

PROTEST AGAINST THE AMERICAN WAR.

I RISE, my lords, to declare my sentiments on this most solemn and serious subject. It has imposed a load upon my mind, which, I fear, nothing can remove; but which impels me to endeavour its alleviation, by a free and unreserved communication of my sentiments.

In the first part of the address I have the honour of heartily concurring with the noble earl who moved it. No man feels sincerer joy than I do; none can offer more genuine congratulation on every accession of strength to the Protestant succession. I therefore join in every congratulation on the birth of another princess, and the happy recovery of her Majesty. But I must stop here. My courtly complaisance will carry me no further. I will not join in congratulation on misfortune and disgrace. I cannot concur in a blind and servile address, which approves, and endeavours to sanctify, the monstrous measures which have heaped disgrace and misfortune upon us. This, my lords, is a perilous and tremendous moment! It is not a time for adulation. The smoothness of flattery cannot now avail; cannot save us in this rugged and awful crisis. It is now necessary to instruct the throne in the language of truth. We must dispel the delusion and the darkness which envelope it; and display, in its full danger and true colours, the ruin that is brought to our doors.

This, my lords, is our duty. It is the proper function of this noble assembly, sitting, as we do, upon our honours in this House, the hereditary council of the crown. Who is the minister, *where* is the minister, that has dared to suggest to the throne the contrary, unconstitutional language this day delivered from it? The accustomed language from the throne has been application to Parliament for advice, and a reliance on its constitutional advice and assistance. As it is the right of Parliament to give, so it is the duty of the crown to ask it. But on this day, and in this extreme momentous exigency, no reliance is reposed on our constitutional counsels! no advice is asked from the sober and enlightened care of Parliament! but the crown, from itself and by itself, declares an unalterable determination to pursue measures—and what measures, my lords? The measures that have produced the imminent perils that threaten us; the measures that have brought ruin to our doors.

Can the minister of the day now presume to expect a continuance of support in this ruinous infatuation? Can Parliament be so dead to its dignity and its duty, as to be thus deluded into the loss of the one and the violation of the other? to give an unlimited credit and support for the steady perseverance in measures not proposed for our parliamentary advice, but dictated and forced upon us—in measures, I say, my lords, which have reduced this late flourishing empire to ruin and contempt?

"But yesterday,
And England might have stood against the world:
Now none so poor to do her reverence."

I use the words of a poet; but though it be poetry, it is no fiction. It is a shameful truth, that not only the power and strength of this country are wasting away and expiring, but her well-earned glories, her true honour, and substantial dignity are sacrificed. France, my lords, has insulted you; she has encouraged and sustained America; and whether America be wrong or right, the dignity of this country ought to spurn at the officious insult of French interference. The ministers and ambassadors of those who are called rebels and enemies are in Paris; in Paris they transact the reciprocal interests of America and France. Can there be a more mortifying insult? Can even our ministers sustain a more humiliating disgrace? Do they dare to resent it? Do they presume even to hint a vindication of their honour, and the dignity of the State, by requiring the dismission of the plenipotentiaries of America? Such is the degradation to which they have reduced the glories of England! The people whom they affect to call contemptible rebels, but whose growing power has at last obtained the name of enemies; the people with whom they have engaged this country in war, and against whom they now command our implicit support in every measure of desperate hostility; this people, despised as rebels, or acknowledged as enemies, are abetted against you, supplied with every military store, their interests consulted, and their ambassadors entertained, by your inveterate enemy! and our ministers dare not interpose with dignity or effect. Is this the honour of a great kingdom? Is this the indignant spirit of England, who "but yesterday" gave law to the house of Bourbon? My lords, the dignity of nations demands a decisive conduct in a situation like this. Even when the greatest prince that perhaps this country ever saw filled our throne, the requisition of a Spanish general on a similar subject was attended to, and complied with. For, on the spirited remonstrance of the Duke of Alva, Elizabeth found herself obliged to deny the Flemish exiles all countenance, support, or even entrance into her dominions; and the Count le Marque, with his few desperate followers, were expelled the kingdom. Happening to arrive at the Brille, and finding it weak in defence, they made themselves masters of the place; and this was the foundation of the United Provinces.

My lords, this ruinous and ignominious situation, where we cannot act with success, nor suffer with honour, calls upon us to remonstrate in the strongest and loudest language of truth, to rescue the ear of Majesty from the delusions which surround it. The desperate state of our arms abroad is in part known. No man thinks more highly of them than I do. I love and honour the English troops. I know their virtues and their valour. I know they can achieve anything except impossibilities; and I know that the conquest of English America is an impossibility. You cannot, I venture to say it, you cannot conquer America. Your armies last war effected everything that could be effected; and what was it? It cost a numerous army under the command of a most able general,* now a noble lord in this House, a long and laborious campaign, to expel five thousand Frenchmen from French America. My lords, *you cannot conquer America.* What is your present situation there? We do not know the worst; but we know that in three campaigns we have done nothing and suffered much. Besides the sufferings, perhaps total loss of the northern force;† the best-appointed army that ever took the field, commanded by Sir William Howe, has retired from the American lines. He was obliged to relinquish his attempt, and with great delay and danger to adopt a new and distant plan of operations. We shall soon know, and in any event have reason to lament, what may have happened since. As to conquest, therefore, my lords, I repeat, it is impossible. You may swell every expense, and every effort, still more extravagantly; pile and accumulate every assistance you can buy or borrow; traffic and barter with every little pitiful German prince that sells and sends his subjects to the shambles of a foreign prince; your efforts are for ever vain and impotent: doubly so from this mercenary aid on which you rely. For it irritates, to an incurable resentment, the minds of your enemies, to overrun them with the mercenary sons of rapine and plunder; devoting them and their possessions to the rapacity of hireling cruelty. If I were an American, as I am an Englishman, while a foreign troop was landed in my country, I never would lay down my arms—never—never—never!

Your own army is infected with the contagion of these illiberal allies. The spirit of plunder and of rapine is gone forth among them. I know it—and notwithstanding what the noble earl,* who moved the address, has given as his opinion of our American army, I know from authentic information, and the most experienced officers, that our discipline is deeply wounded. Whilst this is notoriously our sinking situation, America grows and flourishes: whilst our strength and discipline are lowered, hers are rising and improving.

But, my lords, who is the man that, in addition to these disgraces and mischiefs of our army, has dared to authorize and associate to our arms the tomahawk and scalping-knife of the savage? to call into civilized alliance the wild and inhuman savage of the woods; to delegate to the merciless Indian the defence of disputed rights, and to wage the horrors of his barbarous war against our brethren? My lords, these enormities cry aloud for redress and punishment. Unless thoroughly done away, it will be a stain on the national character. It is a violation of the constitution. I believe it is against law. It is not the least of our national misfortunes that the strength and character of our army are thus impaired. Infected with the mercenary spirit of robbery and rapine; familiarized to the horrid scenes of savage cruelty, it can no longer boast of the noble and generous principles which dignify a soldier; no longer sympathize with the dignity of the royal banner, nor feel the pride, pomp, and circumstance of glorious war, "that make ambition virtue!" What makes ambition virtue? The sense of honour. But is the sense of honour consistent with a spirit of plunder, or the practice of murder? Can it flow from mercenary motives, or can it prompt to cruel deeds? Besides these murderers and plunderers, let me ask our ministers, what other allies have they acquired? What other powers have they associated to their cause? Have they entered into alliance with the king of the gypsies? Nothing, my lords, is too low or too ludicrous to be consistent with their counsels.

The independent views of America have been stated and asserted as the foundation of this address. My lords, no man wishes for the due dependence of America on this country more than I do. To preserve it, and not confirm that state of independence into which your measures hitherto have driven them, is the object which we ought to unite in attaining. The Americans, contending for their rights against arbitrary exactions, I love and admire. It is the struggle of free and virtuous patriots;

---

* Lord Amherst, then Sir Jeffery Amherst.
† General Burgoyne's army.

* Lord Percy.

but contending for independency and total disconnection from England, as an Englishman, I cannot wish them success. For, in a due constitutional dependency, including the ancient supremacy of this country in regulating their commerce and navigation, consists the mutual happiness and prosperity both of England and America. She derived assistance and protection from us; and we reaped from her the most important advantages. She was, indeed, the fountain of our wealth, the nerve of our strength, the nursery and basis of our naval power. It is our duty, therefore, my lords, if we wish to save our country, most seriously to endeavour the recovery of these most beneficial subjects: and in this perilous crisis, perhaps the present moment may be the only one in which we can hope for success. For in their negotiations with France they have, or think they have, reason to complain, though it be notorious that they have received from that power important supplies and assistance of various kinds, yet it is certain they expected it in a more decisive and immediate degree. America is in ill-humour with France on some points that have not entirely answered her expectations. Let us wisely take advantage of every possible moment of reconciliation. Besides, the natural disposition of America herself still leans towards England; to the old habits of connection and mutual interest that united both countries. This *was* the established sentiment of all the continent, and still, my lords, in the great and principal part, the sound part of America, this wise and affectionate disposition prevails ; and there is a very considerable part of America yet sound—the middle and the southern provinces. Some parts may be factious and blind to their true interests; but if we express a wise and benevolent disposition to communicate to them those immutable rights of nature, and those constitutional liberties, to which they are equally entitled with ourselves; by a conduct so just and humane, we shall confirm the favourable, and conciliate the adverse. I say, my lords, the rights and liberties to which they are equally entitled with ourselves; but no more. I would participate to them every enjoyment and freedom which the colonizing subjects of a free state can possess, or wish to possess; and I do not see why they should not enjoy every fundamental right in their property, and every original substantial liberty, which Devonshire or Surrey, or the county I live in, or any other county in England, can claim; reserving always, as the sacred right of the mother country, the due constitutional dependency of the colonies. The inherent supremacy of the State in regulating and protecting the navigation and commerce of all her subjects, is necessary for the mutual benefit and preservation of every part, to constitute and preserve the prosperous arrangement of the whole empire.

The sound parts of America, of which I have spoken, must be sensible of these great truths, and of their real interests. America is not in that state of desperate and contemptible rebellion which this country has been deluded to believe. It is not a wild and lawless banditti, who, having nothing to lose, might hope to snatch something from public convulsions. Many of their leaders and great men have a great stake in this great contest. The gentleman who conducts their armies, I am told, has an estate of four or five thousand pounds a year; and when I consider these things, I cannot but lament the inconsiderate violence of our penal acts, our declarations of treason and rebellion, with all the fatal effects of attainder and confiscation.

As to the disposition of foreign powers which is asserted to be pacific * and friendly, let us judge, my lords, rather by their actions and the nature of things than by interested assertions. The uniform assistance supplied to America by France suggests a different conclusion. The most important interests of France, in aggrandizing and enriching herself with what she most wants, supplies of every naval store from America, must inspire her with different sentiments. The extraordinary preparations of the house of Bourbon, by land and by sea, from Dunkirk to the Straits, equally ready and willing to overwhelm these defenceless islands, should rouse us to a sense of their real disposition, and our own danger. Not five thousand troops in England!—hardly three thousand in Ireland! What can we oppose to the combined force of our enemies? Scarcely twenty ships of the line fully or sufficiently manned, that any admiral's reputation would permit him to take the command of. The river of Lisbon in the possession of our enemies! The seas swept by American privateers! Our channel trade torn to pieces by them! In this complicated crisis of danger, weakness at home, and calamity abroad, terrified and insulted by the neighbouring powers, unable to act in America, or acting only to be destroyed, where is the man with the forehead to promise or hope for success in such a situation? or from perseverance in the measures that have driven us to it? Who has the forehead to do so? Where is that man? I should be glad to see his face.

You cannot *conciliate* America by your present measures. You cannot *subdue* her by your present, or by any measures. What, then, can you do? You cannot conquer; you cannot gain; but you can *address*. You can lull the fears and anxieties of the moment into an ignorance of the danger that should produce them. But, my lords, the time demands the

---

* In the King's speech.

language of truth. We must not now apply the flattering unction of servile compliance, or blind complaisance. In a just and necessary war, to maintain the rights or honour of my country, I would strip the shirt from my back to support it. But in such a war as this, unjust in its principle, impracticable in its means, and ruinous in its consequences, I would not contribute a single effort, nor a single shilling. I do not call for vengeance on the heads of those who have been guilty : I only recommend to them to make their retreat. Let them walk off; and let them make haste, or they may be assured that speedy and condign punishment will overtake them. My lords, I have submitted to you, with the freedom and truth which I think my duty, my sentiments on your present awful situation. I have laid before you the ruin of your power, the disgrace of your reputation, the pollution of your discipline, the contamination of your morals, the complication of calamities, foreign and domestic, that overwhelm your sinking country. Your dearest interests, your own liberties, the constitution itself, totters to the foundation. All this disgraceful danger, this multitude of misery, is the monstrous offspring of this unnatural war. We have been deceived and deluded too long. Let us now stop short. This is the crisis—the only crisis,* of time and situation, to give us a possibility of escape from the fatal effects of our delusions. But if, in an obstinate and infatuated perseverance in folly, we slavishly echo the peremptory words this day presented to us, nothing can save this devoted country from complete and final ruin. We madly rush into multiplied miseries and "confusion worse confounded."

Is it possible, can it be believed, that ministers are yet blind to this impending destruction? I did hope that, instead of this false and empty vanity, this overweening pride, engendering high conceits and presumptuous imaginations, that ministers would have humbled themselves in their errors, would have confessed and retracted them, and by an active, though a late repentance, have endeavoured to redeem them. But, my lords, since they had neither sagacity to foresee, nor justice nor humanity to shun, these oppressive calamities; since not even severe experience can make them feel, nor the imminent ruin of their country awaken them from their stupefaction, the guardian care of Parliament must interpose. I shall, therefore, my lords, propose to you an amendment to the address to his Majesty, to be inserted immediately after the two first paragraphs of congratulation on the birth of a princess, to recommend an immediate cessation of hostilities, and the commencement of a treaty to restore peace and liberty to America, strength and happiness to England, security and permanent prosperity to both countries. This, my lords, is yet in our power; and let not the wisdom and justice of your lordships neglect the happy, and perhaps the only, opportunity. By the establishment of irrevocable law, founded on mutual rights, and ascertained by treaty, these glorious enjoyments may be firmly perpetuated. And let me repeat to your lordships, that the strong bias of America, at least of the wise and sounder parts of it, naturally inclines to this happy and constitutional reconnection with you. Notwithstanding the temporary intrigues with France, we may still be assured of their ancient and confirmed partiality to us. America and France cannot be congenial. There is something decisive and confirmed in the honest American, that will not assimilate to the futility and levity of Frenchmen.

My lords, to encourage and confirm that innate inclination to this country, founded on every principle of affection, as well as consideration of interest; to restore that favourable disposition into a permanent and powerful reunion with this country; to revive the mutual strength of the empire; again to awe the house of Bourbon, instead of meanly truckling, as our present calamities compel us, to every insult of French caprice and Spanish punctilio; to re-establish our commerce; to re-assert our rights and our honour; to confirm our interests, and renew our glories for ever,—a consummation most devoutly to be endeavoured, and which, I trust, may yet arise from reconciliation with America,—I have the honour of submitting to you the following amendment, which I move to be inserted after the two first paragraphs of the address:—

"And that this House does most humbly advise and supplicate his Majesty to be pleased to cause the most speedy and effectual measures to be taken for restoring peace in America; and that no time may be lost in proposing an immediate cessation of hostilities there, in order to the opening of a treaty for the final settlement of the tranquillity of these invaluable provinces, by a removal of the unhappy causes of this ruinous civil war; and by a just and adequate security against the return of the like calamities in times to come. And this House desire to offer the most dutiful assurances to his Majesty that they will, in due time, cheerfully co-operate with the magnanimity and tender goodness of his Majesty, for the preservation of his people, by such explicit and most solemn declarations, and provisions of fundamental and revocable laws, as may be judged necessary for the

---

* It cannot escape observation with what urgent anxiety the noble speaker presses this point throughout his speech—the critical necessity of instantly treating with America. But the warning voice was heard in vain ; the address triumphed ; Parliament adjourned ; ministers enjoyed the festive recess of a long Christmas ; and America ratified her alliance with France.

ascertaining and fixing for ever the respective rights of Great Britain and her colonies."

In the course of this debate, Lord Suffolk, secretary for the northern department, undertook to defend the employment of the Indians in the war. His lordship contended that, besides its policy and necessity, the measure was also allowable on principle; for that "it was perfectly justifiable to use all the means that God and nature put into our hands!"

I AM ASTONISHED! (exclaimed Lord Chatham, as he rose)—shocked! to hear such principles confessed—to hear them avowed in this House, or in this country: principles equally unconstitutional, inhuman, and unchristian!

My lords, I did not intend to have encroached again upon your attention; but I cannot repress my indignation. I feel myself impelled by every duty. My lords, we are called upon as members of this House, as men, as Christian men, to protest against such notions standing near the throne, polluting the ear of Majesty. "That God and nature put into our hands!" I know not what ideas that lord may entertain of God and nature; but I know that such abominable principles are equally abhorrent to religion and humanity. What! to attribute the sacred sanction of God and nature to the massacres of the Indian scalping-knife—to the cannibal savage torturing, murdering, roasting, and eating; literally, my lords, *eating* the mangled victims of his barbarous battles! Such horrible notions shock every precept of religion, divine or natural, and every generous feeling of humanity. And, my lords, they shock every sentiment of honour; they shock me as a lover of honourable war, and a detester of murderous barbarity.

These abominable principles, and this more abominable avowal of them, demand the most decisive indignation. I call upon that right reverend bench, those holy ministers of the Gospel, and pious pastors of our church; I conjure them to join in the holy work, and vindicate the religion of their God. I appeal to the wisdom and the law of this learned bench to defend and support the justice of their country. I call upon the bishops to interpose the unsullied sanctity of their lawn; upon the learned judges to interpose the purity of their ermine to save us from this pollution. I call upon the honour of your lordships to reverence the dignity of your ancestors, and to maintain your own. I call upon the spirit and humanity of my country to vindicate the national character. I invoke the genius of the constitution. From the tapestry that adorns these walls, the

* Lord Effingham.— Lord Effingham Howard was Lord High Admiral of England against the Spanish Armada, the destruction of which was represented in the tapestry on the walls of the old House of Lords.

NO. X.

immortal ancestor of this noble lord * frowns with indignation at the disgrace of his country. In vain he led your victorious fleets against the boasted Armada of Spain; in vain he defended and established the honour, the liberties, the religion, the *Protestant religion*, of this country, against the arbitrary cruelties of Popery and the Inquisition, if these more than Popish cruelties and inquisitorial practices are let loose among us; to turn forth into our settlements, among our ancient connections, friends, and relations, the merciless cannibal, thirsting for the blood of man, woman, and child! to send forth the infidel savage—against whom? Against your Protestant brethren; to lay waste their country, to desolate their dwellings, and extirpate their race and name, with these horrible hell-hounds of savage war!—*hell-hounds, I say, of savage war*. Spain armed herself with blood-hounds to extirpate the wretched natives of America; and we improve on the inhuman example even of Spanish cruelty: we turn loose these savage hell-hounds against our brethren and countrymen in America, of the same language, laws, liberties, and religion; endeared to us by every tie that should sanctify humanity.

My lords, this awful subject, so important to our honour, our constitution, and our religion, demands the most solemn and effectual inquiry. And I again call upon your lordships, and the united powers of the State, to examine it thoroughly and decisively, and to stamp upon it an indelible stigma of the public abhorrence. And I again implore those holy prelates of our religion to do away these iniquities from among us. Let them perform a lustration; let them purify this House, and this country, from this sin.

My lords, I am old and weak, and at present unable to say more; but my feelings and indignation were too strong to have said less. I could not have slept this night in my bed, nor reposed my head on my pillow, without giving this vent to my eternal abhorrence of such preposterous and enormous principles.

MEN who early attain eminence repose in their first creed. They neglect the progress of the human mind subsequent to its adoption, and when, as in the present case, it has burst forth into action, they regard it as a transient madness, worthy only of pity or derision. They mistake it for a mountain torrent that will pass away with the storm that gave it birth. They know not that it is the stream of human opinion *in omne volubilis ævum*, which the accession of every day will swell, which is destined to sweep into the same oblivion the resistance of learned sophistry, and of powerful oppression.—*Mackintosh.*

WILLIAM PITT.

Born 1759. Died 1806.

[NAPOLEON BUONAPARTE, on his return from Egypt, having dissolved the Directorial Government (Nov. 9, 1799), sent a letter to King George III., urging him to join with him in restoring peace. This overture was declined by Lord Grenville, as was a second from M. Talleyrand, and the subject became a matter for debate in both Houses.

An Address of a warlike character, in favour of the rejection of the overtures, was proposed by Lord Grenville, and carried in both Houses.

The following is an extract from Mr. Pitt's speech on the occasion (delivered Feb. 3, 1800), containing, in support of the Address, a masterly summary of Napoleon's career up to that time, and a by no means unjust though stern estimate of his principles.]

THE FIRST CONSUL OF THE FRENCH REPUBLIC.

HAVING taken a view of what the state of France was, let us now examine what it is. In the first place, we see, as has been truly stated, a change in the description and form of the sovereign authority; a supreme power is placed at the head of this nominal republic, with a more open avowal of military despotism than at any former period; with a more open and undisguised abandonment of the names and pretences under which that despotism long attempted to conceal itself. The different institutions, republican in their form and appearance, which were before the instruments of that despotism, are now annihilated; they have given way to the absolute power of one man, concentrating in himself all the authority of the State, and differing from other monarchs only in this, that, as my honourable friend* truly stated it, he wields a sword instead of a sceptre. What, then, is the confidence we are to derive either from the frame of the government, or from the character and past conduct of the person who is now the absolute ruler of France?

Had we seen a man, of whom we had no previous knowledge, suddenly invested with the sovereign authority of the country; invested with the power of taxation, with the power of the sword, the power of war and peace, the unlimited power of commanding the resources, of disposing of the lives and fortunes, of every man in France; if we had seen, at the same moment, all the inferior machinery of the revolution, which, under the variety of successive shocks, had kept the system in motion, still remaining entire, all that, by requisition and plunder, had given activity to the revolutionary system of finance, and had furnished the means of creating an army, by converting every man who was of age to bear arms into a soldier, not for the defence of his own country, but for the sake of carrying unprovoked war into surrounding countries; if we had seen all the subordinate instruments of Jacobin power subsisting in their full force, and retaining (to use the French phrase) all their original organization; and had then observed this single change in the conduct of their affairs, that there was now one man with no rival to thwart his measures, no colleague to divide his powers, no council to control his operations, no liberty of speaking or writing, no expression of public opinion to check or influence his conduct; under such circumstances, should we be wrong to pause, or wait for the evidence of facts and experience, before we consented to trust our safety to the forbearance of a single man, in such a situation, and to relinquish those means of defence which have hitherto carried us safe through all the storms of the revolution? if we were to ask what are the principles and character of this stranger, to whom fortune has suddenly committed the concerns of a great and powerful nation?

But is this the actual state of the present question? Are we talking of a stranger of whom we have heard nothing? No, sir; we have heard of him; we, and Europe, and the world, have heard both of him and of the satellites by whom he is surrounded; and it is impossible to discuss fairly the propriety of any answer which could be returned to his overtures of negotiation, without taking into consideration the inferences to be drawn from his personal character and conduct. I know it is the fashion with some gentlemen to represent any reference to topics of this nature as invidious and irritating; but the truth is, that they rise unavoidably out of the very nature of the question. Would it have been possible for ministers to discharge their duty, in offering their advice to their Sovereign, either for accepting or declining negotiation, without taking into their account the reliance to be placed on the disposition and the principles of the person on whose disposition and principles the security to be obtained by treaty must, in the present circumstances, principally depend? or would they act honestly or candidly towards Parliament and towards the country, if, having been guided by these considerations, they forbore to state publicly and distinctly the real grounds which have influenced their decision; and if, from a false delicacy and groundless timidity, they purposely declined an examination of a point, the most essential towards enabling Parliament to form a just determination on so important a subject?

What opinion, then, are we led to form of the pretensions of the Consul to those particular qualities which, in the official note, are represented as affording us, from his personal character, the surest pledge of peace? We are told, this is his *second attempt* at general pacification. Let us see, for a moment, how this *second attempt* has been conducted. There

---

* Mr. Canning.

is, indeed, as the learned gentleman has said, a word in the first declaration which refers to general peace, and which states this to be the second time in which the Consul has endeavoured to accomplish that object. We thought fit, for the reasons which have been assigned, to decline altogether the proposal of treating, under the present circumstances; but we, at the same time, expressly stated that, whenever the moment for treaty should arrive, we would in no case treat but in conjunction with our allies. Our general refusal to negotiate at the present moment did not prevent the Consul from renewing his overtures; but were they renewed for the purpose of general pacification? Though he had hinted at general peace in the terms of his first note; though we had shown, by our answer, that we deemed negotiation, even for general peace, at this moment inadmissible; though we added that even at any future period we would treat only in conjunction with our allies; what was the proposal contained in his last note? To treat, not for *general peace*, but for a *separate peace* between Great Britain and France.

Such was the second attempt to effect *general pacification:* a proposal for a *separate* treaty with Great Britain. What had been the first? The conclusion of a *separate* treaty with Austria; and, in addition to this fact, there are two anecdotes connected with the conclusion of this treaty, which are sufficient to illustrate the disposition of this pacificator of Europe. This very treaty of Campo Formio * was ostentatiously professed to be concluded with the Emperor for the purpose of enabling Buonaparte to take the command of the army of England, and to dictate a separate peace with this country on the banks of the Thames. But there is this additional circumstance, singular beyond all conception, considering that we are now referred to the treaty of Campo Formio as a proof of the personal disposition of the Consul to general peace: he sent his two confidential and chosen friends, Berthier and Monge, charged to communicate to the Directory this treaty of Campo Formio; to announce to them that one enemy was humbled, that the war with Austria was terminated, and, therefore, that now was the moment to prosecute their operations against this country. They used, on this occasion, the memorable words, "*The Kingdom of Great Britain and the French Republic cannot exist together.*" This, I say, was the solemn declaration of the deputies and ambassadors of Buonaparte himself, offering to the Directory the firstfruits of this first attempt at general pacification.

So much for his disposition towards general pacification: let us look next at the part he has taken in the different stages of the French revolution, and let us then judge whether we are to look to him as the security against revolutionary principles; let us determine what reliance we can place on his engagements with other countries, when we see how he has observed his engagements to his own. When the constitution of the third year was established under Barras, that constitution was imposed by the arms of Buonaparte, then commanding the army of the Triumvirate in Paris. To that constitution he then swore fidelity. How often he has repeated the same oath I know not; but twice, at least, we know that he has not only repeated it himself, but tendered it to others, under circumstances too striking not to be stated.

Sir, the House cannot have forgotten the revolution of the 4th of September, which produced the dismissal of Lord Malmesbury from Lisle. How was that revolution procured? It was procured chiefly by the promise of Buonaparte (in the name of his army) decidedly to support the Directory in those measures which led to the infringement and violation of everything that the authors of the constitution of 1795, or its adherents, could consider as fundamental, and which established a system of despotism inferior only to that now realized in his own person. Immediately before this event, in the midst of the desolation and bloodshed of Italy, he had received the sacred present of new banners from the Directory; he delivered them to his army with this exhortation: "Let us swear, fellow-soldiers, by the manes of the patriots who have died by our side, eternal hatred to the enemies of the constitution of the third year:" that very constitution which he soon after enabled the Directory to violate, and which, at the head of his grenadiers, he has now finally destroyed. Sir, that oath was again renewed, in the midst of that very scene to which I have last referred: the oath of fidelity to the constitution of the third year was administered to all the members of the assembly then sitting (under the terror of the bayonet), as the solemn preparation for the business of the day; and the morning was ushered in with swearing attachment to the constitution, that the evening might close with its destruction.

If we carry our views out of France, and look at the dreadful catalogue of all the breaches of treaty, all the acts of perfidy at which I have only glanced, and which are precisely commensurate with the number of treaties which the republic has made (for I have sought in vain for any one which it has made, and which it has not broken); if we trace the history of them all from the beginning of the revolution to the present time, or if we select those which have been accompanied by the most atrocious cruelty,

---

* Signed March 17, 1797.

and marked the most strongly with the characteristic features of the revolution, the name of Buonaparte will be found allied to more of them than that of any other that can be handed down in the history of the crimes and miseries of the last ten years. His name will be recorded with the horrors committed in Italy, in the memorable campaign of 1796 and 1797, in the Milanese, in Genoa, in Modena, in Tuscany, in Rome, and in Venice.

His entrance into Lombardy was announced by a solemn proclamation, issued on the 27th of April, 1796, which terminated with these words: "Nations of Italy! the French army is come to break your chains; the French are the friends of the people in every country; your religion, your property, your customs shall be respected." This was followed by a second proclamation, dated from Milan, 20th of May, and signed "Buonaparte," in these terms: "Respect for property and personal security, respect for the religion of countries; these are the sentiments of the government of the French republic, and of the army of Italy. The French, victorious, consider the nations of Lombardy as their brothers." In testimony of this fraternity, and to fulfil the solemn pledge of respecting property, this very proclamation imposed on the Milanese a provisional contribution to the amount of twenty millions of livres, or near one million sterling; and successive exactions were afterwards levied on that single State to the amount, in the whole, of near six millions sterling. The regard to religion and to the customs of the country was manifested with the same scrupulous fidelity. The churches were given up to indiscriminate plunder. Every religious and charitable fund, every public treasure, was confiscated. The country was made the scene of every species of disorder and rapine. The priests, the established form of worship, all the objects of religious reverence, were openly insulted by the French troops; at Pavia, particularly, the tomb of St. Augustine, which the inhabitants were accustomed to view with peculiar veneration, was mutilated and defaced. This last provocation having roused the resentment of the people, they flew to arms, surrounded the French garrison, and took them prisoners, but carefully abstained from offering any violence to a single soldier. In revenge for this conduct, Buonaparte, then on his march to the Mincio, suddenly returned, collected his troops, and carried the extremity of military execution over the country: he burnt the town of Benasco, and massacred eight hundred of its inhabitants; he marched to Pavia, took it by storm, and delivered it over to general plunder, and published, at the same moment, a proclamation, of the 26th of May, ordering his troops to shoot all those who had not laid down their arms, and taken an oath of obedience, and to burn every village where the *tocsin* should be sounded, and to put its inhabitants to death.

The transactions with Modena were on a smaller scale, but in the same character. Buonaparte began by signing a treaty, by which the Duke of Modena was to pay twelve millions of livres, and neutrality was promised him in return; this was soon followed by the personal arrest of the duke, and by a fresh extortion of two hundred thousand sequins; after this he was permitted, on the payment of a further sum, to sign another treaty, called a *Convention de Sureté*, which of course only the prelude to the repetition of similar exactions.

Nearly at the same period, in violation of the rights of neutrality, and of the treaty which had been concluded between the French republic and the Grand Duke of Tuscany in the preceding year, and in breach of a positive promise given only a few days before, the French army forcibly took possession of Leghorn, for the purpose of seizing the British property which was deposited there, and confiscating it as prize; and shortly after, when Buonaparte agreed to evacuate Leghorn in return for the evacuation of the Island of Elba, which was in the possession of the British troops, he insisted upon a separate article, by which, in addition to the plunder before obtained by the infraction of the law of nations, it was stipulated that the Grand Duke should pay to the French the expense which they had incurred by this invasion of his territory.

In the proceedings towards Genoa we shall find not only a continuation of the same system of extortion and plunder (in violation of the solemn pledge contained in the proclamations already referred to), but a striking instance of the revolutionary means employed for the destruction of independent governments. A French minister was at that time resident at Genoa, which was acknowledged by France to be in a state of neutrality and friendship. In breach of this neutrality, Buonaparte began, in the year 1796, with the demand of a loan; he afterwards, from the month of September, required and enforced the payment of a monthly subsidy, to the amount which he thought proper to stipulate; these exactions were accompanied by repeated assurances and protestations of friendship; they were followed, in May, 1797, by a conspiracy against the government, fomented by the emissaries of the French embassy, and conducted by the partisans of France, encouraged, and afterwards protected, by the French minister. The conspirators failed in their first attempt; overpowered by the courage and voluntary exertions of the inhabitants, their force was dispersed, and many of their number were arrested. Buonaparte instantly considered the defeat of the conspirators as an act of aggression against the French republic;

he dispatched an aide-de-camp with an order to the Senate of this independent state; first, to release all the French who were detained; secondly, to punish those who had arrested them; thirdly, to declare that they had no share in the insurrection; and fourthly, to disarm the people. Several French prisoners were immediately released, and a proclamation was preparing to disarm the inhabitants, when, by a second note, Buonaparte required the arrest of the three Inquisitors of State, and immediate alterations in the constitution; he accompanied this with an order to the French minister to quit Genoa if his commands were not immediately carried into execution; at the same moment his troops entered the territory of the republic, and shortly after the councils, intimidated and overpowered, abdicated their functions. Three deputies were then sent to Buonaparte to receive from him a new constitution: on the 6th of June, after the conferences at Montebello, he signed a convention, or rather issued a decree, by which he fixed the new form of their government; he himself named provisionally all the members who were to compose it, and he required the payment of seven millions of livres, as the price of the subversion of their constitution and their independence. These transactions require but one short comment: it is to be found in the official account given of them at Paris, which is in these memorable words: "General Buonaparte has pursued the only line of conduct which could be allowed in the representative of a nation, which has supported the war only to procure the solemn acknowledgment of the right of nations to change the form of their government. He contributed nothing towards the revolution of Genoa, but he seized the first moment to acknowledge the new government, as soon as he saw that it was the result of the wishes of the people."

It is unnecessary to dwell on the wanton attacks against Rome under the direction of Buonaparte himself, in the year 1796, and in the beginning of 1797, which led first to the treaty of Tolentino, concluded by Buonaparte, in which, by enormous sacrifices, the Pope was allowed to purchase the acknowledgment of his authority as a sovereign prince; and secondly, to the violation of that very treaty, and to the subversion of the Papal authority by Joseph Buonaparte, the brother and the agent of the general, and the minister of the French republic to the Holy See. A transaction accompanied by outrages and insults towards the pious and venerable Pontiff (in spite of the sanctity of his age and the unsullied purity of his character), which even to a Protestant seemed hardly short of the guilt of sacrilege.

But of all the disgusting and tragical scenes which took place in Italy, in the course of the period I am describing, those which passed at Venice are perhaps the most striking and the most characteristic. In May, 1796, the French army, under Buonaparte, in the full tide of its success against the Austrians, first approached the territories of this republic, which, from the commencement of the war, had observed a rigid neutrality. Their entrance on these territories was, as usual, accompanied by a solemn proclamation in the name of their general. "Buonaparte to the Republic of Venice. It is to deliver the finest country in Europe from the iron yoke of the proud house of Austria, that the French army has braved obstacles the most difficult to surmount. Victory in union with justice has crowned its efforts. The wreck of the enemy's army has retired behind the Mincio. The French army, in order to follow them, passes over the territory of the Republic of Venice; but it will never forget that ancient friendship unites the two republics. Religion, government, customs, and property shall be respected. That the people may be without apprehension, the most severe discipline shall be maintained. All that may be provided for the army shall be faithfully paid for in money. The general-in-chief engages the officers of the Republic of Venice, the magistrates, and the priests, to make known these sentiments to the people, in order that confidence may cement that friendship which has so long united the two nations, faithful in the path of honour as in that of victory. The French soldier is terrible only to the enemies of his liberty and his government. Buonaparte."

This proclamation was followed by exactions similar to those which were practised against Genoa, by the renewal of similar professions of friendship, and the use of similar means to excite insurrections. At length, in the spring of 1797, occasion was taken from disturbances thus excited, to forge, in the name of the Venetian government, a proclamation hostile to France; and this proceeding was made the ground for military execution against the country, and for effecting by force the subversion of its ancient government, and the establishment of the democratic forms of the French Revolution. This revolution was sealed by a treaty, signed in May, 1797, between Buonaparte and commissioners appointed on the part of the new and revolutionary government of Venice. By the second and third secret articles of this treaty, Venice agreed to give as a ransom, to secure itself against all farther exactions or demands, the sum of three millions of livres in money, the value of three millions more in articles of naval supply, and three ships of the line; and it received in return the assurances of the friendship and support of the French republic. Immediately after the signature of this treaty, the arsenal, the library, and the Palace of St. Marc, were ransacked and plundered, and heavy additional contributions were imposed upon its inhabitants; and, in not more than four months afterwards, this very republic of Venice, united by alliance to France, the creature of Buonaparte himself, from whom it had received the present of French liberty, was by the same Buonaparte transferred, under the treaty of Campo Formio, to "that iron yoke of the proud house of Austria," to deliver it from which he had represented, in his first proclamation, to be the great object of all his operations.

Sir, all this is followed by the memorable expedition into Egypt, which I mention, not merely because it forms a principal article in the catalogue of those acts of violence and perfidy in which Buonaparte has been engaged; not merely because it was an enterprise peculiarly his own, of which he was himself the planner, the executor, and the betrayer; but chiefly because, when from thence he retires to a different scene to take possession of a new throne, from which he is to speak upon an equality with the kings and governors of Europe, he leaves behind him, at the moment of his departure, a specimen, which cannot be mistaken, of his principles of negotiation. The intercepted correspondence, which has been alluded to in this debate, seems to afford the strongest ground to believe that his offers to the Turkish government to evacuate Egypt were made solely with a view "*to gain time;*" that the ratification of any treaty on this subject was to be delayed, with the view of finally eluding its performance, if any change of circumstances favourable to the French should occur in the interval. But whatever gentlemen may think of the intention with which these offers were made, there will at least be no question with respect to the credit due to those professions by which he endeavoured to prove, in Egypt, his pacific dispositions. He expressly enjoins his successor strongly and steadily to insist in all his intercourse with the Turks, that he came to Egypt with no hostile design, and that he never meant to keep possession of the country; while, on the opposite page of the same instructions, he states in the most unequivocal manner his regret at the discomfiture of his favourite project of colonizing Egypt, and of maintaining it as a territorial acquisition. Now, sir, if in any note addressed to the Grand Vizier, or the Sultan, Buonaparte had claimed credit for the sincerity of his professions, that he forcibly invaded Egypt with no view hostile to Turkey, and solely for the purpose of molesting the British interests; is there any one argument now used to induce us to believe his present professions to us, which might not have been equally urged on that occasion to the Turkish Government? Would not those professions have been equally supported by solemn asseverations, by the same reference which is now made to personal character, with this single difference, that they would then have been accompanied with one instance less of that perfidy, which we have had occasion to trace in this very transaction?

It is unnecessary to say more with respect to the credit due to his professions, or the reliance to be placed on his general character: but it will, perhaps, be argued, that, whatever may be his character, or whatever has been his past conduct, he has now an interest in making and preserving peace. That he has an interest in making peace is at best but a doubtful proposition, and that he has an interest in preserving it is still more uncertain. That it is his interest to negotiate, I do not indeed deny; it is his interest above all to engage this country in separate negotiation, in order to loosen and dissolve the whole system of confederacy on the Continent; to palsy, at once, the arms of Russia or of Austria, or of any other country that might look to you for support; and then either to break off his separate treaty, or, if he should have concluded it, to apply the lesson which is taught in his school of policy in Egypt; and to revive, at his pleasure, those claims of indemnification which *may have been reserved to some happier period.*

This is precisely the interest which he has in negotiation; but on what grounds are we to be convinced that he has an interest in concluding and observing a solid and permanent pacification? Under all the circumstances of his personal character, and his newly-acquired power, what other security has he for retaining that power but the sword? His hold upon France is the sword, and he has no other. Is he connected with the soil, or with the habits, the affections, or the prejudices of the country? He is a stranger, a foreigner, and an usurper; he unites in his own person everything that a pure republican must detest; everything that an enraged Jacobin has abjured; everything that a sincere and faithful Royalist must feel as an insult. If he is opposed at any time in his career, what is his appeal? *He appeals to his fortune;* in other words, to his army and his sword. Placing, then, his whole reliance upon military support, can he afford to let his military renown pass away, to let his laurels wither, to let the memory of his achievements sink in obscurity? Is it certain that with his army confined within France, and restrained from inroads upon her neighbours, he can maintain, at his devotion, a force sufficiently numerous to support his power? Having no object but the possession of absolute dominion, no passion but military glory, is it certain that he can feel such an interest in permanent peace as would justify us in laying down our arms, reducing our expense, and relinquishing our means of security, on the faith of his engagements? Do we believe that after the conclusion of peace he would not still sigh over the lost trophies of Egypt, wrested from him by the celebrated victory of Aboukir, and the brilliant exertions of that heroic band of British seamen, whose influence and example rendered the Turkish troops invincible at Acre? Can he forget that the effect of these exploits enabled Austria and Russia, in one campaign, to recover from France all which she had acquired by his victories, to dissolve the charm which, for a time, fascinated Europe, and to show that their generals, contending in a just cause, could efface, even by their success and their military glory, the most dazzling triumphs of his victories and desolating ambition?

Can we believe, with these impressions on his mind, that if, after a year, eighteen months, or two years, of peace had elapsed, he should be tempted by the appearance of a fresh insurrection in Ireland, encouraged by renewed and unrestrained communication with France, and fomented by the fresh infusion of Jacobin principles; if we were at such a moment without a fleet to watch the ports of France, or to guard the coasts of Ireland, without a disposable army, or an embodied militia, capable of supplying a speedy and adequate reinforcement, and that he had suddenly the means of transporting thither a body of twenty or thirty thousand French troops; can we believe that at such a moment his ambition and vindictive spirit would be restrained by the recollection of engagements, or the obligation of treaty? Or, if in some new crisis of difficulty and danger to the Ottoman empire, with no British navy in the Mediterranean, no confederacy formed, no force collected to support it, an opportunity should present itself for resuming the abandoned expedition to Egypt, for renewing the avowed and favourite project of conquering and colonizing that rich and fertile country, and of opening the way to wound some of the vital interests of England, and to plunder the treasures of the East, in order to fill the bankrupt coffers of France,—would it be the interest of Buonaparte, under such circumstances, or his principles, his moderation, his love of peace, his aversion to conquest, and his regard for the independence of other nations—would it be all, or any of these that would secure us against an attempt, which would leave us only the option of submitting without a struggle to certain loss and disgrace, or of renewing the contest which we had prematurely terminated, and renewing it without allies, without preparation, with diminished means, and with increased difficulty and hazard?

Hitherto I have spoken only of the reliance which we can place on the professions, the character, and the conduct of the present First Consul; but it remains to consider the stability of his power. The revolution has been marked throughout by a rapid succession of new depositaries of public authority, each supplanting his predecessor: what grounds have we as yet to believe that this new usurpation, more odious and more undisguised than all that preceded it, will be more durable? Is it that we rely on the particular provisions contained in the code of the pretended constitution, which was proclaimed as accepted by the French people, as soon as the garrison of Paris declared their determination to exterminate all its enemies, and before any of its articles could even be known to half the country, whose consent was required for its establishment?

I will not pretend to inquire deeply into the nature and effects of a constitution, which can hardly be regarded but as a farce and a mockery. If, however, it could be supposed that its provisions were to have any effect, it seems equally adapted to two purposes; that of giving to its founder, for a time, an absolute and uncontrolled authority, and that of laying the certain foundation of future disunion and discord, which, if they once prevail, must render the exercise of all the authority under the constitution impossible, and leave no appeal but to the sword.

Is then military despotism that which we are accustomed to consider as a stable form of government? In all ages of the world it has been attended with the least stability to the persons who exercised it, and with the most rapid succession of changes and revolutions. The advocates of the French Revolution boasted, in its outset, that by their new system they had furnished a security for ever, not to France only, but to all countries in the world, against military despotism; that the force of standing armies was vain and delusive; that no artificial power could resist public opinion; and that it was upon the foundation of public opinion alone that any government could stand. I believe that, in this instance, as in every other, the progress of the French Revolution has belied its professions; but so far from its being a proof of the prevalence of public opinion against military force, it is, instead of the proof, the strongest exception from that doctrine which appears in the history of the world. Through all the stages of the revolution military force has governed; public opinion has scarcely been heard. But still I consider this as only an exception from a general truth; I still believe that, in every civilized country (not enslaved by a Jacobin faction), public opinion is the only sure support of any government. I believe this with the more satisfaction, from a conviction that if this contest is happily terminated, the established governments of Europe will stand upon that rock firmer than ever; and whatever may be the defects of any particular constitution, those who live under it will prefer its continuance to the experiment of changes which may plunge them in the unfathomable abyss of revolution, or extricate them from it, only to expose them to the terrors of military despotism. And to apply this to France, I see no reason to believe that the present usurpation will be more permanent than any other military despotism, which has been established by the same means, and with the same defiance of public opinion.

What, then, is the inference I draw from all that I have now stated? Is it that we will in no case treat with Buonaparte? I say no such thing. But I say, as has been said in the answer returned to the French note, that we ought to wait for *experience, and the evidence of facts*, before we are convinced that such a treaty is admissible. The circumstances I have stated would well justify us if we should be slow in being convinced: but, on a question of peace and war, everything depends upon degree, and upon comparison. If, on the one hand, there should be an appearance that the policy of France is at length guided by different maxims from those which have hitherto prevailed; if we should hereafter see signs of stability in the government, which are not now to be traced; if the progress of the allied army should not call forth such a spirit in France, as to make it probable that the act of the country itself will destroy the system now prevailing; if the danger, the difficulty, the risk of continuing the contest, should increase, while the hope of complete ultimate success should be diminished; all these, in their due place, are considerations which, with myself and (I can answer for it) with every one of my colleagues, will have their just weight. But at present these considerations all operate one way; at present there is nothing from which we can presage a favourable disposition to change in the French councils. There is the greatest reason to rely on powerful co-operation from our allies; there are the strongest marks of a disposition in the interior of France to active resistance against this new tyranny; and there is every ground to believe, on reviewing our situation, and that of the enemy, that if we are ultimately disappointed of that complete success which we are at present entitled to hope, the continuance of the contest, instead of making our situation comparatively worse, will have made it comparatively better.

If, then, I am asked, how long are we to persevere in the war? I can only say that no period can be accurately assigned beforehand. Considering the importance of obtaining complete security for the objects for which we contend, we ought not to be discouraged too soon: but on the other hand, considering the importance of not impairing and exhausting the radical strength of the country, there are limits beyond which we ought not to persist, and which we can determine only by estimating and comparing fairly, from time to time, the degree of security to be obtained by treaty, and the risk and disadvantage of continuing the contest.

LORD PLUNKET.
Born 1764. Died 1854.

[ROBERT EMMET, at whose trial the following speech was delivered, was the son of an eminent physician, who himself was known to be in principle a violent antagonist to the Union. Robert's brother had formed one of the band of the United Irishmen, who formed the Irish Rebellion of 1798, and Robert himself was expelled from the University of Dublin for political intrigues.

There is no doubt that Emmet had great hopes of being aided by the French in his scheme for establishing an independent government, and possibly received promises on the subject during his stay on the Continent after leaving Dublin, as he is known to have had interviews with Buonaparte and Talleyrand.

However this might be, and whatever may have been his hopes of success, there is no doubt that his schemes were wild and undigested, and that he did not meet with the assistance which he expected from his friends. Added to the folly, to use no worse term, of his plans, his temper was so rash and inconsiderate, and his resolution and obstinacy so determined, that at the head of about 80 men he commenced his proceedings with a demonstration in Dublin, on the 23rd of July, 1803. The murder of Viscount Kilwarden and his nephew, who unfortunately encountered the insurgents in their march, and a few skirmishes with the soldiery, were the beginning and end of this foolish conspiracy.

The ringleaders, Roche, Kearney, Kirwan, Rourke, Redmond, Russel, and Emmet suffered death for their treason.

The youth, bravery, and elevated spirit of Emmet; the undaunted resolution which he showed on his trial, and the eloquent speech which he then delivered, have caused him to be considered as little less than a martyr by his countrymen, and have won him sympathy from people of all nations and principles wherever his short, sad, foolish history has been told.

As Mr. Hooy, the editor of the collection of Plunket's speeches, from which the following extract is taken, well and eloquently observes:

"The life of Robert Emmet is one of the most affecting episodes in Irish history. Of all the United Irishmen, there is not one who has left a memory invested with so much sympathy at home and abroad. His last speech has been ever since his death a gospel of rebellion against England. Even in the American schools it is as popular a recitative as Patrick Henry's defiances; and Robert Emmet trampling on the British crown figured as often on a western signboard, thirty years ago, as General Jackson. There was such purity, chivalry, and devotion in his nature—his life, his love, his death, are full of a romance so true and so touching —that in thinking of him, men unconsciously elevate his character above the poor failure—an hour's scuffle with the police and the picquet, stained by an atrocious murder—which history asserts his insurrection to have been. They wonder how that wild attempt can have won for its leader a character like Bayard's; but so it is."

Emmet was tried before a special commission, presided over by Lord Norbury, on the 19th of September, 1803, and he was executed on the following day.

His speech before alluded to will be found following that of his prosecutor.]

TRIAL OF ROBERT EMMET.

MY LORDS and gentlemen of the jury, you need not entertain any apprehension that at this hour of the day I am disposed to take up a great deal of your time, by observing upon the evidence which has been given. In truth, if this were an ordinary case, and if the object of this prosecution did not include some more momentous interests than the mere question of the guilt or innocence of the unfortunate gentleman who stands a prisoner at the bar, I should have followed the example of his counsel, and should have declined making any observation upon the evidence. But, gentlemen, I do feel this to be a case of infinite importance indeed. It is a case important, like all others of this kind, by involving the life of a fellow-subject; but it is doubly—and tenfold important, because from the evidence which has been given in the progress of it, the system of this conspiracy against the laws and constitution of the country has been developed in all its branches; and in observing upon the conduct of the prisoner at the bar, and in bringing home the evidence of his guilt, I am bringing home guilt to a person who, I say, is the centre, the life-blood and soul of this atrocious conspiracy.

* * * *

Gentlemen, what was the part which the prisoner took in that night of horror I will not attempt to insinuate to you. I hope and trust in God, for the sake of himself, his fame, his eternal welfare, that he was incapable of being a party to the barbarities which were committed—I do not mean to insinuate that he was—but that he headed this troop, and was present while some shots were fired, has been proved by uncontroverted testimony. At what time he quitted them—whether from prudence, despair, or disgust, he retired from their bands, is not proved by evidence upon the table; but from the moment of the discomfiture of his project, we find him again concealed. We trace him with the badges of rebellion glittering upon his person, attended by the two other consuls, Quigley, the bricklayer, and Dowdall, the clerk—whether for concealment or to stimulate the wretched peasantry to other acts of insurrection, you will determine; we first trace him to Doyle's and then to Bagnall's; one identifies him, the other, from her fears, is incapable of doing so. But the same party, in the same uniforms, go to her house, until the apprehension of detection drove them from her. When he could no longer find shelter in the mountains, nor stir up the inhabitants of them, he again retires to his former obscure lodging, the name of Ellis is abandoned, the regimental coat is abandoned, and again he assumes the name of Hewitt. What is his conduct in this concealment? He betrays his apprehensions of being taken up by government. For what? Has any explanation been given to show what it could be, unless for rebellious practices? There he plans a mode of escape, refusing to put his name upon the door. You find him taken a reluctant prisoner, twice attempting to escape, and only brought within the reach of the law by force and violence. What do you find then? Has he been affecting to disguise his object, or that his plan was less dignified than his motive—that of treason? No such thing. He tells young Palmer that he was in Thomas Street that night—he confesses the treason—he boasts of his uniform, part of which was upon his person when he was taken. He acknowledges all this to the young man in the house—a witness, permit me to remark, not carried away by any excess of over-zeal to say anything to the injury of the prisoner, and therefore to his testimony, so far as it affects the prisoner, you may, with a safe conscience, afford a reasonable degree of credit.

Under what circumstances is he taken? In the room in which he was—upon a chair near the door is found an address to the government of the country; and in the very first paragraph of that address, the composer of it acknowledges himself to be at the head of a conspiracy for the overthrow of the government, which he addresses, telling them, in diplomatic language, what conduct the undersigned will be compelled to adopt, if they shall presume to execute the law. He is the leader, whose nod is a fiat, and he warns them of the consequences!

Gentlemen of the jury, you will decide whether the prisoner at the bar or Mrs. Palmer was the person who denounced those terms, and this vengeance against the government. What is found upon him? A letter written by a brother conspirator consulting him upon the present posture of the rebellion, their future prospects, and the probability of French assistance, and also the probable effects of that assistance, if it should arrive. What farther is found at the depôt?—and everything found there, whether coming out of the desk which he appears to have used and resorted to, or in any other part of the place which he commanded, is evidence against him. You find a treatise upon the art of war, framed for the purpose of drilling the party who were employed to effect this rebellion; but of war they have proved that they are incapable of knowing anything but its ferocities and its crimes; you find two proclamations, detailing systematically and precisely the views and objects of this conspiracy; and you find a manuscript copy of one of them, with interlineations, and other marks of its being an original draft. It will be for you to consider who was the framer of it —the man who presided in the depôt, and regulated all the proceedings there; or whether it was framed by Dowdall, the clerk, by Quigley, the bricklayer, or by Stafford, the baker, or any of the illiterate victims of the ambition of this young man who have been convicted in this court, or whether it did not flow from his pen, and was dictated by his heart.

Gentlemen, with regard to this mass of accumulated evidence, forming irrefragable proof of the guilt of the prisoner, I conceive no man capable of putting together two ideas can have a doubt. Why then do I address you, or why should I trespass any longer upon your time and your attention? Because, as I have already mentioned, I feel this to be a case of great public expectation — of the very last national importance; and because, when I am prosecuting a man, in whose veins the very life-blood of this conspiracy flowed, I expose to the public eye the utter meanness and insufficiency of its resources. What does it avow itself to be? A plan, not to correct the excesses or reform the abuses of the government of the country; not to remove any specks of imperfection which might have grown upon the surface of the constitution, or to restrain the overgrown power of the crown; or to restore any privilege of parliament; or to throw any new security around the liberty of the subject. No; but it plainly and boldly avows itself to be a plan to separate Great Britain from Ireland, uproot the monarchy, and establish "a free and independent republic in Ireland," in its place! To sever the connection between Great Britain and Ireland! Gentlemen, I should feel it a waste of words and of public time, were I addressing you or any person within the limits of my voice, to talk of the frantic desperation of the plan of any man who speculates upon the dissolution of that empire, whose glory and whose happiness depend upon its indissoluble connection. But were it practicable to sever that connection, to untie the links which bind us to the British constitution, and to turn us adrift upon the turbulent ocean of revolution, who could answer for the existence of this country, as an independent power, for a year? God and nature have made the two countries essential to each other—let them cling to each other to the end of time, and their united affection and loyalty will be proof against the machinations of the world.

But how was this to be done? By establishing "a free and independent republic!" High-sounding name! I would ask, whether the man who used it understood what he meant? I will not ask what may be its benefits, for I know its evils. There is no magic in the name. We have heard of "free and independent republics," and have since seen the most abject slavery that ever groaned under iron despotism growing out of them.

Formerly, gentlemen of the jury, we have seen revolutions effected by some great call of the people, ripe for change and unfitted by their habits for ancient forms; but here from the obscurity of concealment and by the voice of that pigmy authority, self-created and fearing to show itself, but in arms under cover of the night, we are called upon to surrender a constitution which has lasted for a period of one thousand years. Had any body of the people come forward, stating any grievance or announcing their demand for a change? No; but while the country is peaceful, enjoying the blessings of the constitution, growing rich and happy under it, a few desperate, obscure, contemptible adventurers in the trade of revolution form a scheme against the constituted authorities of the land, and by force and violence to overthrow an ancient and venerable constitution, and to plunge a whole people into the horrors of civil war!

If the wisest head that ever lived had framed the wisest system of laws which human ingenuity could devise—if he were satisfied that the system were exactly fitted to the disposition of the people for whom he intended it, and that a great proportion of that people were anxious for its adoption—yet give me leave to say, that under all these circumstances of fitness and disposition, a well-judging mind and a humane heart would pause awhile and stop upon the brink of his purpose, before he would hazard the peace of the country, by resorting to force for the establishment of his system; but here, in the frenzy of a distempered ambition, the author of this proclamation conceives the project of "a free and independent republic;" he at once flings it down, and he tells every man in the community, rich or poor, loyal or disloyal, he must adopt it at the peril of being considered an enemy to the country, and of suffering the pains and penalties attendant thereupon.

And how was this revolution to be effected? The proclamation conveys an insinuation that it was to be effected by their own force, entirely independent of foreign assistance. Why? Because it was well known that there remained in this country few so depraved, so lost to the welfare of their native land, who would not shudder at forming an alliance with France; and therefore the people of Ireland are told, "the effort is to be entirely your own, independent of foreign aid." But how does this tally with the time when the scheme was first hatched—the very period of the commencement of the war with France? How does this tally with the fact of consulting in the depôt about co-operating with the French, which has been proved in evidence? But, gentlemen, out of the proclamation I convict him of duplicity. He tells the government of the country not to resist their mandate, or think that they can effectually suppress rebellion, by putting down the present attempt, but that "they will have to crush a greater exertion, rendered still greater by foreign assistance;" so that upon the face of the proclamation they avowed, in its naked deformity, the abominable plan of an alliance with the usurper of the French throne, to overturn the ancient constitution of the land, and to substitute a new republic in its place.

Gentlemen, so far I have taken up your time with observing upon the nature and extent of the conspiracy; its objects and the means by which they proposed to effectuate them. Let me now call your attention to the pretexts by which they seek to support them. They have not stated what particular grievance or oppression is complained of, but they have travelled back into the history of six centuries—they have raked up the ashes of former cruelties and rebellions, and upon the memory of them, they call upon the good people of this country to embark into similar troubles; but they forgot to tell the people, that until the infection of new-fangled French principles was introduced, this country was for an hundred years free from the slightest symptom of rebellion, advancing in improvement of every kind beyond any example, while the former animosities of the country were melting down into a general system of philanthropy and cordial attachment to each other. They forget to tell the people whom they address that they have been enjoying the benefit of equal laws, by which the property, the person, and constitutional rights and privileges of every man are abundantly protected. They have not pointed out a single instance of oppression. Give me leave to ask any man who may have suffered himself to be deluded by those enemies of the law, what is there to prevent the exercise of honest industry and enjoying the produce of it? Does any man presume to invade him in the enjoyment of his property? If he does, is not the punishment of the law brought down upon him? What does he want? What is it that any rational friend to freedom could expect, that the people of this country are not fully and amply in the possession of? And therefore when those idle stories are told of six hundred years' oppression, and of rebellions prevailing when this country was in a state of ignorance and barbarism, and which have long since passed away, they are utterly destitute of a fact to rest upon; they are a fraud upon feeling, and are the pretext of the factious and ambitious, working upon credulity and ignorance.

Let me allude to another topic: they call for revenge on account of the removal of the parliament. Those men who, in 1798, endeavoured to destroy the parliament, now call upon the loyal men, who opposed its transfer, to join them in rebellion; an appeal vain and fruitless. Look around and see with what zeal and loyalty they rallied round the throne and constitution of the country. Whatever might have been the difference of opinion heretofore among Irishmen upon some points, when armed rebels appeared against the laws and public peace, every minor difference was annihilated in the paramount claim of duty to our king and country.

So much, gentlemen, for the nature of this conspiracy and the pretexts upon which it rests. Suffer me, for a moment, to call your attention to one or two of the edicts published by the conspirators. They have denounced, that if a single Irish soldier, or in more faithful description, Irish rebel, shall lose his life after the battle is over, quarter is neither to be given nor taken. Observe the equality of the reasoning of these promulgers of liberty and equality. The distinction is this: English troops are permitted to arm in defence of the government and the constitution of the country, and to maintain their allegiance; but if an Irish soldier, yeoman, or other loyal person, who shall not within the space of fourteen days from the date and issuing forth of their sovereign proclamation, appear in arms with them; if he presumes to obey the dictates of his conscience, his duty, and his interest—if he has the hardihood to be loyal to his sovereign and his country, he is proclaimed a traitor, his life is forfeited, and his property is confiscated. A sacred palladium is thrown over the rebel cause, while, in the same breath, undistinguishing vengeance is denounced against those who stand up in defence of the existing and ancient laws of the country. For God's sake, to whom are we called upon to deliver up, with only fourteen days to consider of it, all the advantages we enjoy? Who are they who claim the obedience? The prisoner is the principal: I do not wish to say anything harsh of him; a young man of considerable talents, if used with precaution, and of respectable rank in society, if content to conform himself to its laws. But when he assumes the manner and the tone of a legislator, and calls upon all ranks of people, the instant the provisional government proclaim in the abstract a new government, without specifying what the new laws are to be, or how the people are to be conducted and managed—but that the moment it is announced, the whole constituted authority is to yield to him; it becomes an extravagance bordering upon frenzy: this is going beyond the example of all former times. If a rightful sovereign were restored, he would forbear to inflict punishment upon those who submitted to the king *de facto*, but here there is no such forbearance. We who have lived under a king, not only *de facto* but *de jure* in possession of the throne, are called upon to submit ourselves to the prisoner—to Dowdall, the vagrant politician—to the bricklayer, to the baker, the old-clothes-man, the hodman, and the ostler. These are the persons to whom this proclamation, in its majesty and dignity, calls upon a great people to yield obedience, and a powerful government to give "a prompt, manly, and sagacious acquiescence to their just and unalterable determination!" "We call upon the British government not to be so mad as to oppose us." Why, gentlemen, this goes beyond all serious discussion; and I mention it merely to show the contemptible nature of this conspiracy, which hoped to have set the entire country in a flame. When it was joined by nineteen counties from north to south, catching the electrical spark of revolution, they engaged in the conspiracy—the general, with his lieutenant-general, putting himself at the head of the forces, collected not merely from the city, but from the neighbouring counties; and when all their strength is collected, voluntary and forced, they are stopped in their progress, in the first glow of their valour, by the honest voice of a single peace officer, at which the provincial forces were disconcerted and alarmed, but ran like hares, when one hundred soldiers appeared against them.

Gentlemen, why do I state these facts? Is it to show that the government need not be vigilant, or that our gallant countrymen should relax in their exertions? By no means; but to induce the miserable victims who have been misled by those phantoms of revolutionary delusion, to show them that they ought to lose no time in abandoning a cause which cannot protect itself, and exposes them to destruction, and to adhere to the peaceful and secure habits of honest industry. If they knew it, they have no reason to repine at their lot. Providence is not so unkind to them in casting them in that humble walk in which they are placed. Let them obey the law and cultivate religion, and worship their God in their own way. They may prosecute their labour in peace and tranquillity; they need not envy the higher ranks of life, but may look with pity upon that vicious despot who watches with the sleepless eye of disquieting ambition, and sits a wretched usurper trembling upon the throne of the Bourbons. But I do not wish to awaken any remorse, except such as may be salutary to himself and the country, in the mind of the prisoner. But when he reflects that he has stooped from the honourable situation in which his birth, talents, and his education placed him, to debauch the minds of the lower orders of ignorant men with the phantoms of liberty and equality, he must feel that it was an unworthy use of his talents; he should feel remorse for the consequences which ensued, grievous to humanity and virtue, and should endeavour to make all the atonement he can, by employing the little time which remains for him in endeavouring to undeceive them.

Liberty and equality are dangerous names to make use of; if properly understood, they mean enjoyment of personal freedom under the equal protection of the laws; and a genuine love of liberty inculcates a friendship for our friends, our king, and country—a reverence for their lives, an anxiety for their safety; a feeling which advances from private to public life, until it expands and swells into the more dignified name of philanthropy and philosophy. But in the cant of modern philosophy, these affections which form the ennobling distinctions of man's nature are all thrown aside; all the vices of his character are made the instrument of moral good—an abstract quantity of vice may produce a certain quantity of moral good. To a man whose principles are thus poisoned and his judgment perverted the most flagitious crimes lose their names; robbery and murder become moral good. He is taught not to startle at putting to death a fellow-creature, if it be represented as a mode of contributing to the good of all. In pursuit of those phantoms and chimeras of the brain, they abolish feelings and instincts, which God and nature have planted in our hearts for the good of human kind. Thus by the printed plan for the establishment of liberty and a free republic, murder is prohibited and proscribed; and yet you heard how this caution against excesses was followed up by the recital of every grievance that ever existed, and which could excite every bad feeling of the heart, the most vengeful cruelty and insatiate thirst of blood.

Gentlemen, I am anxious to suppose that the mind of the prisoner recoiled at the scenes of murder which he witnessed, and I mention one circumstance with satisfaction: it appears he saved the life of Farrell; and may the recollection of that one good action cheer him in his last moments! But though he may not have planned individual murders, that is no excuse to justify his embarking in treason, which must be followed by every species of crimes. It is supported by the rabble of the country, while the rank, the wealth, and the power of the country are opposed to it. Let loose the rabble of the country from the salutary restraints of the law, and who can take upon him to limit their barbarities? Who can say, he will disturb the peace of the world and rule it when wildest? Let loose the winds of heaven, and what power less than omnipotent can control them? So it is with the rabble; let them loose, and who can restrain them? What claim, then, can the prisoner have upon the compassion of a jury, because in the general destruction which his schemes necessarily produce he did not meditate individual murder? In the short space of a quarter of an hour, what a scene of blood and horror was exhibited! I trust that the blood which has been shed in the streets of Dublin upon that night, and since upon the scaffold, and which may hereafter be shed, will not be visited upon the head of the prisoner. It is not for me to say what are the limits of the mercy of God, or what a sincere repentance of those crimes may effect; but I do say, that if this unfortunate young gentleman retains any of the seeds of humanity in his heart, or possesses any of those qualities which a virtuous education in a liberal seminary must have planted in his bosom, he will make an atonement to his God and his country, by employing whatever time remains to him in warning his deluded countrymen from persevering in their schemes. Much blood has been shed, and he perhaps would have been immolated by his followers if he had succeeded. They are a bloodthirsty crew, incapable of listening to the voice of reason, and equally incapable of obtaining rational freedom, if it were wanting in this country, as they are of enjoying it. They imbrue their hands in the most sacred blood of the country, and yet they call upon God to prosper their cause, as it is just!—But as it is atrocious, wicked, and abominable, I most devoutly invoke that God to confound and overwhelm it.

SPEECH OF ROBERT EMMET.

MY LORDS,—What have I to say that sentence of death should not be passed on me according to law? I have nothing to say that can alter your predetermination, nor that will become me to say, with any view to the mitigation of that sentence which you are here to pronounce, and I must abide by. But I have that to say, which interests me more than life, and which you have laboured (as was necessarily your office in the present circumstances of this oppressed country) to destroy. I have much to say, why my reputation should be rescued from the load of false accusation and calumny which has been heaped upon it. I do not imagine that, seated where you are, your minds can be so free from impurity as to receive the least impression from what I am going to utter. I have no hopes that I can anchor my character in the breast of a Court constituted and trammelled as this is. I only wish, and it is the utmost I expect, that your Lordships may suffer it to float down your memories untainted by the foul breath of prejudice, until it finds some more hospitable harbour to shelter it from the storm by which it is at present buffeted.

Were I only to suffer death, after being adjudged guilty by your tribunal, I should bow in silence, and meet the fate that awaits me without a murmur; but the sentence of the law which delivers my body to the executioner, will, through the ministry of that law, labour in its own vindication to consign my character to obloquy; for there must be guilt somewhere, whether in the sentence of the Court or in the catastrophe, posterity must determine. A man in my situation, my lords, has not only to encounter the difficulties of fortune, and the force of power over minds which it has corrupted or subjugated, but the difficulties of established prejudice; the man dies, but his memory lives. That mine may not perish—that it may live in the respect of my countrymen, I seize upon this opportunity to vindicate myself from some of the charges alleged against me. When my spirit shall be wafted to a more friendly port—when my shade shall have joined the bands of those martyred heroes who have shed their blood on the scaffold and in the field, in defence of their country and of virtue, this is my hope—I wish that my memory and name may animate those who survive me, while I look down with complacency on the destruction of that perfidious Government which upholds its domination by the blasphemy of the Most High; which displays its power over man as over the beasts of the forest; which sets man upon his brother, and lifts his hand in the name of God, against the throat of his fellow who believes or doubts a little more than the Government standard—a Government steeled to barbarity by the cries of the orphans and the tears of the widows which it has made.

[Here Lord Norbury interrupted Mr. Emmet; saying, that the mean and wicked enthusiasts who felt as he did were not equal to the accomplishment of their wild designs.]

I appeal to the Immaculate God. I swear by the throne of Heaven—before which I must shortly appear—by the blood of the murdered patriots who have gone before me, that my conduct has been, through all this peril and through all my purposes, governed only by the convictions which I have uttered, and by no other view than that of their cure, and the emancipation of my country from the superinhuman oppression under which she has so long and too patiently travailed; and I confidently and assuredly hope that wild and chimerical as it may appear, there is still union and strength in Ireland to accomplish this most noble enterprise.

Of this I speak with the confidence of immense knowledge, and with the consolation that appertains to that confidence. Think not, my lords, I say this for the petty gratification of giving you a transitory uneasiness; a man who never yet raised his voice to assert a lie will not hazard his character with posterity by asserting a falsehood on a subject so important to his country, and on an occasion like this. Yes, my lords, a man who does not wish to have his epitaph written until his country is liberated, will not leave a weapon in the power of envy, nor a pretence to impeach the probity which he means to preserve even in the grave to which tyranny consigns him.

[Here he was again interrupted by the Court.]

Again, I say, what I have spoken was not intended for your lordships, whose situation I commiserate rather than envy—my expressions were for my countrymen; if there is an Irishman present, let my last words cheer him in the hour of affliction.

[Here he was again interrupted. Lord Norbury said he did not sit there to hear treason.]

I have always understood it to be the duty of a judge, when a prisoner has been convicted, to pronounce the sentence of the law; I have also understood the judges sometimes think it their duty to hear with patience, and to speak with humanity, to exhort the victims of the laws, and to offer with tender benignity their opinions of the motives by which he was actuated in the crime of which he was adjudged guilty. That a judge has thought it his duty so to have done, I have no doubt; but where is the boasted freedom of your institutions? Where is the vaunted impartiality, clemency, and mildness of your Courts of Justice, if an unfortunate prisoner, whom your policy, and not your justice, is about to deliver into the hands of the executioner, is not suffered to explain his motives sincerely and truly, and to vindicate the principles by which he was actuated?

My lords, it may be a part of the system of angry justice to bow a man's mind by humiliation to the proposed ignominy of the scaffold—but worse to me than the purposed shame, or the scaffold's terrors, would be the shame of such foul and unfounded imputations as have been laid against me in this Court. You, my lord, are a judge; I am the supposed culprit; I am a man, you are a man also: by a revolution of power we might change places, though we never could characters. If I stand at the bar of this Court, and dare not vindicate my character, what a farce is your justice! If I stand at this bar and dare not vindicate my character, how dare you calumniate it? Does the sentence of death, which your unhallowed policy inflicts on my body, also condemn my tongue to silence and my reputation to reproach? Your executioner may abridge the period of my existence, but whilst I exist I shall not forbear to vindicate my character and motives from your aspersions; and as a man, to whom fame is dearer than life, I will make the last use of that life in doing justice to that reputation which is to live after me, and which is the only legacy I can leave to those I honour and love, and for whom I am proud to perish.

As men, my lords, we must appear on the great day at one common tribunal, and it will then remain for the Searcher of all hearts to show a collective universe, who was engaged in the most virtuous actions or attached by the purest motives—by the country's oppressors, or—

[Here he was again interrupted, and told to listen to the sentence of the law.]

My lords, will a dying man be denied the legal privilege of exculpating himself in the eyes of the community of an undeserved reproach thrown upon him during his trial, by charging him with ambition, and attempting to cast away, for a paltry consideration, the liberties of his country? Why did your lordships insult me? or rather, why insult justice in demanding of me why sentence of death should not be pronounced? I know, my lord, that form prescribes that you should ask the question—the form also prescribes the right of answering. This, no doubt, may be dispensed with, and so might the whole ceremony of the trial, since sentence was already pronounced at the Castle before the jury was empannelled. Your lordships are but the priests of the oracle, and I submit; but I insist on the whole of the forms.

[Here the Court desired him to proceed.]

I am charged with being an emissary of France. An emissary of France! and for what end? It is alleged I wish to sell the independence of my country! and for what end? Was this the object of my ambition?—and is this the mode by which a tribunal of justice reconciles contradictions? No, I am no emissary; and my ambition was to hold a place among the deliverers of my country—not in power, not in profit, but in the glory of the achievement. Sell my country's independence! and for what? Was it for a change of masters? No, but for ambition! Oh, my country! was it personal ambition that could influence me? Had it been the soul of my actions, could I not, by my education and fortune—by the rank and consideration of my family—have placed myself among the proudest of my oppressors? My country was my idol; to it I sacrificed every selfish, every endearing sentiment, and for it I now offer up my life. O God! No, my lord; I acted as an Irishman, determined on delivering his country from the yoke of a domestic faction, which is its joint partner and perpetrator in the parricide, for the ignominy of existing with an exterior of splendour and a conscious depravity: it was the wish of my heart to extricate my country from the doubly-riveted despotism. I wished to place her independence beyond the reach of any power on earth—I wished to exalt her to that proud station in the world.

Connections with France were indeed intended—but only as far as mutual interest would sanction or require. Were they to assume any authority inconsistent with the purest independence, it would be the signal for its destruction; we sought aid, and we sought it as we had assurance we should obtain it—as auxiliaries in war and allies in peace.

Were the French to come as invaders or enemies, uninvited by the wishes of the people, I should oppose them to the utmost of my strength. Yes, my countrymen, I should advise you to meet them on the beach with a sword in one hand and a torch in the other; I would meet them with all the destructive fury of war, and I would animate my countrymen to immolate them in their boats, before they had contaminated the soil of my country. If they succeeded in landing, and if forced to retire before superior discipline, I would dispute every inch of ground, burn every blade of grass, and the last entrenchment of liberty should be my grave. What I could not do myself, if I should fall, I should leave as a last charge to my countrymen to accomplish, because I should feel conscious that life any more than death is unprofitable when a foreign nation holds my country in subjection.

But it was not an enemy that the succours of France were to land. I looked indeed for the succours of France; but I wished to prove to France and to the world, that Irishmen deserved to be assisted; that they were indignant at slavery, and ready to assert the right and independence of their country.

I wished to procure for my country the guarantee which Washington procured for America. To procure an aid which by its example would be as important as its valour—disciplined, gallant, pregnant with science and experience; who would perceive the good and polish the rough points of our character; they would come to us as strangers and leave us as friends, after sharing our perils and elevating our destiny. These were my objects—not to receive new taskmasters, but to expel old tyrants. These were my views, and these only became Irishmen. It was for these ends I sought aid from France, because France, even as an enemy, could not be more implacable than the enemy already in the bosom of my country.

[Here he was interrupted by the Court.]

I have been charged with that importance in the efforts to emancipate my country as to be considered the keystone of the combination of Irishmen, or, as your lordship expressed it, "the life and blood of the conspiracy;" you do me honour over much; you have given to the solution all the credit of a superior. There are men engaged in the conspiracy who are not only superior to me, but even to your own estimation of yourself, my lord; before the splendour of whose genius and virtues I should bow with respectful deference, and who would think themselves dishonoured to be called would not disgrace themse blood-stained hand.

[Here he was int

What, my lord! shall passage to that scaffold, v which you are only the inte has erected for my murder, able for all the blood that in this struggle of the o oppressor? Shall you tell be so very a slave as not t

I do not fear to appro Judge, to answer for the life, and am I to be appal mere remnant of mortality who, if it were possible innocent blood that you unhallowed ministry in one lordship might swim in it.

[Here the Judge i

Let no man dare, when me with dishonour; let memory, by believing that in any cause but of my c independence, or that I minion of power in the miseries of my countrymen the Provisional Government no inference can be tortur nance barbarity or debasen jection, humiliation, or trea would not have submitted to the same reason that I wo domestic oppressor. In th I would have fought on country, and its enemy s passing over my lifeless who lived but for my co subjected myself to the dan watchful oppressor and grave, only to give my cou and my country their ind be loaded with calumny, resent or repel it? No, G

If the spirits of the illu pate in the concern and ca dear to them in this tra dear and venerable shade o look down with scrutiny your suffering son, and see moment deviated from morality and patriotism wl to instil into my youthful I am now to offer up my li

My lords, you are impa —the blood which you seel the artificial terrors that st it circulates warmly and r channels which God create but which you are bent to so grievous that they cry to Heaven. Be ye patient! I have but a few words more to say. I am going to my cold and silent grave; my lamp of life is nearly extinguished; my race is run; the grave opens to receive me, and I sink into its bosom! I have but one request to ask at my departure from this world; it is the charity of its silence! Let no man write my epitaph; for as no man who knows my motives dare now vindicate them, let not prejudice or ignorance asperse them. Let them and me repose in obscurity and peace, and my tomb remain uninscribed, until other times and other men can do justice to my character. When my country takes her place among the nations of the earth—then, and not till then—let my epitaph be written. I HAVE DONE.

JOHN PYM.
Born 1584. Died 1643.

[THE speech which follows is by the illustrious John Pym, member for Tavistock in almost all the parliaments of Charles I., and the bold leader of the House of Commons during the great struggle that preceded the parliamentary wars. So popular indeed was he as an orator in his day, that he was emphatically styled "King Pym." His eloquence was of that bluff and nervous order most suited to the stirring times in which he lived, and proved of good service to the Commons in conducting the impeachments which were so frequent and so necessary during the tyrannous and arbitrary reign of the 1st Charles. The occasion of the speech here given was the impeachment of George Villiers, the proud and ambitious Duke of Buckingham, whose evil influence in the counsels of the King doubtless brought on so many of the mistakes and misfortunes into which Charles I. afterwards fell.

Buckingham's son, of the same name, was the unprincipled minister and favourite of Charles II. It may be added, Pym's speech was delivered in 1626, and that will itself best explain the grounds of the impeachment.]

CHARGE AGAINST THE DUKE OF BUCKINGHAM.

MY LORDS,—The matter of fact needs no proof, being so notorious; and therefore I shall insist only upon the consequence which made this fact of the duke's a grievance in the commonwealth; and conclude with strengthening the whole with some precedents.

Every offence presupposes a duty: the first work is to show the duke was bound to do otherwise. I need to allege nothing else but that he was a sworn counsellor and servant to the king, and so ought to have preferred his master's honour and service before his own pride, in seeking to ennoble his own relations.

There are some laws peculiar, according to the temper of several states; there are other laws that are so essential and co-natural with government, that being broken, all things run into confusion.

Such is that law of suppressing vice and encouraging virtue by apt punishments and rewards.

Whosoever moves the king to give honour, which is a double reward, binds himself to make good a double proportion of merit in that party that is to receive it; the first of value and excellency, the second of continuance.

As this honour lifts them above others, so should they have virtue beyond others; and as it is also perpetual, not ending with their persons, but depending upon their posterity, so there ought to be, in the first root of this honour, some such active merit to the commonwealth, as may transmit a vigorous example to their successors to raise them to an imitation of the like.

I forbear reflections on those persons to whom this article collaterally relates, since the commands I have received from the Commons concern the Duke of Buckingham only; I shall therefore leave the first point concerning the offence, and come to the next point, viz., the grievance, which in the articles is expressed in three respects.

First, Prejudicial to the noble barons.

Secondly, To the king, by disabling him from rewarding extraordinary virtue.

Thirdly, To the kingdom, which comprehends all.

First. It is prejudicial to this high court of peers. I will not trouble your lordships with recital, how ancient, how famous this degree of barons hath been in the western monarchies. I will only say, the baronage of England hath upheld that dignity, and doth conceive it in a greater height than any other nation.

The lords are great judges, a court of the last resort; they are great commanders of state, not only for the present, but as law-makers and counsellors for the time to come; and this not by delegacy and commission, but by birth and inheritance. If any be brought to be a member of this great body who is not qualified to the performance of such state functions, it must needs prejudice the whole body; as a little water put into a great vessel of wine, which, as it receives spirits from the wine, so doth it leave therein some degrees of its own infirmities and coldness.

Secondly. It is prejudicial to the king; not that it can disable him from giving honour, for that is a power inseparable from the crown; but by making honour ordinary, it becomes an incompetent reward for extraordinary virtue. When men are made noble, they are taken out of the press of the common sort; and how can it choose but fall in estimation, when honour itself is made a press?

Thirdly. It is prejudicial to the kingdom. Histories and records are full of the great assistance which the crown had received from the barons on foreign and domestic occasions; and not only by their own persons, but their retinue and tenants; and therefore they are called by Bracton, *Robur Belli*. How can the crown expect the like from those who have no tenants, and are hardly able to maintain themselves? Besides, this is not all; for the prejudice goes not only privately from thence, in that they cannot give the assistance they ought, but positively, in that they have been a greater burden to the kingdom since, by the gifts and pensions they have received; nay, they will even stand in need to receive more for the future support of their dignities.

This makes the duke's offence greater, that in this weakness and consumption of the state, he hath not been content alone to consume the public treasure, which is the blood and nourishment of the state, but hath brought in others to help him in this work of destruction; and that they might do it the more eagerly by enlarging their honour, he hath likewise enlarged their necessities and appetites.

I shall second this charge with two precedents; the first, 28 Henry VI., in the complaint against the Duke of Suffolk, that he had married his niece to the Earl of Kendal, and procured him £1,000 *per annum* in the duchy of Guyenne: and yet this party was the son of a noble and well-deserving father.

The second, in 17 Edw. IV., an Act of Parliament for the degrading of Thomas Neville, Marquis of Montague, and Duke of Bedford. The reason expressed in the Act is, because he had not a revenue to support that dignity; together with another reason, that when men are called to honour, and have not livelihood to support it, it induceth great poverty, and causeth briberies, extortions, embraceries, and maintenance.

SIR ROBERT PEEL.
Born 1788. *Died* 1850.

[THE following speech, which is here reprinted in its entirety, was delivered by Sir Robert Peel at the grand dinner given in his honour at the Merchant Tailors' Hall in the spring of 1835, and subsequently to his resignation of office after the short-lived ministry of 1834. The conservative principles which he then professed and so gallantly attempted to carry out are well laid down in this address, and their enunciation there, when read in the light of Peel's after career, will be of no small interest to the political student. Sir E. Bulwer Lytton, in his poem of "St. Stephen's," has sketched the character of this statesman in the three following lines:—

"Peel, decorous with his Median quiver,
Though to wound either side humanely loth,
Shot each in turn, and put an end to both."

SPEECH AT THE MERCHANT TAILORS' HALL,
11TH MAY, 1835.

GENTLEMEN, with the deep feelings of pride and satisfaction by which I must necessarily be animated, there does mix, as you may well believe, one painful feeling that springs from the consciousness that any language of mine must be totally inadequate to express the intensity of my sensations in addressing you upon the present occasion. Gentlemen, I well know that these are the trite and ordinary excuses made by all speakers upon occasions like the present; but if you will only place yourselves in my situation, if you will only recollect that I was alone, as it were, in this company, that I remained seated while all the rest of you were standing, that I remained silent while all the rest of you were enthusiastically vociferating your generous approbation, that I was conscious that all your kindly attention, and consideration, and deep feeling were concentrated upon myself,—if you will recollect that I am a public man, that I am a man of the people, that I derive, I will not say my chief, my only strength from public applause and public confidence, that I am moreover a man who looks for no reward for public services excepting only public approbation, who aspires to no dignity except in all honesty and purity the good opinion of his fellow-subjects—the sound good opinion I mean, as distinguished from the paltry and fleeting popularity which may be gained at the moment, even by the weakest and most contemptible, in pandering or succumbing to faction, or even in more meekly and gently attempting at once to flatter and inflame the people's prejudices;—I say, then, that if you will take all these considerations and circumstances into your attention, you may be well able to believe, that although the excuse I have offered you for my deficiency in power adequately to respond to your great kindness may be trite, though it may be the ordinary phraseology of speakers in complimentary assemblages; yet upon this peculiar occasion it is perfectly consistent with truth, that I am unable to do justice to my feelings, in pouring forth to you my heartfelt thanks for the honour which you have conferred upon me.

But let me not be suspected of idle egotism. Let it not be thought that I have been so misled by the suggestions of personal vanity as to attribute to myself, or any deserts of mine, the origin of this meeting, or the feelings which you have this evening expressed. I agree with our worthy chairman in thinking that the address which I received from so large a body of the merchants, bankers, and traders of this city, was a sufficient compliment and reward for any services and exertions of mine. It asserted the principle by which I was animated: it bore with it the true reward of public services—the approbation of my fellow-citizens. I wanted no other demonstration of public feeling; and if I had regarded this meeting as merely a demonstration of personal compliment, I should have almost discouraged it, as being, after the address, a superfluous token of public esteem. No, Sir, the object of this meeting is a demonstration of public feeling in the metropolis. I do think that public interests may be promoted by it. I do think that the impulse which has been given from this centre of the commercial world—the vital impulse must thrill to every extremity of the British empire. I repeat, Sir, that the throes of this mighty heart must send the wholesome life-blood of sound doctrine and good principle to every remote member of the body corporate of the United Kingdom. Gentlemen, I understand that by assembling here to-day, you mean to mark your attachment to the ancient institutions of the country, and your firm resolution to maintain those principles, which are interwoven with the safety of those institutions, and the security and prosperity of this empire. It was incumbent upon you to come forth in this manner, because you do not happen to have any public recognized organ through whom your sentiments could be expressed. When I look round this great meeting, abounding as it does in wealth—abounding in intelligence—abounding in respectability—and reflect that there is not one single member out of the eighteen allotted for the metropolitan districts to represent your opinions, I am not surprised that you should resolve to speak for yourselves. Whatever be the numbers here assembled, they might have been almost indefinitely swelled by fresh accessions. The hall has been taxed to the utmost extent of its accommodation, and if there were room for ten times a greater number of gentlemen within these walls, we should have had them present. And yet you and your friends had not the good fortune to secure, out of the whole eighteen, a single representative by whom your opinions could be spoken, through whom your just and legitimate influence could be exercised in the public councils. In order, therefore, that there should be no misconstruction of your silence, you feel it necessary to speak through other organs than those which the new representative system has provided for you; and in concurrence with this feeling it is that I come forward to lend my humble countenance to this meeting.

And, gentlemen, it is because this is a public occasion, and because we are met to promote a public object, that you will expect from me some further observations, and some allusions to the state of public affairs. Gentlemen, what I shall say will be spoken by me as one of yourselves, not as one anxious for triumph as a party man—still less as a candidate for office: I shall speak to you as a British subject in a private capacity, feeling a tenfold greater interest in the cause of good government than in any emoluments or advantages he could possibly derive from office; a man who has a tenfold greater desire, on public grounds, for the maintenance of the principles he professes and conscientiously believes to be essential to the welfare of the country, than for any benefits, if benefits they can be called, which he could derive from the acquisition of office. I believe indeed that there is no greater mistake than that people situated as I happen to be are so very anxious for office. Some fancy that the wholesome rest of every politician is broken by his feverish longing for office. If I were to speak from my own experience, I should tell a different tale. There is to me and to many others nothing in office, so far as mere personal feelings or interests are concerned, to compensate for its labours and its annoyances, and its deep anxieties, its interruption of domestic repose and happiness. Away, then, Sir, with the ridiculous assertion that men who are really qualified for the first trusts of the state would consent to procure them by any dishonest sacrifice of opinion, to any compromise of character. We hear constantly the professions of great alarm about court intrigue and court favouritism, and base coalitions of public men for the promotion of their private ends. The country quite mistakes the real danger in this respect; the danger is, not that public men, fit for public trusts, and worthy of public confidence, will seek office by unworthy means, but that they will seek excuses for declining it—will refuse to bear the heavy sacrifices of time and labour and repose, which it imposes. That office holds out great advantages to the ambitious minds of some, I will not deny; but are there not out of office equal, if not greater, means of distinction in public life? For myself, in taking office, in submitting to its drudgery, I was urged by nothing but a sense of public duty, and by the desire not to shrink from that obligation which every British subject incurs when called upon to serve his king, to the utmost of his ability and power. I hope that his Majesty has not a more devoted servant than I; but this I can say with truth, that when I entered the king's service I entered it with the consciousness that I neither sought nor desired any favour, any honour, any reward which the king has in his power to bestow. Office is no doubt a legitimate object of ambition. I think it anything but a reflection on a public man to seek it, when he can hold it consistently with his public principles, and when the holding of it will advance those principles; but speaking for myself, I repeat that I do not covet it, and that nothing has reconciled me to it but the imperative sense of public duty. The chief consolation I have had in holding it, the chief reward I retain on relinquishing it, is the proud reflection that I have had the good fortune in being connected in civil life with that illustrious man* whose fame exceeds that of any other conqueror—a man from whom I never have been one moment estranged by any difference on political subjects,

* The Duke of Wellington.

and with whom my connection never has been embittered by the slightest infusion of paltry jealousy. I am gratified by the thought, connected as I have been with him in the civil service of the Crown, I shall have my name transmitted with his to after-ages. This is the chief pride, the dearest gratification of my heart.

But I feel that I have been straying from the subject immediately before us — the present state of public affairs. Allow me to speak to you not as a party man, but as one of yourselves, and to submit to you plain opinions in plain language. I prefer this, and I am sure so will you, to that elaborate concatenation of phrases which is sometimes called eloquence, in which you have the smallest possible quantity of common sense enveloped in the greatest multitude of equivocal words. I say to you, then, that there is danger to the institutions of this country, danger to the mixed and happily balanced form of government under which we have lived and prospered. But it is in your power, and in the power of those who think with you and fill situations in the country corresponding to yours, to avert the danger. It is in your power, by unremitting activity and by the exercise of those functions which the constitution has left to you, to mitigate, if not altogether to remove, the evil. My fixed opinion is, that the danger can be only met by your gaining for your principles an effectual influence in the popular branch of the legislature. We shall only aggravate the evil if we attempt to deceive ourselves as to the nature of the instruments we can employ. Let us not indulge in useless lamentations. Let us waste no time in regretting that which is beyond our remedy. This is quite idle. The first step towards safety is a knowledge of the real source of our strength, a just confidence in it, and a firm resolution to exert it. If we cease to take a desponding view of public affairs, all will be yet well. Though you may not be able to exercise that full share of influence to which you are legitimately entitled, yet hesitate not to strain every nerve to acquire all that can be acquired. Act like Englishmen, and if you will do so, I am confident, from the national spirit and indomitable resolution, that the country will be rescued from the dangers by which it is at present threatened. I warn you that you must not place a firm reliance either upon the prerogative of the Crown—or on the influence or authority of the House of Lords, or on the combined effect of them. The prerogative of the Crown, the authority of the Lords, are constitutionally potent in occasionally controlling the acts or encroachments of the House of Commons; but you must not now-a-days depend upon them as bulwarks which are impassable, and which can be committed without apprehension to the storm and struggle of passion and ambition and the love of change. The government of the country, allow me to tell you, must be mainly conducted with the goodwill and through the immediate agency of the House of Commons. I again say the royal prerogative, the authority of the House of Lords, are most useful, nay, necessary, in our mixed and balanced constitution. But you must not strain those powers. You would not consider that to be worthy of the name of government, which is nothing but a series of jealousies and hostile collisions between two branches of the legislature. You wish to see all branches of the legislature maintaining each its independent authority, but moving, through mutual confidence, in harmonious concert towards the great end of civil society and civil government—the public good. I ask you then, not to underrate, not to misunderstand the power and authority of the House of Commons, not to trust to the controlling checks which may theoretically exist upon that power and authority; but to secure, through the legitimate exercise of constitutional privileges, that degree of influence for your principles in the House of Commons, which will be ten times more powerful for the establishment of what is good, and the resistance of what is evil, than any extrinsic control of the Crown or the House of Lords. On taking office, I avowed my determination to abide by the Reform Bill. I trust I have redeemed that pledge. On this broad constitutional principle my friends and I acted. We acted in the spirit of the Reform Bill, not niggardly, not merely content with a cold assent and submission to its details, but with an honest and generous deference to its spirit and to the authority which it established. When we found, after a patient and sufficient trial, that we had not the confidence of the House of Commons, although the array opposed to us was miscellaneous in the extreme, although the majority was small, we felt it our duty to resign. However strongly we might have opposed the establishment of the new elective system, we now adhered to our pledge. We did not entertain the vain notion of governing the country against a majority of the reformed House of Commons. We refused, indeed, to be obedient instruments in the hands of that majority. We thought it safer for the country to refuse to be so, and, therefore, unable to enforce our own principles, we retired from office. Allow me then to recommend you also to follow this example, to refrain from flattering yourselves with vague and distant hopes of altering the present system —let us not seem, even in thought, to threaten those who have acquired new rights with the forfeiture of that acquisition. Let us stand by the constitution as it exists at present. Let us never hint at alteration, or by our conduct raise a secret doubt, even in the minds of the most suspicious. I venture to prophesy to you that the proposition for change will not come from you. If it comes, it will come from those who clamoured most loudly for the Reform Bill, who demanded the whole bill, and nothing but the bill. Ay, it will come from them, and the moment, perhaps, is not far distant — the moment that they have ascertained the bill is not likely to answer the purposes they had in view — the moment they see it is not potent to exclude the influence of what we call Conservative principles. Let us then declare our readiness to accept in good faith, as a constitutional settlement, the provisions of the Reform Bill, and let us by that declaration fortify ourselves in the resistance to new agitations of the public mind on questions of government, to new innovations on what was called but yesterday by its friends the second charter of our liberties. And while you determine to respect the Reform Bill, prove practically your respect for it by exercising every privilege which it leaves untouched, or which it for the first time confers. There must be no laziness—no apathy—and above all, no despondency. Let each man consider the franchise he possesses not as a personal privilege, but as a public trust, which it is his duty to fulfil.

But I have said enough upon this subject; I do not despair that if we continue to exert ourselves, if we here set an example to the empire, it will, in all its parts, be before long animated by the constitutional and truly English feelings which are here displayed. How, it will be asked, are you to regain your influence in the House of Commons? Not, let me tell you, as your enemies would impute to you, by bribery and corruption and unworthy means, but by going forth with a frank exposition of your principles, and by showing that there is nothing selfish in your support of the institutions under which you live, and of your defence of the rights which you inherited. Let us disclaim all interest in the maintenance of any abuse — let us declare that we are willing to redress any real grievance, and to concur in the application of the best remedy which can possibly be devised for that purpose. We hold that no public office ought to be maintained for the mere purpose of patronage; that public appointments can only be vindicated on the ground of their being necessary to the public service. We want no sinecures. We want no greater amount of salary for the reward of public officers than that which may be sufficient for securing integrity and competence in the discharge of important official duties. Above all, we deny that we are separated by any fancied line of interest, or of pride, or of privilege, from the middling classes of the country. Why, who are we, or at least nine-tenths of those who are here assembled, that any one should tell us that we have an interest separate, or feelings discordant from those of the middling classes of society? If we ourselves don't belong to the middling classes of society, I want to know how wide the interval may be that is presumed to separate us? Speaking in behalf of nine-tenths at least of those assembled within these walls, I say we disclaim any separation from the middling classes of society in this country. O no, we are bound to them by a thousand ramifications of direct personal connection, and common interests and common feelings. If circumstances may appear to have elevated some of us above the rest, to what, I venture to ask, is that elevation owing? It is owing to nothing else but to the exercise, either on our own part or on the part of our immediate forefathers, of those qualities of diligence, of the love of order, of industry, of integrity in commercial dealings, which have hitherto secured to every member of the middle class of society the opportunities of elevation and distinction in this great community; and it is because we stand in our present situation— it is because we owe our elevation in society to the exercise of those qualities, and because we feel that so long as this ancient form of government, and the institutions connected with it, and the principles and feelings which they engender, shall endure, the same elevation will be secured by the same means, that we are resolved, with the blessing of God, to keep clear for others those same avenues that were opened to ourselves, that we will not allow their course to be obstructed by men who want to secure the same advantages by dishonest means—to reach, by some shorter cut, that goal which can be surely attained, but can only be attained, through industry, and patient perseverance, and strict integrity. Gentlemen, what was the charge against myself? It was this, that the king had sent to Rome for the son of a cotton-spinner, in order to make him prime minister of England. Did I feel that a reflection? Did it make me discontented with the state of the laws and institutions of the country? No; but does it not make me, and ought it not make you, gentlemen, anxious to preserve that happy order of things under which the same opportunities of distinction may be ensured to other sons of other cotton-spinners, provided they can establish a legitimate claim on the confidence of their king and country? We are charged with having some interest in the perpetuation of abuses. Why, can there be any one with a greater interest than we have, that the public burdens should be as much lightened as they can possibly be, consistent with the maintenance of the public engagements? We are represented as fattening on the public income. Looking to this company, and to those associated with it in feeling, is there any gain, I ask, connected with the increase of the public burdens that can countervail the interest we have in their reduction. We have a direct, a superior interest to any other in the correction of every abuse and the application of every just principle of just and wise economy.

At the same time, consistently with these feelings, consistently with the determination to correct real abuses, and to promote real economy, we do not disguise that it is our firm resolution to maintain, to the utmost of our power, the limited monarchy of this country, to respect the rights of every branch of the legislature, to maintain inviolate the united Church of England and Ireland, to maintain it as a predominant establishment, meaning by predominance, not the denial of any civil right to other classes of the community, but maintaining the Church in the possession of its property and of all its just privileges. Such is our firm resolution; we will submit to no compromise, and we will exercise every privilege which the constitution has intrusted to us for the legitimate maintenance and support of the constitution in Church and State. This is the appeal we make to the middle classes of the community—to those who are mainly the depositaries of the elective franchise. We tell them that it is not only our determination to resist any direct attack on our institutions, but that we are also resolved that we will not permit the ancient prescriptive government of this country—the mitigated monarchy, consisting of three branches of the legislature—we are determined that we will not allow it to be changed, by plausible and specious propositions of reform, into a democratic republic. We will not allow, if we can prevent it—we will not allow that, through plausible and popular pretexts of improvement and reform, there shall gradually take place such an infusion of democracy into the institutions of this country as shall essentially change their theory and practical character, and shall by slow degrees rob us of the blessings we have so long enjoyed under our limited monarchy, and popular but balanced constitution.

Now, gentlemen, that is what I apprehend we mean by—this is the construction we put upon the term "Conservative principles;" and such is the ground on which we make an appeal to the country at large for the maintenance of those principles. We tell all, in whatever class of life they may be, that they ought to feel as deep an interest in the maintenance of those principles as any of the politicians or men of property who are now within my hearing. The encouragement of industry, the demand for productive labour, depends on the maintenance of those principles. The preservation of order depends on them, the maintenance of that security, which has hitherto led men through honest industry to accumulate property in this country, depends upon them. And now that the feelings excited by political contests and great changes in the electoral system have subsided, I cannot help entertaining a sincere hope and belief, disclaiming any intention of interfering improperly with the political franchise, that there is still that fund of good sense in this community that will enable us, if not to gain a predominating influence in the Commons' House of Parliament, still to acquire that degree of influence that shall control and prevent many bad projects.

My advice to you is, not to permit past differences on political subjects now to prevent a cordial union with those who take a similar view with yourselves on matters of immediately pressing importance. There are many questions on which you formerly differed with others, that are now settled. There are many public men from whose views you formerly dissented, who agree with you that the Reform Bill is not to be made a platform from which a new battery is to be directed against the remaining institutions of this country. If they agree with you in this, the essential practical point; if, wishing with you to correct real abuses, they are still determined to maintain the ancient principles on which the constitution of the country is founded, to protect the interests of order and property, it would be madness to revive old and extinguished differences, and to allow the remembrance of such shadows to obstruct an harmonious and cordial union for the defence and preservation of all that remains.

Gentlemen, I ought to apologize for detaining you so long, and I shall not further prevent my Hon. friend, the chairman, from proceeding in the execution of his remaining duties. But, in conclusion, let me call on you to recollect the associations connected with the place where we are now assembled. From this place a voice* issued in 1793 of memorable moment — a voice in support of the ancient principles of the British monarchy—a voice which encouraged and enabled the ministers of that day to check the contagion of democratic and French principles, then in their ascendant. I call on you to remember the motto under which you are now assembled, *Concordiâ parvæ res crescunt*: to bear in mind, that by acting on the advice which it involves, small as your influence in the public councils may now be, it is capable, by unity of purpose, by cordial concert, and good understanding— by common exertions directed to a common end, it is capable of vast expansion and increase. By your example you will rally around you a thousand hearts to fight in the same righteous cause. Proclaim to the country from this, the metropolis of commerce, that, entertaining principles of moderation in public affairs, you will still stand firm in defence of the ancient walls, and guard the ancient landmarks of the con-

---

* That of Burke.

stitution; that you will rally round the monarchy and protect its just prerogatives; that you will defend the independent exercise of the authority of the House of Lords, and maintain firm and inviolate the rights of the Established Church; that you will stand by, in the emphatic language of the most solemn Acts of Parliament, the Protestant government and the Protestant religion of this country. Yes, elevate that voice in the cause of those principles — principles so moderate, so just, so necessary — and depend upon it, it will be re-echoed from every part of this country, and the pulsation of the heart of the great corporate community will vibrate through every artery of this mighty empire.

THE LATE PRINCE CONSORT.

Born 1819. *Died* 1861.

[THE subjoined estimate of Sir Robert Peel, from the "Addresses" of the late Prince Consort, may appropriately follow our last selection. It occurs in a speech delivered at the banquet given by the Lord Mayor of York and the mayors of the chief cities and towns of the United Kingdom, to the Lord Mayor of London, October 25th, 1850.]

CHARACTER OF SIR ROBERT PEEL.

THE constitution of Sir Robert Peel's mind was peculiarly that of a statesman, and of an English statesman: he was liberal from feeling, but conservative upon principle. Whilst his impulse drove him to foster progress, his sagacious mind and great experience showed him how easily the whole machinery of a state and of society is deranged, and how important, but how difficult also, it is to direct its further development in accordance with its fundamental principles, like organic growth in nature. It was peculiar to him, that in great things, as in small, all the difficulties and objections occurred to him first; he would anxiously consider them, pause, and warn against rash resolutions; but having convinced himself, after a long and careful investigation, that a step was not only right to be taken, but of the practical mode also of safely taking it, it became to him a necessity and a duty to take it: all his caution and apparent timidity changed into courage and power of action, and at the same time readiness cheerfully to make any personal sacrifice which its execution might demand.

Gentlemen, if he has had so great an influence over this country, it was from the nation recognizing in his qualities the true type of the English character, which is essentially practical. Warmly attached to his institutions, and revering the bequests left to him by the industry, wisdom, and piety of his forefathers, the Englishman attaches little value to any theoretical scheme. It will attract his attention only after having been for some time placed before him: it must have been thoroughly investigated and discussed before he will entertain it. Should it be an empty theory, it will fall to the ground during this time of probation; should it survive this trial, it will be on account of the practical qualities contained in it; but its adoption in the end will entirely depend upon its harmonizing with the national feeling, the historic development of the country, and the peculiar nature of its institutions.

THOMAS LORD ERSKINE.

Born 1748. *Died* 1823.

[WE are sorry our space does not allow us to print in its entirety the fine speech of which the conclusion only is here given. It is from beginning to end a great specimen of forensic oratory. The exordium, the examination of the evidence, and the peroration are alike worthy of study.

The "Gordon Riots" are too well known, and the language of our extract too clear, to need any historical explanation of the speaker's position. The speech was delivered before Lord Mansfield, Chief Justice of England, in February, 1781.]

TRIAL OF LORD GEORGE GORDON.

WHAT is the evidence then on which the connection of my noble client with the outrages of the mob is to be proved? Why that they had blue cockades. How absurd! Is he answerable for every man that wears a blue cockade? If a person commits murder in my livery, without my command, counsel, or consent, is the murder mine?

In all cumulative constructive treasons, gentlemen, you are to judge from the tenor of a man's behaviour, not from crooked and disjointed parts of it. *Nemo repente est turpissimus*. No one can possibly be guilty of this crime by a sudden impulse of the mind; Lord George Gordon stands, therefore, upon the evidence at Coachmakers' Hall as pure and white as snow. He stands so upon the evidence of a man who had differed with him as to the expediency of his conduct, yet who swears that, from the time he took the chair till the time which is the subject of inquiry, there was no blame in him.

You, therefore, are bound as Christian men to believe that when he came to St. George's Fields on the memorable morning, he had no hostile intention of repealing a law by rebellion.

But it seems all his behaviour at Coachmakers' Hall was colour and deceit. Let us see, therefore, whether this body of men, when assembled, answered the description of that which I have stated to be the purpose of him who assembled them. Were they a multitude arrayed for terror and force? On the contrary you have heard, upon the evidence of men whose veracity is not to be impeached, that they were sober, decent, quiet, peaceable tradesmen, of the better sort, well-dressed and well-behaved; and that there was not a man among them who had any one weapon, offensive or defensive. Sir Philip Jennings Clerke tells you he went into the fields; that he drove through them, talked to many individuals amongst them, who all informed him that it was not their wish to persecute the Papists, but that they were alarmed for the fate of their religion. He further told you he never saw a more peaceable multitude, and it appears upon the oath of all who were present, that Lord George Gordon went among the crowd exhorting them to peace and quiet.

Mark his conduct, gentlemen, when he heard from Mr. Evans that there was a low riotous set of people assembled in Palace Yard. Mr. Evans, being a member of the Protestant Association, and desirous that nothing tumultuary might happen from the assembly, went in his carriage with Mr. Spinage to St. George's Fields to inform Lord George that there were such people assembled, probably Papists, who were determined to do mischief. The moment he told him of it, whatever his original plan might have been, he instantly changed it on seeing its impropriety. "Do you intend," said Mr. Evans, "to carry up all these men with the petition to the House of Commons?" "No, I do not," he replied. "Will you then give me leave," says Mr. Evans, "to go round to the different divisions, and tell the people it is not your lordship's purpose?" He answered, "By all means." Mr. Evans accordingly went, but it was impossible to guide such a number of people, peaceable as they were. Being all invincibly desirous to go, he was at last obliged to leave the fields, exhausted with heat and fatigue, beseeching them to be peaceable and orderly. At the very time that he left them in perfect harmony and good order, it appears, gentlemen, by the evidence of Sir Philip Jennings Clerke, that Palace Yard was in an uproar, filled with mischievous boys and the lowest dregs of the people.

Gentlemen of the jury, I have all along told you that the crown was aware that it had no case of treason without connecting the noble prisoner with consequences which it was in some luck to find advocates to state without proof to support it. I can only speak for myself, that small as my chance is of ever arriving at that high office, I would not accept of it on the terms of being obliged to produce, as evidence of guilt against a fellow-citizen, that which I have been witness to this day. For Mr. Attorney-General perfectly well knew the innocent and laudable motive with which the protection was given. Yet he produced it to insinuate that Lord George Gordon, knowing himself to be the ruler of those villains, set himself up as saviour from their fury. We called Lord Stormont to explain this matter to you, who told you that Lord George Gordon came to Buckingham House and begged to see the king, saying he might be of great use in quelling the riots. Can there be on earth a greater proof of conscious innocence? For if he had been the wicked mover of them, would he have gone to the king to have confessed it by offering to recall his followers from the mischiefs he had provoked? No! but since a public protest issued by himself and the association reviling the authors of these mischiefs, the Protestant cause was still made the pretext, he thought his public exertions might be useful, as they might tend to remove the prejudices which wicked men had diffused. The king thought so likewise, and therefore, as appears by Lord Stormont, refused to see Lord George till he had given the test of his loyalty by such exertions. But sure I am our gracious sovereign meant no trap for innocence, nor ever recommended it as such to his servants.

Lord George's language was simply this: "The multitude pretend to be perpetrating these acts under the authority of the Protestant petition. I assure your Majesty they are not the Protestant Association, and I shall be glad to be of any service in suppressing them." I say, by God, that man is a ruffian who shall, after this, presume to build upon such honest, artless conduct as an evidence of guilt. But, gentlemen, if Lord George Gordon had been guilty of high treason, as is assumed to-day, in the face of the cabinet and of the whole parliament, how are they to defend themselves from the misprision of suffering such a man to go at large and to approach his sovereign? The man that conceals the perpetration of treason is himself a traitor; but they are all perfectly safe. For nobody thought of treason till fears arising from another quarter bewildered their senses.

The king, therefore, and his servants very wisely accepted my noble friend's promise of assistance, and he flew with honest zeal to fulfil it. Sir Philip Jennings Clerke tells you that he made use of every expression that it was possible for a man in such circumstances to do. He begged them, for God's sake, to disperse and go home; hoped the petition would be granted, but that rioting was not the way to effect it. Sir Philip said he felt himself bound, without being particularly asked, to say everything he could in protection of an injured and innocent man, and repeated again that there was not an art he could possibly make use of that he did not zealously employ; but it was all in vain. "I began," says he, "to tremble for myself; for Lord George read the resolution of the House, which was hostile to them, and said their petition would not be taken into consideration until they were quiet." But did he say, therefore go on to burn and destroy? On the contrary, he helped to pen that motion, and read it to the multitude, as one which he himself had approved. After this he went into the coach with Sheriff Pugh, in the city, and there it was that he publicly signed that protection which has been read in evidence against him, although Mr. Fisher, who now stands in my presence, and who has repeatedly told me that he thought Lord George Gordon to be as innocent as the child unborn, confessed in the privy council, that he himself had granted similar protections to various people, yet was dismissed as having done nothing but his duty.

Such is the plain and simple truth. For this just obedience to His Majesty's request do the king's servants come to-day into this court, where the king is supposed in person to sit, to turn that obedience into the crime of high treason, and to ask you to put the noble prisoner to death for it.

Gentlemen, you have now heard, upon the solemn oaths of honest, disinterested men, a faithful history of the conduct of Lord George Gordon, from the day that he became a member of the Protestant Association to the day that he was committed a prisoner to the Tower, and I have no doubt, from the attention with which I have been honoured, that you have still kept in your minds the principles to which I entreated you would apply the evidence, and that you have measured it all by that standard.

You have therefore only to look back to the whole of it together; to reflect on all you have heard concerning him; to trace him in your recollection through every part of the transaction; and considering it with one liberal view, to ask your own honest hearts, whether you can say that this noble and unfortunate youth is a wicked and deliberate traitor, who deserves by your verdict to suffer a shameful and ignominious death, and to stain the ancient honours of his house for ever.

The crime which the crown would have fixed upon him is, that he assembled the Protestant Association round the House of Commons, not merely to influence and persuade parliament by the earnestness of their supplications, but actually to coerce it by hostile rebellious force. That finding himself disappointed in the success of this coercive policy, he afterwards incited his followers to abolish the legal indulgences to Papists which the object of the petition was to repeal, by the burning of their houses of worship, and the destruction of their property, which ended at last in a general attack on the property of all orders of men, religious and civil, on the public treasures of the nation, and on the very being of the government.

To support a charge of so atrocious and unnatural a complexion, the laws of even arbitrary nations would require the most incontrovertible proof. They would demand either the villain to have been taken in the overt act of wickedness, or if he worked in secret upon others, his guilt to be brought out by the consistent tenor of his conduct, or by the discovery of some plot or conspiracy. The very worst inquisitor that dealt in blood would vindicate the torture at least by plausibility and the semblance of truth.

What evidence then will a jury of Englishmen expect from the servants of the crown, before they deliver up a brother accused before them to ignominy and death? What proof will their consciences exact? What will their plain and manly understandings accept of? What does the immemorial custom of their fathers, and the written law of this land, warrant them in demanding? Nothing less, in any case of blood, than the clearest and most unequivocal proof. But in this case the statute has not even trusted to the humanity and justice of our general law, but has said in plain, rough, expressive terms proveable, that is, says Lord Coke, not upon conjectural presumptions or inferences, or strains of wit, but upon direct and plain proof. For the King, Lords, and Commons, continues that great lawyer, did not use the word *probable*, for then a common argument might have served; but *proveable*, which signifies the highest force of demonstration. Now, what evidence, gentlemen of the jury, does the crown offer to you in compliance with these sound and sacred doctrines of justice? Nothing but a few broken, interrupted, disjointed words, without context or connection, uttered by the speaker in agitation and heat, and heard by those who relate them to you in the midst of tumult and confusion; and even these words, mutilated as they are, in direct opposition to, and inconsistent with, repeated and earnest declarations delivered at the very same time, and on the very same occasion, related to you by a much greater number of persons, and which are absolutely incompatible with the whole tenor of his conduct, proved to you by respectable witnesses, whom we only ceased calling because human life would have been too short to hear the remainder.

What can be added to such observations, which, even if they were clear, carry their own explanation in every one of your minds? Who of us, gentlemen, would be safe, standing at the bar of God, or man, if we were to be judged, not by the regular current of our lives, and conversations, but by detached and unguarded expressions, picked out by malice, and recorded without context or circumstances against us, though directly inconsistent with other expressions delivered at the same time on the same subject, and though repugnant to the whole tenor of our deportment and behaviour. Yet such is the only evidence by which the crown asks you to dip your hands, and to stain your consciences, in the innocent blood of the noble and unfortunate youth who now stands before you. On the mere evidence of *the words* you have heard from their witness, which, even if they had stood uncontroverted by the proofs with which we have swallowed them up, or unexplained by circumstances which destroy their malignity, could not, at the very most, amount in law to more than a breach of the act of tumultuous petitioning, if such an act still exist. For the worst malice of his enemies has not been able to bring out the slightest testimony that he has ever directed, countenanced, or approved rebellious force against the legislature of his country; and without which evidence it is impossible to make a case of treason by the most strained and romantic construction. It is, indeed, astonishing to me that men can keep the natural colour of their cheeks, when they ask for blood in such a case, even if the prisoner had made no defence. But will they still continue to demand it after what they have heard? It is, really, hardly to be presumed!

I will, gentlemen, just remind the Solicitor-General, before he begins his reply, what matter he has to encounter.

That the going up in a body was not even originated by Lord George, but by others in his absence. That when proposed by him, it was unanimously adopted by the whole association, and consequently their act as much as his; not determined in a conclave, but with open doors, and the resolution published to all the world; known to the ministers and magistrates of the country, who did not even signify to him, or to anybody else, that it was dangerous or illegal. That decency and peace were enjoined and commanded; and that the badges of distinction, which are now cruelly turned into the charge of an hostile array against him, were expressly and publicly directed for the prevention of disorder; that there was not even a walking-stick among the populace to disturb the public tranquillity; and that their demeanour was perfectly decent and temperate till it was disgraced by the acts of a villanous banditti, which have been, however, separated from the Protestant Association by the most incontrovertible proof; and which, even if not so separated, could not have affected Lord George but by bringing home their conduct to him.

While the House of Commons was deliberating, he repeatedly entreated the crowd to behave with decency and peace, and to retire to their houses. But my noble friend knew not that he was speaking to the enemies of his cause. When they at last dispersed, no man thought or imagined that treason had been committed; and his lordship was carried home by Sir James Lowther, a gentleman of the first fortune and character, who tells you that on the coach being surrounded by the mob, Lord George beseeched them to be quiet and to disperse, or parliament would never listen to their petition. He then returned to bed, where he lay unconscious that ruffians were ruining him by their disorders in the night. On Monday, he published an advertisement, reviling the authors of these riots; and, as the Protestant cause had been wickedly made the pretext for them, enjoining all who wished well to it to behave like good citizens. Nor has the crown even attempted to prove that he had either given, or that he afterwards gave, secret instructions in opposition to that public admonition. He afterwards begged an audience to receive the King's commands; he waited on the ministers; he attended his duty in parliament; and when the multitude, amongst whom there was not a man of the Associated Protestants, again assembled on the Tuesday, under pretence of the Protestant cause, he offered his services, and read a resolution of the house to them, accompanied with every expostulation which a zeal for peace could possibly inspire; and because he was speaking to ruffians and papists, and not to the authors of the petition, and who therefore would not obey him, how is that to be imputed to him?

He afterwards, agreeably to the King's direction, attended the magistrates in their duty, honestly and honourably exerting all his power to quell the fury of the multitude; which circumstance, to the dishonour of the crown, has been scandalously turned against him. Even the protections which he granted publicly in the coach of the Sheriff of London, whom he was assisting in his office of magistracy, are produced in evidence of his guilt, though protections of a similar nature were, to the knowledge of the whole Privy Council, granted by Mr. Fisher himself, who now stands in my presence unreproved, and who would have explained their tendency, so as to remove every imputation of criminality, had he been examined.

What, then, has produced this trial for high treason, or given it when produced the seriousness and solemnity it wears? What but the inversion of all justice by judging from consequences, instead of from causes and designs! What but the artful manner in which the crown has endeavoured to blend the petitioning in a body, and the zeal with which an animated disposition conducted it, with the melancholy crimes that followed! crimes which the shameful indolence of our magistrates, which the total extinction of all police and government suffered to be committed in broad day, in the delirium of drunkenness, by an unarmed banditti, without a head, without plan or object, and without a refuge from the instant gripe of justice: a horde of ruffians, with whom the Associated Protestants and their president had no manner of connection, and whose cause they overturned, dishonoured, and ruined.

How iniquitous, then, is it to attempt, without evidence, to infect your imaginations, who are upon your oaths dispassionately and disinterestedly to try the offence of merely assembling a multitude with a petition to repeal a law (which has happened so often in all our memories before) by blending it with the subsequent catastrophe, on which every man's mind may be supposed to retain some degree of irritation? This is indeed wicked. It is taking the advantage of all the infirmities of our nature. Do the prosecutors wish you, while you are listening to the evidence, to connect it with consequences in spite of reason and truth, in order to hang the millstone of prejudice round the prisoner's innocent neck? If there be such men, may Heaven forgive them for the attempt, and inspire you with fortitude and wisdom to do your duty to your fellow-citizen, with calm, steady, reflecting minds!

Gentlemen, I have no manner of doubt that you will. I am, indeed, sure you cannot but see (notwithstanding my great inability, increased by a perturbation of mind arising, thank God, from no dishonest cause) that there has been no evidence on the part of the crown to fix the guilt of the late commotions upon my noble client, but that, on the contrary, we have been able to resist the *probability*—I might almost say the *possibility*—of the charge, not only by living witnesses, whom we ceased to call, because the trial would never have ended, but by the evidence of all the blood that has paid the forfeit of that guilt already; which, I will take upon me to say, is the strongest and most unanswerable proof that the combination of natural events ever brought together for the shield of an innocent man. It is, that in the trial of all the black catalogue of culprits who expired on the gibbets, though conducted by the ablest servants of the crown, with an eye, and a laudable eye, to the investigation of the matter which to-day engages your attention, no one fact appeared which showed any plan, any object, any leader. That, finally, out of forty-four thousand persons who signed the petition of the Protestants, or among those who were convicted, tried, or even apprehended on suspicion; or of all the felons that were let loose from prisons, and who assisted in the destruction and plunder of our property, not a single wretch was to be found who could even attempt to save his own life by the plausible promise of giving evidence on the present occasion.

Gentlemen, what can overturn such proof as this? Surely a good man might, without superstition, believe that such an union of events was something more than the natural issues of life, and that the Providence of God was watchful for the protection of innocence and truth. I may now, therefore, relieve you from the pain of hearing me any longer, and be myself relieved from the pain of speaking on a subject which agitates and distresses me. Since, gentlemen, Lord George Gordon stands clear of every hostile act or purpose against the legislature of his country, or the properties of his fellow-subjects—since the whole tenor of his conduct repels the belief of the traitorous purpose charged in the indictment—my task is finished. I shall make no address to your passions. I will not remind you of the long and rigorous imprisonment he has suffered. I will not speak to you of his great youth, of his illustrious birth, and of his uniformly animated and generous zeal in parliament for the constitution of his country. Such topics might be useful in the balance of a doubtful case; yet even then I should have trusted to the honest hearts of Englishmen to have felt them without excitation. At present, the plain and rigid rules of justice and truth are sufficient to entitle me to your verdict, and may God Almighty, who is the sacred author of both, fill your minds with the deepest impressions of them, and with virtue to follow those impressions! You will then restore my innocent client to liberty, and me to that peace of mind, which, since the protection of that innocence in any part depended upon me, I have never known.

LORD PALMERSTON.
Born 1784.

[THE following extract is from a speech delivered by Lord Palmerston on March 1st, 1848, in answer to an attack upon his foreign policy by Mr. Anstey, M.P. for Youghal.]

IN DEFENCE OF HIS FOREIGN POLICY.

NOW, in proceeding to continue the statement which I was interrupted by the necessary adjournment of the House in making the other day, I really feel that I have some apology to make to the House for detaining them with transactions that occurred twenty years ago, at a moment when the public attention is engrossed by matters of the most overpowering importance, and of the most overwhelming interest, succeeding each other with unexampled rapidity, and which, for the moment at least, must throw into the shade all the interest of those long gone by and frequently discussed matters. I have also on my own part to solicit some indulgence from the House, in times like these, when the proper person or corporate body to appoint for such authority as has been imposed upon me, would be the Siamese twins—the one to write all that has to be written, and the other to hear all that he has to hear, and to say all that has to be said. Since this motion has been brought forward, and especially during the last week, I really have not had the time that I should wish to devote to methodise and arrange the whole of the matters referred to by the hon. and learned gentleman (Mr. Anstey) in his speech. I trust, therefore, that any want of arrangement on my part, which is a necessary consequence, perhaps, of the want of arrangement on his part, may be pardoned by the House, who otherwise should not be disposed to excuse such deficiency on the part of those who have any matter to submit to its consideration. The hon. and learned gentleman skipped about from transaction to transaction, and jumbled the various matters adverted to in his notice in such a manner, that the topics of his speech might be likened to the confused mass of luggage brought to the Custom-house by some of the continental steamboats, when no man knows where he is to find his own. Now, the subjects which the notice of the hon. and learned gentleman includes, are 40 in number; they have been already the subject of 139 discussions in Parliament, while the correspondence relative to them is contained in no less than 2,775 folio volumes of office papers. Under these circumstances, the House will readily suppose that I must trust mainly to my recollection in the statements which I shall feel it to be my duty to make them, and that neither in the last week, nor indeed at any time since this notice has been given, has it been in my power to go through, with that minuteness which would be necessary, the multiplied transactions to which the notice relates. I remember a friend of mine mentioning to me the circumstances connected with an accident to a naval officer who was nearly drowned, and afterwards recovered by the ordinary mode of treatment. At the moment of drowning all the events of his past life rushed hurriedly to his recollection. Now, though I have been much threatened and attacked by the hon. and learned gentlemen, I have not been anything like so nearly swamped by him as that all the events of my official life should crowd at one moment to my mental vision. I trust, however, that my memory on all these matters is sufficient to enable me to give to the House such information as will be satisfactory to them. I believe that the best method for me to pursue, will be to take the topics in the order in which they stand on the Notice Paper.

The first of these topics is the Treaty of Adrianople, which appears, in fact, to be the main question to be discussed by the House. With regard to this and all the other topics, I would say that papers concerning them had been laid at the time before Parliament, spontaneously or at the call of Parliament, containing such a statement of the transactions as appeared to the Government sufficient to explain the transactions which had taken place. The hon. and learned member calls in the first resolution for secret papers, of which there are very few; but I may state that with regard to the correspondence generally of Governments, the practice is this—and, I may add, that practice I have invariably followed—the practice and the duty of a Government when diplomatic transactions occur which it is desirable that the House and the country should become acquainted with—the practice is, to lay before Parliament such portions of the diplomatic transactions that have taken place as will convey to Parliament a true and faithful knowledge of all the main and important circumstances that occurred. But it is not the duty of the Government—but, on the contrary, it would be a breach of that duty if it did so—to lay before Parliament such portions of that correspondence as contained mere opinions and confidential communications made by the Foreign Minister to our agents abroad concerning other matters, and the publication of which would be injurious to the public service, and would have the effect of defeating the object which Parliament and the Government ought to have in view. The Minister at a foreign court is bound to tell his Government everything he hears, everything he thinks, everything that is stated to him whether in confidence or not, by the Government with whom he is accredited; and it is manifest that there must be in his despatches a number of communications of various kinds, which, if published, would at once deprive that Minister of all future access to such confidential communications as are essential to the public interest to have made. And I will venture to say that any man who has been at all concerned in these matters, either in the Government or in diplomacy, will at once see that if the rule were acted upon that everything which a foreign Minister writes was strictly to be laid before Parliament, our Minister would soon cease to write anything of benefit or of advantage to the Government or to the country. And when portions of the despatches are withheld, it is not with the wish or the intention or the effect of withholding from Parliament knowledge which it is essential Parliament should possess, but simply for the purpose of not exposing your agent to the certainty of being placed in a position which would deprive him of being at any future time useful to the

Government. Therefore when the hon. and learned gentleman now moves for papers beyond those which have been already produced with respect to these transactions, my answer is—that it is not consistent with my public duty to accede to the demand; but at the same time, if the House choose to appoint a Secret Committee to inquire into the whole subject, I can have no objection whatever to such a course. I have only to say, that if a Secret Committee have to go through the 2,775 volumes of documents, I wish them joy of their task. The Treaty of Adrianople itself has been laid before Parliament.

* * * *

The next motion, or rather two or three motions, relate to transactions of a somewhat similar character—to the Treaty of Unkiar Skelessi, and the communications, on the part of Russia, with the Governments of Turkey, Moldavia, and Wallachia. The Treaty of Unkiar Skelessi has been laid before Parliament. That treaty—as is well known—was no doubt, to a certain degree, forced upon Turkey by the Russian envoy, Count Orloff, under circumstances which rendered it difficult for Turkey to refuse acceding to it. Mehemet Ali had invaded Syria, and had advanced far into Asia Minor, and threatened Constantinople. The Sultan applied to the British Government for assistance; but the British Government was not at that time in a condition to send that assistance. We had not a naval force at our disposal sufficient for the purpose. It was known that Russia had offered assistance. The Russian Government said :—" We know that application has been made to England, and we should prefer that England should interfere; but if England finds it inconvenient to do so, we will give the assistance that is required, and save Constantinople from the attack of Mehemet Ali." That was done, and Russia sent a force which did stop the advance of the Egyptian army; and an arrangement was made between the Sultan and Mehemet Ali, by which Mehemet Ali was to be made Pasha of Egypt, Syria, and a part of Arabia. The British Government were, however, surprised to learn that when the Russian troops quitted the Bosphorus, they carried that treaty away with them. It was, however, a treaty for a limited period—that is to say, for a period of eight years. The most objectionable feature in it was, that the Sultan bound himself to consult with the Russian Government on all the affairs of his empire—that he did, practically, give to the Russian Government a power of interference and dictation in Turkey, both in her internal and external policy, which we thought was not consistent with the independent position which we considered it necessary that Turkey should maintain.

But that treaty was concluded; and whatever might be the objection that England or France was disposed to make to it, it was not competent for either England or France—except by a declaration of war—to compel the parties to annul it. The only course that we felt it was open to us to pursue was to wait until the treaty should expire, and then to endeavour, by friendly communications, to supersede the necessity on which that treaty was founded, by affording to Turkey a larger protection than was given to her by the single engagement with Russia.

Then comes the question of the Treaty of Commerce of 1838, with regard to which I must say, that, though commercial treaties are no novelties in the world, and though the man who negociates one can scarcely have a claim to be ranked with the inventor of printing, or the discoverer of the compass, or other brilliant discoveries, yet I do not wish to detract from the merit which is due to the hon. member for Stafford (Mr. Urquhart) in connection with it.

* * * *

Now, sir, the hon. member said that Russia had not acceded to this treaty. Other Powers did almost immediately after it was signed; but Russia did not, and it is true that for a long time Russia held out for former treaties. But, within the last few years, Russia has acceded, for she has concluded a treaty similar in principle and details to the Treaty of 1838, with one exception—that permission is given to Russia to prohibit the exportation of certain things—to establish a monopoly—and to impose certain restrictions, internal restrictions, upon Russian subjects. The British Government has been much pressed by the Turkish Government to consent to similar restrictions upon British subjects; but, as yet, I have thought it my duty to decline acceding to those requests. We, therefore, stand in this way:— We are bound by the Treaty of 1838, and the Russian Government is upon the same footing, because the Russian Government made its assent to the imposition of these restrictions dependent upon those restrictions being accepted also by other European Powers.

Really, sir, it is hardly worth while to defend the character of my late lamented friend, Mr. Poulett Thompson (Lord Sydenham), from the imputation, in the discharge of his public duty as a responsible minister of the crown, of being swayed either by private interest, family pursuits, or any other motive than by a sense of public duty. Those who knew that man—and every man who knew him must regret his great and serious loss to the public service—must have known that if there was a man that was incapable of swerving from his public duty from any such base and sordid motives as those imputed to him, Lord Sydenham was the man.

I must therefore, sir, beg to be excused from saying any more on that subject.

I can state to the House the differences between the draft of the treaty sent out in consequence of communications between Mr. Urquhart, the Board of Trade, and the Foreign Office, and the treaty concluded by Lord Ponsonby. The draft provided that British goods should pay only the import duty of three per cent., after which they might be transported to, and sold in, any part of the Ottoman dominions, without any further payments. The treaty, in addition to the three per cent. import duty, laid on a further duty of two per cent. upon the transport and sale of goods; and beyond that no other duty is to be paid in any part of the Ottoman dominions. This was one of the things to which in negotiation we were obliged to submit. Nobody can suppose, especially in arranging commercial transactions between two countries, that you can go with a draft treaty in one hand, and a pen in the other, and say to a foreign minister, "There, sir, sign that treaty, or jump out of the window." You cannot do that, therefore you must negotiate. The draft makes no provisions with regard to foreign goods purchased in Turkey by British subjects with the view of their being again sold in Turkey. This was an omission in the draft; but the treaty provides that foreign goods so purchased may be resold upon the same conditions as Turkish goods. The draft allows the Porte to levy upon goods exported a duty not exceeding the rate of three per cent.; and in return it allows British subjects to purchase all kinds of goods in the Ottoman dominions either for resale or exportation, subject only to the payment of the transport duty on such goods, and to the tolls demanded for the maintenance of the roads along which the goods are conveyed; the treaty limits the export duty to three per cent., and admits of duties being levied upon goods purchased by British subjects for resale in Turkey to the same amount as those levied upon subjects of the most favoured nations. It further stipulates with regard to goods re-exported, and which may not have paid interior duties, that British subjects shall pay in lieu of such interior duties one fixed duty of nine per cent. It was a great object with us to abolish these interior duties, which were a great obstacle to the progress of British manufactured goods in Turkey, and which being made arbitrarily at the caprice of the governors of the provinces, were uncertain in their amount, and excessively vexatious in their mode of being levied. The draft provides that no duties shall be levied on goods *in transitu;* the treaty limits the duties on goods *in transitu* to the three per cent. impost. The draft does not allude to the point I am now about to state. The treaty specifies in detail the various ports of the Ottoman empire at which it is applicable, and records the consent of the Porte to other powers settling their commercial matters upon the same basis. Of course it was intended to bring all other powers within the same regulations; and this is the memorandum I have upon the draft. The above seems to be the essential point to be discussed. I think I have now stated enough with regard to the commercial treaty.

The next motion which stands in order is the Treaty of July, 1840. That treaty, the transactions which led to it and which have followed it, have been the subject of much discussion in Parliament; and upon these matters it was my duty to lay upon the table of the House some blue books of no inconsiderable dimensions. I believe, therefore, that Parliament and the country are pretty well supplied with information upon those transactions; and, in fact, if they were not, the subject would require far more time than the indulgence of the House would probably accord to me. In point of fact, there is hardly one of these motions—forty in number—which, to discuss them thoroughly, would not require the whole day. It is clear, therefore, that I can only take the salient points here and there of such objections as struck me to be of force in the course of the hon. and learned gentleman's speech. The history of the treaty of 1840 is simply this: Mehemet Ali wanted to make himself independent; but he saw, with the sagacity that belongs to him, that Egypt alone would not form an independent State; and, therefore, he determined to add to Egypt the whole of Syria and Arabia, and such parts of Asia Minor as he could get. He was prevented in that determination. He was stopped by the Russians. He was persuaded to accept a modified arrangement, by which he became Pasha and Governor of Syria and Egypt; and for a few years he did so, but in the mean time he proceeded to augment his army and to increase his navy, and in 1839 he broke loose again, invaded Asia Minor, and threatened the capital of the Turkish empire. Those familiar with the events of that period will remember the important battles which took place between his forces and the Turkish army, his rapid defeats of the Turks, and the extent to which the Sultan's power was prostrated before the forces of Mehemet Ali. It became then a matter of serious consideration for the Powers of Europe to determine what they should do, and what would be the consequences of the uninterrupted access of the Russians. Europe had for some years, from 1832 down to 1838-9, been continually kept in a state of anxiety upon the subject of Eastern affairs. We were told that Mehemet Ali was going to take Turkey, but the Russians would interpose; that England and France

onstantinople to be occu-
; and that there would be
urope, and that something
ll, negotiation for a long
xplosion; but the explosion
I know it was the opinion
ld have been far better to
ew Arabian monarchy or
l; that we ought to have
s with Mehemet Ali as an
n; and it did not signify to
hether Turkey was in that
not. I certainly was not
e Government was not of
er Powers of Europe were
It did appear to all—
the Turkish empire, as it
idable to none of its neigh-
useful as an element in the
world; that if Turkey was
there would be a scramble
is of her empire, which
o differences between the
nd that a general war, in
d be the result. It was,
tter, for the sake of peace
of Europe, to sustain the
as it was, and to prevent
by the assault of Mehemet
a, Russia, and Prussia, also
We thought at first that
opinion too, for we were in
France upon that subject.
r a long time that the French
osed to go along with us in
e believed necessary. Dif-
or, prevailed at length in
for me to pass judgment
The fact was that the
declared over and over
uld not, without running
nion in that country, make
o any coercive measures for
ing the advance of Mehe-
him to retire from Syria
with Egypt. The hon. and
says that, under these cir-
nch Government proposed
adron to the Dardanelles,
invitation of the French
o. I think that was not a
urse, or one by which any-
voided. Where was the
ger was in Syria. What
e accomplished? To com-
retire from Syria. What
is it to send a squadron to
Squadrons can only act
and to send a squadron to
mpel Mehemet Ali to retire
not very materially have
in view. We certainly

agreed with France, that if anything should pass on the part of Russia (who professed, however, a desire to co-operate with reference to Turkey) of a hostile character, or, if it was thought better, with the view of retaining the independence of Turkey, that naval aid should not be given by Russia alone, but that the flags of England and France should act in conjunction with Russia; and if the Porte should express that opinion, we said we would send such a representative of the naval power of England as might show to the world we were represented by a certain naval force. But I am not conscious that there was anything to do in the Dardanelles except to show ourselves, and to maintain the position which naturally belongs to England in a joint operation. Then the state of the case was this:—The French Government declined to act in the place where action was necessary, but they were willing to act at the place where no action could operate upon the matter at issue. The hon. and learned member, however, then says, that to the astonishment of England, of France, and of all Europe, towards the latter end of the year 1839, Baron Brunow arrived in this country upon a special mission; and the hon. and learned member stated that Baron Brunow arrived for the purpose of putting an end to the mutual distrust which since 1839 had existed between England and Russia. [Mr. ANSTEY: Since 1830.] Well, since 1830. But what then becomes of the charge which the hon. and learned member makes against me of being such a determined instrument in the hands of Russia? He says from 1830 to 1839, during the nine years in which I was in the office I have now the honour to hold, there had been such mutual distrust between the English and the Russian Governments that it was necessary Baron Brunow should be sent as ambassador to represent the real views of the Emperor, in order to remove that distrust. I am satisfied with that statement, which is likely to be true. Of course, many circumstances had contributed to inspire distrust mutually in the minds of the English and the Russian Governments with regard to the views and intentions of each other; and it was the object of Baron Brunow to remove that distrust, and to bring a full explanation of the views of the Emperor, which views, he thought, would be satisfactory to the Government of England. But then, says the hon. and learned gentleman, there was another object in the visit of Baron Brunow. He came to induce England to abandon her alliance with France, and to abandon also the measures taken for maintaining the integrity of Turkey. If the hon. and learned member was perfectly right with regard to the first part of Baron Brunow's instructions, he was as completely wrong in his understanding of the second. So far was Baron Brunow from being charged to endeavour to induce England to break with France, that one of the most explicit parts of the communication he had to make was this:—

"We do not ask for it; we are aware that your position requires you should be well looked after; but we do not wish to exclude France in any degree whatever from the general concert which we desire to see established for the maintenance of the independence of Turkey. All we wish is, that you should fully and perfectly understand that our policy, as much as yours, is the maintenance of Turkey as it is. We are anxious to co-operate with you, and that you should co-operate with us, in maintaining Turkey such as she is, and in preventing the dismemberment of her empire by means of the establishment of a new kingdom in Syria."

Nothing, therefore, could be more frank and honourable towards France, and more directly contrary to that which was asserted by the hon. member, than was the proposition of Baron Brunow. There was, as the hon. and learned gentleman said, a difference of opinion between the British Government and Baron Brunow with regard to the number of ships which should centre at the Dardanelles. That caused a reference to Russia. The Russian Government acceded to what we proposed, and from that moment the distrust which up to that time had existed between Russia and England was removed; and the English Government was convinced—and everything which has since occurred has confirmed that conviction—that the policy of Russia in this matter was the same as the policy of England, namely, to maintain the Turkish empire, and to prevent the Turkish territory being severed. Public opinion in France at that period was so strong, that the French Government was prevented being a party to any coercive measures, even had they so desired, which I am far from asserting; and the French Government said—" If you other powers choose to act, we do not pretend to prevent you, but we say that we cannot be parties to such a proceeding." It is well known that by the gallantry of our admirals and fleet—by Sir Charles Napier in particular, amongst others—those operations were brought in an exceedingly short space of time to a successful issue. The Egyptian troops were compelled to evacuate Syria, and the Pasha was compelled at last to accept the conditions which the Allied Powers offered him— conditions which he thought perfectly compatible with the independence and integrity of the Turkish empire—and conditions which have resulted in removing from that time to this those causes of disturbance and disquiet which for every six months of the six preceding years had placed all the Powers of Europe in imminent jeopardy of wars and broils. Our object was the maintenance of peace by the removal of the dangers by which that peace was threatened; and I contend that the circumstances which have occurred since that time have amply proved that the course which we adopted was well calculated to attain that end. From that time to this, we have heard nothing of the affairs of the Levant, except as regards certain local broils between the Druses and the Maronites. As far as the peace of Europe is concerned, nothing has since occurred calculated to occasion fears for its preservation.

W. J. FOX.

Born 1786. *Died* 1864.

[As specimens of platform eloquence, the lectures and addresses of W. J. Fox, for many years member for Oldham, will, perhaps, for vigour and earnestness bear favourable comparison with any of his time. Mr. Fox was, we believe, of humble origin, but during the anti-Corn Law agitation was a prominent and able platform champion of the objects of the League, whilst at the same time in his life he contributed the celebrated "Letters of a Norwich Weaver Boy" to the newspapers then issued by the Association.

Subsequently he became a preacher in the Unitarian body, after which, to quote the words of a writer in "*Men of the Time*," "he took a position independent of all sectarian denominations," and for many years preached at the Chapel in South Street, Finsbury. It was whilst so engaged that he delivered his "Lectures to the Working Classes," at the National Hall, Holborn, from one of which our selection has been made. His opinions, as will be seen from the extract given, were of the most democratic order; and it was perhaps partly to this cause and to the eloquent audacity with which he avowed them, that his comparative failure in the House of Commons is to be attributed. His presence and manner of delivery were also unfavourable to the chance of his ever becoming a pleasant or attractive orator.]

ON THE APPROACHING ANNIVERSARY OF THE BATTLE OF WATERLOO.

(*From a Lecture delivered* 16*th June*, 1844.)

TWENTY-NINE years have rendered the battle of Waterloo sufficiently remote for its character and consequences to be justly appreciated. Those of us who remember that event seem thereby to belong to another generation. The veterans who celebrate its anniversary are now thinned in their ranks from year to year. The passions and triumphs, hopes and fears of that period, have passed away; the writer of fiction weaves the event into his composition for effect; the historian compares documents, calls up his best power of narrative, and tries his skill in philosophizing; the various interests and combinations of partisanery which then divided the world have become faint and dim; the schoolmaster points to the battle in his chronological table, and instructs his pupil; the mother finds it in her tale-book, and recounts it to her child. And how should the battle of Waterloo be recounted? With what lessons and applications should it be told? How should parents of the working class present it to their children's minds, so as to "point a moral" as well as "adorn a tale," transmit historic truth faithfully, reap wisdom from the event, and preserve the sense of that responsibility under which we teach whatever tends to the formation of character and to the guidance of future conduct; building up the young in the truthfulness, honesty, and patriotism, by which they shall render service in their generation, and do their part faithfully, for the world's improvement.

This is what I will endeavour to show in the present lecture. With what feelings and tendencies should parents instruct their children in the events of those eventful times; how make them best subservient to that which is the great object of all education — the guidance of the mind in the way in which it should go — to the formation of character according to the truest and noblest principles.

Now, in the first instance, it is desirable that the child should be well made to understand what the *battle of Waterloo* was, and what all battles are. It should not be allowed to rest in a mere collocation of words, the thing itself should be realized to the mind, that tremendous thing of twenty-nine years ago. The imagination of the child should be stimulated; he should have pictures placed before his fancy; he should see there the sights and sounds of that awful day. The picture should be presented in its completeness. The ground should be traced to him. The valley, with the opposing hills, upon the one side crowned with wood; the mansion, the industrial farm-house, the land covered with the ripening corn — he should see them all as the sun was shining upon them a day or two before the battle. He should be taught to behold the gathering of those mighty armies, from 150,000 to 200,000, upon the opposite sides, in the pride, pomp, and circumstance of war — their neighing steeds and ponderous artillery, their waving plumes and banners — the glittering array on either side, their pride in their leader, their eagerness for the conflict, and the care and caution with which, by both parties, every arrangement was made for the opening of that fearful scene. The rainy night, the dull and heavy morning — the ceaseless roar of the cannon — the impetuous charge — the rapid retreat — the artillery ranged at different points, and dealing havoc and destruction — the clang of martial music — the shouts of the victors — the screams of the wounded — all, all should be realized, down to the last great struggle — the defeat — the hot pursuit and death dealt on every side upon those who were flying from the field of battle; and then the outburst of victory — the messengers speeded to all parts of Europe — the ringing of bells — the glare of illuminations — the shouting of the congregated multitude for the fortune of the world decided upon that tremendous day.

Yes, the child should realize all this, and should not stop here. The battle should be looked at with the private soldier's eye, as well as with that of the officer. He should be informed of the feeling of those who, through that long drenching night, were shivering, foodless and wearied, — so exhausted that even at the noontide of the following day, when they were ordered to lie down that the cannon-shot might pass over them, some of them fell into deep slumber upon the moist corn-field, amid all the roar of the battle, from which they awoke in the very agonies of death. He should see the field strewed with some 40,000 corpses, heaped together indiscriminately, — men of all nations — English, French, Germans, Prussians, Poles, — all blended there; and then behold the wounded, with shattered limbs, crawling along upon the ranks and piles of dead. He should then be taken to the temporary hospitals, and there behold the lancet of the surgeon as busily at work as had been the sword of the soldier, the task of amputating limbs, extracting bullets, and binding wounds, proceeding for eight days upon that blood-stained field. He should see the roads from the scene of conflict, in the direction of France at least, marked by the corpses of those who were cut down as they fled, scattered here and there, their blood and brains seeming, as it were, inscriptions telling that "This is the march to Paris of the vast armies that professed to be banded for the independence of nations." From this his mind should pass to the bereaved families by thousands and tens of thousands, — the starving orphans and children, the broken-hearted widows, — the consequences entailed upon so many by all the ruinous adjuncts of war. He should imagine, in contrast with the glittering procession — the troops crowned with laurel — the bands playing "See the conquering hero comes!" — the gratulating cheers of the multitudes awaiting their return — another long procession of sable-garbed mourners, with the bitter tears streaming down their cheeks: he should witness the ruined families, the crowded workhouses, jails, and graves, — all these, too, being monuments of the great battle, the glorious victory, of Waterloo.

The parent should blink to his child no portion of truth connected with such events; he should give him no partial or one-sided view of the matter. Look at the field of battle all around. Trace all its consequences from that gloomy centre which, as an orb of darkness and misery, radiates over so many nations. He should impress all this upon the mind of the youth; he should bring together the sufferings of those who perished by hundreds and thousands, of fatigue and famine, more numerous than those who fell upon the battle-field. Thus, having assembled all these attendant circumstances of the battle together, he should bid the child think upon them. He should say to him, "This is battle! Such is war! and such was Waterloo! Understand the event, and then you may proceed to moralize upon its causes and consequences."

"And what was all this for?" will be the natural question of the child. I presume the parent can make no better answer than that this was the completion of a succession of efforts to put down the *French Revolution*— for the second French war was the continuation of the first in spirit and purpose. This was the object at the outset. This was the aim at last to replace the Bourbons upon the throne of France; to bring that country into the condition in which it had been before the revolution; to wipe that event out of history; to sponge it, as it were, from any record in the living and actual state of France and Europe, and make it, as much as possible, what it would have been had that event never occurred. That aim was thought to be accomplished. The victory at Waterloo was deemed the triumphant completion of the war against the French revolution.

But what was, in reality, the French revolution, that nations should have fought against it, or that England especially should have sought its utter extinction? What, I say, was the French revolution? The outbreak of a people down-trodden, starved, insulted, spurned, and scorned, till humanity could bear no more. Any just delineation of the state of France before the revolution,— the wretchedness of its peasantry, the grinding imposts to which they were subjected, the horrible insults to which they were compelled to submit, the licentiousness of its court, the hypocrisy of its church, and the insolence of its nobles: any true picture of France before the revolution is a full justification of the revolution. Apologize for that event! Why, France would infinitely more have needed an apology, had there been no revolution. We should have had to find excuse for a people utterly divesting themselves of the best attributes of our nature; submitting to be worse than brutalized; and with the form of man indicating nothing of that divine spirit within, by which he asserts the dignity of his being, claims his rights, and will not be like the poor worm — trodden upon even without writhing under and against the foot by which he is crushed. Apologize for the French revolution! I say, we must have apologized not only for France, but for human nature, for the course of events, for the plan of the world, and for the Divine Providence itself, had there been no French revolution.

It was to quell this just and inevitable outbreak, to expunge it from history, to reverse all that it had done, to turn back the wheels of time; for this it was that Europe fought; for this did Britain expend its wealth and people; and for this did Wellington triumph at Waterloo.

But then it is said, a mild revolution — a moderate reform — might have been a very good

thing in the then existing circumstances of the French nation; but they were so violent, so headlong, and committed so many outrageous deeds, that the gentleness of many classes in this country utterly recoils from the exhibition under any circumstances whatever. We frequently meet with people who seem to feel like the dandy when he saw the man broken upon the wheel — a cruel punishment, by which in some states a criminal was tied to a large wheel, and the executioner with a massive bludgeon stood over him, banging on his body, a bone cracking at every blow, and the sufferer uttering excruciating groans and yells. "Pray, my dear fellow," said the dandy, "your lot is very hard; but the noise you make is quite vulgar and outrageous." In like manner would these sensitive individuals have had the French people bear their wrongs, and make their changes as tenderly and gingerly, as if a mere turnpike bill had been the sum and substance of the whole matter in discussion, and they could have afforded to set forth in the coolest and calmest manner the wrongs they had endured, and the rights which, as human beings, they desired and claimed. It is not in the nature of things that such should have been the case. The French revolution was a natural reaction, the result of the principles of our being, which work as infallibly under such circumstances as do the mighty powers and elements of the material world in their combination, when the liquid metals and liberated gases are commingling and exploding in the bowels of the earth. When the volcano roars and the earthquake shakes down towns and cities, you cannot then interpose, and say to Nature, "Be moderate, and effect your changes and revolutions more gently than this!" It is not in the elements of things, or in their laws, that such should be the case; nor is it in those of our own being, when the tyranny of ages is to be heaved off from the breast of a nation that it may breathe freely; when humanity starts up to a full sense of the enjoyment of its rights and dignity from a state of degradation — it is not, I say, in the nature of man that this should be done quietly.

"Great evils ask great passions to redress them,
And whirlwinds fitliest scatter pestilence."

Had the French taken counsel of more moderate persons, they would have made a nice little revolution, like that which occurred in England in 1688. Great care would have been taken with the change of persons to alter no principles. One set of people, perhaps, would have moved off from the possession of good things, and another set would have moved into their enjoyment, unless, indeed, the same parties had maintained their standing just by the change and transfer of their allegiance. There might have been a little incidental massacre, like that at Glencoe, or a bit of civil war like that which occurred in Ireland, concluding with a treaty only made to be violated. A little toleration might have been established, and a good deal of penalty inflicted by the side of that toleration. The plan might have been introduced of ruling a country *through* a Parliament, instead of the old plan, without a Parliament. A very gentle land tax might have been laid by the aristocracy upon their own ample estates; a system of corruption and influence might have been substituted for one of prerogative, and that mode of having recourse to public credit been resorted to, by which one generation makes all succeeding generations pay for its own follies, madness, and extravagance.

But then the bad principles of the French revolution rendered it, we are told, a thing to be guarded against. War against principle is at all times a very hopeful undertaking; it will succeed when you can knock down argument with a cannon-ball, and when you can pierce a proposition with a bayonet; but until that happens, war against principle is more likely to lead to the confirmation of such principle than anything else.

But we are told much of the anarchy and atheism of that period. What does that charge mean? Why take the most far-going and free-writing authors who preceded the revolution? Were Voltaire and Rousseau anarchists and atheists? Those who say so know nothing about their writings, or read them with that purblind prejudice which sees what it intends to see, and not what is really before it. Both of those writers did as much against atheism, and with as much effect, as any man that ever graced our bench of bishops.

And then as to the charge of disregard of the rights of property at that time. Why, in the creed even of the Mountain faction, property was a foremost article. Property was as sacred in France through the revolutionary times as it now is in this country; and more sacred than it is at this moment here, if the property in question consists of labour.

In looking at the French revolution, one thing should never be forgotten. The people were driven to it in the first instance. The principles which they laid down were the simplest and the broadest; such as human nature, left to itself, everywhere recognizes.

"A man's a man, for a' that,"

we often say and sing, and no class objects at present to our doing so; and yet that was the principle of the French revolution. " All ye are brethren," is a Christian doctrine; and yet that was the principle of the French revolution. Clothe them in hateful colours as you may, you cannot strip from the eye of posterity the fact that the principles of the French revolution—the principles of liberty, equality, and human rights — are sacred and eternal principles belonging to all morality and religion. They were so judged at the time by men who had eyes to see and hearts to feel; by men like that pure, noble-minded genuine Christian philanthropist, Roscoe, of Liverpool, who hailed the annunciation of such principles with the whole fervour of his soul; and when the National Convention put forth its celebrated Declaration of Rights, invoked all the powers of nature to give it sanction : —

"O catch its high import, ye winds as ye blow,
 O bear it, ye waves, as ye roll:
From the nations that feel the sun's vertical glow,
 To the farthest extremes of the pole.
Equal rights, equal laws to the nations around,
 Peace and freedom, its precepts impart;
And wherever the footsteps of man can be found,
 May he bind the decree on his heart."

Crimes, no doubt, there were — sanguinary and enormous crimes, perpetrated during the course of the French revolution. But, be it remembered that these acts were done in self-defence. The revolution itself was completed peaceably, and no proof whatever is capable of being adduced, that a peaceably accomplished event it would not have remained had it been let alone. But the fact is, there was a ceaseless struggle for a counter-revolution — a struggle carried on continually within, and stimulated from without. The revolution was never secure for a day; there were always persons in different ranks of society plotting. Foreign gold was circulating there to bribe domestic treason; and all Europe in arms was thundering on the frontiers. Is it wonderful that crimes were committed in self-defence in the circumstances in which they were placed? Blockade a man in his own house—bribe his servants—put gun-powder under his bed — set fire to his dwelling already surrounded by banditti — and then you must not be surprised if his conduct is *rather* extravagant, and he becomes somewhat violent. Let there be no exaggeration here. In describing this event, we speak as though the streets of Paris had for years and years flowed with blood. Much there was indeed shed of real noble blood: many fell under the guillotine who deserved statues raised to their honour, and a niche in history — many who, if they had lived in this country at no great distance of time, would have had their chance of being hanged under the reign of terror of William Pitt; for if the French literary, philosophic, and patriotic men suffered, we must not forget that our honest Hardy, and not only men of the shoemaking class, but that our Holcrofts, and Thelwalls, and Horne Tookes — our men of philosophy, literature, art, and genius — were also perilled, and it was by no virtue of the then ruling power that we did not commit some crimes as foul as any of those that stained the progress of the French revolution.

And then as to the number who fell during the revolution. Mr. Carlyle has gone into this subject very appropriately in his celebrated work. When the reign of terror was over, the authentic returns stated the victims to amount to 2,000, and even the emigrants, who took exception to the accuracy of that return, have not calculated more than double the number. Many of the sufferers were distinguished persons, and therefore the crime made a noise all over Europe. But be the number of victims either 2,000 or 4,000, there have been periods when, by the operation of the corn-law monopoly in this country, in one single year as much human life has been destroyed as was sacrificed by the guillotine in the French revolution. The victims of the corn-law are not only more numerous than those of the French revolution, but the kind of death — the abridgment of food, the sinking of the heart, the breaking down into abject poverty — the falling almost from moral compulsion into crime, with all the horrible sensations and agencies that belong to it.— O! these are ten thousand times worse than the sudden stroke of the guillotine which at once destroys sensation.

* * * *

Having thus reviewed the war as antagonistic of the French revolution, and having regarded the events which were adjuncts to it, the child will naturally inquire after its consequences. "What was the use of this grand victory?" will be the question put to the teacher. Well, the battle of Waterloo replaced the Bourbons; and where are they now? The son of Monsieur Egalité is upon the throne of France, and sits there nominally as "the citizen king," by the voice of the people, and not "by the grace of God." The Bourbons reigned fifteen years, and those fifteen years of Bourbon rule required twenty-three years of hard fighting to obtain. For every hour which they reigned over France 100 lives had been sacrificed upon the battle-field, to say nothing of the tears and miseries and the horrors that attend a state of war, and the wretchedness which it propagates to the remotest distances. The reign of an archangel would have been dearly purchased at such a cost as that.

Well, it is said, they triumphed over French principles by the battle of Waterloo. I should like to know what *principles* they conquered. They have not triumphed over my opinion or yours; they have not destroyed the thoughts and tendencies of the people of France. Civil equality is established there, and exists there in a higher degree than in any other country on the face of the earth. There the cabman, if insulted by the marshal, may take his honourable revenge for the insult—this, too, in a land where Voltaire was beaten by hired menials, and refused what was called the satisfaction of a gentleman because he was not of noble origin. Civil equality exists there, and an open career

or talents, which may rise out the accommodations a[n]? are often so necessary in t[he] distinction. The prime m[inister] upon a third floor, and [is] worse on that account. [...] speech — far more so th[an] society which are fostered [in] France, if a man prefer [...] Christ, he says so, and not[h]ing him from society for [...] man is poor and zealous, declaring his principles, h[e] jail; and if he is in highe[r] then he holds his tongue, being identified with an[y] perhaps takes part in enco[ur]secution which makes a j[...] the opinions he holds in h[...] this, they have in France—barrier against counter-re[...] proprietary of 4,000,000 eighty times the number which we have; of course, scale, with such enormous dually possessed of a simi[lar] influence. They have a [...] arising from property in [...] scarcely anything else in [...] the same degree or exten[t] merous, comfortable, bold, men, neither very rich nor to hold their own, and to tr[...] And the fear of the poli[...] property should be subdiv[...] the state of the Irish c[...] them, for nothing of the so[...] they have not to compete absentee landlord; they hav[e] selves in order to get the against starvation in the[...] but they have the world shareholders in the soil up and are just the sort of p[...] assailed, to defend it to th[e]

Well, then, the French [...] down after all. Its princip[les] its practical results are enj[...] extent which makes it n[...] that the country paid for [...] of trouble and a great de[al] how much good, of far le[ss] brought for an instant into blessings we have enumer[...] waged, treasure lavished, bl[...] kept in commotion, and t[he] and improvement been thr[...] of Waterloo was a remar[k...] combination of military tr[...] discomfiture. That war [...] settle Europe, and a prett[y] Spain is not quite tranq[uil] soon settled in a different way from what the allied sovereigns then intended. Holland was settled by the separation of Belgium from it, Ireland was so settled that the very champions of intolerance themselves had to concede Catholic emancipation. England was settled in a way which required the massacre in the north, and which led to the incendiarism of the south— which necessitated the Reform Bill, and which will demand greater changes yet. The struggle, which was maintained with massacre and cannon abroad, not only failed there, but fails here. From day to day we see the indubitable proofs that that strife is not terminated, that the fancied victory is not gained. Although its hero may have most judiciously disposed his troops in Ireland, the spirit of agitation there— Heaven prosper it! — is working its way peacefully, legally, but determinately, towards what I think is due to Ireland — not separation, but justice; freedom, and any degree of legislative independence which it is the will of that nation to require, and which I believe it will obtain— exhibiting the spectacle of the victor of Napoleon becoming the vanquished of Daniel O'Connell.

After a review of the facts and bearings of that memorable time, the parent, I think, will do well to lead his child to moralize upon *war* and the *military profession*. I answer for no one but myself; and, in fact, what I say here I wish ever to be understood as being not only my own personal opinion, but as thrown out not for reception, but for investigation. But in my opinion—and therefore, I should like that point seriously considered by the parent in training his child—the military profession is not an honest one. Christianity, or any other system of morality, ill deserves such a name, if it allows the hiring out of physical strength for the shedding of human blood, at the bidding of others, without having one's own conscience in the matter. Let the parent, if he sees the question in this light, instil into his child's mind these principles, that he may never be likely to become a red-coated slave to others— that he may consider it as the privilege of humanity that we are moral beings—that conscience is inalienable, and that the general, the government, and the monarch, cannot hold that for us, nor dispense with our obedience to its sacred decrees. There is the first obligation of our being—the very soul of duty; and he who puts it out of his power to judge of the justice of the cause in which he is performing " *the duties,*" as they are called, of a soldier, parts with all that divides man from the brute, driven by the agency and the will of another—he places himself in a position so degraded, that we may well blush to see humanity brought down to that level.

The cost of wars and their results in impeding the advancement of civilization, will form another branch of moral disquisition, which the parent should study for himself, and throw light upon for his child. This same French war cost us an addition to our debt of £600,000,000 sterling, and has burdened us with £30,000,000 annually of permanent taxes. The very first year after the establishment of peace all over the world, by this great victory of Waterloo, the estimates were for 170,000 soldiers, to be kept on foot by this country as a standing army. A standing army! What have free states to do with such a thing as that? When I denounce the military profession as unchristian, I may, perhaps, be asked, " Are you, then, for unarming the nation?" No; I would *arm the nation*. It should indeed be the nation. Under such circumstances, if the country was in danger of invasion, every man would turn out at once with his musket upon his shoulder. Give the people institutions which attract their veneration and love; give them laws which administer justice to the millions, and bring it to the door of the poor man's cottage; give them establishments and improvements which secure to all the remuneration of their toil and services to the community — making them as happy as a rightful distribution of the produce and the wealth of a nation can render humanity—and you will have an invincible people, before whom all hireling bands will be scattered as chaff before the wind.

Teach your children lessons such as these, growing out of the events, which may be laid before them in all varieties and forms. It is time to turn them to such account. Truth, goodness, and wisdom—even these may grow as if manured with the blood shed at Waterloo. The evils of the past are fruitful of blessings for the future. Let the page of history be turned with a careful hand — let it be read with an observant eye—pondered with a reflective mind; and rich will the fruit become in stores with which he may endow his son — a noble and worthy heritage, teaching him to judge better than his fathers did of the merit which nations should recompense, and the crimes which they should denounce. Oh, there are those, by their inventions, mitigating toil, who have multiplied the means of enjoyment upon the face of the earth—who, by their discoveries, have aided the advance of science, and let in the light of heaven where all had been as dark as the dungeon. Then there are those whose writings form our intellectual heritage and enrichment. There are the philanthropists who have led society onward, healing the wounded, and strengthening the right-minded. They are the world's benefactors and heroes — those who, by their disinterested exertions, their long and painful study, and their noble sacrifices, have conquered good for humanity. These are the men to whom statues and pillars should be raised — theirs the times around whose record the pen of the historian should glow with unwonted eloquence — these should the voice of public gratulation hail, awarding to them a higher meed of public and lasting gratitude than the best services of the warrior in the field of battle ever won, or ever could possibly deserve. Battles cannot win good of this description: it is by peaceful arts that society advances; it is by the powers of mind, in their benign influence upon the arrangements of life, public institutions, and private character; it is by these that the world gets its good; it is in reference to these that the youthful mind should be trained. As generation after generation sees this matter more clearly, and appreciates more justly the achievements of the distinguished — the peacefully distinguished — in that proportion will honour be awarded to the worthiest; the nation will look back on its train of benefactors with unfeigned veneration, and the anniversaries it will celebrate will be those in which some great discovery or invention has been made for the good of society, or some important advance effected in political liberty, giving to those benefits their permanence and security.

BENJAMIN DISRAELI.
Born 1805. *Living.*

[THE speech which follows, containing, as it does, a fine estimate of the life and character of the late Prince Consort, was delivered by Mr. Disraeli in the House of Commons on its re-assembling in January, 1862, for the first time after the great national loss to which the speaker so eloquently referred. As a specimen of careful and elaborate English it is well worthy of the attention of the oratorical student, but it is not to be looked upon as in any way representative of Mr. Disraeli's accustomed style. Some illustrations of his more vehement moods, and of that brilliant sarcastic force which have, in no small measure, contributed to raise Mr. Disraeli to his present leading position as an orator in the House of Commons, will be given later on in this volume.]

CHARACTER OF THE PRINCE CONSORT.

NO person can be insensible of the fact that the House meets to-night under circumstances very much changed from those which have attended our assembling for many years. Of late, indeed for more than twenty years past, whatever may have been our personal rivalries and our party strifes, there was at least one sentiment in which we all acquiesced, and in which we all shared, and that was a sentiment of admiring gratitude to that throne whose wisdom and goodness so frequently softened the acerbities of our free public life, and so majestically represented the matured intelligence of an enlightened people. All that has changed. He is gone who was the comfort and support of that throne. It has been said that there is nothing which England so much appreciates as the fulfilment of duty. The prince whom we have lost not only was eminent for the fulfilment of his duty, but it was the fulfilment of the highest duty; and it was the fulfilment of the highest duty under the most difficult circumstances. Prince Albert was the consort of his Sovereign. He was the father of one who might be his Sovereign. He was the prime councillor of a realm, the political constitution of which did not even recognise his political existence. Yet, under these circumstances, so difficult and so delicate, he elevated even the throne by the dignity and purity of his domestic life. He framed, and partly accomplished, a scheme of education for the heir of England which proves how completely its august projector had contemplated the office of an English king. In the affairs of state, while his serene spirit and elevated position bore him above all the possible bias of our party life, he showed, upon every great occasion, all the resources, all the prudence, and all the sagacity of an experienced and responsible statesman. I have presumed, sir, to touch upon three instances in which there was on the part of Prince Albert, the fulfilment of duty of the highest character, under circumstances of the greatest difficulty. I will venture to touch upon another point of his character, equally distinguished by the fulfilment of duty; but in this instance the duty was not only fulfilled, but it was created. Although Prince Albert was adopted by this country, he was, after all, but a youth of tender years; yet such was the character of his mind that he at once observed that, notwithstanding all those great achievements which long centuries of internal concord and of public liberty had permitted the energy and enterprise of Englishmen to accomplish, there was still a great deficiency in our national character, and which, if neglected, might lead to the impairing not only of our social happiness, but even the sources of our public wealth,—and that was a deficiency of culture. But he was not satisfied in detecting the deficiency, he resolved to supply it. His plans were deeply laid; they were maturely considered, and notwithstanding the obstacles which they encountered, I am prepared to say they were eminently successful. What might have been his lot had his term completed that which is ordained as the average life of man, it may be presumption to predict. Perhaps he would have impressed upon his age not only his character but his name; but this I think posterity will acknowledge, that he heightened the intellectual and moral standard of this country, that he extended and expanded the sympathies of all classes, and that he most beneficially adapted the productive powers of England to the inexhaustible resources of science and art. It is sometimes deplored by those who loved and admired him, that he was thwarted occasionally in his enterprises, and that he was not duly appreciated in his works. These, however, are not circumstances for regret but for congratulation. They prove the leading and original mind which so long and so advantageously laboured for this country. Had he not encountered these obstacles, had he not been subject to occasional distrust and misrepresentation, it would only have proved that he was a man of ordinary mould and temper. Those who move must change, and those who change must necessarily disturb and alarm prejudices; and what he encountered was only a demonstration that he was a man superior to his age, and admirably adapted to carry out the work he had undertaken. Sir, there is one point, and one point only, on which I would presume for a moment to dwell; and it is not for the sake of you, sir, whom I am now addressing, or for the generation to which we belong, but it is that those who come after us may not misapprehend the nature of this illustrious man. Prince Albert was not a patron. He was not one of those who, by their smiles and by their gold, reward excellence or stimulate exertion. His contributions to the cause of progress and improvement were far more powerful and far more precious. He gave to it his thought, his time, his toil: he gave to it his life. I see in this House many gentlemen—on both sides, and in different parts of it—who occasionally entered with the Prince at those council boards where they conferred and decided upon the great undertakings with which he was connected; and I ask them, without the fear of a denial, whether he was not the leading spirit—whether his was not the mind that foresaw the difficulty, and his the resources that supplied the remedy—whether his was not the courage to overcome apparently insurmountable obstacles, and whether every one who worked with him did not feel that he was the real originator of those great plans of improvement which they contributed to carry out. Sir, we have been asked to-night to condole with the Crown in this great calamity. That is no easy office. To condole in general is the office of those who, without the pale of sorrow, feel for the sorrowing; but in this instance the country is as heart-stricken as its Queen. Yet, in the mutual sensibilities of a Sovereign and a people there is something ennobling, something that elevates the spirit beyond the ordinary claim of earthly sorrow. The counties, and cities, and corporations of the realm, and those illustrious institutions of learning, of science, of art, and of skill, of which he was the highest ornament and the inspiring spirit, have bowed before the throne under this great calamity. It does not become the Parliament of the country to be silent. The expression of our feelings may be late, but even in that lateness some propriety may be observed if to-night we sanction the expression of the public sorrow, and ratify, as it were, the record of a nation's woe. It is with these feelings that I shall support the address in answer to the speech from the throne.

THE EARL OF DERBY.
Born 1799. *Living.*

[IT may perhaps be interesting to compare the subjoined speech by the great leader of the Conservative party in the House of Lords, delivered, as it was, on the same evening and under the same circumstances as that of Mr. Disraeli, which here precedes it. For this reason, and because in some respects it views the character of the Prince Consort from a different standpoint from that of the noble lord's representative in the Commons, it has been added in this place.]

ANOTHER ESTIMATE OF THE PRINCE CONSORT'S CHARACTER.

MY LORDS, the present is an occasion, if ever there was one, on which it is desirable that nothing should occur to mar the harmony, or interfere with the unanimity with which we should carry our address to the throne. One of the main topics of that address is to express our sympathy with her Majesty on that deep affliction with which it has pleased Providence to visit her, and at the same time our sense of the irreparable loss which the country has sustained from that calamity. The lamented Prince Consort was called suddenly, in early manhood, to a station the most exalted and the most perilous, surrounded by every temptation, having at his command every luxury that human heart could wish for. For a period of two-and-twenty years he blamelessly discharged all the duties of a husband and a father. He made his household the model of domestic order and family affection. Placed in a position of the extremest delicacy, he so conducted himself that even the breath of calumny never ventured to insinuate against him the slightest abuse of the influence attaching to his high position. That illustrious Prince, whose loss we all lament, and to whose merits so much justice has been done in such eloquent and feeling terms by the noble lord who moved and my noble friend who seconded the address, was illustrious in the truest and highest sense of the word. Such a term indeed is inadequate to express his worth. He has passed from amongst us in the very prime of life, in the full vigour of bodily activity and intellectual power. But he has not passed away without leaving his mark behind upon the age in which he lived. He never condescended to flatter: on the contrary, upon some occasions he even went to the very verge of indiscretion in pointing out defects; and yet he pursued steadily, silently, and most unostentatiously, that line of life which he had chalked out for himself. He succeeded in establishing an impress of himself, which will long endure, upon the habits, the feelings, and the tastes of this country. Few men have had the opportunity of knowing how wide his Royal Highness's range of study—how few the intervals he allowed to the most harmless and innocent recreations—how assiduously he exercised a mind of more than ordinary natural powers, and more than ordinary cultivation; how he, as it were instinctively, seized upon the main and leading principles of every question submitted to his consideration, and how unfalteringly he worked every question out in its minutest details. My lords, this is not the place to say that ample justice will be done to him, but the country will, day by day, have more ample means of estimating the services which he rendered to the cause of art and science; nor is this the place to speak of the stimulus which he gave by his personal attention and by his unremitting efforts in the promotion of everything which would tend to improve the domestic comfort of the humbler classes of the community, to expand the mind and increase the sphere of intellectual enjoyment, and raise the social and moral condition of every class of her Majesty's subjects. The debt which is due to him from the country on these grounds can hardly be estimated at present, and I fear it will only be estimated in its intensity in the loss of the advantages to which I have referred. But, my lords, this is the place in which one word at least should be said upon a different portion of his life; I mean upon the part which he took with regard to public affairs. Some years ago, I recollect, it was a matter of not unnatural constitutional jealousy that any interference with public affairs should take place from one who was altogether irresponsible to the authorities of the country. My lords, those persons who so argued argued upon a not unnatural constitutional jealousy, but they argued in forgetfulness of the very dictates of human nature, and required that which was rendered impossible by the very constitution of the human mind. For they required what amounted, in fact, to this: that two persons should be living in the closest and most intimate relations, in the most absolute confidence which can subsist between husband and wife, and yet that the opinions of the one should be altogether concealed, and that the thoughts of the one should altogether abstain from a consideration of those topics which, day by day, and hour by hour, must be a subject of engrossing care and anxiety to the other. My lords, the very statement of facts shows the impossibility of meeting the views of those persons who so argued. I should say there was occasion for that jealousy, if in his high position the Prince Consort had ever made himself the tool, or sought to subserve the machinations of political parties in England. I am sure every one who had an opportunity of judging will agree that no one could be more absolutely and entirely free from such imputations, and that the whole of his efforts were directed, irrespective of party altogether, to give his Sovereign and his wife that counsel and advice which he thought most befitting his position. But if it was desirable that there should be this influence between the Sovereign and the Prince Consort on the subject of public affairs, how much more desirable was it that it should be exercised by him with a full knowledge of every political circumstance, of the views brought forward by the Minister, and of all the discussions which took place, than that it should be exercised in private, and with an imperfect knowledge of the grounds upon which certain questions were submitted to her Majesty. And, my lords, I appeal confidently to all who have had the honour to be admitted to that personal intercourse with the Sovereign—which is the highest privilege of a Minister—whether from the presence of his Royal Highness, whether from his calm, and cool, and impartial judgment, whether from his great ability, and the manner in which he applied himself to every topic, they have not been frequently indebted to him for valuable and useful suggestions and for great assistance. In the Prince Consort the Queen has lost not only the husband of her youth, the father of her children, him to whom her youthful affections were freely given and have in maturer years only increased and intensified with conjugal love, but she has also lost the familiar friend, the trusted counsellor, the never-failing adviser, to whom she could look up in every difficulty and in every emergency, and to whom she did look up with that proud humility which none but a woman's heart can know, glorying in the intellectual superiority of him to whom her own will and her own judgment were freely put into subjection. My lords, I do not doubt but that in the affection of the surviving members of her family she has a source of consolation; but in the discharge of public duties she must henceforth tread alone the high and thorny paths of sovereignty—the sustaining hand, the guiding judgment, the never-failing counsellor, are hers no more. And who, my lords, can hear without the deepest emotion how, in the full consciousness of her utter desolation and of her aggravated responsibility, in the very presence of death, in the first moment of that agony of grief, rising as it were beneath the overwhelming weight of that crushing sorrow, she uttered the noble words, that, with God's blessing, she would discharge the duties which were devolving upon her. My lords, I cannot pursue the subject; but of this I am confident, that of those who hear me there is not one who will not join in the fervent prayer to God that she may be strengthened in this noble resolve, and that He who has seen fit to inflict this heavy blow, and to deprive her of him who was on earth her comfort and support, may be Himself her comfort and support in this deep, deep grief. My lords, the words of our address may be inadequate; they are inadequate. But if they convey inadequately, they convey unfailingly, not only the expression of your lordships' unanimous feelings, but the unanimous expression of a nation's devoted loyalty, deep and grateful and loving as it is. My lords, in the presence of this sorrow, I am satisfied it will be the desire of all on both sides of this and the other House of Parliament to contribute all in their power to spare her Majesty one additional care, one additional sorrow, added to those which press so heavily upon her. For my own part, and those with whom I have the honour to act, such, I am sure, will be the spirit in which we shall enter upon the business of this session of Parliament. I earnestly trust, and from the tenour of the speech I am hopeful that her Majesty's Ministers are disposed to meet us in the same spirit; that they are disposed to apply themselves to those useful and practical matters in which all can alike join harmoniously and cordially for the improvement and advancement of our common country; and not only to abstain from bringing forward themselves, but to discourage in others the agitation of topics of more violent controversy and discussion, which, in their possible results, add to the anxieties and to the cares of the Sovereign.

DANIEL O'CONNELL.
Born 1775. *Died* 1847.

[ANY standard collection of speeches would be incomplete without some specimens of the style of the great Irish "Agitator," as he himself delighted to be called. Though not of the highest or noblest type, the eloquence of O'Connell had at the time of its delivery an almost resistless power, and it was said that Lord Derby, in the days of O'Connell Mr. Stanley, was the only man that the great demagogue ever feared in debate. It has, however, been well observed that "his chief characteristic as a daring leader of the people against the existing order of things was the wonderful sagacity with which he could march along the boundary-line of strict legal action without crossing it, or committing either himself or his followers." At the Irish bar he was beyond question the first advocate of his day, whether for oratory or ready adaptation of the law. The speech selected below was delivered at a meeting of the citizens, freemen, and freeholders of the city of Dublin, held at the Royal Exchange, on Tuesday, 18th Sept., 1810, to consider of a petition to the King and Parliament, praying them to take into consideration the repeal of the Act of Union; Sir James Riddell, High Sheriff of the city of Dublin, in the chair. Some other speeches from the same source will be found later in this volume.]

REPEAL OF THE UNION.

[A resolution in favour of an address to the King and the Imperial Parliament, praying a repeal of the Act of Union having been proposed and carried, Mr. O'Connell, on commencing his speech, declared that]

HE offered himself to the meeting with unfeigned diffidence. He was unable to do justice to his feelings on the great national subject on which they had met. He felt too much of personal anxiety to allow him to arrange in anything like order, the many topics which rushed upon his mind, now that, after ten years of silence and torpor, Irishmen began again to recollect their enslaved country. It was a melancholy period, those ten years—a period in which Ireland saw her artificers starved—her tradesmen begging—her merchants become bankrupts—her gentry banished—her nobility degraded. Within that period domestic turbulence broke from day to day into open violence and murder—religious dissensions were aggravated and embittered—credit and commerce were annihilated — taxation augmented in amount and in vexation. Besides the "hangings-off" of the ordinary assizes, we had been disgraced by the necessity that existed for holding two special commissions of death, and had been degraded by one rebellion —and, to crown all, we were at length insulted by being told of our *growing prosperity*. This was not the painting of imagination—it borrowed nothing from fancy—it was, alas! the plain representation of the facts that had occurred—the picture, in sober colours, of the real state of his ill-fated country. There was not a man present but must be convinced that he did not exaggerate a single fact: there was not a man present but must know that more misery existed than he had described. Such being the history of the first ten years of the Union, it would not be difficult to convince any unprejudiced man, that all those calamities had sprung from that measure. Ireland was favoured by Providence with a fertile soil, an excellent situation for commerce, intersected by navigable rivers, indented at every side with safe and commodious harbours, blessed with a fruitful soil, and with a vigorous, hardy, generous, and brave population; how did it happen, then, that the noble qualities of the Irish people were perverted? that the order of Providence was disturbed, and its blessings worse than neglected? The fatal cause was obvious —it was the Union. That these deplorable effects would follow from that accursed measure was prophesied. Before the Act of Union passed, it had been already proved that the trade of the country and its credit must fail as capital was drawn from it; that turbulence and violence would increase, when the gentry were removed to residence in another country; that the taxes should increase in the same proportion as the people became unable to pay them. "But," continued Mr. O'Connell, "neither the argument nor the prophetic fears have ended with our present evils. It has also been demonstrated, that as long as the Union continues, so long must our misfortunes accumulate. The nature of that measure, and the experience of facts which we have now had, leave no doubt of the truth of what has been asserted respecting the future. But, if there be any still incredulous, he can only be of those who submit their reason to authority. To such person, the authority of Mr. John Foster, Chancellor of the Exchequer for Ireland, would probably be conclusive; and Foster has assured us, that final ruin to our country must be the consequence of the Union. I will not dwell on the miseries of my country; I am disgusted with the wretchedness the Union has produced; and I do not dare to trust myself with the contemplation of the accumulation of sorrow that must overwhelm the land, if the Union be not repealed; I beg to call the attention of the meeting to another part of the subject. The Union, sir, was a violation of our national and inherent rights—a flagrant injustice. The representatives whom we had elected for a short period of eight years had no authority to dispose of their country for ever. It cannot be pretended that any direct or express authority to that effect was given to them; and the nature of their delegation excludes all idea of their having any such by implication. They were the servants of the nation, empowered to consult for its good—not its masters, to make traffic and dispose of it at their fantasy or for their profit. I deny that the nation itself had a right to barter its independence, or to commit political suicide; but when our servants destroyed our existence as a nation, they added to the baseness of assassination all the guilt of high treason. The reasoning upon which those opinions are founded is sufficiently obvious. They require no sanction from the authority of any name—neither do I pretend to give them any weight, by declaring them to be conscientiously my own; but if you want authority to induce the conviction that the Union had *injustice* for its principle, and a *crime* for its basis, I appeal to that of his Majesty's present Attorney-General, Mr. Saurin, who, in his place in the Irish Parliament, pledged his character as a lawyer and a statesman, that the Union must be a violation of every moral principle, and that it was a mere question of prudence whether it should not be resisted by force. I also appeal to the opinions of the late Lord High Chancellor of Ireland, Mr. George Ponsonby—of the present Solicitor-General, Mr. Bushe—and of that splendid lawyer, Mr. Plunket. The Union was, therefore, a manifest injustice—and it continues to be unjust at this day; it was a crime, and must be still criminal, unless it shall be ludicrously pretended that crime, like wine, improves by old age, and that time mollifies injustice into innocence. You may smile at the supposition, but in sober sadness you must be convinced that we daily suffer injustice; that every succeeding day adds only another sin to the catalogue of British vice; and that if the Union continues, it will only make crime hereditary, and injustice perpetual. We have been robbed, my countrymen, most foully robbed of our birthright, of our independence. May it not be permitted to us, mournfully to ask how this consummation of evil was perfected? for it was not in any disastrous battle that our liberties were struck down—no foreign invader had despoiled the land; we have not forfeited our country by any crimes—neither did we lose it in any domestic insurrection. No, the rebellion was completely put down before the Union was accomplished: the Irish militia and the Irish yeomanry had put it down. How, then, have we become enslaved? Alas! England that ought to have been to us as a sister and a friend—England, whom we had loved, and fought and bled for—England, whom we have protected, and whom we do protect—England, at a period when out of 100,000 of the seamen in her service, 70,000 were Irish—England stole upon us like a thief in the night, and robbed us of the precious gem of our Liberty; she stole from us 'that which nought enriched her, but made us poor indeed.' Reflect, then, my friends, on the means employed to accomplish this disastrous measure. I do not speak of the meaner instruments of bribery and corruption—we all know that everything was put to sale—nothing profane or sacred was omitted in the Union mart—offices in the revenue, commands in the army and navy, the sacred ermine of justice, and the holy altars of God were all profaned and polluted as the rewards of Union services. By a vote in favour of the Union, ignorance, incapacity, and profligacy obtained certain promotion : and our ill-fated but beloved country was degraded to her utmost limits before she was transfixed in slavery. But I do not intend to detain you in the contemplation of those vulgar means of parliamentary success—they are within the daily routine of official *management;* neither will I direct your attention to the frightful recollection of that avowed fact which is now part of history, that the *rebellion* itself was fomented and encouraged in order to facilitate the Union. Even the rebellion was an accidental and secondary cause—the real cause of the Union lay deeper, but is quite obvious. It is to be found at once in the *religious dissensions* which the enemies of Ireland have created, and continued, and seek to perpetuate amongst ourselves, by telling us off, and separating us into wretched sections and miserable subdivisions; they separated the Protestant from the Catholic, and the Presbyterian from both; they revived every antiquated cause of domestic animosity, and they invented new pretexts of rancour; but above all, my countrymen, they belied and calumniated us to each other—they falsely declared that we hated each other, and they continued to repeat the assertion, until we came to believe it; they succeeded in producing all the madness of party and religious distinctions; and whilst we were lost in the stupor of insanity, they plundered us of our country, and left us to recover at our leisure from the horrid delusion—into which we have been so artfully conducted.

"Such, then, were the means by which the Union was effectuated. It has stripped us of commerce and wealth; it has degraded us, and deprived us not only of our station as a nation, but even of the name of our country; we are governed by foreigners—foreigners make our laws, for were the one hundred members who nominally represent Ireland in what is called the Imperial Parliament, were they really our representatives, what influence could they, although unbought and unanimous, have over the five hundred and fifty-eight English and Scotch members? But what is the fact? Why, that out of the one hundred, such as they are, that sit for this country, more than one-fifth know nothing of us, and are unknown to us. What, for example, do we know about Andrew Strahan, printer to the king? What can Henry Martin, barrister-at-law, care for the rights or liberties of Irishmen? Some of us may, perhaps for our misfortunes, have been compelled to read a verbose pamphlet of James Stevens; but who knows anything of one Crile, one Hughan, one Cackin, or of a dozen more whose names I could mention, only because I have discovered them for the purpose of speaking to you about them? What sympathy can we, in our sufferings, expect from those men? What solicitude for our interests? What are they to Ireland, or Ireland to them? No, we are not represented—we have no effectual share in the legislation—the thing is a mere mockery; neither is the Imperial Parliament competent to legislate for us—it is too unwieldy a machine to legislate with discernment for England alone; but with respect to Ireland, it has all the additional inconvenience that arises from want of interest and total ignorance. Sir, when I talk of the utter ignorance, in Irish affairs, of the members of the Imperial Parliament, I do not exaggerate or mistake; the ministers themselves are in absolute darkness with respect to this country. I undertake to demonstrate it. Sir, they have presumed to speak of the growing prosperity of Ireland. I know them to be vile and profligate—I cannot be suspected of flattering them—yet vile as they are, I do not believe they could have had the audacity to insert in the speech, supposed to be spoken by his Majesty, *that expression*, had they known that, in fact, Ireland was in abject and increasing poverty. Sir, they were content to take their information from a pensioned Frenchman—a being styled Sir Francis D'Ivernois, who, in one of the pamphlets which it is his trade to write, has proved, by excellent samples of vulgar arithmetic, that our manufactures are flourishing, our commerce extending, and our felicity consummate. When you detect the ministers themselves in such gross ignorance, as, upon such authority, to place an insulting falsehood as it were in the mouth of our revered sovereign, what think you can be the fitness of nine minor imps of legislation to make laws for Ireland? Indeed, the recent plans of taxation sufficiently evince how incompetent the present scheme of Parliament is to legislate for Ireland. Had we an Irish Parliament, it is impossible to conceive that they would have adopted taxes at once oppressive and unproductive—ruinous to the country, and useless to the crown. No, sir, an Irish Parliament, acquainted with the state of the country, and individually interested to tax proper objects, would have, even in this season of distress, no difficulty in raising the necessary supplies. The loyalty and good sense of the Irish nation would aid them; and we should not, as now, perceive taxation unproductive of money, but abundantly fertile in discontent. There is another subject that peculiarly requires the attention of the legislature; but it is one which can be managed only by a resident and domestic Parliament—it includes everything that relates to those strange and portentous disturbances which, from time to time, affright and desolate the fairest districts of the island. It is a delicate and difficult subject, and one that would require the most minute knowledge of the causes that produce those disturbances, and would demand all the attention and care of men, whose individual safety was connected with the discovery of a proper remedy. I do not wish to calculate the extent of evil that may be dreaded from the outrages I allude to, if our country shall continue in the hands of foreign empirics and pretenders; but it is clear to a demonstration, that no man can be attached to his king and country, who does not avow the necessity of submitting the control of this political evil, to the only competent tribunal—an Irish Parliament. The ills of this awful moment are not confined to our domestic complaints and calamities. The great enemy* of the liberty of the world extends his influence and his power from the Frozen Ocean to the

---

* Napoleon.

Straits of Gibraltar. He threatens us with invasion from the thousand ports of his vast empire; how is it possible to resist him with an impoverished, divided, and dispirited empire? If, then, you are loyal to your excellent monarch—if you are attached to the last relic of political freedom, can you hesitate to join in endeavouring to procure the remedy for all your calamities—the sure protection against all the threats of your enemy—*the Repeal of the Union?* Yes, restore to Irishmen their country, and you may well defy the invader's force; give back Ireland to her hardy and brave population, and you have nothing to dread from foreign power. It is useless to detail the miseries that the Union has produced, or point out the necessity that exists for its Repeal. I have never met any man who did not deplore this fatal measure, which has despoiled his country; nor do I believe that there is a single individual in the island who could be found even to pretend approbation of that measure. I would be glad to see the face of the man, or rather of the beast, who could dare to say he thought the Union wise or good—for the being who could say so must be devoid of all the feelings that distinguish humanity. With the knowledge that such were the sentiments of the universal Irish nation, how does it happen that the Union had lasted for ten years? The solution of the question was easy. The Union continued only because we despaired of its Repeal. Upon this despair alone had it continued—yet what could be more absurd than such despair? If the Irish sentiment be but once known—if the voice of six millions be raised from Cape Clear to the Giant's Causeway—if the men most remarkable for their loyalty to their king, and attachment to constitutional liberty, will come forward as the leaders of the public voice, the nation would, in an hour, grow too great for the chains that now shackle you, and the Union must be repealed without commotion and without difficulty. Let the most timid amongst us compare the present probability of repealing the Union with the prospect that in the year 1795 existed of that measure being ever brought about. Who, in 1795, thought an Union possible? Pitt dared to attempt it, and he succeeded; it only requires the resolution to attempt its Repeal—in fact, it requires only to entertain the hope of repealing it, to make it impossible that the Union should continue; but that pleasing hope could never exist, whilst the infernal dissensions on the score of religion were kept up. The Protestant alone could not expect to liberate his country—the Roman Catholic alone could not do it—neither could the Presbyterian; but amalgamate the three into the Irishman, and the Union is repealed. Learn discretion from your enemies—they have crushed your country by fomenting religious discord—serve her by abandoning it for ever. Let each man give up his share of the mischief—let each man forsake every feeling of rancour. But I say not this to barter with you, my countrymen—I require no equivalent from you—whatever course you shall take, my mind is fixed—I trample under foot the Catholic claims, if they can interfere with the Repeal; I abandon all wish for emancipation, if it delays that Repeal. Nay, were Mr. Perceval, to-morrow, to offer me the Repeal of the Union, upon the terms of re-enacting the entire penal code, I declare it from my heart, and in the presence of my God, that I would most cheerfully embrace his offer. Let us then, my beloved countrymen, sacrifice our wicked and groundless animosities on the altar of our country—let that spirit which heretofore emanating from Dungannon spread all over the island, and gave light and liberty to the land, be again cherished amongst us—let us rally round the standard of Old Ireland, and we shall easily procure that greatest of political blessings, an Irish King, an Irish House of Lords, and an Irish House of Commons."

JOHN MILTON.
Born 1608. *Died* 1675.

[The next selection, though not strictly a specimen of oratory, yet as representing that high oratorical style of prose of which Milton was so great a master, may well claim a place in this volume.]

Eulogy on Cromwell.

IN speaking of such a man, who has merited so well of his country, I should do nothing, if I only exculpated him from crimes; particularly since it not only so nearly concerns the country, but even myself, who am so closely implicated in the same disgrace, to evince to all nations, and as far as I can, to all ages, the excellence of his character, and the splendour of his renown. Oliver Cromwell was sprung from a line of illustrious ancestors, who were distinguished for the civil functions which they sustained under the monarchy, and still more for the part which they took in restoring and establishing true religion in this country. In the vigour and maturity of his life, which he passed in retirement, he was conspicuous for nothing more than for the strictness of his religious habits and the innocence of his life; and he had tacitly cherished in his breast that flame of piety which was afterwards to stand him in so much stead on the greatest occasions, and in the most critical exigencies. In the last parliament which was called by the King, he was elected to represent his native town; when he soon became distinguished by the justness of his opinions, and the vigour and decision of his counsels. When the sword was drawn, he offered his services, and was appointed to a troop of horse, whose numbers were soon increased by the pious and the good, who flocked from all quarters to his standard; and in a short time he almost surpassed the greatest generals in the magnitude and the rapidity of his achievements. Nor is this surprising; for he was a soldier disciplined to perfection in the knowledge of himself. He had either extinguished, or by habit had learned to subdue, the whole host of vain hopes, fears, and passions, which infest the soul. He first acquired the government of himself, and over himself acquired the most signal victories; so that on the first day he took the field against the external enemy, he was a veteran in arms, consummately practised in the toils and exigencies of war. It is not possible for me, in the narrow limits in which I circumscribe myself on this occasion, to enumerate the many towns which he has taken, the many battles which he has won. The whole surface of the British empire has been the scene of his exploits and the theatre of his triumphs; which alone would furnish ample materials for a history, and want a copiousness of narration not inferior to the magnitude and diversity of the transactions. This alone seems to be a sufficient proof of his extraordinary and almost supernatural virtue, that by the vigour of his genius, or the excellence of his discipline, adapted not more to the necessities of war than to the precepts of Christianity, the good and the brave were from all quarters attracted to his camp, not only as to the best school of military talents, but of piety and virtue; and that during the whole war, and the occasional intervals of peace, amid so many vicissitudes of faction and of events, he retained and still retains the obedience of his troops, not by largesses or indulgence, but by his sole authority, and the regularity of his pay. In this instance his fame may rival that of Cyrus, of Epaminondas, or any of the great generals of antiquity. Hence he collected an army as numerous and as well equipped as any one ever did in so short a time; which was uniformly obedient to his orders, and dear to the affections of the citizens; which was formidable to the enemy in the field, but never cruel to those who laid down their arms; which committed no lawless ravages on the persons or the property of the inhabitants; who, when they compared their conduct with the turbulence, the intemperance, the impiety, and the debauchery of the royalists, were wont to salute them as friends, and to consider them as guests. They were a stay to the good, a terror to the evil, and the warmest advocates for every exertion of piety and virtue. Nor would it be right to pass over the name of Fairfax, who united the utmost fortitude with the utmost courage; and the spotless innocence of whose life seemed to point him out as the peculiar favourite of Heaven. Justly indeed may you be excited to receive this wreath of praise; though you have retired as much as possible from the world, and seek those shades of privacy which were the delight of Scipio. Nor was it only the enemy whom you subdued: but you have triumphed over that flame of ambition and that lust of glory which are wont to make the best and the greatest of men their slaves. The purity of your virtues and the splendour of your actions consecrate those sweets of ease which you enjoy, and which constitute the wished-for haven of the toils of man. Such was the case which, when the heroes of antiquity possessed, after a life of exertion and glory, not greater than yours, the poets, in despair of finding ideas or expressions better suited to the subject, feigned that they were received into Heaven, and invited to recline at the tables of the gods. But whether it were your health, which I principally believe, or any other motive, which caused you to retire, of this I am convinced, that nothing could have induced you to relinquish the service of your country, if you had not known that in your successor liberty would meet with a protector, and England with a stay to its safety, and a pillar to its glory. For while you, O Cromwell, are left among us, he hardly shows a proper confidence in the Supreme who distrusts the security of England; when he sees that you are in so special a manner the favoured object of the divine regard. But there was another department of the war which was destined for your exclusive exertions.

Without entering into any length of detail, I will, if possible, describe some of the most memorable actions, with as much brevity as you performed them with celerity. After the loss of all Ireland, with the exception of one city, you in one battle immediately discomfited the forces of the rebels; and were busily employed in settling the country, when you were suddenly recalled to the war in Scotland. Hence you proceeded with unwearied diligence against the Scots, who were on the point of making an irruption into England with the King in their train: and in about the space of one year, you entirely subdued, and added to the English dominion, that kingdom which all our monarchs, during a period of 800 years, had in vain struggled to subject. In one battle you almost annihilated the remainder of their forces, who, in a fit of desperation, had made a sudden incursion into England, then almost destitute of garrisons, and got as far as Worcester; where you came up with them by forced marches, and captured almost the whole of their nobility. A profound peace ensued;

when we found, though indeed not then for the first time, that you were as wise in the cabinet as valiant in the field. It was your constant endeavour in the senate either to induce them to adhere to those treaties which they had entered into with the enemy, or speedily to adjust others which promised to be beneficial to the country. But when you saw that the business was artfully procrastinated, that every one was more intent on his own selfish interest than on the public good, that the people complained of the disappointments which they had experienced, and the fallacious promises by which they had been gulled, that they were the dupes of a few overbearing individuals, you put an end to their domination. A new parliament is summoned: and the right of election given to those to whom it was expedient. They meet, but do nothing; and, after having wearied themselves by their mutual dissensions, and fully exposed their incapacity to the observation of the country, they consent to a voluntary dissolution. In this state of desolation to which we were reduced, you, O Cromwell! alone remained to conduct the government, and to save the country. We all willingly yield the palm of sovereignty to your unrivalled ability and virtue, except the few among us, who, either ambitious of honours which they have not the capacity to sustain, or who envy those which are conferred on one more worthy than themselves, or else who do not know that nothing in the world is more pleasing to God, more agreeable to reason, more politically just, or more generally useful, than that the supreme power should be vested in the best and the wisest of men. Such, O Cromwell! all acknowledge you to be; such are the services which you have rendered, as the leader of our councils, the general of our armies, and the father of your country. For this is the tender appellation by which all the good among us salute you from the very soul. Other names you neither have nor could endure; and you deservedly reject that pomp of title which attracts the gaze and admiration of the multitude. For what is a title but a certain definite mode of dignity? But actions such as yours surpass, not only the bounds of our admiration, but our titles; and like the points of pyramids, which are lost in the clouds, they soar above the possibilities of titular commendation. But since, though it be not fit, it may be expedient, that the highest pitch of virtue should be circumscribed within the bounds of some human appellation, you endured to receive, for the public good, a title most like to that of the father of your country; not to exalt, but rather to bring you nearer to the level of ordinary men; the title of king was unworthy the transcendent majesty of your character. For if you had been captivated by a name over which, as a private man, you had so completely triumphed and crumbled into dust, you would have been doing the same thing as if, after having subdued some idolatrous nation by the help of the true God, you should afterwards fall down and worship the gods which you had vanquished. Do you, then, sir, continue your course with the same unrivalled magnanimity. It sits well upon you. To you our country owes its liberties, nor can you sustain a character at once more momentous and more august than that of the author, the guardian, and the preserver of our liberties; and hence you have not only eclipsed the achievements of all our kings, but even those which have been fabled of our heroes. Often reflect what a dear pledge the beloved land of your nativity has entrusted to your care; and that liberty which she once expected only from the chosen flower of her talents and her virtues, she now expects from you only, and by you only hopes to obtain. Revere the fond expectations which we cherish, the solicitudes of your anxious country. Revere the looks and the wounds of your brave companions in arms, who, under your banners, have so strenuously fought for liberty; revere the shades of those who perished in the contest. Revere also the opinions and the hopes which foreign States entertain concerning us, who promise to themselves so many advantages from that liberty, which we have so bravely acquired, from the establishment of that new government, which has begun to shed its splendour on the world, which, if it be suffered to vanish like a dream, would involve us in the deepest abyss of shame. And, lastly, revere yourself; and, after having endured so many sufferings and encountered so many perils for the sake of liberty, do not suffer it, now it is obtained, either to be violated by yourself, or in any one instance impaired by others. You cannot be truly free unless we are free too; for such is the nature of things, that he who intrenches on the liberty of others is the first to lose his own and become a slave. But if you, who have hitherto been the patron and tutelary genius of liberty, if you, who are exceeded by no one in justice, in piety, and goodness, should hereafter invade that liberty which you have defended, your conduct must be fatally operative, not only against the cause of liberty, but the general interests of piety and virtue. Your integrity and virtue will appear to have evaporated, your faith in religion to have been small; your character with posterity will dwindle into insignificance, by which a most destructive blow will be levelled against the happiness of mankind. The work which you have undertaken is of incalculable moment, which will thoroughly sift and expose every principle and sensation of your heart, which will fully display the vigour and genius of your character, which will evince whether you really possess those great qualities of piety, fidelity, justice, and self-denial, which made us believe that you were elevated by the special direction of the Deity to the highest pinnacle of power. At once wisely and discreetly to hold the sceptre over three powerful nations, to persuade people to relinquish inveterate and corrupt for new and more beneficial maxims and institutions, to penetrate into the remotest parts of the country, to have the mind present and operative in every quarter, to watch against surprise, to provide against danger, to reject the blandishments of pleasure and the pomp of power; these are exertions compared with which the labour of war is mere pastime; which will require every energy and employ every faculty that you possess; which demand a man supported from above, and almost instructed by immediate inspiration. These and more than these are, no doubt, the objects which occupy your attention and engross your soul; as well as the means by which you may accomplish these important ends, and render our liberty at once more ample and more secure. And this you can, in my opinion, in no other way so readily effect, as by associating in your councils the companions of your dangers and your toils; men of exemplary modesty, integrity, and courage; whose hearts have not been hardened in cruelty and rendered insensible to pity by the sight of so much ravage and so much death, but whom it has rather inspired with the love of justice, with a respect for religion, and with the feeling of compassion, and who are more zealously interested in the preservation of liberty, in proportion as they have encountered more perils in its defence. They are not strangers or foreigners, a hireling rout scraped together from the dregs of the people, but for the most part, men of the better conditions in life, of families not disgraced if not ennobled, of fortunes either ample or moderate; and what if some among them are recommended by their poverty? for it was not the lust of ravage which brought them into the field; it was the calamitous aspect of the times, which in the most critical circumstances, and often amid the most disastrous turns of fortune, roused them to attempt the deliverance of their country from the fangs of despotism. They were men prepared, not only to debate, but to fight; not only to argue in the senate, but to engage the enemy in the field. But, unless we will continually cherish indefinite and illusory expectations, I see not in whom we can place any confidence, if not in these men and such as these. We have the surest and most indubitable pledge of their fidelity in this, that they have already exposed themselves to death in the service of their country; of their piety in this, that they have been always wont to ascribe the whole glory of their successes to the favour of the Deity, whose help they have so suppliantly implored, and so conspicuously obtained; of their justice in this, that they even brought the King to trial, and when his guilt was proved, refused to save his life; of their moderation in our own uniform experience of its effects, and because, if by any outrage they should disturb the peace which they have procured, they themselves will be the first to feel the miseries which it will occasion, the first to meet the havoc of the sword, and the first again to risk their lives for all those comforts and distinctions which they have so happily acquired; and lastly, of their fortitude in this, that there is no instance of any people who ever recovered their liberty with so much courage and success; and therefore let us not suppose that there can be any persons who will be more zealous in preserving it.

THOMAS JEFFERSON.
Born 1743.   *Died* 1826.
(President of the United States, 1801-9.)
EXTRACT FROM INAUGURAL ADDRESS.

DURING the contest of opinion through which we have passed, the animation of discussions and of exertions has sometimes worn an aspect which might impose on strangers, unused to think freely, and to speak and to write what they think; but this being now decided by the voice of the nation, announced according to the rules of the constitution, all will, of course, arrange themselves under the will of the law, and unite in common efforts for the common good. All, too, will bear in mind this sacred principle, that, though the will of the majority is, in all cases, to prevail, that will, to be rightful, must be reasonable; that the minority possess their equal rights, which equal laws must protect, and to violate which would be oppression. Let us then, fellow citizens, unite with one heart and one mind.

Let us restore to social intercourse that harmony and affection, without which liberty, and even life itself, are but dreary things; and let us reflect that, having banished from our land that religious intolerance under which mankind so long bled and suffered, we have yet gained little, if we countenance a political intolerance, as despotic, as wicked, and capable of as bitter and bloody persecutions.

During the throes and convulsions of the ancient world, during the agonizing spasms of infuriated man, seeking, through blood and slaughter, his long-lost liberty, it was not wonderful that the agitation of the billows should reach even this distant and peaceful shore, that this should be more felt and feared by some, and less by others, and should divide opinions as to measures of safety.

But every difference of opinion is not a difference of principle. We have called by different names brethren of the same principle. We are all republicans; we are all federalists. If there be any among us who would wish to dissolve this union, or to change its republican form, let them stand undisturbed, as monuments of the safety with which error of opinion may be tolerated, where reason is left free to combat it.

I know, indeed, that some honest men fear that a republican government cannot be strong; that this government is not strong enough. But would the honest patriot, in the full tide of successful experiment, abandon a government which has so far kept us free and firm, on the theoretic and visionary fear that this government, the world's best hope, may by possibility want energy to preserve itself? I trust not; I believe this, on the contrary, the strongest government on earth.

I believe it the only one where every man, at the call of the law, would fly to the standard of the law, and would meet invasions of the public order as his own personal concern. Sometimes it is said that man cannot be trusted with the government of himself. Can he, then, be trusted with the government of others? or have we found angels, in the form of kings, to govern him? Let history answer this question.

Let us, then, with courage and confidence, pursue our own federal and republican principles; our attachment to union and representative government. Kindly separated, by nature and a wide ocean, from the exterminating havoc of one quarter of the globe; too high minded to endure the degradations of the others; possessing a chosen country, with room enough for our descendants to the thousandth and thousandth generation; entertaining a due sense of our equal right to the use of our own faculties, to the acquisitions of our own industry, to honour and confidence from our fellow citizens. Resulting not from birth, but from our actions, and their sense of them; enlightened by a benign religion, professed, indeed, and practised in various forms, yet all of them inculcating honesty, truth, temperance, gratitude, and the love of man; acknowledging and adoring an overruling Providence, which, by all its dispensations, proves that it delights in the happiness of man here and his greater happiness hereafter; with all these blessings, what more is necessary to make us a happy and prosperous people?

Still one thing more, fellow citizens; a wise and frugal government, which shall restrain men from injuring one another; shall leave them otherwise free to regulate their own pursuits of industry and improvement; and shall not take from the mouth of labour the bread it has earned. This is the sum of good government; and this is necessary to close the circle of our felicities.

GARIBALDI.
Born 1807. *Living.*

[THE following extract is from a letter addressed to the editor of *La Nation Suisse*, by the Liberator of Italy. It breathes forth a fine spirit of patriotism, and is worthy of preservation even in its translated form.]

THE CAUSE OF FREEDOM IN 1864.

I DESIRE to add my name to the four thousand citizens of Geneva who have addressed the United States in favour of the maintenance of the constitution and the abolition of slavery, and I hope in so doing to obtain the approbation of the Liberal press, and of all my fellow-citizens. Glory to Switzerland! That old home of liberty deserves to stand in the vanguard of human emancipation. From a fatality now weighing on nations, we see great peoples grow less, and even disappear, before the lying flattery of despotism, and the champions of freedom become the police of tyranny. Well, let Switzerland take the lead till nations repent. Tyrants pass away: nations are immortal. What avails a minority? We shall conquer by aid of our old traditions; and we shall again see tyranny melt before the popular phalanx as snow before the sun. We shall conquer because we have right, justice, and brotherhood on our side. Let me now call the attention of Switzerland to a great fact. The American republics present to the world the spectacle of the connection of the peoples. An aggression against the Peruvian territory, completed by the Spanish Bourbons, has raised a cry of shame and vengeance from all her sister nations. If the elder sister of republics will send one word of comfort to her suffering sister, it would be a striking contrast to the shameful leaguer of tyrants against liberty, which we now see in Europe. Mind this—Poland swamped by Russia, amid the apathy of all, is the first step to a return to the barbarism of the middle ages. If the "Partition" disgraced the Eighteenth, the destruction of Poland is a lasting blot on the Nineteenth century. Alas! our civilization as yet is but false.

SAMUEL TAYLOR COLERIDGE.
Born 1772. *Died* 1834.

THE PROMULGATION OF TRUTH.

I HAVE explained the good, that is, the natural, consequences of the promulgation of all truths which all are bound to know and to make known. The evils *occasioned* by it, with few and rare exceptions, have their origin in the attempts to suppress or pervert it; in the fury and violence of imposture attacked or undermined in her strongholds, or in the extravagances of ignorance and credulity, roused from their lethargy, and angry at the medicinal disturbance — awakening, not yet broad awake, and thus blending the monsters of uneasy dreams with the real objects on which the drowsy eye had alternately half opened and closed, again half opened and again half closed. This *re-action* of deceit and superstition, with all the trouble and tumult incident, I would compare to a fire which bursts forth from some stifled and fermenting mass on the first admission of light and air. It roars and blows and converts the already spoilt or damaged stuff, with all the straw and straw-like matter near it, first into flame and the next moment into ashes. The fire dies away, the ashes are scattered on all the winds, and what began in worthlessness ends in nothingness. Such are the evils, that is, the casual consequences of the same promulgation.

It argues a narrow or corrupt nature to lose the general and lasting consequences of rare and virtuous energy, in the brief accidents which accompanied its first movements—to sit lightly by the emancipation of the human reason from a legion of devils, in our complaints and lamentations over the loss of a herd of swine! The Cranmers, Hampdens, and Sidneys; the counsellors of our Elizabeth, and the friends of our other great deliverer, the third William,—is it in vain that these have been our countrymen? Are we not the heirs of their good deeds? And what are noble deeds but noble truths realized? As Protestants, as Englishmen, as the inheritors of so ample an estate of might and right, an estate so strongly fenced, so richly planted, by the sinewy arms and dauntless hearts of our forefathers, we have of all others have good cause to trust in the truth, you to follow its pillars of fire through the darkness and the desert, even though its light should but suffice to make us certain of its own presence. If there be elsewhere men jealous of the light, who prophesy an excess of evil over good from its manifestation, we are entitled to ask them, on what experience they ground their bodings? Our own country bears no traces, our own history contains no records, to justify them. From the great eras of national illumination we date the commencement of our main national advantages. The tangle of delusions, which stifled and distorted the growing tree, have been torn away; the parasite weeds, that fed on its very roots, have been plucked up with a salutary violence. To us there remain only quiet duties, the constant care, the gradual improvement, the cautious unhazardous labours of the industrious, though contented gardener, to prune, to engraft, and one by one to remove from its leaves and fresh roots, the slug and the caterpillar. But far be it from us to undervalue with light and senseless detraction, the conscientious hardihood of our predecessors, or even to condemn in them that vehemence, to which the blessings it won for us leave now neither temptation or pretext. That the very terms, with which the bigot or the hireling would blacken the first publishers of political and religious truth, are, and deserve to be, hateful to us, we owe to the effects of its publication. We ante-date the feelings in order to criminate the authors of our tranquillity, opulence, and security. But let us be aware. Effects will not, indeed, immediately disappear with their causes; but neither can they long continue without them. If by the *reception* of truth in the spirit of truth, we *became* what we are; only by the *retention* of it in the same spirit, can we *remain* what we are. The narrow seas that form our boundaries, what were they in times of old? The convenient highway for Danish and Norman pirates. What are they now? Still but "a span of waters." Yet they roll at the base of the inisled Ararat, on which the ark of the Hope of Europe and of civilization rested!

F. W. ROBERTSON.
Born 1816. *Died* 1853.

[THE short extract which follows is from an Address by the late Rev. F. W. Robertson to the members of the Working Men's Institute at Brighton, of which he was, during its early years, the chief ornament and pillar. For large and liberal views on questions affecting the true position of the working classes, the lectures and addresses of this author are amongst the most valuable contributions to modern literature.]

TRUE DEMOCRACY DEFINED.

DEMOCRACY, if it means anything, means government by the people. It has for its very watchword, Equality of all men. Now let us not endeavour to make it ridiculous. I suppose that a sensible democrat does not mean that all individual men are equal in intelligence and worth. He does not mean that the Bushman or the Australian is equal to the Englishman. But he means this—that the original stuff of which all men are made, is equal; that there is no reason why the Hottentot and the Australian may not be cultivated, so that in the lapse of centuries they may be equal to Englishmen. I suppose the democrat would say, there is no reason why the son of a cobbler should not by education become fit to be the prime minister of the land, or take his place on the bench of judges. And I suppose that all free institutions mean this. I suppose they are meant to assert—Let the people be educated; let there be a fair field and no favour; let every man have a fair chance, and then the happiest condition of a nation would be, that when every man had been educated morally and intellectually to his very highest capacity, there should then be selected out of men so trained a Government of the Wisest and the Best.

GEORGE CANNING.

Born 1770. *Died* 1827.

[THE speech which is given below was delivered by Canning, then Secretary for Foreign Affairs, on the 12th of December, 1826, in the House of Commons, and its effect both within and without the House is described by contemporaries as most marvellous. In February of the following year, Canning succeeded Lord Liverpool as Prime Minister, but was not long spared to enjoy either his honours or his life, as he died, worn out both in body and mind, on the 8th of August of the same year.]

ON MOVING THE CONSIDERATION OF THE KING'S MESSAGE ON THE RELATIONS SUBSISTING BETWEEN GREAT BRITAIN AND PORTUGAL.

MR. SPEAKER,—In proposing to the House of Commons to acknowledge, by an humble and dutiful Address, his Majesty's most gracious message on the subject of the relations subsisting between Great Britain and Portugal, and the present condition of the latter state; and, in calling on this House to reply to that communication, in terms which will be, in fact, an echo to the sentiments contained in the royal message, and equally in accordance with the anticipations of his Majesty's government — in doing this, Sir, I cannot but feel that, however confident I may be in the justice of the cause, and accustomed as I am to the policy which it becomes us, in accordance with the recommendations contained in his Majesty's message, to adopt; yet, Sir, I am free to admit, it well becomes a British minister, in recommending a British House of Commons to take any step calculated to bring upon their country the hazards of war, to make use of the language of regret and sorrow that such a necessity should exist.

I assure the House there is not, within its walls, at this moment, any set of men more fully convinced than are his Majesty's ministers— nor any individual more intimately persuaded than he who has now the honour to address you—of the vital importance of the continuance of peace to this country and to the world. [So strongly am I impressed with this opinion, and for reasons of which I will take the liberty before I sit down to adduce to the House, that I am perfectly ready to declare that no question, involving a doubtful success or construction— no consideration of merely present advantage— and, Sir, I will go farther, and add, no anticipation of remote and contingent difficulty could arise, which I should not a thousand times rather completely pass over, or, at least, adjourn, than concur in a measure calling on the government of this country to involve itself in the consequences of a war. But, Sir, there are cases which render the adoption of such a course not merely honourable and beneficial, but also necessary and inevitable, and I am equally certain the present occasion presents such a case; and I feel that what has been acted on in the best times of our history — what has been promulgated by our best statesmen—and what has always received the support and concurrence of successive English parliaments, is an adherence to national faith, and respect for the national honour. These are the two questions which cannot be compromised under any circumstances whatsoever—the cause of national faith, and the cause of national honour. Sir, if I did not consider the present question as completely falling within both these cases—if I was not intimately satisfied that the national faith and the national honour were alike interested on this occasion— I should not dare to address the House of Commons, as I now do, in the full and unlimited confidence (almost amounting to conviction) that the most gracious communication made to parliament by his Majesty, will meet with that reply from parliament which his Majesty expects. Viewing the matter as I do, I shall beg leave to proceed, first, to a simple statement and review of facts, in order the better to bring the case under the cognizance of parliament, in the shortest and clearest form I can devise, and of which the subject itself is susceptible.

Before entering into the consideration of any collateral circumstances connected with the subject, I shall state shortly the situation of the case, which, as it appears to me, resolves itself into a case of national law, and a question of fact. With regard to the fact, on the one hand, that is now to be brought under the consideration of parliament, as it has previously been submitted to the attention of his Majesty's government, Sir, in my mind, it is impossible to consider that fact in any other light than that in which it presented itself to the minds of his Majesty's ministers; and I think it equally impossible for parliament and government (taking such a view of the case) to come to any other decision than that contemplated in his Majesty's message. Among the relations of alliance and amity by which, at different periods of her history, this country has connected herself with the other nations of Europe, there exist no treaties so old in their date—none so constant in their duration — and, I may add, none so precise in the obligations it imposes upon both countries, and so intimately interwoven with the line of policy adopted by Great Britain in its foreign relations, as are the treaties of amity and alliance formed between this country and the kingdom of Portugal. Sir, I may be excused for calling the attention of the House to the fact, that our most remote history contains (I may add, the most brilliant periods of our history are those which contain) notices of the treaties of alliance, amity, and guarantee, subsisting between the King of Great Britain and his Portuguese Majesty. The good understanding thus created between the two countries began early, and has continued long. It has survived a variety of conflicting interests and circumstances, which, in the course of events, from time to time, have naturally and unavoidably arisen. It is much older than the epoch to which I am about to advert, when the good understanding previously subsisting between the two states acquired fresh vigour on the occasion of the present family of Portugal ascending the throne of that kingdom. Anterior to the accession of the house of Braganza to the throne, friendly relations subsisted between Portugal and this country — relations which were continued without interruption, and renewed with sincerity, on, I will say, both parts. It has been adhered to in periods when the faith of other alliances has been shaken; it has been vindicated in those fields of blood and glory which remain among the most brilliant pages of the history of England. Sir, in that alliance we have always been scrupulously faithful. Sometimes, I admit, we have found the treaty burthensome to maintain — of that there can be no question; and many are those who may have wished us to shake it off, and free ourselves from the incumbrance of observing it; but a feeling of national honour, and what I may be allowed to denominate a sentiment of national sympathy, joined to a common interest, and a cause identified with that country, has induced England to persevere, unterrified by the difficulties attendant upon a continuance of the relations subsisting between us and Portugal.

I feel the considerations to which I have more particularly adverted present too narrow and limited a view of the case. It is not only among ages long gone by, and in treaties now superseded by time and the course of events, that traces are discoverable of the relation in which Portugal has been considered to stand in regard to Great Britain; for in the latest compact entered into between the nations of modern Europe, that which now forms the patent law of the civilized world, I allude, Sir, to the convention of Vienna, a similar course was taken in the treaty then entered into between this country and Portugal. At that period, Sir, Great Britain was well aware of the inconveniences which many individuals were fond of representing as arising out of our connection with Portugal; but we were also aware of the credit, and, I will add, advantage derivable from that connection; and we renewed our obligations to uphold and support Portugal, on future occasions, in terms so strong and imperative, as to lay a foundation perfectly adequate to support the present proceeding. The terms of that treaty I will take leave to read to the House previous to calling on it to concur in the vote, with the proposal of which it is my intention to conclude. The third article of the treaty between Great Britain and Portugal, concluded at Vienna on the 22nd of February, 1815, stated, that "the treaty of alliance entered into between his Britannic Majesty and the King of Portugal at Rio de Janeiro, was founded on circumstances of a temporary nature, which had now happily ceased to exist; and, on that ground, the provisions of the treaty should be considered null and void as relating to all the parties interested; however, without prejudice to the ancient and established treaties of alliance, friendship, and guarantee, which had so long and happily subsisted between the two countries: these treaties being now renewed by the high contracting parties, and acknowledged to remain in full force and effect."

In order that the House may fully understand, and accurately appreciate, the effect of the observations which the perusal of this treaty is calculated to excite, I may be permitted to explain the previous circumstances of Portugal, and the condition of the reigning family in that country. In the year 1807, when, by the declaration of Buonaparte, the house of Braganza ceased to reign, the King of Portugal, under the advice of his Britannic Majesty's government, set sail for the Brazils, and established in that country the seat of his monarchy. This step was taken by virtue of a secret convention concluded between this country and Portugal, to the effect, that so long as the House of Braganza remained in that part of their dominions, or in the event of their return, his Britannic Majesty would never acknowledge any other dynasty on the throne of Portugal than the family of Braganza. I may be allowed to remark, that this convention greatly contributed to the furtherance of a proceeding which placed that family beyond the power of Buonaparte, and consequently promoted the ascendancy of British interests in the Peninsula. It was this secret convention that brought about the emigration, and greatly contributed to decide that step by which the royal family of Portugal was removed from the power of France.

The King of Portugal having become established upon his throne, the article ceased to be secret, and became part of the law of nations by the treaty of 1810, and from that time up to the treaty of Vienna, it was clearly understood throughout Europe, that we had determined not to acknowledge any sovereign in Portugal, except a member of the house of Braganza. But that determination arose solely from the supposition that that sovereign would be compelled to a forced residence in Brazil. Beyond this it was not binding upon us, as it was felt that the moment the ground of the obligation ceased, there was an end to the treaty. It happened, in consequence of the happy conclusion of the war, that the option of returning was offered to his Majesty, and as it was felt that the force of such a previous obligation no longer existed, the forcible separation from Portugal not continuing, it was deemed reasonable that we should perform such other obligation as the force of existing treaties rendered imperative upon us. The King of Portugal came into possession of his European dominions, the ground of our former obligation ceased, and the treaty was so far ended. But when that treaty was so far ended, there came another obligation, which I have just now read to the House. That treaty, I may be allowed to say, was repealed without prejudice to other ancient treaties of friendship and alliance; treaties so long and so happily subsisting between the two crowns of Portugal and Great Britain, which were, to a certain extent, renewed by the two high contracting parties, and which are, to this day, of full force and effect. I should also state, that if all the treaties to which this paragraph referred, were, by some convulsion of nature, or some other accident, consigned to total oblivion, I consider Great Britain to be morally bound to fulfil her obligations, and that, in case of necessity, she would be bound, and is bound, to act in the defence of Portugal. But, happily, that is not the case; all the preceding treaties are in existence—they are in the full knowledge of all the civilized nations of the world—they are of easy reference to all mankind—they are known to Spain—to all the continental states of Europe—they are so numerous, and the result of the whole is so clear, that I shall merely select one or two of them, with a view to show the nature of our obligations to our ancient friend and ally—Portugal.

The first to which I shall advert is that concluded in 1661, at the time of the marriage of Charles II. with the Infanta of Portugal. The obligations of that treaty, after reciting the delivering of Bombay, Tangier, and other places, some of which still remained, and some not, to the government to which they were delivered, it was stated, that, in consideration of those grants, which were of so much benefit to the King of Great Britain, he professed, and declared himself, by and with the consent of his privy council, that he would take upon him the defence of Portugal; that he would aid and defend her by sea and by land, with all his power, and in all other manner and respect, even as he would defend England itself. By that treaty it was further conditioned, that, in case of necessity, or any foreign attack, he should send and transport, at his own proper cost and expense, two regiments of horse, of 500 men, and two regiments of foot, of 1,000 men each. There were other various stipulations, amounting to the same effect, which render it unnecessary for me to go farther into it at present.

The next treaty, to which I beg the attention of the House, is that of 1703: it was a tripartite treaty, made between the States-general of Holland, Great Britain, and Portugal, and was contemporaneous with the famous commercial treaty of Methuen, whose provisions still continue to be in full force and effect. By the second article of the treaty of 1703, it was conditioned, that if at any time, and whenever it happened, the Kings of Spain or France, or both, or either of them, should make war on Portugal, or give reason to suspect they had jointly or separately any intention to make war on her or her colonial possessions beyond the seas, her Majesty shall use her good offices to persuade those powers not to make war; but in case those offices should not succeed, the third article provides, that should such interference not be successful, and should war be actually made on Portugal, then the above-named contracting powers declare, that they shall make war on the Kings of Spain or France, or both or either of them; and that, while hostile arms shall be borne against Portugal, they shall provide 12,000 men, armed and equipped, and leave them there while their presence may be deemed necessary. From these articles, the House will perceive the nature, if not the extent, of our ancient obligations to our ally. I am ready to admit, Sir, that either of these treaties might, by time and circumstances, be supposed to have relaxed in their force; or it might be asked, why one party having withdrawn itself from the responsibility, say Holland, for instance, the other should still be considered as bound to adhere to it? It may be said, the language of these treaties is so loose and prodigal, that they could only have originated in good feeling, and that it was out of nature to suppose any one nation would engage to defend another as she would herself. It may be said, there is something so exaggerated in these treaties, that they were never intended to be carried into effect. But with regard to this very treaty of 1703, even if I stood upon it alone; even though the circumstances of Holland had changed; even if her sentiments had changed; if her obligations were either altered or had become obsolete; I need not raise the question whether, the government and sentiments of England not changing, she is now liable or not to perform her obligation? This is not the time to do so, even if I admitted that such a question could have been raised. The objections, if any, should have been taken at the Congress of Vienna, when the eyes of the whole world were open to our relative situation with Portugal; when we proclaimed the existence of our ancient treaties of friendship and alliance, so long subsisting with her; and when they were acknowledged to be of full force and effect. That was the time to object, if objection was thought necessary; and it is not so much on the specific articles of the treaties of 1661 and 1703 that we have acted and continue to act, as on the general spirit of all the treaties, admitted and recognized at the Congress of Vienna. I say Portugal has a right to claim the assistance of Great Britain, as an ally, and call upon her to defend the integrity of her territory. This is the state of the case as to our moral and political obligations towards Portugal; and I am not ashamed to say —I have a right to say—that when Portugal, in the apprehension of a coming storm, applied for our assistance, while we had no hesitation in acknowledging our obligation to afford it, if the *casus fœderis* had once arisen, yet I say that we were bound to wait till we ascertained the fact upon sufficient authority. Whether delay or difficulty interposed, it was not as to the existence of an admitted obligation, but as to the knowledge of the fact having actually taken place, which justified the call for our assistance.

In this stage of our proceedings, I beg to answer incidentally a charge of delay which has been made against his Majesty's government on this very important subject. But, in few words, I can state to the House, there is not the shadow of foundation for any such charge. It was only on Sunday, the 3rd of December, that I received from the Portuguese ambassador the direct and formal demand of assistance from this country. True, long before that time rumours were afloat of an unauthorized description—rumours finding their way from Madrid, where everything was distorted, through the channels of the French press, where everything was again disfigured and perverted, to serve party purposes; but, until the 8th of December, we had not received that accurate information on which alone we could found a communication to parliament. That precise information, on which we could act, only arrived on Friday last. On Saturday, the decision of the government was taken—on Sunday we obtained the sanction of his Majesty —on Monday we came down to parliament— and at this very hour, while I have now the honour of addressing the House, British troops are on their march for Portugal. I trust, therefore, that we are not in justice to be charged with any unseemly delay; but, on the other hand, while we felt the claim of Portugal to be so clear, our obligation to assist her so binding, and the possible consequences of interference so spreading, it was our duty not to give any credit to hearsay or to rumour; but, while admitting the full force of our obligation, we were bound to have the full knowledge of the facts of the case, before we took a step whose consequences no man could precisely calculate. Rumours and reports, as I have just said, were long afloat, of incursions made by Spain upon our ally; but, then, they reached us through channels upon which no man in his senses would found any grave proceeding. In one case, at Madrid, they were put forth to deceive; in others, to conceal; and, coming through the French newspaper press—these rumours, I say, coming through such sources, were not to be relied upon by his Majesty's government, and we therefore waited for authenticated facts, in order to come before parliament with what we might call the truth. In former instances, when parliament was called upon to assist Portugal, the regular and constitutional power of the monarchy was lodged in the breast of the King: the signification of his wish, the expression of his desire, the putting forward his individual claim for assistance, would have been enough; but when it was stated to me that matters had changed, that the constitution was modified and altered, it became my duty to inquire, first, whether the constitution of Portugal authorized the claim; next, if it were competent to the authorities making it to do so, and whether the chambers had given their sanction to the reception of our troops, such as we were to expect for the troops of an old and faithful ally. We were bound to take care, before a single soldier left England, or set his foot upon the shore of Portugal, that the sanction of the executive—of all the proper authorities —should be obtained; and I beg leave again to state, with reference to the charge of delay, which has somewhere or other been brought against his Majesty's ministers, that it was only this morning I received the sanction of the Chambers assembled at Lisbon. So far, then, from any charge of delay being justifiably brought against the government, I can boldly say, had we proceeded faster, we should have acted precipitately, and every caution was necessary to be used, before we involved this country in proceedings, which might prove to be unnecessary by the result, or might expose us to an unpleasant reception of our troops in Portugal. The account which I received to-day of the proceedings of the Chambers at Lisbon, is contained in a despatch from Sir W. A'Court, dated the 29th of November. It states, that the day after the arrival of the news of the entry of the rebels, ministers demanded the extension of their executive powers, an augmentation of the troops, and permission to apply for foreign assistance. The deputies assembled agreed to the demand with acclamation, and a similar spirit operating in the other chamber, the members rose in a body from their seats, expressed their readiness to acquiesce in the call, and many of them offered their personal assistance in the cause of their country. The Duke de Cadaval, the president, was the first who so declared himself, and the minister, who described the proceeding to our ambassador, declared it was a moment worthy of the good days of Portugal.

THE ORATOR.

So far the House will see we have a reasonable guarantee for the good reception of our troops; and then, the next question remaining for our consideration is, has the *casus fœderis* arrived? Bands of Portuguese, armed, equipped, and trained in Spain, had made hostile incursions into Portugal at several points; and what is remarkable in this case is, that the attack on Portugal is not the ground on which the application for British assistance has been complied with. The attack in the south of Portugal was stated in the French papers; but that on Tras os Montes was only received, authentically, this morning, and those on Villa Viciosa no longer ago than Friday. The intelligence of this new fact is the more satisfactory, as it confirmed the facts which were already known. The irruption upon one point of Portugal might be stated to be made by some corps who had escaped the vigilance of the Spanish government; it might be represented as the effort of some stragglers, acting in defiance of Spain: but an attack on the whole line gives that decided and certain character to the aggression which cannot be mistaken.

If a single company of Spanish soldiers, in arms, had crossed the frontier, the hostile aggression would be undoubted; and here the question is, to consider whether persons, clothed and equipped by Spain, and crossing the frontiers, are, or are not, guilty of an attack or invasion of Portugal—forsooth, because they were not Spanish soldiers, or Spanish mercenaries in the employ of Spain; but Portuguese troops, whom Portugal had nurtured, and who, in return, had brought with them devastation into their native land, and that by means furnished by a foreign enemy? Why, it could be but petty and puerile quibbling to say, that this was not an invasion, because the agents were originally from Portugal: and that, therefore, their attack was not to be repelled.

I have already stated, and I now repeat, that it never has been the wish or the pretension of the British government to interfere in the internal concerns of the Portuguese nation. Questions of that kind the Portuguese nation must settle among themselves. But if we were to admit that hordes of traitorous refugees from Portugal, with Spanish arms—or arms furnished or restored to them by Spanish authorities—in their hands, might put off their country for one purpose, and put it on again for another—put it off for the purpose of attack, and put it on again for the purpose of impunity—if, I say, we were to admit this juggle, and either pretend to be deceived by it ourselves, or attempt to deceive Portugal, into a belief that there was nothing of external attack, nothing of foreign hostility, in such a system of aggression—such pretence and attempt would perhaps be only ridiculous and contemptib... acquire a much more ser... being employed as an exc... ancient friendship, and as... rid of the positive stipulati...

This then is the case w... House of Commons. Here... an undoubted pledge of... taken in a corner—not kep... parties—but publicly rec... annals of history, in the... Here are, on the other han... foreign aggression, perpetr... pally through the instrum... traitors; but supported... instigated by foreign coun... foreign ends. Putting t... pledge together, it is impos... should refuse the call that... him; nor can Parliament, I... to enable his Majesty to... obligations. I am willin... question of to-night, and t... the House of Commons up... divested altogether of collo... from which I especially wi... the minds of those who h... the minds of others, to wh... will find its way. If I w... moment, without adding a... no doubt but that I shou... rence of the House in t... mean to propose.

When I state this, it w... House, that the vote for... call upon them is a vot... Portugal, not a vote for w... beg the House to keep thes... distinct in their considerat... I think I have said eno... have now farther to say,... upon the Spanish govern... may be observed that, un... show their conduct to hav... the law of nations, contrar... neighbourhood, contrary,... laws of God and man—with... —still I do not mean to p... *tentiæ*, a possibility of red... It is our duty to fly to the... be the assailant who he... remembered, that in thus f... tions of ancient treaties,... obligation of which all the... according to the universall... tion of the law of nations... upon that assailant, nor gi... much less to any other pow... against ourselves.

Sir, the present situatio... anomalous, and the recent... are crowded with events s...

House will, perhaps, not think that I am unprofitably wasting its time, if I take the liberty of calling its attention shortly and succinctly to those events, and to their influence on the political relations of Europe. It is known that the consequence of the residence of the King of Portugal in Brazil, was to raise the latter country from a colonial to a metropolitan condition; and that from the time when the King began to contemplate his return to Portugal, there grew up in Brazil a desire of independence that threatened dissension, if not something like civil contest, between the European and American dominions of the house of Braganza. It is known also that Great Britain undertook a mediation between Portugal and Brazil, and induced the King to consent to a separation of the two crowns—confirming that of Brazil on the head of his eldest son. The ink with which this agreement was written was scarcely dry, when the unexpected death of the King of Portugal produced a new state of things, which re-united on the same head the two crowns which it had been the policy of England, as well as of Portugal and of Brazil to separate. On that occasion, Great Britain, and another European court closely connected with Brazil, tendered advice to the Emperor of Brazil, now become King of Portugal, which advice it cannot be accurately said that his imperial Majesty followed, because he had decided for himself before it reached Rio de Janeiro; but in conformity with which advice, though not in consequence of it, his imperial Majesty determined to abdicate the crown of Portugal in favour of his eldest daughter. But the Emperor of Brazil had done more. What had not been foreseen—what would have been beyond the province of any foreign power to advise—his imperial Majesty had accompanied his abdication of the crown of Portugal with the grant of a free constitutional charter to that kingdom.

It has been surmised that this measure, as well as the abdication which it accompanied, was the offspring of our advice. No such thing: Great Britain did not suggest this measure. It is not her duty nor her practice to offer suggestions for the internal regulation of foreign states. She neither approved nor disapproved of the grant of a constitutional charter to Portugal: her opinion upon that grant was never required. True it is, that the instrument of the constitutional charter was brought to Europe by a gentleman of high trust in the service of the British government. Sir C. Stuart had gone to Brazil to negociate the separation between that country and Portugal. In addition to his character of plenipotentiary of Great Britain, as the mediating power, he had also been invested by the King of Portugal with the character of his most faithful Majesty's plenipotentiary for the negociation with Brazil. That negociation had been brought to a happy conclusion ; and therewith the British part of Sir C. Stuart's commission had terminated. But Sir C. Stuart was still resident at Rio de Janeiro, as the plenipotentiary of the King of Portugal, for negociating commercial arrangements between Portugal and Brazil. In this latter character it was, that Sir C. Stuart, on his return to Europe, was requested by the Emperor of Brazil to be the bearer to Portugal of the new constitutional charter. His Majesty's government found no fault with Sir C. Stuart for executing this commission; but it was immediately felt, that if Sir C. Stuart were allowed to remain at Lisbon, it might appear, in the eyes of Europe, that England was the contriver and imposer of the Portuguese constitution. Sir C. Stuart was, therefore, directed to return home forthwith : in order that the constitution, if carried into effect there, might plainly appear to be adopted by the Portuguese nation itself, not forced upon them by English interference.

As to the merits, Sir, of the new constitution of Portugal, I have neither the intention, nor the right, to offer any opinion. Personally, I may have formed one; but as an English minister, all I have to say is,—"May God prosper this attempt at the establishment of constitutional liberty in Portugal! and may that nation be found as fit to enjoy and to cherish its new-born privileges, as it has often proved itself capable of discharging its duties amongst the nations of the world !"

I, Sir, am neither the champion nor the critic of the Portuguese constitution. But it is admitted on all hands to have proceeded from a legitimate source—a consideration which has mainly reconciled continental Europe to its establishment : and to us, as Englishmen, it is recommended, by the ready acceptance which it has met with from all orders of the Portuguese people. To that constitution, therefore, thus unquestioned in its origin, even by those who are most jealous of new institutions—to that constitution, thus sanctioned in its outset by the glad and grateful acclamations of those who are destined to live under it—to that constitution, founded on principles in a great degree similar to those of our own, though differently modified — it is impossible that Englishmen should not wish well. But it would not be for us to force that constitution on the people of Portugal, if they were unwilling to receive it, or if any schism should exist amongst the Portuguese themselves, as to its fitness and congeniality to the wants and wishes of the nation. It is no business of ours to fight its battles. We go to Portugal in the discharge of a sacred obligation, contracted under ancient and modern treaties. When there, nothing shall be done by us to enforce the establishment of the constitution; but we must take care that nothing shall be done by others to prevent it from being fairly carried into effect. Internally, let the Portuguese settle their own affairs; but with respect to external force, while Great Britain has an arm to raise, it must be raised against the efforts of any power that should attempt forcibly to control the choice, and fetter the independence of Portugal.

Has such been the intention of Spain? Whether the proceedings which have lately been practised or permitted in Spain, were acts of a government exercising the usual power of prudence and foresight (without which a government is, for the good of the people which live under it, no government at all), or whether they were the acts of some secret illegitimate power—of some furious fanatical faction, overriding the counsels of the ostensible government, defying it in the capital, and disobeying it on the frontiers—I will not stop to inquire. It is indifferent to Portugal, smarting under her wrongs—it is indifferent to England, who is called upon to avenge them—whether the present state of things be the result of the intrigues of a faction, over which, if the Spanish government has no control, it ought to assume one as soon as possible; or of local authorities, over whom it has control, and for whose acts it must, therefore, be held responsible. It matters not, I say, from which of these sources the evil has arisen. In either case, Portugal must be protected; and from England that protection is due.

It would be unjust, however, to the Spanish government, to say, that it is only amongst the members of that government that an unconquerable hatred of liberal institutions exists in Spain. However incredible the phenomenon may appear in this country, I am persuaded that a vast majority of the Spanish nation entertain a decided attachment to arbitrary power, and a predilection for absolute government. The more liberal institutions of countries in their neighbourhood have not yet extended their influence into Spain, nor awakened any sympathy in the mass of the Spanish people. Whether the public authorities of Spain did or did not partake of the national sentiment, there would almost necessarily grow up between Portugal and Spain, under present circumstances, an opposition of feelings, which it would not require the authority or the suggestions of the government to excite and stimulate into action. Without blame, therefore, to the government of Spain—out of the natural antipathy between the two neighbouring nations—the one prizing its recent freedom, the other hugging its traditionary servitude—there might arise mutual provocations, and reciprocal injuries which, perhaps, even the most active and vigilant ministry could not altogether restrain. I am inclined to believe that such has been, in part at least, the origin of the differences between Spain and Portugal. That in their progress they have been adopted, matured, methodized, combined, and brought into more perfect action, by some authority more united and more efficient than the mere feeling disseminated through the mass of the community, is certain; but I do believe their origin to have been as much in the real sentiment of the Spanish population, as in the opinion or contrivance of the government itself.

Whether this be or be not the case, is precisely the question between us and Spain. If, though partaking in the general feelings of the Spanish nation, the Spanish government has, nevertheless, done nothing to embody those feelings, and to direct them hostilely against Portugal; if all that has occurred on the frontiers, has occurred only because the vigilance of the Spanish government has been surprised, its confidence betrayed, and its orders neglected—if its engagements have been repeatedly and shamefully violated, not by its own good will, but against its recommendation and desire—let us see some symptoms of disapprobation, some signs of repentance, some measures indicative of sorrow for the past, and of sincerity for the future. In that case his Majesty's Message, to which I propose this night to return an answer of concurrence, will retain the character which I have ascribed to it—that of a measure of defence for Portugal, not a measure of resentment against Spain.

With these explanations and qualifications, let us now proceed to the review of facts. Great desertions took place from the Portuguese army into Spain, and some desertions took place from the Spanish army into Portugal. In the first instance, the Portuguese authorities were taken by surprise; but, in every subsequent instance, where they had an opportunity of exercising a discretion, it is but just to say, that they uniformly discouraged the desertions of the Spanish soldiery. There exist between Spain and Portugal specific treaties, stipulating the mutual surrender of deserters. Portugal had, therefore, a right to claim of Spain that every Portuguese deserter should be forthwith sent back. I hardly know whether from its own impulse, or in consequence of our advice, the Portuguese government waived its right under those treaties; very wisely reflecting, that it would be highly inconvenient to be placed, by the return of their deserters, in the difficult alternative of either granting a dangerous amnesty, or ordering numerous executions. The Portuguese government, therefore, signified to Spain that it would be entirely satisfied if, instead of surrendering the deserters, Spain would restore their arms, horses, and equipments; and, separating the men from their officers, would remove both from the frontiers into the interior of Spain. Solemn engagements were entered into by the Spanish government to this effect—first with Portugal, next with France, and afterwards with England. Those engagements, concluded one day, were violated the next. The deserters, instead of being disarmed and dispersed, were allowed to remain congregated together near the frontiers of Portugal, where they were enrolled, trained, and disciplined, for the expedition which they have since undertaken. It is plain that in these proceedings there was perfidy somewhere. It rests with the Spanish government to show that it was not with them. It rests with the Spanish government to prove, that if its engagements have not been fulfilled—if its intentions have been eluded and unexecuted, the fault has not been with the government; and that it is ready to make every reparation in its power.

I have said that these promises were made to France and to Great Britain, as well as to Portugal. I should do a great injustice to France if I were not to add, that the representations of that government upon this point with the cabinet of Madrid, have been as urgent, and, alas! as fruitless, as those of Great Britain. Upon the first irruption into the Portuguese territory, the French government testified its displeasure by instantly recalling its ambassador; and it further directed its *chargé d'affaires* to signify to his Catholic Majesty that Spain was not to look for any support from France against the consequences of this aggression upon Portugal. I am bound, I repeat, in justice to the French government, to state, that it has exerted itself to the utmost, in urging Spain to retrace the steps which she has so unfortunately taken. It is not for me to say whether any more efficient course might have been adopted to give effect to their exhortations; but as to the sincerity and good faith of the exertions made by the government of France, to press Spain to the execution of her engagements, I have not the shadow of a doubt: and I confidently reckon upon their continuance.

It will be for Spain, upon knowledge of the step now taken by his Majesty, to consider in what way she will meet it. The earnest hope and wish of his Majesty's government is, that she may meet it in such a manner as to avert any ill consequences to herself, from the measure into which we have been driven by the unjust attack upon Portugal.

Sir, I set out with saying, that there were reasons which entirely satisfied my judgment that nothing short of a point of national faith or national honour would justify, at the present moment, any voluntary approximation to the possibility of war. Let me be understood, however, distinctly, as not meaning to say that I dread a war in a good cause (and in no other may it be the lot of this country ever to engage!) from a distrust of the strength of the country to commence it, or of her resources to maintain it. I dread it, indeed; but upon far other grounds: I dread it from an apprehension of the tremendous consequences which might arise from any hostilities in which we might now be engaged. Some years ago, in the discussion of the negociations respecting the French war against Spain, I took the liberty of adverting to this topic. I then stated that the position of this country in the present state of the world, was one of neutrality, not only between contending nations, but between conflicting principles; and that it was by neutrality alone that we could maintain that balance, the preservation of which I believed to be essential to the welfare of mankind. I then said, that I feared that the next war which should be kindled in Europe, would be a war not so much of armies as of opinions. Not four years have elapsed, and behold my apprehension realized! It is, to be sure, within narrow limits that this war of opinion is at present confined: but it *is* a war of opinion, that Spain (whether as government or as nation) is now waging against Portugal; it is a war which has commenced in hatred of the new institutions of Portugal. How long is it reasonable to expect that Portugal will abstain from retaliation? If into that war this country shall be compelled to enter, we shall enter into it with a sincere and anxious desire to mitigate rather than exasperate—and to mingle only in the conflict of arms, not in the more fatal conflict of opinions. But I much fear that this country (however earnestly she may endeavour to avoid it), could not, in such case, avoid seeing ranked under her banners all the restless and dissatisfied of any nation with which she might come in conflict. It is the contemplation of this new power in any future war, which excites my most anxious apprehension. It is one thing to have a giant's strength, but it would be another to use it like a giant. The consciousness of such strength is, undoubtedly, a source of confidence and security; but in the situation in which this country stands, our business is not to seek opportunities of displaying it, but to content ourselves with letting the professors of violent and exaggerated doctrines on both sides feel, that it is not their interest to convert an umpire into an adversary. The situation of England amidst the struggle of political opinions which agitate more or less sensibly different countries of the world, may be compared to that of the Ruler of the Winds, as described by the poet:—

——" Celsâ sedet Æolus arce,
Sceptra tenens; mollitque animos et temperat iras;
Ni faciat, maria ac terras cœlumque profundum
Quippe ferant rapidi secum, verrantque per auras."

The consequence of letting loose the passions at present chained and confined, would be to produce a scene of desolation which no man can contemplate without horror; and I should not sleep easy on my couch, if I were conscious that I had contributed to precipitate it by a single moment.

This, then, is the reason—a reason very different from fear—the reverse of a consciousness of disability—why I dread the recurrence of hostilities in any part of Europe; why I would bear much, and would forbear long; why I would, as I have said, put up with almost any thing that did not touch national faith and national honour;—rather than let slip the furies of war, the leash of which we hold in our hands—not knowing whom they may reach, or how far their ravages may be carried. Such is the love of peace which the British government acknowledges; and such the necessity for peace which the circumstances of the world inculcate. I will push these topics no farther.

I return, in conclusion, to the object of the Address. Let us fly to the aid of Portugal, by whomsoever attacked, because it is our duty to do so, and let us cease our interference where that duty ends. We go to Portugal, not to rule, not to dictate, not to prescribe constitutions; but to defend and to preserve the independence of an ally. We go to plant the standard of England on the well-known heights of Lisbon. Where that standard is planted, foreign dominion shall not come.

[After an animated debate arising out of the address, in which Messrs. Brougham, Hume, and other leading members of the House took part, Canning replied as follows; and some portions of that reply are amongst the most celebrated passages in modern oratory.]

I rise, Sir, for the purpose of making a few observations, not so much in answer to any general arguments, as in reply to two or three particular objections which have been urged against the Address which I have had the honour to propose to the House.

In the first place, I frankly admit to my honourable friend (Mr. Bankes), the member for Dorsetshire, that I have understated the case against Spain: I have done so designedly—I warned the House that I would do so—because I wished no further to impeach the conduct of Spain than was necessary for establishing the *casus fœderis* on behalf of Portugal. To have gone further—to have made a full statement of the case against Spain—would have been to preclude the very object which I have in view—that of enabling Spain to preserve peace without dishonour.

The honourable gentleman (Mr. Bright) who spoke last, indeed, in his extreme love for peace, proposes expedients which, as it appears to me, would render war inevitable. He would avoid

NO. XVII.

interference at this moment, when Spain may be yet hesitating as to the course which she shall adopt; and the language which he would hold to Spain is, in effect, this: "You have not yet done enough to implicate British faith, and to provoke British honour. You have not done enough, in merely enabling Portuguese rebels to invade Portugal, and to carry destruction into her cities; you have not done enough in combining knots of traitors, whom, after the most solemn engagements to disarm and to disperse them, you carefully re-assembled, and equipped and sent back with Spanish arms, to be plunged into kindred Portuguese bosoms. I will not stir for all these things. Pledged though I am by the most solemn obligations of treaty to resent attack upon Portugal as injurious to England, I love too dearly the peace of Europe to be goaded into activity by such trifles as these. No. But give us a good declaration of war, and then I'll come and fight you with all my heart." This is the honourable gentleman's contrivance for keeping peace. The more clumsy contrivance of his Majesty's government is this:—"We have seen enough to show to the world that Spain authorized, if she did not instigate, the invasion of Portugal;" and we say to Spain, "Beware, we will avenge the cause of our ally, if you break out into declared war; but, in the meantime, we will take effectual care to frustrate your concealed hostilities." I appeal to my honourable friend, the member for Dorsetshire, whether he does not prefer this course of his Majesty's government, the object of which is to nip growing hostilities in the ear, to that of the gallant and chivalrous member for Bristol, who would let aggressions ripen into full maturity, in order that they may then be mowed down with the scythe of a magnificent war.

My honourable friend (Mr. Bankes) will now see why it is that no papers have been laid before the House. The facts which call for our interference in behalf of Portugal are notorious as the noon-day sun. That interference is our whole present object. To prove more than is sufficient for that object, by papers laid upon the table of this House, would have been to preclude Spain from that *locus pœnitentiæ* which we are above all things desirous to preserve to her. It is difficult, perhaps, with the full knowledge which the government must in such cases possess, to judge what exact portion of that knowledge should be meted out for our present purpose, without hazarding an exposure which might carry us too far. I know not how far I have succeeded in this respect; but I can assure the House, that if the time should unfortunately arrive when a further exposition shall become necessary, it will be found, that it was not for want of evidence that my statement of this day has been defective.

K

An amendment has been proposed, purporting a delay of a week, but in effect, intended to produce a total abandonment of the object of the Address; and that amendment has been justified by a reference to the conduct of the government, and to the language used by me in this House, between three and four years ago. It is stated, and truly, that I did not then deny that cause for war had been given by France in the invasion of Spain, if we had then thought fit to enter into war on that account. But it seems to be forgotten that there is one main difference between that case and the present—which difference, however, is essential and all-sufficient. We were then free to go to war, if we pleased, on grounds of political expediency. But we were not then bound to interfere, on behalf of Spain, as we now are bound to interfere on behalf of Portugal, by the obligations of treaty. War might then have been our free choice, if we had deemed it politic—interference on behalf of Portugal is now our duty, unless we are prepared to abandon the principles of national faith and national honour.

It is a singular confusion of intellect which confounds two cases so precisely dissimilar. Far from objecting to the reference to 1823, I refer to that same occasion to show the consistency of the conduct of myself and my colleagues. We were then accused of truckling to France, from a pusillanimous dread of war. We pleaded guilty to the charge of wishing to avoid war. We described its inexpediency, its inconveniences, and its dangers—dangers especially of the same sort of those which I have hinted at to-day; but we declared that, although we could not overlook those dangers, those inconveniences, and that inexpediency, in a case in which remote interest and doubtful policy were alone assigned as motives for war, we would cheerfully affront them all, in a case—if it should arrive—where national faith or national honour were concerned. Well, then, a case has now arisen, of which the essence is faith—of which the character is honour. And when we call upon Parliament, not for offensive war—which was proposed to us in 1823,—but for defensive armament, we are referred to our abstinence in 1823, as disqualifying us for exertion at the present moment; and we are told, that because we did not attack France on that occasion, we must not defend Portugal on this. I, Sir, like the proposers of the amendment, place the two cases of 1823 and 1826 side by side, and deduce from them, when taken together, the exposition and justification of our general policy. I appeal from the warlike preparations of to-day, to the forbearance of 1823, in proof of the pacific character of our counsels; I appeal from the imputed tameness of 1823, to the Message of to-night, in illustration of the nature of those motives, by which a government, generally pacific, may nevertheless be justly roused into action.

Having thus disposed of the objections to the Address, I come next to the suggestions of some who profess themselves friendly to the purpose of it, but who would carry that purpose into effect by means which I certainly cannot approve. It has been suggested, Sir, that we should at once ship off the Spanish refugees now in this country, for Spain; and that we should, by the repeal of the Foreign Enlistment Act, let loose into the contest all the ardent and irregular spirits of this country. Sir, this is the very suggestion which I have anticipated with apprehension, in any war in which this country might be engaged, in the present unquiet state of the minds of men in Europe. These are the expedients, the tremendous character of which I ventured to adumbrate rather than to describe, in the speech with which I prefaced the present motion. Such expedients I disclaim. I dread and deprecate the employment of them. So far, indeed, as Spain herself is concerned, the employment of such means would be strictly, I might say, epigrammatically just. The Foreign Enlistment Act was passed in the year 1819, if not at the direct request, for the especial benefit, of Spain. What right, then, would Spain have to complain if we should repeal it now, for the especial benefit of Portugal?

The Spanish refugees have been harboured in this country, it is true; but on condition of abstaining from hostile expeditions against Spain; and more than once, when such expeditions have been planned, the British government has interfered to suppress them. How is this tenderness for Spain rewarded? Spain not only harbours, and fosters, and sustains, but arms, equips, and marshals the traitorous refugees of Portugal, and pours them by thousands into the bosom of Great Britain's nearest ally. So far, then, as Spain is concerned, the advice of those who would send forth against Spain such dreadful elements of strife and destruction, is, as I have admitted, not unjust. But I repeat, again and again, that I disclaim all such expedients; and that I dread especially a war with Spain, because it is the war of all others in which, by the example and practice of Spain herself, such expedients are most likely to be adopted. Let us avoid that war if we can—that is, if Spain will permit us to do so. But, in any case, let us endeavour to strip any war—if war we must have—of that formidable and disastrous character which the honourable gentleman (Mr. Brougham) has so eloquently described, and which I was happy to hear him concur with me in deprecating, as the most fatal evil by which the world could be afflicted.

Sir, there is another suggestion with which I cannot agree, although brought forward by two honourable members (Sir R. Wilson and Mr. Baring), who have, in the most handsome manner, stated their reasons for approving of the line of conduct now pursued by his Majesty's government. Those honourable members insist that the French army in Spain has been, if not the cause, the encouragement of the late attack by Spain against Portugal; that his Majesty's government were highly culpable in allowing that army to enter into Spain; that its stay there is highly injurious to British interests and honour; and that we ought instantly to call upon France to withdraw it.

There are, Sir, so many considerations connected with those propositions, that were I to enter into them all, they would carry me far beyond what is either necessary or expedient to be stated on the present occasion. Enough, perhaps, it is for me to say, that I do not see how the withdrawing of the French troops from Spain could effect our present purpose. I believe, Sir, that the French army in Spain is now a protection to that very party which it was originally called in to put down. Were the French army suddenly removed at this precise moment, I verily believe that the immediate effect of that removal would be, to give full scope to the unbridled rage of a fanatical faction, before which, in the whirlwind of intestine strife, the party least in numbers would be swept away.

So much for the immediate effect of the demand which it is proposed to us to make, if that demand were instantly successful. But when, with reference to the larger question of a military occupation of Spain by France, it is averred, that by that occupation the relative situation of Great Britain and France is altered; that France is thereby exalted and Great Britain lowered, in the eyes of Europe, I must beg leave to say that I dissent from that averment. The House knows, the country knows, that when the French army was on the point of entering Spain, his Majesty's government did all in their power to prevent it—that we resisted it by all means short of war. I have just now stated some of the reasons why we did not think the entry of that army into Spain a sufficient ground for war; but there was, in addition to those which I have stated, this peculiar reason—that whatever effect a war, commenced upon the mere ground of the entry of a French army into Spain, might have, it probably would not have had the effect of getting that army out of Spain. In a war against France at that time, as at any other, you might, perhaps, have acquired military glory; you might, perhaps, have extended your colonial possessions; you might even have achieved, at great cost of blood and treasure, an honourable peace; but as to getting the French out of Spain, that would have been the one object which you, almost certainly, would not have accomplished. How seldom, in the whole history of the wars of Europe, has any war between two great powers ended in the obtaining of the exact, the identical object, for which the war was begun?

Besides, Sir, I confess I think, that the effects of the French occupation of Spain have been infinitely exaggerated.

I do not blame those exaggerations, because I am aware that they are to be attributed to the recollections of some of the best times of our history; that they are the echoes of sentiments which, in the days of William and Anne, animated the debates, and dictated the votes of the British parliament. No peace was in those days thought safe for this country while the crown of Spain continued on the head of a Bourbon. But were not the apprehensions of those days greatly overstated? Has the power of Spain swallowed up the power of maritime England? Or does England still remain, after the lapse of more than a century, during which the crown of Spain has been worn by a Bourbon—niched in a nook of that same Spain—Gibraltar; an occupation which was contemporaneous with the apprehensions that I have described, and which has happily survived them?

Again, Sir, is the Spain of the present day the Spain of which the statesmen of the times of William and Anne were so much afraid? Is it indeed the nation whose puissance was expected to shake England from her sphere? No, Sir, it was quite another Spain. It was the Spain, within the limits of whose empire the sun never set—it was Spain "with the Indies" that excited the jealousies and alarmed the imaginations of our ancestors.

But then, Sir, the balance of power! The entry of the French army into Spain disturbed that balance, and we ought to have gone to war to restore it! I have already said, that when the French army entered Spain, we might, if we chose, have resisted or resented that measure by war. But were there no other means than war for restoring the balance of power? Is the balance of power a fixed and unalterable standard? Or is it not a standard perpetually varying, as civilisation advances, and as new nations spring up, and take their place among established political communities? The balance of power a century and a half ago was to be adjusted between France and Spain, the Netherlands, Austria, and England. Some years afterwards, Russia assumed her high station in European politics. Some years after that again, Prussia became not only a substantive, but a preponderating monarchy. Thus while the balance of power continued in principle the same, the means of adjusting it became more varied and enlarged. They became enlarged, in proportion to the increased number of considerable states: in proportion, I may say, to the number of weights which might be shifted into the one or the other scale. To look to the policy of Europe in the times of William and Anne, for the purpose of regulating the balance of power in Europe at the present day, is to disregard the progress of events, and to confuse dates and facts which throw a reciprocal light upon each other.

It would be disingenuous, indeed, not to admit that the entry of the French army into Spain was, in a certain sense, a disparagement —an affront to the pride—a blow to the feelings of England. And it can hardly be supposed that the government did not sympathise on that occasion with the feelings of the people. But I deny that, questionable or consurable as the act might be, it was one which necessarily called for our direct and hostile opposition. Was nothing then to be done? Was there no other mode of resistance, than by a direct attack upon France, or by a war to be undertaken on the soil of Spain? What, if the possession of Spain might be rendered harmless in rival hands—harmless as regards us, and valueless to the possessors? Might not compensation for disparagement be obtained, and the policy of our ancestors vindicated by means better adapted to the present time? If France occupied Spain, was it necessary, in order to avoid the consequences of that occupation, that we should blockade Cadiz? No. I looked another way. I sought materials of compensation in another hemisphere. Contemplating Spain, such as our ancestors had known her, I resolved that if France had Spain, it should not be Spain "with the Indies." I called the New World into existence, to redress the balance of the Old.

It is thus, Sir, that I answer the accusation brought against his Majesty's government, of having allowed the French army to usurp and to retain the occupation of Spain. That occupation, I am quite confident, is an unpaid and unredeemed burden to France. It is a burden of which, I verily believe, France would be glad to rid herself. But they know little of the feelings of the French government, and of the spirit of the French nation, who do not know, that, worthless or burdensome as that occupation may be, the way to rivet her in it would be, by angry or intemperate representations, to make the continuance of that occupation a point of honour.

I believe, Sir, there is no other subject on which I need enter into defence or explanation. The support which the Address has received, from all parties in the House, has been such as would make it both unseemly and ungrateful in me to trespass unnecessarily upon their patience. In conclusion, Sir, I shall only once more declare, that the object of the Address which I propose to you is not war;—its object is to take the last chance of peace. If you do not go forth, on this occasion, to the aid of Portugal, Portugal will be trampled down, to your irretrievable disgrace: and then will come war in the train of national degradation. If, under circumstances like these, you wait till Spain has matured her secret machinations into open hostility, you will in a little while have the sort of war required by the pacificators. And who shall say where that war will end?

WILLIAM COBBETT.
Born 1762. Died 1835.

[WILLIAM COBBETT is not a name that stands high in the list of orators, nevertheless so active was he both with voice and pen for many years, that some memorial of this extraordinary man may fairly come within the scope of this work. The specimen of his style which is here given may be studied as strikingly characteristic of his angrier moods, and however little the reader may sympathise with the sentiments expressed, it is impossible to deny the force and fire with which they are set down in the address which follows.]

ADDRESS TO THE INDUSTRIOUS CLASSES.
(On the Causes of Poverty and Misery in the Time of Cobbett.)

THE picture which our country exhibits at this moment, while it sinks our own hearts within us, fills the whole civilized world with wonder and amazement. This country has been famed, in all ages, not only for its freedom and for the security its laws gave to person and property, but for the happiness of its people, for the comfort they enjoyed, for the neatness and goodness of their dress, the good quality and the abundance of their household furniture, bedding, and utensils, and for the excellence and plenty of their food. So that a Lord Chancellor, who four hundred years ago wrote a book on our laws, observes in that book, that, owing to these good laws and the security and freedom they gave, the English people possessed, in abundance, *all things that conduce to make life easy and happy.*

This was the state of our great-grandfathers and great-grandmothers, who little thought of what was to befall their descendants! The very name of England was pronounced throughout the world with respect. That very name was thought to mean high-spirit, impartial justice, freedom, and happiness. What does it mean now? It means that which I have not the power to describe, nor the heart to describe, if I had the power. England now contains the most miserable people that ever trod the earth. It is the seat of greater human suffering, of more pain of body and mind, than was ever before heard of in the world. In countries which have been deemed the most wretched, there never has existed wretchedness equal to that which is now exhibited in this once flourishing, free, and happy country.

In this country the *law* provides that no human being shall suffer from want of food, lodging, or raiment. Our forefathers, when they gave security to property, when they made the laws to give to the *rich* the safe enjoyment of their wealth, did not forget that there must always be some *poor*, and that God wished that the poor should not perish for want, they being entitled to an existence as well as the rich. Therefore, the law said, and it still says, that to make a sure and certain provision for the poor, is required by the first principles of civil society. He who is rich to-day may be poor to-morrow; and he is not to starve because he is become unfortunate.

Upon this principle of common humanity and of natural justice the *Poor-laws* were founded; and those laws give to every one a *right*, a *legal* as well as an equitable right, to be maintained out of the real property of the country, if, from whatever cause, *unable* to obtain a maintenance through his or her own exertions. To receive parish-relief is no *favour!* it is no gift that the relieved person receives; it is what the *law* insures him; and what he cannot be refused without a breach of the law, and without an outrageous act of injustice and oppression.

Such being the law; that is, the law having taken care that relief shall always be at hand for the destitute, the law has forbidden *begging*. It has pointed out to every destitute person the place where he can obtain legal and effectual relief, and, therefore, it has said: "You shall not *beg*. If you beg, you shall be punished." And as we well know, punishment is frequently inflicted for begging.

But what do we see before our eyes at this moment? We see, all over the kingdom, misery existing to such an extent, that the Poor-laws are found insufficient, and that a system of *general beggary* is introduced, under the name of subscriptions, voluntary contributions, soup-shops, and the like, and, in the Metropolis, where our eyes are dazzled with the splendour of those who live on taxes, we see that a society has been formed for raising money to provide a receptacle for the *houseless poor* during the night; that is to say, to give a few hours' shelter to wretched beings, who must otherwise lie down and die in the very streets! To-day we read of a poor man expiring on his removal from one country parish to another. To-morrow we read of a poor woman, driven back from the door of one poor-house in London, carried back to expire in another poor-house before the morning. The next day we read of a man found dead in the street, and nearly a skeleton; while we daily see men harnessed and drawing carts loaded with gravel to repair the highways.

Is this *England?* Can this be *England?* And can these wretched and miserable and degraded objects be *Englishmen?* Yes, this is England; with grief, shame, and indignation we must confess it; but still we must confess that such is now once free and happy England! That same country that was until of late years famed throughout the world for all that was great, good, amiable, and enviable.

This change never can have taken place without *a cause*. There must have been something, and something done *by man*, too, to produce this change, this disgraceful, this distressing, this horrible change. God has not afflicted the country with pestilence or with famine; nor has the land been invaded and ravaged by an enemy. Providence has, of late, been more than ordinarily benevolent to us. Three successive *harvests* of uncommon abundance have blessed, or would have blessed, these islands. *Peace* has been undisturbed. War appears not to have been even thought possible. The sounds of warlike glory have, even yet, hardly ceased to vibrate on our ears. And yet, in the midst of profound peace and abundant harvests, the nation seems to be convulsed with the last struggles of gnawing hunger.

It is *man*, therefore, and not a *benevolent Creator*, who has been the cause of our sufferings, present and past, and of the more horrid sufferings, which we now but reasonably anticipate. To *man*, therefore, must we look for *an account* of these evils, into the cause of which let us, without any want of charity, but, at the same time, without fear and without self-deception, freely inquire.

My good, honest, kind, and industrious country-people, you have long been deceived by artful and intriguing and interested men, who have a *press* at their command, and who, out of taxes raised from your labour, have persuaded you that your sufferings arise from nothing that *man* can cause or *cure*. But have only a little patience with me, and I think that I am able to convince you, that your sufferings and your degradation have arisen from the *weight of taxes imposed on you*, and from *no other cause whatever*.

When you consider that your salt, pepper, soap, candles, sugar, tea, beer, shoes, and all other things are taxed, you must see that you *pay taxes* yourselves; and when you consider that the taxes paid by your richer neighbours disable them from paying you so much in wages as they would otherwise pay you, you must perceive, that taxes are *disadvantageous* to you. In short, it is a fact that no man can deny, that the poverty and misery of the people have gone on increasing precisely in the same degree that the taxes have gone on increasing.

The tax on *salt is fifteen shillings* a bushel. Its cost at the *sea-side*, where a kind Providence throws it abundantly on our shores, is *one shilling*. Owing to the delays and embarrassments arising from the tax, the price comes, at last, to *twenty shillings!* Thus, a bushel of salt, which is about as much as a middling family uses in a year (in all sorts of ways), costs to that family *eighteen shillings*, at least, *in tax!* Now, if an industrious man's family had the eighteen shillings in pocket, instead of paying them in tax, would not that family be the *better* for the change? If, instead of paying sixpence for a pot of beer (if beer a man must have) he had to pay twopence, would not he be fourpence the richer? And if the taxes were light instead of heavy, would not your wages and profits enable you to live better and dress better than you now do?

They who have good health, good luck, and small families, make a shift to go along with this load of taxes. Others bend under it. Others come down to poverty. And a great part of these are pressed to the very earth, some ending their days in workhouses, and others perishing from actual want. The farmers are daily falling into ruin; the little farmers fall first; the big ones become little, and the little ones become paupers, unless they escape from the country, while they have money enough to carry them away. Thousands of men of some property are, at this moment, preparing to quit the country. The *poor* cannot go; so that things, without a great change, will be worse and worse for all that remain, except for those who live upon the taxes.

And how are these taxes *disposed of?* We are told by impudent men, who live on these taxes, that *we*, the payers of the taxes, are become *too learned;* that we have been brought *too near* to the Government; that is to say, that we have got *a peep behind the curtain*. It is well known that a great deal has been said about *educating* the poor. At one time, even the *poverty* was ascribed to a *want of education* amongst the labouring classes. They were *so ignorant*, and that was the cause of their misery. And poor Mr. Whitbread said that the Scotch were better than the English, only because they were *better educated*. But now, behold, we are *too well educated:* we are too knowing; we have approached *too near* to the Government; and therefore *new laws* have been passed to keep us at a greater distance; a *more respectful* distance.

This precaution comes, however, too late. We have had our look behind the curtain. We cannot be again deluded. We cannot be made to *unknow* that which we know. We know that the fruit of our labour is *mortgaged* to those who have lent money to the Government. We know, that to pay the interest of this mortgage—to pay a standing army in time of peace—to pay the tax-gatherers—and to pay placemen and pensioners, we are so heavily taxed, that we can no longer live in comfort, and that many of us are wholly destitute of food, and are brought to our deaths by hunger.

Endeavours have been made to persuade us, that *we* are not hurt by the taxes. It has been said, that taxes *come back* to us, and are a *great blessing* to us. And Mr. Justice Bailey has lately taken occasion to say from the bench, that a *national debt* is a good thing, and even a necessary thing. England did pretty well without a debt for *seven hundred years!* How this matter came to be talked of from the bench I do not know; but for my part I look upon a national debt as the greatest curse that ever afflicted a people. In our country it has made a happy people miserable, and a free people slaves. And I am convinced that, unless that debt be got rid of in some way or other, and that, too, in a short time, this country will fall so low, that a century will not see it revive.

Those who wish to make us believe that it is not the taxes that make us poor and miserable, tell us that they come back to us. This being a grand source of delusion, I will endeavour to explain the matter to you. I have done it many times; but all eyes are not opened at the first operation; and, besides, there are, every month, some young persons who are beginning to read about such things.

Burke, of whom many of you never heard, said that *taxes* were *dews*, drawn up by the blessed sun of government, and sent down again upon the people in refreshing and fructifying *showers*. This was a very pretty description, but very false. For taxes, though they fall in heavy showers upon one part of the community, never return to another part of it. To those who live on taxes, the taxes are, indeed, refreshing and fructifying showers; but to those who pay them, they are a scorching sun and a blighting wind. They draw away the riches of the soil, and they render it sterile and unproductive. But how came this Burke to talk in this way? Why, he was one of those who lived upon the taxes! Very fine and refreshing and fertilizing showers fell upon *him*. He had a pension of *three thousand pounds a year for his life;* his wife, *fifteen hundred pounds a year for her life;* and besides these, he obtained, in 1795, grants of money to be paid yearly to his executors *after his death!* And not a trifle neither; for he took care to get this settled upon *executors*, *two thousand five hundred pounds a year*. The following is a copy of the grant:—

"To the executors of Edmund Burke, £2,500 a year. Granted by two patents, dated 24th October, 1795—One for £1,100 a year, to be paid during the life of Lord Royston, and the Rev. and Hon. Auchild Grey.

The other for £1,340 to be paid during the life of the Princess Amelia, Lord Althorp, and William Cavendish, Esq."

Now, as Mr. Grey is still alive, and as Lord Althorp and Mr. Cavendish are alive, the money is all of it still paid to the executors of Burke; these executors have already received on this account *more than fifty thousand pounds* in principal money; and as there is no probability of the death of the gentlemen above-named, they may yet receive double the sum. Burke's pension, while he was alive, cost the nation about *twenty thousand pounds*; and his wife's about *four thousand pounds*. So that here are about *seventy-four thousand pounds* already paid by the public on account of this one man, and that, too, in *principal money*, without reckoning *interest*!

This, you will allow, must have been to Burke, his wife, and executors, an exceedingly refreshing and fructifying shower! But not so to those who have had to pay this money. It has not tended to refresh us. In the space of twenty-seven years, seventy-four thousand pounds have been taken from us, who pay the taxes, on account of this *one man*. Now, suppose a different mode from the present were used in making us pay taxes. The pensions have, for the last twenty-seven years, amounted to £2,740 a year. Suppose the amount of them to have been raised upon fifty tradesmen, at £54 a year each. Would not each of these tradesmen be now £2,700 poorer than they would have been, if they had not had these "refreshing showers," to send off in dews? Suppose them to be raised upon 400 labourers at about £10 each. Must not these 400 labourers be made poor and miserable, must they not be prevented from saving a penny; and must they not, at last, be brought to the poorhouse by these "refreshing showers?" Is not this as plain as the nose on your face? Is it not plain that this pension to the executors of this man now takes away the means of comfortable living from nearly *four hundred labourers' families?* Has not this been going on for twenty-seven years; and has one single man in Parliament made even an effort to put a stop to it? Has one single man moved even for an inquiry into the matter? And yet the facts are all before the Parliament in their own printed reports!

And what services did this Burke render the country? For to give such a man such enormous sums, there must have been some reason. His services were these: He deserted his party in the Opposition; and he wrote three pamphlets to urge the nation on to war, and to cause it to persevere in the war, against the republicans of France! Which war raised the annual taxes from *sixteen* millions a year in time of peace, to *fifty-three* millions a year in time of peace, and the poor-rates from *two millions* a year to about *twelve millions* a year! These were the services which were so great, that it was not sufficient to give him *three thousand* pounds a year for them during his life-time, but we must still pay the executors *two thousand five hundred pounds* a year; and may have to pay them this for fifty years yet to come!

Need we wonder that we are poor? Need we wonder that we are miserable? Need we wonder that we have, at last, come to see Englishmen harnessed and drawing carts, loaded with gravel? And if we complain of these things, are we to be told that we are seditious? Are we to be told that we wish to destroy the Constitution? Are we to be imprisoned, fined, and banished?

DANIEL WEBSTER.

Born 1782. *Died* 1852.

CHARACTER OF TRUE ELOQUENCE.

WHEN public bodies are to be addressed on momentous occasions, when great interests are at stake, and strong passions excited, nothing is valuable, in speech, farther than it is connected with high intellectual and moral endowments. Clearness, force, and earnestness, are the qualities which produce conviction. True eloquence, indeed, does not consist in speech. It cannot be brought from far. Labour and learning may toil for it, but they will toil in vain. Words and phrases may be marshalled in every way, but they cannot compass it. It must exist in the man, in the subject, and in the occasion. Affected passion, intense expression, the pomp of declamation, all may aspire after it—they cannot reach it. It comes, if it come at all, like the outbreaking of a fountain from the earth, or the bursting forth of volcanic fires, with spontaneous, original, native force. The graces taught in the schools, the costly ornaments, and studied contrivances of speech, shock and disgust men, when their own lives, and the fate of their wives, their children, and their country, hang on the decision of the hour. Then words have lost their power, rhetoric is vain, and all elaborate oratory contemptible. Even genius itself then feels rebuked and subdued, as in the presence of higher qualities. Then patriotism is eloquent; then self-devotion is eloquent. The clear conception, outrunning the deductions of logic, the high purpose, the firm resolve, the dauntless spirit, speaking on the tongue, beaming from the eye, informing every feature, and urging the whole man onward, right onward to his object—this, this is eloquence: or rather it is something greater and higher than all eloquence—it is action, noble, sublime, godlike action.

HENRY GRATTAN.
Born 1750.   Died 1820.

[THE subjoined speech was delivered by Grattan in the House of Commons on the 25th May, 1815, and is a grand specimen of his varied power. In the language of a late eloquent editor of Grattan's speeches (Mr. D. O. Madden) "it may be said with truth, that the speeches of Grattan are a valuable contribution to political philosophy, well meriting the best attention of the statesman, the historian, and the philosopher. The thinking power to be found in all his speeches, combined with his vivid imagery, his singular mastery over rhythm, and the impassioned spirit pervading them, form their distinctive characteristics. There never was such an union of the orator and the sage." Apart from the historical interest which attaches to its subject, the following speech is remarkable also for its lofty and generous estimate of the characters of Fox and Burke, which occurs towards its close.]

THE DOWNFALL OF BUONAPARTE.

SIR, I sincerely sympathize with the honourable gentleman who spoke last in his anxiety on this important question; and my solicitude is increased by a knowledge that I differ in opinion from my oldest political friends. I have further to contend against the additional weight given to the arguments of the noble lord who moved the amendment, by the purity of his mind, the soundness of his judgment, and the elevation of his rank. I agree with my honourable friends in thinking that we ought not to impose a government upon France. I agree with them in deprecating the evil of war; but I deprecate still more the double evil of a peace without securities, and a war without allies. Sir, I wish it was a question between peace and war; but, unfortunately for the country, very painfully to us, and most injuriously to all ranks of men, peace is not in our option; and the real question is, whether we shall go to war when our allies are assembled, or fight the battle when those allies shall be dissipated?

Sir, the French government is war; it is a statocracy, elective, aggressive, and predatory; her armies live to fight, and fight to live; their constitution is essentially war, and the object of that war the conquest of Europe. What such a person as Buonaparte at the head of such a constitution will do, you may judge by what he has done; and, first, he took possession of the greater part of Europe; he made his son King of Rome; he made his son-in-law Viceroy of Italy; he made his brother King of Holland; he made his brother-in-law King of Naples; he imprisoned the King of Spain; he banished the Regent of Portugal, and formed his plan to take possession of the crown of England. England had checked his designs; her trident had stirred up his empire from its foundation; he complained of her tyranny at sea; but it was her power at sea which arrested his tyranny on land — the navy of England saved Europe. Knowing this, he knew the conquest of England became necessary for the accomplishment of the conquest of Europe, and the destruction of her marine necessary for the conquest of England. Accordingly, besides raising an army of 60,000 men for the invasion of England, he applied himself to the destruction of her commerce, the foundation of her naval power. In pursuit of this object, and on his plan of a western empire, he conceived, and in part executed, the design of consigning to plunder and destruction the vast regions of Russia; he quits the genial clime of the temperate zone; he bursts through the narrow limits of an immense empire; he abandons comfort and security, and he hurries to the pole, to hazard them all, and with them the companions of his victories, and the fame and fruits of his crimes and his talents, on speculation of leaving in Europe, throughout the whole of its extent, no one free or independent nation. To oppose this huge conception of mischief and despotism, the great potentate of the north, from his gloomy recesses, advances to defend himself against the voracity of ambition amid the sterility of his empire. Ambition is omnivorous—it feasts on famine and sheds tons of blood, that it may starve in ice, in order to commit a robbery on desolation. The power of the North, I say, joins another prince, whom Buonaparte had deprived of almost the whole of his authority, the King of Prussia, and then another potentate, whom Buonaparte had deprived of the principal part of his dominions, the Emperor of Austria. These three powers, physical causes, final justice, the influence of your victories in Spain and Portugal, and the spirit given to Europe by the achievements and renown of your great commander (the Duke of Wellington), together with the precipitation of his own ambition, combine to accomplish his destruction. Buonaparte is conquered. He who said: " I will be like the Most High:" he who smote the nations with a continual stroke—this short-lived son of the morning, Lucifer, falls, and the Earth is at rest; the phantom of royalty passes on to nothing, and the three kings to the gates of Paris; there they stand, the late victims of his ambition, and now the disposers of his destiny and the masters of his empire; without provocation he had gone to their countries with fire and sword; with the greatest provocation they come to his country with life and liberty; they do an act unparalleled in the annals of history, such as nor envy, nor time, nor malice, nor prejudice, nor ingratitude can efface; they give to his subjects liberty, and to himself life and royalty. This is greater than conquest! The present race must confess their virtues, and ages to come must crown their monuments, and place them above heroes and kings in glory everlasting.

When Buonaparte states the conditions of the treaty of Fontainebleau are not performed, he forgets one of them, namely, the condition by which he lives. It is very true there was a mixture of policy and prudence in this measure; but it was a great act of magnanimity notwithstanding, and it is not in Providence to turn such an act to your disadvantage. With respect to the other act, the mercy shown to his people, I have underrated it; the allies did not give liberty to France, they enabled her to give a constitution to herself, a better constitution than that which, with much laboriousness, and circumspection, and deliberation, and procrastination, the philosophers fabricated, when the Jacobins trampled down the flimsy work, murdered the vain philosophers, drove out the crazy reformers, and remained masters of the field in the triumph of superior anarchy and confusion; better than that, I say, which the Jacobin destroyed, better than that which he afterwards formed, with some method in his madness, and more madness in his method; with such a horror of power, that in his plan of a constitution he left out a government, and with so many wheels that everything was in movement and nothing in concert, so that the machine took fire from its own velocity in the midst of death and mirth, with images emblematic of the public disorder, goddesses of reason turned fool, and of liberty turned fury. At length the French found their advantage in adopting the sober and unaffected security of King, Lords, and Commons, on the idea of that form of government which your ancestors procured by their firmness, and maintained by their discretion. The people had attempted to give the French liberty, and had failed; the wise men (so her philosophers called themselves) had attempted to give liberty to France, and had failed; it remained for the extraordinary destiny of the French to receive their free constitution from kings. This constitution Buonaparte has destroyed, together with the treaty of Fontainebleau, and having broken both, desires your confidence; Russia confided, and was deceived; Austria confided, and was deceived. Have we forgotten the treaty of Luneville, and his abominable conduct to the Swiss? Spain and other nations of Europe confided, and all were deceived. During the whole of this time he was charging on England the continuation of the war, while he was, with uniform and universal perfidy, breaking his own treaties of peace for the purpose of renewing the war, to end it in what was worse than war itself—his conquest of Europe.

But now he repents and will be faithful! he says so, but he says the contrary also: "I protest against the validity of the treaty of Fontainebleau; it was not done with the consent of the people; I protest against everything done in my absence; see my speech to the army and people; see the speech of my council to me." The treaty of Paris was done in his absence; by that treaty were returned the French colonies and prisoners: thus he takes life and empire from the treaty of Fontainebleau, with an original design to set it aside; and he takes prisoners and colonies from the treaty of Paris, which he afterwards sets aside also; and he musters an army, by a singular fatality, in a great measure composed of troops who owe their enlargement, and of a chief who owes his life, to the powers he fights, by the resources of France, who owes to those powers her salvation. He gives a reason for this: "Nothing is good which was done without the consent of the people" (having been deposed by that people, and elected by the army in their defiance). With such sentiments, which go not so much against this or that particular treaty as against the principles of alliance, the question is, whether, with a view to the security of Europe, you will take the faith of Napoleon, or the army of your allies?

Gentlemen maintain, that we are not equal to the contest; that is to say, confederated Europe cannot fight France single-handed. If that be your opinion, you are conquered this moment; you are conquered in spirit: but that is not your opinion, nor was it the opinion of your ancestors. They thought, and I hope transmitted the sentiment as your birth-right, that the armies of these islands could always fight, and fight with success their own numbers. See now the numbers you are to command: by this treaty you are to have in the field what may be reckoned not less than 600,000 men; besides that stipulated army you have at command, what may be reckoned as much more,—I say you and the allies. The Emperor of Austria alone has an army of 500,000 men, of which 120,000 were sent to Italy to oppose Murat, who is now beaten; Austria is not, then, occupied by Murat; Prussia is not occupied by the Saxon, nor Russia by the Pole,—at least, not so occupied that they have not ample and redundant forces for this war; you have a general never surpassed, and allies in heart and confidence. See now Buonaparte's muster: he has lost his external dominions, and is reduced from a population of 100,000,000, to a population of 25,000,000; besides, he has lost the power of fascination, for though he may be called the subverter of kings, he has not proved to be the redresser of grievances. Switzerland has not forgotten, all Europe remembers the nature of his reformation, and that the best reform he introduced was worse than the worst government he subverted. As little can Spain or Prussia forget what was worse even than his reformations, the march of his armies: it was not an army; it was a military government in march, like the Roman legions in Rome's worst time, Italica or Rapax, responsible to nothing, nor God, nor man. Thus he has administered a cure to his partisans for any enthusiasm that might have been annexed to his name, and is now reduced to his resources at home; it is at home that he must feed his armies and find his strength, and at home he wants artillery, he wants cavalry; he has no money, he has no credit, he has no title. With respect to his actual numbers, they are not ascertained, but it may be collected that they bear no proportion to those of the allies.

But gentlemen presume that the French nation will rise in his favour as soon as we enter their country. We entered their country before, but they did not rise in his favour; on the contrary, they deposed him; the article of deposition is given at length. It is said we endeavour to impose a government on France. The French armies elect a conqueror for Europe, and our resistance to this conqueror is called imposing a government on France; if we put down this chief, we relieve France as well as Europe from a foreign yoke, and this deliverance is called the imposition of a government on France. He—he imposed a government on France; he imposed a foreign yoke on France; he took from the French their property by contribution; he took their children by conscription; he lost her empire, and a thing almost unimaginable, he brought the enemy to the gates of Paris. We, on the contrary, formed a project, as appears from a paper of 1805, which preserved the integrity of the French empire; the allies, in 1814, not only preserved the integrity of the empire as it stood in 1792, but gave her her liberty, and they now afford her the only chance of redemption. Against these allies will France now combine, and having received from them her empire as it stood before the war, with additions in consequence of their deposition of Buonaparte, and having gotten back her capital, her colonies, and her prisoners, will she break the treaty to which she owes them; rise up against the allies who gave them; break her oath of allegiance; destroy the constitution she has formed; depose the King she has chosen; rise up against her own deliverance, in support of contribution and conscription, to perpetuate her political damnation under the yoke of a stranger?

Gentlemen say France has elected him. They have no grounds for so saying; he had been repulsed at Antibes, and he lost thirty men; he landed near Cannes the 1st of March, with 1,100. With this force he proceeded to Grasse, Digne, Gap, and on the 7th he entered Grenoble; he there got from the desertion of regiments above 3,000 men and a park of artillery; with this additional force he proceeded to Lyons; he left Lyons with about 7,000 strong, and entered Paris on the 20th, with all the troops of the line that had been sent to oppose him; the following day he reviewed his troops; and nothing could equal the shouts of the army except the silence of the people. This was, in the strictest sense of the word, a military election: it was an act where the army deposed the civil government; it was the march of a military chief over a conquered people. The nation did not rise to resist Buonaparte or to defend Louis, because the nation could not rise upon the army; her mind as well as her constitution was conquered; in fact, there was no nation; everything was army, and everything was conquest. France had passed through all the degrees of political probation, revolution, counter-revolution, wild democracy, intense despotism, outrageous anarchy, philosophy, vanity, and madness; and now she lay exhausted, for horse, foot, and dragoons to exercise her power, to appoint her a master—captain or cornet who should put the brand of his name upon her government, calling it his dynasty, and under this stamp of dishonour pass her on to futurity.

Buonaparte, it seems, is to reconcile everything by the gift of a free constitution. He took possession of Holland, he did not give her a free constitution; he took possession of Spain, he did not give her a free constitution; he took possession of Switzerland, whose independence he had guaranteed, he did not give her a free constitution; he took possession of Italy, he did not give her a free constitution; he took possession of France, he did not give her a free constitution; on the contrary, he destroyed the directorial constitution, he destroyed the consular constitution, and he destroyed the late constitution formed on the plan of England! But now he is, with the assistance of the Jacobins, to give her liberty; that is, the man who can bear no freedom, unites to form a constitution with a body who can bear no government! In the mean time, while he professes liberty, he exercises despotic power, he annihilates the nobles, he banishes the deputies of the people, and he sequesters the property of the emigrants. "Now he is to give liberty!" I have seen his constitution, as exhibited in the newspaper; there are faults innumerable in the frame of it, and more in the manner of accepting it: it is to be passed by subscription without discussion, the troops are to send deputies, and the army is to preside. There is some cunning, however, in making the subscribers to the constitution renounce the house of Bourbon; they are to give their word for the deposition of the king, and take Napoleon's word for their own liberty; the offer imports nothing which can be relied on, except that he is afraid of the allies. Disperse the alliance, and farewell to the liberty of France and the safety of Europe.

Under this head of ability to combat Buonaparte, I think we should not despair.

With respect to the justice of the cause, we must observe, Buonaparte has broken the treaty of Fontainebleau; he confesses it; he declares he never considered himself as bound by it. If, then, that treaty is out of the way, he is as he was before it—at war. As Emperor of the French, he has broken the treaty of Paris; that treaty was founded on his abdication; when he proposes to observe the treaty of Paris, he proposes what he cannot do unless he abdicates.

The proposition that we should not interfere with the government of other nations is true, but true with qualifications. If the government of any other country contains an insurrectionary principle, as France did when she offered to aid the insurrections of her neighbours, your interference is warranted; if the government of another country contains the principle of universal empire, as France did, and promulgated, your interference is justifiable. Gentlemen may call this internal government, but I call this conspiracy; if the government of another country maintains a predatory army, such as Buonaparte's, with a view to hostility and conquest, your interference is just. He may call this internal government, but I call this a preparation for war. No doubt he will accompany this with offers of peace; but such offers of peace are nothing more than one of the arts of war, attended, most assuredly, by charging on you the odium of a long and protracted contest, and with much common-place, and many good saws and sayings of the miseries of bloodshed, and the savings and good husbandry of peace, and the comforts of a quiet life; but if you listen to this, you will be much deceived; not only deceived, but you will be beaten. Again, if the government of another country covers more ground in Europe, and destroys the balance of power, so as to threaten the independence of other nations, this is a cause of your interference. Such was the principle upon which we acted in the best times; such was the principle of the grand alliance; such the triple alliance; and such the quadruple; and by such principles has Europe not only been regulated, but protected. If a foreign government does any of those acts I have mentioned, we have a cause of war; but if a foreign power does all of them, forms a conspiracy for universal empire, keeps up an army for that purpose, employs that army to overturn the balance of power, and attempts the conquest of Europe—attempts, do I say? in a great degree achieves it (for what else was Buonaparte's dominion before the battle of Leipsic?), and then receives an overthrow, owes its deliverance to treaties which give that power its life, and these countries their security (for what did you get from France but security?); if this power, I say, avails itself of the conditions in the treaties which give it colonies, prisoners, and deliverance, and breaks those conditions which give you security, and resumes the same situation which renders this power capable of repeating the same atrocity, has England, or has she not, a right of war?

Having considered the two questions,—that of ability, and that of right,—and having shown that you are justified on either consideration to go to war, let me now suppose that you treat for peace. First, you will have a peace upon a war establishment, and then a war without your present allies. It is not certain that you will have any of them, but it is certain that you will not have the same combination while Buonaparte increases his power by confirmation of his title and by further preparation; so that you will have a bad peace and a bad war. Were I disposed to treat for peace, I would not agree to the amendment, because it disperses your allies and strengthens your enemy, and says to both, we will quit our alliance to confirm Napoleon on the throne of France, that he may hereafter more advantageously fight us, as he did before, for the throne of England.

Gentlemen set forth the pretensions of Buonaparte; gentlemen say that he has given liberty to the press. He has given liberty to publication, to be afterwards tried and punished according to the present constitution of France —as a military chief pleases; that is to say, he has given liberty to the French to hang themselves. Gentlemen say, he has in his dominions abolished the slave trade. I am unwilling to deny him praise for such an act; but if we praise him for giving liberty to the African, let us not assist him in imposing slavery on the European. Gentlemen say, Will you make war upon character? But the question is, will you trust a government without one? What will you do if you are conquered? say gentlemen. I answer, the very thing you must do if you treat,—abandon the Low Countries. But the question is, in which case are you most likely to be conquered—with allies or without them? Either you must abandon the Low Countries, or you must preserve them by arms; for Buonaparte will not be withheld by treaty. If you abandon them, you will lose your situation on the globe; and instead of being a medium of communication and commerce between the new world and the old, you will become an anxious station between two fires—the continent of America, rendered hostile by the intrigues of France; and the continent of Europe, possessed by her arms. It then remains for you to determine, if you do not abandon the Low Countries, in what way you mean to defend them, alone or with allies.

Gentlemen complain of the allies, and say,

they have partitioned such a country, and transferred such a country, and seized on such a country. What! will they quarrel with their ally, who has possessed himself of a part of Saxony, and shake hands with Buonaparte, who proposed to take possession of England? If a prince takes Venice, we are indignant; but if he seizes on a great part of Europe, stands covered with the blood of millions, and the spoils of half mankind, our indignation ceases; vice becomes gigantic, conquers the understanding, and mankind begin by wonder, and conclude by worship. The character of Buonaparte is admirably calculated for this effect; he invests himself with much theatrical grandeur; he is a great actor in the tragedy of his own government; the fire of his genius precipitates on universal empire, certain to destroy his neighbours or himself; better formed to acquire empire than to keep it, he is a hero and a calamity, formed to punish France and to perplex Europe.

The authority of Mr. Fox has been alluded to,—a great authority and a great man; his name excites tenderness and wonder; to do justice to that immortal person you must not limit your view to this country; his genius was not confined to England, it acted three hundred miles off in breaking the chains of Ireland; it was seen three thousand miles off in communicating freedom to the Americans; it was visible, I know not how far off, in ameliorating the condition of the Indian; it was discernible on the coast of Africa in accomplishing the abolition of the slave trade. You are to measure the magnitude of his mind by parallels of latitude. His heart was as soft as that of a woman; his intellect was adamant; his weaknesses were virtues; they protected him against the hard habit of a politician, and assisted nature to make him amiable and interesting. The question discussed by Mr. Fox in 1792, was, whether you would treat with a revolutionary government? The present is, whether you will confirm a military and a hostile one? You will observe that when Mr. Fox was willing to treat, the French, it was understood, were ready to evacuate the Low Countries. If you confirm the present government, you must expect to lose them. Mr. Fox objected to the idea of driving France upon her resources, lest you should make her a military government. The question now is, whether you will make that military government perpetual. I therefore do not think the theory of Mr. Fox can be quoted against us; and the practice of Mr. Fox tends to establish our proposition, for he treated with Buonaparte and failed. Mr. Fox was tenacious of England, and would never yield an iota of her superiority; but the failure of the attempt to treat was to be found, not in Mr. Fox, but in Buonaparte.

On the French subject, speaking of authority, we cannot forget Mr. Burke—Mr. Burke, the prodigy of nature and acquisition. He read everything, he saw everything, he foresaw everything. His knowledge of history amounted to a power of foretelling; and when he perceived the wild work that was doing in France, that great political physician, intelligent of symptoms, distinguished between the access of fever and the force of health; and what other men conceived to be the vigour of her constitution, he knew to be no more than the paroxysm of her madness, and then, prophet-like, he pronounced the destinies of France, and, in his prophetic fury, admonished nations.

Gentlemen speak of the Bourbon family. I have already said, we should not force the Bourbon upon France; but we owe it to departed (I would rather say to interrupted) greatness, to observe, that the House of Bourbon was not tyrannical; under her, everything, except the administration of the country, was open to animadversion; every subject was open to discussion—philosophical, ecclesiastical, and political, so that learning, and arts, and sciences, made progress. Even England consented to borrow not a little from the temperate meridian of that government. Her court stood controlled by opinion, limited by principles of honour, and softened by the influence of manners: and, on the whole, there was an amenity in the condition of France, which rendered the French an amiable, an enlightened, a gallant, and an accomplished race. Over this gallant race you see imposed an Oriental despotism. Their present court (Buonaparte's court) has gotten the idiom of the East as well as her constitution; a fantastic and barbaric expression: an unreality, which leaves in the shade the modesty of truth, and states nothing as it is, and everything as it is not. The attitude is affected, the taste is corrupted, and the intellect perverted. Do you wish to confirm this military tyranny in the heart of Europe? A tyranny founded on the triumph of the army over the principles of civil government, tending to universalize throughout Europe the domination of the sword, and to reduce to paper and parchment, Magna Charta and all our civil institutions. An experiment such as no country ever made, and no good country would ever permit; to relax the moral and religious influences; to set Heaven and Earth adrift from one another, and make God Almighty a tolerated alien in His own creation; an insurrectionary hope to every bad man in the community, and a frightful lesson to profit and power, vested in those who have pandered their allegiance from king to emperor, and now found their pretensions to domination on the merit of breaking their oaths and deposing their sovereign. Should you do anything so monstrous as to leave your allies in order to confirm such a system; should you forget your name, forget your ancestors, and the inheritance they have left you of morality and renown; should you astonish Europe, by quitting your allies to render immortal such a composition, would not the nations exclaim, "You have very providently watched over our interests, and very generously have you contributed to our service, and do you falter now? In vain have you stopped in your own person the flying fortunes of Europe; in vain have you taken the eagle of Napoleon, and snatched *invincibility* from his standard, if now, when confederated Europe is ready to march, you take the lead in the desertion, and preach the penitence of Buonaparte and the poverty of England?"

As to her poverty, you must not consider the money you spend in your defence, but the fortune you would lose if you were not defended; and further, you must recollect you will pay less to an immediate war than to a peace with a war establishment, and a war to follow it. Recollect further, that whatever be your resources, they must outlast those of all your enemies; and further, that your empire cannot be saved by a calculation. Besides, your wealth is only a part of your situation. The name you have established, the deeds you have achieved, and the part you have sustained, preclude you from a second place among nations; and when you cease to be the first you are nothing.

EDMUND BURKE.
The Duty of Representatives.

IT ought to be the happiness and glory of a representative to live in the strictest union, the closest correspondence, and the most unreserved communication with his constituents. Their wishes ought to have great weight with him; their opinion high respect; their business unremitted attention. It is his duty to sacrifice his repose, his pleasures, his satisfactions, to theirs; and above all, ever and in all cases, to prefer their interest to his own. But, his unbiassed opinion, his mature judgment, his enlightened conscience, he ought not to sacrifice to you, to any man, or to any set of men living. These he does not derive from your pleasure; no, nor from the law and the constitution. They are a trust from Providence, for the abuse of which he is deeply answerable. Your representative owes you, not his industry only, but his judgment; and he betrays, instead of serving you, if he sacrifices it to your opinion.

WENDELL PHILLIPS.
Living.

[THE name of Wendell Phillips, together with that of his friend and fellow-labourer, W. Lloyd Garrison, has been for many years past associated with the Abolition Cause in America, of which he has ever been the most eloquent champion. His style, though not such as we are much accustomed to in this country, as will be seen from the address which we quote, is grand and glowing, and in every way admirably suited to the large assemblies which his name and reputation can at any moment call together. The speech which follows was delivered on the 28th January, 1852, before the Massachusetts Anti-Slavery Society, and though somewhat tinctured by the special politics of its time, has sufficient of general interest both in its theme and the treatment of it, to make it appreciable by all English readers.]

Public Opinion on the Abolition Question.

MR. PRESIDENT:—I have been thinking, while sitting here, of the different situations of the Anti-slavery cause now and one year ago, when the last anniversary of this society was held. To some, it may seem that we had more sources of interest and of public excitement on that occasion than we have now. We had with us, during a portion, at least, of that session, the eloquent advocate of our cause on the other side of the water. We had the local excitement and the deep interest which the first horror of the Fugitive Slave Bill had aroused. We had, I believe, some fugitives, just arrived from the house of bondage. It may seem to many that, meeting as we do to-day robbed of all these, we must be content with a session more monotonous and less effectual in arousing the community. But when we look over the whole land; when we look back upon what has taken place in our own Commonwealth, at Christiana, at Syracuse; look at the passage through the country of the great Hungarian; at the present state of the public mind —it seems to me that no year, during the existence of the society, has presented more encouraging aspects to the Abolitionists. The views which our friend (Parker Pillsbury) has just presented, are those upon which, in our most sober calculation, we ought to rely. Give us time, and, as he said, talk is all-powerful. We are apt to feel ourselves over-shadowed in the presence of colossal institutions. We are apt, in coming up to a meeting of this kind, to ask what a few hundred or a few thousand persons can do against the weight of government, the mountainous side of majorities, the influence of the press, the power of the pulpit, the organization of parties, the omnipotence of wealth. At times, to carry a favourite purpose, leading statesmen have endeavoured to cajole the people into the idea that this age was like the past, and that a "rub-a-dub agitation," as ours is contemptuously styled, was only to be despised. The time has been when, as our friend observed, from the steps of the Revere House—yes, and from the depots of New York railroads.—Mr. Webster has described this Anti-slavery movement as a succession of lectures in schoolhouses—the mere efforts of a few hundred men and women to talk together, excite each other, arouse the public, and its only result a little noise. He knew better. He knew better the times in which he lived. No matter where you meet a dozen earnest men pledged to a new idea—wherever you have met them, you have met the beginning of a revolution. Revolutions are not made: they come. A revolution is as natural a growth as an oak. It comes out of the past. Its foundations are laid far back. The child feels; he grows into a man, and thinks; another, perhaps, speaks, and the world acts out the thought. And this is the history of modern society. Men undervalue the Anti-slavery movement, because they imagine you can always put your finger on some illustrious moment in history, and say, here commenced the great change which has come over the nation. Not so. The beginning of great changes is like the rise of the Mississippi. A child must stoop and gather away the pebbles to find it. But soon it swells broader and broader, bears on its ample bosom the navies of a mighty republic, fills the Gulf, and divides a Continent.

I remember a story of Napoleon which illustrates my meaning. We are apt to trace his control of France to some noted victory, to the time when he camped in the Tuileries, or when he dissolved the Assembly by the stamp of his foot. He reigned, in fact, when his hand was first felt on the helm of the vessel of state, and that was far back of the time when he had conquered in Italy, or his name had been echoed over two continents. It was on the day when five hundred irresolute men were met in that Assembly which called itself, and pretended to be, the government of France. They heard that the mob of Paris was coming the next morning, thirty thousand strong, to turn them, as was usual in those days, out of doors. And where did this seemingly great power go for its support and refuge? They sent Tallien to seek out a boy lieutenant—the shadow of an officer —so thin and pallid, that, when he was placed on the stand before them, the President of the Assembly, fearful, if the fate of France rested on the shrunken form, the ashy cheek before him, that all hope was gone, asked, "Young man, can you protect the Assembly?" And the stern lips of the Corsican boy parted only to reply, "I always do what I undertake." Then and there Napoleon ascended his throne; and the next day, from the steps of St. Roche, thundered forth the cannon which taught the mob of Paris, for the first time, that it had a master. That was the commencement of the Empire. So the Anti-slavery movement commenced unheeded in that "obscure hole" which Mayor Otis could not find, occupied by a printer and a black boy.

In working these great changes, in such an age as ours, the so-called statesman has far less influence than the many little men who, at various points, are silently maturing a regeneration of public opinion. This is a reading and thinking age, and great interests at stake quicken the general intellect. Stagnant times have been when a great mind, unchored in error, might snag the slow-moving current of society. Such is not our era. Nothing but Freedom, Justice, and Truth is of any permanent advantage to the mass of mankind. To these society, left to itself, is always tending. In our day, great questions about them have called forth all the energies of the common mind. Error suffers sad treatment in the shock of eager intellects. "Everybody," said Talleyrand, "is cleverer than anybody;" and any name, however illustrious, which links itself to abuses, is sure to be overwhelmed by the impetuous current of that society which (thanks to the press and a reading public) is potent, always, to clear its own channel. Thanks to the Printing-Press, the people now do their own thinking, and statesmen, as they are styled— men in office—have ceased to be either the leaders or the clogs of society.

This view is one that Mr. Webster ridiculed in the depôts of New York. The time has come when he is obliged to change his tone; when he is obliged to retrace his steps—to acknowledge the nature and the character of the age in which he lives. Kossuth comes to this country, penniless, and an exile; conquered on his own soil; flung out as a weed upon the waters; nothing but his voice left; and the Secretary of State must meet him. Now, let us see what he says of his "rub-a-dub agitation," which consists of the voice only—of the tongue, which our friend Pillsbury has described. This is that "tongue" which the impudent statesman declared, from the drunken steps of the Revere House, ought to be silenced—this tongue which was a "rub-a-dub agitation" to be despised, when he spoke to the farmers of New York.

He says, "We are too much inclined to underrate the power of moral influence." Who is? Nobody but a Revere House statesman. "We are too much inclined to underrate the power of moral influence, and the influence of public opinion, and the influence of the principles to which great men—the lights of the world and of the present age—have given their sanction. Who doubts that, in our struggle for liberty and independence, the majestic eloquence of Chatham, the profound reasoning of Burke, the burning satire and irony of Colonel Barré, had influences upon our fortunes here in America? They had influences both ways. They tended, in the first place, somewhat to diminish the confidence of the British ministry in their hopes of success, in attempting to subjugate an injured people. They had influence another way, because all along the coasts of the country—and all our people in that day lived upon the coast—there was not a reading man who did not feel stronger, bolder, and more determined in the assertion of his rights, when these exhilarating accents from the two Houses of Parliament reached him from beyond the seas."

"I thank thee, Jew!" This "rub-a-dub agitation," then, has influence both ways. It diminishes the confidence of the Administration in its power to execute the Fugitive Slave Law, which it has imposed so insolently on the people. It acts on the *reading men* of the nation, and in that single fact is the whole story of the change. Wherever you have a reading people, there every tongue, every press, is a power. Mr. Webster, when he ridiculed in New York the agitation of the Anti-slavery body, supposed he was living in the old feudal times, when a statesman was an integral element in the state, an essential power in himself. He must have supposed himself speaking in those ages when a great man outweighed the masses. He finds now that he is living much later, in an age when the accumulated common-sense of the people outweighs the greatest statesman or the most influential individual. Let me illustrate the difference of our times and the past in this matter, by their difference in another respect. The time has been when men cased in iron from head to foot, and disciplined by long years of careful instruction, went to battle. Those were the days of nobles and knights; and in such times, ten knights, clad in steel, feared not a whole field of unarmed peasantry, and a hundred men-at-arms have conquered thousands of the common people, or held them at bay. Those were the times when Winkelried, the Swiss patriot, led his host against the Austrian phalanx, and finding it impenetrable to the thousands of Swiss who threw themselves on the serried lances, gathered a dozen in his arms, and, drawing them together, made thus an opening in the close-set ranks of the Austrians, and they were overborne by the actual mass of numbers. Gunpowder came, and then any finger that could pull a trigger was equal to the highest born and the best disciplined; knightly armour, and horses clad in steel, went to the ground before the courage and strength which dwelt in the arm of the peasant, as well as that of the prince. What gunpowder did for war, the printing-press has done for the mind, and the statesman is no longer clad in the steel of special education, but every reading man is his judge. Every thoughtful man, the country through, who makes up an opinion, is his jury,

to which he answers, and the tribunal to which he must bow. Mr. Webster, therefore, does not overrate the power of this "rub-a-dub agitation," which Kossuth has now adopted, "stealing our thunder." He does not overrate the power of this "rub-a-dub agitation," when he says, "Another great mistake, gentlemen, is sometimes made. [Yes, in Bowdoin Square!] We think nothing powerful enough to stand before despotic power. There is something strong enough, quite strong enough; and if properly exerted, it will prove itself so; and that is the power of intelligent public opinion." "I thank thee, Jew!" That opinion is formed, not only in Congress, or on hotel steps; it is made also in the school-houses, in the town-houses, at the hearth-stones, in the railroad-cars, on board the steamboats, in the social circle, in these anti-slavery gatherings which he despises. Mark you: *there is nothing powerful enough to stand before it!* It may be a self-styled divine institution; it may be the bank-vaults of New England; it may be the mining interests of Pennsylvania; it may be the Harwich fishermen, whom he told to stand by the Union, because its bunting protected their decks; it may be the factory operative, whom he told to uphold the Union, because it made his cloth sell for half a cent more a yard; it may be a parchment Constitution, or even a Fugitive Slave Bill, signed by Millard Fillmore!!!—no matter, all are dust on the threshing-floor of a reading public, once roused to indignation. Remember this, when you would look down upon a meeting of a few hundreds in the one scale, and the fanatic violence of State Street in the other, that there is NOTHING, Daniel Webster being witness, strong enough to stand against public opinion—and if the tongue and the press are not parents of that, what is?

Napoleon said, "I fear three newspapers more than a hundred thousand bayonets." Mr. Webster now is of the same opinion. "There is not a monarch on earth," he says, "whose throne is not liable to be shaken by the progress of opinion and the sentiment of the just and intelligent part of the people." "I thank thee, Jew!" We have been told often, that it was nothing but a morbid sentiment that was opposed to the Fugitive Slave Bill—it was a sentiment of morbid philanthropy. Grant it all. But take care, Mr. Statesman; cure or change it in time, else it will beat all your dead institutions to dust. Hearts and sentiments are alive, and we all know that the gentlest of Nature's growths or motions will, in time, burst asunder or wear away the proudest dead-weight man can heap upon them. If this be the power of the gentlest growth, let the stoutest heart tremble before the tornado of a people roused to terrible vengeance by the sight of long years of cowardly and merciless oppression, and oft-repeated instances of selfish and calculating apostasy. You may build your Capitol of granite, and pile it high as the Rocky Mountains; if it is founded on or mixed up with iniquity, the pulse of a girl will in time beat it down. "There is no monarch on earth whose throne is not liable to be shaken by the sentiment of the just and intelligent part of the people." What is this but a recantation—doing penance for the impudence uttered in Bowdoin Square? Surely this is the white sheet and lighted torch which the Scotch Church imposed as penance on its erring members. Who would imagine that the same man who said of the public discussion of the slavery question, that it must be put down, could have dictated this sentiment—" It becomes us, in the station which we hold, to let that public opinion, so far as we form it, have free course"? What was the haughty threat we heard from Bowdoin Square a year ago? "This agitation must be put down." Now, "It becomes us, in the station which we hold, to let that public opinion have free course." Behold the great doughface cringing before the calm eye of Kossuth, who had nothing but "rub-a-dub agitation" with which to rescue Hungary from the bloody talons of the Austrian eagle!

This is statesmanship! The statesmanship that says to the Commonwealth of Massachusetts to-day, "Smother those prejudices," and to-morrow, "There is no throne on the broad earth strong enough to stand up against the sentiment of justice." What is that but the "prejudices" of the Commonwealth of Massachusetts against man-hunting? And this is the man before whom the press and the pulpit of the country would have had the Abolitionists bow their heads, and lay their mouths in the dust, instead of holding fast to the eternal principles of justice and right!

It would be idle, to be sure, to base any argument on an opinion of Mr. Webster's. Like the chameleon, he takes his hue, on these subjects, from the air he breathes. He has his "October sun" opinion, and his Faneuil Hall opinions. But the recantation here is at least noticeable; and his testimony to the power of the masses is more valuable as coming from an unwilling witness. The best of us are conscious of being, at times, somewhat awed by the colossal institutions about us, which seem to be opposing our progress. There are those who occasionally weary of this moral suasion, and sigh for something tangible; some power that they can feel, and see its operation. The advancing tide you cannot mark. The gem forms unseen. The granite increases and crumbles, and you can hardly mark either process. The great change in a nation's opinion is the same. We stand here to-day, and if we look back twenty years, we can see a change in public opinion; yes, we can see a great change. Then the great statesmen had pledged themselves not to talk on this subject. They have been made to talk. These hounds have been whipped into the traces of the nation's car, not by *three* newspapers, which Napoleon dreaded, but by *one*. The great parties of the country have been broken to pieces and crumbled. The great sects have been broken to pieces. Suppose you cannot put your finger upon an individual fact; still, in the great result, you see what Webster tells us in his speech: "Depend upon it, gentlemen, that between these two rival powers—the autocratic power, maintained by arms and force, and the popular power, maintained by opinion—the former is constantly decreasing! and, thank God! the latter is constantly increasing. Real human liberty is gaining the ascendant;—[he must feel sad at that!]—and the part which we have to act in all this great drama is to show ourselves in favour of those rights; to uphold our ascendancy, and to carry it on, until we shall see it culminate in the highest heaven over our heads."

Now I look upon this speech as the most remarkable Mr. Webster has ever made on the anti-slavery agitation to which we are devoted —as a most remarkable confession, under the circumstances. I read it here and to you, because, in the circle I see around me, the larger proportion are Abolitionists—men attached to the movement which this meeting represents—men whose thoughts are occasionally occupied with the causes and with the effects of its real progress. I would force from the reluctant lips of the Secretary of State his testimony to the real power of the masses. I said that the day was, before gunpowder, when the noble, clad in steel, was a match for a thousand. Gunpowder levelled peasant and prince. The printing-press has done the same. In the midst of thinking people, in the long run, there are no so-called "great" men. The accumulated intellect of the masses is greater than the heaviest brain God ever gave to a single man. Webster, though he may gather into his own person the confidence of parties, and the attachment of thousands throughout the country, is but a feather's weight in the balance against the average of public sentiment on the subject of slavery. A newspaper paragraph, a county meeting, a gathering for conversation, a change in the character of a dozen individuals—these are the several fountains and sources of public opinion. And, friends, when we gather, month after month, at such meetings as these, we should encourage ourselves with considerations of this kind:—that we live in an age of democratic equality; that, for a moment, a party may stand against the age, but in the end it goes by the board; that the man who launches a sound argument, who sets on two feet a startling fact, and bids it travel from Maine to Georgia, is just as certain that in the end he will change the government, as if, to destroy the Capitol, he had placed gunpowder under the Senate-chamber. Natural philosophers tell us, that if you will only multiply the simplest force into enough time, it will equal the greatest. So it is with the slow intellectual movement of the masses. It can scarcely be seen, but it is a constant movement: it is the shadow on the dial; never still, though never seen to move; it is the tide, it is the ocean, gaining on the proudest and strongest bulwarks that human art or strength can build. It may be defied for a moment, but in the end Nature always triumphs. So the race, if it cannot drag a Webster along with it, leaves him behind and forgets him. The race is rich enough to afford to do without the greatest intellects God ever let the Devil buy. Stranded along the past, there are a great many dried mummies of dead intellects, which the race found too heavy to drag forward.

I hail the almighty power of the tongue. I swear allegiance to the omnipotence of the press. The people never err. "*Vox populi, vox Dei*"—the voice of the people is the voice of God. I do not mean this of any single verdict which the people of to-day may record. In time, the selfishness of one class neutralizes the selfishness of another. The interests of one age clash against the interests of another; but in the great result the race always means right. The people always mean right, and in the end they will have the right. I believe in the twenty millions—not the twenty millions that live now, necessarily—to arrange this question of slavery, which priests and politicians have sought to keep out of sight. They have kept it locked up in the Senate-chamber, they have hidden it behind the communion-table, they have appealed to the superstitious and idolatrous veneration for the State and the Union to avoid this question, and so have kept it from the influence of the great democratic tendencies of the masses. But change all this, drag it from its concealment, and give it to the people; launch it on the age, and all is safe. It will find a safe harbour. A man is always selfish enough for himself. The soldier will be selfish enough for himself; the merchant will be selfish enough for himself; yes, he will be willing to go to hell to secure his own fortune, but he will not be ready to go there to make the fortune of his neighbour. Rarely is any man willing to sacrifice his own character for the benefit of his neighbour; and whenever we shall be able to show this nation that the interests of a class, not of the whole, the interests of a portion of the country, not of the masses, are subserved by holding our fellow-men in bondage, then we shall spike the guns of the enemy, or get their artillery on our side.

I want you to turn your eyes from institutions to men. The difficulty of the present day and with us, is, we are bullied by institutions. A man gets up in the pulpit, or sits on the bench, and we allow ourselves to be bullied by the judge or the clergyman, when, if he stood side by side with us, on the brick pavement, as a simple individual, his ideas would not have disturbed our clear thoughts an hour. Now the duty of each anti-slavery man is simply this—Stand on the pedestal of your own individual independence, summon those institutions about you, and judge them. The question is deep enough to require this judgment of you. This is what the cause asks of you, my friends; and the moment you shall be willing to do this, to rely upon yourselves, that moment the truths I have read from the lips of one whom the country regards as its greatest statesman, will shine over your path, assuring you that out of this agitation, as sure as the sun shines at noonday, the future character of the American government will be formed.

If we lived in England, if we lived in France, the philosophy of our movement might be different, for there stand accumulated wealth, hungry churches, and old nobles—a class which popular agitation but slowly affects. To these public opinion is obliged to bow. We have seen, for instance, the agitation of 1848 in Europe, deep as it was, seemingly triumphant as it was, for six months, retire, beaten, before the undisturbed foundations of the governments of the Continent. You recollect, no doubt, the tide of popular enthusiasm which rolled from the Bay of Biscay to the very feet of the Czar, and it seemed as if Europe was melted into one republic. Men thought the new generation had indeed come. We waited twelve months, and "the turrets and towers of old institutions—the church, law, nobility, government—reappeared above the subsiding wave." Now there are no such institutions here; no law that can abide one moment when popular opinion demands its abrogation. The government is wrecked the moment the newspapers decree it. The penny papers of this State in the Sims case did more to dictate the decision of Chief Justice Shaw, than the Legislature that sat in the State House, or the statute-book of Massachusetts. I mean what I say. The penny papers of New York do more to govern this country than the White House at Washington. Mr. Webster says we live under a government of laws. He was never more mistaken, even when he thought the anti-slavery agitation could be stopped. We live under a government of men—and morning newspapers. Bennett and Horace Greeley are more really Presidents of the United States than Millard Fillmore. Daniel Webster himself cannot even get a nomination. Why? Because, long ago, the ebbing tide of public opinion left him a wreck, stranded on the side of the popular current.

We live under a government of men. The Constitution is nothing in South Carolina, but the black law is everything. The law that says the coloured man shall sit in the jury-box in the city of Boston is nothing. Why? Because the Mayor and Aldermen, and the Selectmen of Boston, for the last fifty years, have been such slaves of colorphobia, that they did not choose to execute this law of the Commonwealth. I might go through the statute-book, and show you the same result. Now if this be true against us, it is true for us. Remember, that the penny papers may be starved into anti-slavery, whenever we shall put behind them an anti-slavery public sentiment. Wilberforce and Clarkson had to vanquish the moneyed power of England, the West-India interest, and overawe the peerage of Great Britain, before they conquered. The settled purpose of the great middle class had to wait till all this was accomplished. The moment we have the control of public opinion—the women and the children, the school-houses, the school-books, the literature, and the newspapers—that moment we have settled the question.

Men blame us for the bitterness of our language and the personality of our attacks. It results from our position. The great mass of the people can never be made to stay and argue a long question. They must be made to feel it, through the hides of their idols. When you have launched your spear into the rhinoceros hide of a Webster or a Benton, every Whig and Democrat feels it. It is on this principle that every reform must take for its text the mistakes of great men. God gives us great scoundrels for texts to anti-slavery sermons. See to it, when Nature has provided you a monster like Webster, that you exhibit him—himself a whole menagerie—throughout the country. It is not often, in the wide world's history, that you see a man so lavishly gifted by nature, and called, in the concurrence of events, to a position like that which he occupied on the 7th of March, surrender his great power, and quench the high hopes of his race. No man, since the age of Luther, has ever held in his hand, so palpably, the destinies and character of a mighty people. He stood like the Hebrew prophet betwixt the living and the dead. He had but to have upheld the cross of common truth and honesty, and the black dishonour of two hundred years would have been effaced for ever. He bowed his vassal head to the temptations of the flesh and of lucre. He gave himself up into the lap of the Delilah of slavery, for the mere promise of a nomination, and the greatest hour of the age was bartered away,—not for a mess of pottage, but for the *promise* of a mess of pottage,—a promise, thank God! which is to be broken. I say it is not often that Providence permits the eyes of twenty millions of thinking people to behold the fall of another Lucifer, from the very battlements of Heaven, down into that "lower deep of the lowest deep" of hell. On such a text, how effective should be the sermon!

Let us see to it, that, in spite of the tenderness of American prejudice, in spite of the morbid charity that would have us rebuke the sin, but spare the sinner, in spite of this effeminate Christianity, that would let millions pine, lest one man's feelings be injured,—let us see to it, friends, that we be "harsh as truth and uncompromising as justice;" remembering always, that every single man set against this evil may be another Moses, every single thought you launch may be the thunders of another Napoleon from the steps of another St. Roche; remembering that we live not in an age of individual despotism, when a Charles the Fifth could set up or put down the slave-trade, but surrounded by twenty millions, whose opinion is omnipotent,—that the hundred gathered in a New England school-house may be the hundred who shall teach the rising men of the other half of the continent, and stereotype Freedom on the banks of the Pacific; remembering and worshipping reverentially the great American idea of the omnipotence of "thinking men," of the "sentiment of justice," against which no throne is potent enough to stand, no Constitution sacred enough to endure. Remember this, when you go to an antislavery gathering in a school-house, and know that, weighed against its solemn purpose, its terrible resolution, its earnest thought, Webster himself, and all huckstering statesmen, in the opposite scale, shall kick the beam. Worshipping the tongue, let us be willing, at all times, to be known throughout the community as the all-talk party. The age of bullets is over. The age of men armed in mail is over. The age of thrones has gone by. The age of statesmen—God be praised! *such* statesmen—is over. The age of thinking men has come. With the aid of God, then, every man I can reach I will set *thinking* on the subject of slavery. The age of reading men has come. I will try to imbue every newspaper with Garrisonianism. The age of the masses has come. Now, Daniel Webster counts one. Give him joy of it!— but the "rub-a-dub agitation" counts at least twenty,—nineteen better. Nineteen, whom no chance of nomination tempts to a change of opinions once a twelvemonth; who need no Kossuth advent to recall them to their senses.

What I want to impress you with is, the great weight that is attached to the opinion of everything that can call itself a man. Give me anything that walks erect, and can read, and he shall count one in the millions of the Lord's sacramental host, which is yet to come up and trample all oppression in the dust. The weeds poured forth in nature's lavish luxuriance, give them but time, and their tiny roots shall rend asunder the foundations of palaces, and crumble the Pyramids to the earth. We may be weeds in comparison with those marked men; but in the lavish luxuriance of that nature which has at least allowed us to be "thinking, reading men," I learn, Webster being my witness, that there is no throne potent enough to stand against us. It is morbid enthusiasm this that I have. Grant it. But they tell us that this heart of mine, which beats so unintermittedly in the bosom, if its force could be directed against a granite pillar, would wear it to dust in the course of a man's life. Your Capitol, Daniel Webster, is marble, but the pulse of every humane man is beating against it. God will give us time, and the pulses of men shall beat it down. Take the mines, take the Harwich fishing-skiffs, take the Lowell mills, take all the coin and the cotton, still the day must be ours, thank God, for the hearts—the hearts are on our side!

There is nothing stronger than human prejudice. A crazy sentimentalism like that of Peter the Hermit hurled half of Europe upon Asia, and changed the destinies of kingdoms. We may be crazy. Would to God he would make us all crazy enough to forget for one moment the cold deductions of intellect, and let these hearts of ours beat, beat, beat, under the promptings of a common humanity! They have put wickedness into the statute-book, and its destruction is just as certain as if they had put gunpowder under the Capitol. That is my faith. That it is which turns my eye from the ten thousand newspapers, from the forty thousand pulpits, from the millions of Whigs, from the millions of Democrats, from the might of sect, from the marble government, from the iron army, from the navy riding at anchor, from all that we are accustomed to deem great and potent,—turns it back to the simplest child or woman, to the first murmured protest that is heard against bad laws. I recognize in it the great future, the first rumblings of that volcano destined to overthrow these mighty preparations, and bury in the hot lava of its full excitement all this laughing prosperity which now rests so secure on its side.

All hail, Public Opinion! To be sure, it is a dangerous thing under which to live. It rules to-day in the desire to obey all kinds of laws, and takes your life. It rules again in the love of liberty, and rescues Shadrach from Boston Court-House. It rules to-morrow in the manhood of him who loads the musket to shoot down — God be praised! — the man-hunter, Gorsuch. It rules in Syracuse, and the slave escapes to Canada. It is our interest to educate this people in humanity, and in deep reverence for the rights of the lowest and humblest individual that makes up our numbers. Each man here, in fact, holds his property and his life dependent on the constant presence of an agitation like this of anti-slavery. Eternal vigilance is the price of liberty: power is ever stealing from the many to the few. The manna of popular liberty must be gathered each day, or it is rotten. The living sap of to-day outgrows the dead rind of yesterday. The hand intrusted with power becomes, either from human depravity or *esprit de corps*, the necessary enemy of the people. Only by continual oversight can the democrat in office be prevented from hardening into a despot: only by unintermitted agitation can a people be kept sufficiently awake to principle not to let liberty be smothered in material prosperity. All clouds, it is said, have sunshine behind them, and all evils have some good result; so slavery, by the necessity of its abolition, has saved the freedom of the white race from being melted in the luxury or buried beneath the gold of its own success. Never look, therefore, for an age when the people can be quiet and safe. At such times Despotism, like a shrouding mist, steals over the mirror of Freedom. The Dutch, a thousand years ago, built against the ocean their bulwarks of willow and mud. Do they trust to that? No. Each year the patient, industrious peasant gives so much time from the cultivation of his soil and the care of his children to stop the breaks and replace the willow which insects have eaten, that he may keep the land his fathers rescued from the water, and bid defiance to the waves that roar above his head, as if demanding back the broad fields man has stolen from their realm.

Some men suppose that, in order to the people's governing themselves, it is only necessary, as Fisher Ames said, that the "Rights of Man be printed, and that every citizen have a copy." As the Epicureans, two thousand years ago, imagined God a being who arranged this marvellous machinery, set it going, and then sunk to sleep. Republics exist only on the tenure of being constantly agitated. The anti-slavery agitation is an important, nay, an essential part of the machinery of the state. It is not a disease nor a medicine. No; it is the normal state,—the normal state of the nation. Never, to our latest posterity, can we afford to do without prophets, like Garrison, to stir up the monotony of wealth, and re-awake the people to the great ideas that are constantly fading out of their minds,—to trouble the waters, that there may be health in their flow. Every government is always growing corrupt. Every Secretary of State is, by the very necessity of his position, an apostate. I mean what I say. He is an enemy to the people, of necessity, because the moment he joins the government, he gravitates against that popular agitation which is the life of a republic. A republic is nothing but a constant overflow of lava. The principles of Jefferson are not up to the principles of to-day. It was well said of Webster, that he knows well the Hancock and Adams of 1776, but he does not know the Hancocks and Adamses of to-day. The republic which sinks to sleep, trusting to constitutions and machinery, to politicians and statesmen, for the safety of its liberties, never will have any. The people are to be waked to a new effort, just as the Church has to be regenerated in each age. The anti-slavery agitation is a necessity of each age, to keep ever on the alert this faithful vigilance, so constantly in danger of sleep. We must live like our Puritan fathers, who always went to church, and sat down to dinner, when the Indians were in their neighbourhood, with their musket-lock on the one side and a drawn sword on the other.

If I had time or voice to-night, I might proceed to a further development of this idea, and I trust I could make it clear, which I fear I have not yet done. To my conviction, it is Gospel truth, that, instead of the anti-slavery agitation being an evil, or even the unwelcome cure of a disease in this government, the youngest child that lives may lay his hand on the youngest child that his grey hairs shall see, and say: "The agitation was commenced when the Declaration of Independence was signed; it took its second tide when the Anti-slavery Declaration was signed in 1833,—a movement, not the cure, but the diet of a free people,—not the homœopathic or the allopathic dose to which a sick land has recourse, but the daily cold water and the simple bread, the daily diet and absolute necessity, the manna of a people wandering in the wilderness." There is no Canaan in politics. As health lies in labour, and there is no royal road to it but through toil, so there is no republican road to safety but in constant distrust. "In distrust," said Demosthenes, "are the nerves of the mind." Let us see to it that these sentinel nerves are ever on the alert. If the Alps, piled in cold and still sublimity, be the emblem of Despotism, the ever-restless ocean is ours, which, girt within the eternal laws of gravitation, is pure only because never still.

THE ROYAL PARDON.

THE legal and proper mercy of a King of England may remit the punishment, but not stop the trial.—*Junius.*

RICHARD COBDEN.
Born 1800. Living.

[THE name of Richard Cobden at once suggests the great movements with which it is so inseparably associated; foremost among these being Free Trade, the Corn Laws, and the operations of the Peace Party. Moreover, his "unadorned eloquence," since first that phrase was uttered by Sir Robert Peel, has always found not a few appreciative listeners, both in the House of Commons and the country at large. We need, therefore, offer no excuse for adding to this collection a specimen of Mr. Cobden's oratory, which, though neither lofty nor rhetorical in its style, yet for plain business-like and withal concentrated force, has seldom been surpassed. In early life Mr. Cobden was chiefly engaged in commercial pursuits; but having entered Parliament as member for Stockport in 1841, with few intermissions, he has been actively employed in political affairs ever since. The Speech which we have here selected was delivered at a great meeting of the Peace Party held in Exeter Hall on the 30th of October, 1849, and responsive to the Congress that had taken place in Paris in August of the same year, and as a clear declaration of the cardinal points of that creed which Mr. Cobden has so long espoused, has an interest quite independent of the style in which it is composed.

At the meeting where this speech was made, many foreigners, as well as many of the eminent men of our own country, were present and addressed the assembly, Mr. William Ewart occupying the chair.]

SPEECH AT EXETER HALL, 30TH OF OCT., 1849.

THE resolution which has been put into my hnds is:—

"That this meeting receives, with the highest satisfaction, the assurances of sympathy in this great movement, as conveyed in the letters which have been read from the Archbishop of Paris, from MM. Lamartine, Victor Hugo, Emile de Girardin, and other distinguished foreigners; and it hails with delight the presence of the gentlemen who have honoured this assembly with their attendance on the present occasion, and trusts that their visits to this country will prove to them a source of personal gratification, and that it will tend to advance the period when national animosities shall be for ever forgotten, and peace and good will prevail throughout the world."

It is now, I believe, exactly two years since this island was frighted from its propriety by the cry of an impending invasion from France. You all remember how great was the alarm on that occasion. We were terrified with the threat of the French army marching in at one end of London, and the Horse Guards marching out at the other. You know that the highest military authority in the country swelled the chorus of that alarm. You recollect that orders were given to improve our coast defences, to add to our steam fleet, to put in motion our squadron of evolution, and to prepare to repel the attack of these hostile Frenchmen from our shores. Well, and what said the men of peace on that occasion? I can say of myself that it was that wicked cry, that consummation of a warlike system, that brought me into the ranks of the peace party of this country. We held our public meetings, and we protested that we did not regard the French as brigands, or as pirates—that we had faith that they had no intention whatever of making a wanton attack upon our shores. But we did more. We proposed to go and see these fierce and warlike people. Whilst the brave men, who trust to their armed forces, were digging steam-docks, launching steam-ships, and putting their coast defences in order, the men of peace were making their preparations to cross the Channel, and hold out the right hand of friendship and confidence to the French people. And we come to tell you that we have paid that visit, and that the hand we tendered has been most cordially grasped. We have now the pleasure of seeing here a deputation from France; and it is in honour of those gentlemen, and of the other foreigners who are present, that we meet here to-day. In your name, and in the terms of this motion, I beg to tender them our hearty welcome.

When I look back, only for two years, and remember the arguments that were then adduced, openly and publicly, not only in our newspapers, but in our public assemblies,—when I remember the disparaging, insulting, suspicious language, that was applied to the people of France,—when I recollect how every man was decried who ventured even a surmise that it was possible the great mass of the French people were not disposed for war—and when I think of the altered tone of those same journals which have, within the last month, complained that the French people—who, they had told us, were ready to break forth upon their neighbours, the moment Louis Philippe should die—are too pacific now, and cease to take any interest in foreign politics at all, I am tempted to ask, will these organs of the press learn a little modesty for the future? Will the lessons of these two short years have no effect upon them? Do they think the English people have memories? Will they be more diffident after this exposure? I will wait till to-morrow morning before I offer an opinion.

My esteemed friend (Mr. Samuel Gurney), who has just spoken, has dwelt upon the most exalted and sacred view of this question. I join with him in paying homage to those principles of Christianity which he has so well enforced. When I became a party to the peace movement, it was with the conviction that the principles of peace, enjoined in the New Testament, would be advocated on the highest religious grounds, by men, more competent by study, and more entitled by position and by profession, to deal with those arguments than myself. But I am very much afraid—and our esteemed friend Mr. Gurney, himself, will, I think, agree with me—that those arguments are not alone sufficient to convince the politicians of the day. I am very sorry to say it, but I believe that that letter of Mr. Gurney, in which he gave his opinion as to the financial consequences of this warlike system, had more effect upon the minds of the politicians and influential statesmen of this country, than all th[e] made, or ever could ma[ke] religious feelings. Havin[g] deal with, and secular obje[ct] must bear in mind that, [the] sanction of Christianity f[or] must seek the accomplishm[ent by] human means, for God doe[s not in] our day, to work miracles, w[ill] plish his ends without the[...] when I find myself in the r[...] like this, I prefer to take [...] what the enemy calls our v[...] show, as a practical ma[n] (leaving to others the defe[...] nable position on which Mr. [Gurney] himself), not only that the a[rguments] statesmen of the day may [...] they may be utterly demo[...] ground. One of the highes[t] diplomacy. Now, who are t[hese?] Have the politicians, who [...] that the French were comi[ng...] striving to revive the old er[a...] proved the best diplomat[ists of] peace, who went over to P[aris with] sarcasms, whilst holding ou[t friend]ship to the French? W[hat of] affairs in the east of Eu[rope at this] moment? The question [has] been lately raised, in conne[xion] of the East. We have h[eard of] the designs of a great nort[hern power] what has the maintenance [of peace] On the cordial good und[erstanding of] France and England. W[ithout a] good understanding betwee[n those] who, two years ago, cried [out for] war, and more steam-dock[s as the] way of maintaining the e[mpire,] arming yourselves, and [...] bristle with cannon! No, [we] went over in confidence [with] faith in the French peopl[e that] they had justice and m[agnanimity of] national character,—it was [that] severed the good underst[anding of the] two countries; and it is t[he] between France and Engla[nd that prevents] war between Russia and [...] Let us hear no more boast[s,] let us hear no more taun[ts at our] party, as though they had [no] view. What is the first es[sential of] Finance. What must be t[he opinion of our oppo]nents, if we try them by the [...] position just now? There [is no hope] in the country for financ[ial relief if] the peace party have anti[cipated the] field; for there can be no [reduction] material reduction of taxat[ion except owing] to our principle of diminis[hed...]

ccautions against war than
selves constantly armed to
the amount of our expendi-
, besides those of war, and
? Let us bring our financial
ad tell them what it is, in
', our expenditure, in round
our millions sterling; out
n millions were expended
ebts for past wars, or the
stablishments. More than
taxation goes to pay the
esent war establishments.
of fifty-four paid the whole
government, the civil list,
Queen's establishment, the
ustice, the poor-law office,
ne and foreign secretaries—
ole cost of conducting the
vil government. Is it not
r plan of financial reform
ion, which does not include
g the warlike expenditure?
e only practical party?
eing always under arms,
oment a misunderstanding
at nations, like individuals,
isputes by arbitration. It
s very good in theory, but
All we want the persons,
racticable, to do, is, to try.
t confidence in their judg-
word for anything I want
vay. I want them to try,
ucceed, then we will, at all
edit for having done their
besides bringing forward
ion, I intend to endeavour
n Secretary to try to pre-
ountries to join with us in
at of our naval and military
n, that if we all discontinue
le ships, we shall all of us
relative position with our
e now occupy. There is no
in our own country, or in
us, who will dissent from
have made this suggestion
ion with public men, here
n statesmen, as to our own;
ie admission, that it would
a stop to this expenditure;
a most desirable financial
e propose that some one
begin the good work, should
even make a proposal to
simultaneously, this saving
the prevention of increase,
them, or any one of them,
ur navy has been kept up
ce to France. We have
as France has increased

hers; and so far from proposing, as I want them to do, that both countries should cease from adding to their armaments, our government sends spies to the French dockyards, and no sooner is a fresh keel laid down there, or a fresh forge set up, than my Lords of the Admiralty avail themselves of the pretext to lay down a fresh keel, or set up a fresh forge, here. Was ever such folly as this perpetrated in individual life? There is not a private trader amongst us who could carry on his business on the same principles that the governments of England and France carry on theirs, without finding his way into the Insolvent Court; and I am satisfied, that if these governments continue in the same course, financial difficulties and bankruptcy await them, and they will go into the *Gazette*, without deserving a certificate at the hands of their people.

Already, however, the progress of discussion on this subject, has been attended with some results. Two years ago, we were told that great armies and navies were kept up as a means of defending countries against powerful neighbours. But such is the force of truth, elicited by the progress of discussion on this subject, it is admitted now, by the very parties who vilified us then for taking the same position, that war between two nations is not the evil to be feared; but, say they, it is insurrectionary movements—wars of rebellion, which have to be guarded against. If such be the truth, all I have to say is, that the system of keeping up armies of hundreds of thousands of soldiers to keep down the people, does not answer the purpose of those who enforce it. The system has been tried long enough, and has been proved a failure. When, two years ago, I was unable to attend the Peace Congress at Brussels, I put down on paper the statement that there were at that time, in the aggregate, two millions of armed men in the pay of the different governments of Europe. What has since happened? Why, in spite of these armed myriads, revolutions have swept so fiercely the continent that there is scarcely a throne which has not been shaken to its base, though protected by this array of bayonets. Some of these thrones have, more or less, recovered their equilibrium; but, instead of their occupants trying some new system, in place of that which they have found so entire a failure, they have only set about increasing their armies, so that, where there were three soldiers two years ago, there are now, I should say, four. I have often been puzzled, in trying to conjecture what can be the motives of the old governments of Europe in adhering to this absurd course; and, fairly at a loss to account for it, upon any rational or honest grounds, I have really sometimes been half inclined to doubt whether they have not designedly sought to bring their finances into such utter confusion—such hopeless bankruptcy—that no other form of government can be found willing to undertake the labour and risk of their restoration. It is a puerile illustration; but boys at school, you know, when they have an apple or a cake that they want to keep all to themselves, rub it over with dirt, in order to disgust their school-fellows—and, even so it is, I suspect, with the old governments I speak of. It is no wonder, that, seeing the persistence of their rulers in such an absurd and disastrous career, the more ignorant portion of the people of Europe should have doubts whether society be not altogether founded on false principles, and, in their despair, advocate the policy of digging up the very foundations of the social edifice. It is we, the maligned Utopists—the advocates of reduced warlike establishments, who have, alone, proposed a remedy for these disorders.

I am not going into the question of the internal affairs of other countries. If any particular nation has a fancy to be taxed for the maintenance of an army of three or four hundred thousand soldiers, for its own oppression, I am not going to interfere with the fancy. But I would point out that these standing armies are not raised and maintained out of the immediate pockets of the people; they are paid for by loans. And, if we want really to prevent governments from keeping up these large armaments, our mode must be to raise such a public opinion in England, and elsewhere, as shall dissuade individuals from lending their money to those governments. We have already struck a blow at the system: Austria has, indeed, got a loan; but the money was not advanced by Holland or by England; a fact which must satisfactorily prove that the right spirit has dawned upon us. The loan has been chiefly subscribed for by the bankers of Vienna; and, as treasury bonds and inconvertible paper have been taken in payment, it really amounts to little more than a funding of part of the floating debt, at a high rate of interest; and the estimation in which the loan is held generally, is sufficiently demonstrated by the fact, that, before the bonds were issued, they were at a discount of one per cent. There is now another great northern power in the market. Russia, I see from yesterday's paper, is indirectly applying for a loan. The great Czar has sent forth his ukase, in which he invites people to give him credit for three or four millions sterling, in the shape of treasury bonds; and I am delighted to perceive, from the very ukase itself, that the loan is needed "to cover the expense of the war lately carried on in Hungary." After this, what becomes of the boast about the wealth of this power? Did we not hear, the other day, that rich Russia, liberal Russia, had taken up two millions of the Austrian loan, had given the Pope

£500,000, and the Gran
£250,000? Don't be gulle
thing of the kind. I dec
long investigation into
government, that I would
investment for my child
stock, which the *bulls* and
and selling in the City fo
over, I know men, of more
in Russian affairs, who wo
bid than mine. From th
heart, I thank heaven, t
in its Divine Providence,
huge standing armies of
men, there will also be a
and a discontented people.
consequences, under God'
that, even in this world,
policy meets with retrib
should be much less san
the expectation of realizing
It is by the emphatic
principles, at meetings li
the cause we have espouse
It is from these platforms
is created, and the policy
determined.

I am especially anxiou
pudiate and denounce th
ference in the domestic a
countries. We boast that,
house, who has not viola
country, is his castle, whi
burglar. What shall w
burglary of nations, when
governing state is invade
and stronger nation, un
pretext of the weaker c
Upon no principle of jus
foreign power interfere, by
affairs of another and ind
until this is thoroughly r
upon, by the governments
can, practically, be no secu
among nations. I say thi
interference of Russia wit
land with Spain, of Franc
has been, indeed, a doctri
country, with relation to
affected me more poignant
circumstance of recent da
forth from this country—n
but by the mouth of the
that, by the law of natio
vernment had a right to c
power to aid it in puttin
pleased to call the rebellio
this is a question, not of
but of the responsibility of
governed. The boy Emp
pelled from his most imp
the right, it is said, to ca

cut the throats of his own subjects. If this be admitted, there is an end of the responsibility of governments to their people. In England, we have maintained, since 1688, the principle that the people are the sovereign source of power. Suppose that, at some future period—the supposition, under existing circumstances, is impossible—the English people were to come into conflict with their sovereign, and that he was defeated, as was the case with the Austrian government in Hungary, is it pretended that, in such a case, the sovereign would be justified in calling in the Turks, for example, to her aid, as Austria had called in Russia? Yet this is the principle advocated by those who approve the Russian intervention in Hungary. A large proportion of the daily press of this country has been hounding on the Cossacks in their brutal invasion—their cruel treatment of a more civilized and freer people. I reflect, with humiliation, as an Englishman, upon the part which these journals have taken upon this subject during the last few months—and I implore the men now present, who represent foreign countries on this occasion, to believe me when I assure them that these papers do not represent the public opinion or heart of this country. Let the Peace Congress, which is spreading its roots and its branches, far and wide, throughout the world, proclaim these four cardinal principles in faith and heart—arbitration instead of war; a simultaneous reduction of armaments; the denunciation of the right of any nation to interfere, by force, in the domestic affairs of any other nation; the repudiation of loans to warlike governments. Let these cardinal points be adhered to, and, with the Divine blessing, which cannot fail to be vouchsafed to so good a work, perseverance will ensure an eventful triumph to the friends of peace.

CROSBY (LORD MAYOR) AT THE BAR OF THE HOUSE OF COMMONS ON A CHARGE OF CONTUMACY.

I ASK no favour of this House—I crave no mercy. I am ready to go to my noble friend at the Tower, if the House shall order me. My conscience is clear, and tells me that I have kept my oath, and done my duty to the city, of which I have the honour to be chief magistrate, and to my country. I will never betray the privileges of the citizens, nor the rights of the people. I have no apology to make for having acted uprightly, and I fear not any resentment in consequence of such conduct. I will through life continue to obey the dictates of honour and conscience, to give my utmost support to every part of the constitution of this kingdom; and the event I shall always leave to heaven, at all times ready to meet my fate.

EDWARD LORD THURLOW.
Born 1732. Died 1806.

[THE Duke of Grafton having reproached Lord Thurlow with his plebeian extraction, and his recent admission into the peerage, Lord Thurlow rose from the woolsack, and advanced slowly to the place from which the chancellor generally addresses the house; then fixing on the duke the look of Jove when he grasps the thunder, in a level tone of voice, he spoke as follows; and, in the words of an American critic, "The effect of this speech, both within the walls and out of them, was prodigious. It gave Lord Thurlow an ascendancy in the house which no chancellor had ever possessed; it invested him, in public opinion, with a character of independence and honour; and this, though he was ever on the unpopular side in politics, made him always popular with the people."]

SPEECH IN THE HOUSE OF LORDS, IN REPLY TO THE DUKE OF GRAFTON.

I AM amazed at the attack the noble duke has made on me. Yes, my lords [*considerably raising his voice*], I am amazed at his grace's speech. The noble duke cannot look before him, behind him, or on either side of him, without seeing some noble peer who owes his seat in this house to his successful exertions in the profession to which I belong. Does he not feel that it is as honourable to owe it to these, as to being the accident of an accident? To all these noble lords the language of the noble duke is as applicable and as insulting as it is to myself. But I do not fear to meet it single and alone. No one venerates the peerage more than I do: but, my lords, I must say, that the peerage solicited me, not I the peerage. Nay more: I can say, and will say, that as a peer of Parliament, as Speaker of this right honourable House, as keeper of the great seal, as guardian of his Majesty's conscience, as Lord High Chancellor of England, nay, even in that character alone in which the noble duke would think it an affront to be considered,—as A MAN, I am at this moment as respectable,—I beg leave to add,—I am at this time as much respected, as the proudest peer I now look down upon.

THE HONOUR OF THE CROWN, AND THAT OF THE PEOPLE, IDENTIFIED.

THE King's honour is that of his people. Their real honour and real interest are the same. This is no vain punctilio. A clear, unblemished character comprehends, not only the integrity that will not offer, but the spirit that will not submit to, an injury; and whether it belongs to an individual, or to a community, it is the foundation of peace, of independence, and of safety. Private credit is wealth; public honour is security. The feather that adorns the royal bird supports his flight. Strip him of his plumage, and you fix him to the earth.—*Junius.*

JOHN PHILPOT CURRAN.

Born 1750.   *Died* 1817.

[The following passages are extracted from a speech in defence of Archibald Hamilton Rowan, delivered in the Court of King's Bench, in Ireland, on the 29th of January, 1794. The Attorney-General filed an information against Mr. Rowan, in which he was charged, as Secretary to the Society of United Irishmen at Dublin, with having published a false, malicious, and seditious libel against the Government. Despite the splendid eloquence of Curran exerted on his behalf, the accused was convicted, and on conviction fined £500, and sentenced to two years' imprisonment. Rowan subsequently made his escape to America, whence he returned after some years to receive the King's pardon, and enjoy the last years of a long life in his native country. A full account of the trial of Rowan, and all the circumstances connected with it, may be found in an admirable work by the late Charles Phillips, entitled " Curran and his Contemporaries."]

DEFENCE OF MR. ROWAN.

THIS paper, gentlemen, insists upon the necessity of emancipating the Catholics of Ireland, and that is charged as part of the libel. If they had waited another year, if they had kept this prosecution impending for another year, how much would remain for a jury to decide upon, I should be at a loss to discover. It seems as if the progress of public reformation was eating away the ground of the prosecution. Since the commencement of the prosecution, this part of the libel has unluckily received the sanction of the legislature. In that interval our Catholic brethren have obtained that admission, which it seems it was a libel to propose: in what way to account for this I am really at a loss. Have any alarms been occasioned by the emancipation of our Catholic brethren? Has the bigoted malignity of any individuals been crushed? Or has the stability of the government, or has that of the country, been weakened? Or is one million of subjects stronger than four millions? Do you think that the benefit they received should be poisoned by the sting of vengeance? If you think so, you must say to them, "You have demanded emancipation, and you have got it; but we abhor your persons, we are outraged at your success; and we will stigmatize by a criminal prosecution the relief which you have obtained from the voice of your country." I ask you, gentlemen, do you think, as honest men anxious for the public tranquillity, conscious that there are wounds not yet completely cicatrized, that you ought to speak this language at this time to men who are too much disposed to think that in this very emancipation they have been saved from their own parliament by the humanity of their sovereign? Or do you wish to prepare them for the revocation of those improvident concessions? Do you think it wise or humane at this moment to insult them, by sticking up in a pillory the man who dared to stand forth their advocate? I put it to your oaths, do you think that a blessing of that kind, that a victory obtained by justice over bigotry and oppression, should have a stigma cast upon it by an ignominious sentence upon men bold and honest enough to propose that measure? To propose the redeeming of religion from the abuses of the church, the reclaiming of three millions of men from bondage, and giving liberty to all who had a right to demand it; giving, I say, in the so much censured words of this paper, giving "universal emancipation!" I speak in the spirit of the British law, which makes liberty commensurate with and inseparable from British soil; which proclaims even to the stranger and the sojourner, the moment he sets his foot upon British earth, that the ground on which he treads is holy, and consecrated by the genius of "universal emancipation." No matter in what language his doom may have been pronounced; no matter what complexion incompatible with freedom, an Indian or an African sun may have burnt upon him; no matter in what disastrous battle his liberty may have been cloven down; no matter with what solemnities he may have been devoted upon the altar of slavery; the first moment he touches the sacred soil of Britain, the altar and the god sink together in the dust; his soul walks abroad in her own majesty; his body swells beyond the measure of his chains, that burst from around him, and he stands redeemed, regenerated, and disenthralled, by the irresistible genius of "universal emancipation."

[Here Mr. Curran was interrupted by a sudden burst of applause from the court and bail. Silence, however, was restored after some minutes.]

Gentlemen, I am not such a fool as to ascribe any effusion of this sort to any merit of mine. It is the mighty theme, and not the inconsiderable advocate, that can excite interest in the hearer! What you hear is but the testimony which nature bears to her own character; it is the effusion of her gratitude to that power, which stamped that character upon her.

And, gentlemen, permit me to say, that if my client had occasion to defend his cause by any mad or drunken appeals to extravagance or licentiousness, I trust in God I stand in that situation, that, humble as I am, he would not have resorted to me to be his advocate. I was not recommended to his choice by any connection of principle or party, or even private friendship; and saying this, I cannot but add, that I consider not to be acquainted with such a man as Mr. Rowan, a want of personal good fortune.

Gentlemen, upon this great subject of reform and emancipation there is a latitude and boldness of remark, justifiable in the people, and necessary to the defence of Mr. Rowan, for which the habits of professional studies, and technical adherence to established forms, have rendered me unfit. It is, however, my duty, standing here as his advocate, to make some few observations to you, which I conceive to be material.

Gentlemen, you are sitting in a country which has a right to the British constitution, and which is bound by an indissoluble union with the British nation. If you were now even at liberty to debate upon that subject; if you even were not by the most solemn compacts, founded upon the authority of your ancestors and of yourselves, bound to that alliance, and had an election now to make; in the present unhappy state of Europe, if you had been heretofore a stranger to Great Britain, you would now say, we will enter into society and union with you;

Una salus ambobus erit, commune periclum.

But to accomplish that union, let me tell you, you must learn to become like the English people; it is vain to say, you will protect their freedom if you abandon your own. The pillar whose base has no foundation, can give no support to the dome under which its head is placed; and if you profess to give England that assistance which you refuse to yourselves, she will laugh at your folly, and despise your meanness and insincerity. Let us follow this a little further, I know you will interpret what I say with the candour in which it is spoken. England is marked by a natural avarice of freedom, which she is studious to engross and accumulate, but most unwilling to impart, whether from any necessity of her policy, or from her weakness, or from her pride, I will not presume to say; but that so is the fact, you need not look to the east, or to the west, you need only look to yourselves.

In order to confirm that observation, I would appeal to what fell from the learned counsel for the crown, that notwithstanding the alliance subsisting for two centuries past between the two countries, the date of liberty in one goes no further back than the year 1784.

If it required additional confirmation, I should state the case of the invaded American, and the subjugated Indian, to prove that the policy of England has ever been to govern her connections more as colonies, than as allies; and it must be owing to the great spirit indeed of Ireland if she shall continue free. Rely upon it, she will ever have to hold her course against an adverse current; rely upon it, if the popular spring does not continue strong and elastic, rely upon it, a short interval of debilitated nerve and broken force will send you down the stream again, and reconsign you to the condition of a province.

If such should become the fate of your constitution, ask yourselves what must be the motive of your government? It is easier to govern a province by a faction, than to govern a co-ordinate country by co-ordinate means. I do not say it is now, but it will be always thought easiest by the managers of the day, to govern the Irish nation by the agency of such a faction, as long as this country shall be found willing to let her connection with Great Britain be preserved only by her own degradation. In such a precarious and wretched state of things, if it shall ever be found to exist, the true friend of Irish liberty, and British connection, will see, that the only means of saving both must be, as Lord Chatham expressed it, the infusion of new health and blood into the constitution. He will see how deep a stake each country has in the liberty of the other; he will see what a bulwark he adds to the common cause, by giving England a co-ordinate and co-interested ally, instead of an oppressed, enfeebled, and suspected dependant; he will see how grossly the credulity of Britain is abused by those who make her believe that her solid interest is promoted by our depression; he will see the desperate precipice to which she approaches by such a conduct, and with an animated and generous piety he will labour to avert her danger. But, gentlemen of the jury, what is likely to be his fate? The interest of the sovereign must be for ever the interest of his people, because his interest lies beyond his life; it must live in his fame, it must live in the tenderness of his solicitude for an unborn posterity; it must live in that heart-attaching bond by which millions of men have united the destinies of themselves and their children with his, and call him by the endearing appellation of king and father of his people.

But what can be the interest of such a government as I have described? Not the interest of the king, not the interest of the people, but the sordid interest of the hour; the interest in deceiving the one, and in oppressing and deforming the other; the interest of unpunished rapine and unmerited favour: that odious and abject interest, that prompts them to extinguish public spirit in punishment or in bribe; and to pursue every man, even to death, who has sense to see and integrity and firmness enough to abhor and to oppose them. What, therefore, I say, gentlemen, will be the fate of the man who embarks in an enterprise of so much difficulty and danger? I will not answer it. Upon that hazard has my client put everything that can be dear to man;—his fame, his fortune, his person, his liberty, and his children; but with what event your verdict only can answer, and to that I refer your country.

Gentlemen, there is a fourth point remaining. Says this paper, "For both these purposes, it appears necessary that provincial conventions should assemble preparatory to the convention of the Protestant people. The delegates of the

Catholic body are not justified in communicating with individuals, or even bodies of inferior authority, and therefore an assembly of a similar nature and organization is necessary to establish an intercourse of sentiment, and uniformity of conduct, an united cause and an united nation. If a convention on the one part does not soon follow, and is not soon connected with that on the other, the common cause will split into the partial interest; the people will relax into inattention and inertness; the union of affection and exertion will dissolve, and, too probably, some local insurrection, instigated by the malignity of our common enemy, may commit the character and risk the tranquillity of the island, which can be obviated only by the influence of an assembly arising from, assimilated with the people, and whose spirit may be, as it were, knit with the soul of the nation; unless the sense of the Protestant people be on their part as fairly collected and as judicially directed, unless individual exertion consolidates into collective strength, unless the particles unite into mass, we may perhaps serve some person or some party for a little, but the public not at all; the nation is neither insolent, nor rebellious, nor seditious; while it knows its rights, it is unwilling to manifest its powers; it would rather supplicate the administration to anticipate revolution, by well-timed reform, and to save their country in mercy to themselves."

Gentlemen, it is with something more than common reverence, it is with a species of terror that I am obliged to tread this ground. But what is the idea put in the strongest point of view? We are willing not to manifest our powers, but to supplicate administration, to anticipate revolution, that the legislature may save the country in mercy to itself.

Let me suggest to you, gentlemen, that there are some circumstances which have happened in the history of this country, that may better serve as a comment upon this part of the case than any I can make. I am not bound to defend Mr. Rowan as to the truth or wisdom of the opinions he may have formed. But if he did really conceive the situation of the country such as that the not redressing her grievances might lead to a convulsion, and of such an opinion not even Mr. Rowan is answerable here for the wisdom, much less shall I insinuate any idea of my own upon so awful a subject; but if he did so conceive the fact to be, and acted from the fair and honest suggestion of a mind anxious for the public good, I must confess, gentlemen, I do not know in what part of the British constitution to find the principle of his criminality.

But, gentlemen, be pleased further to consider, that he cannot be understood to put the fact on which he argues on the authority of his assertion. The condition of Ireland was as open to the observation of every other man as to that of Mr. Rowan; what then does this part of the publication amount to? In my mind, simply to this: "The nature of oppression in all countries is such, that although it may be borne to a certain degree, it cannot be borne beyond that degree; you find it exemplified in Great Britain; you find the people of England patient to a certain point, but patient no longer. That infatuated monarch James II. experienced this; the time did come when the measure of popular suffering and popular patience was full; when a single drop was sufficient to make the waters of bitterness to overflow. I think this measure in Ireland is brimful at present; I think the state of representation of the people in parliament is a grievance; I think the utter exclusion of three millions of people is a grievance of that kind that the people are not likely long to endure, and the continuation of which may plunge the country into that state of despair which wrongs exasperated by perseverance never fail to produce." But to whom is even this language addressed? Not to the body of the people, on whose temper and moderation, if once excited, perhaps not much confidence could be placed; but to that authoritative body whose influence and power would have restrained the excesses of the irritable and tumultuous; and for that purpose expressly does this publication address the volunteers. "We are told that we are in danger; I call upon you, the great constitutional saviours of Ireland, defend the country to which you have given political existence, and use whatever sanction your great name, your sacred character, and the weight you have in the community, must give you to repress wicked designs, if any there are.

"We feel ourselves strong; the people are always strong; the public chains can only be riveted by the public hands. Look to those devoted regions of southern despotism, behold the expiring victim on his knees, presenting the javelin recking with his blood to the ferocious monster who returns it into his heart. Call not that monster the tyrant, he is no more than the executioner of that inhuman tyranny which the people practise upon themselves, and of which he is only reserved to be a later victim than the wretch he has sent before. Look to a nearer country, where the sanguinary characters are more legible; whence you almost hear the groans of death and torture. Do you ascribe the rapine and murder of France to the few names that we are execrating here? Or do you not see that it is the frenzy of an infuriated multitude abusing its own strength, and practising those hideous abominations upon itself? Against the violence of this strength let your virtue and influence be our safeguard."

What criminality, gentlemen of the jury, can you find in this? what at any time? But I ask you, peculiarly at this momentous period, what guilt can you find in it? My client saw the scene of horror and blood which covers almost the face of Europe: he feared that causes, which he thought similar, might produce similar effects, and he seeks to avert those dangers by calling the united virtue and tried moderation of the country into a state of strength and vigilance. Yet this is the conduct which the prosecution of this day seeks to punish and stigmatize. And this is the language for which this paper is reprobated to-day, as tending to turn the hearts of the people against their sovereign, and inviting them to overturn the constitution. Let us now, gentlemen, consider the concluding part of this publication: it recommends a meeting of the people to deliberate on constitutional methods of redressing grievances. Upon this subject I am inclined to suspect that I have in my youth taken up crude ideas, not founded, perhaps, in law; but I did imagine that when the Bill of Rights restored the right of petitioning for the redress of grievances, it was understood that the people might boldly state among themselves that grievances did exist; that they might lawfully assemble themselves in such manner as they might deem most orderly and decorous. I thought I had collected it from the greatest luminaries of the law. The power of petitioning seemed to me to imply the right of assembling for the purpose of deliberation. The law requiring a petition to be presented by a limited number seemed to me to admit that the petition might be prepared by any number whatever, provided in doing so they did not commit any breach or violation of the public peace. I know that there has been a law passed in the Irish parliament of last year, which may bring my former opinion into a merited want of authority. That law declares that no body of men may delegate a power to any smaller number, to act, think, or petition for them. If that law had not passed, I should have thought that the assembling by a delegated convention was recommended, in order to avoid the tumult and disorder of a promiscuous assembly of the whole mass of the people. I should have conceived before that act that any law to abridge the orderly appointment of the few to consult for the interest of the many, and thus force the many to consult by themselves or not at all, would in fact be a law not to restrain but to promote insurrection: but that law has spoken, and my or or must stand corrected. Of this, however, let me remind you, you are to try this part of the publication by what the law was then, not by what it is now. How was it understood until last session of parliament? You have both in England and Ireland, for the last ten years, these delegated meetings. The volunteers of Ireland in 1782 met by delegation; they framed a plan of parliamentary reform; they presented it to the representative wisdom of the nation; it was not received, but no man ever dreamed that it was not the undoubted right of the subject to assemble in that manner. They assembled by delegation at Dungannon; and to show the idea then entertained of the legality of their public conduct, that same body of volunteers was thanked by both houses of parliament, and their delegates most graciously received at the throne. The other day, you had delegated representatives of the Catholics of Ireland, publicly elected by the members of that persuasion, and sitting in convention in the heart of your capital, carrying on an actual treaty with the existing government, and under the eye of your own parliament, which was then assembled; you have seen the delegates from that convention carry the complaints of their grievances to the foot of the throne, from whence they brought back to that convention the auspicious tidings of that redress which they had been refused at home.

Such, gentlemen, have been the means of popular communication and discussion, which until the last session have been deemed legal in this country; as, happily for the sister kingdom, they are yet considered there.

I do not complain of this act as any infraction of popular liberty; I should not think it becoming in me to express any complaint against a law when once become such. I observe only that one mode of popular deliberation is thereby taken utterly away, and you are reduced to a situation in which you never stood before. You are living in a country where the constitution is rightly stated to be only ten years old; where the people have not the ordinary rudiments of education. It is a melancholy story, that the lower orders of the people here have less means of being enlightened than the same class of people in any other country. If there be no means left by which public measures can be canvassed, what will be the consequence? Where the press is free, and discussion unrestrained, the mind, by the collision of intercourse, gets rid of its own asperities, a sort of insensible perspiration takes place, by which those acrimonies, which would otherwise fester and inflame, are quietly dissolved and dissipated. But now, if any aggregate assembly shall meet, they are censured; if a printer publishes their resolutions, he is punished; rightly, to be sure, in both cases, for it has been lately done. If the people say, Let us not create tumult, but meet in delegation, they cannot do it. If they are anxious to promote parliamentary reform in that way, they cannot do it; the law of the last session has for the first time declared such meetings to be a crime. What then remains? Only the liberty of the press, that sacred palladium, which no influence, no power, no minister, no government, which nothing but the depravity, or folly, or corruption of a jury, can ever destroy. And what calamity are the people saved from by having public communication left open to them? I will tell you, gentlemen, what they are saved from, and what the government is saved from; I will tell you also to what both are exposed by shutting up that communication. In one case sedition speaks aloud and walks abroad; the demagogue goes forth, the public eye is upon him, he frets his busy hour upon the stage; but soon either weariness, or bribe, or punishment, or disappointment, bear him down, or drive him off, and he appears no more. In the other case, how does the work of sedition go forward? Night after night the muffled rebel steals forth in the dark, and casts another and another brand upon the pile, to which, when the hour of fatal maturity shall arrive, he will apply the flame. If you doubt of the horrid consequences of suppressing the effusion even of individual discontent, look to those enslaved countries where the protection of despotism is supposed to be secured by such restraints, even the person of the despot there is never in safety. Neither the fears of the despot, nor the machinations of the slave have any slumber, the one anticipating the moment of peril, the other watching the opportunity of aggression. The fatal crisis is equally a surprise upon both; the decisive instant is precipitated without warning, by folly on the one side, or by frenzy on the other, and there is no notice of the treason till the traitor acts. In those unfortunate countries (one cannot read it without horror) there are officers whose province it is to have the water, which is to be drunk by their rulers, sealed up in bottles, lest some wretched miscreant should throw poison into the draught.

But, gentlemen, if you wish for a nearer and more interesting example, you have it in the history of your own revolution; you have it at that memorable period, when the monarch found a servile acquiescence in the ministers of his folly, when the liberty of the press was trodden under foot, when venal sheriffs returned packed juries to carry into effect those fatal conspiracies of the few against the many, when the devoted benches of public justice were filled by some of those fondlings of fortune, who, overwhelmed in the torrent of corruption at an early period, lay at the bottom like drowned bodies, while soundness or sanity remained in them; but at length becoming buoyant by putrefaction, they rose as they rotted, and floated to the surface of the polluted stream, where they were drifted along, the objects of terror, and contagion, and abomination.

In that awful moment of a nation's travail, of the last gasp of tyranny, and the first breath of freedom, how pregnant is the example? The press extinguished, the people enslaved, and the prince undone.

As the advocate of society, therefore, of peace, of domestic liberty, and the lasting union of the two countries, I conjure you to guard the liberty of the press, that great sentinel of the state, that grand detector of public imposture; guard it, because when it sinks, there sinks with it, in one common grave, the liberty of the subject and the security of the crown.

Gentlemen, I am glad that this question has not been brought forward earlier; I rejoice for the sake of the court, of the jury, and of the public repose, that this question has not been brought forward till now. In Great Britain analogous circumstances have taken place. At the commencement of that unfortunate war which has deluged Europe with blood, the spirit of the English people was tremblingly alive to the terror of French principles; at that moment of general paroxysm, to accuse was to convict. The danger loomed larger to the public eye from the misty medium through which it was surveyed. We measure inaccessible heights by the shadows which they project; where the lowness and the distance of the light form the length of the shade.

There is a sort of aspiring and adventurous credulity, which disdains assenting to obvious truths, and delights in catching at the improbability of circumstances, as its best ground of faith. To what other cause, gentlemen, can you ascribe that, in the wise, the reflecting, and the philosophic nation of Great Britain, a printer has been gravely found guilty of a libel, for publishing those resolutions to which the present minister of that kingdom had actually subscribed his name? To what other cause can you ascribe, what in my mind is still more astonishing, in such a country as Scotland, a nation cast in the happy medium between the spiritless acquiescence of submissive poverty, and the sturdy credulity of pampered wealth; cool and ardent, adventurous and persevering; winning her eagle flight against the blaze of every science, with an eye that never winks, and a wing that never tires; crowned as she is with the spoils of every art, and decked with the wreath of every muse; from the deep and scrutinizing researches of her Humes, to the sweet and simple, but not less sublime and pathetic morality of her Burns—how from the bosom of a country like that, genius and character, and talents, should be banished to a distant barbarous soil; condemned to pine under the horrid communion of vulgar vice and base-born profligacy, for twice the period that ordinary calculation gives to the continuance of human life? But I will not further press any idea that is painful to me, and I am sure must be painful to you; I will only say, you have now an example, of which neither England nor Scotland had the advantage; you have the example of the panic, the infatuation, and the contrition of both. It is now for you to decide whether you will profit by their experience of idle panic and idle regret, or whether you meanly prefer to palliate a servile imitation of their frailty, by a paltry affectation of their repentance. It is now for you to show that you are not carried away by the same hectic delusions, to acts, of which no tears can wash away the fatal consequences, or the indelible reproach.

Gentlemen, let me suggest another observation or two. If still you have any doubt as to the guilt or innocence of the defendant, give me leave to suggest to you what circumstances you ought to consider in order to found your verdict. You should consider the character of the person accused, and in this your task is easy. I will venture to say there is not a man in this nation more known than the gentleman who is the subject of this prosecution, not only by the part he has taken in public concerns, and which he has taken in common with many, but still more so by that extraordinary sympathy for human affliction, which, I am sorry to think, he shares with so small a number. There is not a day that you hear the cries of your starving manufacturers in your streets, that you do not also see the advocate of their sufferings—that you do not see his honest manly figure, with uncovered head, soliciting for their relief, searching the frozen heart of charity for every string that can be touched by compassion, and urging the force of every argument and every motive, save that which his modesty suppresses—the authority of his own generous example. Or if you see him not there, you may trace his steps to the private abode of disease and famine and despair, the messenger of Heaven, bearing with him food and medicine and consolation. Are these the materials of which you suppose anarchy and public rapine to be formed? Is this the man on whom to fasten the abominable charge of goading on a frantic populace to mutiny and bloodshed? Is this the man likely to apostatize from every principle that can bind him to the state; his birth, his property, his education, his character, and his children? Let me tell you, gentlemen of the jury, if you agree with his prosecutors in thinking that there ought to be a sacrifice of such a man on such an occasion—and upon the credit of such evidence you are to convict him—never did you, never can you, give a sentence consigning any man to public punishment with less danger to his person or to his fame: for where could the hireling be found to fling contumely or ingratitude at his head, whose private distresses he had not laboured to alleviate, or whose public condition he had not laboured to improve?

I cannot, however, avoid adverting to a circumstance that distinguishes the case of Mr. Rowan from that of a late sacrifice in a neighbouring kingdom.*

The severer law of that country, it seems, and happy for them that it should, enables them to remove from their sight the victim of their infatuation; the more merciful spirit of our law deprives you of that consolation; his sufferings must remain for ever before your eyes, a continual call upon your shame and your remorse. But those sufferings will do more; they will not rest satisfied with your unavailing contrition, they will challenge the great and paramount inquest of society, the man will be weighed against the charge, the witness, and the sentence; and impartial justice will demand, why has an Irish jury done this deed? The moment he ceases to be regarded as a criminal he becomes of necessity an accuser; and let me ask you, what can your most zealous defenders be prepared to answer to such a charge? When your sentence shall have sent him forth to that stage which guilt alone can render infamous, let me tell you, he will not be like a little statue upon a mighty pedestal, diminishing by elevation; but he will stand a striking and imposing object upon a monument, which, if it does not and it cannot record the atrocity of his crime, must record the atrocity of his conviction. And upon this subject, credit me when I say, that I am still more anxious for you than I can possibly be for him. I cannot but feel the peculiarity of your situation. Not the jury of his own choice, which the law of England allows, but which ours refuses;† collected in that box by a person, certainly no friend to Mr. Rowan, certainly not very deeply interested in giving him a very impartial jury. Feeling this, as I am persuaded you do, you cannot be surprised, however you may be distressed at the mournful presage, with which an anxious public is led to fear the worst from your possible determination. But I will not, for the justice and honour of our common country, suffer my mind to be borne away by such melancholy anticipation; I will not relinquish the confidence that this day will be the period of his sufferings; and, however

---

* Alluding to the banishment of Muir, Palmer, and others.

† In making up the jury, Mr. Rowan was not allowed the same right of challenge which is enjoyed in England.

merciless he has been hitherto pursued, that your verdict will send him home to the arms of his fans, ... ishes of his country. But if, ... Heaven forbid, it hath still been unfortunately determined, that because he has not bent to power and authority, because he would not bow down before the golden calf and worship it, he is to be bound and cast into the furnace, I do trust in God that there is a redeeming spirit in the constitution, which will be seen to walk with the sufferer through the flames, and to preserve him unhurt by the conflagration.

A SKETCH OF CURRAN.

The personal appearance and manner of Curran have been thus described by his friend and biographer, C. Phillips:—" Mr. Curran was of short stature, with a swarthy complexion, and 'an eye that glowed like a live coal.' His countenance was singularly expressive, and as he stood before a jury, he not only read their hearts with a searching glance, but he gave them back his own in all the fluctuations of his feelings, from laughter to tears. His gesture was bold and impassioned; his articulation was uncommonly distinct and deliberate; the modulations of his voice were varied in a high degree, and perfectly suited to the widest range of his eloquence."

LORD STANLEY.
Born 1826. Living.

[Lord Stanley, the eldest son of the present Earl of Derby, is better known as a statesman and administrator than as an orator. Nevertheless, his speeches, both in and out of Parliament, are so representative of that luminous insight which he has brought to bear on all the great political questions of his age, and so suggestive, from the practical sagacity with which they abound, that no work attempting to exhibit the Parliamentary eloquence of the present time would be complete without some illustration of his style. The present extract forms the greater part of a speech delivered in the Town Hall of King's Lynn on the 19th of October, 1864, before a large number of the electors and non-electors of that borough, for which he has been member for many years past. Though treating chiefly of questions of the day, and the existing relations of political affairs, the speech may be looked on and studied as a fine model for the clear survey and unflinching account of his stewardship which every enlightened representative should be prepared to offer to his constituents when public occasion requires them at his hands. Any criticism on the oratorical style of Lord Stanley will be best afforded by posterity. The following speech has been, by the extreme courtesy of Lord Stanley, revised before publication in this volume.]

SPEECH AT KING'S LYNN, 19TH OCT., 1864.

MR. MAYOR and gentlemen; I have come here for the purpose of addressing to you a few remarks on the present state of public affairs, in accordance with a promise made long ago and at the request of many here present whom I hope I may reckon among my friends. I say this that I may not seem to occupy your time unnecessarily, and I suppose I need offer no excuse for not having stood before you in this room either last autumn or the autumn before. The truth is, that the last three years, however eventful in the history of Europe and of America, have been years of singular peace and calm, as regards the people of these islands. It is not difficult to see to what that peace has been owing. Great material prosperity; absence in general of distress among the people, with one notable exception,—and in that case it was distress relieved with a care and success never witnessed before on so large a scale; a well-founded belief that any measure really called for by public opinion will be passed, and that so far our constitution answers the purpose for which it was framed; the removal in the last thirty years of nearly all the principal grievances which in the days of the old Reform Bill stirred men's minds; stirring events abroad drawing off attention from home affairs; perhaps also a kind of political scepticism encouraged, if not created, by the success of a government which is practically absolute in France; and by the crisis through which the greatest republic of the world is passing;—these in my mind are the causes of the state of things which exists now, which perplexes politicians of the old school, and disgusts those who confound agitation with progress. Some of these causes, no doubt, are temporary; but others are permanent in their character. I do not expect the absolute calm of the last four or five years to continue; but neither do I believe we shall return to the somewhat feverish and excited condition of the public mind which prevailed with few intermissions from 1830 to the time of the Crimean war. Nor do I, for my part, regret this. It is quite right to ascertain from time to time that your house is in good order, the foundation safe and the roof water-tight; but a man may do that without passing his life in examining every crack in the plaster and testing the soundness of every plank and beam; or, to put it in another way, I would say that those are not the healthiest men who are always thinking about their health. And, as it is with individuals, so it is with states. Political institutions are a means and not an end; and if peace is kept abroad, if life and property are protected at home, if the revenue is fairly collected and economically spent, and if individual freedom is left to every man, as far as is consistent with the rights of others, to do the best he can for himself and his neighbours, I believe the state has discharged the principal functions which it can with advantage undertake. And I think in our day it is one of the duties of a man of sense, whether he calls himself a Liberal or a Conservative, to watch that the state does not, as all continental governments without an exception do, extend its control far beyond those which are its legitimate and natural occupations. Now let me say after this preface that I do not mean to ask you to follow me in what is called a review of the session. What is done is done, and neither praise nor fault-finding can alter it. We may, then, leave the past alone; our business is with the present and with the future. There is only one past debate to which I shall refer, and I notice it because it seems likely, in a great degree, to influence the present policy of the country. We had a discussion last July on the conduct of foreign affairs. The ostensible object of that debate was to take the sense of the House as to whether the Danish negotiations had been mismanaged; but the object with which many members went into it, I among the rest, was to obtain from Parliament a distinct and decided expression of opinion in favour of a policy of non-intervention in continental disputes. In that we perfectly succeeded. The feeling upon that point came nearer to unanimity than I ever recollect to have been the case in Parliament upon any occasion equally important. I believe the feeling of the country went the same way, and unless I greatly mistake, the debate of July, 1864, will mark the beginning of a new epoch in the history of British diplomacy. Only do not let us feel too confident that the victory is gained. We have everybody's reason, with very few exceptions, in favour of a policy of peace; but cases are likely to arise in which the feelings and political passions of many men will be on the other side; and caution and care will still be necessary, lest what has been gained in 1864 should be lost in future years. Now, perhaps, I ought to guard myself in speaking of a policy of non-intervention. I do not mean that England should never give advice nor ever express an opinion upon questions not affecting her own interests; but I say that that should be done without menace, or the semblance of menace; it should be done in such a way as not to hold out hopes to one party, or threats to another, that force is intended to be used. Inasmuch, too, as under such circumstances, advice which is importunately obtruded is likely to be received with no great respect, I think it ought to be given only on rare and important occasions, when there is a reasonable hope that the parties concerned may be willing to accept it, or when the national conscience and feeling requires a protest on the part of our Government. Now there are at this time four leading questions in public affairs, which are likely to occupy attention for some years to come: First, there is the American war, as to which the duty of strict and absolute neutrality is, to my mind, plain; and, for my part, I do not wish to violate that neutrality, even to the extent of an impression of sympathy with one side or with the other. I speak of it simply as an observer, and if I were to venture upon prediction, which is always hazardous, I should say that I see no prospect of its early close. When two nations are worked up to a pitch of mutual hatred in which their own losses cease to affect them, if only they can inflict a greater loss upon the enemy, nothing will separate them except the utter exhaustion of one or the other. The time for that has not yet come. Neither party, as I believe, is half beaten yet; and considering the determination which the North has shown, I think it likely, as I did three years ago, that with their enormous superiority of force, they will occupy and overrun in the end the whole territory of the South. The North may succeed so far as to gratify their feeling of revenge and their desire of supremacy; but when they have done that their political difficulties will begin. I cannot realise the manner in which a republican community of 20,000,000 can hold consistently with its own principles of government, or indeed with any principles of free government, another community of 6,000,000 or 7,000,000, utterly disaffected to their rule. That is the real perplexity of the American future. As to the drain of men and money, I do not think, in comparison, much of it. The overflow of Europe will fill up all gaps in the population, and although I should be almost equally sorry to be a creditor either of the North or of the South, yet a country with the gigantic natural resources of America cannot be permanently ruined. All we can do—all we ought to do—is to let them fight it out. We are not in any way responsible for the war; we did not make it or advise it; and we know for certain that any offer of English mediation would be repelled as an insult, and probably be ascribed to interested motives. Our concern in the question, as the thing has turned out, is really more one of humanity than of self-interest. Taking into account the state of the markets in 1860, and setting against the cotton famine the opening of new markets elsewhere, and the gain to India, I doubt if, on the whole, we have been serious losers by this war. There is next the question of Italy; and as to that, I think we see our way more clearly than we did two or three years since. The Italian people have undoubtedly shown moderation and good sense under considerable difficulties; and they have their reward, for I think it is impossible to doubt that Rome, or at least the Roman territory, will pass into their hands at no very distant date. The late arrangement with France comes to this—that the Pope may hold his own if he can, his debts being paid for him, and time being given him to organize an army of his own. Now even if the Italian Government were disposed to observe that treaty strictly,—and probably they will observe it only in the letter,—

they cannot prevent a rising in Rome itself, and they cannot prevent over that extent of frontier, money, and arms, and volunteers being poured in. And then the question remains whether any army which the Pope can maintain on his own account, supported as he may be indirectly by Austria and Spain, but not openly assisted by any European state, will suffice to put down a rising. I do not think we in England can easily understand the extreme importance which the Italians attach to the possession of what, after all, is an unhealthy and decaying town, possessing no peculiar military or commercial advantages, and with nothing to recommend it except an historical name. But if they think it worth while on that account to quarrel with the bulk of their clergy (who form in Italy a powerful class) and their adherents, and to incur the ill-will of the Catholic powers, I think the choice will shortly be in their own hands. For Venice they will have to wait considerably longer. It is impossible that they can long maintain an army upon its present footing; they are at this moment spending 50 per cent. above their income, and the alternative before them is plain—either to disarm in part and to adopt frankly a policy of peace, or to involve themselves in a fresh war with Austria, the issue of which would be exceedingly doubtful. For my own part, accepting Italy as a fact, and wishing well to its people and government, I hope they will adopt the former and not the latter course. Most states desire to extend their frontiers, but it is a bad bargain to do that at the cost of national bankruptcy; and if to accomplish that object they have, as they probably would have, to call in foreign aid, they would almost certainly be expected to pay for it in the same way that they did before, and that would, I think, be a transaction not very edifying on the score of political morality, and not very conducive to the maintenance of tranquillity in Europe. There is another part of Europe in which we shall probably see great changes before long—I mean Germany. It is clear that the clumsy scheme of a German Federation has in practice broken down, and it is equally clear that the mutual rivalry of Austria and Prussia, to say nothing of the jealousies of foreign powers, will make it impossible for all Germany to be united for any purpose or in any manner as a single community. The only remaining alternative is either that the smaller states should unite among themselves for purposes of mutual protection, in which case they would be dependent upon France to a great extent, or that, according to their geographical position and their political tendencies, they should connect themselves, some with Austria and some with Prussia, so as to be, for diplomatic and military purposes, practically annexed to those countries. The latter alternative is, in my opinion, the

more likely one to be the result; and in that case I sincerely hope that England will not interfere, even by her advice, to prevent it. The existence of those petty German sovereignties is useless: they multiply, as we have seen, the risk of war; they serve, as far as I can perceive, no single political purpose; and the sooner they disappear from the map of Europe, in my judgment, the better. The fourth question of which I spoke is that of the East. It does not press at this moment, and therefore I shall only touch it in passing. I believe the breaking up of the Turkish empire to be only a question of time, and probably not of a very long time. The Turks have played their part in history; they have had their day, but that day is over; and I confess I do not understand, except it be from the influence of old diplomatic traditions, the determination of our older statesmen to stand by Turkish rule, whether it be right or wrong. I think we are making for ourselves enemies of races which will very soon become in eastern countries the dominant; we are keeping back countries by whose improvement we, as the great traders of the world, shall be the principal gainers; and we are doing this for no earthly advantage, either present or prospective. I admit that England has an interest, and a very strong one, in the neutrality of Egypt; and some interest also, although to a less extent, in Constantinople not falling into the hands of any great European power; but these two points set aside, I can conceive no injury arising to Great Britain from any transfer of power which may affect the Turkish empire; and, although that is not a practical question at the present moment, I have a very strong idea that before long it will become so. Now, in regard to colonial matters, apart from two questions—one, that of the African settlements, and the other that of colonial defences, on both of which I shall touch as matters of finance—there is only one subject which need interest us greatly at home,—I mean the relations among themselves of the colonies composing the two great groups of Australia and of British North America. In British North America there is a strong movement now in progress in favour of federation— or rather, in favour of union in some shape. In Australia the same feeling is beginning to arise, though it has not expressed itself so strongly, or assumed so practical a form. I think that both in one case and in the other that tendency ought to be encouraged. We know, whatever our wish about it may be, that these colonies must at no very distant date be independent states. We have no interest except in their strength and well-being. We see practically in America the danger of a federal union, hastily and loosely patched up between separate and sovereign states, each naturally jealous of its own independence We have in practice settled the relations of the colonies to the mother country; and the work remaining to us to do is to help them to settle their relations with one another. By so doing we shall strengthen the British empire, while they remain connected with us, and when they cease to be our dependencies we shall obtain more cordial and more powerful allies. I do not know if it is worth while to mention here that unlucky quarrel which has sprung up between the home authorities and those of Australia on the subject of transportation. The case is briefly this: we continue to send a certain number of convicts yearly to Western Australia. That we have an undoubted right to do, and the West Australians themselves do not complain. But when the sentences of these men are expired, they emigrate to the other Australian colonies, and they introduce there a dangerous and a degraded population. Against that the inhabitants of those other colonies protest, and they say (I think with perfect truth) that if you turn these men loose upon any part of that continent, they are sure to find their way to every other. Now, there is some irritation—I am afraid I must say a great deal of irritation—on this subject, and I think not unreasonably, and I mention it because it seems to me that this is a matter on which it would be utter folly for England to stand upon her legal rights. We know that before long the West Australians themselves will object, as all the other colonists have done, to receive our felons. When that happens, we must discontinue sending them. It is only, therefore, a question of sending them for a few years, and the number whom we so send out is small. Under these circumstances, I think it would be wise for the English Government to yield at once, and to declare that transportation to Australia shall cease. They will have to make that concession, at any rate, before long; and it is surely wiser and better to do it while we can do it freely and with a good grace.

* * * *

Now, there is one question of great importance at all times, but one on which you will hardly expect me to enter into detail to-day— I mean that which relates to the franchise. It is useless to discuss that matter until we know whether anything is likely to be done or attempted in that direction by the present Cabinet. How that may be I do not know, and possibly at this moment they themselves do not. But I do know this—that while a very small measure would not satisfy that party from whom the demand for action proceeds, a large measure is quite impossible to be carried, except in a state of popular feeling very different from that which exists at the present moment. It is quite idle to think that where the question in dispute is the transfer of power from one class to another, you can settle the matter after a little friendly discussion in a way that will satisfy everybody. Any man who expects that will be disappointed. There are many persons here who remember the year 1832. At that time the whole of the middle and lower classes, with the exception of an inconsiderable minority, were on one side, and on the other only a few hundred persons interested in the maintenance of the rotten boroughs. Yet that Reform Bill was not carried without a struggle, which agitated the country from one end to the other. It is not the upper, it is the middle class, the owners of the greater part of the property of the country, and by far the most powerful class in it, that exercises political supremacy at the present day. They are not likely to part with that of their own free will (at least if they do, it will be a thing new in history), and I see no such movement on the part of the working classes as would be likely to overbear that resistance which must be expected. I do not think that the Conservative party have anything to reproach themselves with on this subject. They were expected by Parliament and by the public to make in 1858-9 some proposal which should be in the nature of a compromise. They made it, they failed, and they withdrew from power. Their successors have made a similar attempt; they failed also, and they have stayed where they were. Now, my opinions on this question are what they were in 1859; but if it is to be dealt with at all, it cannot be settled without a dissolution of Parliament, and therefore any person who may want to have from me a detailed explanation of what I should or what I should not support will be quite sure to have his opportunity. But it does not follow, even if this whole question be left untouched, that Parliament need remain idle. We have a vast mass of miscellaneous work on hand, quite enough to occupy our attention for years to come. Our law still, after many reforms, perhaps the most cumbrous and complicated in Europe, wants to be consolidated and simplified. That is a process involving, no doubt, labour, and requiring that it should be placed in the hands of persons in whom Parliament shall have confidence; but otherwise it is a task not especially difficult. We have that extraordinary system of purchased commissions in the army, which I firmly expect to see done away with,— at least so far as regards the higher grades. We have the question of parish or union rating for Poor Law purposes; and connected with that is that intricate problem of the law of settlement. We know that the administration of our great public charities is faulty, and I cannot conceive of a better investment of time and labour than would be a Parliamentary inquiry into at least the chief of them, with a view to utilize the immense resources at their disposal. We have a licensing system which satisfies nobody, and the reform of which was recommended by a committee of the House of Commons ten years ago. In Ireland and Scotland the laws which regulate marriage are in a state only fit for a barbarous country. It cannot be said that what is called the private legislation of Parliament is in a condition altogether satisfactory, though, as to that, I must frankly admit that though I see the evil, I do not find it easy to suggest a remedy. Then our patent laws want amending, if the privilege of granting patents for inventions is to be retained, and that is in itself a question for serious discussion. A Commission has been appointed, on which I have the honour to sit, to inquire into the laws relating to capital punishment. And, whatever opinion may exist as to the limits within which that punishment should be inflicted, I think almost everyone agrees as to the inconvenience of having cases, as they are now, privately tried over again in the Home Office, after they have been publicly tried by a judge and jury. Well, I might go on almost indefinitely with a list of questions that require to be dealt with or discussed; but these are enough as a sample. You will see that there is plenty of work which you may put upon us, and I only wish that you, the constituencies, would look a little more sharply after us, and make sure that we do it. Idleness is not Conservatism; economy and administrative improvement are just as much the interest of those classes whose position and associations render them Conservative as of any others; and if, as I believe, the country does not desire organic change, it as little wishes for a state of utter lethargy and stagnation. Regulated activity disarms agitation; apathy and neglect create it. And now, gentlemen, you will be glad to hear that I am drawing to a close of what has necessarily been a very long and I fear a very tedious survey. I am not fond of long speeches; my only excuse must be that the ground to be travelled over is extensive, and that in view of an election, and probably of a contest, I do not want any voter in this town to say that he has been either deluded or left in the dark as to the opinions of his representative. There are two classes of subjects which I have left untouched: those relating to India, which, however important, I could not make interesting, or, perhaps, even intelligible, to gentlemen who may hear of them for the first time; and questions relating to ecclesiastical subjects, in regard to which, although there may be a good deal of talk, it does not seem to me that Parliament is inclined to take any active step. But as to those, or indeed any other matters within my power, I shall be glad to answer any questions that may be put to me. Party politics, as you know, I do not deal in upon these occasions. In the House of Commons, it is almost inevitable, if a man wishes to do anything, that he should act with a political party; but there has never been a time in my memory when more party spirit had so little life in it. The reason, I believe, is this,—that between moderate Conservatives and moderate Liberals, the differences are slight, and those who represent extreme opinions on either side were never fewer, and never exercised less influence than at present. There may be an extreme Tory party, though I never saw it, nor do I know what its views are. There is, no doubt, a Democratic party, but it is a small minority in the House of Commons. All between represents shades of opinion which merge almost imperceptibly into one another, the most reasonable men, in my belief, being generally found near the middle. That is a state of things which is embarrassing to many people, but not, so far as I can see, injurious to the country. It may be that those who are now in what is called opposition, may be called upon to take their turn of power. If they are, I hope and believe that they will use it wisely. But one advantage I am afraid they will not have — I greatly doubt whether they will be treated with as much patience and as much forbearance as during the last five years has been exhibited by them towards their rivals. But, whoever may administer affairs, it is opinion that governs. Opinion is the stream, and politicians, with all respect to them, are the straws that float upon it. It is opinion that governs, and I believe the opinion in England was never more moderate than now in regard to home affairs; never more resolute as to the maintenance of peace abroad; never more willing to deal with practical and proved abuses; but never less inclined to undervalue the merits of the institutions under which we live. And now, once more, let me apologise for the length of this address; let me thank you for the kindness of your reception; and let me express a hope that the political tie which now connects us may long remain unbroken. Broken by my fault I hope it may not be; broken by my choice I assure you it never shall be.

SHERIDAN, ON BURKE.

"To whom I look up with homage—whose genius is commensurate with his philanthropy, whose memory will stretch beyond the fleeting objects of any little partial temporary shuffling, through the whole range of human knowledge, and honourable aspirations after human good, as large as the system which forms life, as large as those objects which adorn it—a gentleman whose abilities, happily for the glory of the age in which we live, are not entrusted to the perishable eloquence of the day, but will live to be the admiration of that hour when all of us shall be mute, and most of us forgotten."

THOMAS WENTWORTH, EARL OF STRAFFORD.

Born 1593. *Died* 1641.

[Thomas Wentworth, the ill-fated Earl of Strafford, came of an ancient family in Yorkshire, and was created a peer by Charles I. For a time, his high genius associated itself with the popular cause; but it afterwards fell under the fatal influences of the Court, and he then advocated some of its most despotic measures. His career and fall are alike too much matter of history to be enlarged on here. Suffice it to say, that he was, in 1640, accused by the popular party in the Commons of an attempt to subvert the fundamental laws of the realm, and the impeachment was carried up to the bar of the House of Lords on the 18th of November in the same year. Subsequently a Bill of Attainder was passed against him, and, abandoned by his king, he suffered death on the scaffold, 12th May, 1641. What follows here is his last defence before the House of Lords. We are indebted to the admirable work on British Eloquence, by Dr. Goodrich, an American author, for the arrangement and annotation of this speech.]

DEFENCE BEFORE THE HOUSE OF LORDS, 13TH OF APRIL, 1641.*

MY LORDS,—This day I stand before you charged with high treason. The burden of the charge is heavy, yet far the more so because it hath borrowed the authority of the House of Commons. If they were not interested, I might expect a no less easy, than I do a safe, issue. But let neither my weakness plead my innocence, nor their power my guilt. If your lordships will conceive of my defences, as they are in themselves, without reference to either party—and I shall endeavour so to present them—I hope to go hence as clearly justified by you, as I now am in the testimony of a good conscience by myself.

My lords, I have all along, during this charge, watched to see that poisoned arrow of treason, which some men would fain have feathered in my heart; but, in truth, it hath not been my quickness to discover any such evil yet within my breast, though now, perhaps, by sinister information, sticking to my clothes.

They tell me of a twofold treason, one against the statute, another by the common law; this direct, that consecutive; this individual, that accumulative; this in itself, that by way of construction.

As to this charge of treason, I must and do acknowledge, that if I had the least suspicion of my own guilt, I would save your lordships the pains. I would cast the first stone. I would pass the first sentence of condemnation against myself. And whether it be so or not, I now refer to your lordships' judgment and deliberation. You, and you only, under the care and protection of my gracious master, are my judges. Under favour, none of the Commons are my peers, nor can they be my judges. I shall ever celebrate the providence and wisdom of your noble ancestors, who have put the keys of life and death, so far as concerns you and your posterity, into your own hands. None but your own selves, my lords, know the rate of your noble blood; none but yourselves must hold the balance in disposing of the same.*

I shall now proceed in repeating my defences as they are reducible to the two main points of treason. And,

I. For treason against the statute, which is the only treason in effect, there is nothing alleged for that but the fifteenth, twenty-second, and twenty-seventh articles.

[Here the Earl brought forward the replies which he had previously made to these articles, which contained all the charges of individual acts of treason. The fifteenth article affirmed that he had "inverted the ordinary course of justice in Ireland, and given immediate sentence upon the lands and goods of the King's subjects, under pretence of disobedience; had used a military way for redressing the contempt, and laid soldiers upon the lands and goods of the King's subjects, to their utter ruin." There was a deficiency of proofs as to the facts alleged. The Earl declared that "the customs of England differed exceedingly from those of Ireland; and therefore, though ceasing of men might seem strange here, it was not so there;" and that "nothing was more common there than for the governors to appoint soldiers to put all manner of sentences into execution," as he proved by the testimony of Lord Dillon, Sir Adam Loftus, and Sir Arthur Teringham.

The twenty-seventh article charged him with having, as lieutenant-general, charged on the county of York eightpence a day for supporting the train-bands of said county during one month, when called out; and having issued his warrants without legal authority for the collection of the same. The Earl replied that "this money was freely and voluntarily offered by them of Yorkshire, in a petition; and that he had done nothing but on the petition of the county, the King's special command, and the connivance, at least, of the Great Council, and upon a present necessity for the defence and safety of the county, when about to be invaded from Scotland."

The twenty-second and twenty-third articles were the most pressing. Under these he was charged with saying in the Privy Council that "the Parliament had forsaken the King; that the King ought not to suffer himself to be overmastered by the stubbornness of the people; and that, if his Majesty pleased to employ forces, he had some in Ireland that might serve to reduce this kingdom," "thus counselling to his Majesty to put down Parliament, and subvert the fundamental laws of the kingdom by force and arms. To this the Earl replied, (1.) That there was only one witness adduced to prove these words, viz., Sir Henry Vane, secretary of the Council, but that two or more wit-

---

* There are in the Parliamentary History two reports of this speech—one by Whitlocke, and the other by some unknown friend of Strafford. As each has important passages which are not contained in the other, they are here combined by a slight modification of language, in order to give more completeness to this masterly defence.

* Strafford had no chance of acquittal except by inducing the Lords, from a regard to their dignity and safety, to rise above the influence of the Commons as his prosecutors, and of the populace who surrounded Westminster Hall by thousands, demanding his condemnation. In this view, his exordium has admirable dexterity and force. He reverts to the same topic in his peroration, assuring them, with the deepest earnestness and solemnity (and, as the event showed, with perfect truth), that if they gave him up, they must expect to perish with him in the general ruin of the peerage.

nesses are necessary by statute to prove a charge of treason. (2.) That the others who were present, viz., the Duke of Northumberland, the Marquis of Hamilton, Lord Cottington, and Sir Thomas Lucas, did not, as they deposed under oath, remember these words. (3.) That Sir Henry Vane had given his testimony as if he was in doubt on the subject, saying "as I do remember," and " such or such like words," which admitted the words might be "*that* kingdom," meaning Scotland.]

II. As to the other kind, viz., constructive treason, or treason by way of *accumulation;* to make this out, many articles have been brought against me, as if in a heap of mere felonies or misdemeanours (for they reach no higher) there could lurk some prolific seed to produce what is treasonable! But, my lords, when a thousand misdemeanours will not make one felony, shall twenty-eight misdemeanours be heightened into treason?

I pass, however, to consider these charges, which affirm that I have designed the overthrow both of religion and of the State.

1. The first charge seemeth to be used rather to make me odious than guilty; for there is not the least proof alleged—nor *could* there be any —concerning my confederacy with the Popish faction. Never was a servant in authority under my lord and master more hated and maligned by these men than myself, and that for an impartial and strict execution of the laws against them; for observe, my lords, that the greater number of the witnesses against me, whether from Ireland or from Yorkshire, were of that religion. But for my own resolution, I thank God I am ready every hour of the day to seal my dissatisfaction to the Church of Rome with my dearest blood.

Give me leave, my lords, here to pour forth the grief of my soul before you. These proceedings against me seem to be exceeding rigorous, and to have more of prejudice than equity—that upon a supposed charge of hypocrisy or errors in religion, I should be made so odious to three kingdoms. A great many thousand eyes have seen my accusations, whose ears will never hear that, when it came to the upshot, those very things were not alleged against me! Is this fair dealing among Christians? But I have lost nothing by that. Popular applause was ever nothing in my conceit. The uprightness and integrity of a good conscience ever was, and ever shall be, my continual feast; and if I can be justified in your lordships' judgments from this great imputation —as I hope I am, seeing these gentlemen have thrown down the bucklers—I shall account myself justified by the whole kingdom, because absolved by you who are the better part, the very soul and life of the kingdom.

2. As for my designs against the State, I dare plead as much innocency as in the matter of religion. I have ever admired the wisdom of our ancestors, who have so fixed the pillars of this monarchy that each of them keeps a due proportion and measure with the others—have so admirably bound together the nerves and sinews of the State, that the straining of any one may bring danger and sorrow to the whole economy. The prerogative of the Crown and the propriety of the subject have such natural relations, that this takes nourishment from that, and that foundation and nourishment from this. And so, as in the lute, if any one string be wound up too high or too low, you have lost the whole harmony; so here the excess of prerogative is oppression—of pretended liberty in the subject is disorder and anarchy. The prerogative must be used as God doth His omnipotence, upon extraordinary occasions; the laws must have place at all other times. As there must be prerogative because there must be extraordinary occasions, so the propriety of the subject is ever to be maintained, if it go in equal pace with the other. They are fellows and companions that are, and ever must be, inseparable in a well-ordered kingdom; and no way is so fitting, so natural to nourish and entertain both, as the frequent use of Parliaments, by which a commerce and acquaintance is kept up between the King and his subjects.*

These thoughts have gone along with me these fourteen years of my public employments, and shall, God willing, go with me to the grave! God, his Majesty, and my own conscience, yea, and all of those who have been most accessory to my inward thoughts, can bear me witness that I ever did inculcate this, that the happiness of a kingdom doth consist in a just poise of the King's prerogative and the subject's liberty, and that things could never go well till these went hand in hand together. I thank God for it, by my master's favour, and the providence of my ancestors, I have an estate which so interests me in the commonwealth, that I have no great mind to be a slave, but a subject. Nor could I wish the cards to be shuffled over again, in hopes to fall upon a better set; nor did I ever nourish such base and mercenary thoughts as to become a pander to the tyranny and ambition of the greatest man living. No! I have, and ever shall, aim at a fair but bounded liberty; remembering always that I am a freeman, yet a subject—that I have rights, but under a monarch. It hath been my misfortune, now when I am grey-headed, to be charged by the mistakers of the times, who are so highly bent that all appears to them to be in the extreme for monarchy which is not for themselves. Hence it is, that designs, words, yea, intentions, are brought out as demonstrations of my mis-

---

* Strafford was generally regarded as the secret author of the King's aversion to Parliaments, which had led him to dispense with their use for many years. Hence the above declaration, designed to relieve him from the effects of this prejudice.

demeanours. Such a multiplying-glass is a prejudicate opinion!

The articles against me refer to expressions and actions—my expressions either in Ireland or in England, my actions either before or after these late stirs.

(1.) Some of the expressions referred to were uttered in private, and I do protest against their being drawn to my injury in this place. If, my lords, words spoken to friends in familiar discourse, spoken at one's table, spoken in one's chamber, spoken in one's sick bed, spoken, perhaps, to gain better reason, to gain one's self more clear light and judgment by reasoning—if these things shall be brought against a man as treason, this (under favour) takes away the comfort of all human society. By this means we shall be debarred from speaking—the principal joy and comfort of life—with wise and good men, to become wiser and better ourselves. If these things be strained to take away life, and honour, and all that is desirable, this will be a silent world! A city will become a hermitage, and sheep will be found among a crowd and press of people! No man will dare to impart his solitary thoughts or opinions to his friend and neighbour!

Other expressions have been urged against me, which were used in giving counsel to the King. My lords, these words were not wantonly or unnecessarily spoken, or whispered in a corner; they were spoken in full council, when, by the duty of my oath, I was obliged to speak according to my heart and conscience in all things concerning the King's service. If I had forborne to speak what I conceived to be for the benefit of the King and the people, I had been perjured toward Almighty God. And for delivering my mind openly and freely, shall I be in danger of my life as a traitor? If that necessity be put upon me, I thank God, by His blessing, I have learned not to stand in fear of him who can only kill the body. If the question be whether I must be traitor to man or perjured to God, I will be faithful to my Creator. And whatsoever shall befall me from popular rage or my own weakness, I must leave it to that Almighty Being, and to the justice and honour of my judges.

My lords, I conjure you not to make yourselves so unhappy as to disable your lordships and your children from undertaking the great charge and trust of this commonwealth. You inherit that trust from your fathers. You are born to great thoughts. You are nursed for the weighty employments of the kingdom. But if it be once admitted that a counsellor, for delivering his opinion with others at the council board, *candide et caste*, with candour and purity of motive, under an oath of secrecy and faithfulness, shall be brought into question, upon some misapprehension or ignorance of law—if every word that he shall speak from sincere and noble intentions shall be drawn against him for the attainting of him, his children and posterity—I know not (under favour I speak it) any wise or noble person of fortune who will, upon such perilous and unsafe terms, adventure to be counsellor to the King. Therefore I beseech your lordships so to look on me, that my misfortune may not bring an inconvenience to yourselves. And though my words were not so advised and discreet, or so well weighed as they ought to have been, yet I trust your lordships are too honourable and just to lay them to my charge as high treason. Opinions may make a heretic, but that they make a traitor I have never heard till now.

(2.) I am come next to speak of the actions which have been charged upon me.

[Here the Earl went through with the various overt acts alleged, and repeated the sum and heads of what had been spoken by him before. In respect to the twenty-eighth article, which charged him with "a malicious design to engage the kingdoms of England and Scotland in a national and bloody war," but which the managers had not urged in the trial, he added more at large, as follows:]

If that one article had been proved against me, it contained more weighty matter than all the charges besides. It would not only have been treason, but villainy, to have betrayed the trust of his Majesty's army. But as the managers have been sparing, by reason of the times, as to insisting on that article, I have resolved to keep the same method, and not utter the least expression which might disturb the happy agreement intended between the two kingdoms. I only admire how I, being an incendiary against the Scots in the twenty-third article, am become a confederate with them in the twenty-eighth article! how I could be charged for betraying Newcastle, and also for fighting with the Scots at Newburne, since fighting against them was no possible means of betraying the town into their hands, but rather to hinder their passage thither! I never advised war any farther than, in my poor judgment, it concerned the very life of the King's authority, and the safety and honour of his kingdom. Nor did I ever see that any advantage could be made by a war in Scotland, where nothing could be gained but hard blows. For my part, I honour that nation, but I wish they may ever be under their own climate. I have no desire that they should be too well acquainted with the better soil of England.

My lords, you see what has been alleged for this constructive, or rather destructive, treason. For my part, I have not the judgment to conceive that such treason is agreeable to the fundamental grounds either of reason or of law. Not of reason, for how can that be treason in the lump or mass, which is not so in any of its parts? or how can that make a thing treasonable which is not so in itself? Not of law, since neither statute, common law, nor practice hath from the beginning of the government ever mentioned such a thing.

It is hard, my lords, to be questioned upon a law which cannot be shown! Where hath this fire lain hid for so many hundred years, without smoke to discover it, till it thus bursts forth to consume me and my children? My lords, do we not live under laws? and must we be punished by laws before they are made? Far better were it to live by no laws at all; but to be governed by those characters of virtue and discretion which Nature hath stamped upon us, than to put this necessity of divination upon a man, and to accuse him of a breach of law before it is a law at all! If a waterman upon the Thames split his boat by grating upon an anchor, and the same have no buoy appended to it, the owner of the anchor is to pay the loss; but if a buoy be set there, every man passeth upon his own peril. Now, where is the mark, where is the token set upon the crime, to declare it to be high treason?

My lords, be pleased to give that regard to the peerage of England as never to expose yourselves to such moot points—such constructive interpretations of law. If there must be a trial of wits, let the subject matter be something else than the lives and honour of peers! It will be wisdom for yourselves and your posterity to cast into the fire these bloody and mysterious volumes of constructive and arbitrary treason, as the primitive Christians did their books of curious arts; and betake yourselves to the plain letter of the law and statute, which telleth what is and what is not treason, without being ambitious to be more learned in the art of killing than our forefathers. These gentlemen tell us that they speak in defence of the commonwealth against my arbitrary laws. Give me leave to say it, I speak in defence of the commonwealth against their arbitrary treason!

It is now full two hundred and forty years since any man was touched for this alleged crime to this height before myself. Let us not awaken those sleeping lions to our destruction, by taking up a few musty records that have lain by the walls for so many ages, forgotten or neglected.

My lords, what is my present misfortune may be for ever yours! It is not the smallest part of my grief that not the crime of treason, but my other sins, which are exceeding many, have brought me to this bar; and, except your lordships' wisdom provide against it, the shedding of my blood may make way for the tracing out of yours. You, your estates, your posterity, lie at the stake!

For my poor self, if it were not for your lordships' interest, and the interest of a saint in heaven, who hath left me here two pledges on earth—[at this his breath stopped, and he shed tears abundantly in mentioning his wife]—I should never take the pains to keep up this ruinous cottage of mine. It is loaded with such infirmities, that in truth I have no great pleasure to carry it about with me any longer. Nor could I ever leave it at a fitter time than this, when I hope that the better part of the world would perhaps think that by my misfortunes I had given a testimony of my integrity to my God, my King, and my country. I thank God, I count not the afflictions of the present life to be compared to that glory which is to be revealed in the time to come!

My lords! my lords! my lords! something more I had intended to say, but my voice and my spirit fail me. Only I do in all humility and submission cast myself down at your lordships' feet, and desire that I may be a beacon to keep you from shipwreck. Do not put such rocks in your own way, which no prudence, no circumspection can eschew or satisfy, but by your utter ruin! And so, my lords, even so, with all tranquillity of mind, I submit myself to your decision. And whether your judgment in my case—I wish it were not the case of you all—be for life or for death, it shall be righteous in my eyes, and shall be received with a *Te Deum laudamus*, we give God the praise.

EDMUND BURKE.
Born 1730. Died 1797.

[The magnificent speech which follows this note was delivered by Burke, in the House of Commons, on the 28th February, 1785, and remains as one of the finest memorials of its author's genius. The occasion of its delivery was a memorable debate arising out of a motion made by Fox, relative to the affairs of the East India Company. Certain debts, amounting in all to an enormous sum of money, having been alleged to be due from the Nabob of Arcot to some of the Company's servants, for various services conferred on that potentate, over a long period of years, and the claim having been admitted by the Board of Control, Fox attempted, by his motion, to arrest the payment. Pitt, however, was at that time Prime Minister; and despite the combined energies of Burke and Fox, the motion was defeated, and the ministry victorious. It was, however, in a great measure, in consequence of the failure of Fox's motion in this matter that Burke proceeded to the last great labour of his life—the impeachment of Warren Hastings—many of the grounds for which impeachment may be discovered from a careful reading of the speech we have here reprinted. Though extending to a great length, the speech, with the exception of certain portions, which, being almost purely statistical, have been omitted from our pages, is here reproduced in its entirety; and where it has been found absolutely necessary to curtail it, an attempt has been made to supply the omission by a short *resumé*, which, it is hoped, will leave the reader in full possession of the thread of the discourse, without burdening him with too elaborate figures and details. It may be remarked here, that this speech is one of those especially recommended by Lord Brougham for the study of the young orator.—See page 2 of this work.]

On the Nabob of Arcot's Debts.

MR. SPEAKER:—The times we live in have been distinguished by extraordinary events. Habituated, however, as we are, to uncommon combinations of men and of affairs, I believe nobody recollects anything more surprising than the spectacle of this day. The right hon. gentleman (Henry Dundas) whose conduct is now in question formerly stood forth in this house the prosecutor of the worthy baronet (Sir T. Rumbold) who spoke after him. He charged him with several grievous acts of malversation in office; with abuses of a public trust of a great and heinous nature. In less than two years we see the situation of the parties reversed; and a singular revolution puts the worthy baronet in a fair way of returning the prosecution in a recriminatory bill of pains and penalties, grounded on a breach of public trust, relative to the government of the very same part of India. If he should undertake a bill of that kind, he will find no difficulty in conducting it with a degree of skill and vigour fully equal to all that have been exerted against him.

But the change of relation between these two gentlemen is not so striking as the total indifference of their deportment under the same unhappy circumstances. Whatever the merits of the worthy baronet's defence might have been, he did not shrink from the charge. He met it with manliness of spirit and decency of behaviour. What would have been thought of him if he had held the present language of his old accuser? When articles were exhibited against him by that right honourable gentleman, he did not think proper to tell the house that we ought to institute no inquiry, to inspect no paper, to examine no witness. He did not tell us (what at the time he might have told us with some show of reason) that our concerns in India were matters of delicacy; that to divulge anything relative to them would be mischievous to the State. He did not tell us that those who would inquire into his proceedings were disposed to dismember the empire. He had not the presumption to say that for his part, having obtained in his Indian presidency the ultimate object of his ambition, his honour was concerned in executing with integrity the trust which had been legally committed to his charge; that others, not having been so fortunate, could not be so disinterested; and therefore their accusations could spring from no other source than faction, and envy to his fortune.

Had he been frontless enough to hold such vain, vapouring language in the face of a grave, a detailed, a specified matter of accusation, whilst he violently resisted everything which could bring the merits of his cause to the test; had he been wild enough to anticipate the absurdities of this day; that is, had he inferred, as his late accuser has thought proper to do, that he could not have been guilty of malversation in office, for this sole and curious reason, that he had been in office; had he argued the impossibility of his abusing his power on this sole principle, that he had power to abuse, he would have left but one impression on the mind of every man who heard him, and who believed him in his senses—that in the utmost extent, he was guilty of the charge.

But, Sir, leaving these two gentlemen to alternate as criminal and accuser upon what principles they think expedient, it is for us to consider, whether the Chancellor of the Exchequer, and the Treasurer of the Navy, acting as a Board of Control, are justified by law or policy in suspending the legal arrangements made by the court of directors, in order to transfer the public revenues to the private emolument of certain servants of the East India Company, without the inquiry into the origin and justice of their claims, prescribed by an Act of Parliament.

It is not contended that the Act of Parliament did not expressly ordain an inquiry. It is not asserted that this inquiry was not, with equal precision of terms, specially committed under particular regulations to the court of directors. I conceive, therefore, the Board of Control have no right whatsoever to intermeddle in that business. There is nothing certain in the principles of jurisprudence if this be not undeniably true, that when a special authority is given to any persons by name, to do some particular act, that no others, by virtue of general powers, can obtain a legal title to intrude themselves into that trust, and to exercise those special functions in their place. I therefore consider the intermeddling of ministers in this affair as a downright usurpation. But if the strained construction by which they have forced themselves into a suspicious office (which every man, delicate with regard to character, would rather have sought constructions to avoid) were perfectly sound and perfectly legal, of this I am certain, that they cannot be justified in declining the inquiry which had been prescribed to the court of directors. If the Board of Control did lawfully possess the right of executing the special trust given to that court, they must take it as they found it, subject to the very same regulations which bound the court of directors. It will be allowed that the court of directors had no authority to dispense with either the substance or the mode of inquiry prescribed by the Act of Parliament. If they had not, where in the Act did the Board of Control acquire that capacity? Indeed, it was impossible they should acquire it. What must we think of the fabric and texture of an Act of Parliament which should find it necessary to prescribe a strict inquisition; that should descend into minute regulations for the conduct of that inquisition; that should commit this trust to a particular description of men, and in the very same breath should enable another body, at their own pleasure, to supersede all the provisions the Legislature had made, and to defeat the whole purpose, end, and object of the law? This cannot be supposed even of an Act of Parliament conceived by the ministers themselves, and brought forth during the delirium of the last session.

My honourable friend has told you in the speech which introduced his motion, that fortunately this question is not a great deal involved in the labyrinths of Indian detail. Certainly not. But if it were, I beg leave to assure you that there is nothing in the Indian detail which is more difficult than in the detail of any other business. I admit, because I have some experience of the fact, that for the interior regulation of India, a minute knowledge of India is requisite. But on any specific matter of delinquency in its government, you are as capable of judging as if the same thing were done at your door. Fraud, injustice, oppression, peculation, engendered in India, are crimes of the same blood, family, and cast, with those that are born and bred in England. To go no farther than the case before us: you are just as competent to judge whether the sum of four millions sterling ought, or ought not, to be passed from the public treasury into a private pocket, without any title except the claim of the parties, when the issue of fact is laid in Madras, as when it is laid in Westminster. Terms of art, indeed, are different in different places; but they are generally understood in none. The technical style of an Indian treasury is not one jot more remote than the jargon of our own exchequer, from the train of our ordinary ideas, or the idiom of our common language. The difference, therefore, in the two cases is not in the comparative difficulty or facility of the two subjects, but in our attention to the one, and our total neglect of the other. Had this attention and neglect been regulated by the value of the several objects, there would be nothing to complain of. But the reverse of that supposition is true. The scene of the Indian abuse is distant indeed; but we must not infer that the value of our interest in it is decreased in proportion as it recedes from our view. In our politics, as in our common conduct, we shall be worse than infants if we do not put our senses under the tuition of our judgment, and effectually cure ourselves of that optical illusion which makes a briar at our nose of greater magnitude than an oak at five hundred yards distance.

I think I can trace all the calamities of this country to the single source of our not having had steadily before our eyes a general, comprehensive, well-connected, and well-proportioned view of the whole of our dominions, and a just sense of their true bearings and relations.

After all its reductions, the British empire is still vast and various. After all the reductions of the House of Commons, stripped as we are of our brightest ornaments, and of our most important privileges, enough are yet left to furnish us, if we please, with means of showing to the world that we deserve the superintendence of as large an empire as this kingdom ever held, and the continuance of as ample privileges as the House of Commons, in the plenitude of its power, had been habituated to assert. But if we make ourselves too little for the sphere of our duty; if, on the contrary, we do not stretch and expand our minds to the compass of their object, be well assured that everything about us will dwindle by degrees, until at length our concerns are shrunk to the dimensions of our minds. It is not a predilection to mean, sordid, home-bred cares that will avert the consequences of a false estimation of our interest, or prevent the shameful dilapidation into which a great, mighty empire must fall, by mean reparations upon mighty ruins.

I confess I feel a degree of disgust, almost leading to despair, at the manner in which we are acting in the great exigencies of our country. There is now a bill in this house, appointing a rigid inquisition into the minutest detail of our offices at home. The collection of sixteen millions annually; a collection on which the public greatness, safety, and credit have their reliance; the whole order of criminal jurisprudence, which holds together society itself, have at no time obliged us to call forth such powers; no, nor anything like them. There is not a principle of the law and constitution of this country that is not subverted to favour the execution of that project. And for what is all this apparatus of bustle and terror? Is it because anything substantial is expected from it? No. The stir and bustle itself is the end proposed. The eye-servants of a short-sighted master will employ themselves, not on what is most essential to his affairs, but on what is nearest to his ken. Great difficulties have given a just value to economy; and our minister of the day must be an economist, whatever it may cost us. But where is he to exert his talents? At home, to be sure; for where else can he obtain a profitable credit for their exertion? It is nothing to him whether the object on which he works under her eye be promising or not. If he does not obtain any public benefit, he may make regulations without end. Those are sure to: pay in present expectation, whilst the effect is at a distance, and may be the concern of other times and other men. On these principles he chooses to suppose (for he does not pretend more than to suppose) a naked possibility, that he shall draw some resource out of crumbs dropped from the trenchers of penury; that something shall be laid in store from the short allowance of revenue officers, overloaded with duty, and famished for want of bread; by a reduction from officers who are at this very hour ready to barter the treasury with what breaks through stone walls for an increase of their appointments. From the marrowless bones of these skeleton establishments, by the use of every sort of cutting, and of every sort of fretting tool, he flatters himself that he may chip and rasp an empirical alimentary powder, to diet into some similitude of health and substance the languishing chimeras of fraudulent reformation.

Whilst he is thus employed according to his policy and to his taste, he has not leisure to inquire into those abuses in India that are drawing off money by millions from the treasures of this country, which are exhausting the vital juices from members of the state, where the public inanition is far more sorely felt than in the local exchequer of England. Not content with winking at these abuses, whilst he attempts to squeeze the laborious ill-paid drudges of English revenue, he lavishes in one act of corrupt prodigality upon those who never served the public in any honest occupation at all, an annual income equal to two-thirds of the whole collection of the revenues of this kingdom.

Actuated by the same principle of choice, he has now on the anvil another scheme, full of difficulty and desperate hazard, which totally alters the commercial relation of two kingdoms; and what end soever it shall have, may bequeath a legacy of heart-burning and discontent to one of the countries, perhaps to both, to be perpetuated to the latest posterity. This project is also undertaken on the hope of profit. It is provided, that out of some (I know not what) remains of the Irish hereditary revenue, a fund at some time, and of some sort, should be applied to the protection of the Irish trade. Here we are commanded again to task our faith, and to persuade ourselves that out of the surplus of deficiency, out of the savings of habitual and systematic prodigality, the minister of wonders will provide support for this nation, sinking under the mountainous load of two hundred and thirty millions of debt. But whilst we look with pain at his desperate and laborious trifling; whilst we are apprehensive that he will break his back in stooping to pick up chaff and straws, he recovers himself in an elastic bound, and with a broadcast swing of his arm, he squanders over his Indian field a sum far greater than the clear produce of the whole hereditary revenue of the kingdom of Ireland.

Strange as this scheme of conduct in the ministry is, and inconsistent with all just policy, it is still true to itself, and faithful to its own perverted order. Those who are bountiful to crimes will be rigid to merit, and penurious to service. Their penury is even held out as a blind and cover to their prodigality. The economy of injustice is to furnish resources for the fund of corruption. Then they pay off their protection to great crimes and great criminals, by being inexorable to the paltry frailties of little men; and their modern flagellants are sure, with a rigid fidelity, to whip their own enormities on the vicarious back of every small offender.

It is to draw your attention to economy of quite another order—it is to animadvert on offences of a far different description, that my honourable friend has brought before you the motion of this day. It is to perpetuate the abuses which are subverting the fabric of your empire, that the motion is opposed. It is therefore with reason (and if he has power to carry himself through, I commend his prudence) that the right honourable gentleman makes his stand at the very outset, and boldly refuses all parliamentary information. Let him admit but one step towards inquiry, and he is undone. You must be ignorant, or he cannot be safe. But before his curtain is let down, and the shades of eternal night shall veil our eastern dominions from our view, permit me, Sir, to avail myself of the means which were furnished in anxious and inquisitive times, to demonstrate out of this single act of the present minister what advantages you are to derive from permitting the greatest concern of this nation to be separated from the cognizance, and exempted even out of the competence of Parliament. The greatest body of your revenue, your most numerous armies, your most important commerce, the richest sources of your public credit (contrary to every idea of the known settled policy of England), are on the point of being converted into a mystery of state. You are going to have one-half of the globe hid even from the common liberal curiosity of an English gentleman. Here a grand revolution commences. Mark the period, and mark the circumstances. In most of the capital changes that are recorded in the principles and system of any government, a public benefit of some kind or other has been pretended. The revolution commenced in something plausible; in something which carried the appearance at least of punishment of delinquency or correction of abuse. But here, in the very moment of the conversion of a department of British government into an Indian mystery, and in the very act in which the change commences, a corrupt private interest is set up in direct opposition to the necessities of the nation. A diversion is made of millions of the public money from the public treasury to a private purse. It is not into secret negotiations for war, peace, or alliance, that the House of Commons is forbidden to inquire. It is a matter of account; it is a pecuniary transaction; it is the demand of a suspected steward upon ruined tenants and an embarrassed master that the Commons of Great Britain are commanded not to inspect. The whole tenor of the right honourable gentleman's argument is consonant to the nature of his policy. The system of concealment is fostered by a system of falsehood. False facts, false colours, false names of persons and things, are its whole support.

Sir, I mean to follow the right honourable gentleman over that field of deception, clearing what he has purposely obscured, and fairly stating what it was necessary for him to misrepresent. For this purpose it is necessary you should know with some degree of distinctness a little of the locality, the nature, the circumstances, the magnitude of the pretended debts on which this marvellous donation is founded, as well as of the persons from whom and by whom it is claimed.

[Here Mr. Burke entered into details relative to the alleged accumulation of the debts, and then resumed:]

Sir, at this moment it will not be necessary to consider the various operations which the capital and interest of this debt have successively undergone. I shall speak to these operations when I come particularly to answer the right honourable gentleman on each of the heads, as he has thought proper to divide them. But this was the exact view in which these debts first appeared to the court of directors and to the world. It varied afterwards. But it never appeared in any other than a most questionable shape. When this gigantic phantom of debt first appeared before a young minister, it naturally would have justified some degree of doubt and apprehension. Such a prodigy would have filled any common man with superstitious fears. He would exorcise that shapeless, nameless form, and by everything sacred would have adjured it to tell by what means a small number of slight individuals, of no consequence or situation, possessed of no lucrative offices, without the command of armies, or the known administration of revenues, without profession of any kind, without any sort of trade sufficient to employ a pedlar, could have, in a few years (to some even in a few months) amassed treasures equal to the revenues of a respectable kingdom? Was it not enough to put these gentlemen, in the noviciate of their administration, on their guard, and to call upon them for a strict inquiry (if not to justify them in a reprobation of those demands without any inquiry at all), that when all England, Scotland, and Ireland had for years been witness to the immense sums laid out by the servants of the Company in stocks of all denominations, in the purchase of lands, in the buying and building of houses, in the securing quiet seats in Parliament, or in the tumultuous riot of contested elections, in wandering throughout the whole range of those variegated modes of inventive prodigality which sometimes have excited our wonder, sometimes roused our indignation, that after all India was four millions still in debt to them? India in debt to them! For what? Every debt for which an equivalent of some kind or other is not given, is on the face of it a fraud. What is the equivalent they have given? What equivalent had they to give? What are the articles of commerce or the branches of manufacture which those gentlemen have carried hence to enrich India? What are the sciences they beamed out to enlighten it? What are the arts they introduced to cheer and to adorn it? What are the religions, what the moral institutions they have taught among that people as a guide to life, or as a consolation when life is to be no more, that there is an eternal debt, a debt "still paying, still to owe," which must be bound on the present generation of India, and entailed on their mortgaged posterity for ever? A debt of millions, in favour of a set of men, whose names, with few exceptions, are either buried in the obscurity of their origin and talents, or dragged into light by the enormity of their crimes.

In my opinion, the courage of the minister was the most wonderful part of the transaction, especially as he must have read, or rather the right honourable gentleman says he has read for him, whole volumes upon the subject. The volumes, by the way, are not by one-tenth part so numerous as the right honourable gentleman has thought proper to pretend, in order to frighten you from inquiry; but in these volumes, such as they are, the minister must have found a full authority for a suspicion (at the very least) of everything relative to the great fortunes made at Madras. What is that authority? Why, no other than the standing authority for all the claims which the ministry has thought fit to provide for—the grand debtor—the Nabob of Arcot himself. Hear that prince, in the letter written to the court of directors, at the precise period, whilst the main body of these debts were contracting. In his letter he states himself to be, what undoubtedly he is, a most competent witness to this point. After speaking of the war with Hyder Ali in 1768 and 1769, and of other measures which he censures (whether right or wrong it signifies nothing), and into which he says he had been led by the Company's servants, he proceeds in this manner —"If all these things were against the real interests of the Company, they are ten thousand times more against mine, and against the prosperity of my country, and the happiness of my people, for your interests and mine are the same. What were they owing to them? To the private views of a few individuals, who have enriched themselves at the expense of your influence and of my country; for your servants have no trade in this country, neither do you pay them high wages, yet in a few years they return to England with many lacs of pagodas. How can you or I account for such immense fortunes, acquired in so short a time, without any visible means of getting them?"

When he asked this question, which involves its answer, it is extraordinary that curiosity did not prompt the Chancellor of the Exchequer to that inquiry which might come in vain recommended to him by his own Act of Parliament. Does not the Nabob of Arcot tell us in so many words, that there was no fair way of making the enormous sums sent by the Company's servants to England? And do you imagine that there was or could be more honesty and good faith in the demand for what remained behind in India? Of what nature were the transactions with himself? If you follow the train of his information, you must see that if these great sums were at all lent, it was not property, but spoil, that was lent; if not lent, the transaction was not a contract, but a fraud. Either way, if light enough could not be furnished to authorize a full condemnation of these demands, they ought to have been left to the parties who best knew and understood each other's proceedings. It was not necessary that the authority of government should interpose in favour of claims whose very foundation was a defiance of that authority, and whose object and end was its entire subversion.

It may be said that this letter was written by the Nabob of Arcot in a moody humour, under the influence of some chagrin. Certainly it was, but it is in such humours that truth comes out. And when he tells you from his own knowledge, what every one must presume, from the extreme probability of the thing, whether he told it or not, one such testimony is worth a thousand that contradict that probability, when the parties have a better understanding with each other, and when they have a point to carry that may unite them in a common deceit.

If this body of private claims of debt, real or devised, were a question, as it is falsely pretended, between the Nabob of Arcot as debtor, and Paul Benfield and his associates as creditors, I am sure I should give myself but little trouble about it. If the hoards of oppression were the fund for satisfying the claims of bribery and peculation, who would wish to interfere between such litigants. If the demands were confined to what might be drawn from the treasures which the Company's records uniformly assert that the Nabob is in possession of; or if he had mines of gold or silver, or diamonds (as we know that he has none), these gentlemen might break open his hoards, or dig in his mines without any disturbance from me. But the gentlemen on the other side of the house know as well as I do, and they dare not contradict me, that the Nabob of Arcot and his creditors are not adversaries, but collusive parties, and that the whole transaction is under a false colour and false names. The litigation is not, nor ever has been, between their rapacity and his hoarded riches. No, it is between him and them combining and confederating on one side, and the public revenues, and the miserable inhabitants of the ruined country, on the other. These are the real plaintiffs and the real defendants in the suit. Refusing a shilling from his hoards for the satisfaction of any demand, the Nabob of Arcot is always ready, nay, he earnestly, and with eagerness and passion, contends for delivering up to these pretended creditors his territory and his subjects. It is, therefore, not from treasuries and mines, but from the food of your unpaid armies, from the blood withheld from the veins, and whipt out of the backs of the most miserable of men, that we are to pamper extortion, usury, and peculation, under the false names of debtors and creditors of state.

[The speaker then proceeded to review, in the most searching manner, the several classes of creditors, and their respective claims on the Nabob, animadverting in the strongest terms on their acknowledgment by the ministry. He then continued:]

But what corrupt men, in the fond imaginations of a sanguine avarice, had not the confidence to propose, they have found a Chancellor of the Exchequer in England hardy enough to undertake for them. He has cheered their drooping spirits. He has thanked the peculators for not despairing of their commonwealth. He has told them they were too modest. He has replaced the twenty-five per cent. which, in order to lighten themselves, they had abandoned in their conscious terror. Instead of cutting off the interest, as they had themselves consented to do, with the fourth of the capital, he has added the whole growth of four years' usury of twelve per cent. to the first overgrown principal; and has again grafted on this meliorated stock a perpetual annuity of six per cent. to take place from the year 1781. Let no man hereafter talk of the decaying energies of nature. All the acts and monuments in the records of peculation, the consolidated corruption of ages, the patterns of exemplary plunder in the heroic times of Roman iniquity, never equalled the gigantic corruption of this single act. Never did Nero, in all the insolent prodigality of despotism, deal out to his prætorian guards a donation fit to be named with the largess showered down by the bounty of our Chancellor of the Exchequer on the faithful band of his Indian sepoys.

The right honourable gentleman (Mr. Dundas) lets you freely and voluntarily into the whole transaction. So perfectly has his conduct confounded his understanding, that he fairly tells you, that through the course of the whole business he has never conferred with any but the agents of the pretended creditors. After this, do you want more to establish a secret understanding with the parties—to fix, beyond a doubt, their collusion and participation in a common fraud?

If this were not enough, he has furnished you with other presumptions that are not to be shaken. It is one of the known indications of guilt to stagger and prevaricate in a story, and to vary in the motives that are assigned to conduct. Try these ministers by this rule. In their official dispatch, they tell the presidency of Madras, that they have established the debt for two reasons: first, because the Nabob (the party indebted) does not dispute it; secondly, because it is mischievous to keep it longer afloat, and that the payment of the European creditors will promote circulation in the country. These two motives (for the plainest reasons in the world) the right honourable gentleman has this day thought fit totally to abandon. In the first place, he rejects the authority of the Nabob of Arcot. It would indeed be pleasant to see him adhere to this exploded testimony. He next, upon grounds equally solid, abandons the benefits of that circulation, which was to be produced by drawing out all the juices of the body. Laying aside, or forgetting these pretences of his dispatch, he has just now assumed a principle totally different, but to the full as extraordinary. He proceeds upon a supposition, that many of the claims may be fictitious. He then finds that in a case where many valid and many fraudulent claims are blended together, the best course for their discrimination is indiscriminately to establish them all. He trusts (I suppose), as there may not be a fund sufficient for every description of creditors, that the best warranted claimants will exert themselves in bringing to light those debts which will not bear an inquiry. What he will not do himself, he is persuaded will be done by others; and for this purpose he leaves to any person a general power of excepting to the debt. This total change of language, and prevarication in principle, is enough, if it stood alone, to fix the presumption of unfair dealing. His dispatch assigns motives of pol.. concord, trade, and circulation. His speech p.oc.....ms discord and litigations, and proposes, as the ultimate end, detection.

But he may shift his reasons; and wind and turn as he will, confusion waits him at all his doubles. Who will undertake this detection? Will the Nabob? But the right honourable gentleman has himself this moment told us, that no prince of the country can by any motive be prevailed upon to discover any fraud that is practised upon him by the Company's servants. He says, what (with the exception of the complaint against the cavalry loan) all the world knows to be true; and without that prince's concurrence, what evidence can be had of the fraud of any the smallest of these demands? The ministers never authorized any person to enter into his exchequer and to search his records. Why then this shameful and insulting mockery of a pretended contest? Already contests for a preference have arisen among these rival bond creditors. Has not the Company itself struggled for a preference for years, without any attempt at detection of the nature of those debts with which they contended? Well is the Nabob of Arcot attended to in the only specific complaint he has ever made. He complained of unfair dealing in the cavalry loan. It is fixed upon him with interest on interest; and this loan is excepted from all power of litigation.

This day, and not before, the right honourable gentleman thinks that the general establishment of all claims is the surest way of laying open the fraud of some of them. In India this is a reach of deep policy. But what would be thought of this mode of acting on a demand upon the treasury in England? Instead of all this cunning, is there not one plain way open, that is, to put the burthen of the proof on those who make the demand? Ought not the ministry to have said to the creditors, "The person who admits your debt stands excepted to as evidence; he stands charged as a collusive party, to hand over the public revenues to you for sinister purposes? You say, you have a demand of some millions on the Indian treasury; prove that you have acted by lawful authority; prove at least that your money has been bonâ fide advanced; entitle yourself to my protection by the fairness and fulness of the communications you make." Did an honest creditor ever refuse that reasonable and honest test?

There is little doubt that several individuals have been seduced by the purveyors to the Nabob of Arcot to put their money (perhaps the whole of honest and laborious earnings) into their hands, and that at such high interest as, being condemned at law, leaves them at the mercy of the great managers whom they trusted. These seduced creditors are probably persons of no power or interest either in England or India, and may be just objects of compassion. By ta'i-g, i, this arrangement, no measures for discrimi......uon and uiscovery, the fraudulent and the fair are in the first instance confounded in one mass. The subsequent selection and distribution is left to the Nabob. With him the agents and instruments of his corruption, whom he sees to be omnipotent in England, and who may serve him in future, as they have done in times past, will have precedence, if not an exclusive preference. These leading interests domineer, and have always domineered, over the whole. By this arrangement, the persons seduced are made dependent on their seducers; honesty (comparative honesty at least) must become of the party of fraud, and must quit its proper character, and its just claims, to entitle itself to the alms of bribery and peculation.

[Here, again, Mr. Burke entered minutely into a question of accounts, disputing the accuracy of the claims put forward, and alleging fraud in the pretended creditors; after which he proceeded as follows:]

It is impossible (at least I have found it impossible) to fix on the real amount of the pretended debts with which your ministers have thought proper to load the Carnatick. They are obscure; they shun inquiry; they are enormous. That is all you know of them.

That you may judge what chance any honourable and useful end of government has for a provision that comes in for the leavings of these gluttonous demands, I must take it on myself to bring before you the real condition of that abused, insulted, racked, and ruined country; though in truth my mind revolts from it; though you will hear it with horror; and I confess I tremble when I think on these awful and confounding dispensations of Providence. I shall first trouble you with a few words as to the cause.

The great fortunes made in India in the beginnings of conquest, naturally excited an emulation in all the parts, and through the whole succession of the Company's service. But in the Company it gave rise to other sentiments. They did not find the new channels of acquisition flow with equal riches to them. On the contrary, the high flood-tide of private emolument was generally in the lowest ebb of their affairs. They began also to fear that the fortune of war might take away what the fortune of war had given. Wars were accordingly discouraged by repeated injunctions and menaces; and, that the servants might not be bribed into them by the native princes, they were strictly forbidden to take any money whatsoever from their hands. But vehement passion is ingenious in resources. The Company's servants were not only stimulated, but better instructed by the prohibition. They soon fell upon a contrivance which answered their purposes far better than the methods which were forbidden; though in this also they violated an ancient, but they thought an abrogated order. They reversed their proceedings. Instead of receiving presents, they made loans. Instead of carrying on wars in their own name, they contrived an authority at once irresistible and irresponsible, in whose name they might ravage at pleasure; and being thus freed from all restraint, they indulged themselves in the most extravagant speculations of plunder. The cabal of creditors who have been the object of the late bountiful grant from his Majesty's ministers, in order to possess themselves, under the name of creditors and assignees, of every country in India, as fast as it should be conquered, inspired into the mind of the Nabob of Arcot (then a dependant on the Company of the humblest order) a scheme of the most wild and desperate ambition, that I believe ever was admitted into the thoughts of a man so situated. First, they persuaded him to consider himself as a principal member in the political system of Europe. In the next place they held out to him, and he readily imbibed the idea of, the general empire of Hindostan. As a preliminary to this undertaking, they prevailed on him to propose a tripartite division of that vast country: one part to the Company, another to the Marattas, and the third to himself. To himself he reserved all the southern part of the great peninsula, comprehended under the general name of the Deccan.

On this scheme of their servants, the Company was to appear in the Carnatick in no other light than as a contractor for the provision of armies, and the hire of mercenaries for his use, and under his direction. This disposition was to be secured by the Nabob's putting himself under the guarantee of France, and by the means of that rival nation, preventing the English for ever from assuming an equality, much less a superiority, in the Carnatick. In pursuance of this treasonable project (treasonable on the part of the English), they extinguished the Company as a sovereign power in that part of India; they withdrew the Company's garrisons out of all the forts and strongholds of the Carnatick; they declined to receive the ambassadors from foreign courts, and remitted them to the Nabob of Arcot; they fell upon and totally destroyed the oldest ally of the Company, the King of Tanjore, and plundered the country to the amount of near five millions sterling; one after another, in the Nabob's name, but with English force, they brought into a miserable servitude all the princes and great independent nobility of a vast country. In proportion to these treasons and violences, which ruined the people, the fund of the Nabob's debt grew and flourished.

Among the victims to this magnificent plan of universal plunder, worthy of the heroic avarice of the projectors, you have all heard (and he has made himself to be well remembered) of an Indian chief called Hyder Ali Khan. This man possessed the western, as the Company, under the name of the Nabob of Arcot, does the eastern division of the Carnatick. It was among the leading measures in the design of this cabal (according to their own emphatic language) to extirpate this Hyder Ali. They declared the Nabob of Arcot to be his sovereign, and himself to be a rebel, and publicly invested their instrument with the sovereignty of the kingdom of Mysore. But their victim was not of the passive kind. They were soon obliged to conclude a treaty of peace and close alliance with this rebel, at the gates of Madras. Both before and since that treaty, every principle of policy pointed out this power as a natural alliance; and on his part, it was courted by every sort of amicable office. But the cabinet council of English creditors would not suffer their Nabob of Arcot to sign the treaty, nor even to give to a prince, at least his equal, the ordinary titles of respect and courtesy. From that time forward, a continued plot was carried on within the divan, black and white, of the Nabob of Arcot, for the destruction of Hyder Ali. As to the outward members of the double, or rather treble government of Madras, which had signed the treaty, they were always prevented by some overruling influence (which they do not describe, but which cannot be misunderstood) from performing what justice and interest combined so evidently to enforce.

When at length Hyder Ali found that he had to do with men who either would sign no convention, or whom no treaty and no signature could bind, and who were the determined enemies of human intercourse itself, he decreed to make the country possessed by these incorrigible and predestinated criminals a memorable example to mankind. He resolved, in the gloomy recesses of a mind capacious of such things, to leave the whole Carnatick an everlasting monument of vengeance; and to put perpetual desolation as a barrier between him and those against whom the faith which holds the moral elements of the world together was no protection. He became at length so confident of his force, so collected in his might, that he made no secret whatsoever of his dreadful resolution. Having terminated his disputes with every enemy, and every rival, who buried their mutual animosities in their common detestation against the creditors of the Nabob of Arcot, he drew from every quarter whatever a savage ferocity could add to his new rudiments in the arts of destruction; and compounding all the materials of fury, havoc, and desolation, into one black cloud, he hung for a while on the declivities of the mountains. Whilst the authors of all these evils were idly and stupidly gazing on this menacing meteor, which blackened all their horizon, it suddenly burst, and poured down the whole of its contents upon the plains of the Carnatick. Then ensued a scene of woe, the like of which no eye had seen, no heart conceived, and which no tongue can adequately tell. All the horrors of war before known or heard of, were mercy to that new havoc. A storm of universal fire blasted every field, consumed every house, destroyed every temple. The miserable inhabitants, flying from their flaming villages, in part were slaughtered; others, without regard to sex, to age, to the respect of rank, or sacredness of function; fathers torn from children, husbands from wives, enveloped in a whirlwind of cavalry, and amidst the goading spears of drivers, and the trampling of pursuing horses, were swept into captivity, in an unknown and hostile land. Those who were able to evade this tempest, fled to the walled cities. But escaping from fire, sword, and exile, they fell into the jaws of famine.

The alms of the settlement, in this dreadful exigency, were certainly liberal, and all was done by charity that private charity could do; but it was a people in beggary; it was a nation which stretched out its hands for food. For months together these creatures of sufferance, whose very excess and luxury in their most plenteous days had fallen short of the allowance of our austerest fasts, silent, patient, resigned, without sedition or disturbance, almost without complaint, perished by a hundred a day in the streets of Madras; every day seventy at least laid their bodies in the streets, or on the glacis of Tanjore, and expired of famine in the granary of India. I was going to awake your justice towards this unhappy part of our fellow-citizens by bringing before you some of the circumstances of this plague of hunger. Of all the calamities which beset and waylay the life of man, this comes the nearest to our heart, and is that wherein the proudest of us all feels himself to be nothing more than he is; but I find myself unable to manage it with decorum; these details are of a species of horror so nauseous and disgusting; they are so degrading to the sufferers and to the hearers; they are so humiliating to human nature itself, that, on better thoughts, I find it more advisable to throw a pall over this hideous object, and to leave it to your general conceptions.

For eighteen months without intermission this destruction raged from the gates of Madras to the gates of Tanjore; and so completely did these masters in their art, Hyder Ali and his more ferocious son, absolve themselves of their impious vow, that when the British armies traversed, as they did, the Carnatick for hundreds of miles in all directions, through the whole line of their march they did not see one man, not one woman, not one child, not one four-footed beast of any description whatever. One dead, uniform silence reigned over the whole region. With the inconsiderable exceptions of the narrow vicinage of some few forts, I wish to be understood as speaking literally. I mean to produce to you more than three witnesses, above all exception, who will support this assertion in its full extent. That hurricane of war passed through every part of the central provinces of the Carnatick. Six or seven districts to the north and to the south (and these not wholly untouched) escaped the general ravage.

The Carnatick is a country not much inferior in extent to England. Figure to yourself, Mr. Speaker, the land in whose representative chair you sit, figure to yourself the form and fashion of your sweet and cheerful country, from Thames to Trent, north and south, and from the Irish to the German sea, east and west, emptied and embowelled (may God avert the omen of our crimes!) by so accomplished a desolation. Extend your imagination a little further, and then suppose your ministers taking a survey of this scene of waste and desolation; what would be your thoughts if you should be informed, that they were computing how much had been the amount of the excises, how much the customs, how much the land and malt tax, in order that they should charge (take it in the most favourable light) for public service, upon the relics of the satiated vengeance of relentless enemies, the whole of what England had yielded in the most exuberant seasons of peace and abundance? What would you call it? To call it tyranny, sublimed into madness, would be too faint an image; yet this very madness is the principle upon which the ministers at your right hand have proceeded in their estimate of the revenues of the Carnatick, when they were providing, not supply for the establishments of its protection, but rewards for the authors of its ruin.

Every day you are fatigued and disgusted with this cant, "The Carnatick is a country that will soon recover, and become instantly as prosperous as ever." They think they are talking to innocents, who will believe that by sowing of dragons' teeth, men may come up ready grown and ready armed. They who will give themselves the trouble of considering (for it requires no great reach of thought, no very profound knowledge) the manner in which mankind are increased and countries cultivated, will regard all this raving as it ought to be regarded. In order that the people, after a long period of vexation and plunder, may be in a condition to maintain government, government must begin by maintaining them. Here the road to economy lies not through receipt, but through expense; and in that country nature has given no short cut to your object. Men must propagate, like other animals, by the mouth. Never did oppression light the nuptial torch; never did extortion and usury spread out the genial bed. Does any of you think that England, so wasted, would, under such a nursing attendance, so rapidly and cheaply recover? But he is meanly acquainted with either England or India who does not know that England would a thousand times sooner resume population, fertility, and what ought to be the ultimate secretion from both, revenue, than such a country as the Carnatick.

The Carnatick is not by the bounty of nature a fertile soil. The general size of its cattle is proof enough that it is much otherwise. It is some days since I moved that a curious and interesting map, kept in the India House, should be laid before you. The India House is not yet in readiness to send it; I have therefore brought down my own copy, and there it lies for the use of any gentleman who may think such a matter worthy of his attention. It is indeed a noble map, and of noble things; but it is decisive against the golden dreams and sanguine speculations of avarice run mad. In addition to what you know must be the case in every part of the world (the necessity of a previous provision of habitation, seed, stock, capital), that map will show you, that the use of the influences of Heaven itself are in that country a work of art. The Carnatick is refreshed by few or no living brooks or running streams, and it has rain only at a season; but its product of rice exacts the use of water subject to perpetual command. This is the national bank of the Carnatick, on which it must have a perpetual credit, or it perishes irretrievably. For that reason, in the happier times of India, a number almost incredible of reservoirs have been made in chosen places throughout the whole country; they are formed for the greater part of mounds of earth and stones, with sluices of solid masoury; the whole constructed with admirable skill and labour, and maintained at a mighty charge. In the territory contained in that map alone I have been at the trouble of reckoning the reservoirs, and they amount to upwards of eleven hundred, from the extent of two or three acres to five miles in circuit. From these reservoirs currents are occasionally drawn over the fields, and these watercourses again call for a considerable expense to keep them properly scoured and duly levelled. Taking the district in that map as a measure, there cannot be in the Carnatick and Tanjore fewer than ten thousand of these reservoirs of the larger and middling dimensions, to say nothing of those for domestic services, and the use of religious purification. These are not the enterprises of your power, nor in a style of magnificence suited to the taste of your minister. These are the monuments of real kings, who were the fathers of their people; testators to a posterity which they embraced as their own. These are the grand sepulchres built by ambition; but by the ambition of an insatiable benevolence, which, not contented with reigning in the dispensation of happiness during the contracted term of human life, had strained with all the reachings and graspings of a vivacious mind, to extend the dominion of their bounty beyond the limits of nature, and to perpetuate themselves through generations of generations, the guardians, the protectors, the nourishers of mankind.

Long before the late invasion, the persons who are objects of the grant of public money now before you, had so diverted the supply of the pious funds of culture and population, that everywhere the reservoirs were fallen into a miserable decay. But after those domestic enemies had provoked the entry of a cruel foreign foe into the country, he did not leave it until his revenge had completed the destruction begun by their avarice. Few, very few indeed, of these magazines of water that are not either totally destroyed, or cut through with such gaps as to require a serious attention and much cost to re-establish them as the means of present subsistence to the people and of future revenue to the state.

What, Sir, would a virtuous and enlightened ministry do on the view of the ruins of such works before them?—on the view of such a chasm of desolation as that which yawned in the midst of those countries to the north and south, which still bore some vestiges of cultivation? They would have reduced all their most necessary establishments; they would have suspended the justest payments; they would have employed every shilling derived from the producing to reanimate the powers of the unproductive parts. While they were performing this fundamental duty, whilst they were celebrating these mysteries of justice and humanity, they would have told the corps of fictitious creditors, whose crimes were their claims, that they must keep an awful distance; that they must silence their inauspicious tongues; that they must hold off their profane unhallowed paws from this holy work; they would have proclaimed with a voice that should make itself heard, that on every country the first creditor is the plough; that this original, indefeasible claim supersedes every other demand.

This is what a wise and virtuous ministry would have done and said. This, therefore, is what our minister could never think of saying or doing. A ministry of another kind would have first improved the country, and have thus laid a solid foundation for future opulence and future force. But on this grand point of the restoration of the country, there is not one syllable to be found in the correspondence of our ministers; from the first to the last they felt nothing for a land desolated by fire, sword, and famine;

their sympathies took another direction; they were touched with pity for bribery, so long tormented with a fruitless itching of its palms; their bowels yearned for usury, that had long missed the harvest of its returning months; they felt for peculation, which had been for so many years raking in the dust of an empty treasury; they were melted into compassion for rapine and oppression, licking their dry, parched, unbloody jaws. These were the objects of their solicitude. These were the necessities for which they were studious to provide.

[The speaker here took a survey of the revenue of the Carnatick at the time of the alleged contracting of the debts and afterwards, with a view of disproving the existence of the creditors' claims as set forth by the ministry, and then resumed:]

But I, Sir, who profess to speak to your understanding and to your conscience, and to brush away from this business all false colours, all false appellations, as well as false facts, do positively deny that the Carnatick owes a shilling to the Company, whatever the Company may be indebted to that undone country. It owes nothing to the Company, for this plain and simple reason—the territory charged with the debt is their own. To say that their revenues fall short, and owe them money, is to say they are in debt to themselves, which is only talking nonsense. The fact is, that by the invasion of an enemy and the ruin of the country, the Company, either in its own name, or in the names of the Nabob of Arcot and the Rajah of Tanjore, has lost for several years what it might have looked to receive from its own estate. If men were allowed to credit themselves, upon such principles anyone might soon grow rich by this mode of accounting. A flood comes down upon a man's estate in the Bedford Level of a thousand pounds a year, and drowns his rent for ten years. The chancellor would put that man into the hands of a trustee, who would gravely make up his books, and for this loss credit himself in his account for a debt due to him of £10,000. It is, however, on this principle the Company makes up its demands on the Carnatick. In peace they go the full length, and indeed more than the full length, of what the people can bear for current establishments; then they are absurd enough to consolidate all the calamities of war into debts, to metamorphose the devastations of the country into demands upon its future production. What is this but to avow a resolution utterly to destroy their own country, and to force the people to pay for their sufferings to a government which has proved unable to protect either the share of the husbandman or their own? In every lease of a farm, the invasion of an enemy, instead of forming a demand for arrear, is a release of rent; nor for that release is it at all necessary to show, that the invasion has left nothing to the occupier of the soil, though in the present case it would be too easy to prove that melancholy fact. I therefore applauded my right honourable friend, who, when he canvassed the Company's accounts, as a preliminary to a bill that ought not to stand on falsehood of any kind, fixed his discerning eye and his deciding hand on these debts of the company, from the Nabob of Arcot and Rajah of Tanjore, and at one stroke expunged them all, as utterly irrecoverable; he might have added as utterly unfounded.

On these grounds I do not blame the arrangement this day in question, as a preference given to the debt of individuals over the Company's debt. In my eye it is no more than the preference of a fiction over a chimera; but I blame the preference given to those fictitious private debts over the standing defence and the standing government. It is there the public is robbed. It is robbed in its army; it is robbed in its civil administration; it is robbed in its credit; it is robbed in its investment which forms the commercial connection between that country and Europe. There is the robbery.

But my principal objection lies a good deal deeper. That debt to the company is the pretext under which all the other debts lurk and cover themselves. That debt forms the foul putrid mucus, in which are engendered the whole brood of creeping ascarides, all the endless involutions, the eternal knot, added to a knot of those inexpungable tape-worms which devour the nutriment, and eat up the bowels of India. It is necessary, Sir, you should recollect two things; first, that the Nabob's debt to the Company carries no interest. In the next place you will observe, that whenever the Company has occasion to borrow, she has always commanded whatever she thought fit at eight per cent. Carrying in your mind these two facts, attend to the process with regard to the public and private debt, and with what little appearance of decency they play into each other's hands a game of utter perdition to the unhappy natives of India. The Nabob falls into an arrear to the Company. The Presidency presses for payment. The Nabob's answer is, I have no money. Good. But there are soucars who will supply you on the mortgage of your territories. Then steps forward some Paul Benfield, and from his grateful compassion to the Nabob, and his filial regard to the Company, he unlocks the treasures of his virtuous industry; and for a consideration of twenty-four or thirty-six per cent. on a mortgage of the territorial revenue, becomes security to the Company for the Nabob's arrear.

All this intermediate usury thus becomes sanctified by the ultimate view to the Company's payment. In this case would not a plain man ask this plain question of the Company: If you knew that the Nabob must annually mortgage his territories to your servants to pay his annual arrear to you, why is not the assignment or mortgage made directly to the Company itself? By this simple obvious operation, the Company would be relieved, and the debt paid without the charge of a shilling interest to that prince. But if that course should be thought too indulgent, why do they not take that assignment with such interest to themselves as they pay to others, that is, eight per cent.? Or, if it were thought more advisable (why it should I know not) that he must borrow, why do not the Company lend their own credit to the Nabob for their own payment? That credit would not be weakened by the collateral security of his territorial mortgage. The money might still be had at eight per cent. Instead of any of these honest and obvious methods, the Company has for years kept up a show of disinterestedness and moderation, by suffering a debt to accumulate to them from the country powers without any interest at all; and at the same time have seen before their eyes, on a pretext of borrowing to pay that debt, the revenues of the country charged with an usury of 20, 24, 36, and even 48 per cent., with compound interest, for the benefit of their servants. All this time they know that by having a debt subsisting without any interest, which is to be paid by contracting a debt on the highest interest, they manifestly rendered it necessary to the Nabob of Arcot to give the private demand a preference to the public; and by binding him and their servants together in a common cause, they enable him to form a party to the utter ruin of their own authority, and their own affairs. Thus their false moderation, and their affected purity, by the natural operation of everything false, and everything affected, becomes pander to the unbridled debauchery and licentious lewdness of usury and extortion.

In consequence of this double game, all the territorial revenues have, at one time or other, been covered by those locusts, the English soucars. Not one single foot of the Carnatick has escaped them; a territory as large as England. During these operations, what a scene has that country presented! The usurious European assignee supersedes the Nabob's native farmer of the revenue; the farmer flies to the Nabob's presence to claim his bargain; whilst his servants murmur for wages, and his soldiers mutiny for pay. The mortgage to the European assignee is then resumed, and the native farmer replaced; replaced, again to be removed on the new clamour of the European assignee. Every man of rank and landed fortune being long since extinguished, the remaining miserable last cultivator, who grows to the soil, after having his back scored by the farmer, has it again flayed by the whip of the assignee, and is thus by a ravenous, because a short-lived, succession of claimants, lashed from oppressor to oppressor, whilst a single drop of blood is left as the means of extorting a single grain of corn. Do not think I paint. Far, very far from it; I do not reach the fact, nor approach to it. Men of respectable condition, men equal to your substantial English yeomen, are daily tied up and scourged to answer the multiplied demands of various contending and contradictory titles, all issuing from one and the same source. Tyrannous exaction brings on servile concealment; and that again calls forth tyrannous coercion. They move in a circle, mutually producing and produced, till at length nothing of humanity is left in the government, no trace of integrity, spirit, or manliness in the people, who drag out a precarious and degraded existence under this system of outrage upon human nature. Such is the effect of the establishment of a debt to the Company, as it has hitherto been managed, and as it ever will remain, until ideas are adopted totally different from those which prevail at this time.

Your worthy ministers, supporting what they are obliged to condemn, have thought fit to renew the Company's old order against contracting private debts in future. They begin by rewarding the violation of the ancient law; and then they gravely re-enact provisions, of which they have given bounties for the breach. This inconsistency has been well exposed. But what will you say to their having gone the length of giving positive directions for contracting the debt which they positively forbid?

[Again Mr. Burke entered on statistical explanations and proofs, with reference to the Carnatick ; passing on afterwards to the conduct of the ministry with reference to Tanjore.]

Such is the state to which the Company's servants have reduced that country. Now come the reformers, restorers, and comforters of India. What have they done? In addition to all these tyrannous exactions, with all these ruinous debts in their train, looking to one side of an agreement whilst they wilfully shut their eyes to the other, they withdraw from Tanjore all the benefits of the treaty of 1762, and they subject that nation to a perpetual tribute of forty thousand a year to the Nabob of Arcot; a tribute never due, or pretended to be due to *him*, even when he appeared to be something; a tribute, as things now stand, not to a real potentate, but to a shadow, a dream, an incubus of oppression. After the Company has accepted in subsidy, in grant of territory, in remission of rent, as a compensation for their own protection, at least two hundred thousand pounds a-year, without discounting a shilling for that receipt, the ministers condemn this harrassed nation to be tributary to a person who is himself, by their own arrangement, deprived of the right of war or peace, deprived of the power of the sword, forbidden to keep up a single regiment of soldiers, and is therefore wholly disabled from all protection of the country which is the object of the pretended tribute. Tribute hangs on the sword. It is an incident inseparable from real sovereign power. In the present case to suppose its existence, is as absurd, as it is cruel and oppressive. And here, Mr. Speaker, you have a clear exemplification of the use of those false names, and false colours, which the gentlemen who have lately taken possession of India choose to lay on for the purpose of disguising their plan of oppression. The Nabob of Arcot, and Rajah of Tanjore, have in truth and substance, no more than a merely civil authority, held in the most entire dependence on the Company. The Nabob, without military, without federal capacity, is extinguished as a potentate; but then he is carefully kept alive as an independent and sovereign power, for the purpose of rapine and extortion—for the purpose of perpetuating the old intrigues, animosities, usuries, and corruptions.

It was not enough that this mockery of tribute was to be continued without the correspondent protection, or any of the stipulated equivalents, but ten years of arrear, to the amount of £400,000 sterling, is added to all the debts of the Company, and to individuals in order to create a new debt, to be paid (if at all possible to be paid, in whole or in part), only by new usuries; and all this for the Nabob of Arcot, or rather for Mr. Benfield, and the corps of the Nabob's creditors and their soucars. Thus these miserable Indian princes are continued in their seats, for no other purpose than to render them in the first instance objects of every species of extortion, and in the second, to force them to become, for the sake of a momentary shadow of reduced authority, a sort of subordinate tyrants, the ruin and calamity, not the fathers and cherishers of their people.

But take this tribute only as a mere charge (without title, cause, or equivalent) on this people. What one step has been taken to furnish grounds for a just calculation and estimate of the proportion of the burthen and the ability? None; not an attempt at it. They do not adapt the burthen to the strength; but they estimate the strength of the bearers by the burthen they impose. Then what care is taken to leave a fund sufficient to the future reproduction of the revenues that are to bear all these loads? Every one but tolerably conversant in Indian affairs, must know that the existence of this little kingdom depends on its control over the river Cavery. The benefits of Heaven to any community ought never to be connected with political arrangements, or made to depend on the personal conduct of princes; in which the mistake, or error, or neglect, or distress, or passion of a moment on either side, may bring famine on millions, and ruin an innocent nation perhaps for ages. The means of the subsistence of mankind should be as immutable as the laws of nature, let power and dominion take what course they may. Observe what has been done with regard to this important concern. The use of this river is indeed at length given to the Rajah, and a power provided for its enjoyment at his own charge; but the means of furnishing that charge (and a mighty one it is) are wholly cut off. This use of the water, which ought to have no more connection than clouds and rains, and sunshine, with the politics of the Rajah, the Nabob, or the Company, is expressly contrived as a means of enforcing demands and arrears of tribute. This horrid and unnatural instrument of extortion had been a distinguishing feature in the enormities of the Carnatick politics, that loudly called for reformation. But the food of a whole people is by the reformers of India conditioned on payments from its prince, at a moment that he is overpowered with a swarm of their demands, without regard to the ability of either prince or people. In fine, by opening an avenue to the irruption of the Nabob of Arcot's creditors and soucars, whom every man who did not fall in love with oppression and corruption on an experience of the calamities they produced, would have raised wall before wall, and mound before mound, to keep from a possibility of entrance, a more destructive enemy than Hyder Ali is introduced into that kingdom. By this part of their arrangement, in which they establish a debt to the Nabob of Arcot, in effect and substance, they deliver over Tanjore, bound hand and foot, to Paul Benfield, the old betrayer, insulter, oppressor, and seburge of a country, which has for years been an object of an unremitted, but unhappily an unequal struggle, between the bounties of Providence to renovate, and the wickedness of mankind to destroy.

The right honourable gentleman (Mr. Dundas) talks of the fairness in determining the territorial dispute between the Nabob of Arcot and the prince of that country, when he superseded the determination of the directors, in whom the law had vested the decision of that controversy. He is in this just as feeble as he is in every other part. But it is not necessary to say a word in refutation of any part of his argument. The mode of the proceeding sufficiently speaks the spirit of it. It is enough to fix his character as a judge that he never heard the directors in defence of their adjudication, nor either of the parties in support of their respective claims. It is sufficient for me, that he takes from the Rajah of Tanjore by this pretended adjudication, or rather from his unhappy subjects, £40,000 a-year of his and their revenue, and leaves upon his and their shoulders all the charges that can be made on the part of the Nabob, on the part of his creditors, and on the part of the Company, without so much as hearing him as to right or to ability. But what principally induces me to leave the affair of the territorial dispute between the Nabob and the Rajah to another day, is this, that both the parties being stripped of their all, it, little signifies under which of their names the unhappy, undone people are delivered over to the merciless soucars, the allies of that right honourable gentleman and the Chancellor of the Exchequer. In them ends the account of this long dispute of the Nabob of Arcot and the Rajah of Tanjore. The right honourable gentleman is of opinion, that his judgment in this case can be censured by none but those who seem to act as if they were paid agents to one of the parties. What does he think of his Court of Directors? If they are paid by either of the parties, by which of them does he think they are paid? He knows that their decision has been directly contrary to his. Shall I believe that it does not enter into his heart to conceive, that any person can stendily and actively interest himself in the protection of the injured and oppressed, without being well paid for his service? I have taken notice of this sort of discourse some days ago, so far as it may be supposed to relate to me. I then contented myself, as I shall now do, with giving it a cold, though a very direct, contradiction. Thus much I do from respect to truth. If I did more, it might be supposed, by my anxiety to clear myself, that I had imbibed the ideas, which, for obvious reasons, the right honourable gentleman wishes to have received concerning all attempts to plead the cause of the natives of India, as if it were a disreputable employment. If he had not forgotten, in his present occupation, every principle which ought to have guided him, and I hope did guide him, in his late profession, he would have known, that he who takes a fee for pleading the cause of distress against power, and manfully performs the duty he has assumed, receives an honourable recompense for a virtuous service. But if the right honourable gentleman will have no regard to fact in his insinuations, or to reason in his opinions, I wish him at least to consider, that if taking an earnest part with regard to the oppressions exercised in India, and with regard to this most oppressive case of Tanjore in particular, can ground a presumption of interested motives, he is himself the most mercenary man I know. His conduct indeed is such that he is on all occasions the standing testimony against himself. He it was that first called to that case the attention of the House; the reports of his own committee are ample and affecting upon that subject; and as many of us as have escaped his massacre, must remember the very pathetic picture he made of the sufferings of the Tanjore country, on the day when he moved the unwieldy code of his Indian resolutions. Has he not stated over and over again in his reports, the ill treatment of the Rajah of Tanjore (a branch of the royal house of the Marattas, every injury to whom the Marattas felt as offered to themselves) as a main cause of the alienation of that people from the British power? And does he now think, that to betray his principles, to contradict his declarations, and to become himself an active instrument in those oppressions which he had so tragically lamented, is the way to clear himself of having been actuated by a pecuniary interest, at the time when he chose to appear full of tenderness to that ruined nation?

The right honourable gentleman is fond of parading on the motives of others, and on his own. As to himself, he despises the imputations of those who suppose that anything corrupt could influence him in this his unexampled liberality of the public treasure. I do not know that I am obliged to speak to the motives of the ministry, in the arrangements they have made of the pretended debts of Arcot and Tanjore. If I prove fraud and collusion with regard to public money on those right honourable gentlemen, I am not obliged to assign their motives; because no good motives can be pleaded in favour of their conduct. Upon that case I stand: we are at issue; and I desire to go to trial. This, I am sure, is not loose railing, or mean insinuation, according to their low and degenerate fashion, when they make attacks on the measures of their adversaries. It is a regular and juridical course; and, unless I choose, nothing can compel me to go further.

But since these unhappy gentlemen have dared to hold a lofty tone about their motives, and affect to despise suspicion, instead of being careful not to give cause for it, I shall beg leave to lay before you some general observations on what I conceive was their duty in so delicate a business.

If I were worthy to suggest any line of prudence to that right honourable gentleman, I would tell him, that the way to avoid suspicion in the settlement of pecuniary transactions, in which great frauds have been very strongly presumed, is, to attend to these few plain principles:
—First, to hear all parties equally, and not the managers for the suspected claimants only. Not to proceed in the dark—but to act with as much publicity as possible. Not to precipitate decision. To be religious in following the rules prescribed in the commission under which we act. And, lastly, and above all, not to be fond of constraining constructions, to force a jurisdiction, and to draw to ourselves the management of a trust in its nature invidious and obnoxious to suspicion, where the plainest letter of the law does not compel it. If these few plain rules are observed, no corruption ought to be suspected; if any of them are violated, suspicion will attach in proportion. If all of them are violated, a corrupt motive of some kind or other will not only be suspected, but must be violently presumed.

[At this point Mr. Burke stepped aside, as it were, to direct attention to the part taken in reference to the alleged debts by certain servants of the India Company, named Benfield and Atkinson, proceeding thence to the conclusion of this great oration as follows:]

I confine myself to the connection of ministers, mediately or immediately, with only two persons concerned in this debt. How many others, who support their power and greatness within and without doors, are concerned originally, or by transfers of those debts, must be left to general opinion. I refer to the reports of the select committee for the proceedings of some of the agents in these affairs, and their attempts, at least, to furnish ministers with the means of buying general courts, and even whole parliaments, in the gross.

I know that the ministers will think it little less than acquittal, that they are not charged with having taken to themselves some part of the money of which they have made so liberal a donation to their partizans, though the charge may be indisputably fixed upon the corruption of their politics. For my part, I follow their crimes to that point to which legal presumptions and natural indications lead me, without considering what species of evil motive tends most to aggravate or to extenuate the guilt of their conduct. But if I am to speak my private sentiments, I think that in a thousand cases for one it would be far less mischievous to the public, and full as little dishonourable to themselves, to be polluted with direct bribery, than thus to become a standing auxiliary to the oppression, usury, and peculation of multitudes, in order to obtain a corrupt support to their power. It is by bribing, not so often by being bribed, that wicked politicians bring ruin on mankind. Avarice is a rival to the pursuits of many. It finds a multitude of checks, and many opposers, in every walk of life. But the objects of ambition are for the few; and every person who aims at indirect profit, and therefore wants other protection than innocence and law, instead of its rival becomes its instrument. There is a natural allegiance and fealty due to this domineering paramount evil, from all the vassal vices, which acknowledge its superiority, and readily militate under its banners; and it is under that discipline alone that avarice is able to spread to any considerable extent, or to render itself a general public mischief. It is therefore no apology for ministers that they have not been bought by the East India delinquents, but that they have only formed an alliance with them for screening each other from justice, according to the exigency of their several necessities. That they have done so is evident; and the junction of the power of office in England, with the abuse of authority in the East, has not only prevented even the appearance of redress to the grievances of India; but I wish it may not be found to have dulled, if not extinguished, the honour, the candour, the generosity, the good nature, which used formerly to characterize the people of England. I confess I wish that some more feeling than I have yet observed for the sufferings of our fellow-creatures and fellow-subjects in that oppressed part of the world, had manifested itself in any one quarter of the kingdom, or in any one large description of men.

That these oppressions exist, is a fact no more denied, than it is resented as it ought to be. Much evil has been done in India under the British authority. What has been done to redress it? We are no longer surprised at anything. We are above the unlearned and vulgar passion of admiration. But it will astonish posterity, when they read our opinions in our actions, that after years of inquiry we have found out that the sole grievance of India consisted in this, that the servants of the Company there had not profited enough of their opportunities, nor drained it sufficiently of its treasures; when they shall hear that the very first and only important act of a commission specially named by Act of Parliament, is to charge upon an undone country, in favour of a handful of men in the humblest ranks of the public service, the enormous sum of perhaps four millions of sterling money.

It is difficult for the most wise and upright government to correct the abuses of remote delegated power, productive of unmeasured wealth, and protected by the boldness and strength of the same ill-gotten riches. These abuses, full of their own wild native vigour, will grow and flourish under mere neglect. But where the supreme authority, not content with winking at the rapacity of its inferior instruments, is so shameless and corrupt as openly to give bounties and premiums for disobedience to its laws; when it will not trust to the activity of avarice in the pursuit of its own gains; when it secures public robbery by all the careful jealousy and attention with which it ought to protect property from such violence; the commonwealth then is become totally perverted from its purposes; neither God nor man will long endure it; nor will it long endure itself. In that case, there is an unnatural infection, a pestilential taint fermenting in the constitution of society, which fever and convulsions of some kind or other must throw off; or in which the vital powers, worsted in an unequal struggle, are pushed back upon themselves, and by a reversal of their whole functions, fester to gangrene, to death; and instead of what was but just now the delight and boast of the creation, there will be cast out in the face of the sun, a bloated, putrid, noisome carcass, full of stench and poison, an offence, a horror, a lesson to the world.

In my opinion, we ought not to wait for the fruitless instruction of calamity to inquire into the abuses which bring upon us ruin in the worst of forms, in the loss of our fame and virtue. But the right honourable gentleman (Mr. Dundas) says, in answer to all the powerful arguments of my honourable friend—" that this inquiry is of a delicate nature, and that the state will suffer detriment by the exposure of this transaction." But it is exposed; it is perfectly known in every member, in every particle, and in every way, except that which may lead to a remedy. He knows that the papers of correspondence are printed, and that they are in every hand.

He and delicacy are a rare and singular coalition. He thinks that to divulge our Indian politics may be highly dangerous. He! the mover! the chairman! the reporter of the committee of secrecy! he that brought forth in the utmost detail, in several vast, printed folios, the most recondite parts of the politics, the military, the revenues of the British Empire in India. With six great chopping bastards, each as lusty as an infant Hercules, this delicate creature blushes at the sight of his new bridegroom, assumes a virgin delicacy; or, to use a more fit as well as a more poetic comparison, the person so squeamish, so timid, so trembling lest the winds of heaven should visit too roughly, is expanded to broad sunshine, exposed like the sow of imperial augury, lying in the mud with all the prodigies of her fertility about her, as evidence of her delicate amours—

Triginta capitum fœtus enixa jacebat,
Alba solo recubans albi circum ubera nati.

Whilst discovery of the misgovernment of others led to his own power, it was wise to inquire; it was safe to publish; there was then no delicacy; there was then no danger. But when his object is obtained, and in his imitation he has outdone the crimes that he had reprobated in volumes of reports, and in sheets of bills and penalties, then concealment becomes prudence; and it concerns the safety of the state that we should not know, in a mode of parliamentary cognizance, what all the world knows but too well, that is, in what manner he chooses to dispose of the public revenues to the creatures of his politics.

The debate has been long, and as much so

on my part, at least as on the part of those who have spoken before me. But long as it is, the more material half of the subject has hardly been touched on; that is, the corrupt and destructive system to which this debt has been rendered subservient, and which seems to be pursued with at least as much vigour and regularity as ever. If I considered your case or my own, rather than the weight and importance of this question, I ought to make some apology to you, perhaps some apology to myself, for having detained your attention so long. I know on what ground I tread. This subject, at one time taken up with so much fervour and zeal, is no longer a favourite in this House. The House itself has undergone a great and signal revolution. To some the subject is strange and uncouth; to several harsh and distasteful; to the relics of the last Parliament it is a matter of fear and apprehension. It is natural for those who have seen their friends sink in the tornado which raged during the last shift of the monsoon, and have hardly escaped on the planks of the general wreck—it is but too natural for them, as soon as they make the rocks and quicksands of their former disasters, to put about their new-built barks, and, as much as possible, to keep aloof from this perilous lee shore.

But let us do what we please to put India from our thoughts, we can do nothing to separate it from our public interest and our national reputation. Our attempts to banish this importunate duty will only make it return upon us again and again, and every time in a shape more unpleasant than the former. A government has been fabricated for that great province; the right honourable gentleman says, that, therefore, you ought not to examine into his conduct. Heavens! what an argument is this! We are not to examine into the conduct of the direction, because it is an old government: we are not to examine into this Board of Control, because it is a new one. Then we are only to examine into the conduct of those who have no conduct to account for. Unfortunately, the basis of this new government has been laid on old condemned delinquents, and its superstructure is raised out of prosecutors turned into protectors. The event has been such as might be expected. But if it had been otherwise constituted; had it been constituted even as I wished, and as the mover of this question had planned, the better part of the proposed establishment was in the publicity of its proceedings; in its perpetual responsibility to Parliament. Without this check, what is our government at home, even awed, as every European government is, by an audience formed of the other states of Europe, by the applause or condemnation of the discerning and critical company before which it acts? But if the scene on the other side of the globe, which tempts, invites, almost compels to tyranny and rapine, be not inspected with the eye of a severe and unremitting vigilance, shame and destruction must ensue. For one, the worst event of this day, though it may deject, shall not break or subdue me. The call upon us is authoritative. Let who will shrink back, I shall be found at my post. Baffled, discountenanced, subdued, discredited, as the cause of justice and humanity is, it will be only the dearer to me. Whoever, therefore, shall at any time bring before you anything towards the relief of our distressed fellow-citizens in India, and towards a subversion of the present most corrupt and oppressive system for its government, in me shall find a weak, I am afraid, but a steady, earnest, and faithful assistant.

LOUIS KOSSUTH.
Born 1802. *Living.*
EUROPEAN FREEDOM.

IT is said of Pyrrhus, the king of Epirus, that he sent a messenger to ancient Rome, who, on his return, reported to his master that he had seen a city of kings, where every man was as much a king as the king of Epirus himself. So I may say that I have seen the public opinion of the English people pronounced in such wise, that, as Lord Brougham, I believe, once said, in the voice of the people the thunder of the Almighty was felt. I have received a most kind greeting at Southampton, and addresses have been sent to me from all parts of the kingdom so numerous, that in reading and answering them I have some idea of the public opinion of England; but I see that public opinion incarnated in the great demonstrations of London, Birmingham, and Manchester; and those demonstrations loudly proclaim, " Ye oppressed nations of Europe, be of good cheer; the hour of delivery is at hand." I have experienced enough in my public life to know that public opinion which is pronounced by the people of England, in that cause of which I am one of the humble representatives, may be dissimulated for a while, it may be jeered at, but at last obeyed it must be; because England is a constitutional country, and in a constitutional country the public opinion is caused by law, by right, by constitution, to give direction to Government and Parliament. I know what power public opinion has a right to claim in this glorious land; and, because I know it, I may be permitted to say that I thank the people of England and the people of Manchester for their great aid in the cause of humanity, not in my own name only, but in the name of oppressed nations. Since my arrival on England's happy shores, I have had a continual opportunity of hearing the pronunciation of that public opinion in respect of a question, the solution of which is ostensibly marked out by Providence to be the test of our time—a question which will decide the fate of mankind for centuries. This question is not only of scanty, partial interest; it is not only a noble commiseration for the misfortunes of individuals, or of one country; it is a question of national interest, in which every country, every people, is equally interested. I say equally interested. There may be a difference as to the succession of time at which one or the other nation will be affected by the inevitable consequences of this question. But, affected they will all be, one a day sooner, another a day later—it is a mere question of time. And no country, no nation, however proud its position, and chiefly none within the boundaries of the Christian family and of European civilization, can avoid a share of the consequences of this comprehensive question, which will be the proximate fate of humanity. I scarcely need to say this comprehensive question is, whether Europe should be ruled by the principle of freedom or by the principle of despotism. To bring more home in a practical way to your generous hearts that idea of freedom, the question is, whether Europe shall be ruled by the principle of centralization or by the principle of self-government. Because self-government is freedom, and centralization is absolutism. What! shall freedom die away for centuries, and mankind become nothing more than a blind instrument for the ambition of a few; or shall the brand of servitude be wiped away from the brow of humanity? Woe, a thousandfold woe, to every nation which, confident in its proud position of to-day, so carelessly regards this all-comprehensive struggle for these great principles! It is the mythical struggle between heaven and hell. To be blessed or to be damned is the lot of all; there is no transition between heaven and hell. Woe, a thousandfold woe, to every nation which will not embrace within its sorrows and its cares the future, but only the passing moment of the present time. As the sun looms through the mist before it rises, so the future is seen in the events of the present day. There are some who endeavour to contract the expressions of sympathy which I have the honour to meet, to the narrow scale of personality. They would fain make believe that there is nothing more in these demonstrations than a matter of fashion —a transitory ebullition of popular feeling, passing away like a momentary bubble, or, at the utmost, the tribute of approbation to the bravery of a gallant people in a just cause, and of consolation to their unmerited misfortunes. But I say it is not so. I say that the very source of this demonstration is the instinctive feeling of the people, that the destiny of mankind is come to a turning-point for centuries. It is the cry of alarm upon the ostensible approach of universal danger. It is the manifestation of the instinct of self-preservation roused by the instinctive knowledge of the fact, that the decisive struggles for the destinies of Europe draw so near, and that no people, no country, can remain unaffected by the issue of this great struggle of principles. We have been told that the despotic governments of Europe have become weak; that the despotic governments of Europe feel their approaching death; and if it be so, I hope the struggle so called forth will be the last in mankind's history. In stating this case as I conceive it, I say it is not my individuality, it is not my presence which has roused any new feeling, any new sentiment. I am nothing but the opportunity which elicited the hidden spark—the opportunity at which the instinctive apprehension of approaching danger to nations, burst forth in a loud cry of alarm. Else how can a sophist explain the fact of the universality of these demonstrations, not restricted to my presence, not restricted to a climate, not restricted to the peculiar character of a people, not restricted to a society's organization, but spreading through the world like the pulsation of one heart, or like the spark from an electric battery!

J. B. GOUGH.

Born 1817. *Living.*

The Cause of Temperance

OUR enterprise is in advance of the public sentiment, and those who carry it on are glorious iconoclasts, who are going to break down the drunken Dagon worshipped by their fathers. Count me over the chosen heroes of this earth, and I will show you men that stood alone—ay, alone, while those they toiled, and laboured, and agonized for, hurled at them contumely, scorn, and contempt. They stood alone; they looked into the future calmly and with faith; they saw the golden beam inclining to the side of perfect justice; and they fought on amidst the storm of persecution. In Great Britain they tell me when I go to see such a prison:—"There is a dungeon in which such a one was confined;" "Here, among the ruins of an old castle, we will show you where such a one had his ears cut off, and where another was murdered." Then they will show me monuments towering up to the heavens:— "There is a monument to such a one; there is a monument to another." And what do I find? That the one generation persecuted and howled at these men, crying "Crucify them! crucify them!" and dancing round the blazing faggots that consumed them; and the next generation busied itself in gathering up the scattered ashes of the martyred heroes and depositing them in the golden urn of a nation's history. Oh, yes! the men that fight for a great enterprise are the men that bear the brunt of the battle, and "He who seeth in secret"—seeth the desire of his children, their steady purpose, their firm self-denial—"will reward them openly," though they may die and see no sign of the triumphs of their enterprise.

Our cause is a progressive one. I read the first constitution of the first temperance society formed in the State of New York in 1809, and one of the bye-laws stated, "Any member of this association who shall be convicted of intoxication shall be fined a quarter of a dollar, except such act of intoxication shall take place on the 4th of July, or any other regularly appointed military muster." We laugh at that now; but it was a serious matter in those days: it was in advance of the public sentiment of the age. The very men that adopted that principle were persecuted: they were hooted and pelted through the streets, the doors of their houses were blackened, their cattle mutilated. The fire of persecution scorched some men so, that they left the work. Others worked on, and God blessed them. Some are living to-day; and I should like to stand where they stand now, and see the mighty enterprise as it rises before them. They worked hard. They lifted the first turf—prepared the bed in which to lay the corner-stone. They laid it amid persecution and storm. They worked under the surface; and men almost forgot that there were busy hands laying the solid foundation far down beneath. By-and-by they got the foundation above the surface, and then commenced another storm of persecution. Now we see the superstructure—pillar after pillar, tower after tower, column after column, with the capitals emblazoned with "Love, truth, sympathy, and good will to men." Old men gaze upon it as it grows up before them. They will not live to see it completed, but they see in faith the crowning cope-stone set upon it. Meek-eyed women weep as it grows in beauty; children strew the pathway of the workmen with flowers. We do not see its beauty yet—we do not see the magnificence of its superstructure yet —because it is in course of erection. Scaffolding, ropes, ladders, workmen ascending and descending, mar the beauty of the building; but by-and-by, when the hosts who have laboured shall come up over a thousand battle-fields waving with bright grain never again to be crushed in the distillery—through vineyards, under trellised vines, with grapes hanging in all their purple glory never again to be pressed into that which can debase and degrade mankind—when they shall come through orchards, under trees hanging thick with golden, pulpy fruit never to be turned into that which can injure and debase—when they shall come up to the last distillery and destroy it; to the last stream of liquid death and dry it up; to the last weeping wife and wipe her tears gently away; to the last little child and lift him up to stand where God meant that man should stand; to the last drunkard and nerve him to burst the burning fetters and make a glorious accompaniment to the song of freedom by the clanking of his broken chains—then, ah! then will the cope-stone be set upon it, the scaffolding will fall with a crash, and the building will start in its wondrous beauty before an astonished world. The last poor drunkard shall go into it and find a refuge there; loud shouts of rejoicing shall be heard, and there shall be joy in heaven, when the triumphs of a great enterprise shall usher in the day of the triumphs of the cross of Christ. I believe it; on my soul, I believe it. Will you help us? That is the question. We leave it with you. Good night.

OLIVER CROMWELL.

Born 1599. Died 1658.

[CROMWELL was not by any means an eloquent man in the ordinary sense of the term, but the following second extract finds its place here as a specimen of the speech of a great man, peculiarly characteristic of his mind, and illustrative of a political and moral situation unique in the history of the world. It is taken from his address to the first Parliament (commonly called the Barebones Parliament) summoned by him after the dissolution of the Rump on the 4th July, 1653, as edited by Mr. Carlyle.

It may not be out of place here to quote what Mr. Carlyle himself says respecting this speech :—

"Intelligent readers have found intelligibility in this speech of Oliver's: but to one who has had to read it as a painful Editor, reading every fibre of it with magnifying-glasses, has to do,—it becomes all glowing with intelligibility, with credibility; with the splendour of genuine Veracity and heroic Depth and Manfulness;—and seems, in fact, as Oliver's speeches generally do, to an altogether singular degree, the express image of the soul it came from !—Is not this the end of all speaking, and wagging of the tongue in every conceivable sort, except the false and accursed sorts? Shall we call Oliver a *bad* Speaker, then? Shall we not, in a very fundamental sense, call him a good Speaker ?"]

The Little Parliament.

IN my pilgrimage, and some exercises I have had abroad, I did read that Scripture often, Forty-first of Isaiah; where God gave me, and some of my fellows, encouragement "as to" what He would do there and elsewhere; which He hath performed for us. He said, "He would plant in the wilderness the cedar, the shittah tree, and the myrtle, and the oil tree; and He would set in the desert the fir tree, and the pine tree, and the box tree together." For what end will the Lord do all this? "That they may see, and know, and consider, and understand together, that the hand of the Lord hath done this;"—that it is He who hath wrought all the salvations and deliverances we have received. For what end? To see, to know, and understand together, that He hath done and wrought all this for the good of the Whole Flock. Therefore, I beseech you—but I think I need not—have a care of the Whole Flock! Love the sheep, love the lambs; love all, tend all, cherish and countenance all, in all things that are good. And if the poorest Christian, the most mistaken Christian, shall desire to live peaceably and quietly under you,—I say, if any should desire but to lead a life of godliness and honesty, let him be protected.

I think I need not advise, much less press you, to endeavour the Promoting of the Gospel; to encourage the Ministry;* such a Ministry, and such Ministers as be faithful in the Land; upon whom the true character is. Men that have received the Spirit, which Christians will be able to discover, and do "the will of;" men that "have received Gifts from Him who is ascended up on high, who hath led captivity captive, to *give* gifts to men,"† even for this same work of the Ministry! And truly the Apostle, speaking in another place, in the Twelfth of the Romans, when he has summed up all the mercies of God, and the goodness of God; and discoursed, in the former Chapters, of the foundations of the Gospel, and of those things that are the subject of those first Eleven Chapters,—he beseecheth them to "present their bodies a living sacrifice." He beseecheth them that they would not esteem highly of themselves, but be humble and sober-minded, and not stretch themselves beyond their line; and also that they would have a care for those that "had received gifts" to the uses there mentioned. I speak not,—I thank God it is far from my heart,—for a Ministry deriving itself from the Papacy, and pretending to that which is so much insisted on, "Succession." The true Succession is through the Spirit—given in its measure. The Spirit is given for that use, "To make proper Speakers-forth of God's eternal Truth;" and that's right Succession. But I need not discourse of these things to you; who, I am persuaded, are taught of God, much more and in a greater measure than myself, concerning those things.

Indeed I have but one word more to say to you; though in that perhaps I shall show my weakness: it's by way of encouragement to go on in this Work. And give me leave to begin thus. I confess I never looked to see such a Day as this—it may be nor you neither—when Jesus Christ should be so owned as He is, this day, in this Work. Jesus Christ is owned this day by the Call of you; and you own Him, by your willingness to appear for Him. And you manifest this, as far as poor creatures may do, to be a Day of the Power of Christ. I know you well remember that Scripture, "He makes His People willing in the day of His power."* God manifests this to be the Day of the Power of Christ; having, through so much blood, and so much trial as hath been upon these Nations, made this to be one of the great issues thereof: To have His People called to the Supreme Authority. He makes this to be the greatest mercy, next to His own Son. God hath owned His Son; and He hath owned you, and made you own Him. I confess I never looked to have seen such a day; I did not. Perhaps you are not known by face to one another; indeed I am confident you are strangers, coming from all parts of the Nation as you do: but we shall tell you that indeed we have not allowed ourselves the choice of one person in whom we had not this good hope, That there was in him faith in Jesus Christ, and love to all His People and Saints.

Thus God hath owned you in the eyes of the world; and thus, by coming hither, you own Him: and, as it is in Isaiah xliii. 21,—it's an high expression; and look to your own hearts whether, now or hereafter, God shall apply it to *you:* "This People," saith God, "I have formed for Myself, that they may show forth my praise." I say, it's a memorable passage; and, I hope, not unfitly applied: the Lord apply it to each of your hearts! I shall not descant upon the words; they are plain: indeed you are as like the "forming of God" as ever people were. If a man should tender a Book to you to swear you upon, I dare appeal to all your consciences, Neither directly nor indirectly did you seek for your coming hither. You have been passive in coming hither; being *called*—and indeed that's an active work—though not on your part! "This People have *I formed:*" consider the circumstances by which you are "called" hither; through what strivings—through what blood you are come hither—where neither you nor I, nor no man living, three months ago, had any thought to have seen such a company taking upon them, or rather being called to take, the Supreme Authority of this Nation! Therefore, own your call! Indeed, I think it may be truly said that there never was a Supreme Authority consisting of such a Body, above One hundred and forty, I believe; never such a Body that came into the Supreme Authority before, under such a notion as this, in such a way of owning God, and being owned by Him. And therefore I may also say, never such a "People" so "formed," for such a purpose, were thus called before.

---

* Preaching Clergy.   † Ephesians iv. 8.

* Psalm cx. 3, a favourite Psalm of Oliver's.

If it were a time to compare your standing with that of those that have been "called" by the Suffrages of the People—which who can tell how soon God may fit the People for such a thing? None can desire it more than I! Would all were the Lord's People; as it was said, "Would all the Lord's People were Prophets." I would all were fit to be called. It ought to be the longing of our hearts to see men brought to own the Interest of Jesus Christ. And give me leave to say: If I know anything in the world, what is there likelier to win the People to the interest of Jesus Christ, to the love of Godliness (and therefore what stronger duty lies on you, being thus called), than an humble and godly conversation? So that they may see that you love them; that you lay yourselves out, time and spirits, for them! Is not this the likeliest way to bring them to their liberties? And do not you, by this, put it upon God to find out times and seasons for you; fit seasons by putting forth His Spirit? At least you convince them that, as men fearing God have fought them out of their bondage under the Regal Power, so men fearing God do now rule them in the fear of God, and take care to administer Good unto them. But this is some digression. I say, own your call; for it is of God! Indeed, it is marvellous, and it hath been unprojected. It's not long since either you or we came to know of it. And indeed this hath been the way God dealt with us all along, To keep things from our eyes all along, so that we have seen nothing in all His dispensations, long beforehand;—which is also a witness, in some measure, to our integrity. I say, you are called with a high calling. And why should we be afraid to say or think, That *this* may be the door to usher in the Things that God has promised; which have been prophesied of; which He has set the hearts of His People to wait for and expect? We know who they are that shall war with the Lamb, "against His enemies:" they shall be "a people called, and chosen and faithful." And God hath, in a Military way—we may speak it without flattering ourselves, and I believe you know it—He hath appeared with them, with that same "People," and for them; and now in these Civil Powers and Authorities does not He appear? These are not ill prognostications of the God we wait for. Indeed I do think somewhat is at the door: we are at the threshold;—and therefore it becomes us to lift up our heads, and encourage ourselves in the Lord. And we have thought, some of us, That it is our duties to *endeavour* this way; not merely to *look* at that Prophecy in Daniel, "And the Kingdom shall not be delivered to another people," and passively wait. Truly God hath brought this to your hands, by the owning of your call; blessing the Military Power. The Lord hath directed their hearts to be instrumental to call you; and set it upon our hearts to deliver over the Power "to another people." But I may appear to be beyond my line here; these things are dark. Only, I desire my thoughts to be exercised in these things, and so I hope are yours.

Truly seeing things are thus, that you are at the edge of the Promises and Prophecies. At least, if there were neither Promise nor Prophecy, yet you are carrying on the best things, you are endeavouring after the best things; and, as I have said elsewhere, if I were to choose any servant, the meanest Officer for the Army or the Commonwealth, I would choose a godly man that hath principles. Especially where a trust is to be committed. Because I know where to *have* a man that hath principles. I believe if any one of you should choose a servant, you would do thus. And I would all our Magistrates were so chosen:—this may be done; there may be good effects of this! Surely it's our duty to choose men that fear the Lord, and will praise the Lord: such hath the Lord "formed for Himself;" and He expects no praises from *other* than such.

This being so, truly it puts me in mind of another Scripture, that famous Psalm, Sixty-eighth Psalm; which indeed is a glorious Prophecy, I am persuaded, of the Gospel Churches—it may be, of the Jews also. There it prophesies that "He will bring His People again from the depths of the Sea, as once He led Israel through the Red Sea." And it may be, as some think, God will bring the Jews home to their station "from the isles of the sea," and answer their expectations "as from the depths of the sea." But, at all events, sure I am, when the Lord shall set up the glory of the Gospel Church, it shall be a gathering of people as "out of deep waters," "out of the multitude of waters;" such are His People, drawn out of the multitudes of the Nations and People of this world. And truly that Psalm is very glorious in many other parts of it: When He gathers them, "great was the company" of them that publish His word. "Kings of Armies did flee apace, and she that tarried at home divided the spoil;" and "Although ye have lain among the pots, yet shall ye be as the wings of a dove, covered with silver, and her feathers with yellow gold." And indeed the triumph of that Psalm is exceeding high and great; and God is accomplishing it. And the close of it—that closeth with my heart, and I do not doubt with yours, "The Lord shakes the hills and mountains, and they reel." And God hath a Hill too; "an high Hill as the Hill of Bashan: and the chariots of God are twenty thousand, even thousands of Angels, and God will dwell upon this Hill for ever!"

CHARLES JAMES FOX.

Born 1749. Died 1806.

[For a clear understanding of the speeches which are given below it may be necessary to offer a short sketch of the circumstances under which they were delivered, and also of the historical events which immediately preceded them. For this purpose we cannot do better than quote the concise statement of affairs contained in a recent popular History of England, as follows:—"Papers relative to an apprehended rupture between Great Britain and Russia having been laid before the House on the 6th of February, 1792, there arose out of them several debates, in which the spirit of party was strongly displayed. On the 13th of February, Mr. Grey loudly complained that ministers had not produced the preliminaries said to have been adjusted between the Russian and Turkish negotiators, and that large sums had been unnecessarily spent in fitting out an armament. A week later Mr. Grey moved for a more ample production of papers regarding various portions of the recent diplomacy of ministers, arguing that the whole of the correspondence was necessary, if they wished to justify the steps they had taken. Pitt, who was then Prime Minister, resisted the demand, conceiving that sufficient had been disclosed to make the House acquainted with all the essential parts of the business, and asserting that confidence was due to the administration until their capacity or integrity was impeached. On the 29th of February, the subject was revived by Mr. Whitbread, then member for Bedford, who moved the following resolutions:—'That no arrangement respecting Oczakow and its district appears to have been capable of affecting the political or commercial interests of this country, so as to justify any hostile interference on the part of Great Britain between Russia and the Porte; and that the interference of Great Britain for the purpose of preventing the cession of the said fortress and its district to the Empress of Russia has been wholly unsuccessful, and that His Majesty's ministers, in endeavouring, by means of an armed force, to compel the Empress of Russia to abandon her claim to Oczakow and its district, and in continuing an armament after the object for which it had been proposed was relinquished, had been guilty of gross misconduct, tending to incur unnecessary expenses, and to diminish the influence of the British nation in Europe.' Many members, amongst whom were Windham and Sheridan, took part in the debate; but the two most remarkable speeches were delivered by the great rivals, Pitt and Fox. On the second evening of the debate (1st of March, 1792), the House being extremely clamorous for Fox, he rose and gave utterance to the splendid speech which we have here reprinted, and in which he made one of his most terrific attacks upon Pitt. To give, therefore, a connected interest to the reading of this speech, we have here added Pitt's explanation, and Fox's subsequent reply; and, as a fine passage of arms between the two political rivals, this debate is well worthy of the space which it occupies in our columns. It may also be remembered that this speech of Fox is one of those specimens of eloquence referred to by Lord Brougham in his letter to Macaulay (see p. 2), as being most deserving of attentive study and imitation. It is also amongst the best reported of Fox's addresses in .Parliament, the majority of which have come down to us in the third person. That of Pitt's, which follows, is not so ample, but is sufficiently full to give a clear view of the arguments he used and the energy with which they were enforced. It may be added that the great minister was again triumphant, and Mr. Whitbread's resolutions were negatived by a large majority."]

THE RUSSIAN ARMAMENT.

AFTER the challenge which was thrown out to me, in the speech of the right honourable gentleman (Mr. Dundas), last night, I did consider it my duty to trouble you somewhat at length on this important question. But before I enter into the consideration of it, I will explain why I did not obey a call made in the beginning of the day, and repeated several times, in a manner not very consistent either with the freedom of debate, or with the order which the right honourable gentleman himself has prescribed for the discussion of this day. Why any members should think themselves entitled to call on an individual in that way, I know not; but why I did not yield to the call is obvious. It was said by an honourable gentleman last night to be the wish of the right honourable gentleman to hear all that could be said on the subject, before he should rise to enter into his defence. If so, it certainly would not become me to prevent him from hearing any other gentleman who might be inclined to speak on the occasion; and as he particularly alluded to me, I thought it respectful to give way to gentlemen, that I might not interrupt the course which he has chosen for himself, as it seems he reserves himself till I have spoken. This call on me is of a singular nature. A Minister is accused of having rashly engaged the country in a measure, by which we have suffered disaster and disgrace, and when a motion of censure is made, he chooses to reserve himself, and speak after every one, that no means may be given to reply to his defence—to expose its fallacy, if fallacious—or to detect its misrepresentations, if he shall choose to misrepresent what may be said. If the right honourable gentlemen is truly desirous of meeting the charges against him, and he has confidence in his ability to vindicate his conduct, why not pursue the course which would be manly and open? Why not go into a committee, as was offered him by the honourable gentleman who made the motion (Mr. Whitbread), in which the forms of this House would have permitted members on each side to answer whatever was advanced by the other, and the subject would have received the most ample discussion? Instead of this honourable course, he is determined to take all advantages. He screens himself by a stratagem which no defendant in any process in this country could enjoy; since no man put upon his defence in any court of justice could so contrive as not only to prevent all reply to his defence, but all refutation of what he may assert—all explanation of what he may misrepresent. Such are the advantages which the right honourable gentleman is determined to seize in this moment of his trial; and to confess the truth, never did man stand so much in need of every advantage! never was there an occasion in which a Minister was exhibited to this House in circumstances so ungracious as those under which he stands before it in the present moment! For what is our precise situation? Last session of Parliament we had no fewer than four debates upon the question of the armament, in which the right honourable gentleman involved this country, without condescending to explain the object which he had in view. The minority of this House stood forth against the monstrous measure of involving the country, without unfolding the reason. The Minister proudly and obstinately refused, and called on the majority to support him. We gave our opinion at large on the subject, and with effect, as it turned out, on the public mind. On that of the right honourable gentleman, however, we are not successful; for what was his conduct? He replied to us, "I hear what you say; I could answer all your charges; but I know my duty to my King too well to submit at this moment to expose the secrets of the State, and to lay the reasons before you of the measure on which I demand your confidence. I choose rather to lie for a time under all the imputations which you may heap against me, trusting to the explanations which will come at last." Such was explicitly his language. However I might differ from the right honourable gentleman in opinion, I felt for his situation. There was in this excuse some shadow of a reason on which it might be possible to defend him, when the whole of his conduct came to be inquired into. I thought it hard to goad him, when, perhaps, he considered it as unsafe to expose what he was doing. But when the conclusion of the negotiation had loosed him from his fetters, when he had cast off the trammels that bound him, I thought that, like the horse described by Homer (if I remembered, I would quote the lines), exulting in the fresh pastures after he had freed himself from the bridle, the right honourable gentleman would have been eager to meet us with every sort of explanation and satisfaction. I thought that, restrained by no delicacy, and panting only for the moment that was to restore him to the means of developing, of expatiating upon, every part of his conduct that was mysterious, of, clearing up that which had been reprobated, of repelling on the heads of his adversaries those very accusations with which they had loaded him—the right honourable gentleman would have had but one wish, that of coming forward in a bold and manly manner, and endeavouring to make his cause good against us, in the face of the world. Has he done so? has he even given us the means of inquiring fully and fairly into his conduct? No such thing. He lays before us a set of papers, sufficient, indeed, as I shall contend, to found a strong criminal charge for misconduct against him, but evidently mutilated, garbled, and imperfect, with a view of precluding that full inquiry which his conduct demands, and which we had every reason to expect he would not have shrunk from on this day. We call for more; they are denied us. Why? "Because," say the gentlemen on the other side, "unless the papers now before you show there is ground for accusation, and unless you agree to accuse, it is not safe or proper to grant you more." But is this a *defence* for the right honourable gentleman? Do these papers exculpate him? Directly the reverse. *Primâ facie*, they condemn him. They afford us, in the first instance, the proof of disappointment. They show us that we have not obtained what we armed to obtain, and they gave us no justification of the right honourable gentleman for that disappointment. I have heard much ingenuity displayed, to maintain that there was no guilt. But what is the fallacy of this argument? When we called for papers during the Spanish negotiation, we were answered, "The negotiation was pending, and it was unsafe to grant them." Very well. But when it was over, and the same reasons for withholding them could not be said to exist, we were told, "Look to the result—the nation is satisfied with what we have got, and you must lay a ground of criminality before we can admit your principle of calling for papers." Thus we were precluded from all inquiry into that business; but now the right honourable gentleman, conscious that the country feels somewhat differently, admits the ground of criminality to have been laid by producing those documents on your table, imperfect as they are. It is from his own confession, therefore, that I am to pronounce him guilty, until he proves himself not to be so; and it is enough for me to contend, that the papers now before us afford him, *primâ facie*, no justification; but, on the contrary, afford strong proof of his guilt, inasmuch as they evince a complete failure in the object he armed to obtain. Sir, the right honourable gentleman is sensible how much these circumstances render it necessary for him to take every possible advantage his situation can give him; instead, therefore, of showing himself anxious to come forward, or thinking it his duty to explain why it was inconvenient or impolitic for him to state last year the true grounds on which he had called upon us to arm, what was the object of that armament, and why he had abandoned it, he lays a few papers on the table, and contents himself with an appeal unheard of before. "If you have anything to say against me, speak out, speak all—I will not say a word till you have done—let me hear you one after another—I will have all the advantage of the game—none of you shall come behind me—for as soon as you have all thrown forth what you have to say, I will make a speech, which you shall not have an opportunity to contradict, and I will throw myself on my majority, that makes you dumb for ever." Such is the situation in which we stand, and such is the course which the right honourable gentleman thinks it honourable to pursue!

I cheerfully yield to him the ground he

chooses to occupy, and submit to the call addressed personally to myself (although, perhaps, not in a manner very decorous), of stating to the House what I have to offer, before the right honourable gentleman will open his lips.

Having made these preliminary observations on the manner in which this business has been conducted, I will proceed frankly to state the reasons upon which I found the vote of censure in which I shall this night agree. Much argument has been used on topics, not unfit, indeed, to be mixed with this question, but not necessary; topics which undoubtedly may be incidentally taken up, but which are not essential to the discussion. In this class I rank what has been said upon the balance of Europe. Whether the insulated state of policy which disdained all continental connection whatever, as adopted at the beginning of the present reign—whether the system of extensive foreign connection, so eagerly insisted on by a young gentleman who spoke yesterday for the first time—or whether, as I am inclined to suspect is the true and wise course, the medium between these two be our interest, are certainly very proper topics to be discussed, but as certainly not essential topics to this question. Of the three, I certainly think the middle line the true political course of this country; I think that, in our situation, every continental connection is to be determined by its own merits. I am one of those who think that a total inattention to foreign connections might be, as it has proved, very injurious to this country. But if I am driven to choose between the two extremes—between that of standing insulated and aloof from all foreign connection, and trusting for defence to our own resources, and that system, as laid down in the speech of an honourable gentleman who distinguished himself so much last night, to the extent to which he pressed it—I do not hesitate to declare that my opinion is for the first of those situations. I should prefer even total disunion to that sort of connection, to preserve which we should be obliged to risk the blood and the resources of the country in every quarrel and every change that ambition or accident might bring about in any part of the continent of Europe. But in the question before us, I deny that I am driven to either of these extremes. The honourable gentleman, who spoke with all the open ingenuousness as well as the animation of youth, seemed himself to dread the extent to which his own doctrines would lead him: he failed, therefore, to sustain the policy of the system he described, in that part where it can alone apply—namely, to the degree which it is necessary for us to support a balance of power. Holland, for instance, he states to be our natural ally. Granted. "To preserve Holland, and that she may not fall into the arms of France, we must make an alliance with Prussia." Good. But Prussia may be attacked by Austria. Then we must make an alliance with the Ottoman Porte, that they may fall on Austria. Well, but the Porte may be attacked by Russia. Then we must make an alliance with Sweden, that he may fall on Russia. By the way, I must here remind him, that he totally forgot even to mention Poland, as if that country, now become in some degree able to act for itself, from the change in its constitution, was of no moment, or incapable of influencing in any manner upon this system of treaties and attacks. His natural ingenuity pointed out to him, that in casting up the account of all this, it would not produce a favourable balance for England, and he evaded the consequence of his own principle by saying, that perhaps Russia would not attack the Porte; for when we speculate on extreme cases (says the honourable gentleman), we have a right to make allowances: it is fair to expect that when we are in alliance with the Porte, Russia will feel too sensibly the importance of the commercial advantages she enjoys by her intercourse with this country, to risk the loss of them by an attack on the Porte. Are we, then, to suppose that, in that scene of universal contest and warfare, this ambitious Power, that is perpetually and systematically, as it has been reproached her, aiming at the destruction of the Porte, and while the rest of Europe has been at peace, has been in a state of restless and unceasing hostility with her, will then be the only Power at peace, and let slip so favourable an opportunity of destroying her old enemy, simply because she is afraid of losing the trade with you in the Baltic? If the honourable gentleman means to state this as a rational conjecture, I would ask him to look to the fact. Did her sense of these advantages restrain her in the late war, or compel her to desist from the demands she made before we began to arm? Certainly not. We find, from the documents before us, that she adhered to one uniform, steady course, from which neither the apprehension of commercial loss, nor the terrors of our arms, influenced her one moment to recede. What, then, are we to conclude from this intricate system of balances and counter-balances, and these dangerous theories with which the honourable gentleman seemed to amuse himself? Why, that these are speculations too remote from our policy; that in some parts, even according to the honourable gentleman's argument, they may be defective, after all; and consequently, that if the system he builds upon it fails in one of its possibilities, it fails in the whole of them. Such must ever be the fate of systems so nicely constructed. But it is not true that the system necessary to enable this country to derive the true benefit from the Dutch alliance, ought to be founded upon those involved and mysterious politics which make it incumbent upon us, nay, which prove its perfection, by compelling us to stand forward the principals in every quarrel, the Quixotes of every enterprise, the agitators in every plot, intrigue, and disturbance, which are every day arising in Europe, to embroil one state of it with another. I confess that my opinions fall infinitely short of these perilous extremes; that possibly my genius is too scanty, and my understanding too limited and feeble, for the contemplation of their consequences, and that I can speculate no farther than on connections immediately necessary to preserve us, safe and prosperous, from the power of our open enemies, and the encroachment of our competitors: that this I hold to be the only test by which the merits of an alliance can be tried, which I should esteem either valuable or useless in proportion to its strict adherence to this principle. I did think, for instance, that when the intrigues of France threatened to deprive us of our ancient ally, Holland, it was wise to interfere, and afterwards to form an alliance by which that evil might be prevented. But every step beyond the alliance we then formed, every link in the chain of confederacies so largely expatiated upon by the gentlemen on the other side, brings us more and more remote from its true principle; the broad and clear lines of your policy become narrower and less distinct, until they are carried at last to an extremity of Europe, where every trace of them is lost.

Other topics have been introduced into the discussion. The beginning of the war between Russia and the Porte has been referred to. What possible connection that has with our armament I know not; but of that I shall have occasion to speak by-and-by.

I come, however, Sir, to a question more immediately before us, and that is, the value and importance annexed, in the minds of his Majesty's Ministers, to the fortress of Oczakow; and here I must beg leave to say, that they have not once attempted to answer the arguments so judiciously and ably enforced by my honourable friend who made this motion. It was explicitly stated by the gentlemen on the other side, as the only argument for our interference at all, that the balance of Europe was threatened with great danger if Oczakow was suffered to remain in the hands of Russia. Of no less importance did Ministers last year state this fortress of Oczakow, than as if it were indeed the *talisman** on which depended the fate of the whole Ottoman Empire.

---

* This was an allusion to a part of Mr. Grey's speech, who had quoted a passage from Mr. Hastings' narrative of the Benares Expedition, to much the same effect.

But if this, from their own admission, was true last year, what has happened to alter its value? If it then excited the alarms of his Majesty's Ministers for the safety of Europe, what can enable them now to tell us that we are perfectly secure? If it was true that her bare possession of Oczakow would be so dangerous, what must be the terror of Europe when they saw our negotiators put Russia into the way of seizing even Constantinople itself? This was the strong argument of my honourable friend (Mr. Whitbread), and which he maintained with such solid reasoning, that a shadow of an answer has not been given to it. To illustrate the value of Oczakow, however, one honourable gentleman (Mr. Grant) went back to the reign of Elizabeth—nay, to the days of Philip and Demosthenes. He told me that when Demosthenes, urging the Athenians to make war on Philip, reproached them with inattention to a few towns he had taken, the names of which they scarcely knew, telling them that those towns were the keys by which he would in time invade and overcome Greece, he gave them a salutary warning of the danger that impended. But if the opponents of that great orator had prevailed—if they had succeeded in inducing their countrymen to acquiesce in the surrender not only of those towns, but of considerably more, as in the present instance, with what face would he afterwards have declared to his countrymen, "True it was that these sorry and nameless towns were the keys to the Acropolis itself, but you have surrendered them; and what is the consequence? You are now in a state of the most perfect security—you have now nothing to fear—you have now the prospect of sixteen years of peace before you!" I ask, Sir, what would have been the reception even of Demosthenes himself, if he had undertaken to support such an inconsistency?

Let us try this, however, the other way. In order to show that his Majesty's Ministers merit the censure which is proposed, I will admit that the preservation of the Turks is necessary for the security of a balance of power. I trust, at the same time, that this admission, which I make merely for the argument, will not be disingenuously quoted upon me, as hypothetical statements too commonly are, for admissions of fact. What will the right honourable gentleman gain by it? The Turks, by his arrangement, are left in a worse situation than he found them in; for, previous to his interference, if Russia had gone to Constantinople, he would have been unfettered by the stipulations which bind him now, and he and his ally might have interfered to save the Porte from total destruction. Now, however, the possible and total extirpation of the Ottoman power is made to depend on a point so precarious as their accepting the proposal which the right honourable gentleman thought fit to agree to for them, within the space of four months. And what is this proposal? Why, that the Turks should give up not only the object of the war they had begun, but this very Oczakow, which of itself was sufficient, in the hands of Russia, to overturn the balance. If, therefore, it was so important to recover Oczakow, it is not recovered, and Ministers ought to be censured. If unimportant, they ought never to have demanded it. If so unimportant, they ought to be censured for arming; but if so important as they have stated it, they ought to be censured for disarming without having gotten it. Either way, therefore, the argument comes to the same point, and I care not on which side the gentlemen choose to take it up; for whether Oczakow be, as they told us last year, the key to Constantinople, on the preservation of which to Turkey the balance of Europe depended, or, as they must tell us now, of no comparative importance, their conduct is equally to be condemned for disarming, and pusillanimously yielding up the object, in the first instance; for committing the dignity of their Sovereign, and hazarding the peace of their country, in the second. But they tell us, it is unfair to involve us in this dilemma; there was a middle course to be adopted. Oczakow was certainly of much importance; but this importance was to be determined upon by circumstances. Sir, we are become nice, indeed, in our political arithmetic! In this calculating age, we ascertain to a scruple what an object is really worth. Thus it seems that Oczakow was worth an armament, but not worth a war: it was worth a threat, but not worth carrying that threat into execution. Sir, I can conceive nothing so degrading and dishonourable as an argument such as this. To hold out a menace, without ever seriously meaning to enforce it, constitutes, in common language, the true description of a bully; applied to the transactions of a nation, the disgrace is deeper, and the consequences fatal to its honour. Yet such is the precise conduct the King's Ministers have made the nation to hold in the eyes of Europe, and which they defend by an argument which, if urged in private life, would stamp a man with the character of a coward and a bully, and sink him to the deepest abyss of infamy and degradation. Sure I am, that this distinction never suggested itself to the reflection of a noble Duke, whose conduct throughout the whole of this business has evinced the manly character of his mind, unaccustomed to such calculations! From him we learn the fact. He said, in his place, that his colleagues thought it fit to risk a threat to recover Oczakow, but would not risk a war for it. Such conduct was not for him! It might suit the characters of his colleagues in office; it could not his. But they say, it might be worth a war with the public opinion, but worth nothing without it. I cannot conceive any case in which a great and wise nation, having committed itself by a menace, can withdraw that menace without disgrace. The converse of the proposition I can easily conceive—that there may be a place, for instance, not fit to be asked at all, but which, being asked for, and with a menace, it is fit to insist upon. This undoubtedly goes to make a nation, like an individual, cautious of committing itself, because there is no ground so tender as that of honour. How do Ministers think on this subject? Oczakow was everything by itself, but when they added to Oczakow the honour of England, it became nothing. Oczakow, by itself, threatened the balance of Europe; Oczakow and honour weighed nothing in the scale. Honour is, in their political arithmetic, a *minus* quantity, to be subtracted from the value of Oczakow. Sir, I am ashamed to state this reasoning; nor can I reflect on the foul stain it has fixed on the English name, without feeling mortified and humbled indeed! Their late colleague, the noble Duke (the Duke of Leeds), urged his sentiments with the feelings that became him; feelings that form a striking contrast to those that actuate the right honourable gentlen He told his country, that when he had made his mind to the necessity of demanding Oczal it was his opinion that it might have l obtained without a war; but having once manded it, he felt it his duty not to shrink f the war that might ensue from the rejectic that demand, and preferred the resignatic his office to the retracting that opinion. different was the conduct of the right hon able gentleman, though his advice was the s and small were the scruples he felt in turnis the honour of his Sovereign, whose name pledged to this demand, and afterwards obli him to recede from it.

They tell us, however, and seem to value themselves much upon it, that in abandoning the object for which they had armed, they acted in conformity to public opinion. Sir, I will fairly state my sentiments on this subject too. It certainly is right and prudent to consult the public opinion; it is frequently wise to attend even to public prejudices, on subjects of such infinite importance as whether they are to have war or peace. But if, in the capacity of a vant to the Crown, I were to see, or strong imagine that I saw, any measures going for that threatened the peace or prosperity of country, and if the emergency were so pre as to demand the sudden adoption of a dec course to avert the mischief, I should not tate one moment to act upon my own opi If the public opinion did not happen to sq with mine; if, after pointing out to them danger, they did not see it in the same with me, or if they conceived that an remedy was preferable to mine, I should consider it as due to my King, due to my country, due to my own honour, to retire, that they might pursue the plan which they thought better, by a fit instrument—that is, by a man who thought with them. Such would be my conduct on any subject where conscientiously I could not surrender my opinion. If the case was doubtful, or the emergency not so pressing, I should be ready, perhaps, to surrender my opinion to that of the public; but one thing is most clear in such an event as this—namely, that I ought to give the public the means of forming an opinion.

Do I state this difference fairly? If I do, and if the gentlemen over against me will admit that in the instance before us the public opinion ought to have influenced them, it follows that the public opinion ought to have been consulted before we were committed in the eyes of Europe, and that the country ought to have had the means and the information necessary to form their judgment upon the true merits of this question. Did the King's Ministers act thus? Did they either take the public opinion, or did they give us the means of forming one? Nothing like it. On the 28th of March, the message was brought down to this House; on the 29th, we passed a vote of approbation, but no opinion was asked from us, no explanation was given us; so far from it, we were expressly told our advice was not wanted—that we had nothing to do with the prerogative of the Crown to make war—that all our business was to give confidence. So far with regard to this House; and I cannot help thinking this conduct somewhat hard upon the majority, who certainly might have counted for something in the general opinion, when the right honourable gentleman was collecting it, if he meant fairly so to do. I grant, indeed, that there are many ways by which the feeling and temper of the public may be tolerably well known out of this House, as well as in it. I grant that the opinion of a respectable meeting at Manchester, of a meeting at Norwich, of a meeting at Wakefield, of public bodies of men in different parts of England, might give the right honourable gentleman a correct idea of the public opinion. Permit me to say also, that in the speeches of the minority of this House he might find also the ground of public opinion—both what might give it rise, and what might give it countenance. But was the majority of this House the only body whose opinions were not worth consulting? "I travelled to Norwich, to York, Manchester, Wakefield, for opinions," will the right honourable gentleman say? "I listened to the minority, I looked to Lord Stormont, to the Earl of Guildford; but as to you, my trusty majority, I did not look to you! I had other business for you! It is not your office to give opinions; your business is to confide! You must pledge yourself, in the first instance, to all I can ask from you, and perhaps some time in the next year I may condescend to let you know the grounds on which you are acting." Such is the language he holds to us, if his conduct were to be explained by words; and a conduct more indecent or preposterous is not easily to be conceived. For it is neither more nor less than to tell us—"When I thought the Ottoman Power in danger, I asked for an armament to succour it. You approved and granted it to me. The public sense was against me, and without minding you, I yielded to that sense. My opinion, however, remains still the same; though it must be confessed, that I led you into giving a sanction to my schemes by a species of reasoning which it appears the country has saved itself by resisting. But they were to blame. I yet think that the exact contrary of what was done ought to have been done; and that the peace and safety of Europe depended upon it. But never mind how you voted, or how directly opposite to the general opinion, with which I complied, was that opinion I persuaded you to support. Vote now that I was right in both—in the opinion I still maintain, and in my compliance with its opposite. The peace of Europe is safe; I keep my place, and all is right again." But, after all, the right honourable gentleman did not act from any deference to the public opinion; and to prove this, I have but to recall to your recollection dates. The message was brought down, as I said before, on the 28th of March; and in less than a week—I believe in four days—afterwards, before it was possible to collect the opinion of any one public body of men, their whole system was reversed. The change, therefore, could not come from the country, even had they been desirous of consulting it. But I have proved that they were not desirous to have any opinion from any quarter; they came down with their purposes masked and veiled to this House, and tried all they could to preclude inquiry into what they were doing. These are not the steps of men desirous of acting by opinion. I hold it, however, to be now acknowledged that it was not the public opinion, but that of the minority in this House, which compelled the Ministers to relinquish their ill-advised projects; for a right honourable gentleman who spoke last night (Mr. Dundas) owned the truth in his own frank way. "We certainly," said he, "do not know that the opinion of the public was against us; we only know that a great party in this country was against us, and therefore we apprehended that though one campaign might have been got through, at the beginning of the next session they would have interrupted us in procuring the supplies." I believe I quote the right honourable gentleman correctly; and here, Sir, let me pause, and thank him for the praise which he gives the gentlemen on this side the House. Let me indulge the satisfaction of reflecting, that though we have not the emoluments of office nor the patronage of power, yet we are not excluded from great influence on the measures of Government. We take pride to ourselves that at this moment we are not sitting in a Committee of Supply, voting enormous fleets and armies to carry into execution this calamitous measure. To us he honestly declares this credit to be due; and the country will, no doubt, feel the gratitude they owe us for having saved them from the miseries of war. An honourable gentleman, indeed (Mr. Jenkinson), has told us that our opposition to this measure in its commencement occasioned its having been abandoned by the Ministers; but he will not allow us the merit of having saved the country from a war by our interposition, but charges us with having prevented their obtaining the terms demanded, which would have been got without a war. I am glad to hear this argument; but must declare, in the name of the minority, that we think ourselves most unfairly treated by it, and forced into a responsibility that belongs in no manner whatsoever to our situation. The right honourable gentleman, when repeatedly pressed on this subject during the last session, was uniform in affirming that he had reasons for his conduct, to his mind so cogent and unanswerable, that he was morally certain of the indispensable necessity of the measures he was pursuing. He has said the same since, and to this hour continues his first opinion. If, therefore, the right honourable gentleman thought so, and thought at the same time that our arguments were likely to mislead the country from its true interests, why did he continue silent? If public opinion was so necessary for him, that without it, as he tells us now, he could not proceed a single step, why did he suffer us to corrupt the passions, to blind and to pervert the understandings of the public to a degree that compelled his sacrifice of this essential measure? Why did he quietly, and without concern, watch the prevalence of our false arguments? Why did he sanction their progress, by never answering them, when he knew the consequence must necessarily be to defeat his dearest object, and put the safety of his country to the hazard? Why did he not oppose some antidote to our poison? But having neglected to do this (because of his duty to preserve State secrets, as he would have us believe), what shadow of a right, what possible pretext has he to come forward now, and accuse us for thwarting his views, or to cast the responsibility of his failure and disgrace upon us, whose arguments he never answered, and to whom he obstinately and invariably refused all sort of information, by which we might have been enabled to form a better judgment, and possibly to agree with him on this subject? The right honourable gentleman, however (Mr. Dundas), judges more fairly of us; and I thank him for the handsome acknowledgment he paid to the true character of the gentlemen on this side of the House; for, by owning that because we did not happen to approve of this armament it was abandoned, he owns another fact, that we are not what another honourable gentleman (Mr. Steele) chose to represent us—an indiscriminate faction, that disapproves of everything, right and wrong. This is clearly manifest from his own admissions; for giving up when they found we disapproved, they must have begun in the idea that we should approve. We approved in the case of Holland, and in the case of Spain. In the first case we did so, because the rectitude of the thing was so clear and manifest, as that every well-wisher to England must approve. We did so in the case of Spain, because the objects were explained to us—the insult given, and the reparation demanded, were both before us. But had the right honourable gentleman any right, because we agreed to the Dutch and Spanish armaments, to anticipate the consent of the Opposition to this? It was insulting to impute the possibility to us. What! agree to take the money out of the pockets of the people, without an insult explained, or an object held up! It is said the object was stated, and that the means only were left to conjecture—that the *object* proposed to the House was an armament to make a peace, and Oczakow was supposed to be the *means* by which that peace was to be effected. Sir, it is almost constantly my misfortune to be differing from the right honourable gentleman about the import of the words *object* and *means*. In my way of using these words, I should have directly transposed them, and called the armament the *means* of effecting peace, and Oczakow the *object* of that armament. And the event proves that Ministers thought as I do; for they gave up that object because they knew they could get the end they proposed by their armament without it. This object, indeed, whatever was its importance —whether it was or was not, as we have alternately heard it asserted and denied, the key of Constantinople, nay, as some wild and fanciful people had almost persuaded themselves, the key to our possessions in the East Indies—the King's Ministers have completely renounced, and see by their conduct to have cared very little wh became of that or Constantinople itself. balance of Europe, however, is perfectly they tell us; and on that point we have noth more to apprehend. The enormous accessio power to Russia, from the possession of (kow, so far from affecting Great Britain, i likely, according to what the Ministers assure us, to disturb the tranquillity of her nearest neighbours. That Oczakow, therefore, was at any time an object sufficient to justify their interference, I have stated many reasons for concluding will not, be alleged this night. Some of the gentlemen on the other side, indeed, have advanced other grounds, and told us (I confess it is for the first time) that in this war the Empress of Russia was the aggressor; that on her part the war was offensive; and that it became us to interfere to stop her progress. They tell us of various encroachments in the Cuban, of hostilities systematically carried on in violation of treaties, and many other instances, not one of which they have attempted to prove by a single document, or have rested on any other foundation than their own assertions. But to these, Sir, I shall oppose the authority of Ministers themselves; for in one of the despatches of the Duke of Leeds to Mr. Whitworth, he desires him to communicate to the Court of Petersburg, that if they will consent to make peace with the Turks on the *status quo*, the allies will consent to guarantee the Crimea to them, "*the object of the war*," as he states it to be. I desire no further proof than this that we always considered the Turks as the aggressors; for it follows that where any place, in the possession of one Power, is made the object of a war by another, the Power claiming that object is the aggressor. If, for example, we were at war with Spain, and Gibraltar the object, Spain of course would be the aggressor; the contrary if the Havannah were the object. The King of England, therefore, by the despatch which I have quoted, has, in words and in fact, acknowledged the Turks to have been the aggressors in this war, by making pretensions to a province solemnly ceded to Russia in the year 1783. I can scarcely think that Ministers mean to contend that cession by treaty does not give right to possession. Where are we to look, therefore, to ascertain the right of a country to any place or territory, but to the *last treaty*? To what would the opposite doctrine lead? France might claim Canada, ceded in 1763; or we Tobago, ceded in 1783. It might be urged that they took advantage of our dispute with our own colonies, and that the treaty gave no right. Canada, Jamaica, everything might be questioned. Where would be the peace of Europe if these doctrines were to be acted on? Every country must continue in a state of endless perplexity, armament, and preparations. But, happily for mankind, a different principle prevails in the law of nations; there the last treaty gives the right, and upon that we must aver, that if, as the despatch says, the Crimea was the object, the Turk was the aggressor.

What therefore was the right claimed by the right honourable gentleman to enter into this dispute? I will answer: the right of a proud man, anxious to play a lofty part. France had gone off the stage—the character of the miserable disturber of empires was vacant, and he resolved to boast and vapour, and play his anti-tricks and gestures on the same theatre. And what have been the first effects of this new experiment upon the British nation? That, in the pride and zenith of our power, we have miserably disgraced ourselves in the eyes of Europe—that the name of his Majesty has been sported with, and stained; that the people of England have been inflamed, their commerce disturbed, the most valuable citizens dragged from their houses, and half a million of money added to the public burdens. And here, Sir, in justice to my own feelings, I cannot pass over wholly in silence the fate of that valuable body of our fellow-citizens, who are more particularly the victims of these false alarms, and by whom the most bitter portion of the common calamity must be borne. I am compelled to admit that every State has a right, in the season of danger, to claim the services of all or any of its members; that the "*salus populi, suprema lex est.*" Tenderness and consideration in the use of such extensive powers is all I can recommend to those whose business it is to call them into action. But here I must lament, in common with every feeling mind, that unnecessary barbarity which dragged them from their homes, deprived them of their liberty, and tore them from the industrious exercise of those modes of life by which they earned support for their families, wantonly, cruelly, and without pretext, because without the smallest intention of employing them. The gentlemen well know what I state to be a fact; for they know that their system was changed, and their object abandoned, before even they had begun to issue press-warrants.

I return, Sir, to the disgraceful condition in which the right honourable gentleman has involved us. Let us see whether what I have said on this point be not literally true. The Empress of Russia offered, early in the year 1790, to depart from the terms she had at first thrown out—namely, that Bessarabia, Wallachia, and Moldavia, should be independent of the Ottoman power. This, it appears, she yielded upon the amicable representations of the allied Powers, and substituted in the room of them those conditions which have since been conceded to her—namely, that the Dniester should be the boundary between the two empires, and all former treaties should be confirmed. "Then," say Ministers, "if we gained this by simple negotiation, what may we not gain by an armament?" Thus judging of her pusillanimity by their own, they threatened her. What did she do? Peremptorily refused to depart one atom from her last conditions; and these, I assert, were in the possession of his Majesty's Ministers long before the armament: they knew not only this early in the month of March, but likewise the resolution of the Empress not to rise in her demands, notwithstanding any farther success that might attend her arms. The memorial of the Court of Denmark, which they have, for reasons best known to themselves, refused us, but which was circulated in every court and published in every newspaper in Europe, fully informed them of these matters. But the King's Ministers, with an absurdity of which there is no example, called upon the country to arm. Why? Not because they meant to employ the armament against her, but in the fanciful hope that because, in an amicable negotiation, the Empress had been prevailed upon not to press the demand of Wallachia, Moldavia, and Bessarabia, as independent sovereignties, they should infallibly succeed by arming, and not employing that armament, in persuading her to abandon all the rest! And what was the end? Why, that after pledging the King's name in the most deliberate and solemn manner; after lofty vapouring, menacing, promising, denying, turning and turning again; after keeping up the parade of an armament for four months, accompanied with those severe measures, to be regretted even when necessary, to be reprobated when not, the right honourable gentleman crouches humbly at her feet; entreats, submissively supplicates of her moderation that she will grant him some small trifle of what he asks, if it is but by way of a boon; and finding at last that he can get nothing, either by threats or his prayers, gives up the whole, precisely as she insisted upon having it.

The right honourable gentleman, however, is determined that this House shall take the whole of this disgrace upon itself. I heard him, with much delight, on a former day, quote largely from that excellent and philosophical work, "The Wealth of Nations." In almost the first page of that book he will find it laid down as a principle, that by a division of labour in the different occupations of life, the objects to which it is applied are perfected, time is saved, dexterity improved, and the general stock of science augmented: that by joint effort and reciprocal accommodation the severest tasks are accomplished, and difficulties surmounted too stubborn for the labour of a single hand. Thus, in the building of a great palace, we observe the work to be parcelled out into different departments, and distributed and subdivided into various degrees, some higher, some lower, to suit the capacities and condition of those who are employed in its construction. There is the architect, that invents the plan, and erects the stately columns; there is the dustman and the nightman, to clear away the rubbish. The right honourable gentleman applies these principles to his politics, and in the division and cast of parts for the job we are now to execute for him, has reserved for himself the higher and more respectable share of the business, and leaves all the dirty work to us. Is he asked why the House of Commons made the armament last year? he answers, "The House of Commons did not make the armament! I made it. The House of Commons only approved it." Is he asked why he gave up the object of the armament after he had made it? "I did not give it up!" he exclaims. "I think the same of its necessity as ever; it is the House of Commons that gives it up; it is the House that supports the nation in their senseless clamour against my measures; it is to this House that you must look for the shame and guilt of your disgrace." To himself he takes the more conspicuous character of menacer. It is he that distributes provinces and limits empires; while he leaves to this House the humbler office of licking the dust and begging forgiveness.

"Not mine these groans—
These sighs that issue, or these tears that flow."

"I am forced into these submissions by a low, contracted, grovelling, mean-spirited, and ignorant people!" But this is not all. It rarely happens that in begging pardon, when men determine upon that course, they have not some benefit in view, or that the profit to be got is not meant to counterbalance, in some measure, the honour to be sacrificed. Let us see how the right honourable gentleman managed this. On the first indication of hostile measures against Russia, 135 members of this House divided against the adoption of them. This it was, according to a right honourable gentleman who spoke in the debate yesterday (Mr. Dundas), that induced Ministers to abandon their first object; but not like the Duke of Leeds, who candidly avowed that if he could have once brought himself to give up the claim of Oczakow, he would not have stood out for the razing its fortifications, or any such terms. The Ministers determined that the nation at least shall reap no benefit from the reversal of their system. "You have resisted our projects," say they; "you have discovered and exposed our incapacity; you have made us the ridicule of Europe, and such we shall appear to posterity; you have defeated, indeed, our intentions of involving you in a war; but *you* shall not be the gainers by it! *you* shall not save your money! We abandon Oczakow, as you compel us to do; but we will keep up the armament, if it is only to spite you!" Determined to act this disgraceful part, their next care was to do it in the most disgraceful manner; and as they had dragged Parliament and their King through the dirt and mire, they resolved to exhibit them in this offensive plight to the eyes of Europe. To do this they did not care to trust to the minister we had at Petersburg — a gentleman distinguished for amiable manners, and by the faithful, the vigilant, and the able discharge of his duty. Why was the management of the negotiation taken from him? Was he too proud for this service? No man is too proud to do his duty; and of all our foreign ministers, Mr. Whitworth I should think the very last to whom it could be reproached that he is remiss in fulfilling the directions he receives in their utmost strictness. But a new man was to be found; one whose reputation for talents and honour might operate, as they hoped, as a sort of set-off against the incapacity he was to cure, and the national honour he was deputed to surrender. Was it thus determined, because in looking round their diplomatic body there was no man to be selected from it whose character assimilated with the dirty job he was to execute? As there was honour to be sacrificed, a stain to be fixed upon the national character, engagements to be retracted, and a friend to be abandoned, did it never occur to them that there was *one man* upon their diplomatic list who would have been pronounced by general acclamation thoroughly qualified in soul and qualities for this service? Such a person they might have found, and not so occupied as to make it inconvenient to employ him; they would have found him absent from his station, under the pretence of attending his duty in this House, though he does not choose often to make his appearance here. Instead of this, however, they increased the dishonour that they doomed us to suffer, by sending a gentleman endowed with every virtue and accomplishment; who had acquired, in the service of the Empress of Russia at an early period of his life, a character for bravery and enterprise that rendered him personally esteemed by her, and in whom fine talents and elegant manner, ripened by habit and experience, had confirmed the flattering promise of his youth. Did they think that the shabbiness of their message was to be done away by the worth of the messenger? If I were to send an humiliating apology to any person, would it change its quality by being entrusted to Lord Rodney, Admiral Pigot, my honourable friend behind me (General Burgoyne), Lord Cornwallis, Sir Henry Clinton, Sir William Howe, or any other gallant and brave officer? Certainly not.

It was my fortune, in very early life, to have set out in habits of particular intimacy with Mr. Fawkener, and however circumstances may have intervened to suspend that intimacy—circumstances arising from wide differences in political opinion—they never have altered the sentiments of private esteem which I have uniformly felt for him; and with every amiable and conciliating quality that belongs to man, I know him to be one from whom improper submissions are the least to be expected. Well, sir, these gentlemen, Mr. Whitworth and Mr. Fawkener, commence the negotiation, by the offer of three distinct propositions, each of them better than the other, and accompany it with an expression somewhat remarkable—namely, that this negotiation is to be as unlike all the others as possible, and to be "founded in perfect candour." To prove this, they submit at once to the Russian ministers "all that their instructions enable them to propose." Who would not have imagined, according to the plain import of these words, that unless the Empress had assented to one of these propositions, all amicable interposition would have been at an end, and war the issue? The "perfect candour" promised in the beginning of their note, leads them to declare explicitly, that unless the fortifications of Oczakow be razed, or the Turks are allowed as an equivalent to keep both the banks of the Dneister, the allies cannot propose any terms to them. What answer do they receive? An unequivocal rejection of every one of their propositions; accompanied, however, with a declaration, to which I shall soon return, that the navigation of that river shall be free to all the world, and a reference to those maxims of policy which have invariably actuated the Empress of Russia in her intercourse with neutral nations, whose commerce she has at all times protected and encouraged. With this declaration the British plenipotentiaries declare themselves perfectly contented; nay more, they engage, that if the Turks should refuse these conditions, and continue obstinate longer than four months, the allied Courts "will abandon the termination of the war to the events it may produce." And here ends for ever all care for the Ottoman empire, all solicitude about the balance of power. The right honourable gentleman will interpose no farther to save either, but rests the whole of a measure once so indispensable to our safety, upon this doubtful issue, whether the Turks will accept in December those very terms which, in July, the British Ministers could not venture to propose to them!

Sir, we may look in vain to the events of former times for a disgrace parallel to what we have suffered. Louis the Fourteenth, a monarch often named in our debates, and whose reign exhibits more than any other the extremes of prosperous and of adverse fortune, never, in the midst of his most humiliating distresses, stooped to so despicable a sacrifice of all that can be dear to man. The war of the succession, unjustly began by him, had reduced his power, had swallowed up his armies and his navies, had desolated his provinces, had drained his treasures, and deluged the earth with the blood of the best and most faithful of his subjects Exhausted by his various calamities, he offered at one time to his enemies to relinquish all the objects for which he had begun the war: that proud monarch sued for peace, and was content to receive it from our moderation. But when it was made a condition of that peace, that he should turn his arms against his grandson, and compel him by force to relinquish the throne of Spain—humbled, exhausted, conquered as he was, misfortune had not yet bowed his spirit to conditions so hard as these. We know the event: he persisted still in the war, until the folly and wickedness of Queen Anne's Ministers enabled him to conclude the peace of Utrecht, on terms considerably less disadvantageous even than those he had himself proposed. And shall *we*, sir, the pride of our age, the terror of Europe, submit to this humiliating sacrifice of our honour? Have *we* suffered a defeat at Blenheim? Shall we, with our increasing prosperity, our widely-diffused capital, our navy, the just subject of our common exultation, overflowing coffers, that enable us to give back to the people what, in the hour of calamity, we were compelled to take from them; flushed with a recent triumph over Spain, and yet more than all, while our old rival and enemy was incapable of disturbing us, shall it be for us to yield to what France disdained in the hour of her sharpest distress, and exhibit ourselves to the world, the sole example in its annals of such an abject and pitiful degradation?

But gentlemen inform us now, in justification, as I suppose they mean it, of all these measures, that to effect a peace between Russia and the Porte was only the ostensible cause of our armament, or at least was not the sole cause; and that Ministers were under some apprehension lest the Emperor, if the allies were to disarm, should insist on better terms from the Turks than he had agreed to accept by the convention of Reichenbach. This I cannot believe. When his Majesty sends a message to inform his Parliament that he thinks it necessary to arm for a specific purpose, I cannot suppose that a falsehood has been put into his Majesty's mouth; and that the armament which he proposes as necessary for one purpose, is intended for another. If the right honourable gentleman shall tell me that although the war between Russia and the Porte was the real cause of equipping the armament, yet that being once equipped, it was wise to keep it up when no longer wanted on that account, because the Emperor seemed inclined to depart from the convention of Reichenbach; then I answer, that it was his duty to have come with a second message to Parliament, expressly stating this new object, with the necessary information, to enable the House to judge of its propriety. Another of the arguments for continuing the armament after the object was relinquished is, that Russia might have insisted on harder terms, not conceiving herself bound by offers which we had refused to accept. I perfectly agree with gentlemen, that after the repeated offer of those terms on the part of Russia, and the rejection of them by us, the Empress was not bound to adhere to them in all possible events and contingencies. If the war had continued, she would have had a right to farther indemnification for the expense of it. But was it not worth the Minister's while to try the good faith of the Empress of Russia, after she had so solemnly pledged herself to all Europe that she would not rise in her demands? The experiment would have been made with little trouble; by the simple expedient of sending a messenger to ask the question. The object of his armament would have suffered little by the delay, as an answer from the Russian Court might have been had in five or six weeks. Was it reasonable in Ministers to suppose that, because in the early part of the negotiation the Empress had shown so much regard to us as actually to give up whatever pretensions she had formed to other provinces of the Turkish empire, solely with the view of obtaining our concurrence to the principle on which she offered to make peace, she would revert to those very pretensions the instant she had obtained that concurrence on our part, for the benefit of which she had sacrificed them? Surely, as I have said, it was worth while to make the experiment; but simple and obvious as this was, a very different course was adopted. Oczakow, indeed, was relinquished before the armament began, as we may find by comparing the date of the press-warrants with that of the Duke of Leeds's resignation. As soon as the King's message was delivered to Parliament, a messenger was dispatched to Berlin with an intimation of the resolution to arm. This, perhaps, was rashly done, as they might have foreseen that the measure would probably meet with opposition, and much time could not have been lost by waiting the event of the first debate. No sooner was the division known than a second messenger was sent off to overtake and stop the despatches of the first; and this brings me to another argument, which I confess appears to me very unlikely to help them out. They tell us that the King of Prussia having armed in consequence of our assurances of support, we could not disarm before we knew the sentiments of the Court of Berlin, without the imputation of leaving our ally in the lurch. Did we wait for the sentiments of that Court to determine whether Oczakow was to be given up or not? Sir, when that measure was resolved upon, the right honourable gentleman actually had abandoned his ally; and that such was the general sense of the Court of Berlin, I believe can be testified by every Englishman who was there at the time. No sooner did the second messenger arrive, and the contents of his despatches become known, than a most general indignation rose against the conduct of the right honourable gentleman; and I am well enough informed on the subject to state to this House, that not an Englishman could show his face in that capital without exposing himself to mortification, perhaps to insult. But, between the 28th of March, when the message was brought down to this House, and the 2nd or 3rd of April, when the second messenger was dispatched with the news that Ministers had abandoned the object of it, the armament could not have been materially advanced. Why then was it persisted in? The right honourable gentleman cannot argue that he kept up the armament in compliance with his engagements with Prussia, when the armament, in fact, did not exist, and when it had been begun but four or five days previous to his renouncing the object of it. That could not have been his motive. What then was the motive? Why, that he was too proud to own his error, and valued less the money and tranquillity of the people than the appearance of firmness, when he had renounced the reality. False shame is the parent of many crimes. By false shame a man may be tempted to commit a murder, to conceal a robbery. Influenced by this false shame, the Ministers robbed the people of their money, the seamen of their liberty, their families of support and protection; and all this to conceal that they had undertaken a system which was not fit to be pursued. If they say that they did this, apprehensive that without the terror of an armament Russia would not stand to the terms which they had refused to accept, they do no more than acknowledge that by the insolence of their arming, and the precipitancy of their submission, they had either so provoked her resentment or excited her contempt, that she would not even condescend to agree to her own propositions when approved by them. But however they might have thought her disposed to act on this subject, it was at least their duty to try whether such would have been her conduct or not.

To prove that the terms to which they agreed at last were the same with those they before rejected, all I feel it necessary for me to observe is, that the free navigation of the river Dniester, the only novelty introduced into them, was implied in proposing it as a boundary; for it is a well-known rule, that the boundary between two powers must be as free to the one as to the other. True, says the Minister, but we have got the free navigation for the subjects of other powers, particularly for those of Poland. If this be an advantage, it is an advantage he has gained by concession; for if he had not agreed that the river should be the boundary, the navigation would not have been free. The Turks offered no such stipulation, had they been put in possession of both the banks; besides which, as a noble duke whom I have already quoted well observed, it is an advantage whatever may be its value, which can subsist only in time of peace. It is not, I suppose, imagined that the navigation will be free in time of war. They have then got nothing that deserves the name of a "modification," a term, I must here observe, the use of which is not justified even by the original memorial, where the sense is more accurately expressed by the French word "*radoucissement*." Was it then for some *radoucissement* that they continued their armament? Was it to say to the Empress, when they had conceded everything, "We have given you all you asked, give us something that we may hold out to the public, something that we may use against the minority; that minority whom we have endeavoured to represent as your allies. We have sacrificed our allies, the Turks, to you; you can do no less than sacrifice your allies, the minority, to us!" If I had been to advise the Empress on the subject, I would have counselled her: Grant the British Minister something of this sort. I would even have advised her to raze the fortifications of Oczakow if he had insisted on it; I would have appealed from her policy to her generosity, and said, Grant him this as an apology, for he stands much in need of it. His whole object was to appear to gain something, no matter what, by continuing the armament; and even in this last pitiful and miserable object he has failed. If, after all, I ask whether these terms are contained in the peace that we have concluded for the Turks, or rather which the Turks concluded for themselves, the answer is, "We have no authentic copy of it." Is this what we have got by our arms, by distressing our commerce, dragging our seamen from their homes and occupations, and squandering our money? Is this the efficacy of our interference, and the triumph of our wisdom and our firmness? The Turks have at length concluded a peace, of which they do not even condescend to favour us with a copy, so that we know what it is only by report; and the balance of Europe, late in so much danger, and of so much importance, is left for them to settle without consulting us! Is it for this that we employed such men as Mr. Fawkener and Mr. Whitworth? They were sent to negotiate for the materials of a speech, and failed. But what are the complaints that private friendship has a right to make to those of an insulted public? Half a million of money is spent, the people alarmed and interrupted in their proper pursuits by the apprehension of a war, and for what? For the restoration of Oczakow? No; Oczakow is not restored. To save the Turks from being too much humbled? No; they are now in a worse situation than they would have been had we never armed at all. If Russia had persevered in that system of encroachment of which she is accused, we could, as I observed before, then have assisted them unembarrassed. We are now tied down by treaties and fettered by stipulations; we have even guaranteed to Russia what we before said it would be unsafe for the Turks to yield, and dangerous to the peace of Europe for Russia to possess. This is what the public have got by the armament. What, then, was the private motive?

> Scilicet, ut Turno contingat regia conjux,
> Nos, animæ viles, inhumata infletaque turba,
> Sternamur campis——

The Minister gained, or thought he was to gain, an excuse for his rashness and misconduct, and to purchase this excuse was the public money and the public quiet wantonly sacrificed. There are some effects which, to combine with their causes, is almost sufficient to drive men mad! That the pride, the folly, the presumption of a single person, shall be able to involve a whole people in wretchedness and disgrace is more than philosophy can teach mortal patience to endure. Here are the true weapons of the enemies of our constitution! Here may we search for the source of those seditious writings meant either to weaken our attachment to the constitution, by depreciating its value, or that loudly tell us we have no constitution at all! We may blame, we may reprobate such doctrines, but while we furnish those who circulate them with arguments such as these; while the example of this day shows us to what degree the fact is true, we must not wonder if the purposes they are meant to answer be but too successful.

They argue that a constitution cannot be right where such things are possible, much less so when they are practised without punishment. This, sir, is a serious reflection to every man who loves the constitution of England. Against the vain theories of men, who project fundamental alterations upon grounds of more speculative objection, I can easily defend it; but when they recur to these facts, and show me how we may be doomed to all the horrors of war by the caprice of an individual, who will not even condescend to explain his reasons, I can only fly to this House, and exhort you to rouse from your lethargy of confidence into the active mistrust and vigilant control which is your duty and your office.

Without recurring to the dust to which the Minister has been humbled, and the dirt he has been dragged through, if we ask for what has the peace of the public been disturbed? for what is that man pressed and dragged like a felon to a service that should be honourable? We must be answered, For some three-quarters of a mile of barren territory on the banks of the Dniester! In the name of all we value give us, when such instances are quoted in derogation of our constitution, some right to answer, that these are not its principles, but the monstrous abuses intruded into its practice. Let it not be said that because the executive power, for an adequate and evident cause, may adopt measures that require expense without consulting Parliament, we are to convert the exception into a rule, to reverse the principle; and that it is now to be assumed that the people's money may be spent for any cause, or for none, without either submitting the exigency to the judgment of their representatives, or inquiring into it afterwards, unless we can make out ground for a criminal charge against the executive Government. Let us disclaim these abuses and return to the constitution. I am not one of those who lay down rules as universal and absolute, because I think there is hardly a political or moral maxim which is universally true, but I maintain the general rule to be, that before the public money be voted away, the occasion that calls for it should be fairly stated, for the consideration of those who are the proper guardians of the public money. Had the Minister explained his system to Parliament before he called for money to support it, and Parliament had decided that it was not worth supporting, he would have been saved the mortification and disgrace in which his own honour is involved, and by being furnished with a just excuse to Prussia for withdrawing from the prosecution of it, have saved that of his Sovereign and his country, which he has irrecoverably tarnished. Is unanimity necessary to his plans? He can be sure of it in no manner, unless he explains them to this House, who are certainly much better judges than he is of the degree of unanimity with which they are likely to be received. Why, then, did he not consult us? Because he had other purposes to answer in the use he meant to make of his majority. Had he opened himself to the House at first, and had we declared against him, he might have been stopped in the first instance. Had we declared for him, we might have held him too firmly to his principle, to suffer his receding from it as he has done. Either of these alternatives he dreaded. It was his policy to decline our opinions, and to exact our confidence, that thus having the means of acting either way, according to the exigencies of his personal situation, he might come to Parliament and tell us what our opinions ought to be; which set of principles would be most expedient to shelter him from inquiry, and from punishment. It is for this he comes before us with a poor and pitiful excuse, that for want of the unanimity he expected, there was reason to fear, if the war should go to a second campaign, that it might be obstructed. Why not speak out, and own the real fact? He feared that a second campaign might occasion the loss of his place. Let him keep but his place, he cares not what else he loses. With other men, reputation and glory are the objects of ambition; power and place are coveted but as the means of these. For the Minister, power and place are sufficient of themselves. With them he is content; for them he can calmly sacrifice every proud distinction that ambition covets, and every noble prospect to which it points the way!

Sir, there is yet an argument which I have not sufficiently noticed. It has been said, as a ground for his defence, that he was prevented from gaining what he demanded by our opposition; and, but for this, Russia would have complied, and never would have hazarded a war. Sir, I believe the direct contrary, and my belief is as good as their assertion, unless they will give us some proof of its veracity. Until then, I have a right to ask them, what if Russia had not complied? Worse and worse for him! He must have gone on, redoubling his menaces and expenses, the Empress of Russia continuing inflexible as ever, but for the salutary opposition which preserved him from his extremity of shame. I am not contending that armaments are never necessary to enforce negotiations; but it is one, and that not the least, of the evils attending the right honourable gentleman's misconduct, that by keeping up the parade of an armament never meant to be employed, he has, in a great measure, deprived us of the use of this method of negotiating whenever it may be necessary to apply it effectually. For if you propose to arm in concert with any foreign Power, that Power will answer, "What security can you give me that you will persevere in that system? You say you cannot go to war unless your people are unanimous." If you aim to negotiate against a foreign Power, that Power will say, "I have only to persist; the British Minister may threaten, but he dare not act—he will not hazard the loss of his place by a war." A right honourable gentleman (Mr. Dundas), in excuse for withholding papers, asked what foreign Power would negotiate with an English Cabinet if their secrets were likely to be developed and exposed to the idle curiosity of a House of Commons? I do not dread such a consequence; but if I must be pushed to extremes, if nothing were left me but an option between opposite evils, I should have no hesitation in choosing. "Better have no dealings with them at all," I should answer, "if the right of inquiry into every part of a negotiation they think fit, and of knowing why they are to vote the money of their constituents, be denied the House of Commons." But there is something like reason why no foreign Power will negotiate with us, and that a much better reason than a dread of disclosing their secrets, in the right honourable gentleman's example. I declare, therefore, for the genius of our constitution, against the practice of his Majesty's Ministers: I declare that the duties of this House are, vigilance in preference to secrecy, deliberation in preference to dispatch. Sir, I have given my reasons for supporting the motion for a vote of censure on the Minister. I will listen to his defence with attention, and I will retract wherever he shall prove me to be wrong.

MR. CHANCELLOR PITT said, the vehemence and violence which had been employed, and the splendid eloquence of the right honourable gentleman who had just sat down, had called the attention of this House to the subject now before it. His eloquence, for whatever purpose it was directed, was always powerful; and he was happy that his arguments on this debate had been brought forward, and that he had taken the opportunity, at a time when it was fully awake, to draw their attention to his sentiments. He was also happy in the circumstance of the adjourned debate, as it had allowed the House to go more fully into the subject, and it was with peculiar satisfaction to him that, after having heard stated everything that had been said on a former evening, as well as on this, he now rose with a very different temper, and a different view from that right honourable gentleman, to recall the attention of the House from that brilliant display of language, and that forcible appeal which had been made to their passions and imaginations, to what appeared to him to be the proper subject before them, and the real point in dispute between them, and upon which their judgment ought to be exercised; and then he should leave the whole to the deliberate wisdom and impartial justice which he was confident that House would exercise on this important subject, in which our national policy was involved, and on a point particularly affecting the character of the deliberative, as well as the executive part of Government.

In stating the grounds on which he should have to call the attention of the House, after it had heard the arguments of the right honourable gentleman, and also after having heard the debate of the preceding night, to which he had satisfaction in reverting, he should endeavour to be as clear and as concise as possible; and notwithstanding the eloquence with which they had just heard one side of the subject maintained, he still referred with confidence to the principles developed in the debate of the day before, and in a speech, which was still in the recollection of the House, and regarded as a specimen of that clear eloquence, strong sense, justness of reasoning, and extensive knowledge, which he believed was wholly unexampled in any public assembly on a first essay, and would do honour to the most practised speaker or statesman that ever delivered his sentiments within the walls of that House.

In stating whatever occurred to him on this subject, and the grounds he should lay before the House, he begged to say, that he did not feel it necessary to enter into the grounds of some of the reasoning which the House had heard in the course of this debate; because the general question of system was one part necessarily connected with the merits of the exercise of that system, and because it was impossible to separate the conduct of Ministers from the principle on which they acted, before the armament which formed the matter of dispute was entered into; and having done so, then he should proceed to state the grounds on which the subject was taken up on that system. That part, therefore, which went to separate those two points was unnecessary, and being no material part of the debate, he should therefore dismiss all consideration of that sort of reasoning, as the paying attention to that distinction would only create confusion in considering the real points before the House. He should therefore take the liberty of confining the subject to its real limits, as they appeared to him; in the course of which he should lay it down as an argument, that the measure in question was founded on policy, and that success was not unreasonably to be expected in the issue.

The way in which the question was to be debated appeared to him to be, first, by desiring the House to recollect the principle of the measure, or the foundation of our continental connection; and then the policy, under all the circumstances of the case. These points would be governed by the relative situation of the country with regard to its alliances with foreign Powers; by a consideration of the danger and inconvenience to which it might have been exposed by an extension of the maritime power of Russia. The wisdom or folly of the whole system would, in a great measure, depend on what was called the balance of power in Europe.

Many gentlemen seemed to think that the question of the balance of power had been improperly introduced into the subject, and that it had nothing to do with the discussion of this case, but was totally inapplicable. These points, indeed, were not strenuously maintained, and therefore need not be dwelt upon; but he noticed them, not for any particular application they had to the subject, but for the sake of the principle which the re tation of those sentiments tended to suppo The foundation of the matter, which he sho urge to the House, rested on this: the gene balance of power, as applicable in the case the arguments on the whole of the subject, h by some been the object of argumentat attack, and decried, and by others treated w affected ridicule; but on the regular discussi of this, much, in his opinion, depended. had heard it allowed that the balance of pow was a question in which both sides of the Hou agreed in principle. Gentlemen on the oth' side admitted the necessity of maintaining tl balance, and said that they differed only degree; and yet the length to which th carried their arguments against interferen would, notwithstanding this admission, defe the very principle which they affect to suppor and thus the system which they pretend favour could not regularly be applied at all.

When gentlemen admitted that there w such a thing as the balance of power, what w it but saying, that if we are ourselves, or if o ally is, in a situation of danger from the ove growth of another Power, we should, from du regard to the tranquillity of Europe, use ou endeavours to check the growth of that Power and indeed they might be engaged themselve immediately in the calamity of a war by neglect ing this principle, when applied to one all only. He did not mean immediately in th sense of time; but that we ourselves migh become the objects of attack, in consequence of inattention to the principle of the balance of power. Whether this was material to Great Britain, or to any of her allies, at the time of the armament, was another question which h should not endeavour to argue there; that would come much better in another stage of the argument. The point which he had there to contend was, that the principle of the balance of power was such as they ought to regard with vigilance and attention, because they were so deeply interested in its consequences. And what he objected to on the part of gentlemen, who argued on the other side, was, that what they admitted in terms on the subject, they denied in substance; and he believed that no one nation in Europe would for a moment be secure in its tranquillity, if the spirit of these doctrines was to be the governing principle of its council. He was persuaded that, notwithstanding all they had heard to the contrary, the balance of power was a thing on which depended much of the happiness of the world, because, though in some particular instances it led nations to war, it contributed, on the whole, to promote the general tranquillity, and to render wars of ambition less frequent and less destructive. This principle being admitted, and it could not reasonably be denied, the first question then would be, whether the situation of the Turkish empire was such as to be affected in any great degree by the projects of the Imperial Court; and if so, whether this would, in fact, or probably might, have any effect on the balance of power in Europe? Whether that kingdom was indebted to this for any and what degree of intervention in its favour? Whether that intervention was rightly employed? Whether it was carried as far as, under all the circumstances, was prudent and wise, and no farther? These were the questions on which the whole of the debate would turn, and on which he hoped the justice of the House would decide.

He had heard it very much contended in the debate, which made it necessary for him to trouble the House so much upon the subject, that the balance of power, as applied to the Turkish empire, was a wild and chimerical idea. Indeed, it was contended the last year specifically, that the whole of the question of the balance of power was irrelevant. Gentlemen did not choose to go to that length in the course of the present discussion; and yet the right honourable gentleman who had spoken last went, if he was not mistaken with respect to what he had said, very nearly to that extreme. He went very near to the point of contending, that if the Turkish empire were destroyed, it would have no effect on the balance of power in Europe, and would be a matter of total indifference in that respect to the other Powers of Europe. He believed, however, that if this was his opinion, he would find himself singular in that idea.

He should not, for the purposes of his defence, enter much at length into the nature of the empire of Turkey; but it was material to the House, for the proper understanding of the subject in dispute, to reflect for a while on the system of the alliance. They would remember that they had formed an alliance with the Court of Prussia, and that it was due to the interest of that Power that England, as its ally, should not neglect to notice and to check the sudden growth of a maritime Power which might, and probably would, be an inconvenient neighbour to that Power. It was of importance to England itself, as a maritime Power, independent of all alliance with any other; and as to the necessity there was of regarding the Porte as a Power to be the object of attention to Europe, he believed that it would be found, that from the earliest periods of the Turkish empire down to the present, it had been held essential to the balance of power, that no other should be suffered to have too great a maritime ascendancy over this Power. France, ever since the reign of Francis I., had been considered as forming a very material part of the balance of power of Europe. In this country, since the reign of King William, in every memorable era, down to the present period, it had been regarded in the same light. The principal Powers of Europe had entertained the same opinion of it. Its importance to the balance of Europe was held out by the best authors who had written upon the subject: it was remarked by Montesquieu; nor had it been ever denied by any author of any authority whatever. If this were true in general, how much more so must it be of the Turkish empire, when considered as threatened by the ascendancy of so great a maritime Power as that of Russia. Indeed, Russia of itself, to any Power, if suffered to increase its naval strength, would be very formidable, and destroy that balance on which, they all allowed, so much depended. Was it not wise, then, for this country to interfere for the purpose of checking the growth of this formidable Power? The time might come when they would not have that in their power; and although, for the happiness of mankind, Providence seemed to have ordained that empires, when they became of an unwieldy size, worked their own destruction, yet it was wise in them to do all they could to prevent the excessive growth. And here he believed it would be granted him, that the progress of Russia was great and rapid, and the character of the Empress, whatever virtues she might possess, not entirely free from ambition.

Of the truth of this they had some recent specimens, and the House would, he hoped, see that if no interference had taken place on their part between those contending parties, that the advantages which the Empress would have gained over the Turkish empire would have given her the entire command of the Black Sea. He affirmed, then, that not only as an ally of Prussia, but also on the general principle of self-preservation, interference was dictated.

Having stated distinctly his opinion on the principle of the balance of power, that it applied to Turkey as well as to any other Power, and that the interest of this maritime country, which must be affected by the aggrandizement of Russia, even independent of any alliance, in consequence of our alliance with the Court of Berlin, became still more immediately connected, and that these considerations could not be separated, the question then was, Whether there was a serious and reasonable apprehension of danger towards them or their ally, so as to render interference, and to render a prevention of the farther aggrandizement, a rational policy on the part of England; and whether Ministers were to be accused of having gone so far in the risks they entered into, for what appeared to them at least to be for the future advantage of the country ?

Their conduct, in the first instance, was certainly not censurable ; for as to the commencement of the interference, it was at the request of her Imperial Majesty. She desired that they, in conjunction with their ally, the Court of Berlin, would represent to the Porte the moderation of her demands. Those demands were, that Bessarabia, Moldavia, and Wallachia should be ceded to her; and this requisition her Imperial Majesty was pleased to term a specimen of her moderation. Now, he wished the House to reflect what would have been the consequence, and whether it would not have been to the disadvantage of the Turkish empire? and he thought this point so clear, that he might leave it to the House without farther comment.

He agreed with the right honourable gentleman who spoke last, that the last actual attack was unquestionably commenced on the Empress by the Turks, and that the claims of the Turks, taken by themselves, were unjust, and not included in any treaty ; but then the point of offensive or defensive war was not the question to be considered by those who were to interfere for the sake of preserving the balance of power, nor was the actual commencement of hostility the real aggression between states ; these points were often governed by a consideration of the system adopted by either party. There was a regular system on the part of Russia for an encroachment on the Turks. This, he believed, was the origin of the dispute between the parties, and if so, it was not very material, even on the point of justice, much less on the system of the balance of power, who struck the first blow; and that, but for their interference, the final accomplishment of the views of the Empress would have followed, was a point which he believed would not be denied. If it could be denied, the intervention of this country had in this case been successful; if their representations had been such as to induce Russia to desist from part of her project, how could it be said they had gained nothing? Was the compelling the Empress to give up Moldavia, Wallachia, and Bessarabia nothing? These, she originally stipulated, should be ceded to her instead of Oczakow; and because the other object was not obtained, were the Ministers to be censured? They armed for the obtaining what appeared to them necessary ; but all their object was not obtained, and for this he should state reasons hereafter.

Gentlemen, when they argued upon the value of Oczakow, seemed to him to be wide of the real point to be considered. The truth was, that it was not of any great value as to its population or its commerce, but it was relatively so as a fortress which commanded the Dneister; and so formidable was it to ships navigating this river, that they must pass within the reach of the guns of the fortress. He did not state this place to be of great value, but he stated it to be important as a point to be gained by the Empress on her system of ambition. If he was right in the principle, namely, that it was a point worth contending for, it followed, of course, that it was their duty to resist the scheme of ambition of this Imperial Princess ; and where there was a probability of success, he would ask any man in this country whether the object intended to be gained was not worth the risk ? He would ask any man, if he was put into their situation, to determine for himself, whether he would not suffer the inconvenience, or the hazard of the miscarriage of the project, for the sake of what he had reason to hope he would gain ?

The object that was to be attained by the arming, though not worth all, was worth some risks. The contest between them was only with regard to the application of the principle ; feeling, as he did feel, the justice of this balance of power, to undergo a small inconvenience in order to avoid a greater, this principle had been admitted and recognised in many of the most brilliant periods of the history of the country. It was a principle which had been constantly acted upon from the time the country began to hold any rank amidst the surrounding nations of Europe.

It was the duty of the King's Ministers to compare the changes that had happened with that principle, to compare the means with the end, the difficulty of the object with the prospect of obtaining it, and its importance when obtained. He conceived he did his duty in advising the relinquishment of the object when he thought it could only be procured at too high a price. It had been said by some people that the sense of the nation was against the measure, and that, therefore, the King's Ministers had abandoned their plan ; others had alleged that they had abandoned their original idea on account of the opposition of that House,—that was, of 135 gentlemen. Neither the one nor the other of these was true. It was a measure of a certain degree of importance, and was worth the going to a certain specific length, but was not worth the going farther. It had been asserted, that after they had engaged in the war, they ought not to have changed their opinion, although that was a circumstance that took place almost in the history of every war. It might happen, that they would be disappointed in certain objects, and they would not then sacrifice more than the object was worth. But how were the circumstances altered ?—some were alarmed at the expenses, which created great apprehensions in the country. He did not find fault with any opinion that had been delivered from real conviction. By these, and a number of similar circumstances, the difficulties of the war were increased, and therefore they took into their most serious consideration the difficulty of obtaining their object, and compared it with the real value of it when obtained. But had it not been for that opposition, that which was by that means unattainable, in his judgment, might have been obtained at no greater expense. He should say, that the opposition, instead of claiming to themselves the merit of preventing this country from being plunged into a war, had prevented the establishment of peace in so solid and so substantial a manner as might otherwise have taken place in the country.

As to the cause of the Empress having refused to comply with their terms, he believed that the resistance of her Imperial Majesty to the requisitions of our Court was owing in part to the arguments used by opposition in this country. He did not mean to call in question the propriety of any Member of Parliament delivering his opinion, although the effect might afterwards turn out to be against the interest of his country, if he should, at the time of delivering his sentiments, be of opinion that greater inconvenience would arise to the State from his concealing than from his stating his opinion. He did not mean to blame this, even although it might be apparent that the effect of delivering such an opinion would be attended with a certain degree of inconvenience to the country, by embarrassing Government.

Such opinions were delivered on this subject, and he was of opinion that they had contributed to increase the disposition of the Empress to a resistance to our requisitions; but he did not charge opposition with any principle hostile to the State. He was bound to admit the purity of their motives, unless he could prove the contrary; and other evidence than their own professions he could not have. But whatever might be their opinions, he must say, that as far as they had any tendency, they did tend to induce the Empress to refuse to comply with the requisitions of this country. It could not be disputed but they did tend to diminish the effect of their intervention; and but for those opinions, he firmly believed that their negotiation would have been successful. This was mere matter of opinion; but he could not help saying that such was the situation of Russia, and such the situation of this country, that with a small additional expense, they should have had it in their power—for they had the means—of inducing her Imperial Majesty to comply with their terms. That this was certain he did not affirm; but he affirmed there was ground for the country to expect it. He asserted that the division in the country encouraged the temper of resistance in Russia, and if to save expense was right, they should have done so; but, unfortunately, the enemy of the country was encouraged by an opposition who took merit to themselves for rendering that useless which, but for their effort, would have been attended with success, and that, in his opinion, without much expense; and they now triumphed in what they had done. But he did not envy them their triumph; it was not a triumph over the enemies of their country, but over the Council of the King. And now, as he was on the subject of triumph and of popularity, he must observe, that if he and his right honourable friend (Mr. Dundas) were to go to the capital of the empire, whom opposition had thus served, certain he was that they would not be found in any place of glory between two orators (alluding to the bust of Mr. Fox placed by the Empress between those of Demosthenes and Cicero); and that he did not believe that if he were to go to the capital of the empire whose interest they had been endeavouring to protect, that he would receive the same sort of address from the Grand Vizier as that which which was read yesterday by an honourable member of this House. Indeed, he did not know what to think of that composition. Of its authenticity he could say nothing. The honourable gentleman told nothing of it but that which he was pleased to read of it. Whether he read the whole of it—what was its date—from whom it came—to whom—and why —he could not possibly guess. All he could say was that, having inquired of the persons most likely to be able to inform him, he had not been able to find out any such paper, or anything at all like it.

The honourable gentlemen on the opposite side had laid much stress upon a question which they had very frequently put to Ministers during the discussion: Why did they not disarm the moment that they knew the terms upon which Russia would conclude a peace with the Porto? and they had all along argued that the only reason which he and his colleagues had given for that conduct was, that they were afraid that Russia might increase her demands or make new claims if they had disarmed. That this was the only ground of their conduct he completely denied, because he conceived that no person acquainted in any degree with the actual situation of Europe at the time could be ignorant that there were other reasons that ought to claim attention, and which, to have overlooked, would have been a failure of duty and a total disregard to the interests of the country. The next point that he must notice was the management of the negotiation, which had been so much misrepresented by the other side of the House, and which, he was of opinion, could be fully justified, and would be so, in the opinion of the House, on the result. He should, therefore, not follow the right honourable gentleman into a detail of particulars during its progress, because he conceived it to be perfectly unnecessary; and if the conduct of Ministers had produced such advantages, or greater than the country expected from the negotiation, he left it to the House and the country to determine what degree of censure was due to them. On the point of censure, the right honourable gentleman and his friends seemed to have made up their minds so completely that he had declared, whether the reasons for arming were right or wrong, they were equally wrong and equally deserving of censure. This he considered as a species of argument which, however ingeniously put, could have little weight; for that Ministers, whether they were right or wrong in their object for arming, ought to be censured, was a doctrine that even the most unsuccessful result of a negotiation could not justify. There next occurred to his recollection a part of the right honourable gentleman's speech, which he was sorry was not omitted, but which he could not allow to pass without a reply. He meant his allusion to the gentleman who was sent as a Minister to Russia—a person in whom Ministers had every reason to confide, and who justly merited the compliments which the right honorable gentleman bestowed upon him; but the allusion made to another person, or rather the attack made upon him in his absence, was highly improper, and, in his opinion, very unlike the usual liberality of the right honourable gentleman; and he would say in the presence of the House, and to the public, that there was no man whatever who had been in the diplomatic line, to whom this country owed more than to the honourable person alluded to; the services he had performed the country could be no stranger to, and the exercise of his abilities would always be of importance when called into action. With regard to the importance of Oczakow, the right honourable gentleman seemed to have barred that question being brought to issue, because, as he had remarked just before, he had said, that whether it was, or was not, of importance to the balance of power in Europe, it could, in no shape whatever, be a ground for interference between Russia and the Ottoman Porte; and by this manner of arguing he did maintain, that the whole jet of all the arguments of the right honourable gentleman and his friends, both on this and the former nights of discussion, came to this, that he would, upon the question of the Russian armament, admit any premises, provided the conclusions tended to censure Ministers, although the very first of the resolutions brought forward stated directly that Oczakow was not of sufficient importance to require interference. To establish this, great pains had been taken to impress upon the House a belief that they had been guilty of the grossest iniquity, and most unwarrantable treachery towards their allies. That they had stimulated Turkey to the war in which she had been engaged, a fact which he disclaimed, and which could not be made good. That they had deserted Sweden at a critical juncture, which likewise he would not allow; and that by their interference and mediation nothing had been gained or secured to Prussia. That their intervention in the affairs of Brabant was improper; and that wherever they had employed their influence, or wished to favour an ally, they had met with disgrace, and their allies with disappointment. Upon this subject he was perfectly at ease, nor did he conceive that there were any just grounds to reproach Ministers upon. As to the duplicity in their negotiations, which had been ascribed to the system of continental alliance, he did not believe the House had gone with the right honourable gentleman on that point. He must therefore say, that with regard to the moderation of the first terms offered by the Empress, and the propriety of acceding to those they finally got, that matter being so fully in possession of the House, he left it to their judgment. As to their motives, he could likewise rely, that they should be judged by their actions, whatever were their reasons, both on that and every other occasion where the interest of the country was concerned; and he owned that his chief hopes were rested upon the advantages that had been gained by the system both of foreign and domestic policy, which his Majesty's Ministers had pursued, and the actual prosperity of the country, to whatever causes gentlemen might ascribe it. He wished for no discretionary power, that was not necessary for the functions of the situation in which he might be placed, and he knew, as well as anybody, that the conduct of the present time, good or bad, must affect posterity. Having stated the leading grounds for his opposition to the resolutions moved, he must contend, that if any obloquy attended the measures of Government in the Russian negotiation, it proceeded from misrepresentation. From what motives that misrepresentation proceeded, he did not mean to give any opinion; and should content himself with relying upon a liberal and just decision of the House, after they had fairly and fully considered every circumstance that could enable them to decide upon his conduct, and those who acted with him."

TO THIS, FOX REPLIED AS FOLLOWS:—" I do assure the House that I mean to confine myself strictly to explanation, having heard nothing from the right honourable gentleman to make me retract the censure which, in my opinion, his conduct demands. But I wish the House to recollect, that when, at the beginning of the last session, I asked for what purpose a part of the armament provided against Spain was kept up, I was told, that it arose from the situation of Europe, and was necessary for the protection of our homeward-bound West-India merchantmen: but neither did I then understand, nor by anything that fell from me, give gentlemen reason to think I understood, that force to be destined to act against Russia. The right honourable gentleman's insinuation, therefore, that I knew of and approved the keeping up an armament to awe the Empress, is totally void of foundation.

With regard to what the right honourable gentleman has chosen to introduce into his speech, respecting compliments and honours conferred on me by the Empress of Russia, I am ready now, and at all times, to declare, that if any foreign sovereign, in friendship with my country, shall pay me the compliment to think well of me, and testify it by those marks of distinction to which he has alluded, I shall feel myself highly gratified by such distinction. With regard to Russia, it has ever been my opinion, that hers was the Power in Europe, I will scarcely except even Holland, with whom the cultivation of reciprocal ties of friendship, both commercial and political, was most natural, and of the greatest consequence to this country. For the uniformity of this opinion, Sir, I appeal to my whole conduct, whether in office or out of it. At the close of the American war, I thought Russia the Power whose naval force, joined with ours, might effectually counterbalance the united navies of the House of Bourbon. The gentlemen on the other side have opportunities of knowing to what degree I endeavoured to give effect to this opinion. When I was again in office, I refused to concur in remonstrances to the Court of Petersburg against the seizure of the Crimea. I appeal farther to the sentiments delivered by me in this House, when I added my voice to those of the right honourable gentleman's supporters, in applauding the success of the measures taken to assist the Stadtholder in 1787; when, in avowing my approbation of what was done, I gave, as my principal reason for that approbation, the option it placed in our power at that moment of forming alliances on the Continent, which might render the advantages we got by our interference permanent; and when I distinctly named Russia as one of those whom it was of the highest importance to cultivate. These have ever been my sentiments, and I have seen nothing in what has recently happened to make me change them. I thought it necessary to say thus much in answer to the hints and insinuations thrown out from the right honourable gentleman opposite to me: as to any farther reply, I should deem it wholly superfluous, even were I permitted to make any, as the right honourable gentleman has chosen to avoid noticing almost every material argument I addressed to the House."

FRANCIS LORD JEFFREY.

Born 1773. Died 1850.

DEPENDENCE OF KINGS.

KINGS have no power of their own; and, even in the purest despotisms, they are the mere organs or directors of that power which they who truly possess the physical and intellectual force of the nation may choose to put at their disposal; and are at all times, and under every form of monarchy, entirely under the control of that only virtual and effective power. There is at bottom, therefore, no such thing as an unlimited monarchy; or indeed as a monarchy that is potentially either more or less limited than every other. All kings *must* act by the consent of that order or portion of the nation which can really command all the rest, and may generally do whatever these substantial masters do not disapprove of. But as it is their power which is truly exerted in the name of the sovereign, so, it is not so much a necessary consequence as an identical proposition to say, that where they are clearly opposed to the exercise of that power, the king has no means whatever of asserting the slightest authority. This is the universal law, indeed, of all governments; and though the different constitution of society, in the various stages of its progress, may give a different character to the controlling power, the principles which regulate its operation are substantially the same in all. There is no room, therefore, for the question, whether there should be any control on the power of a king, or what that control should be; because, as the power really is not the king's, but belongs inalienably to the stronger part of the nation itself, whether it derive that strength from discipline, talents, numbers, or situation, it is impossible that it should be exercised at his instigation, without the concurrence, or acquiescence at least, of those in whom it is substantially vested.

STATE CONVULSIONS—WHY TO BE DREADED.

In the shipwreck of a State, trifles float and are preserved; while everything solid and valuable sinks to the bottom, and is lost for ever!—*Junius.*

JOSEPH MAZZINI.

Born 1809. Living.

[Some specimen of the eloquence of Joseph Mazzini, whose genius and life have perhaps been more misrepresented than those of any other man of his times, may well find a place amongst the few translations which appear in this volume. The subjoined address was delivered by Signor Mazzini, at Milan, on the 25th of July, 1848, at the request of the "National Association," on the occasion of a solemn commemoration of the anniversary of the death of the brothers Bandiera. Attilio and Emilio Bandiera, of high patrician Venetian descent, were the sons of Baron Bandiera, Rear-admiral in the Austrian service. In the month of February, 1844, they were denounced to their father, and to the Austrian government, as conspirators for Italian liberty, by one T. V. Micciarelli. They fled to Corfu. From Corfu they planned a descent upon Calabria, deceived into false hopes of exciting an insurrection there, by spies of the Neapolitan Government. A traitor was placed among them. He quitted them on their landing, on the 16th of June, and betrayed them. They were surrounded and taken prisoners, after a severe struggle, at San Giovanni, in Fiore, on the 19th. On the 25th they were shot at Cosenza, with seven of their companions. For a more complete account of the brothers Bandiera, see an article by Signor Mazzini in the *People's Journal* of February 28th, 1846, and his pamphlet, entitled "Ricordi dei Fratelli Bandiera." Published by Rolandi, Berners Street, London.]

TO THE MEMORY OF THE MARTYRS OF COSENZA.

WHEN I was commissioned by you, young men, to proffer, in this temple, a few words consecrated to the memory of the brothers Bandiera and their fellow-martyrs at Cosenza, I thought that some one of those who heard me might perhaps exclaim with noble indignation, "Why thus lament over the dead? The martyrs of liberty are only worthily honoured by winning the battle they have begun; Cosenza, the land where they fell, is enslaved; Venice, the city of their birth, is begirt with strangers. Let us emancipate them, and until that moment let no words pass our lips save those of war."

But another thought arose and suggested to me, "Why have we not conquered? Why is it that whilst they fight for independence in the North of Italy, liberty is perishing in the South? Why is it that a war which should have sprung to the Alps with the bound of a lion, has dragged itself along for four months with the slow uncertain motion of the scorpion surrounded by the circle of fire? How has the rapid and powerful intuition of a people newly arisen to life been converted into the weary helpless effort of the sick man turning from side to side?" Ah! had we all arisen in the sanctity of the idea for which our martyrs died; had the holy standard of their faith preceded our youth to battle; had we reached that unity of life which was in them so powerful, and made of our every thought an action, and of our every action a thought; had we devoutly gathered up their last words in our hearts, and learned from them that Liberty and Independence are one; that God and the People, Country and Humanity, are the two inseparable terms of the device of every people striving to become a nation; that Italy can only exist, one and holy, in the equality and love of all her children, great in the worship of eternal Truth, and consecrated to a lofty mission, a moral priesthood among the peoples of Europe—we should not now have war, but victory; Cosenza would not be compelled to venerate the memory of her martyrs in secret, nor Venice be restrained from honouring them with a monument; and we here gathered together might gladly invoke those sacred names, without uncertainty as to our future destiny, or a cloud of sadness on our brows, and might say to those precursor souls, "Rejoice, for your spirit is incarnate in your brethren, and they are worthy of you."

The idea which they worshipped, young men, does not as yet shine forth in its full purity and integrity upon your banner. The sublime programme which they dying bequeathed to the rising Italian generation, is yours; but mutilated, broken up into fragments by the false doctrines which, elsewhere overthrown, have taken refuge amongst us. I look around, and I see the struggles of desperate populations, an alternation of generous rage and of unworthy repose; of shouts for freedom and of formulæ of servitude, throughout all parts of our peninsula; but the heart of the country, where is it? What unity is there in this unequal and manifold movement—where is the word which should dominate the hundred diverse and opposing counsels which mislead or seduce the multitude? I hear words usurping the national omnipotence—"the Italy of the North"—"the League of the States"—"federative compacts between princes;" but ITALY, where is it? Where is the common country—the country which the Bandiera hailed as thrice initiator of a new era of European civilization? Intoxicated with our first victories, improvident for the future, we forgot the idea revealed by God to those who suffer; and God has punished our forgetfulness by deferring our triumph. The Italian movement, my brethren, is, by decree of Providence, that of Europe. We arise to give a pledge of moral progress to the European world. But neither political fictions, nor dynastic aggrandizements, nor theories of expediency, can transform or renovate the life of the peoples. Humanity lives and moves through faith; great principles are the guiding stars of Europe towards the future. Let us turn to the graves of our martyrs, and ask from the inspiration of those who died for us all, the secret of victory in the adoration of a principle of a faith. The Angel of Martyrdom and the Angel of Victory are brothers; but the one looks up to heaven, the other looks down to earth, and it is only when, from epoch to epoch, their eyes meet between earth and heaven, that creation is embellished with a new life, and a people arises, evangelist or prophet, from the cradle or the tomb.

I will now, young men, sum up to you, in a few words, the faith of our martyrs: their external life is known to you all, it is now matter of history; I need not recall it to you.

The faith of the brothers Bandiera, which was and is our own, was based upon a few simple incontrovertible truths, which few indeed venture to declare false, but which are, nevertheless, forgotten or betrayed by most.

God and the people. God at the summit of the social edifice; the people, the universality of our brethren, at the base. God, the Father and educator; the people, the progressive interpreter of his law.

No true society can exist without a common belief and a common aim. Religion declares the belief and the aim. Politics regulate society in the practical realization of that belief, and prepare the means of attaining that aim. Religion represents the principle, politics the application.

There is but one sun in heaven for all the earth. There is but one law for those who people the earth. It is alike the law of the human being, and the law of collective humanity. We are placed here below, not for the capricious exercise of our own individual faculties—faculties and liberty are *the means*, and not *the end*—not to work out our own happiness upon earth; happiness can only be reached elsewhere, and there God works for us; but to consecrate our existence to the discovery of a portion of the divine law; to practise it as far as our individual faculties and circumstances allow, and to diffuse the knowledge and the love of it among our brethren. We are here below to endeavour fraternally to build up the unity of the human family, so that the day may come when it may represent "a single sheepfold, with a single shepherd;" the Spirit of God, the law. To aid our search after truth, God has given to us tradition, the voice of anterior humanity, and the voice of our own conscience. Wheresoever these accord is truth, wheresoever they are opposed is error. To attain a harmony and consistency between the conscience of the individual and the conscience of humanity, no sacrifice is too great. Family, city, country, and humanity are but different spheres in which to exercise our activity and our power of sacrifice towards this great aim. God watches from above the inevitable progress of humanity, and from time to time He raises up the great in genius, in love, in thought, or in action, as priests of His truth, and guides to the multitude on their way.

These principles, indicated in their letters, in their proclamations, and in their conversation, with a profound consciousness of the mission entrusted by God to the individual and to humanity, were to Attilio and Emilio Bandiera and their fellow-martyrs the guide and comfort of a weary life; and, when men and circumstances had alike betrayed them, sustained them in death, in religious serenity and calm, and in the certainty of their immortal hopes in the future of Italy. The immense energy of their souls arose from the intense love which informed their faith. And could they now rise from the grave and speak to you, they would, believe me, address you, though with a power very different from that which is given to me, in counsel not unlike this which I now offer to you.

Love! Love is the flight of the soul towards God, towards the great, the sublime, and the beautiful, which are the shadow of God upon earth. Love your family, the partner of your life, those around you ready to share your joys and sorrows, the dead who were dear to you, and to whom you were dear. But let your love be the love taught you by Dante and by us, the love of souls that aspire together; and do not grovel on the earth in search of a felicity which it is not the destiny of the creature here to reach; do not yield to a delusion which inevitably would degrade you into egotism. To love, is to promise, and to receive a promise for the future. God has given us love, that the weary soul may give and receive support upon the way of life. It is a flower which springs up on the path of duty, but which cannot change its course. Purify, strengthen, and improve yourselves by loving. Ever act—even at the price of increasing her earthly trials—so that the sister soul united to your own may never need, here or elsewhere, to blush through you or for you. The time will come when from the height of a new life, embracing the whole past, and comprehending its secret, you will smile together at the sorrows you have endured, the trials you have overcome.

Love your country. Your country is the land where your parents sleep, where is spoken that language in which the chosen of your heart, blushing, whispered the first word of love; it is the house that God has given you, that by striving to perfect yourselves therein, you may prepare to ascend to him. It is your name, your glory, your sign among the peoples. Give to it your thought, your counsel, your blood. Raise it up, great and beautiful, as foretold by our great men. And see that you leave it uncontaminated by any trace of falsehood, or of servitude, unprofaned by dismemberment. Let it be one, as the thought of God. You are twenty-four millions of men, endowed with active, splendid faculties, with a tradition of glory, the envy of the nations of Europe; an immense future is before you, your eyes are raised to the loveliest heaven, and around you smiles the loveliest land in Europe; you are encircled by the Alps and the sea, boundaries marked out by the finger of God for a people of giants. And you must be such, or nothing. Let not a man of that twenty-four millions remain excluded from the fraternal bond which shall join you together; let not a look be raised to that heaven, which is not that of a free man. Let Rome be the ark of your redemption, the temple of your nation. Has she not twice been the temple of the destinies of Europe? In Rome two extinct worlds, the Pagan and the Papal, meet each other like the double jewels of a diadem; and you must draw from thence a third world, greater than the other two. From Rome, the Holy City, the City of Love (Amor), the purest and wisest among you, elected by the vote, and strengthened by the inspiration of a whole people, shall give forth the pact that shall unite us in one, and represent us in the future alliance of the peoples. Until then you have no country, or you have it contaminated.

Love humanity. You can only ascertain your own mission from the aim placed by God before humanity at large. God has given you your country as cradle, humanity as mother, and you can only love your brethren of the cradle in loving your common mother. Beyond the Alps, beyond the sea are other peoples, now fighting or preparing to fight, the holy fight of independence, of nationality, of liberty: other peoples striving by different routes to reach the same goal—improvement, association, and the foundation of an authority which shall put an end to moral anarchy, and link again earth to heaven, and which mankind may love and obey without remorse or shame. Unite with them, they will unite with you. Do not invoke their aid where your single arm can suffice to conquer; but say to them, that the hour will shortly sound for a terrible struggle between right and blind force, and that in that hour you will ever be found with those who have raised the same banner as yourselves.

And love, young men, love and reverence above everything the Ideal. The Ideal is the word of God, superior to every country, superior to humanity; it is the country of the spirit, the city of the soul, in which all are brethren who believe in the inviolability of thought, and in the dignity of our immortal soul; and the baptism of this fraternity is martyrdom. From that high sphere spring the *principles* which alone can redeem the peoples. Arise for them! and not from impatience of suffering, or dread of evil. Anger, pride, ambition, and the desire of material prosperity are arms common to the peoples and their oppressors; and, even should you conquer with them to-day, you will fall again to-morrow; but principles belong to the peoples alone, and their oppressors can find no arms to oppose to them. Adore enthusiasm. Worship the dreams of the virgin soul, and the visions of early youth, for they are the perfume of Paradise, which the soul preserves in issuing from the hands of its Creator. Respect above all things your conscience; have upon your lips the truth that God has placed in your hearts, and, while working together in harmony in all that tends to the emancipation of our soil, even with those who differ from you, yet ever bear erect your own banner, and boldly promulgate your faith.

Such words, young men, would the martyrs of Cosenza have spoken had they been living amongst you. And here, where perhaps, invoked by our love, their holy spirits hover near us, I call upon you to gather them up in your hearts, and to make of them a treasure, amid the storms that yet threaten you, but which, with the name of our martyrs on your lips, and their faith in your hearts, you will overcome.

God be with you, and bless Italy.

TREMENDOUSNESS OF WAR.

As if war was a matter of experiment! As if you could take it up or lay it down as an idle frolic! As if the dire goddess that presides over it, with her murderous spear in hand, and her gorgon at her breast, was a coquette to be flirted with! We ought with reverence to approach that tremendous divinity that loves courage, but commands counsel. War never leaves where it found a nation. It is never to be entered into without mature deliberation; not a deliberation lengthened out into a perplexing indecision, but a deliberation leading to a sure and fixed judgment. When so taken up, it is not to be abandoned without reason as valid, as fully, and as extensively considered. Peace may be made as unadvisedly as war. Nothing is so rash as fear; and the counsels of pusillanimity very rarely put off, whilst they are always sure to aggravate, the evils from which they would fly.—*Burke.*

NATIONAL HONOUR—SACRED AS FEMALE VIRTUE.

To depart, in the minutest article, from the nicety and strictness of punctilio, is as dangerous to national honour as to female virtue. The woman who admits of one familiarity, seldom knows where to stop, or what to refuse; and when the counsels of a great country give way in a single instance—when they once are inclined to submission—every step accelerates the rapidity of the descent.—*Junius.*

RICHARD LALOR SHEIL.
Born 1791. Died 1851.

[The speech from which the following extracts are chosen was delivered on the 27th of January, 1844, in the Court of Queen's Bench, Dublin, on behalf of Mr. John O'Connell, who, with his father, the notorious Daniel O'Connell, and several other conjutors, was indicted for political conspiracy and sedition. The trial commenced on the 15th of January, after a long preliminary delay, and no less than 24 days were consumed in the examination of witnesses and the speeches of counsel, Fitzgibbon, Whiteside, and others of the leading advocates at the Irish Bar being heard on behalf of their respective clients. Daniel O'Connell conducted his own defence; but despite all the eloquence expended on the case, the jury, on the 12th of February, returned a verdict of Guilty against all the defendants. Some delay, however, having arisen out of proceedings on motion for a new trial and other causes, judgment was not pronounced till the 30th of May, when O'Connell was sentenced to a year's imprisonment and a fine of £2,000; the others (with the exception of the Rev. Thomas Tierney, on whom judgment was remitted) to nine months' imprisonment and a fine of £50 each, and all were bound over to keep the peace for seven years. Upon these sentences the defendants were at once committed to prison; but on the 9th of August, Sheil, Lord John Russell, and others, called upon Government to release them from imprisonment, and in consequence of their appeal, the House of Lords, on the 4th of February, reversed the judgment on Mr. O'Connell and his co-defendants. The prisoners were at once released from confinement; but one not unimportant result of the trial was, that the agitation for repeal of the Union, and other extreme measures advocated by the party of O'Connell, was much abated. The speech of Sheil is of great length, and therefore the exordium, peroration, and other of the more important passages in it are all that can be given here. It is, however, hoped that the line of argument adopted by the advocate will still be sufficiently clear to render the speech, in its present form, a good specimen of his powers.]

DEFENCE OF MR. JOHN O'CONNELL.

I AM counsel for Mr. John O'Connell. The importance of this case is not susceptible of exaggeration, and I do not speak in the language of hyperbole when I say that the attention of the empire is directed to the spot in which we are assembled. How great is the trust reposed in you—how great is the task which I have undertaken to perform? Conscious of its magnitude, I have risen to address you, not unmoved, but undismayed; no—not unmoved—for at this moment how many incidents of my own political life come back upon me, when I look upon my great political benefactor, my deliverer, and my friend; but of the emotion by which I acknowledge myself to be profoundly stirred, although I will not permit ·lf-to be subdued by it, solicitude forms no I have great reliance upon you—upon ascendancy of principle over prejudice in minds; and I am not entirely without ..ice upon myself. I do not speak in the language of vain-glorious self-complacency when I say this. I know that I am surrounded by men infinitely superior to me in every forensic, and in almost every intellectual qualification. My confidence is derived, not from any overweening estimate of my own faculties, but from a thorough conviction of the innocence of my client. I know, and I appear in some sort not only as an advocate but a witness before you. I know him to be innocent of the misdeeds laid to his charge. The same blood flows through their veins—the same feelings circulate through their hearts: the son and the father are in all political regards the same, and with the father I have toiled in no dishonourable companionship for more than half my life in that great work, which it is his chief praise that it was conceived in the spirit of peace—that in the spirit of peace it was carried out—and that in the spirit of peace it was brought by him to its glorious consummation. I am acquainted with every feature of his character, with his thoughts, hopes, fears, aspirations. I have—if I may venture to say—a full cognizance of every pulsation of his heart. I know—I am sure as that I am a living man—that from the sanguinary misdeeds imputed to him he shrinks with abhorrence. It is this persuasion—profound, impassioned—and I trust that it will prove contagious—which will sustain me in the midst of the exhaustion incidental to this lengthened trial; will enable me to overcome the illness under which I am at this moment labouring; will raise me to the height of this great argument, and lift me to a level with the lofty topics which I shall have occasion to treat in resisting a prosecution, to which in the annals of criminal jurisprudence in this country no parallel can be found. Gentlemen, the Attorney-General, in a statement of eleven or twelve hours' duration, read a long series of extracts from speeches and publications, extending over a period of nearly nine months. At the termination of every passage which was cited by him, he gave utterance to expressions of strong resentment against the men by whom sentiments so noxious were circulated, in language most envenomed. If, gentlemen of the jury, his anger was not simulated; if his indignation was not merely official; if he spoke as he felt, how does it come to pass that no single step was ever taken by him for the purpose of arresting the progress of an evil represented by him to be so calamitous? He told you that the country was traversed by incendiaries who set fire to the passions of the people; the whole fabric of society, according to the Attorney-General, for the last nine months has been in a blaze; wherefore then did he stand with folded arms to gaze at the conflagration? Where were the Castle fire-engines—where was the indictment—and of *ex officio* information what had become? Is there not too much reason to think that a project was formed, or rather that a plot was concocted, to decoy the traversers, and that a connivance, amounting almost to sanction, was deliberately adopted as a part of the policy of the government, in order to betray the traversers into indiscretions of which advantage was, in due time, to be taken? I have heard it said that it was criminal to tell the people to "bide their time;"* but is the government to "bide its time," in order to turn popular excitement to account? The public prosecutor who gives an indirect encouragement to agitation, in order that he may afterwards more effectually fall upon it, bears some moral affinity to the informer, who provokes the crime from whose denunciation his ignominious livelihood is derived. Has the Attorney-General adopted a course worthy of his great office—worthy of the ostensible head of the Irish bar, and the representative of its intellect in the House of Commons? Is it befitting that the successor of Saurin, and of Plunket, who should "keep watch and ward" from his high station over the public safety, should descend to the performance of functions worthy only of a commissary of the French police; and in place of being the sentinel, should become the "Artful Dodger" of the state? But what, you may ask, could be the motive of the right honourable gentleman for pursuing the course he has adopted, and for which no explanation has been attempted by him? He could not have obtained any advantage signally serviceable to his party by prosecuting Mr. Duffy or Dr. Gray for strong articles in their newspapers; or by prosecuting Mr. Steele or Mr. Tierney for attending unlawful assemblies. He did not fish with lines—if I may avail myself of an illustration derived from the habits of my constituents at Dungarvan—but cast a wide and nicely constructed trammel-net, in order that by a kind of miraculous catch he might take the great agitator-leviathan himself, a member of parliament—Mr. Steele, three editors of newspapers, and a pair of priests, in one stupendous haul together. But there was another object still more important to be gained. Had the Attorney-General prosecuted individuals for the use of violent language, or for attending unlawful meetings, each individual would have been held responsible for his own acts; but in a prosecution for conspiracy, which is open to every one of the objections applicable to constructive treason, the acts and the speeches of one man are given in evidence against another, although the latter may have been at the distance of a hundred miles when the circumstances used against him as evidence, and of which he had no sort of cognizance, took place. By prosecuting Mr. O'Connell for a conspiracy, the Attorney-General treats him exactly as if he were the editor of the *Nation*, the editor of the *Freeman*, and the editor of the *Pilot*. Indeed, if five or six other editors of newspapers in the country had been joined as

traversers, for every line in their newspapers Mr. O'Connell would be held responsible. There is one English gentleman, I believe, upon that jury. If a prosecution for a conspiracy were instituted against the Anti-Corn Law League in England, would he not think it very hard indeed that Mr. Cobden and Mr. Bright should be held answerable for every article in the *Chronicle*, in the *Globe*, and in the *Sun*? How large a portion of the case of the Crown depends upon this implication of Mr. O'Connell with three Dublin newspapers? He is accused of conspiring with men who certainly never conspired with each other. For those who know anything of newspapers are aware that they are mercantile speculations—the property in them is held by shares—and that the very circumstance of their being engaged in the same politics alienates the proprietors from each other. They pay their addresses to the same mistress, and cordially detest each other. I remember to have heard Mr. Barnes, the celebrated editor of the *Times* newspaper, once ask Mr. Rogers what manner of man was a Mr. Tomkins? to which Mr. Rogers replied, "he was a dull dog, who read the *Morning Herald*." Let us turn for a moment from the repeal to the anti-repeal party. You would smile, I think, at the suggestion that Mr. Murray Mansfield * and Mr. Remmy Sheehan † should enter into a conspiracy together. Those gentlemen would be themselves astonished at the imputation. Suppose them to be both members of the Conservative Association; would that circumstance be sufficient to sustain, in the judgment of men of plain sense, the charge of conspiracy upon them? Gentlemen, the relation in which Mr. Duffy, Mr. Barrett, and Dr. Gray stood to the Repeal Association, is exactly the same as that in which Mr. Staunton, the proprietor of the *Weekly Register*, stood towards the Catholic Association. He was paid for his advertisements, and his newspaper contained emancipation news, and was sent to those who desired to receive it. Mr. Stannton is now a member of the Repeal Association; he will tell you that his connection with that body is precisely of the same character as that which existed with the celebrated body to which I have referred; he will prove to you, that over his paper Mr. O'Connell exercises no sort of control, and that all that is done by him in reference to his paper, is the result of his own free and unbiassed will. The speeches made at the Association and public meetings were reported by him in the same manner as in the other public journals; he is not a conspirator; the Government have not treated him as such. Why? Because there were no poems in his

---

* One of the songs of the *Nation* is entitled "Bide your Time."

* The proprietor of the *Evening Packet*.
† The proprietor of the *Evening Mail*. Both high Conservatives.

paper like "The Memory of the Dead,"* which, although in direct opposition to the feelings of Mr. O'Connell, and which he had frequently expressed, is now used in evidence against him. Gentlemen, I have said enough to you to show how formidable is this doctrine of conspiracy—of legal conspiracy—which is so far removed from all notions of actual conspiracy, to show you further how cautious you ought to be in finding eight of your fellow-citizens guilty of that charge. The defendants are indicted for conspiracy, and for nothing else. No counts are inserted for attending unlawful assemblies. The Attorney-General wants a conviction for a conspiracy, and nothing else. He has deviated in these particulars from English usage. In indictments for a conspiracy, counts for attending unlawful assemblies are in England uniformly introduced. English juries have almost uniformly manifested an aversion to find men guilty of a conspiracy. Take Henry Hunt's case as an example. When that case was tried England was in a perilous condition. It had been proved before a secret committee of the House of Commons, of which the present Earl of Derby, the father of Lord Stanley, was the chairman, that large bodies of men were disciplined at night in the neighbourhood of Manchester, and made familiar with the use of arms. An extensive organization existed. Vast public assemblies were held, accompanied with every revolutionary incident in furtherance of a revolutionary object—yet, an English jury would not find Henry Hunt guilty of a conspiracy, but found him guilty, on the fourth count of the indictment, for attending an unlawful assembly. Some of the Chartists were not found guilty of a conspiracy, but were found guilty upon counts from which the word "conspiracy" is left out. Gentlemen, the promises of Mr. Pitt, when the Union was carried, have not been fulfilled — the prospects presented by him in his magnificent declamation have not been realized; but, if in so many other regards we have sustained a most grievous disappointment—if English capital has not adventured here—if Englishmen have preferred sinking their fortunes in the rocks of Mexico, rather than embark them in speculations connected with this fine but unfortunate country—yet, from the Union let one advantage be at all events derived: Let English feelings—let English principles—let English love of justice—let English horror of oppression—let English detestation of foul play—let English loathing of constructive crime, find its way amongst us. But, thank God, it is not to England that I am driven exclusively to refer for a salutary example of the aversion of twelve honest men to prosecutions for conspiracy. You remember the prosecution of Forbes, and of Handwich, and other Orangemen of an inferior class, under Lord Wellesley's administration; they were guilty of a riot in the theatre, but they were charged with having entered into a great political confederacy to upset Lord Wellesley's government, and to associate him with the "exports of Ireland." The Protestant feeling of Ireland rose—addresses were poured in from almost every district in the country, remonstrating against a proceeding which was represented as hostile to the liberties of the country, and as a great stretch of the prerogative of the crown. The jury did their duty, and refused to convict the traversers. The Irish Catholics at that time, heated by feelings of partisanship, were rash enough to wish for a conviction. Fatal mistake! A precedent would have been created, which would soon have been converted into practice against themselves. Gentlemen, we are living in times of strange political vicissitude. God forbid that I should ever live to see the time—(for I hate to see ascendancy of every kind)—God forbid that I should ever live to see the time, or that our children should ever live to see the time, when there shall be arrayed four Catholic judges at a trial at bar upon that bench, when the entire of the Government bar who shall be engaged in a public prosecution shall be Roman Catholic; and when a Catholic Crown solicitor shall strike eleven Protestants from the special jury list, and leave twelve Roman Catholics in that box. I reassert it, and exclaim again, in all the sincerity of my heart, that I pray that such a spectacle never shall be exhibited in this, the first criminal court in the land. I know full well the irrepressible tendency of the power to abuse. We have witnessed strange things, and strange things we may yet behold. It is the duty, the solemn duty—it is the interest, the paramount interest—of every one of us, before and above everything else, to secure the great foundations of liberty—in which we all have an equal concern —from invasion, and to guard against the creation of a precedent which may enable some future Attorney-General to convert the Queen's Bench into a star-chamber, and commit a further inroad upon the principles of the constitution. Gentlemen, it is my intention to show you that my client is not guilty of any of the conspiracies charged in the indictment; and in doing so I shall have occasion to advert to the several proceedings that have been adopted by the Government, and to the evidence that has been laid before you. But before I proceed to that head of the division which I have traced out for myself, I shall show you what the object of my client really was; I shall show you that that object was a legal one, and that it was by legal means that he endeavoured to attain it. The Attorney-General, in a speech

---

* This song was set out at full in the indictment.

of considerable length—but not longer than the greatness of the occasion amply justified—adverted to a great number of diversified topics, quoted the speeches of Sir Robert Peel and of Lord John Russell—adverted to the report of the secret committee of the House of Lords in 1797, and referred to the great era of Irish Parliamentary independence, 1782. That he should have been so multifarious and discursive, I do not complain. In a case of this incalculable importance we should look for light wherever it can be found. I shall go somewhat farther than the year 1782; but do not imagine that I mean to enter into any lengthened narrative or elaborate expatiation. Long tracts of time may be swiftly traversed. I do not think that any writer has given a more accurate or more interesting account of the first struggle of Ireland for the assertion of her rights than Sir Walter Scott. He was a Tory. He was bred and born, perhaps, in some disrelish for Ireland; but when he came amongst us, his opinions underwent a material alteration. The man who could speak of Scotland in those noble lines which were cited in the course of this trial, with so much passionate attachment, made a just allowance for those who felt for the land of their birth the same just emotion. In his life of Swift, he says, Molyneux, the friend of Locke and of liberty, published in 1698, "The case of Ireland being bound by Act of Parliament in England, stated," in which he showed with great force, "that the right of legislation, of which England made so oppressive a use, was neither justifiable by the plea of conquest, purchase, or precedent, and was only submitted to from incapacity of effectual resistance. The temper of the English House of Commons did not brook these remonstrances. It was unanimously voted that these bold and pernicious assertions were calculated to shake the subordination and dependence of Ireland, as united and annexed for ever to the Crown of England; and the vote of the House was followed by an address to the Queen, complaining that although the woollen trade was the staple manufacture of England, over which her legislation was accustomed to watch with the utmost care, yet Ireland, which was dependant upon, and protected by, England, not contented with the linen manufacture, the liberty whereof was indulged to her, presumed also to apply her credit and capital to the weaving of her own wool and woollen cloths, to the great detriment of England. Not a voice was raised in the British House of Commons to contradict maxims equally impolitic and tyrannical. In acting upon these commercial restrictions, wrong was heaped upon wrong, and insult was added to injury—with this advantage on the side of the aggressors, that they could intimidate the people of Ireland into silence by raising, to drown every complaint, the cry of 'rebel,' and 'Jacobite.'" When Swift came to Ireland in 1714, he at first devoted himself to literary occupations; but at length his indignation was aroused by the monstrous wrongs which were inflicted upon his country. He was so excited by the injustice which he abhorred, that he could not forbear exclaiming to his friend Delany, "Do not the villanies of men eat into your flesh?" In 1720, he published a proposal for the use of Irish manufacture, and was charged with having endeavoured to create hostility between different classes of his Majesty's subjects—one of the charges preferred in this very indictment. At that time the judges were dependant upon the Crown. They did not possess that "fixity of tenure" which is a security for their public virtue. They are now no longer, thank God, "tenants at will." They may be mistaken—they may be blinded by strong emotions—but corrupt they cannot be. The circumstance detailed in the following passage in the life of Swift could not by possibility occur in modern times. "The storm which Swift had driven was not long in bursting. It was intimated to Lord Chief Justice Whitshed by a person in great office" (this, if I remember right, was the expression used by Mr. Ross, in reference to a great unknown, who sent him here), "that Swift's pamphlet was published for the purpose of setting the two kingdoms at variance; and it was recommended that the printer should be prosecuted with the uttermost rigour. Whitshed was not a person to neglect such a hint, and the arguments of Government were so successful that the grand juries of the county and city presented the Dean's pamphlet as a seditious, factious, and virulent libel. Waters, the printer, was seized and forced to give great bail; but, upon his trial, the jury, though some pains had been bestowed in selecting them, brought him in not guilty; and it was not until they were worn out by the Lord Chief Justice, who detained them eleven hours, and sent them nine times to reconsider their verdict, that they, at length, reluctantly left the matter in his hands, by a special verdict; but the measures of Whitshed were too violent to be of service to the Government; men's minds revolted against his iniquitous conduct." Sir Walter Scott then proceeds to give an account of the famous Drapier's Letters. After speaking of the first three, Sir Walter Scott says, "It was now obvious, from the temper of Ireland, that the true point of difference between the two countries might safely be brought before the public. In the Drapier's fourth letter, accordingly, Swift boldly treated of the royal prerogative, of the almost exclusive employment of natives of England in places of trust and emolument in Ireland; of the dependence of that kingdom upon England, and the power assumed, contrary to truth, reason, and justice, of binding her by the laws of a parliament in which she had no representation." And, gentlemen, is it a question too bold of me to ask, whether if Ireland have no effective representation—if the wishes and feelings of the representatives of Ireland upon Irish questions are held to be of no account—if the Irish representation is utterly merged in the English, and the Minister does not, by a judicious policy, endeavour to counteract it—as he might, in the opinion of many men, effectually do—is not the practical result exactly the same as if Ireland had not a single representative in Parliament? Gentlemen, Swift addressed the people of Ireland upon this great topic, in language as strong as any that Daniel O'Connell has employed. "The remedy," he says, "is wholly in your hands. . . . By the laws of God, of nations, and of your country, you are, and ought to be, as free a people as your brethren in England." "This tract," says Sir Walter Scott, "pressed at once upon the real merits of the question at issue, and the alarm was instantly taken by the English Government, the necessity of supporting whose domination devolved upon Carteret, who was just landed; and accordingly a proclamation was issued offering £300 reward for the discovery of the author of the Drapier's fourth letter, described as a wicked and malicious pamphlet, containing several seditious and scandalous passages, highly reflecting upon his Majesty and his Ministers, and tending to alienate the affections of his good subjects in England and Ireland from each other." Sir Walter, after mentioning one or two interesting anecdotes, says,—" When the bill against the printer of the Drapier's Letters was about to be presented to the grand jury, Swift addressed to that body a paper entitled "Seasonable Advice," exhorting them to remember the story of the Leyone mode by which the wolves were placed with the sheep, on condition of parting with their shepherds and mastiffs, after which they ravaged the flock at pleasure." A few spirited verses, addressed to the citizens at large, and enforcing similar topics, are subscribed by the Drapier's initials, and are doubtless Swift's own composition, alluding to the charge that he had gone too far in leaving the discussion of Wood's project, to treat of the alleged dependence of Ireland. He concludes in these lines—

If, then, oppression has not quite subdued
At once your prudence and your gratitude—
If you yourselves conspire not your undoing—
And don't deserve and won't bring down your ruin—
If yet to virtue you have some pretence—
If yet you are not lost to common sense,
Assist your patriots in your own defence;
That stupid cant, " He went too far," despise,
And know that to be brave is to be wise;
Think how he struggled for your liberty,
And give him freedom while yourselves are free.

At the same time was circulated the memorable and apt quotation from Scripture by a Quaker (I do not know, gentlemen, whether his name was Robinson, but it ought to have been)—" And the people said unto Saul, shall Jonathan die who hath wrought thy great salvation in Israel? God forbid! As the Lord liveth there shall not one hair of his head fall to the ground, for he hath wrought with God this day; so the people rescued Jonathan, and he died not." Thus admonished by verse, law, and Scripture, the grand jury assembled. It was in vain that the Lord Chief Justice Whitshed, who had denounced the Dean's former tract as seditious, and procured a verdict against the prisoner, exerted himself upon a similar occasion. The hour for intimidation was passed. Sir Walter Scott, after detailing instances of the violence of Whitshed, and describing the rest of the Dean's letters, says :—" Thus victoriously terminated the first grand struggle for the independence of Ireland. The eyes of the kingdom were now moved with one consent upon the man by whose unbending fortitude and pre-eminent talent this triumph was accomplished. The Drapier's head became a sign; his portrait was engraved, worn upon handkerchiefs, struck upon medals, and displayed in every possible manner as the *Liberator* of Ireland." Well might that epithet " grand" be applied to the first great struggle of the people of Ireland by that immortal Scotchman, who was himself so " grand of soul," and who of mental loftiness, as well as of the magnificence of external nature, had a perception so fine—and well might our own Grattan, who was so great and so good, in referring to his own achievement in 1782, address to the spirit of Swift and to the spirit of Molyneux his enthusiastic invocation—and may not I, in such a cause as this, without irreverence, offer up my prayer, that of the spirit by which the soul of Henry Grattan was itself inflamed, every remnant in the bosoms of my countrymen may not be extinguished. A prosecution was not instituted against the great conspirators of 1782. The English minister had been taught in the struggles between England and her colonies a lesson from adversity, that schoolmistress, the only one from whom ministers ever learn anything—who charges so much blood, so much gold, and such torrents of tears, for her instructions. In reading the history of that time, and in tracing the gradual descent of England from the tone of despotic dictation to the reluctant acknowledgment of disaster, and to the ignominious confession of defeat, how many painful considerations are presented to us! If in time—if the English minister in time had listened to the eloquent warnings of Chatham, or to the still more oracular admonitions of Edmund Burke, what a world of woe would have been avoided! By some fatality, England was first demented, and then was lost. Her repentance followed her perdition. The colonies were lost; but Ireland was saved by the timely recognition of the great principle on which her independence was founded. No Attorney-General was found bold enough to prosecute Flood and Grattan for a conspiracy. With what scorn would twelve Irishmen have repudiated the presumptuous functionary by whom such an enterprise should have been attempted. Irishmen then felt that they had a country; they acted under the influence of that instinct of nationality, which, for his providential purposes, the author of nature has implanted in us. We were then a nation—we were not broken into fragments by those dissensions by which we are at once enfeebled and degraded. If we were eight millions of Protestants (and, Heaven forgive me, there are moments when, looking at the wrongs done to my country, I have been betrayed into the guilty desire that we all were); but, if we were eight millions of Protestants, should we be used as we are? Should we see every office of dignity and emolument in this country filled by the natives of the sister island? Should we see the just expenditure requisite for the improvement of our country denied? Should we see the quit and crown rents of Ireland applied to the improvement of Charing Cross, or of Windsor Castle? Should we submit to the odious distinctions between Englishmen and Irishmen introduced into almost every act of legislation? Should we bear with an Arms Bill, by which the Bill of Rights is set at nought? Should we brook the misapplication of a Poor Law? Should we allow the Parliament to proceed as if we had not a voice in the legislature? Should we submit to our present inadequate representation? Should we allow a new tariff to be introduced, without giving us the slightest equivalent for the manifest loss we have sustained? And should we not peremptorily require that the Imperial Parliament should hold periodical sessions for the transaction of Irish business in the metropolis of a powerful, and, as it then would be, an undivided country? But we are prevented by our wretched religious distinctions from co-operating for a single object, by which the honour and substantial interests of our country can be promoted. Fatal, disastrous, detestable distinctions! Detestable, because they are not only repugnant to the genuine spirit of Christianity, and substitute for the charities of religion the rancorous antipathies of sect; but because they practically reduce us to a colonial dependency, make the Union a name, substitute for a real union a tie of parchment which an event might sunder—convert a nation into an appurtenance, make us the footstool of the Minister, the scorn of England, and the commiseration of the world. Ireland is the only country in Europe in which abominable distinctions between Protestant and Catholic are permitted to continue. In Germany, where Luther translated the Scriptures; in France, where Calvin wrote the Institutes; ay, in the land of the Dragonades and the St. Bartholomews; in the land from whence the forefathers of one of the judicial functionaries of this court, and the first ministerial officer of the court, were barbarously driven—the mutual wrongs done by Catholic and Protestant are forgiven and forgotten, while we, madmen that we are, arrayed by that fell fanaticism which, driven from every other country in Europe, has found a refuge here, precipitate ourselves upon each other in those encounters of sectarian ferocity in which our country, bleeding and lacerated, is trodden under foot. We convert the Island, that ought to be one of the most fortunate in the sea, into a receptacle of degradation and suffering; counteract the designs of Providence, and enter into a conspiracy for the frustration of the beneficent designs of God.

[Mr. Sheil here took a rapid survey of the growth of the national feeling up to the time of O'Connell, passing on to vindicate the policy and professions of the chief defendant throughout the whole course of his career, and attempting to prove the alleged seditious meetings not to be such as they were represented in the indictment.]

I have already called attention to the fact that none of the gentry of the country were brought forward to state what the character of these meetings was. All the official persons examined—among whom were several of the high constables of the various districts—concurred in stating that there was no violation of the peace at any of them. Indeed, the assertion of the Attorney-General was, that the peace was kept—kept with the malevolent intention of enabling the whole population to rise at a given time, and establish a republic, of which Mr. O'Connell was to be the head. Forty-one of these meetings were held—all of the same character; and at length a proclamation was determined on and issued for the purpose of putting a stop to the Clontarf meeting. You have heard the remarks of Mr. O'Connell, in reference to the course adopted towards that meeting, and to me they appear extremely reasonable. Notice of that meeting had been given for three weeks, yet the proclamation was not published until the day before that on which it was to have taken place. Mr. O'Connell did not charge the government, when acting in this way, and delaying its measures till the last moment, with being capable of such an atrocious and destructive attempt on the lives of the people, as might have been perpetrated by sending the army amongst an unarmed populace, if the meeting had taken place.

Such an event might have taken place; and it is to be regretted that a more timely warning, one that would have removed all doubt and uncertainty, was not given. I pass this consideration by, and come to another point. It is a usual practice—a rule, in fact—that when a privy council is to assemble, summonses are directed to be issued to all privy councillors being within the vicinity of the city of Dublin. On this occasion, such summonses were not issued. I am given to understand that Chief Baron Brady, who is in the habit of attending at councils, was not summoned. The Right Honourable Anthony Richard Blake, a Roman Catholic gentleman, who was appointed Chief Remembrancer of the Exchequer under a Tory administration — the intimate friend of the Marquis Wellesley—a man who had never appeared in public assemblies, or interfered in the proceedings of public meetings—a man who had never uttered an inflammatory harangue in his life—that gentleman did not receive a summons. I will make no comment on this omission of the government on this occasion, but such undoubtedly is the fact. I have told you who did not receive summonses, and I shall proceed to state who did receive them. The Recorder of the city of Dublin—by whom the jury-list was to be revised—he received a summons. In his department it was that an event most untoward, as respects the traversers, befell. It was suggested in this court that the jury-list possibly might have been mutilated or decimated—for decimation it was—by an accident—perhaps by a rat, as was suggested by one of the court. I am far from suggesting that there was any intentional foul play in this decimation; but that a large portion of the list was omitted is beyond a doubt. I state the fact and make no comment on it. Well, an application was made for the names of the witnesses on the back of the document, on behalf of the traversers. One of the judges declared he thought it matter of right; another of the judges intimated his opinion that it would be advisable for the crown to furnish the list within a reasonable time. From that day to this the list has never been given. The list of jurors is drawn by ballot; there are eleven Catholics upon it. They are struck off. The trial comes on. A challenge is put in to the array, upon the ground that one-tenth, or very nearly one-tenth, of the jury-list was suppressed. One of the court expresses an opinion that the challenge is a good one. His brethren differ from him; but when in a trial at bar, at the instance of the crown, one of the judges gives an intimation so unequivocal as to the construction of the jury-list, perhaps it would have been more advisable for the crown to have discharged the order for a special jury, and to have directed the high sheriff of the city to have returned a panel. I mention these incidents, gentlemen, in order that your feeling that the traversers have been deprived of some of those contingent benefits given them by the law, should give them an equivalent for any loss which they may have sustained in your anxious performance of your sacred duty. At length, in the midst of profound silence, the Attorney-General states the case for the crown, and consumes eleven hours in doing so. I was astonished at his brevity, for the pleading on which his speech was founded is the very Behemoth of indictments, which, as you see, "upheaves its vastness" on that table. Nothing comparable in the bigness of its gigantic dimensions has ever yet been seen. The indictment in Hardy's case, whose trial lasted ten or eleven days, does not exceed three or four pages; but this indictment requires an effort of physical force to lift it up. Combined with this indictment was a tremendous bill of particulars in keeping with it. Gentlemen, the Attorney-General, as I have already observed to you at the outset of these observations, denounced the traversers at the close of almost every sentence that was uttered by him; but it struck me that it was only in reference to two of these charges that he broke forth in a burst of genuine and truly impassioned indignation. The first of those charges was—a conspiracy to diminish the business of a court of law. How well the great Lord Chatham exclaimed—I remember to have read it somewhere, but I forget where—"Shake the whole constitution to the centre, and the lawyer will sit tranquil in his cabinet; but touch a single thread in the cobwebs of Westminster-hall, and the exasperated spider crawls out in its defence." The second great hit of the right honourable gentleman was made when he charged Mr. O'Connell with a deplorable ignorance of law, in stating certain prerogatives of the crown. With respect, gentlemen, to the arbitration courts, the Society of Friends are as liable to an indictment for conspiracy as the defendants. The regulations under which the Quaker arbitration system is carried on will be laid before you; and the opinions of Lord Brougham, who has always been the strenuous advocate of the arbitration system, will, I am sure, have their due weight upon you. With regard to Mr. O'Connell's alleged mistake, respecting the power of the crown to issue writs—what is it after all but a project for swamping the House of Commons, analogous to that of Sir James Graham and my Lord Stanley for swamping the House of Lords? The plain truth is this—the Sovereign has the abstract right to create new boroughs. But the exercise of that right might be regarded as inconsistent with the principles of the constitution. Lord Denman and one of his late Majesty's law advisers in the House of

Commons distinctly asserted the right to issue writs; and although that opinion was reprehended by Sir Charles Wetherell, I believe that of its being strict law there can be little doubt. But the real question between the Attorney-General and the traversers, and the only one to which you will be disposed to pay much regard, was raised by the Attorney-General when he said that there existed a dangerous conspiracy, of which the object was to prepare the great body of the people to rise at a signal and to erect a sanguinary republic, of which Daniel O'Connell should be the head. Gentlemen, how do men proceed who engage in a guilty enterprise of this kind? They bind each other by solemn oaths. They are sworn to secrecy, to silence, to deeds, or to death. They associate superstition with atrocity, and heaven is invoked by them to ratify the covenants of hell. They fix a day, an hour, and hold their assemblages in the midst of darkness and of solitude, and verify the exclamation of the conspirator, in the language of the great observer of our nature:—

Oh, Conspiracy,
Where wilt thou find a cavern dark enough
To hide thy monstrous visage?

How have the repeal conspirators proceeded? Every one of their assemblages have been open to the public. For a shilling, all they said, or did, or thought, were known to the Government. Everything was laid bare and naked to the public eye; they stripped their minds in the public gaze. No oaths, no declaration, no initiation, no form of any kind was resorted to. They did not even act together. Mr. Duffy, proprietor of the *Nation*, did not attend a single meeting in the country. My client attended only three; Mr. Tierney, the priest, attended no more than one. It would have been more manly on the part of the Attorney-General to have indicted Dr. Higgins or Dr. Cantwell, or, as he was pleased to designate them, Bishop Higgins and Bishop Cantwell. Well, why did he not catch a bishop—if not Cantwell, at all events Higgins? For three months we heard nothing but "Higgins, Higgins, Higgins." The *Times* was redolent of Higgins; sometimes he was Lord Higgins, then he was Priest Higgins, afterwards Mr. Higgins. But wherefore is not this redoubted Higgins indicted, or why did you not assail the great John of Tuam himself? He would not have shrunk from your persecution, but, with his mitre on his head and his crozier in his hand, he would have walked in his pontifical vestments into gaol, and smiled disdainfully upon you. But you did not dare to attack him, but fell on a poor Monaghan priest, who only attended one meeting, and only made one speech about the "Yellow Ford," for which you should not include him in a conspiracy, but should make him professor of rhetoric at Maynooth. Gentlemen, an enormous mass of speeches delivered by Mr. O'Connell within the last nine months has been laid before you. I think, however, you will come to the conclusion that they are nothing more than a repetition of the opinions which he expressed in 1810; and when you come to consider them in detail, you will, I am sure, be convinced that these speeches were not merely interspersed with references to peace and order, with a view to escape from the law, but that there runs, through the entire mass of thought that came from the mind of Mr. O'Connell, a pervading love of order, and an unaffected sentiment of abhorrence for the employment of any other than loyal, constitutional, and pacific means for the attainment of his object. He attaches fully as much importance to the means as to the end. He declares that he would not purchase the repeal of the Union at the cost of one drop of blood. He announces that the moment the Government calls upon him to disperse his meetings, these meetings shall be dispersed. He does but ask "the Irish nation to back him;" for from that backing he anticipates the only success to which, as a good subject, as a good citizen, and as a good Christian, he could aspire. But if, gentlemen, it be suggested that in popular harangues obedience to the laws and submission to authority are easily simulated, I think I may fearlessly assert that of the charges preferred against him his life affords the refutation. A man cannot wear the mask of loyalty for forty-four years; however skilfully constructed, the vizor will sometimes drop off, and the natural truculence of the conspirator must be disclosed. You may have heard many references made to the year 1798, and several stanzas of a long poem have been read to you, in order to fasten them on Mr. O'Connell. It was in 1798 that the celebrated man was called to the bar, who was destined to play a part so conspicuous on the theatre of the world. He was in the bloom of youth—in the full flush of life—the blood bounded in his veins, and in a frame full of vigour was embodied an equally elastic and athletic mind. He was in that season of life when men are most disposed to high and daring adventure. He had come from those rocks and mountains of which a description so striking has appeared in the reports of the speeches which have been read to you. He had listened, as he says, to the great Atlantic, whose surge rolls unbroken from the coast of Labrador. He carried enthusiasm to romance; and of the impressions which great events are calculated to make upon minds like his, he was peculiarly susceptible. He was unwedded. He had given no hostages to the State. The conservative affections had not tied their ligaments tender, but indissoluble, about his heart. There was at that time an enterprise on foot, guilty, and deeply guilty, indeed, but not wholly hopeless. The peaks that overhang the Bay of Bantry are dimly visible from Iveragh. What part was taken in that dark adventure by this conspirator of sixty-nine? Curran was suspected—Grattan was suspected. Both were designated as traitors unimpeached; but on the name of Daniel O'Connell a conjecture never lighted. And can you bring yourselves to believe that the man who turned with abhorrence from the conjuration of 1798 would now, in an old age, which he himself has called not premature, engage in an insane undertaking, in which his u life, and the lives of those who are dearer   him than himself, and the lives of hundreds of thousands of his countrymen, would, beyond all doubt, be sacrificed? Can you bring yourselves to believe that he would blast the laurels, which it is his boast that he has won without the effusion of blood—that he would drench the land of his birth, of his affections, and of his redemption, in a deluge of profitless massacre, and that he would lay prostrate that great moral monument which he has raised so high that it is visible from the remotest region of the world? What he was in 1798 he is in 1844. Do you believe that the man who aimed at a revolution would repudiate French assistance and denounce the present dynasty of France? Do you think that the man who aimed at revolution, would hold forth to the detestation of the world the infamous slavery by which the great transatlantic republic, to her everlasting shame, permits herself to be degraded? Or, to come nearer home, do you think that the man who aimed at revolution would have indignantly repudiated the proffered junction with the English Chartists? Had a combination been effected between the Chartists and the Repealers, it would have been more than formidable. At the head of that combination, in England, was Mr. Feargus O'Connor, once the associate and friend of Daniel O'Connell. The entire of the lower orders in the North of England were enrolled in a powerful organization. A league between the Repealers and the Chartists might have been at once effected. Chartism uses its utmost and most clandestine efforts to find its way into this country. O'Connell detects and crushes it. Of the charges proferred against him, am I not right when I exclaim that his life contains the refutation? To the charge that Mr. O'Connell and his son conspired to excite animosity amongst her Majesty's subjects, the last observation that I have made to you is more peculiarly applicable. Gentlemen, Mr. O'Connell and his co-religionists have been made the objects of the fiercest and the coarsest vituperation; and yet I defy the most acute and diligent scrutiny of the entire of the speeches put before you, to detect a single expression—one solitary phrase—which reflects in the remotest degree upon the Protestant religion. He has left all the contumely heaped upon the form of Christianity which he professes utterly unheeded, and the Protestant Operative Society has not provoked a retort; and every angry disputant has, without any interposition on his part, been permitted to rush in "where angels fear to tread." The religion of Mr. O'Connell teaches him two things—charity towards those who dissent from him in doctrine, and forgiveness of those who do him wrong. You recollect (it is from such incidents that we are enabled to judge of the characters and feelings of men)—you remember to have heard in the course of the evidence frequent reference made to Sir Bradley King. The unfortunate man had been deprived of his office, and all compensation was denied him. He used to stand in the lobby of the House of Commons, the most desolate and hopeless-looking man I ever saw. The only one of his old friends that stuck to him was Baron Lefroy. But Baron Lefroy had no interest with the Government. Mr. O'Connell saw Bradley King, and took pity on him. Bradley King had been his fierce political, almost his personal antagonist. Mr. O'Connell went to Lord Althorpe, and obtained for Bradley King the compensation which had been refused him. I remember having read a most striking letter addressed by Sir Abraham Bradley King to Mr. O'Connell, and asked him for it. He could not at first put his hand upon it; but, while looking for it, he mentioned that soon after the death of the old Dublin alderman, an officer entered his study, and told him that he was the son-in-law of Sir Abraham, who had a short time before his death, called him to his bedside, and said:—" When I shall have been buried, go to Daniel O'Connell, and tell him that the last prayer of a grateful man was offered up for him, and that I implored heaven to avert every peril from his head." Mr. O'Connell found the letter—you will allow me to read it:—

"Barrett's Hotel, Spring Gardens,
"4th Aug., 1832.

"My dear Sir,—The anxious wish for a satisfactory termination of my cause, which your continued and unwearied efforts for it have ever indicated, is at length accomplished; the vote of compensation passed last night.

"To Mr. Lefroy and yourself am I indebted for putting the case in the right light to my Lord Althorpe, and for his lordship's consequent candid and straightforward act, in giving me my just dues, and thus restoring myself and family to competence, ease, and happiness.

"To you, Sir, to whom I was early and long politically opposed—to you, who nobly forgetting this continued difference of opinion, and who, rejecting every idea of party feeling or party spirit, thought only of my distress, and sped to succour and support me, how can I express my gratitude? I cannot attempt it. The reward, I feel, is to be found only in your own breast, and I assure myself that the generous feelings of a noble mind will cheer you on to that prosperity and happiness, which a discriminating Providence holds out to those who protect the helpless, and sustain the falling.

"For such reward and happiness to you and yours, my prayers shall be offered fervently, while the remainder of my days, passing, I trust, in tranquillity, by a complete retirement from public life, and in the bosom of my family, will constantly present to me the grateful recollection of one to whom I am mainly indebted for so desirable a closing of my life. Believe me, my dear Sir, with the greatest respect and truth, your faithful servant,

"ABRAHAM BRADLEY KING.

"To Daniel O'Connell, Esq., M.P."

You may deprive him of liberty—you may shut him out from the face of nature, you may inter him in a dungeon, to which a ray of the sun never yet descended; but you never will take away from him the consciousness of having done a good and a noble action, and of being entitled to kneel down every night he sleeps, and to address to his Creator the divinest portion of our Redeemer's prayer. The man to whom that letter was addressed, and the son of the man to whom that letter was addressed, are not guilty of the sanguinary intents which have been ascribed to them, and of this they "put themselves upon their country." Rescue that phrase from its technicalities—let it no longer be a fictitious one; if we have lost our representation in the Parliament, let us behold it in the jury-box, and that you participate in the feelings of millions of your countrymen let your verdict afford a proof. But it is not to Ireland that the aching solicitude with which the result of this trial is intently watched will be confined. There is not a great city in Europe in which, upon the day when the great intelligence shall be expected to arrive, men will not stop each other in the public way, and inquire whether twelve men upon their oaths have doomed to incarceration the man who gave liberty to Ireland? Whatever may be your adjudication, he is prepared to meet it. He knows that the eyes of the world are upon him—and that posterity—whether in a gaol or out of it—will look back to him with admiration; he is almost indifferent to what may befall him, and is far more solicitous for others at this moment than for himself. But I—at the commencement of what I have said to you—I told you that I was not unmoved, and that many incidents of my political life, the strange alternations of fortune through which I have passed, had come back upon me. But now the bare possibility at which I have glanced, has, I acknowledge, almost unmanned me. Shall I, who stretch out to you in behalf of the son the hand whose fetters the father has struck off, live to cast my eyes upon that domicile of sorrow, in the vicinity of this great metropolis, and say, "'Tis there they have immured the Liberator of Ireland, with his fondest and best-beloved child?" No! it shall never be! You will not consign him to the spot to which the Attorney-General invites you to surrender him. When the spring shall have come again, and the winter shall have passed—when the spring shall have come again, it is not through the windows of a prison-house that the father of such a son, and the son of such a father, shall look upon those green hills on which the eyes of many a captive have gazed so wistfully in vain, but in their own mountain home again they shall listen to the murmurs of the great Atlantic; they shall go forth and inhale the freshness of the morning air together; "they shall be free of mountain solitudes;" they will be encompassed with the loftiest images of liberty upon every side; and if time shall have stolen its suppleness from the father's knee, or impaired the firmness of his tread, he shall lean on the child of her that watches over him from heaven, and shall look out from some high place far and wide into the island whose greatness and whose glory shall be for ever associated with his name. In your love of justice—in your love of Ireland—in your love of honesty and fair play—I place my confidence. I ask you for an acquittal, not only for the sake of your country, but for your own. Upon the day when this trial shall have been brought to a termination, when, amidst the hush of public expectancy, in answer to the solemn interrogatory which shall be put to you by the officer of the court, you shall answer, "Not guilty," with what a transport will that glorious negative be welcomed! How will you be blessed, adored, worshipped; and when retiring from this scene of excitement and of passion, you shall return to your own tranquil homes, how pleasurably will you look upon your children, in the consciousness that you will have left them a patrimony of peace by impressing upon the British Cabinet, that some other measure, besides a state prosecution, is necessary for the pacification of your country!

There is no extremity of distress, which, of itself, ought to reduce a great nation to despair. —*Junius.*

JOHN WILKES.

Born 1727. Died 1797.

[This man, celebrated as a wit, profligate, and patriot, is entitled to some honour at the hands of posterity for the bold manner in which he declaimed against the lamentable war with our (at that time) American Colonies, and the liberty which he was instrumental in obtaining for the press to publish the speeches delivered in the Houses of Parliament. However we may abhor his principles, we must at least give him credit for consistency in carrying them out; and however just we may consider his first expulsion from the House of Commons for his abominable "Essay on Woman," we must agree with him in the injustice with which he was denied his seat in Parliament (after his second expulsion), on the ground that the fact of his having been expelled rendered him incapable of being re-elected to serve in the same Parliament, a principle which strikes at the foundation of our political liberty.

The following speech will explain itself, and is a good specimen of his plain and straightforward oratory. It was delivered on the 22nd February, 1775, but the object for which it strove was not attained for many years after.]

THE MIDDLESEX ELECTIONS.

THE motion, which I shall have the honour of submitting to the House, affects, in my opinion, the very vitals of this constitution, the great primary sources of the power of the people, whom we represent, and by whose authority only, delegated to us for a time, we are a part of the legislative body of this kingdom. The proceedings of the last Parliament, in the business of the Middlesex elections, gave a just alarm to almost every elector in the nation. The fatal precedent then attempted to be established was considered as a direct attack on the inalienable rights of the people. Many of the most respectable bodies in this kingdom expressed their abhorrence of those arbitrary measures. They proceeded so far as to petition the Crown for the dissolution of that Parliament, as having been guilty of a flagrant abuse of their trust. Above 60,000 of our fellow subjects, freeholders of the realm, carried their complaints to the foot of the throne; a number surely deserving the highest regard, at least from a Minister, whose whole attention was not engrossed by the 6,000 borough electors, who return a majority for him to this House. The people, sir, were in a ferment, which has not yet subsided. They made my cause their own, for they saw all the powers of Government exerted against the constitution, which was wounded through my sides, and the envenomed shafts of a wicked administration pointed at our laws and liberties no less than at a hated individual. The plan was carried on for some years with a spirit of malevolence and rancour, which would have disgraced the very worst, but with a perseverance which would have done honour to the best cause. I do not mean, sir, to go through an irksome detail of the various persecutions and injuries, which that person suffered, I hope with a becoming fortitude. I have forgiven them. All the great powers of the State were at one time combined to pour their accumulated vengeance on me. The two Houses of Parliament chose me as the most acceptable victim, which could be sacrificed at the shrine of their court idolatry, and even imperial Jove pointed his thunder-bolts, * red with uncommon wrath, at my devoted head. I was scorched, but not consumed. The broad shield of the law protected me. A generous public, and my noble friends, the freeholders of Middlesex, the ever steady friends of liberty and their country, poured balm into my wounds. They are healed so that scarcely a scar remains. But, sir, I feel, I deeply feel the wounds given to the constitution. They are still bleeding, and this House only can heal them, as well as restore the constitution to its former state of purity, health, and vigour. May I be permitted to point out the mode of cure, and the salutary methods which I think you ought to apply? Before I proceed to the remedy, I shall beg the indulgence of the House to state the case with precision and accuracy. I hope they will forgive a dry, but candid and short, narrative of the principal facts, because I mean to argue from them. I will give them as briefly as possible, and with all the impartiality of a bystander.

Mr. Wilkes was first elected for the county of Middlesex, on the 28th of March, 1768. He was expelled the 3rd of February, 1769, and the second time chosen, without opposition, the 16th day of the same month. On the day following the election was vacated, and he was declared by a majority of the House *incapable* of being elected into that Parliament. Notwithstanding this resolution of the House, he was a third time, on the 16th of March, elected without opposition; for I suppose the ridiculous attempt of a Mr. Dingley, who had not a single freeholder to propose, or vote for him, can hardly be called an opposition. That election, however, was declared void the next day. On the 13th of April, Mr. Wilkes was a fourth time elected by a majority of 1,143 votes against Mr. Luttrell, who had only 296. The same day this House voted, "that Mr. Luttrell ought to have been returned." On the 29th of April, a petition was presented to the House from the freeholders of Middlesex by a worthy baronet, † who is not only an honour to this House, but to human nature; notwithstanding which the House on the 8th of May resolved, "that Henry Lawes Luttrell, Esquire, is duly elected a Knight of the shire to serve

---

* In Junius's letter to the King of Dec. 19, 1769, it is said, "the destruction of one man [Mr. Wilkes] has been now, for many years, the sole object of your Government."

† Sir George Savile, Baronet, Member for Yorkshire.

in this present Parliament for the county of Middlesex."

These, sir, are the great outlines, the leading facts. I will not trouble the Clerk to read all the resolutions, to which I have alluded. They are fresh, I am persuaded, in the memories of gentlemen. I only call for that of Feb. 17, 1769, respecting incapacity as the certain consequence of expulsion.

[The Clerk read the Resolution.]

Now, sir, I think it fair to state to the House the whole of what I intend to move in consequence of the facts stated, and the resolution just read. The first motion I intend is, " that the resolution of this House of the 17th of February, 1769, ' that John Wilkes, Esquire, having been, in this session of Parliament, expelled this House, was, and is, incapable of being elected a member to serve in this present Parliament,' be expunged from the journals of this House, as being subversive of the rights of the whole body of electors of this kingdom." This I hold of necessity to restore the constitution, which that resolution tears up by the roots. I shall then, if I succeed—if justice and a reverence for the constitution prevail in this Parliament—proceed to the other motion, "That all the declarations, orders, and resolutions of this House, respecting the election of John Wilkes, Esquire, for the county of Middlesex, as a void election, the due and legal election of Henry Lawes Luttrell, Esquire, into the last Parliament, for the county of Middlesex, and the incapacity of John Wilkes, Esquire, to be elected a Member to serve in the said Parliament, be expunged from the journals of this House, as being subversive of the rights of the whole body of electors of this kingdom."

The words of the resolution of the 17th of February, 1769, which I mean more particularly to combat, are " was and is incapable," and the explanation of them the same day in the order for a new writ, " in the room of John Wilkes, Esquire, who is adjudged incapable of being elected a Member to serve in this present Parliament." In the first formation of this Government, in the original settlement of our constitution, the people expressly reserved to themselves a very considerable part of the legislative power, which they consented to share jointly with a King and House of Lords. From the great population of our island this right could not be claimed and exercised personally, and therefore the many were compelled to delegate that power to a few, who thus were chosen their deputies and agents only, their representatives. It follows from the very idea of a choice, that such choice must be free and uncontrolled, admitting of no restrictions, but the law of the land, to which the King and the Lords are equally subject, and what must arise from the nature of the trust.

A Peer of Parliament, for instance, cannot be elected a Member of the House of Commons, because he already forms a part of another branch of the same legislative body. A lunatic has a natural incapacity. Other instances might be mentioned, but these two are sufficient. The freedom of election is then the common right of the people of England, their fair and just share of power; and I hold it to be the most glorious inheritance of every subject of this realm, the noblest, and, I trust, the most solid part of that beautiful fabric, the English constitution. Here I might lean, sir, on the most respectable authorities which can be cited, the supreme judicature of this kingdom, and the venerable judges of former ages, as well as of our own times. " I met them accidentally this morning in the course of my reading," as an old friend * of Wilkes and Liberty, now, alas! lost to every sense of duty to his country, frequently tells another great assembly, that he accidentally meets in this manner all his tiresome quotations. The House of Peers, sir, in the case of Ashby and White, in 1704, determined " a man has a right to his freehold by the common law; and the law having annexed his right of voting to his freehold, it is of the nature of his freehold, and must depend upon it." On the same occasion likewise they declared, " it is absurd to say the electors' right of choosing is founded upon the law and custom of Parliament. It is an original right, part of the constitution of the kingdom, as much as a Parliament is, and from whence the persons elected to serve in Parliament do derive their authority, and can have no other but that which is given to them by those that have the original right to choose them." The greatest law authorities, both ancient and modern, agree in the opinion that every subject of the realm, not disqualified by law, is eligible of common right. Lord Coke, Lord Chief Justice Holt, and Mr. Justice Blackstone, are the only authorities which I shall cite. I regard not, sir, the slavish, courtly doctrines propagated by lawyers in either House of Parliament, as to the rights of the subject, no more than I do as to what they pronounce high treason and rebellion. Such doctrines are delivered here only to be reported elsewhere. These men have their reward. But the venal tongue of a prostitute advocate or judge is best answered by the wise and sober pen of the same man, when, in a former cool moment, unheated by party rage or faction, after the

* The Duke of Grafton. Junius, in a letter to his Grace, of May 30, 1769, says, " you complained . . . . that your friend, Mr. Wilkes, who had suffered so much for the party, had been abandoned to his fate . . . . as for Mr. Wilkes, it is, perhaps, the greatest misfortune of his life, that you should have so many compensations to make in the closet for your former friendship with him. Your gracious master understands your character, and makes you a persecutor, because you have been a friend."

fullest deliberation, he gave to the nation, to the present age, and to posterity, a fair and impartial detail of their undoubted rights, and when he laid down in clear and express terms the plain law of the land. Lord Coke says, "He which is eligible of common right cannot be disabled by the said ordinance in Parliament, unless it had been by Act of Parliament." Lord Chief Justice Holt declares, "The election of knights belong to the freeholders of counties, and it is an original right, vested in and inseparable from the freehold, and can no more be severed from their freehold, than their freehold itself can be taken away." Mr. Justice Blackstone, in the first book of his "Commentaries on the Laws of England," has the following words:—"Subject to these restrictions and disqualifications, every subject of the realm is eligible of common right." This common right of the subject, sir, was violated by the majority of the last House of Commons; and I affirm that they, and in particular, if I am rightly informed, the noble Lord with the blue riband * committed by that act high treason against Magna Charta. This House only, without the interference of the other parts of the Legislature, took upon them to make the law. They adjudged me incapable of being elected a Member to serve in that Parliament, although I was qualified by the law of the land; and the noble Lord declared in this House, "If any other candidate had only six votes, he would seat him for Middlesex." I repeat it, sir, this violence was a direct infringement of Magna Charta, high treason against the sacred charter of our liberties. The words, to which I allude, ought always to be written in letters of gold. "No freeman shall be disseized of his freehold, or liberties, or free customs, unless by the lawful judgment of his peers, or by the law of the land." By the conduct of that majority, and of the noble Lord, they assumed to themselves the power of making the law, and at the same moment invaded the rights of the people, the King, and the Lords. The two last tamely acquiesced in the exercise of a power, which had been in a great instance fatal to their predecessors, had put an end to their very existence; but the people, sir, and in particular the spirited freeholders of this county, whose ruling passion is the love of liberty, have not yet forgiven the attack on their rights. So dangerous a precedent of usurped power, which may in future times be cited and adopted in practice by a despotic Minister of the Crown, ought to be expunged from the journals of this House.

I have heard and read much of precedents to justify the proceedings of the last House of Commons. I own, sir, I value very little the doctrine of precedents. There is scarcely any new villany under the sun. A precedent can never justify any action in itself wicked, a robbery, for instance, on the heaths of Hounslow or Bagshot, of which there are innumerable precedents. The basest actions may be justified by precedents drawn from bad times and bad men. The sole question is, whether this power is not a direct usurpation on the rights of the people? If that is proved, I care not how long the usurpation has continued, how often practised. It is high time to put an end to it. It was the case of General Warrants. One precedent, however, the most insisted upon, I must take notice of, because it is said fully to come up to the point, but in my opinion in almost every part it proves the contrary of what it has been brought to support. I mean the remarkable case of Mr. Walpole, in 1711, a period in which the rankest Tory principles were countenanced more than in any other of our history prior to 1760. The case, sir, has been so partially quoted, even by a person * whose sole merit here was an assumed accuracy, which he never possessed, that I shall desire it may be read to the House from the journals.

[The Clerk read]

"Resolved, that Robert Walpole, Esquire, having been this session of Parliament committed a prisoner to the Tower of London, and expelled this House, for an high breach of trust in the execution of his office, and notorious corruption when Secretary at War, was and is incapable of being elected a member to serve in the present Parliament."

Now, sir, I must observe, that even that House of Commons, at an era so hostile to the liberties not only of England but of Europe, did not venture to adjudge Mr. Walpole incapable of being elected a member to serve in that Parliament only because he was expelled; but in the body of the resolution itself they added another reason, which would be trifling if the former was sufficient and adequate to the point, "the high breach of trust in the execution of his office, and notorious corruption when Secretary at War." As trustees for the nation, they assigned a public cause, which must interest every member of the community. In the case of Mr. Wilkes, the last House of Commons declared, "that John Wilkes, Esq., having been in this session of Parliament expelled this House, was and is incapable of being elected a member to serve in this present Parliament." The having been expelled, whether justly or unjustly, is the only reason which they gave to the world. I shall not yet, sir, dismiss

---

* By "the noble Lord with the blue riband," Lord North was intended by Mr. Wilkes; but the expression referred to was made use of by his father, Lord Strange, and not by him.

* Jeremiah Dyson, Esq., formerly Clerk of the House of Commons.

the case of Mr. Walpole. It will prove another proposition maintained by me, it will show the injustice of the late House of Commons in seating Mr. Luttrell as representative for the county of Middlesex. The fact was, that the House in Queen Anne's time having expelled Mr. Walpole, ordered immediately the issuing of a new writ. At the subsequent election Mr. Walpole was again returned. A Mr. Taylor, who had a minority of votes, petitioned; but the election was vacated. Had the doctrine propagated by the late majority, and by the noble lord with the blue riband, been just well founded, Mr. Taylor ought to have been the sitting member, the House should have resolved that he ought to have been returned, and that the grossest injustice had actually been committed against him. But even that Parliament, whose memory the nation execrates, stopped short in their career of iniquity, and did not proceed to such enormous wickedness. It was reserved for the present era, when shame has lost its blush. Mr. Luttrell was for some years permitted to sit here as representing the county of Middlesex, although a great majority of the freeholders abhorred and reprobated the idea of his representing them, on every public occasion declared it, and in their petition to this House gave the record of it under their hands to all posterity.

Sir, when the strong, unanswerable reasons on which any doctrine is founded bear me out, I care little about precedents. I recollect, however, another instance in more auspicious times, when a glorious monarch defended the constitution which he had restored. It directly meets the objection so much relied upon, " that expulsion necessarily implies incapacity." It is the last which I shall desire the clerk to read. I wish him to turn to the journals of February 20, 1698.

[The Clerk read]

"Resolved, that Richard Wollaston, Esquire, being a member of the House of Commons, and having since been concerned and acted as a receiver of the duties upon houses, as also upon births, marriages, and burials, contrary to the act, made in the fifth and sixth years of his Majesty's reign, for granting several duties upon salt, beer, ale, and other liquors, be expelled this House."

Now, Sir, I defy all the subtlety of the most expert court lawyer among us, all the sophistry of the bar, to reconcile Mr. Wollaston's case with the favourite court tenet, " that expulsion necessarily implies incapacity." The fact is ascertained, and indeed admitted, that a new writ did issue for the borough of Whitchurch, in Hampshire, and that Mr. Wollaston was re-elected, and sat in the same Parliament.

Incapacity, therefore, in the same Parliament does not necessarily follow expulsion.

I am ready to admit, that where a clear legal incapacity exists, all votes given to a person incapacitated are thrown away, if they are knowingly given to him. But, sir, I beg leave to assert, that this was not the case in the Middlesex business. Mr. Wilkes was qualified by the law of the land; and the freeholders, who perfectly understood the clear point of law, as well as their own rights, expressly declared in the petition presented on the 29th of April, 1769, to the House, "Your petitioners beg leave to represent to this honourable House, that the said Henry Lawes Luttrell had not the majority of legal votes at the said election, nor did the majority of the freeholders, when they voted for John Wilkes, Esq., mean thereby to throw away their votes, or to waive their right of representation; nor would they by any means have chosen to be represented by the said Henry Lawes Luttrell, Esq. Your petitioners therefore apprehend he cannot sit as the representative of the said county in Parliament, without a manifest infringement of the rights and privileges of the freeholders thereof."

This House, sir, is created by the people, as the other is by the King. What right can the majority have to say to any county, city, or borough, you shall not have a particular person to be your representative, only because he is obnoxious to us, when he is qualified by law? Every county, city, or borough has an equal right with all other counties, cities, and boroughs, to its own choice, to its own distinct deputy in the great council of the nation. Each is free and independent, invested with precisely the same powers.

I do not mean, sir, now to enter into the argument, whether it may not be fit to give this House the power of expulsion in the first instance, for very flagrant and infamous crimes, either committed, or of which the member may be convicted, subsequent to his election. The sending the member back to his constituents on such ground might be considered as an appeal to the people. If, however, his constituents should differ in opinion from the majority of this House, if they should think him fit to be re-elected, he ought to be admitted, because he claims his seat under the same authority by which every member holds the privilege of sitting and voting here, a delegation from the people, their free choice. The first appeal to the constituents might in many cases appear just and reasonable. The appeal certainly lies to them, for they are the fountain of this power. We exercise their right. By their representation only we are a House of Parliament. They have the right of choosing for themselves, not a majority here for them.

Sir, I will venture to assert, that the law

of the land, by which all courts of judicature are equally bound, is overturned by the power lately exercised by a majority of a House of Commons. The right of election by law is vested in the freehold. It is not placed in you, but in other hands; in those of the freeholders, or the constituents. Your predecessors not only robbed a particular county of its noblest privileges, but they changed the constitution of a House of Commons. The freeholders of this county and the nation abhorred the proceeding, and poured their execrations on the treacherous authors. From us not only they, but the law and constitution, now expect a full reparation of the injury, by rescinding the resolution.

This usurpation, if acquiesced under, would be attended with the most alarming consequences. If you can reject those disagreeable to a majority, and expel whom you please, the House of Commons will be *self-created* and *self-existing*. You may expel till you approve, and thus in effect you nominate. The original idea of this House being the representative of the commons of the realm will be lost. The consequences of such a principle are dangerous in the extreme. A more forcible engine of despotism cannot be put into the hands of a Minister. I wish gentlemen would attend to the plain consequences of such proceedings, and consider how they may be brought home to themselves. A member hated or dreaded by the Minister is accused of a crime, for instance, of being the author of what he thinks a libel. I select this case as being the crime least likely to be committed by any one gentleman of the present majority of this House. No proof whatever is given on oath before you, because you cannot administer an oath, except in the cases provided for by Act of Parliament. You determine the *fact* however, and thus the Minister begins with invading the rights of juries. Before any trial, he gets the paper voted a libel, and the member he wishes expelled is voted to be the author, which is a *fact* this House is not competent to try and determine. *Expulsion* means always, as it is pretended, *incapacity*. The member is accordingly adjudged *incapable*. He cannot in consequence be re-elected, and thus is totally excluded from Parliament. By such manoeuvres a minister may garble a House of Commons till not a single enemy of his own, or friend of his country, is left here, and the representation of the people in a great degree annihilated. Corruption had not lent despotism wings to fly so high in the reign of Charles I., or the minister of that day would have been contented with expelling Hampden and the four other heroes, because they had immediately been adjudged *incapable*, and thereby incapacitated from thwarting in Parliament the arbitrary measures of a wicked court. My expulsion was an easy victory over liberty and the constitution. It went with wonderful expedition through all the forms of this House, for it was known to be a measure previously adopted in the cabinet, whose members have through the present reign frequently dared to deliberate on the invasion of the dearest rights of their country.

Upon all these considerations, sir, in order to quiet the minds of the people, to restore our violated constitution to its original purity, to vindicate the injured rights of this county in particular, and of all the electors of this kingdom, and that not the least trace of the violence and injustice of the last Parliament in this important cause may disgrace our records, I humbly move, "That the resolution of this House of the 17th of February, 1769, that John Wilkes, Esq., having been in this session or Parliament expelled this House, *was* and *is* incapable of sitting in the present Parliament, be expunged from the journals of this House, as being subversive of the rights of the whole body of electors of this kingdom."

People and Parliament.

Let the commons in Parliament assembled be one and the same thing with the commons at large. The distinctions that are made to separate us are unnatural and wicked contrivances. Let us identify, let us incorporate, ourselves with the people. Let us cut all the cables and snap the chains which tie us to an unfaithful shore, and enter the friendly harbour that shoots far out into the main its moles and jetties to receive us. "War with the world, and peace with our constituents." Be this our motto and our principle. Then, indeed, we shall be truly great. Respecting ourselves, we shall be respected by the world. At present all is troubled, and cloudy, and distracted, and full of anger and turbulence, both abroad and at home; but the air may be cleared by this storm, and light and fertility may follow it. Let us give a faithful pledge to the people, that we honour indeed the crown, but that we *belong* to them; that we are their auxiliaries, and not their task-masters—the fellow-labourers in the same vineyard—not lording over their rights, but helpers of their joy: that to tax them is a grievance to ourselves; but to cut off from our enjoyments to forward theirs, is the highest gratification we are capable of receiving.—*Burke.*

A Shallow Financier.

He must be a miserable statesman who voluntarily, by the same act, increases the public expense, and lessens the means of supporting it.—*Junius.*

PATRICK HENRY.

Born 1736. *Died* 1799.

[The great American lawyer and statesman from one of whose speeches a few extracts are here given, made his first appearance before the Law Courts of Virginia on the 1st of December, 1763, and at once very greatly distinguished himself by his logic and eloquence. In 1765 he was elected a representative in the Virginian Legislature, and soon became a leader of the Revolutionary party. According to Jefferson, "he gave the earliest impulse to the ball of the Revolution." After the Declaration of Independence, the State of Virginia elected Henry its first Governor. The following passages are from a speech of Patrick Henry, on the expediency of adopting the Federal constitution, delivered in the Convention of Virginia, June 5th, 1788.]

ON THE EXPEDIENCY OF ADOPTING THE FEDERAL CONSTITUTION.

MR. CHAIRMAN,—I am much obliged to the very worthy gentleman for his encomium. I wish I were possessed of talents, or possessed of anything, that might enable me to elucidate this great subject. I am not free from suspicion: I am apt to entertain doubts: I rose yesterday to ask a question, which arose in my own mind. When I asked that question, I thought the meaning of my interrogation was obvious: the fate of this question and of America may depend on this. Have they said, we, the States? Have they made a proposal of a compact between States? If they had, this would be a confederation: it is otherwise most clearly a consolidated government. The question turns, sir, on that poor little thing—the expression, we, the people, instead of the States of America. I need not take much pains to show that the principles of this system are extremely pernicious, impolitic, and dangerous. Is this a monarchy, like England—a compact between prince and people; with checks on the former to secure the liberty of the latter? Is this a confederacy, like Holland—an association of a number of independent states, each of which retains its individual sovereignty? It is not a democracy, wherein the people retain all their rights securely. Had these principles been adhered to, we should not have been brought to this alarming transition, from a confederacy to a consolidated government. We have no detail of those great considerations which, in my opinion, ought to have abounded before we should recur to a government of this kind. Here is a revolution as radical as that which separated us from Great Britain. It is as radical, if, in this transition, our rights and privileges are endangered, and the sovereignty of the States relinquished. And cannot we plainly see that this is actually the case? The rights of conscience, trial by jury, liberty of the press, all your immunities and franchises, all pretensions to human rights and privileges, are rendered insecure, if not lost, by this change so loudly talked of by some,

and inconsiderately by others. Is this tame relinquishment of rights worthy of freemen? Is it worthy of that manly fortitude that ought to characterize republicans? It is said eight states have adopted this plan. I declare that if twelve states and a half had adopted it, I would, with manly firmness, and in spite of an erring world, reject it.

You are not to inquire how your trade may be increased, nor how you are to become a great and powerful people, but how your liberties can be secured; for liberty ought to be the direct end of your government. Is it necessary for your liberty that you should abandon those great rights by the adoption of this system? Is the relinquishment of the trial by jury and the liberty of the press necessary for your liberty? Will the abandonment of your most sacred rights tend to the security of your liberty? Liberty, the greatest of all earthly blessings—give us that precious jewel, and you may take everything else.

* * * * * *

I shall be told I am continually afraid; but, sir, I have strong cause of apprehension. In some parts of the plan before you, the great rights of freemen are endangered, in other parts absolutely taken away. How does your trial by jury stand? In civil cases gone—not sufficiently secured in criminal—this best privilege is gone. But we are told that we need not fear, because those in power, being our representatives, will not abuse the powers we put in their hands. I am not well versed in history, but I will submit to your recollection whether liberty has been destroyed most often by the licentiousness of the people, or by the tyranny of rulers. I imagine, sir, you will find the balance on the side of tyranny. Happy will you be if you miss the fate of those nations, who, omitting to resist their oppressors, or negligently suffering their liberty to be wrested from them, have groaned under intolerable despotism!

Most of the human race are now in this deplorable condition. And those nations who have gone in search of grandeur, power, and splendour, have also fallen a sacrifice, and been the victims of their own folly. While they acquired those visionary blessings, they lost their freedom.

My great objection to this government is, that it does not leave us the means of defending our rights, or of waging war against tyrants. It is urged by some gentlemen, that this new plan will bring us an acquisition of strength; an army, and the militia of the States. This is an idea extremely ridiculous: gentlemen cannot be in earnest. This acquisition will trample on your fallen liberty. Let my beloved Americans guard against that fatal lethargy that has pervaded the universe. Have we the means of resisting disciplined armies, when our only defence, the militia, is put into the hands of Congress?

The honourable gentleman said that great danger would ensue if the convention rose without adopting this system. I ask, where is that danger? I see none. Other gentlemen have told us, within these walls, that the Union is gone—or that the Union will be gone. Is not this trifling with the judgment of their fellow-citizens? Till they tell us the ground of their fears I will consider them as imaginary. I rose to make inquiry where those dangers were; they could make no answer. I believe I never shall have that answer. Is there a disposition in the people of this country to revolt against the dominion of laws? Has there been a single tumult in Virginia? Have not the people of Virginia, when labouring under the severest pressure of accumulated distresses, manifested the most cordial acquiescence in the execution of the laws? What could be more lawful than their unanimous acquiescence under general distresses? Is there any revolution in Virginia? Whither is the spirit of America gone? Whither is the genius of America fled? It was but yesterday when our enemies marched in triumph through our country. Yet the people of this country could not be appalled by their pompous armaments; they stopped their career, and victoriously captured them. Where is the peril now compared to that?

Some minds are agitated by foreign alarms. Happily for us, there is no real danger from Europe: that country is engaged in more arduous business: from that quarter there is no cause of fear: you may sleep in safety for ever for them. Where is the danger? If, sir, there was any, I would recur to the American spirit to defend us—that spirit which has enabled us to surmount the greatest difficulties; to that illustrious spirit I address my most fervent prayer, to prevent our adopting a system destructive to liberty.

Let not gentlemen be told that it is not safe to reject this government. Wherefore is it not safe? We are told there are dangers; but those dangers are ideal; they cannot be demonstrated. To encourage us to adopt it, they tell us that there is a plain easy way of getting amendments. When I come to contemplate this part, I suppose that I am mad, or that my countrymen are so. The way to amendment is, in my conception, shut.

* * * * *

The honourable gentleman's observations, respecting the people's right of being the agents in the formation of this government, are not accurate, in my humble conception. The distinction between a national government and a confederacy is not sufficiently discerned. Had the delegates, who were sent to Philadelphia, a power to propose a consolidated government instead of a confederacy? Were they not deputed by States, and not by the people? The assent of the people, in their collective capacity, is not necessary to the formation of a federal government. The people have no right to enter into leagues, alliances, or confederations; they are not the proper agents for this purpose: states and sovereign powers are the only proper agents for this kind of government. Show me an instance where the people have exercised this business: has it not always gone through the legislatures? I refer you to the treaties with France, Holland, and other nations: how were they made? Were they not made by the States? Are the people, therefore, in their aggregate capacity, the proper persons to form a confederacy? This, therefore, ought to depend on the consent of the legislatures; the people having never sent delegates to make any proposition of changing the government. Yet I must say, at the same time, that it was made on grounds the most pure; and perhaps I might have been brought to consent to it, so far as to the change of government; but there is one thing in it which I never would acquiesce in. I mean, the changing it into a consolidated government, which is so abhorrent to my mind.

The honourable gentleman then went on to the figure we make with foreign nations; the contemptible one we make in France and Holland, which, according to the substance of my notes, he attributes to the present feeble government. An opinion has gone forth, we find, that we are a contemptible people: the time has been when we were thought otherwise. Under this same despised government, we commanded the respect of all Europe: wherefore are we now reckoned otherwise? The American spirit has fled from hence; it has gone to regions where it has never been expected; it has gone to the people of France, in search of a splendid government—a strong energetic government. Shall we imitate the example of those nations who have gone from a simple to a splendid government? Are those nations more worthy of our imitation? What can make an adequate satisfaction to them for the loss they have suffered in attaining such a government—for the loss of their liberty? If we admit this consolidated government, it will be because we like a great and splendid one. Some way or other we must be a great and mighty empire: we must have an army and a navy, and a number of things. When the American spirit was in its youth, the language of America was different: liberty, sir, was then the primary object. We are descended from a people whose government was founded on liberty; our glorious forefathers, of Great Britain, made liberty the foundation of everything. That country is become a great, mighty, and splendid nation; not because their government is strong and energetic; but, sir, because liberty is its direct end and foundation. We drew the spirit of liberty from our British ancestors; by that spirit we have triumphed over every difficulty. But now, sir, the American spirit, assisted by the ropes and chains of consolidation, is about to convert this country into a powerful and mighty empire. If you make the citizens of this country agree to become the subjects of one great consolidated empire of America, your government will not have sufficient energy to keep them together: such a government is incompatible with the genius of republicanism. There will be no checks, no real balances, in this government. What can avail your specious, imaginary balances; your rope-dancing, chain-rattling, ridiculous, ideal checks and contrivances? But, sir, we are not feared by foreigners; we do not make nations tremble. Would this constitute happiness, or secure liberty? I trust, sir, our political hemisphere will ever direct its operations to the security of those objects. Consider our situation, sir; go to the poor man; ask him what he does; he will inform you that he enjoys the fruits of his labour, under his own fig-tree, with his wife and children around him in peace and security. Go to every other member of the society: you will find the same tranquil ease and content; you will find no alarms or disturbances! Why, then, tell us of dangers, to terrify us into an adoption of this new form of government? And yet who knows the dangers that this new system may produce? They are out of the sight of the common people; they cannot foresee latent consequences. I dread the operation of it on the middling and lower classes of people; it is for them I fear the adoption of this system.

* * * * * *

The next clause of the Bill of Rights tells you, "that all power of suspending law, or the execution of laws, by any authority, without the consent of the representatives of the people, is injurious to their rights and ought not to be exercised." This tells us that there can be no suspension of government or laws without our own consent; yet this constitution can counteract and suspend any of our laws that contravene its oppressive operation; for they have the power of direct taxation, which suspends our Bill of Rights; and it is expressly provided that they can make all laws necessary for carrying their powers into execution; and it is declared paramount to the laws and constitutions of the States. Consider how the only remaining defence we have left is destroyed in this manner. Besides the expenses of maintaining the Senate and other house in as much splendour as they please, there is to be a great and mighty president, with very extensive powers—the powers of a king. He is to be supported in extravagant magnificence; so that the whole of our property may be taken by this American government, by laying what taxes they please, giving themselves what salaries they please, and suspending our laws at their pleasure.

I might be thought too inquisitive, but I believe I should take up but very little of your time in enumerating the little power that is left to the government of Virginia; for this power is reduced to little or nothing. Their garrisons, magazines, arsenals, and forts, which will be situated in the strongest places within the States—their ten miles square, with all the fine ornaments of human life, added to their powers and taken from the States, will reduce the power of the latter to nothing.

The voice of tradition I trust will inform posterity of our struggles for freedom. If our descendants be worthy the name of Americans, they will preserve and hand down to their latest posterity the transactions of the present times; and though I confess my exclamations are not worthy the hearing, they will see that I have done my utmost to preserve their liberty; for I never will give up the power of direct taxation but for a scourge. I am willing to give it conditionally; that is, after noncompliance with requisitions. I will do more, sir, and what I hope will convince the most sceptical man that I am a lover of the American Union; that in case Virginia shall not make punctual payment, the control of our custom-houses, and the whole regulation of trade, shall be given to Congress; and that Virginia shall depend on Congress even for passports, till Virginia shall have paid the last farthing, and furnished the last soldier.

Nay, sir, there is another alternative to which I would consent; even that they should strike us out of the Union, and take away from us all federal privileges till we comply with federal requisitions; but let it depend upon our own pleasure to pay our money in the most easy manner for our people. Were all the States, more terrible than the mother country, to join against us, I hope Virginia could defend herself; but, sir, the dissolution of the Union is most abhorrent to my mind. The first thing I have at heart is American liberty; the second thing is American union; and I hope the people of Virginia will endeavour to preserve that union. The increasing population of the Southern States is far greater than that of New England; consequently, in a short time, they will be far more numerous than the people of that country. Consider this, and you will find this State more particularly interested to support American liberty, and not bind our posterity by an improvident relinquishment of our rights. I would give the best security for a punctual compliance with requisitions; but I beseech gentlemen, at all hazards, not to grant this unlimited power of taxation.

* * * * *

This constitution is said to have beautiful features; but when I come to examine these features, sir, they appear to me horribly frightful. Among other deformities, it has an awful squinting; it squints towards monarchy: and does not this raise indignation in the breast of every true American? Your President may easily become king. Your senate is so imperfectly constructed, that your dearest rights may be sacrificed by what may be a small minority; and a very small minority may continue for ever unchangeably this government, although horridly defective. Where are your checks in this government? Your strongholds will be in the hands of your enemies. It is on a supposition that your American governors shall be honest, that all the good qualities of this government are founded; but its defective and imperfect construction puts it in their power to perpetrate the worst of mischief, should they be bad men. And, sir, would not all the world, from the eastern to the western hemisphere, blame our distracted folly in resting our rights upon the contingency of our rulers being good or bad? Show me that age and country where the rights and liberties of the people were placed on the sole chance of their rulers being good men, without a consequent loss of liberty. I say that the loss of that dearest privilege has ever followed, with absolute certainty, every such mad attempt.

If your American chief be a man of ambition and abilities, how easy will it be for him to render himself absolute! The army is in his hands, and, if he be a man of address, it will be attached to him; and it will be the subject of long meditation with him to seize the first auspicious moment to accomplish his design. And, sir, will the American spirit solely relieve you when this happens? I would rather infinitely—and I am sure most of this convention are of the same opinion—have a king, lords, and commons, than a government so replete with such insupportable evils. If we make a king, we may prescribe the rules by which he shall rule his people, and interpose such checks as shall prevent him from infringing them; but the President in the field, at the head of his army, can prescribe the terms on which he shall reign master, so far that it will puzzle any American ever to get his neck from under the galling yoke.

I cannot, with patience, think of this idea. If ever he violates the laws, one of two things will happen: he will come at the head of his army to carry everything before him; or, he will give bail, or do what Mr. Chief Justice will order him. If he be guilty, will not the recollection of his crimes teach him to make one bold push for the American throne? Will not the immense difference between being master of everything, and being ignominiously tried and punished, powerfully excite him to make this bold push? But, sir, where is the existing force to punish him? Can he not, at the head of his army, beat down every opposition? Away with your President! We shall have a king; the army will salute him monarch; your militia will leave you, and assist in making him king, and fight against you; and what have you to oppose this force? What will then become of you and your rights? Will not absolute despotism ensue?

WILLIAM WINDHAM.

Born 1750. *Died* 1810.

[Of the oratorical style of Windham, Canning is reported to have said, that if it was not the most eloquent, it certainly was the most insinuating that he had heard in the House of Commons. The following short speech, which is reprinted verbatim, was delivered in Parliament at the close of the year 1806, when Windham, in his official capacity of Secretary at War, called the attention of the House of Commons to the victory which had been achieved on the plains of Maida by a small body of troops under the command of Sir John Stuart. As representing that chivalrous spirit in which Windham always advocated any measure tending to increase either the glory or welfare of the British Army, this speech has now a deeper meaning and interest than were given to it even by the stirring circumstances by which it was inspired.]

ON MOVING THE THANKS OF THE HOUSE TO SIR JOHN STUART AFTER THE BATTLE OF MAIDA, 22ND DEC., 1806.

SIR,—In pursuance of my notice on Friday last, I rise to move that the thanks of this House be given to Major-General Sir John Stuart, and to the officers and men who served under him in the glorious battle of Maida. In saying this, I conceive, indeed, I have said all that is strictly necessary, in order to carry with me the unanimous concurrence of the House; and so lively, so proper, and so general a feeling has manifested itself on this subject throughout the country, that I feel assured the motion will be received, not only with unanimity in Parliament, but with marked and complete approbation from all Englishmen.

Sir, I may safely venture to pronounce the action to which I am referring to have been one of the most distinguished exploits that has ever graced the annals of this or any other country.

Every man must be so impressed with its character and importance, that it is altogether unnecessary for me to dwell upon its value. If I venture to say anything upon the subject, it is purely from an impulse to give indulgence to my feelings. The character of the exploit itself, and the advantages which have flowed from it, must present themselves to the sober reflection of every man; and indeed, this House and the country at large have already, by their admiration and gratitude, pronounced upon the value of the glorious achievement. Amongst the various views in which this victory can be considered, there is not one which does not raise it to a level even with the memorable days of Cressy, of Poitiers, and of Agincourt. In mentioning these scenes of British fame and valour, I cannot omit to remark one peculiar character which belongs to this distinguished service, namely, the accession it has produced to our stock of national glory—the most valuable possession of a great people. Other services may make a greater figure, in relation to their effect in adding to national importance, by acquisitions of strength, resources, or territory, though not of a character to call for the sort of honours and distinctions merited by achievements of this kind. In this respect, the value and importance of the engagement is highly augmented, even in the midst of those splendid and brilliant triumphs to which this country has been so much accustomed. The glory acquired in this action has not often been equalled, nor ever surpassed, in the records of military renown.

Of what value it is to keep up this high character for military spirit—how necessary it is to encourage it with every honourable distinction of public approbation and gratitude—how impossible it is for any great country to preserve its character and independence without the possession of such feelings—these are topics upon which I feel that it is unnecessary for me to dwell; but if ever there was a period of the world when a strong military feeling was required for the preservation of the greatness and glory of a country, this is that period. We have reached an age when the whole world has become, as it were, one universal camp; when all nations are occupied with military views, military fame, and military services; when these warlike pursuits are substituted in the place of the civil arts of life; when no country can be safe that does not cultivate them, and when any country that rejects them can no longer hope to preserve its independence. We are come to that state of society when, as has been well said, "the soldier is abroad;" when, in the language of the poet, "man and steel, the soldier and his sword," are the only productions of a country that can be looked to with confidence for its protection and security.

Sir, it is not because we have lost any part of the military spirit or character of the country, that I dwell with such pride on the value of this exploit; certainly not. This country has never forfeited its just character for military superiority. Yet, from the circumstances under which the war has been hitherto carried on, and the pre-eminence of our great and glorious naval actions, we have not had the same opportunities of distinguishing our arms by land as by sea. The nations of the continent, too, as if their humiliation found relief in the opinion, seem to have been glad to persuade themselves that our military power, in the largest sense of the word, is wholly confined to naval operations. They seem to think that this country is, I shall not say proportionably weak, but that it is not proportionably strong by land as by sea. Now, it is the immediate tendency and effect of the battle of Maida to meet these opinions, and to correct the error in which they have originated; for it is impossible to contemplate this glorious exploit in all its circumstances, and not give way to a feeling of triumph at the superiority of national valour displayed in it.

Yet it may be said that it was not by naked valour that the skill, the discipline, and the experience of the veteran troops of the enemy were to be overcome. It results from the experience of this action that British disciplined troops possess a decided superiority over those of the enemy. Many persons in this country appear to entertain, and in their writings avow, the opinion, that the troops of the enemy are superior to the British. This opinion is flattering to the enemy; but I trust that it has not gone far in the country, and I am convinced that it has not made any impression upon the people or the army. British soldiers are strangers to any feelings that would prevent them, whenever they come in contact with the enemy upon nearly equal terms, from making British valour as conspicuous by land as by sea.

Sir, it is a general opinion that all our naval exploits have been achieved by a superiority of experienced discipline and skill; but I cannot subscribe to such a position. Many of those heroic achievements, which have raised the glory of our navy to the highest pitch, have been effected by the naked valour of Britons, without the aid of skill or discipline. Of this description are the exploits performed in boarding ships, in cutting out vessels from under the protection of batteries, and in various other operations performed by British seamen on shore, in every one of which the native valour of our own countrymen is uniformly triumphant. There are no such instances to be found recorded in the military annals of other nations. Yet our enemies have persuaded other countries that they are as superior to us by land, as we are to them by sea; and this delusion seems hitherto to have prevailed. But the battle of Maida has broken the charm: every circumstance of its progress, the conduct of the officers, and the bravery of the men, have established the ascendancy of British valour, and maintained that superiority which in all ages this country has really and justly possessed. Let me but appeal, in proof of this, to the determination of Sir John Stuart to advance with his inferior force to the attack even of the strong position of the enemy, in case that enemy had not advanced to meet him. The issue of the action that ensued proved to the General and to the troops of the enemy, who arrogated to themselves a superiority over all the troops of the world, that they were not invincible—that they could not withstand the valour of British troops, when fairly opposed to them in action; and yet, from whatever causes (certainly not from want of courage in their adversaries), the events of the late war have contributed to countenance this opinion of their being invincible. They conquered because they thought they could conquer. "*Possunt quia posse videntur.*" This victory, however, has dissolved the spell. It has been obtained, in the face of Europe, in the view of the nation for whose interest the expedition was undertaken, and has proved to the world, in a manner not to be disguised or concealed, that French troops are inferior to British.

It is here necessary to take some precaution for guarding against any possible misconstruction of my meaning. Nothing can be further from my intention than to represent this exploit as exclusively glorious for the reputation of the British arms. The whole of the campaign in Egypt was equally conspicuous for the lustre it cast upon the military character of the British nation. The achievement now under our consideration condenses into a single action all the same merits that were displayed in every operation of that glorious campaign. It is a lesson to this country, to the enemy, and to the world, of the comparative value of British and of French troops, and it thoroughly confirms the decisive superiority of British valour. There never was an action so perfectly framed, so completely calculated, in all its circumstances, to establish this important truth. I cannot more forcibly illustrate this fact than by adopting the eloquent language of Sir John Stuart. "It seemed," said the gallant General, in his dispatch, "as if the prowess of the two nations was to be brought to trial before the world." Certainly no action under any circumstances could be better calculated for such a trial. If two sets of philosophers had undertaken to make an experiment, by doing away everything extraneous to their process, they could not have succeeded more accurately. In the first part of the action the two armies advanced against each other with the bayonet; an operation which, though much talked of, very seldom takes place between great bodies of men. Every circumstance, even in the most minute detail, that had happened previously to the shock, concurred to bring the courage and intrepidity of the two rival nations to the trial. The contest was decided, not by any superiority of corporal strength, but by the predominance of personal intrepidity. Both armies advanced firmly to the charge, until within half a yard of each other. In this moment of perilous trial, British resolution and valour held out, and the enemy shrunk back with panic from the terrible contest. It will not be improper for me to state here, that hardly any of our men were wounded by the bayonet.

Sir, I fear I have to apologize to the House for having trespassed so long on their attention; but really the theme is so pleasing that I cannot refrain from dwelling upon it with peculiar satisfaction. The detail of the action exhibits merits of all sorts, equally honourable to the skill of the officers and to the firmness and valour of the soldiers. Having been led thus far by the natural pleasure which one feels in speaking of so grateful a subject, I shall detain the House no longer than while I can relate to them some circumstances respecting the action which are not generally known.

By the circumstances which I am about to state to you, it will appear that this victory has been more decisive, and the defeat of the enemy more complete, than was at first supposed. Sir John Stuart correctly stated the amount of his own force as under 5,000 men; but when he wrote his dispatch he had not the means of accurately ascertaining the force of the enemy. He estimated it as approaching to 7,000, but he would have been right in stating it at nearly 8,000 men. This fact has been discovered from returns found upon the persons of some of the officers who fell. The next circumstance I have to mention relates to the amount of the enemy's loss. Sir John Stuart stated the numbers of the killed at 700; but it was afterwards ascertained, by observations made upon the spot, that there were killed in the action not fewer than 1,300 men. Fifteen hundred prisoners were the immediate fruit of the action, and a considerable number more fell into our hands from the consequences of it. So that thus a number nearly equal to the whole British force has been disposed of by this brilliant victory. Another consequence of the exploit has been, to set the Calabrians free from the presence of the enemy, and totally to break up the force of General Regnier in those provinces, amounting to 13,000 men.

It is not necessary, perhaps, to dwell so much

on the advantages which have resulted from this battle, but the glory that has been acquired in it I consider of infinitely greater importance than any of its immediate benefits. This it is which will carry the effect of this brilliant exploit beyond its temporary fame, by placing above the reach of doubt the military renown of the country. He who gives glory to his country gives it that which is far more valuable to it than any acquisition whatever. Glory alone is not to be taken away by time or accident. Ships, territories, possessions, may be wrested from a country, but the mode of acquiring them can never be forgotten, and the glory of the conquest is independent of all accidents. The acquisitions that were the consequences of the glorious days of Cressy and Poitiers have long since passed into other hands, but the glory of those illustrious achievements still adheres to the British name, and is immortal. It is that fine extract, that pure essence which endures to all ages, while the grosser parts, the residuum, may pass away, and be lost in the course of time. On this ground it is that I trust the victory of Maida will stand as high as any exploit upon the records of our military achievements, and that the glory of General Stuart and his brave army will survive to the latest posterity, unless the country shall at any future time sink into such a state of degradation that the memory of former glory will become a reproach to existing degeneracy. Yet even at a period so degraded as that which I am supposing, the recollection of the victory of Maida would be calculated to rouse a degenerate race to emulate the glory of their ancestors. The name of General Stuart will justly be ranked amongst the foremost in our military annals.

Sir, I have felt pleasure in dwelling upon the various merits of this brilliant exploit, because it has revived and resuscitated, as it were, that half of our national character which has been called in question, and because it has proved that Britons have the same superiority over the enemy by land that they have by sea. I will conclude by moving,

1st. That the thanks of this House be given to Major-General Sir John Stuart, Knight of the most honourable Order of the Bath, for the distinguished ability displayed by him on the 4th of July last, in the brilliant action on the plains of Maida, which terminated in the signal and total defeat of the superior forces of the enemy.

2nd. That the thanks of this House be given to Brigadier-General the Honourable George Lowry Cole, Brigadier-General William Palmer Ackland, and the several other officers, for their distinguished exertions on the 4th of July last, in the brilliant action on the plains of Maida, which terminated in the signal and total defeat of the superior forces of the enemy; and that Major-General Sir John Stuart do signify the same to them.

3rd. That this House doth highly approve of and acknowledge the distinguished valour and discipline displayed by the non-commissioned officers and private soldiers of the forces serving on the 4th of July last, under the command of Major-General Sir John Stuart, in the brilliant victory obtained on the plains of Maida, and that the same be signified to them by the commanding officers of the several corps, who are desired to thank them for their gallant and exemplary conduct.

MARIE ANTOINETTE.

It is now sixteen or seventeen years since I saw the Queen of France; then the Dauphiness, at Versailles; and surely never lighted on this orb, which she hardly seemed to touch, a more delightful vision. I saw her just above the horizon, decorating and cheering the elevated sphere she just began to move in—glittering like the morning star, full of life, and splendour, and joy. Oh! what a revolution! and what a heart must I have, to contemplate without emotion that elevation and that fall! Little did I dream when she added titles of veneration to those of enthusiastic, distant, respectful love, that she should ever be obliged to carry the sharp antidote against disgrace concealed in that bosom; little did I dream that I should have lived to see such disasters fallen upon her in a nation of gallant men, in a nation of men of honour, and of cavaliers. I thought ten thousand swords must have leaped from their scabbards to avenge even a look that threatened her with insult. But the age of chivalry is gone! That of sophisters, economists, and calculators has succeeded; and the glory of Europe is extinguished for ever! Never, never more shall we behold that generous loyalty to rank and sex, that proud submission, that dignified obedience, that subordination of the heart which kept alive, even in servitude itself, the spirit of an exalted freedom. The unbought grace of life, the cheap defence of nations, the nurse of manly sentiment and heroic enterprise, is gone! It is gone, that sensibility of principle, that chastity of honour, which felt a stain like a wound, which inspired courage whilst it mitigated ferocity, which ennobled whatever it touched, and under which vice itself lost half its evil, by losing all its grossness.—*Burke.*

Men, till a matter be done, wonder that it can be done; and as soon as it is done, wonder again that it was no sooner done.—*Bacon.*

LORD LYNDHURST.

Born 1772. Died 1863.

[The oratorical style of John Singleton Copley, first and last Lord Lyndhurst was so well described by an able critic writing in the *Times* newspaper, shortly after the death of his great subject, that we cannot do better than quote a portion of his remarks here. "Many orators," he observes, "have exceeded Lord Lyndhurst in the brilliancy of particular passages; but in the art of treating a subject as a whole, and leaving on his audience his own impression of the whole and of every part, he is, as far as we know, unrivalled. He disdained ornament, exaggeration, or metaphor; his language was clear, precise, and elegant; but such as might have been expected rather from a cotemporary of Demosthenes, than an English orator of the nineteenth century. He was his own best critic, and had cultivated his taste up to the standard of his other intellectual powers. He was neither dazzled by vanity, nor misled by passion; his temper was as serene as his intellect was clear, and his speeches left little or nothing upon which his antagonists could found an attack or an answer. Indeed, whoever has heard Lord Lyndhurst on a great occasion, has probably enjoyed the very best opportunity which modern times afford of estimating the style and manner of the great orators of classical antiquity." Sir Bulwer Lytton also, in his fine descriptive poem of "St. Stephen's," from which quotation has already been made in this volume, alludes with admiration to what he there styles "Lyndhurst's lofty sense." These encomiums, high as they are, will, we think, be fully borne out by the speech which we have here given. As will be observed on reading it, this was one of those celebrated Sessional Reviews which Lord Lyndhurst, in the zenith of his power and fame, was in the habit of delivering, and which were always looked forward to as among the most characteristic features of the Parliamentary year. The occasion of its delivery was in the autumn of 1839, and shortly after Lord Melbourne's return to power, that minister having tendered his resignation on the previous 8th of May, but again assumed office on the 10th of the same month. The speech, though necessarily treating chiefly of the topics of the time, is perhaps as good an illustration of the speaker's own peculiar manner as could be found in the wide range of his addresses, which have, we believe, never yet been published in a collected form. We may add that, as a pamphlet, it passed through more than twenty editions, and is now reprinted in its entirety.]

A REVIEW OF THE SESSION. DELIVERED IN THE HOUSE OF LORDS, 23RD AUGUST, 1839.

I AM anxious, my lords, to call your attention, in pursuance of the notice I gave yesterday, to the proceedings of the two Houses of Parliament during the present session. As far as I am personally concerned, the task is by no means an agreeable one; but I have undertaken it as a duty—in some sort as a duty which I owe to the noble Viscount (Melbourne), and in pursuance also, in some degree, of an intimation which I received from him in a former period of this session. Your lordships may, perhaps, recollect that when the Irish Municipal Bill was under discussion, I stated to your lordships, in considerable detail, some circumstances relative to the tardy, unsteady course of this bill through the other House of Parliament. The noble viscount, on a subsequent day, with reference to that statement, and also some similar remarks made by my noble and learned friend opposite (Lord Brougham), said that was an unfair course of observation; that I ought to consider, not that particular case alone, but that I should take into account the general proceedings and measures of the Government. My lords, I felt at that time the propriety of the observations made by the noble viscount; and I shall, therefore, in pursuance of that intimation, in justice to the subject, and in justice to the noble viscount himself, call your lordships' attention to the entire proceedings of the present session of Parliament, in order that, when the case is fairly before you, stated with perfect plainness and simplicity on my part, your lordships may be in a condition to judge how far her Majesty's Ministers are entitled to your confidence—how far they can be considered as capable of conducting the affairs of this country in a manner suitable to the extent and importance of this mighty empire. My lords, in directing your attention to this subject, there is one thing that is very remarkable. Your lordships will find, that during the first five months of the session, not a single bill of any importance whatever, passed the two Houses of Parliament. Legislation was a perfect blank. My lords, it seems that her Majesty's Ministers, either from want of energy or want of confidence from the other House of Parliament, are, while that House can be considered as fairly representing the country, incapable of dealing with it and conducting the business of the Government. It is not until the benches have become empty, not until 550 members, as we are told, have quitted the metropolis, and the House consists of little more than a Government board, are they roused from their supineness, or able to conduct in any form whatever the legislation of the country. This, my lords, is a striking illustration of a statement made by anticipation by my noble friend, the noble duke below, when he asked, at a former period, with reference to a House of Commons composed as the present is—how is the King's Government to be carried on? The anticipation of the noble duke has been amply verified by the result; for as long as the House of Commons continues to be a House of Commons, or the form of the representation of the country what it is, the Queen's Government cannot be carried on, and it is not until it ceases to assume that shape that anything like legislation can be conducted through that House by her Majesty's Ministers. My lords, I consider the fair mode of examining the question I am about to submit to your lordships is, to refer, in the first instance, to her Majesty's speech, which must be considered, of course, as the speech of the Ministers, pronounced at the opening of this session. My lords, I look to that speech for the purpose of ascertaining what were the views of the Government, and what the measures they considered essential to the interests of the country; and looking to the Queen's speech with that view, let us inquire to what extent the pledges given in it have been redeemed by her Majesty's Government. In that speech, my lords, there are four principal points to which the attention of Parliament was particularly directed. The Irish Municipal Bill, we were told, was essential to the interests of that part of the empire; we were called to take measures for the purpose of settling the important affairs of Canada; we were told that to carry into effect the recommendations of the Ecclesiastical Commissioners was a matter of great urgency; we were further told that it was a matter of the greatest importance that we should direct our attention to measures for the more speedy and certain administration of justice. These, my lords, were the prominent topics of her Majesty's speech; and I am desirous of leading your lordships through the course of the proceedings of this session, to show how far these particular objects, to which our attention was expressly directed, have been realized. And first, my lords, with respect to the Irish Municipal Bill. It is not my intention to enter into any details on that question. It came up to your lordships' House; it was amended in a manner to make it correspond or nearly with the bill of last session. What was the course pursued by the noble viscount? What was the objection he made and put in front of the battle with respect to the amendments proposed by your lordships? One amendment was made with respect to the freemen; and it is a remarkable circumstance, showing how forgetful noble lords opposite must be of the past history of this bill—exactly the same amendment was made last session; it met with no opposition from Government; it went down to the other House of Parliament; although many objections were urged against the bill in its amended shape in the House of Commons, none whatever was made against that clause: and yet now, so inconsistent were Ministers with themselves, that the amendment which before had been acquiesced in, to which no objection was even whispered by the Government, was put prominently forward, in very front of the battle, as a ground for rejecting the bill! This is not all. Another amendment was propounded and opposed with great zeal and earnestness. That amendment was with respect to the mode of choosing the sheriffs. It turned out that three years ago the noble viscount himself made, in a former bill, precisely the same amendment, and defended it upon just and constitutional grounds; but now, because the amendment proceeded from this side of the House, the noble viscount turned round and gave it his most decided opposition. So much, my lords, for the consistency of her Majesty's Ministers, and the manner in which they have treated this bill. I ascribe it to thoughtlessness, to indifference, a want of recollection, a carelessness about a measure they told us in the speech from the throne was so "essential" to the interests of Ireland. But there was another amendment made by your lordships, the effect of which was to strike out a number of clauses that had been introduced into the bill for the first time in the House of Commons. These clauses were never heard of till the present year; they related to the grand jury cess, the powers of which were to be transferred to the town-councils. They were not even introduced into the bill when it was first brought into the House of Commons; but in that memorable committee of the 19th of April, they were for the first time ingrafted on the bill. We objected to that alteration; we said, let the law in this respect remain as it is; we struck out those clauses. The noble viscount told us it would defeat the bill in another place. I said that is impossible; it is an assumption of privilege and power to which we never can subscribe. You introduce clauses which you call money clauses, and ingraft them on a bill; we strike them out, and say let the law remain as it is, and we are told that is to be fatal to the whole measure. When the bill went down to the other House, those clauses did prove fatal to the measure; but it is worthy of remark, that at the very time these clauses were objected to, it was stated that they might be the subject of a separate bill. They ought to have been the subject of a separate bill. To ingraft them, to tack them on the Municipal Bill was an attack on the privileges of this House. My lords, it was a clumsy attack, and if done with design, could only have been intended to keep on foot something that might be considered in some quarters as a grievance of which the Government might avail themselves as occasion might require. Her Majesty's Ministers are themselves responsible for the loss of this bill. The tacking of such clauses to such a bill was a clumsy act; it was advised by Ministers, and led to the loss of the measure. They, therefore, have defeated a measure calculated, according to their own statement, to promote the interests of Ireland. So much, my lords, with respect to the first measure alluded to in her Majesty's speech from the throne. Now, as to the second —the measures called for by the state of Canada—we all felt that nothing could be more pressing and more urgent than the necessity for taking that most important matter into consideration early in the session. Every hour's delay we felt, and what has since occurred has confirmed the propriety of our opinion, added to the difficulty of the subject. Noble lords hastened up to this house from all parts of the country and the continent for the purpose of being present at the earliest moment during the discussion of this important question. But nothing was done. A few personal discussions took place, and the matter ended. At last, however, at an advanced period of the session, we were told that the plan for settling the Canadas was matured—the plan came forth. A constitution was to be provided for the two provinces, which were to be united into one; the plan was to come into effect at the expiration of three years—in 1842. The temporary government was to be continued till that time, and then it became, as a matter of course, necessary, from the extension of the temporary government, that some further powers should be given to the Governor, in order to provide for local improvement. Thus the matter rested, and continued for some time in suspense. Intimation, however, was given, that there would be an opposition to the measure proposed by Ministers. It was found it would be a vigorous opposition. The measure as to the constitution was abandoned. We were told it was abandoned in consequence of information that had suddenly been received from Canada. What that information was has never been communicated to your lordships or the other House of Parliament; and anybody that will take the pains to trace the proceedings in Canada for the last six months will find that nothing had occurred at that period to alter the state of things with reference to that country as far as related to this measure. With the bill fell also the other part of the scheme, which was, to continue the temporary government for a period of three years. But then it was necessary that something should be done — that at least there should be an appearance of legislating for Canada. Therefore it was that that bill, that fragment of a measure, which passed the other House of Parliament, was submitted to your consideration; but so little importance did her Majesty's Ministers attach to it, that even the noble lord who had the conduct of the measure was utterly unacquainted with its provisions, and could not explain them to your lordships. It must be desirable, if the temporary government of Canada should be prolonged for three years, to give extended powers to the Governor for the purpose of preventing improvements from being at a stand-still; but as the bill is now framed, legislation will not take place until the next spring, when it will be incumbent on your lordships to legislate again on Canada, because in the course of the next year the powers of the Governor under the former bill expire. The bill was altogether idle and unnecessary. It was introduced merely for the purpose of making a show of legislation. So much, my lords, for the redemption of their pledge—so much for the conduct of her Majesty's Government on this important, grave, serious subject—the settlement of the affairs of Canada! With respect, my lords, to the third subject referred to in her Majesty's speech, there is an absolute blank—there is not even a show of legislation. We were to take measures for carrying into effect the recommendation of the Ecclesiastical Commissioners. A bill was brought into the other House of Parliament for that purpose; it was read a second time; it proceeded on a false assumption of facts; it was abandoned; nothing has been done with respect to it. In the speech from the throne it is described as a measure most urgently called for; the recommendation was followed up to the stage I have announced, and by the act of the Ministers themselves, the measure was abandoned; they have done nothing on the subject. The fourth topic, my lords, referred to in the Queen's speech was one of the first importance. Measures were said to be in preparation to provide for the more certain and speedy administration of justice—a subject, my lords, of paramount importance. What has been done in that respect? As in the case of the recommendation of the Ecclesiastical Commissioners, literally nothing! My lords, upwards of two months ago I thought it my duty to call your attention most seriously to the state of the business of the Court of Chancery. There is no court, there are no proceedings in any court, to which the recommendation of the commissioners so strongly applied as to the Court of Chancery. I brought that case under your lordships' consideration. I stated the immense arrear of business in that court, and the remedy that was required. The terms I made use of with respect to the state of that court were, that it had become grievous and intolerable. A noble and learned friend of mine, the Master of the Rolls (Lord Langdale), adverting to those terms, said they were strong terms; but they were not strong enough to denote and describe the extent of the evil, and it is impossible to form an adequate idea of the cruelty of this system, unless you direct your attention to some particular case; then only will you find, by its details, how individuals, how families are ruined, and their prospects blighted, by the magnitude of the evil. Don't let it be supposed for a moment that I am finding fault with the learned judges of that court: they are all persons faithful in the discharge of their respective duties—vigorous, active, able men. But they have no power to cope with the evil: the force of the court for that purpose is not sufficient—that is avowed by every one; and when I brought the matter forward, I stated a plan for the purpose of remedying the evil, which I understood was assented to by my noble and learned friend on the woolsack and by her Majesty's Ministers. It was assented to by my noble and learned friend opposite (Lord Brougham); and I did expect—I understood we had something like a pledge, that some bill would be brought in during the present session of Parliament for remedying the intolerable evil complained of. It was stated by my noble and learned friend on the woolsack, that I did not go far enough; but he was willing, as I understood, to try what I proposed, which, to a considerable extent, would remedy the evil of the present system; but from that time to this, we have heard nothing from her Majesty's Ministers on the subject. They have not touched this grievance, this intolerable grievance. The more speedy and certain administration of justice was stated to be a matter of the first importance in the Queen's speech; the attention of your lordships and of Ministers was directed to the subject; we had a kind of pledge that it would be immediately attended to; from that time to the present no steps whatever have been taken to carry the pledge into effect. But, my lords, it may be said that Ministers have been engaged upon other measures for reforming the law and rendering the administration of justice both speedy and certain. I look around in vain for anything as the fruit and result of their labour, if labour it can be called. I find no bill has been introduced into this house, or passed the two houses, on the subject. None has been presented to us for consideration. The whole is a blank! There is, indeed, a measure which has been lingering through Parliament for three sessions, relative to bankrupt estates in Scotland, and to which no opposition was offered in this house. There was also a bill for the purpose of increasing the salaries and making some trifling alterations in the Supreme Court of Scotland. But neither of these bills apply to England: with respect to England, there has been no attempt to redeem the pledge which her Majesty's Ministers held out in the speech from the throne. With respect to a subject which they themselves considered of so much importance, they have done nothing to effect the more speedy and certain administration of justice. Seeing the noble baron on the woolsack, it occurs to me that this supineness has extended also to him. The noble baron directed a commission to inquire into the state of the Court of Chancery within his jurisdiction: no report has yet been made, nothing has been done; matters stand precisely where they did. My Lords, I have now gone through the particulars of the Queen's speech. I have stated to you what were the promises and pledges of her Majesty's Ministers at the commencement of the session; and I have shown you what has been the performance, or rather I should say, the absence of all performance, on their part. What is the conclusion to be drawn from such a state of things?—Obviously this: Her Majesty's Ministers, at the commencement of the session, threw out deliberately, and in terms, a statement of the opinion which they entertained as to what measures of legislation the interests of the country required; they stated in substance, by being parties to that speech, that the country had a right to expect from a vigorous and an able Administration that these measures should be carried into effect. Not one of them has been accomplished! They have, by pursuing this course, pronounced their own condemnation. They have pronounced judgment on themselves — *habes confitentem reum;* and yet, my lords, these Ministers still continue to hold the reins of government without being able to guide the vessel of the state.

———— Versate diu, quid ferre recusent
Quid valeant humeri

is good advice, not to poets alone; it applies, above all, to persons in the situation of the noble viscount. To undertake the management of the affairs of a great empire without having vigour, capacity, or confidence of Parliament to carry through such measures as are necessary to the interests of the country, is considered by the constitution of these realms a high misdemeanour, rendering the parties liable to be proceeded against by impeachment. And yet this is the course which has been pursued by the present Government. So much then, my lords, as to the measures referred to in the Queen's speech. The Ministers found that it was necessary to attempt something—something to captivate a portion at least of their followers; and it occurred to them that nothing was so well adapted to that purpose as some measure on the subject of general education—a matter, my lords, of the first importance, and deeply interesting to the welfare of the country. What course would an enlightened, able, and straightforward Ministry have pursued with respect to this important subject? They had an example set them by my noble and learned friend opposite, who pursued the very course I am about to point out. It was their duty to have prepared a bill, and to have given time for the consideration of its details, not only in Parliament, but also out of doors. That was the course which a manly, able, and constitutional Government would have pursued; but such a course would not have consisted either with the feelings, or the principles, or even the habits, of her Majesty's present advisers. They left the plain, beaten highroad, in order to deviate, as is their custom, into obscure and tortuous by-paths. Availing themselves of, and at the same time abusing, the confidence which your lordships are always inclined to place in the other House of Parliament, they proceeded, by a vote of that House, carried only by a majority of two, to appoint a committee of general instruction to superintend the great national affair of education. This policy they pursued for the express, I had almost said the avowed, purpose of excluding your lordships from all deliberation on this most important of all-important subjects. Looking at the composition of your lordships' House, do I say too much, when I say that no assembly in the world is better qualified to consider, to discuss, and to advise on such a subject than the House of Peers of this realm? Yet the policy—the little policy I must call it—of her Majesty's Ministers has been to exclude you, my lords, from all consideration of it, and to proceed exclusively on the vote of the other House of Parliament. Of whom, then, I would ask you, does this committee of education consist? There is, first of all, her Majesty's Chancellor of the Exchequer; then there is the noble viscount at the head of the Board of Works, who generally does the work of Government in this House; then there is the noble Secretary of State for the Home Department; and lastly, as a matter of course, there is the noble President of the Council. This is the board of public instruction; this is the board which has to form a plan and to digest a scheme for the superintendence of the general education of this mighty nation. I entertain the greatest possible respect for these individuals in their private capacity; yet I must say of them, in their public capacity, that they are not a body nor a description of individuals who would have been selected, either by the nation or by individuals, for the management of a scheme of education of this character. We find, my lords, in their very first publication, that one of them is ignorant, grossly ignorant, of the very forms of the art which he has undertaken to superintend. What, my lords, was their very first act? They published a scheme of little importance, if considered by itself—it was circulated throughout the country, and it met with signal, nay, with universal reprobation; and that too, not only in England, but also in the more northerly parts of this island. So strong was the feeling excited against it, that though her Majesty's Ministers endeavoured to bribe the General Assembly of the Church of Scotland by giving them the disposal of three hundred livings, they passed a unanimous vote in condemnation of the scheme of Government. Your lordships then thought it to be your duty to address the throne upon the subject; not because you had been treated with indignity by her Majesty's Ministers, but because you thought that you ought to be consulted, and to form part of the body by which a general system of education was to be established. You addressed the throne, my lords, and I rejoice that you did so, and for this reason, that we discovered thereby what are the objects and designs contemplated by her Majesty's advisers. It might have been supposed that this board of instruction was a mere transient body, appointed to dispose of a sum of 30,000*l*. intrusted to its disposal by a vote of the House of Commons; but the answer which the noble viscount advised her Majesty to give to our address lets us into the secret that this system is intended to be permanent; for it tells us that the proceedings of the board are to be laid annually on the table of both Houses of Parliament. You are establishing, then, by a vote of the House of Commons alone, a permanent system of education, and a permanent scheme for the superintendence of that system. As to the other part of the answer which the noble viscount advised her Majesty to give to our address, it is a mere mockery, though I can hardly suppose that it was intended to be so by the noble viscount. You complained, my lords, that you had not been consulted, and that you had not been allowed to exercise any judgment upon the subject; and what did the noble viscount advise her Majesty to say to you in reply?— "Oh, you shall have ample time given you for exercising your judgment, for the proceedings of the board shall be annually laid on your table, and submitted to you for consideration." Now, my lords, what did every man in the realm suppose to be your meaning when you spoke of exercising your judgment on this subject? You meant, and it was known that you meant, a judgment coupled with control—not a judgment without fruit, not a judgment unaccompanied by any practical result. It was then a sneer and a mockery—for I will not use a more harsh expression—it was a sneer and a mockery to tell you that you should be enabled to exercise your judgment upon these annual reports, though I can hardly bring myself to suppose that it was intended to be such by the noble viscount. I pass, my lords, from this subject to another of no inconsiderable importance—to another measure of legislation. The subject to which I have just adverted was a measure of legislation by one House of Parliament, for which your lordships may indeed find a precedent, but it is a precedent drawn from times of tumult and disorder, which I am sure that the noble viscount will not wish to repeat. I come now to another measure of legislation—the first Jamaica Bill. Let us look, my lords, a little closely to the history of that measure.—We had interfered with the privileges of the Colonial Assembly of Jamaica on internal legislation without necessity. The Colonial Assembly did what they thought that they were entitled to do, in consequence of our interference, and what they had often done before successfully under similar circumstances. They presented an address to the Crown, and they stated in that address, that they would proceed to no work of legislation except such as related to the maintenance of public credit until they received an answer to that address. The consequence was, that they were immediately prorogued, and that they were kept under prorogation, and that they never afterwards had an opportunity to do anything in the way of legislation. What, then, did her Majesty's Ministers advise, under such circumstances? Any redress of alleged grievances? Any retractation of rights asserted? Any communication with the Colonial Assembly whatever? No—nothing but a bill to annihilate for ever the constitution of Jamaica. I say, a bill to annihilate the constitution of Jamaica for ever; for, though that bill was nominally intended for nothing more than the suspension of that constitution for five years, every one is aware that the practical result of such a measure would have been its complete extinction at the end of that period. That measure, however, was too strong and too despotic even for the other House of Parliament. A reformed House of Commons—itself a representative assembly—could not consent to abolish another representative assembly, which had been long established in one of our colonies. The bill, on its second reading, was only carried by a majority of five. It was, therefore, considered as lost, and so in point of substance it was. What was the course pursued by her Majesty's Ministers upon hearing of that catastrophe? They stated that, in their opinion, they no longer possessed the confidence of the House of Commons (they never had possessed the confidence of your lordships); and as to the people, they then felt that they had no longer the confidence of the nation at large. They, therefore tendered the resignation of their offices to her Majesty, and that resignation was accepted. The history of the few days subsequent to that event I pass over, for it forms no part of the matter which I have to offer to your lordships; besides it was so fully laid before you by a noble duke, who himself acted a considerable part in it, and was analyzed in so able and masterly a manner by my noble and learned friend on the opposite benches, that the recollection of the whole subject must be fresh in your memories, and I will not impair the effect of it by any representations of my own. There is, however, one point connected with it to which I am anxious to call the attention of your lordships. Her Majesty's Ministers, I repeat, tendered their resignation—that resignation was accepted, and it was understood that they only held office until their successors were appointed. Then commenced the communications for forming another administration. Before they had terminated, these Ministers, who only held office until their successors were appointed, interposed, advised her Majesty, dictated her notes, and were themselves the negotiators with their political opponents. The outgoing Ministers the negotiators with their successors! The result was this—that the Ministers, who only held office until their successors were appointed, at last went the whole length of advising her Majesty to reinstate them in the Government. I say that Ministers gave her Majesty that advice; for such was the result to which all their conduct evidently tended. Such a course of proceeding was never before known to occur in the history of England, and I trust in God that it never will occur again. What, my lords, was the first act of this new Government? Their first act was to draw up a minute, historically formed, argumentatively formed, legally formed; and the unconstitutional character of it was only to be equalled by its folly, its extravagance, and its insolence. Ministers, I have before said, were reinstated in their respective offices. They declared, previously to their reinstatement, that they had lost the confidence of Parliament and of the country. I now ask your lordships what they have done since they have been reinstated in office to regain that forfeited confidence? I say that every act which they have since done, every circumstance with which they have since been connected, has only lowered them still further in the opinion of the public. So far from gaining increased confidence in the House of Commons, all their proceedings have tended to weaken and degrade them more and more. But it was necessary for them to make another experiment for the recovery of public confidence, and therefore they brought in their second Jamaica bill. What, my lords, was the pretence for it? To continue certain laws which were about to expire in that colony. The bill was drawn up with that view, and with that pretence; but other clauses were grafted upon it, equally pernicious in principle with the bill which Ministers had abandoned. That bill, on its second reading, was passed by a majority of ten. So that when Ministers had only a majority of five, they confessed that they had forfeited the confidence of the House of Commons; and when they had got a majority of ten, they ventured to suppose that they had recovered the confidence which they before admitted that they had unwittingly forfeited. They felt that their situation was uncomfortable and uneasy, and that it was necessary for them to do something more to retain the confidence of their party, and the question which occurred to them as most likely to accomplish that object was the question of the ballot. It was impossible that there could be a subject of greater importance. After the Reform Bill, it was one of the most interesting questions that could be submitted to the consideration of Parliament. If ever there was a measure on which it was incumbent that the Government should act as a Government, it was on this very measure of the ballot. The opinion of the Government, as a Government, was well known respecting it; but it was thought that it would be useful in recovering their lost influence in the House of Commons, and so the Government made the ballot an open question. An open question! Most shabby proceeding! There was, however, a double advantage in it: it was to gain them votes in the House of Commons, and it was to afford some members of the Cabinet an opportunity of winning the regard of their constituents; and therefore it was, that in spite of the reluctance of the noble viscount and some of his colleagues, it was made an open question. But when it came under the consideration of the House of Commons, and when a noble member of the Cabinet let out the secret that he had voted for making it an open question as the best way of defeating it, then its intense shabbiness was completely beaten by its still more intense hypocrisy. I cannot, my lords, congratulate the noble viscount on any accession of strength that has accrued to his administration from the course he has pursued upon this question of the ballot. When the second Jamaica bill was passed, the 9th of July had arrived. Up to that day not one bill of any great consequence had passed. All was a blank. We had passed, it was true, the Mutiny Bill; we had passed the Annual Indemnity Bill; we had passed nine money bills, of ordinary course and character; we had passed twelve or fourteen other bills, some for the amendment, some for the continuance, of former bills, and others for trifling and unimportant matters, to which no opposition could be, or indeed was, made in either House of Parliament. Such, my lords, was the state of things on the 9th of July. Still the table of the House of Commons was covered with bills, at once numerous and important. It became, therefore, necessary to inquire what the Government intended to do with them. The session was on the point of expiring, and honourable members were naturally anxious to return to their homes. Were, then, the bills on the table to be proceeded with or not? I find, my lords, by a paper that has been laid upon your lordships' table, that as soon as this intimation was given to her Majesty's Ministers, they abandoned with breathless haste measure after measure. A bill was introduced for the registration of voters in England. What became of it? It was abandoned. A similar bill was introduced for the registration of voters in Scotland. What became of it? It was abandoned. The Fictitious Votes Bill (Scotland)—a bill of great importance to that country? Abandoned. The Preparation of Writs (Scotland)? Abandoned. The Registration of Leases (Scotland)? Abandoned. The Heritable Securities (Scotland)? Abandoned. The District Sessions Bill? Abandoned. The District Prison Bill? Abandoned. The Town Councils Bill? Abandoned. The Ecclesiastical Duties and Revenues Bill? Abandoned. The Factories' Regulation Bill—a bill frequently discussed in both Houses of Parliament, and of vast importance to the interests of humanity? Abandoned. The Collection of Rates Bill, the County Courts Bill, the Embankments in Ireland Bill, and many other bills of different descriptions? All, all were abandoned, because Ministers found it impossible, from not being possessed of either energy, vigour, character, capacity, or the confidence of the House of Commons, to carry them through Parliament during the present session. But another measure, on which I have no doubt that in the speech at the close of the session no inconsiderable reliance will be placed, requires me to call the particular attention of your lordships to it. That measure is the Postage measure. That measure in a former session was ridiculed, not only by the retainers, but also by some of the members of Government. It was abused by them in good set terms, and was denounced as absolutely impracticable. It was said, and with great boldness and vehemence—"In the present state of the revenue, will you consent to abandon another million for a more haphazard experiment?" All this, I repeat, was said, not only by the retainers of Government, but also by their leaders. But the measure was pressed on her Majesty's advisers by their supporters out of doors—and Ministers had neither energy, nor vigour, nor character, nor capacity, nor the confidence of Parliament, wherewith to resist this pressure from without; and, therefore, in spite of their past protestations, and in spite of their better judgment, they resolved to persevere with their scheme for reducing the rate of postage. But, after taking that resolution, what do your lordships suppose was their first step? Not having the courage or the ability to look the measure directly in the face, they hit, as they fancied, upon a contrivance to get rid of it by a side wind; and her Majesty's Chancellor of the Exchequer, with that singular ingenuity which distinguishes his character, thought that if he could introduce in his bill a clause that would be distasteful to the House, he should be enabled to get rid of it altogether. In consequence, he introduced a clause into it, containing a pledge that Parliament would make good any deficiency which might be occasioned in the public revenue by the adoption of his new project. That clause proved, as he anticipated that it would prove, distasteful to the House, and it was zealously and strenuously opposed. It was said, and said justly, by the opponents of the clause, that such a pledge was unnecessary;

for if the revenue proved deficient, it would be the duty of the House of Commons to make that deficiency good. It happened, however, that in spite of all the artifices of the Chancellor of the Exchequer, and in spite of all his able and dexterous manœuvres, the Postage measure passed through all its stages in the House of Commons. But then was raised another cry by the retainers of Government—"Oh! the Lords will never suffer the revenue to be reduced in this precipitate manner. The bill must be discussed in the House of Lords, and in the House of Lords it is sure to be defeated." Well, the bill did come on for discussion here—and I am speaking within the mark when I say, that when it came on I never saw the opposite benches with a thinner attendance. That, however, was not all. The noble viscount introduced the bill to the notice of your lordships, and moved its second reading. He argued against the measure with all the force, with all the talent, with all the knowledge of the world which always distinguish him; and, after he had expatiated on and exhausted all his topics, he concluded by saying, "However, as the bill is wished for out of doors, I now move its second reading." We considered it, my lords, as a measure of finance—which we must either reject altogether or accept altogether—and, therefore, as there were some good points in the bill it was passed, *reluctante* the noble viscount, and has now become the law of the land. My lords, in pursuing the course which I have chalked out for myself, I come now to another bill of very deep interest indeed—I mean the bill for the suppression of the slave trade. When that bill was first introduced into the House of Commons, I made a point of reading with great care and attention all the treaties existing between this country and Portugal, and also all the correspondence which has passed between our Ministers and those of the Court of Lisbon on the subject; and the conclusion to which I came, after a careful perusal of all those documents, was, that Portugal had violated all the engagements which she had made with this country, and, what was more, that she had never entertained the slightest intention to fulfil them. But, then, I also found that what was so clear now, was not a whit the less clear two years ago. And I now say, that her Majesty's Ministers deserted their duty, and forgot what was due to the honour and character of their country, in not calling upon Portugal two years ago to fulfil the engagements into which she had entered with us. I say, further, that they might by the blockade of the port of Lisbon, or by other similar measures of energy and vigour, have compelled Portugal to the fulfilment of her engagements with us two years ago. And what, my lords, would have been the consequence of such a proceeding? That some hundreds of thousands of lives, which have since been sacrificed in the slave-trade, would have been saved to humanity, and that we should have had a certain, an ordinary, and a correct course to pursue, instead of that doubtful, uncertain, and unusual course which the noble viscount has introduced. I, therefore, give her Majesty's Ministers no credit for the measure which they have introduced; on the contrary, I complain of their great tardiness, and of their utter want of efficiency to discharge their duty towards their Sovereign and their country. My lords, I have now brought you down to an advanced period of the session. The 9th of August arrived, and then a huge flight of bills, the οἱ πολλοι of legislation, were introduced into the House of Commons—some of them mischievous—some of them unconstitutional—some of them jobbing, but a great mass of them harmless and inoffensive, which met with no opposition there, and cannot meet with any opposition here. It appears as if her Majesty's Ministers were determined to make up by number what they wanted in the weight and quality of their legislative measures. Am I expressing myself, my lords, too strongly? Be yourselves the judges. The first of these measures that came before you was the Metropolitan Police Courts Bill. By this bill the patronage of the appointments of magistrates at salaries of 1,200*l.* a-year, was to be given to the Secretary of State for the Home Department; but that clause was struck out of the bill by your lordships. There was another provision of the bill, which, in my view of the subject, was of an unconstitutional character —viz., the abolition of the trial by jury in a particular description of crimes. This was the first attempt of such a nature ever made in this country, except during the times of the usurpation, from which the noble viscount at the head of the Government seems very much inclined to draw his precedents. Instead of a jury, a magistrate, appointed by the Crown, paid by the Crown, and removable at pleasure by the Crown, was substituted; and with regard to the offences of stealing goods, and receiving stolen goods, not only was there no limit to his jurisdiction as regards the amount, but the sole person who was to judge whether a party should or should not have the benefit of trial by jury was this very magistrate, appointed, paid, and removable by the Crown. Such was the bill as it passed through the Reformed House of Commons. It was sent up here at the close of the session, and your lordships, acting wisely and constitutionally, struck out that provision. That was one of the measures of this class. Another was the Admiralty Bill, by which the salary of the judge was increased to 4,000*l.* a-year, and by which a learned gentleman being a political partizan, most inflexible in his adherence to Ministers on all occasions, was, notwithstanding this increase of salary, still to retain his seat in Parliament. Other alterations of a most extensive character were proposed to be effected by that bill, and at a period of the session when it was impossible for your lordships to give them due consideration, and your lordships determined to reject the bill. Another measure was brought up to your Lordships' House, which, I think, constituted the most scandalous job ever presented to the consideration of Parliament. When I state what that measure was, your lordships, I am sure, will not think that the terms I use are by any means too strong: I allude to the Sale of Spirits (Ireland) Bill. A bill had been introduced into the other House of Parliament for electoral purposes, having for its object to alter a law which had been adopted by Parliament in order to protect public morals. This bill was so distasteful to the other House that there was no chance of its ever passing; and what do your lordships suppose was the course pursued? The Chancellor of the Exchequer had a bill for the sale of spirits, which had passed through its various stages up to the third reading. Then it was, when nobody expected such a proceeding, that the Chancellor of the Exchequer allowed the person who introduced the bill I have just referred to, to ingraft that bill, at the third reading, on the Government measure, and thus it passed in the House of Commons by a contrivance as base as has ever occurred in the history of legislation. It is unnecessary for me to say, that this addition to the bill of the Government was thrown out by this House, without any attempt being made to defend it, for the whole proceeding was one which would not bear consideration or argument for a moment. But what was the real cause and secret of the bill I have described having been embodied in the Government measure? Why, it was felt to be convenient, with respect to an ulterior measure, to conciliate the patron of that bill, and therefore it was that this extraordinary consent was given to ingraft it on the bill of the Chancellor of the Exchequer. But shabbiness of this kind always fails, and it failed signally in this instance, for when that other measure—the bill relating to the charter of the bank of Ireland—which appears to have been in contemplation at the time this proceeding took place, came on for discussion, that individual, who, it was hoped, would, by this intrigue and manœuvre, be conciliated, turned round and opposed it, and upon that measure, which was so important that the Government ought to have retired if they were not able to carry it, they were defeated, and the bill was abandoned. With respect to the rest of the bills, which were, as I have described them, the sweepings of office, they were dealt out like cards on the table by the noble viscount opposite, who superseded every other office in the Ministry but his own, and did the whole business of the Government in this House. They were submitted with little explanation, and met with no opposition. Such is their history, and such the course of proceeding pursued. But there is another class of bills—three in number—which calls for a few observations. These were the last bills of the session. One of them has been discussed to-night, the others have been considered on former evenings, and they relate to the establishment of a police force at Manchester, Bolton, and Birmingham. They are temporary measures; but why were they produced; and why were they passed through Parliament? Because the Ministers, in granting charters to those three particular towns, were so careless and indifferent in their proceedings, that doubts are entertained as to the validity of the charters which are now under consideration in the courts of law. These bills, therefore, were rendered necessary in consequence of the bungling of Ministers themselves; and they, then, are not entitled to take praise for their introduction. There were, however, other considerations which unfortunately called for the passing of these bills. They were felt to be requisite on account of the tumults and disturbances which have taken place in the northern parts of this island, and for which I consider the Ministers as deeply responsible. They first roused the people. They first sent forth the watchword—"Agitate, agitate, agitate!" and they are responsible for the consequences which followed. Agitation was convenient to place them in power, and up to a certain point it was necessary to maintain them in power. They wished that the flood might go thus far and no farther; that at this point the proud waves should be stayed. But in cases of this kind it is found much easier to let loose the tempest than afterwards to enchain or direct it. This has always been the result of such a course of action. Ambitious men make use of multitudes for their own ambitious purposes, and for the attainment of their own personal objects. They ride into power on the shoulders of the people, and it then becomes inconvenient that that tumult and violence to which they owe their own elevation should continue. They then feel it to be necessary to coerce and restrain agitation, and their deluded followers discover, for the first time, that they are the dupes and victims of those who, on former occasions, had eulogized and encouraged their proceedings. The history of the present Government is of this description. We all remember the period when the noble lord at the head of the Home Department received an address from 150,000 persons assembled in the neighbourhood of Birmingham. With affected humility, for—

Lowliness is young Ambition's ladder,

the noble lord received that address—"he was utterly undeserving of the great honour conferred on him"—"he was deeply grateful for it," and then it was that the noble lord drew a parallel between the proceedings of that meeting and the proceedings of the House of Lords, designating the one as the voice of reason, and the other as the whisper of a faction. Are you surprised at what has followed? Are you astonished at the result? It is only the natural consequence, and I should have been surprised if it had been otherwise. I have now gone through the business of the session as far as my recollection serves me; I have executed the task which I undertook to perform; I have done it with plainness and simplicity, according to my accustomed manner, and, I trust, with scrupulous accuracy and without the slightest degree of exaggeration; and I now put it to your lordships, as a question, whether the Ministers, who have thus conducted themselves in matters of legislation during the last seven months, can enjoy the confidence of Parliament; and whether you are of opinion that they are capable of conducting the affairs of this mighty empire in a manner suitable to its wants and necessities, and such as you are entitled to expect from Ministers of the Crown. I am confident as to what your lordships' opinion and decision must be. I stated in the outset that in bringing this matter under your lordships' consideration, I conceived I was discharging a duty; it has been no grateful task for me; but I have performed it faithfully and to the best of my ability.

SIR JOHN ELIOT.
Born 1590. Died 1629.

[The following speech, which is a fine specimen of the oratory of the time, was delivered in the year 1628, and has been well commented upon by Hazlitt in his valuable but now scarce work, entitled "The Eloquence of the British Senate." We may, therefore, here quote with propriety the note that appears in that collection. "This," he remarks, "is a noble instance of parliamentary eloquence; for the strength and closeness of the reasoning, for the clearness of the detail, for the earnestness of the style, it is admirable: it, in some places, reminds one strongly of the clear, plain, convincing, irresistible appeals of Demosthenes to his hearers. There is no affectation of wit, no studied ornament, no display of fancied superiority; his whole heart and soul are in his subject, he is full of it; his mind seems, as it were, to surround and penetrate every part of it; nothing diverts him from his purpose, or interrupts the course of his reasoning for a moment. The force and connection of his ideas give vehemence to his expressions, and he convinces others, because he is thoroughly impressed with the truth of his own opinions."]

SPEECH IN THE HOUSE OF COMMONS, 1628.

MR. SPEAKER,—We sit here as the great council of the king, and in that capacity it is our duty to take into consideration the state and affairs of the kingdom; and, when there is occasion, to give a true representation of them by way of counsel and advice, with what we conceive necessary or expedient for them.

In this consideration I confess many a sad thought hath affrighted me, and that not only in respect of our dangers from abroad, which yet I know are great, as they have been often pressed and dilated to us, but in respect of our disorders here at home, which do inforce those dangers, and by which they are occasioned: for I believe I shall make it clear unto you, that both at first, the cause of these dangers were our disorders, and our disorders now are yet our greatest dangers; and not so much the potency of our enemies, as the weakness of ourselves does threaten us: and that saying of the father may be assumed by us, *non tam potentia sua quam negligentia nostra*. Our want of true devotion to heaven, our insincerity and doubling in religion, our want of councils, our precipitate actions, the insufficiency or unfaithfulness of our generals abroad, the ignorance or corruptions of our ministers at home, the impoverishing of the sovereign, the oppression and depression of the subject, the exhausting of our treasures, the waste of our provisions, consumption of our ships, destruction of our men, these make the advantage to our enemies, not the reputation of their arms; and if in these there be not reformation, we need no foes abroad; time itself will ruin us.

To show this more fully, I believe you will all hold it necessary, that they seem not an aspersion on the state, or imputation on the Government, as I have known such motions misinterpreted; but far is this from me to propose, who have none but clear thoughts of the excellency of the king, nor can have other ends but the advancement of his Majesty's glory. I shall desire a little of your patience extraordinary to open the particulars, which I shall do with what brevity I may, answerable to the importance of the cause and the necessity now upon us; yet with such respect and observation to the time, as I hope shall not be thought troublesome.

For the first, then, our insincerity and doubling in religion is the greatest and most dangerous disorder of all others; this hath never been unpunished, and of this we have many strong examples of all states and in all times, to awe us. What testimony doth it want? Will you have authority of books? Look on the collections of the committee for religion; there is too clear an evidence. See then the commission procured for composition with the Papists of the north: mark the proceedings thereupon, and you will find them to little less amounting than a toleration in effect; the slight payments, and the easiness in them, will likewise show the favour that is intended.

Will you have proofs of men? Witness the hopes, witness the presumptions, witness the reports of all the Papists generally; observe the dispositions of commanders, the trust of officers, the confidence in secretaries to employments in this kingdom, in Ireland and elsewhere. These all will show it hath too great a certainty; and to this add but the incontrovertible evidence of that all powerful hand, which we have felt so sorely, that gave it full assurance; for as the heavens oppose themselves to us for our impiety, so it is we that first opposed the heavens.

For the second, our want of councils, that great disorder in a state, with which there cannot be stability. If effects may show their causes, as they are often a perfect demonstration of them, our misfortunes, our disasters serve to prove it, and the consequences they draw with them. If reason be allowed in this dark age, the judgment of dependencies and foresight of contingencies in affairs do confirm it; for if we view ourselves at home, are we in strength, are we in reputation equal to our ancestors? If we view ourselves abroad, are our friends as many, are our enemies no more? Do our friends retain their safety and possessions? Do not our enemies enlarge themselves, and gain from them and us? To what counsel owe we the loss of the Palatinate, where we sacrificed both our honour and our men sent thither, stopping those greater powers appointed for that service, by which it might have been defensible. What counsel gave direction to the late action, whose wounds are yet bleeding; I mean the expedition to Rhee, of which there is yet so sad a memory in all men? what design for us, or advantage to our state could that import? You know the wisdom of your ancestors, and the practice of their times, how they preserved their safeties: we all know, and have as much cause to doubt as they had, the greatness and ambition of that kingdom, which the old world could not satisfy. Against this greatness and ambition, we likewise know the proceedings of that princess, that never to be forgotten, excellent queen, Elizabeth, whose name, without admiration, falls not into mention even with her enemies; you know how she advanced herself, and how she advanced the nation in glory and in state; how she depressed our enemies, and how she upheld her friends; how she enjoyed a full security, and made them our scorn, who now are made our terror!

Some of the principles she built on were these; and if I mistake, let reason and our statesmen contradict me.

First, to maintain in what she might, an unity in France, that the kingdom being at peace within itself, might be a bulwark to keep back the power of Spain by land.

Next, to preserve an amity and league between that state and us, that so we might come in aid of the Low Countries, and by that means receive their ships and help them by sea.

This treble cord, so working between France, the States, and England, might enable us, as occasion should require, to give assistance unto others; and by this means the experience of that time doth tell us, that we were not only free from those fears that now possess and trouble us, but then our names were fearful to our enemies. See now what correspondency our actions had with this; square our conduct by these rules; it did induce, as a necessary consequence, a division in France between the Protestants and their king, of which there is too woeful and lamentable experience. It hath made an absolute breach between that state and us, and so entertains us against France, and France in preparation against us, that we have nothing to promise to our neighbours, nay, hardly to ourselves. Nay, observe the time in which it was attempted, and you shall find it not only varying from those principles, but directly contrary and opposite *ex diametro* to those ends, and such, as from the issue and success, rather might be thought a conception of Spain, than begotten here with us.

[Here there was an interruption made by Sir Humphry May (Chancellor of the Duchy, and one of the Privy Council) expressing a dislike; but the House ordered Sir John Eliot to go on; whereupon he proceeded thus:—]

Mr. Speaker, I am sorry for this interruption, but much more sorry if there hath been occasion; wherein as I shall submit myself wholly to your judgment, to receive what censure you should give me if I have offended, so, in the integrity of my intentions, and clearness of my thoughts, I must still retain this confidence, that no greatness shall deter me from the duties which I owe to the service of my king and country; but that, with a true English heart, I shall discharge myself as faithfully and as really, to the extent of my poor power, as any man whose honours or whose offices most strictly oblige him.

You know the dangers Denmark is in, and how much they concerned us; what in respect of our alliance and the country; what in the importance of the Sound; what an advantage to our enemies the gain thereof would be! what loss, what prejudice to us by this disunion; we breaking upon France; France enraged by us; and the Netherlands at amazement between both! neither could we intend to aid that luckless king, whose loss is our disaster.

Can those now, that express their troubles at the hearing of these things, and have so often told us, in this place, of their knowledge in the conjunctures and disjunctures of affairs, say, they advised in this? was this an act of council, Mr. Speaker? I have more charity than to think it, and unless they made a confession of it themselves, I cannot believe it.

For the next—the insufficiency and unfaithfulness of our generals (that great disorder abroad)—what shall I say? I wish there were not cause to mention it; and but out of the apprehension of the danger that is to come, if the like choice hereafter be not prevented, I could willingly be silent; but my duty to my sovereign, my service to this House, and the safety and honour of my country, are above all respects; and what so nearly trenches to the prejudice of this, must not, shall not be forborne.

At Cadiz, then, in that first expedition we made, when we arrived and found a conquest ready, the Spanish ships, I mean, fit for the satisfaction of a voyage, and of which some of the chiefest, then there themselves, have since assured me that the satisfaction would have been sufficient either in point of honour, or in point of profit: why was it neglected? why was it not achieved, it being of all hands granted, how feasible it was?

After, when with the destruction of some of our men, and with the exposition of some others, who (though their fortune since has not been such) by chance came off, when, I say, with the loss of our serviceable men, that unserviceable fort was gained, and the whole army landed, why was there nothing done? Why was there nothing attempted? If nothing was intended, wherefore did they land? If there was a service, wherefore were they shipped again? Mr. Speaker, it satisfies me too much in this, when I think of their dry and hungry march into that drunken quarter (for so the soldiers termed it) where was the period of their journey; so that divers of our men, being left as a sacrifice to the enemy, that labour was at an end.

For the next undertaking at Rhee, I will not trouble you much, only this in short: was not that whole action carried against the judgment and opinion of those officers that were of the council? was not the first, was not the last, was not all, in the landing, in the intrenching, in the continuance there, in the assault, in the retreat, without their assent? Did any advice take place of such as were of the council? If there should be made a particular inquisition thereof these things will be manifest and more. I will not instance the manifesto that was made for the reason of these arms; nor by whom, nor in what manner, nor on what grounds it was published, nor what effects it hath wrought, drawing, as it were, almost the whole world into league against us; nor will I mention the leaving of the wines, the leaving of the salt, which were in our possession, and of a value, as it is said, to answer much of our expense; nor that great wonder which no Alexander or Cæsar ever did, the enriching of the enemy by courtesies, when our soldiers wanted help; nor the private intercourse and parleys with the fort, which continually were held. What they intended may be read in the success; and upon due examination thereof, they would not want their proofs.

For the last voyage to Rochelle, there needs no observations : it is so fresh in memory; nor will I make an inference or corollary on all. Your own knowledge shall judge what truth or what sufficiency they express. For the next, the ignorance and corruption of our ministers, where can you miss of instances? If you survey the court, if you survey the country; if the church, if the city be examined; if you observe the bar, if the bench, if the ports, if the shipping, if the land, if the seas: all these will render you variety of proofs, and that, in such measure and proportion, as shows the greatness of our disease to be such, that if there be not some speedy application for remedy, our case is almost desperate.

Mr. Speaker, I fear I have been too long in these particulars that are past, and am unwilling to offend you, therefore in the rest I shall be shorter; and in that which concerns the impoverishing of the king, no other arguments will I use, than such as all men grant.

The exchequer, you know, is empty, and the reputation thereof gone; the ancient lands are sold; the jewels pawned; the plate engaged; the debts still great; almost all charges, both ordinary and extraordinary, borne up by projects: what poverty can be greater? what necessity so great? what perfect English heart is not almost dissolved into sorrow for this truth?

For the oppression of the subject, which, as I remember, is the next particular I proposed, it needs no demonstration; the whole kingdom is a proof; and for the exhausting of our treasures, that very oppression speaks it. What waste of our provisions, what consumption of our ships, what destruction of our men have been, witness that journey to Algiers—witness that with Mansfield—witness that to Cadiz—witness the next—witness that to Rhee—witness the last (I pray God we may never have more such witnesses); witness likewise the Palatinate—witness Denmark—witness the Turks—witness the Dunkirkers—witness all. What losses we have sustained! how we are impaired in munition, in ships, in men!

It is beyond contradiction that we were never so much weakened, nor ever had less hope how to be restored.

These, Mr. Speaker, are our dangers; these are they which do threaten us; and these are like the Trojan horse brought in cunningly to surprise us. In these do lurk the strongest of our enemies, ready to issue on us, and if we do not speedily expel them, these are the signs, these the invitations to others; these will so prepare their entrance, that we shall have no means left of refuge or defence; for if we have these enemies at home, how can we strive with those that are abroad? if we be free from these, no other can impeach us: our ancient English virtue, like the old Spartan valour, cleared from these disorders, our being in sincerity of religion and once made friends with heaven, having maturity of councils, sufficiency of generals, incorruption of officers, opulency in the king, liberty in the people, repletion in treasure, plenty of provisions, reparation of ships, preservation of men—our ancient English virtue, I say, thus rectified, will secure us; and unless there be a speedy reformation in these, I know not what hopes or expectations we can have.

These are the things, sir, I shall desire to have taken into consideration; that as we are the great council of the kingdom; and have the apprehension of these dangers, we may truly represent them unto the king; whereunto I conceive we are bound by a treble obligation, of duty to God, of duty to his Majesty, and of duty to our country.

And therefore, I wish it may so stand with the wisdom and judgment of the House, that they may be drawn into the body of a remonstrance, and in all humility expressed, with a prayer unto his Majesty, that for the safety of himself, for the safety of the kingdom, and for the safety of religion, he will be pleased to give us time to make perfect inquisition thereof, or to take them into his own wisdom, and there give them such timely reformation as the necessity and justice of the case doth import.

And thus, sir, with a large affection and loyalty to his Majesty, and with a firm duty and service to my country, I have suddenly (and it may be with some disorder) expressed the weak apprehensions I have, wherein, if I have erred, I humbly crave your pardon, and so submit myself to the censure of the House.

ENVY.

The envious man is in pain upon all occasions which ought to give him pleasure. The relish of his life is inverted; and the objects which administer the highest satisfaction to those who are exempt from this passion, give the quickest pangs to those who are subject to it. All the perfections of their fellow-creatures are odious. Youth, beauty, and wisdom, are provocations of their displeasure. What a wretched and apostate state is this! to be offended with excellence, and to hate a man because we approve him. The condition of the envious man is the most emphatically miserable; he is not only incapable of rejoicing in another's merit or success, but lives in a world wherein all mankind are in a plot against his quiet, by studying their own happiness and advantage.—*Steele.*

SIR EDWARD BULWER LYTTON, BART.

Born 1805. *Living.*

[It is not often that the name of the successful novelist or the accomplished poet finds a place in the list of conspicuous orators. This rare honour, however, has long and worthily been accorded to the distinguished subject of the present notice. Sir Edward Bulwer Lytton has now, for many years past, been a prominent member in the English House of Commons, and though seldom speaking, except on great and special occasions of political interest, has won for himself no mean reputation as a statesman as well as rhetorician. His eloquence is, perhaps, too studied and elaborate in its cast to be well suited for the ordinary purposes of debate; but in the treatment of some great theme, such as he delights to discuss, his impassioned reasoning has a marvellous and masterly effect. The speech which we have here given as an illustration of his style was made in the House of Commons, on Tuesday, Dec. 19th, 1854, on the discussion of the Foreign Enlistment Act, the second reading of which had been moved by Lord John Russell, when Sir Bulwer Lytton rose to move as an amendment, that the bill be read a second time that day six months. The original motion was nevertheless, after a long discussion, carried by a considerable majority.]

SPEECH AGAINST THE SECOND READING OF THE FOREIGN ENLISTMENT BILL, 1854.

SIR,—In rising to oppose the second reading of this bill, I feel, indeed, that I require more than the ordinary indulgence of the House; for if even upon trivial occasions it would be with great diffidence that I would offer any comment or reply to a speech from the noble lord, that diffidence must be painfully increased upon an occasion so important, and when the task I have undertaken compels me to rise immediately after so eminent an authority and so consummate a debater. But I trust at least that it will not be necessary for me, or for any gentleman on this side of the House, or indeed on either, to declare our readiness to support the Crown in the resolute prosecution of a war in which the honour of England is pledged to a cause which we believe to be identified with the interests of civilization itself. But if the honour of England be pledged to this quarrel, I am not willing that other nations and posterity should receive our confession that, at its very onset, our own native spirit, nay, even our own military training, were incompetent to encounter the struggle. The noble lord has carried us back to former wars, on which he has expatiated with complacency on the aid we derived from the employment of foreign mercenaries. I shall follow him, as I proceed, through the precedents he advances, and I trust to prove that they have served less to advance his argument than to divert the House from the question that is really at issue. Meanwhile, he cannot deny that in this war, at least, up to the present moment, with inadequate numbers, and at every disadvantage, we have sufficed to fight our own battles and earn our own laurels; and the noble lord has vouchsafed not one reason to show why we should henceforth prefer to win our victories by proxy. That expression may seem exaggerated, considering the small proportion of foreign force to be employed; but honour is not so intolerable a burden that we should fee foreign soldiers to ease ourselves of the slightest portion of that load. My objections to this bill are very broad but very few, and I shall endeavour to state them in as few words as possible. What is it on which you now mainly rely to continue this war with vigour, no matter at what sacrifice and cost? Not so much on the extent of our territory, the amount of our population, the wealth of our resources, as on the ardour of the people; on that spirit of nationality which, we are told by the Minister of War, rises against every danger and augments in proportion to the demand on its energies. It is that ardour you are about to damp—it is that spirit of nationality to which this bill administers both discouragement and affront. The noble lord says our difficulty is at the commencement. What is the commencement? One burst of popular enthusiasm? And in the midst of that enthusiasm, at a time when we are told by the Secretary-at-War that you get recruits faster than you can form them into regiments—you say to the people of this empire, "Your rude and untutored valour does not suffice for the prowess of England, and we must apply to the petty principalities of Europe for the co-operation of their more skilful and warlike subjects." I say that this is an unwise and, I maintain it to be, an unnecessary blow upon the vital principle that now sustains your cause, and brings to your army more men than you know how to employ. And if anything could make this war unpopular, it would be the sight of foreign soldiers quartered and drilled in any part of these kingdoms, paid by the taxes extorted from this people, and occupying barracks of which the paucity is your excuse for not having embodied more of the militia of our native land. Do you mean to say it will not make a difference in the temper of the middle and working classes, now nobly prepared for any pecuniary sacrifice, whether they pay the cost of an army of their own countrymen, who repay them by deeds which make us more proud of the English name, or whether they are to pay foreigners, who may be equally brave, may perform equal service, but whose glory will only compliment our wealth at the expense of our manhood—only prove that we were rich enough to consign to foreign hirelings that standard which a handful of English soldiers had planted on the heights of Alma, and rescued from barbarian numbers on the plains of Inkerman? What, sir, is the reason assigned for this bill besides that learned array of historical precedents to which I shall come afterwards—that, whatever the ardour of our people, it requires time to drill them, to convert raw recruits into disciplined soldiers? Sir, there is some force in that argument, but it confers a grave censure on the Government; it proves all that has been said of their want of activity and foresight, that during the eighteen months in which war—this great, this "protracted war"—was foreseen by all England except its chief Minister—that, during the nine months or so in which we have been actually engaged in hostilities, the Government should not already have raised and drilled a sufficient number of reserve to dispense at least with this first instalment of 10,000 foreigners. Why, if you will compute the time elapsed ever since the Battle of the Alma—the time devoted in preparing this thoughtful and deliberate bill—in corresponding with foreign princes (if the bill pass), in enlisting your foreign soldiers, bringing them hither, and then, it seems, fitting them for service—if you would compute all this time, from first to last, employed in getting together these foreign troops, you would have leisure to drill and send out double the number of your own countrymen. I ask you this question—I press for a reply—you say you require these foreign soldiers for an immediate emergency—that you want them to send out in the interval which you employ in drilling English recruits; that is your main argument—tell me then, plainly, in how short a time do you calculate that they will be raised, imported, organized, despatched to the Crimea? You are bound to show that it will be within a shorter time than you can raise, drill, and send out an equal number of native troops. Can you show this? I might defy you to do it; but until you have shown it, your argument has no ground on which to stand. But it seems to me strange that these practised warriors—so superior to ourselves in all military craft and discipline—are first to be imported to England, and finish their martial education upon English ground. As it has been pertinently said elsewhere, "this is not the shortest road to the Crimea"—you can send these troops from the continent without coming to Parliament at all; why, then, not send them at once to the Crimea from whatever place abroad you collect them? Make your depot anywhere you please out of the British dominions. There is this advantage in that course—you have reasons of your own to draw these mercenaries from quarters which you do not think it discreet to state openly to Parliament. Well, then, you should have sufficient confidence in those reasons to act entirely on your own official responsibility; thus you will neither openly exhibit to the public that spectacle of foreign hirelings within these realms, always so intolerable to the national feelings, nor call upon the House of Commons to sanction, for reasons not plainly before it, a degradation to the spirit of the people we represent. Sir, now look to the extraordinary want of consideration, and, I must say, to the slovenly haste with which the provisions of this bill are devised and matured. Its first introduction led at once to the alarm that these foreigners were intended to supply the place of the native defenders, not only of English honour abroad, but of English security at home; that, in short, they should supply the place of the militia, and the British forces removed from this country. That supposition was indignantly denied. In spite of such denial, the Minister charged with the conduct of the bill finds the public persist in that alarm, for he says that "he hears with surprise from several quarters that such an impression unquestionably prevails out of doors," and then he condescends to look into the bill itself, and is bound to confess that, by the wording of it, it might be perverted to such a purpose. What! in a bill embracing such delicate questions, so nearly touching the keystone of all free institutions, surely the wording ought to have been so deliberately concocted that it should not harbour a phrase which a people jealous of freedom could misinterpret, and which some future Ministers, of more dangerous character than these, might distort into a precedent that would jeopardise the liberties of the country or risk the security of the throne. And then, even as to the number of men required, so little calculation was made, although the noble lord tells us that this is a main reason why we are now summoned, and we might presume that your calculations would be somewhat carefully prepared, that it is an object of indifference whether it be 15,000 or 10,000, and the latter number is at once exchanged for the former. How then can you blame us if we presume to doubt your prudence, your deliberate foresight, your practical ability to conduct this war, when even in this bill, which you have had such leisure to prepare, we see all this blundering in the terms that involve a momentous constitutional principle, and all this careless indecision as to the amount of the force you require? And still more may we doubt your prudence, when, for the sake of so miserable a succour as 10,000 foreign bayonets, or rather for the object of landing and drilling them within these dominions, you, who tell us of the advantage of unanimity, resolve to force on a measure which you were blind indeed if you did not foresee would be unpopular out of doors— which at once necessitates the strongest opposition—which you carried by a petty majority through one House of Parliament—and which, if you carry it through the other, will be such a thorn in your side that I venture to doubt whether you will ever have the courage to use the power you now ask at our hands. Nay, sir, so little had the Minister who introduced elsewhere the measure even examined the constitutional principles which it involves, that he prefaced the bill by observing that the power to enlist and introduce into this country foreign soldiers, without application to Parliament, was formerly considered to be vested in the Crown. I am sure that the Lord President of the Council would warmly deny that our great constitutional authorities have admitted that this was ever, at any period of our history, the acknowledged prerogative of the sovereigns of this country. We all know that William III. sent a message to this House, requesting, in somewhat humble terms, that his Dutch troops should be allowed to remain, and that the House of Commons refused the request. You may say that was in time of peace; but I know that Lord Camden held the doctrine that, neither in peace nor in war, could foreign troops be admitted into this country without the sanction of an Act of Parliament. I know that Mr. Fox declared that, if the Crown ever did possess such a power, we had a constitution in words and not in reality. I can well conceive the indignation with which the Whigs of the last age, who are authorities so high with the Lord President of the Council, would have heard, if now living, such a doctrine —such a remark emanating from a Minister of War, who sits in the same cabinet with the leader of the Whigs. Sir, I could not pass over that rash assertion of a great officer of the Crown on a point essential to the vindication of the freedom of our ancestors and the principles of our ancient constitution. But your bill is amended—the more obnoxious clause is removed: I grant now that all constitutional forms are complied with; I find no fault with you there. But I say, that while adhering to all constitutional forms, you ought not to tamper with something so hostile to the constitutional spirit as the introduction of foreign troops, unless you can establish the closest precedent in parallel cases, or, make out a plea of paramount and urgent necessity. Now, first, as to the precedents cited by the noble lord. I am almost ashamed to repeat what every one knows, namely, that the precedent you would draw from the enlistment of Germans in 1804 and 1806 is wholly inapplicable to the present case. Look to the period of the great French war. Our sovereign was not only King of Great Britain—he was Elector of Hanover. His interests and ours were identified with the German Powers, except, indeed, Prussia, which at that time, influenced, first, by her guilty designs on the partition of Poland, and afterwards by the hope of obtaining Hanover as a reward for neutrality, did, in the opinion of all dispassionate historians, by her selfish inertness and procrastination, paralyze the arms of the other allies, and give to the common foe that gigantic power of which Prussia was afterwards the most signal victim. I trust that Prussia is wiser now; that she will not again amuse other and nobler confederacies by her tortuous diplomacy, cripple their energies by dissimulating lethargy, nor require, at the last, the assistance of their arms to free herself from the ruin in which selfish indifference to the common cause once involved her very existence as a nation. But at that time the enlistment of German soldiers in this country was, at least, natural enough, though even the memory of their gallantry in the field, which deserves all we can say of it, has not, you see, sufficed to render that enlistment popular. The noble lord refers to the debate of 1804, in which Mr. Francis, afterwards Sir Philip, took part. Ay, but he did not tell you the excuse which the then Secretary-at-War made to the objections Mr. Francis indignantly urged. The excuse was this:—"The enlistment of German soldiers was only a measure of providing for a certain number of men who were subjects of the same sovereign, and had been forced to leave their country." Who can say that this is a parallel instance? It is true that other foreigners were enlisted, but they were chiefly from those German nations which had the most cordial sympathy with the English cause. But now, indeed, although we should be proud to have a sincere and hearty alliance with the German courts, it is at least premature to believe that their interests, their objects in the war, are cordially and permanently identified with our own. And if we would render the Germans as popular in England as I hope they yet may be, we could not more defeat that object than by exhibiting German soldiers as substitutes for English valour upon English ground. But the noble lord goes back to the time of Marlborough, nay he says that in all our former wars foreign troops have been employed. Yes; but when they were employed with honour, they were the auxiliary forces of our open allies, and officered by the rank, the chivalry, the military renown of nations in the closest sympathy with ourselves, and were not mere free lances, under unknown and mercenary captains. I say, when they have been employed with honour. For where, indeed, an aid, similar to that which you now demand, has been obtained, wherever foreign princes have been subsidized, and their subjects hired by English gold to take part in the struggles with which they had no English sympathies—there the historian pauses to vent his scorn on the princes who thus sell the blood of their subjects, and his grief at the degradation of England in the blood-money she pays to the hirelings—these are not precedents to follow, but examples to shun. The noble lord reads to us the speech of the Duke of Wellington, and, by a most ingenious perversion of logic, wishes us to believe that, when the Duke said only one-third of our army was British, the rest were mercenaries, like those whom your bill would enlist. Why, sir, they were the Spanish and Portuguese, fighting in defence of their native soil. Who rejects the assistance of worthy allies? Who maintains that England should fight for the world singlehanded? Can the noble lord not comprehend the distinction involved? Here armies of various states combine in a course dear to all. There one state contributes to the general standard, not its own native valour and zeal, but a mercenary band whose valour gives it no glory, whose zeal has no motive but pay. This is what I meant when I said, "Honour was not so intolerable a burden that we should fee foreign soldiers to ease ourselves of its load." We are proud to share honour with the Frenchman, with the Turk, with any people that cooperate in our cause and participate our feelings. That is to share honour with others. Here you ask us to sell a part of that honour which were otherwise our share. The noble lord has stated the advantages conferred on our own army by the German troops in the French war. I grant them fully. I have heard great military authorities say that the German cavalry—especially under the command of the consummate officers it then possessed, such as Arranschild and Victor Alten—taught us how to charge and when to pull up. But the times are changed. Surely since then we have learnt all that they could teach us. How could German officers improve the charge of the Greys and Enniskillens at Balaklava, or that wondrous and stedfast gallantry of the Light Brigade, which brought two hundred out of six hundred men from the midst of the Russian cavalry, and squares of infantry supported by cross batteries of twenty pieces of cannon? Sir, we have learned more from the Germans than instruction in the art of war. We have been indebted to them for noble lessons in the arts of peace. Every cultivator of literature and science must cherish a deep and grateful affection for the German people, and a warm hope in their ultimate coalition with ourselves. Of this initiatory treaty with Austria I will say nothing at present; but if it does lead to an earnest and binding alliance, no man but must welcome a Power which can bring to the common cause from 300,000 to 500,000 men, and which—always assuming it to be sincere—would be our most convenient and our strongest guarantee for the maintenance of those territorial conditions on which any future peace must be based. I should rejoice yet more to learn that Prussia adopts the example of Austria—an example alleged, but still prospective—and contrasts, by her future sincerity, the guileful policy her Court espoused at the commencement of the French war. Between ourselves and the German people, of which Prussia is one of the great representatives, there is so kindred a community of race, of commercial interests, of all that belongs to intellectual interchange, that it would seem to me something monstrous, something out of the course of nature, if Prussia, the great centre of Germanic intelligence—Prussia, with that glorious capital of Berlin, in which philosophy and science have ripened every thought that could most ridicule and abhor the fanatic pretences with which a mock crusader would mask usurpation—that Prussia should sink from the rank among civilized States to which she was raised by the genius of Frederick the Great, and affect to have no vital interest in a war that would roll back from the borders of Europe the tide of a Tartar inundation—the supposition is preposterous! And I will not yet believe that a people which boasts universal education could be induced by any king, however able or beloved, to desert the ramparts which now protect from Attilas and Timours the destinies of the human race. But if we are to bring about a cordial friendship with the families of the German people, in Heaven's name let it be in a mode worthy of them and us. Let us have nations openly for our allies, and not this contraband levy from the surplus forces of their petty princes. Sir, indeed, no one has yet told us where these troops are to come from, and, what is still more important, where, after all, these foreign soldiers have really learned anything more than the holiday part of war—where have been the recent campaigns and wars in which they have exhibited their prowess and acquired their military experience? To hear what is said of the superior merits and seasoned hardihood of these foreigners, one might suppose they were the identical ten thousand who accomplished the retreat of Xenophon, instead of being merely, I suppose, men who have gone through the formal routine of the Landwehr, and seen no more of actual service, nor encountered any greater trial to the nerves, than the stout labourers you enlist in Kilkenny or Yorkshire. But are you sure you will get even trained soldiers—even the men who have gone through the drill of the Landwehr? I doubt it. From all I hear of the composition of that body, I suspect you will obtain only raw recruits—recruits as raw as you can raise in England at less cost, and in a shorter time. But it has been sought to gain some sort of popular favour to this measure—sought not, indeed, by Ministers, for they will not condescend to court popularity, but by their friends out of doors—by implying that the furtive and ulterior object of the Bill is to enlist men who are actuated by a nobler motive than that of ordinary soldiers, and first among all unfortunate refugees, the exiled Poles. But this idea has been so completely scouted by the First Minister of the Crown—it has been so expressly declared that the consent of foreign sovereigns for the enlistment of their subjects is to be obtained—that I shall not waste the time of the House in arguing that supposition. I know not, indeed, what sovereigns now sharing among them the ancient kingdom of Poland you could apply to for permission to form Polish recruits into separate battalions, with all the hopes that Polish recruits would entertain. But on this point I would only say, that if, in spite of the present intention of Ministers—seeing that their intentions are more liable to change than those of ordinary mortals—if you do hereafter establish a legion of Polish or other refugees, at least beforehand make up your mind what are to be the definite objects of the war. If, indeed, among those objects, as the war proceeds, you do see your way to the restitution of Poland among the free States of Europe, say so manfully, and there are few Englishmen who would not rejoice at the possibility of such a barrier to Russian encroachment, and such a reparation to the fraud and violence of a former age. Then, indeed, Poles would be more than our soldiers—they would become our allies, and they would be as welcome to our country, as they would be our brothers in the field. But if you have no idea of such an enterprise, or if you would indolently trust the resuscitation of Poland in the pages of European history to that chapter in human fate with which you appear most familiar—the chapter of accidents—then I say, beware how you wilfully lend yourselves to false hopes, or incur the stain of insincerity with all whom you invite to your standard, not for the sake of pay, but from the expectation of freedom. It would be in vain to say you did not deliberately sanction such hopes; that the Poles must silence their beating hearts, and bo but the unreasoning machines of your military drill. That idea is against the first law of human nature. Every Pole whom you form into regiments would say that you had led him to unavailing slaughter, unless you had made it one object of your war to plant your standard on the citadel of Warsaw. And, do let the House remember that the number of these foreign soldiers, from first to last, is unlimited. It is the peculiarity of this Bill that, while for the commencement of the war, in which you say they are alone required, the force is most paltry and inadequate, yet hereafter, when you say they will not be wanted, the number swells and increases, and is altogether undefined; it is 10,000 men at a time; but the Bill establishes a perpetual depôt of reserve, and, as soon as one set are dispatched to the field, another may be prepared here to succeed them; so that we can form no conceivable guess as to the number you will employ and ultimately disband. Suppose, then, hereafter, you do form Polish battalions, and peace comes, and the Poles have still no country, what is to become of the large bands of armed malcontents you will leave on the surface of Europe, and who cannot quietly melt, like your own soldiers, into the ranks of peaceful citizens? Whatever you do, then, I implore you, for the sake of justice to Poland—for the honour of English sincerity and plain dealing—and for the cause of social order throughout Europe—to decide, before you may enlist battalions of exiled patriots, how far you will venture to extend the definite objects of this war. Sir, it may be quite competent to honourable gentlemen to extend the discussion of this Bill, which is one cause that now brings us together, into a survey of the general conduct of the war, of which you call this an essential measure. I have no such intention. I do not desire to reiterate former charges, nor set into adroit display every casual detail of inexperience or omission; on the contrary, I heard with pleasure the eloquent speech the other night of the Secretary at War—a pleasure, not only at his eloquence, but caused by a feeling more worthy of him and me, because he seemed to me satisfactorily to dispose of many charges connected with his own department; not, indeed, made in this House, but which had excited a painful impression out of doors. I cheerfully recognize in the Cabinet many who have won those high names in the service of their country which give them the noblest stake in its honour and its welfare; nor is there, indeed, one in the Cabinet —I might say in all the Government—of whom I would speak in other terms than those of personal respect. But still, it is not always a motley, and, possibly, sometimes a discordant, combination of able and worthy men which suffices to constitute an able and worthy Cabinet, even in times of peace; and for the fitting and spirited conduct of war it does require a promptitude, a decision, a rapid and comprehensive foresight, which can only come from an unity of purpose and of object; and that unity the conflicting speeches of Ministers have already notoriously belied. Take but a single instance—take the last. Compare the sanguine terms in which the treaty with Austria is paraded by one Minister elsewhere, with the cautious scepticism as to its actual value, "its important results," which has been expressed by the organ of the Government in this House. And here I must make one observation in connexion both with all that this treaty may lead to, and also with the conduct of the war. It has been assumed, on a recent occasion, by the First Minister of the Crown,* that Government was blamed for its reluctance to go to war, as exhibited in preliminary negotiations. This is not strictly the fact. What we presume to regret, if not to blame, is, that in those preliminary negotiations the sentiment of the people, which so deeply resented the first disguised aggression on Turkish independence, was never fairly represented to the Russian Emperor, and that if the language held by our Ministers at the first, without being at all more threatening, had been more frank and plain-spoken, you would have had a better chance of preserving peace than you could have by complimenting the Russian Czar on his moderation and sincerity, after he had openly proposed the subdivision of the Turkish dominions, and after he had deceived your credulity by representing large military preparations as an innocent mode of moral coercion. It may be well to remember this, should a treaty with Austria lead to new overtures for peace. If so, Government are sure of success. They have only carefully to remember the spirit with which they conducted former negotiations, and to conduct the future in a spirit diametrically the reverse. It is not true that we blame the Ministers for not going to war till all parties were prepared to support it; but what we regret—if we dare not blame—is, that the only persons unprepared for the war are the very Ministers charged with its conduct; and so unprepared were they, that the best excuse for all deficiencies is, that they engaged in an indefinite war against a formidable enemy, with military preparations so little raised above the ordinary establishments of peace, and on the niggard hypothesis that its cost could be defrayed out of our annual income. And now, when the public are perhaps indulgently disposed to receive your tardy assumption of energy, braced up at the last moment, at the commencement of winter, as a partial indemnity for your, at least, comparative indolence during the precious months of summer and autumn—who could foresee that one of the gigantic efforts of your collective patriotism, reserved as a surprise, so pleasing and prodigious that, although we are now told by the noble lord it is the main reason why we meet, it is not even alluded to in the speech from the Throne —who could foresee that this gigantic effort— this grand surprise—was to be this begging petition to petty potentates for 10,000 soldiers? What! has it come to this? In an empire, on which we are told that the sun never sets, the national council is hastily summoned to prepare and parade all its military power. One Minister tells us his recruits are more than he can manage; another says we could bring a million soldiers into the field—some day or other; and then, when all the world is breathless to know what you are about to bring forth, *nascitur ridiculus mus*, out creeps this proposal to borrow or crimp from the foreigner 10,000

* See Lord Aberdeen's speech at the Mansion House, Nov. 9th, 1854.

troops to be drilled in these realms. This grand profession of redundant strength, and this curious confession of absolute want, remind me of the adventurer who boasted to an acquaintance he picked up at a coffee-house of the immense wealth he possessed at a distance—his castles in the north, and his lands in the west, and his shares in the copper mines of Cornwall, and the gold mines of Peru—and when he had worked up his listener to the highest point of prospective gratitude as to what he might expect from the munificence of a friend of such boundless resources, suddenly clapped his hand to his pocket and said, "By-the-by, I have a little bill to pay at the bar; you don't happen to have such a thing as tenpence-halfpenny about you?" Whatever way I look at this proposed Bill, I can see nothing to justify and excuse it. I have said that there is no parallel case of precedent. Now, let us ask, what is your plea of necessity? And here, sir, I find my own opinions so lucidly and moderately stated by a great man whose authority must have the utmost weight with gentlemen opposite, that I will read what was said in this House by the late Lord Grey, then Mr. Grey. He said, "On urgent occasions it may be proper to introduce foreign troops into this country, but it should never be done except in cases of extreme and proved necessity, and never should be suffered to be done without being watched with that constitutional jealousy which is the best part of the character of this House, and the best security for the rights and liberties of the people." Now let me pause, and appeal to the generous candour of honourable gentlemen opposite, if these words, from one of the greatest statesmen who ever adorned your opinions, do not justify the jealousy with which we regard this Bill; and, whether we are right or wrong in that jealousy, if they do not amply vindicate us from the unworthy charge of wishing to obstruct the general preparations for the war, because we cavil at the introduction of foreign soldiers? Mr. Grey went on to observe that, "though he was not ready to deny that, for the purpose of our own defence, we should sometimes employ foreign troops, yet he could not help thinking that the wisest course for us would be to rely on what had been emphatically called the energy of an armed nation." So, then, where is this case of urgent and proved necessity—necessity for our own defence? You have not argued it as a necessity; the noble lord has not done so: he is too much of an Englishman for that. It is only argued at most as a question of convenience—the convenience of drilling or organizing the troops in this country; and I say that it does not seem to me a convenience that is worth the purchase. Sir, it was not unreasonably asked elsewhere, "How will this proposition be regarded by the enemy?" What a pretext do you give to the Emperor of Russia to represent to his subjects the correctness of his estimate of the shopkeeping spirit of Great Britain. "Compare," he will say, "their braggart talk in their Houses of Parliament, their boast of the popular enthusiasm, their willingness to contribute their best blood to the cause for which they fight, with the simple fact that before the first year is out they are compelled to apply to the fifth-rate Powers of Europe for 10,000 foreign soldiers, on the pretence—nay, on the confession—that they are not a military nation; that they have not had time since this war began to drill a sufficient number of recruits for an army; which at the battle of Inkermann could only bring 8,000 men fit for service into the field." I don't desire to stand thus either before the enemy or before our allies, and I say that this is not the best mode to remove the hesitation of Austria and Prussia. I am convinced that we have men of our own, even at this moment, in spite of all previous delays, prepared to fight our own battle. You tell us you have already sent large reinforcements to the Crimea. You sent them weeks and months ago. Of course, ever since you have been raising and drilling more. You have had ample leisure. You have leisure still to drill into active service the recruits you obtain from a population so brave, so robust, and so proverbially quick of comprehension as that of Great Britain and Ireland. I deny altogether, that the drafts you will take from our labouring population will derange the channels of agricultural or other industry. We have plenty to spare from a population of nearly thirty millions. The suspension of many industrial occupations on railways and elsewhere, caused by the war, releases a large number of the stoutest portion of our labourers. You may find employment in the army for many more of the marines, now idle at a distance; you may make use of the native forces in India; above all, you have only to rely on our militia—to give fair play to that magnificent nursery of soldiers. I don't presume to offer you advice in details—I say only, go into the market of war with the best spirit of trade. Your best and nearest market is at home. Get there the best article you can; it is the cheapest in the long run. I remember that in 1779, when the ports of France and Spain bristled with hostile ships, when American privateers were seen with impunity in the Channel, that Lord Harcourt offered to Ireland 4,000 foreign troops in lieu of a greater number sent to America. What was the answer of the Irish Parliament? Sir, they rejected the proposal; they declared "that they were competent to defend themselves, or that they were not worth defending." That noble answer, which became the representatives of Ireland, may equally become the United Parliament of the three kingdoms; and what was the practical result of that refusal? Why, the result of refusing 4,000 foreign soldiers was, that 50,000 volunteers immediately presented themselves. Talk of our men being raw recruits: why, how many of those who dashed through the Russian armaments, who braved with equal fortitude unparalleled sufferings, of disease, of climate, of a defective commissariat, were the new recruits you affect to depreciate? That material which a British army has so successfully tested is the material on which a British Parliament may be content to rely. Those labourers and sons of labourers whom the leader of this House eulogized in terms of such just and such noble eloquence; those men—those raw recruits, equally daring in the charge, and calm as veterans under the attack; those men, so patient in their sufferings, and so humane to the foe,—those are the material for your army. You have tried it; keep to it. Without disparagement to the soldiers you may collect from Germany, Switzerland, Sweden, Poland, anywhere abroad, I say we have proved sufficiently that this is not the moment in which we need tax our countrymen in order to arm the foreigner for our defence. Do you ask me what proof? Alma, Balaklava, Inkermann! I say that any deficiencies in the mere mechanism of the drill are quickly got over with officers so skilful as ours; I say that even the raw recruits, before they have joined your standard, have already gone through a more precious discipline than three years of lifeless ceremonials can give to the soldiers of a despotic conscription. They have gone, from their cradles, through the discipline of hardy habits, of patient endurance, of indomitable conviction in the strength of their own right arms—that is the discipline with which armies soon learn to be invincible, and without which men may be faultless in the drill, but valueless in the field. Sir, with these views, and trusting they may not be altogether distasteful to the patriotism of the House, I move that this bill be read a second time this day six months.

NATIONS NOT PERMANENTLY INFLUENCED BY FRIENDSHIPS.

As to the romantic notion that nations or governments are much or permanently influenced by friendships, and God knows what, why, I say that those who maintain those romantic notions, and apply the intercourse of individuals to the intercourse of nations, are indulging in a vain dream. The only thing which makes one government follow the advice and yield to the counsel of another, is the hope of benefit to accrue from adopting it, or the fear of the consequences of opposing it.—*Palmerston.*

JOHN CALDWELL CALHOUN.
Born 1782. *Died* 1850.

[J. C. Calhoun, one of whose best speeches we here reprint, may worthily take rank among the most forcible and conspicuous of American orators. Of Irish extraction, and availing himself of the best education of his time, he displayed in early life those qualities of mind which made his after career so brilliant; and very shortly after he entered Congress, "the young Carolinian" was hailed as one of the master-spirits of his age. After serving many of the highest offices of state, in 1825 he was promoted to the Vice-Presidency, and, with but slight intermission, as Secretary of State and Senator, was engaged in the service of the Republic till his death, in 1850. On the style of his oratory we cannot do better than quote the words of Daniel Webster, contained in one of his addresses in the Senate of the United States, in which he bore a generous testimony to the genius and character of Calhoun. "His eloquence," says Webster, "or the manner of his exhibition of his sentiments in public bodies, was part of his intellectual character. It grew out of the qualities of his mind. It was plain, strong, terse, condensed, concise; sometimes impassioned, still always serene. Rejecting ornament, not often seeking far for illustration, his power consisted in the plainness of his propositions, in the closeness of his logic, and in the earnestness and energy of his manner. These were the qualities which enabled him through a long course of years to speak often, yet always command attention." In addition to his official labours, Calhoun also found leisure for the composition of two masterly political works—the one, "A Disquisition on Government;" the other, a "Discourse on the Constitution and Government of the United States." He will, however, be best remembered for his patriotism, and the eloquence with which he expressed it. The speech which follows was delivered in the House of Representatives of the United States, on the 12th of December, 1811, on the second resolution reported by the Committee of Foreign Relations. Near the end of November, 1811, the Committee on Foreign Relations submitted a report, which, after an able examination of the causes of war with Great Britain, concluded by recommending to the House the adoption of a series of resolutions, among which was the following :—

2. *Resolved,* "That an additional force of ten thousand regular troops ought to be immediately raised, to serve for three years; and that a bounty in lands ought to be given to encourage enlistments."

This resolution having been amended in Committee of the Whole, by omitting the word *ten,* was reported to the House. An animated debate ensued: a majority of the Committee avowed their object to be a preparation for war. The principal speaker in the opposition was John Randolph, to whom Mr. Calhoun seems to have confined his reply. The resolution was finally adopted.]

SPEECH ON INCREASE OF THE ARMY.

MR. SPEAKER:—I understood the opinion of the Committee on Foreign Relations differently from what the gentleman from Virginia (Mr. Randolph) has stated to be his impression. I certainly understood that the Committee recommended the measures now before the House as a preparation for war; and such, in fact, was its express resolve, agreed to, I believe, by every member except that gentleman. I do not attribute any wilful misstatement to him, but consider it the effect of inadvertency or mistake. Indeed, the report could mean nothing but war or empty menace. I hope no member of this House is in favour of the latter. A bullying, menacing system has everything to condemn, and nothing to recommend it. In expense it almost rivals war. It excites contempt abroad, and destroys confidence at home. Menaces are serious things; and ought to be resorted to with as much caution and seriousness as war itself; and should, if not successful, be invariably followed by it. It was not the gentleman from Tennessee (Mr. Grundy) who made this a war question. The resolve contemplates an additional regular force; a measure confessedly improper but as a preparation for war, but undoubtedly necessary in that event.

Sir, I am not insensible to the weighty importance of the proposition, for the first time submitted to this House, to compel a redress of our long list of complaints against one of the belligerents. According to my mode of thinking, the more serious the question, the stronger and more unalterable ought to be our convictions before we give it our support. War, in our country, ought never to be resorted to but when it is clearly justifiable and necessary; so much so, as not to require the aid of logic to convince our understandings, nor the ardour of eloquence to inflame our passions. There are many reasons why this country should never resort to war but for causes the most urgent and necessary. It is sufficient that, under a government like ours, none but such will justify it in the eyes of the people; and were I not satisfied that such is the present case, I certainly would be no advocate of the proposition now before the House.

Sir, I might prove the war, should it ensue, justifiable, by the express admission of the gentleman from Virginia;—and necessary, by facts undoubted, and universally admitted; such as he did not pretend to controvert. The extent, duration, and character of the injuries received; the failure of those peaceful means heretofore resorted to for the redress of our wrongs, are my proofs that it is necessary. Why should I mention the impressment of our seamen; depredations on every branch of our commerce, including the direct export trade, continued for years, and made under laws which professedly undertake to regulate our trade with other nations; negotiation resorted to, again and again, till it is become hopeless; the restrictive system persisted in to avoid war, and in the vain expectation of returning justice? The evil still grows, and, in each succeeding year, swells in extent and pretension beyond the preceding. The question, even in the opinion and by the admission of our opponents, is reduced to this single point—Which shall we do, abandon or defend our own commercial and maritime rights, and the personal liberty of our citizens employed in exercising them? These rights are vitally attacked, and war is the only means of redress. The gentleman from Virginia has suggested none, unless we consider the whole of his speech as recommending patient and resigned submission as the best remedy. Sir, which alternative this House will embrace, it is not for me to say. I hope the decision is made already, by a higher authority than the voice of any man. It is not for the human tongue to instil the sense of independence and honour. This is the work of nature; a generous nature that disdains tame submission to wrongs.

This part of the subject is so imposing as to enforce silence, even on the gentleman from Virginia. He dared not deny his country's wrongs, or vindicate the conduct of her enemy. Only one part of his argument had any, the most remote relation to this point. He would not say we had not a good cause for war, but insisted that it was our duty to define that cause. If he means that this House ought, at this stage of its proceedings, or any other, to specify any particular violation of our rights to the exclusion of all others, he prescribes a course which neither good sense nor the usage of nations warrants. When we contend, let us contend for all our rights—the doubtful and the certain, the unimportant and essential. It is as easy to struggle, or even more so, for the whole as for a part. At the termination of the contest, secure all that our wisdom and valour and the fortune of the war will permit. This is the dictate of common sense; such also is the usage of nations. The single instance alluded to—the endeavour of Mr. Fox to compel Mr. Pitt to define the object of the war against France—will not support the gentleman from Virginia in his position. That was an extraordinary war for an extraordinary purpose, and was not governed by the usual rules. It was not for conquest or for redress of injury, but to impose a government on France which she refused to receive—an object so detestable that an avowal dared not be made.

Sir, I might here rest the question. The affirmative of the proposition is established. I cannot but advert, however, to the complaint of the gentleman from Virginia when he was first up on this question. He said he found himself reduced to the necessity of supporting the negative side of the question, before the affirmative was established. Let me tell the gentleman that there is no hardship in his case. It is not every affirmative that ought to be proved. Were I to affirm that the House is now in session, would it be reasonable to ask for proof? He who would deny its truth, on him would be the proof of so extraordinary a negative. How then could the gentleman, after his admissions, with the facts before him and the country, complain? The causes are such as to warrant, or rather make indispensable, in any nation not absolutely dependent, to defend its rights by force. Let him, then, show the reasons why we ought not so to defend ourselves. On him lies the burden of proof. This he has attempted; he has endeavoured to support his negative. Before I proceed to answer him particularly, let m call the attention of the House to one circumstance; that is, that almost the whole of his arguments consisted of an enumeration of evils always incident to war, however just and necessary; and which, if they have any force, are calculated to produce unqualified submission to every species of insult and injury. I do not feel myself bound to answer arguments of this description; and if I should touch on them, it will be only incidentally, and not for the purpose of serious refutation.

The first argument of the gentleman which I shall notice, is the unprepared state of the country. Whatever weight this argument might have in a question of immediate war, it surely has little in that of preparation for it. If our country is unprepared, let us remedy the evil as soon as possible. Let the gentleman submit his plan, and if a reasonable one, I doubt not it will be supported by the House. But, sir, let us admit the fact and the whole force of the argument. I ask, whose is the fault? Who has been a member for many years past, and seen the defenceless state of his country, even near home, under his own eyes, without a single endeavour to remedy so serious an evil? Let him not say, "I have acted in a minority." It is no less the duty of the minority than a majority to endeavour to defend the country. For that purpose we are sent here, and not for that of opposition.

We are next told of the expenses of the war, and that the people will not pay taxes. Why not? Is it from want of means? What! with 1,000,000 tons of shipping; a commerce of $100,000,000 annually; manufactures yielding a yearly product of $150,000,000; and agriculture of thrice that amount, shall we be told the country wants capacity to raise and support ten thousand or fifteen thousand additional regulars? No; it has the ability—that is admitted—and will it not have the disposition? Is not the cause a just and necessary one? Shall we then utter this libel on the people? Where will proof be found of a fact so disgraceful? It is answered: In the history of the country twelve or fifteen years ago. The case is not parallel. The ability of the country is greatly increased since. The whisky tax was unpopular. But on this, as well as my memory serves me, the objection was not to the tax or its amount, but to the mode of collection. The people were startled by the number of officers; their love of liberty shocked by the multiplicity of regulations. We, in the spirit of imitation, copied from the most oppressive part of European laws on the subject of taxes, and imposed on a young and virtuous people all the severe provisions made necessary by corruption and long-practised evasions. If taxes should become necessary, I do not hesitate to say the people will pay cheerfully. It is for their government and their cause, and it would be their interest and their duty to pay. But it may be, and I believe was said, that the people will not pay taxes because the rights violated are not worth defending; or that the defence will cost more than the gain. Sir, I here enter my solemn protest against this low and "calculating avarice" entering this hall of legislation. It is only fit for shops and counting-houses, and ought not to disgrace the seat of power by its squalid aspect. Whenever it touches sovereign power, the nation is ruined. It is too short-sighted to defend itself. It is a compromising spirit, always ready to yield a part to save the residue. It is too timid to have in itself the laws of self-preservation. It is never safe but under the shield of honour. There is, sir, one principle necessary to make us a great people—to produce not the form, but real spirit of union—and that is, to protect every citizen in the lawful pursuit of his business. He will then feel that he is backed by the government; that its arm is his arm; and will rejoice in its increased strength and prosperity. Protection and patriotism are reciprocal. This is the way which has led nations to greatness. Sir, I am not versed in this calculating policy; and will not, therefore, pretend to estimate in dollars and cents the value of national independence. I cannot measure in shillings and pence the misery, the stripes, and the slavery of our impressed seamen; nor even the value of our shipping, commercial and agricultural losses, under the orders in council, and the British system of blockade. In thus expressing myself I do not intend to condemn any prudent estimate of the means of a country before it enters on a war. This is wisdom—the other, folly. The gentleman from Virginia has not failed to touch on the calamity of war, that fruitful source of declamation by which humanity is made the advocate of submission. If he desires to repress the gallant ardour of our countrymen by such topics, let me inform him that true courage regards only the cause—that it is just and necessary, and that it contemns the sufferings and dangers of war. If he really wishes to promote the cause of humanity, let his eloquence be addressed to Lord Wellesley or Mr. Perceval, and not the American Congress. Tell them, if they persist in such daring insult and injury to a neutral nation, that, however inclined to peace, it will be bound in honour and safety to resist; that their patience and endurance, however great, will be exhausted; that the calamity of war will ensue, and that they, in the opinion of the world, will be answerable for all its devastation and misery. Let a regard to the interests of humanity stay the hand of injustice, and, my life on it, the gentleman will not find it difficult to dissuade his country from rushing into the bloody scenes of war.

We are next told of the dangers of war. I

believe we are all ready to acknowledge its hazards and misfortunes; but I cannot think we have any extraordinary danger to apprehend, at least none to warrant an acquiescence in the injuries we have received. On the contrary, I believe no war can be less dangerous to the internal peace or safety of the country. But we are told of the black population of the Southern States. As far as the gentleman from Virginia speaks of his own personal knowledge, I shall not question the correctness of his statement. I only regret that such is the state of apprehension in his particular part of the country. Of the southern section, I too have some personal knowledge; and can say that in South Carolina no such fears in any part are felt. But, sir, admit the gentleman's statement; will a war with Great Britain increase the danger? Will the country be less able to suppress insurrection? Had we anything to fear from that quarter (which I do not believe), in my opinion the period of the greatest safety is during a war; unless, indeed, the enemy should make a lodgment in the country. Then the country is most on its guard; our militia the best prepared; and our standing army the greatest. Even in our revolution no attempts at insurrection were made by that portion of our population; and however the gentleman may alarm himself with the disorganizing effects of French principles, I cannot think our ignorant blacks have felt much of their baneful influence. I dare say more than one-half of them never heard of the French Revolution.

But as great as he regards the danger from our slaves, the gentleman's fears end not there—the standing army is not less terrible to him. Sir, I think a regular force raised for a period of actual hostilities cannot properly be called a standing army. There is a just distinction between such a force and one raised as a permanent peace establishment. Whatever would be the composition of the latter, I hope the former will consist of some of the best materials of the country. The ardent patriotism of our young men, and the reasonable bounty in land which is proposed to be given, will impel them to join their country's standard, and to fight her battles; they will not forget the citizen in the soldier, and in obeying their officers, learn to contemn their government and constitution. In our officers and soldiers we will find patriotism no less pure and ardent than in the private citizen; but if they should be depraved as represented, what have we to fear from twenty-five thousand or thirty thousand regulars? Where will be the boasted militia of the gentleman? Can one million of militia be overpowered by thirty thousand regulars? If so, how can we rely on them against a foe invading our country? Sir, I have no such contemptuous idea of our militia—their untaught bravery is sufficient to crush all foreign and internal attempts on their country's liberties.

But we have not yet come to the end of the chapter of dangers. The gentleman's imagination, so fruitful on this subject, conceives that our constitution is not calculated for war, and that it cannot stand its rude shock. This is rather extraordinary. If true, we must then depend upon the commiseration or contempt of other nations for our existence. The constitution, then, it seems, has failed in an essential object, "to provide for the common defence." No, says the gentleman from Virginia, it is competent for a defensive, but not for an offensive war. It is not necessary for me to expose the error of this opinion. Why make the distinction in this instance? Will he pretend to say that this is an offensive war; a war of conquest? Yes, the gentleman has dared to make this assertion; and for reasons no less extraordinary than the assertion itself. He says our rights are violated on the ocean, and that these violations affect our shipping and commercial rights, to which the Canadas have no relation. The doctrine of retaliation has been much abused of late by an unreasonable extension; we have now to witness a new abuse. The gentleman from Virginia has limited it down to a point. By his rule, if you receive a blow on the breast, you dare not return it on the head; you are obliged to measure and return it on the precise point on which it was received. If you do not proceed with this mathematical accuracy, it ceases to be just self-defence: it becomes an unprovoked attack.

In speaking of Canada, the gentleman from Virginia introduced the name of Montgomery with much feeling and interest. Sir, there is danger in that name to the gentleman's argument. It is sacred to heroism. It is indignant of submission! It calls our memory back to the time of our revolution—to the Congress of '74 and '75. Suppose a member of that day had risen and urged all the arguments which we have heard on this subject; had told that Congress,—your contest is about the right of laying a tax; and that the attempt on Canada had nothing to do with it; that the war would be expensive; that danger and devastation would overspread our country, and that the power of Great Britain was irresistible,—with what sentiment, think you, would such doctrines have been then received? Happily for us, they had no force at that period of our country's glory. Had such been then acted on, this hall would never have witnessed a great people convened to deliberate for the general good; a mighty empire, with prouder prospects than any nation the sun ever shone on, would not have risen in the west. No; we would have been base subjected colonies; governed by that imperious rod which Britain holds over her distant provinces.

The gentleman from Virginia attributes the preparation for war to everything but its true cause. He endeavoured to find it in the probable rise in the price of hemp. He represents the people of the Western States as willing to plunge our country into war from such interested and base motives. I will not reason on this point. I see the cause of their ardour, not in such unworthy motives, but in their known patriotism and disinterestedness.

No less mercenary is the reason which he attributes to the Southern States. He says that the Non-Importation Act has reduced cotton to nothing, which has produced a feverish impatience. Sir, I acknowledge the cotton of our plantations is worth but little; but not for the cause assigned by the gentleman from Virginia. The people of that section do not reason as he does; they do not attribute it to the efforts of their government to maintain the peace and independence of their country. They see, in the low price of their produce, the hand of foreign injustice; they know well, without the market to the continent, the deep and steady current of supply will glut that of Great Britain; they are not prepared for the colonial state to which again that Power is endeavouring to reduce us, and the manly spirit of that section of our country will not submit to be regulated by any foreign Power.

The love of France and the hatred of England have also been assigned as the cause of the present measures. France has not done us justice, says the gentleman from Virginia, and how can we, without partiality, resist the aggressions of England? I know, sir, we have still causes of complaint against France; but they are of a different character from those against England. She professes now to respect our rights, and there cannot be a reasonable doubt but that the most objectionable parts of her decrees, as far as they respect us, are repealed. We have already formally acknowledged this to be a fact. But I protest against the principle from which his conclusion is drawn. It is a novel doctrine, and nowhere avowed out of this House, that you cannot select your antagonist without being guilty of partiality. Sir, when two invade your rights, you may resist both or either at your pleasure. It is regulated by prudence and not by right. The stale imputation of partiality for France is better calculated for the columns of a newspaper than for the walls of this House.

The gentleman from Virginia is at a loss to account for what he calls our hatred to England. He asks how can we hate the country of Locke, of Newton, Hampden, and Chatham; a country having the same language and customs with ourselves, and descending from a common ancestry. Sir, the laws of human affections are steady and uniform. If we have so much to attach us to that country, potent indeed must be the cause which has overpowered it. Yes, there is a cause strong enough; not in that occult courtly affection which he has supposed to be entertained for France; but it is to be found in continued and unprovoked insult and injury—a cause so manifest that the gentleman from Virginia had to exert much ingenuity to overlook it. But the gentleman, in his eager admiration of that country, has not been sufficiently guarded in his argument. Has he reflected on the cause of that admiration? Has he examined the reasons of our high regard for her Chatham? It is his ardent patriotism, the heroic courage of his mind, that could not brook the least insult or injury offered to his country, but thought that her interest and honour ought to be vindicated at every hazard and expense. I hope, when we are called upon to admire, we shall also be asked to imitate. I hope the gentleman does not wish a monopoly of those great virtues for England.

The balance of power has also been introduced as an argument for submission. England is said to be a barrier against the military despotism of France. There is, sir, one great error in our legislation. We are ready, it would seem from this argument, to watch over the interests of foreign nations, while we grossly neglect our own immediate concerns. This argument of the balance of power is well calculated for the British Parliament, but not at all suited to the American Congress. Tell the former that they have to contend with a mighty Power; and that if they persist in insult and injury to the American people, they will compel them to throw their whole weight into the scale of their enemy. Paint the danger to them, and if they will desist from injuring us, we, I answer for it, will not disturb the balance of power. But it is absurd for us to talk about the balance of power, while they, by their conduct, smile with contempt at what they regard our simple, good-natured vanity. If, however, in the contest it should be found that they underrate us—which I hope and believe—and that we can affect the balance of power, it will not be difficult for us to obtain such terms as our rights demand.

I, sir, will now conclude by adverting to an argument of the gentleman from Virginia, used in debate on a preceding day. He asked, why not declare war immediately? The answer is obvious—because we are not yet prepared. But, says the gentleman, such language as is here held will provoke Great Britain to commence hostilities. I have no such fears. She knows well that such a course would unite all parties here,—a thing which, above all others, she most dreads. Besides, such has been our past conduct, that she will still calculate on our patience and submission until war is actually commenced.

NICHOLAS, CARDINAL WISEMAN.

Born 1802. *Died* 1865.

[Cardinal Wiseman, for many years the most conspicuous Catholic dignitary in this country, and from one of whose addresses we here give a short extract, was, if not a great orator, at least an accomplished speaker, and during the course of his most active life delivered several lectures on literary and artistic subjects, which may well be read as good specimens of platform eloquence. From one of these, being the second of two discourses on the Home Education of the Poor, delivered at St. Martin's Hall in the year 1854, our present selection is made.]

POETRY FOR THE POOR.

DO not be startled if I say boldly, that it is absolutely necessary to create a poetry for the poor. It does not exist. A poetry of a twofold character—a poetry of narrative, and a poetry of song. It may be said that this belongs to a more ancient and more romantic period, that we have come to the days of practical utility, and that to fill the people's thoughts and minds with works simply of imagination, with melodious verse, however beautiful, is assisting them in no way to the great aims of their existence here. It will not be helping them forward in the duties of this world. This I will venture most completely to deny. The people will have poetry, whether it pleases us or not. They will have their songs, they will have their ballads; and if you do not furnish to them such as are worthy, not merely of rational, but of Christian beings; if you do not supply them with a stock of such literature as will not taint them, but, on the contrary, will cultivate and elevate them, you must be content to see them pick up their songs in the street, and buy such as we know by description only: for they are such as none of you would allow for a moment to contaminate your domestic circles.

In other times, in our own country, we are all aware that even the more homely duties of agriculture were made familiar to the ploughman and the labourer in verse; that the "Hundred Points of Good Husbandry," or the "Shepherd's Calendar," or other productions of such writers as Tusser, were familiar in the mouths of the people, because they had in them their best instruction, for the times, in agriculture. And, indeed, even as yet, there are numbers of those old jingles and rhymes which have passed into proverbs, and are familiar to the mouths of the people; such as their prognostics of weather, their anticipations of changes in it, the description of the time and season for performing agricultural operations. These are yet described by them in rhyme, because they have come down from old poets, who thought they could not better impress on the minds of the people, most of whom at that time could not read, the lessons of what was their art, than by thus, in some part, embodying and embalming them in homely verse. But, besides this, there is a power in the songs or poetry of a people which has been felt in every age, and may act either perniciously or most profitably.

I need hardly allude to ancient times. I need not speak of the influence which the bard or minstrel exercised almost upon the destinies of empires; but even in modern prosaic times we have witnessed what striking effects have followed from the power of the Muse. It is certain that in France many national ideas and attachments were kept firmly rooted in the minds of the people by the songs of Beranger. And we should not lose sight of that old saying of an eminent man, "Let me have the writing of the people's songs, and I care not who has the making of their laws." So powerfully was it felt, that the power over the people of the gentle charms of song which goes at once to the affections, was such that it might even sway the legislation of the country. Germany, in our times, has given proof of the minstrel's power. During the late Continental war, when all Germany was aroused as one people, there arose likewise a poet who embodied in himself the whole of this national feeling, who vividly committed this feeling to verse, which put into the mouths equally of the soldier and the peasant, national sentiments of unity and of bravery. And so Körner, by his "Lyre and Sword," proved how truly it was possible to entwine the laurel round the blade without dulling its edge, and that a man might have in his heart at once the tenderness of the bard and the courage of the warrior. For if his life was that of the poet, his end was that of a soldier on the field. And later still, it is well known to all what a powerful enthusiasm was excited through the whole of Germany, a few years ago, by the celebrated song of "The Rhine;" which made the whole nation, or rather that great alliance of nations that are bound together merely by the spell of a common mother tongue, unite themselves into a firm bond of resistance to any possible invasion. And this bond was woven by their poetical sympathies being excited for that noble river, which they had always considered to be the peculiar property and exclusive ornament of their own country. Even among barbarous tribes, too, the effect is the same. The independent feeling of the Albanian mountaineer has been kept up (though it led to a desultory sort of warfare), in great measure, by the collection of native patriotic songs, full of wild beauty, loved by their soldiers and their shepherds, which made them feel that, at every cost, they must preserve their independence amidst the free air of their own rugged homes.

In our own country has it not been so? In the time of the civil war, who does not know what influence the cavalier songs had among those who espoused the royal cause, and what pains were taken to make them known and sung, even after peace was restored, as the means of keeping alive in the breast the peculiar loyalty which was then required? And, in later times, who can forget that "Song of the Shirt," which was in everybody's mouth? What a beneficial influence did not that song exercise upon the rich in favour of the poor! How it awoke more kindly feeling in favour of an oppressed class of society than article upon article in the newspapers, or speeches or pamphlets, though proceeding from men of genius or learning, had been able to raise.

Then shall it not be the case with our people too? Is it not important, is it not necessary, that we should provide for them likewise this poetical literature, without which, I may say, no country has ever been thoroughly civilized as yet? And I really must say I firmly believe that if, at this crisis, there had been ready songs for the people—at this moment of war, so new to us in our generation—which, without exciting any unchristian sentiment of hatred or animosity, should have raised a just indignation against the perfidy of our enemies—should have made the people enthusiastic in their feelings for our army and navy—should have been full of loyal devotion to the Crown, and determination to preserve its honour—this war could not have been the dull and dead thing it has been. And, more: I think that one might even recommend the Chancellor of the Exchequer to have such songs prepared. For if we are to go on for a long period with war-taxes, if such songs were in the mouth, every hour, of the people in every hamlet and every field, they would be the best auxiliary to the tax-gatherer, and at least neutralize some portion of that grumbling and complaining which we all acknowledge to be, at his approach, characteristic of our race.

But some will say, "That is all very well; you can set men to write books, you can put a history into the hand of a clever man, and say, 'Reduce me these nine volumes to one short manual;' and if he *is* a clever man he will do it. But an old axiom says that you cannot make a poet; you cannot call a man, of whatever genius, and say to him, 'Sit down and write me a volume of such poetry as the people will love and sing.'" I own it. But we are not unprovided with the required means. And I say that he will show himself the greatest and the noblest-hearted poet, who will be the most ready to come to our assistance in such a cause. When the celebrated Göethe was one day wandering through the fields, he heard a peasant singing one of his beautiful lays—that which begins, "Kennst du das Land?"—which Byron has imitated in "Know ye the Land?"—and he said that that tribute to his poetic genius, of being in the ploughman's mouth, was to him more, and flattered him more, than all the elaborate criticisms of the learned, and the court and homage of the sovereigns throughout Germany; and that for the first time he now felt that he was a poet. And why, I would ask—why should the lays of ancient Rome be alone thought worthy of that flowing and glowing pen,* which has shed such a charm about them in addition to that which they had received from legendary history? Are not, on the contrary, the home thoughts and the home deeds of this our island worthy to be made familiar as household words to the poor, and to be read or recited in the evening as tales of the hearth and of the heart?

Then, as to our songs, can we be in want of authors for them? There is one genius who belongs certainly to both the hemispheres, though it was not ours that gave him birth—one who, by his keen perception and his warm love of whatever is great or beautiful in nature, whether it be in "forests primeval," or upon the sparkling shores of Salerno—who, by his intimate acquaintance with the depths, with the flexibilities, and, what is still more, with the simplicity of our language—who especially, by that warm and affectionate appreciation of what is true and noble, and honourable and tender in life—whether among the high or among the low—seems eminently calculated to give to the people, and to the world, that which we so much want. And much as we may have admired such creations of poetic genius as "Elsie," or "Evangeline," I am sure we might anticipate still greater pleasure from a collection of the people's songs from the muse of Longfellow.

But such words would require a music worthy of them. Now, standing as I do in this hall, with you as my audience, in a splendid edifice, the greatest and noblest that private enterprize has yet raised to the muse of song,† I am sure it is due to him who has done so much for the people, to express not only admiration for that peculiar talent which he has developed in the creation and propagation of his great work, but gratitude for having conferred upon society a great boon, as he has done, by eliciting a new means of recreation, a fresh source of cheerfulness, capable of exercising upon multitudes a refining and an inspiring influence. For I believe that the progress of music in our time, its great simplification, immense diffusion, and its practical

---

* Macaulay.
† St. Martin's Hall, built by Mr. Hullah.

introduction into such new spheres of life, is one of the most characteristic and noblest symptoms of the interest which this age takes in the good and happiness of the poorer classes. And yet shall I venture to say that something more has to be done? In the village school, in the small country choral union, the elements are but units, which are soon dissolved and removed one from the other. After they have sung in chorus joyfully, whether sacred or profane songs—I use the word, of course, without meaning reproach—each returns home. It is as if one string had been removed from the harp—it carries not away its power of harmony. I think it is of the utmost importance that, in addition to the choral music which is now so general, there should be also a system of melody taught—that is, of songs adapted to given tunes, which may be easily carried away by each hearer. I would have, in other words, every child, when he goes home in the evening from his school, to be there as a cricket upon the hearth, cheering the whole house, making his humble cottage vocal with his fresh and his joyful lay. And then I should not be even content with this. Why should it be, gentlemen, that the highest description which poetry can give of the music of our agricultural pursuits, cannot go beyond making our ploughman whistle at his work, while the Italian vine-dresser is naturally expected to make the whole valley ring and the hills echo with his thrilling and vivid ritornello? I would have the English agricultural peasant a songster, as well as him of southern climes; and therefore when a boy has finished his education, I would have him bear in his memory a stock of songs which should cheer his toil for life—songs full of affection towards everything around him, literally filling his heart with love of his home, making him believe it to be, however humble, to him the happiest and most sacred spot on earth; love of the very earth itself, which submits to his rude handling, and repays the labour of his hands and the sweat of his brow by filling his arms with the teeming abundance of its womb—love of the various domestic creatures that look up to him for their sustenance, and see in him their providence, and pay him back abundantly by the food and the clothing which they give him—love for nature in every form, making it always appear to him fair; whether it be in the storm or in the sunshine, in the gloom of winter or in the bloom of summer—always the same, glowing and joyful; but however bright, ever showing him, piercing through all brightness by its superior brilliancy, beaming over upon him, through every part of her, the face of a gracious and a bountiful God.

RICHARD B. SHERIDAN.

Born 1751. Died 1816.

[We here present the reader with the sad relics o that mighty speech, before alluded to in our note to another speech by Mr. Sheridan (*vide* p. 41), of which Burke declared that it was the most astonishing effort of eloquence, argument, and wit united, of which there was any record or tradition ; of which Fox said, "All that he had ever heard, all that he had ever read, when compared with it, dwindled into nothing, and vanished like vapour before the sun ;" and of which Pitt said that it possessed everything that genius and art could furnish to agitate and control the human mind. Its effects were so extraordinary, that the House was adjourned after a considerable pause, the members having come to the resolution that they were then too much excited to vote dispassionately. Sheridan's summing-up of the same charge against Warren Hastings, in June, 1788, extending as it did over four days, was, perhaps, a yet more extraordinary exhibition of his power ; it is, however, too long to be within the compass of this work. Burke's estimate of that speech may, nevertheless, be well subjoined here, as representing a splendid estimate of his eloquence by the greatest of his contemporaries. His words are :—" He has this day surprised the thousands, who hung with rapture on his accents, by such an array of talents, such an exhibition of capacity, such a display of powers, as are unparalleled in the annals of oratory ; a display that reflected the highest honour upon himself, lustre upon letters, renown upon Parliament, glory upon the country. Of all species of rhetoric, of every kind of eloquence that has been witnessed or recorded, either in ancient or modern times ; whatever the acuteness of the bar, the dignity of the senate, the solidity of the judgment seat, and the sacred morality of the pulpit have hitherto furnished ; nothing has surpassed, nothing has equalled what we have this day heard in Westminster Hall. No holy seer of religion, no sage, no statesman, no orator, no man of any literary description whatever, has come up, in the one instance, to the pure sentiments of morality, or in the other, to that variety of knowledge, force of imagination, propriety and vivacity of allusion, beauty and elegance of diction, strength and copiousness of style, pathos and sublimity of conception, to which we have this day listened with ardour and admiration. From poetry up to eloquence, there is not a species of composition of which a complete and perfect specimen might not, from that single speech, be culled and collected."]

CONFISCATION OF THE TREASURES OF THE BEGUM PRINCESSES OF OUDE.

MR. SHERIDAN commenced his speech by observing, that had it been possible to have received, without a violation of the established rules of Parliament, the paper* which the honourable member (Mr. Dempster) had just now read, he should willingly have receded from any forms of the House, for the purpose of obtaining new lights, and farther illustration on the important subject then before them; not indeed that on the present occasion he found himself so ill prepared, as merely, for this reason, to be prevented from proceeding to the discharge of his duty; neither, to speak freely, was he inclined to consider any explanatory additions to the evidence of Sir Elijah Impey so much framed to elucidate, as to perplex and contra-

---

* A paper relative to and explanatory of certain depositions of Sir Elijah Impey had been read by Mr. Dempster.

dict. Needless to his present purpose was it for him to require Sir Elijah legally to recognize what had been read in his name by the honourable gentleman. In fact, neither the informality of any subsisting evidence, nor the adducement of any new explanations from Sir Elijah Impey, could make the slightest impression upon the vast and strong body of proof which he should now bring forward against Warren Hastings. Yet, if any motive could so far have operated upon him as to make him industriously seek for renewed opportunities of questioning Sir Elijah, it would result from his fresh and indignant recollection of the low and artful stratagem of delivering to the members, and others, in this last period of parliamentary inquiry, printed handbills of defence, the contents of which bespoke a presumptuous and empty boast of completely refuting all which at any time had, or even could be advanced against Mr. Hastings, on the subject of the fourth article in the general charge of a right honourable member (Mr. Burke). But even this was far beneath his notice. The rectitude and strength of his cause were not to be prejudiced by such pitiful expedients; nor should he waste a moment in counteracting measures which, though insidious, were proportionately frivolous and unavailing. Nor would he take up the time of the committee with any general arguments to prove that the subject of the charge, which it fell to his lot to bring forward, was of great moment and magnitude. The attention which Parliament had paid to the affairs of India for many sessions past, the voluminous productions of their committees on that subject, the various proceedings in that House respecting it, their own strong and pointed resolutions, the repeated recommendation of his Majesty, and their reiterated assurances of paying due regard to those recommendations, as well as various acts of the Legislature, were all of them undeniable proofs of the moment and magnitude of the consideration, and incontrovertibly established this plain, broad fact, that Parliament directly acknowledged that the British name and character had been dishonoured and rendered detested throughout India by the malversation and crimes of the principal servant of the East India Company. That fact having been established beyond all question by themselves, and by their own acts, there needed no argument, on his part, to induce the committee to see the importance of the subject about to be discussed on that day, in a more striking point of view, than they themselves had held it up to public observation. There were, he knew, persons without doors who affected to ridicule the idea of prosecuting Mr. Hastings, and who, not inconsistently, redoubled their exertions in proportion as the prosecution became more serious, and to increase their sarcasms upon the subject, by asserting that Parliament might be more usefully employed; that there were matters of more immediate moment to gain their attention; that a commercial treaty with France had been just concluded, and that it was an object of a vast and comprehensive nature, and of itself sufficient to engross their attention. To all this he would oppose these questions. Was Parliament misspending its time by inquiring into the oppressions practised on millions of unfortunate persons in India, and endeavouring to bring the daring delinquent, who had been guilty of the most flagrant acts of enormous tyranny and rapacious peculation, to exemplary and condign punishment? Was it a misuse of their functions to be diligent in attempting, by the most effectual means, to wipe off the disgrace affixed to the British name in India, and to rescue the national character from lasting infamy? Surely no man, who felt either for the one or the other, would think a business of greater moment or magnitude could occupy his attention, or that the House could with too much steadiness, too ardent a zeal, or too industrious a perseverance, pursue its object. Their conduct in this respect, during the course of the preceding year, had done them immortal honour, and proved to all the world that, however degenerate an example of Englishmen some of the British subjects had exhibited in India, the people of England, collectively speaking, and acting by their representatives, felt, as men should feel on such an occasion; that they were anxious to do justice, by redressing injuries and punishing offenders, however high their rank, however elevated their station. Their indefatigable exertions in committees appointed to inquire concerning the affairs of India; their numerous, elaborate, and clear reports; their long and interesting debates, their solemn addresses to the throne, their rigorous legislative acts, their marked detestation of that novel and base sophism in the principles of judicial inquiry (constantly the language of the Governor-General's servile dependents), that crimes might be compounded, that the guilt of Mr. Hastings was to be balanced by his successes, that fortunate events were a full and complete set-off against a system of oppression, corruption, breach of faith, peculation, and treachery; and finally, their solemn and awful judgment that, in the case of Benares, Mr. Hastings' conduct was a proper object of parliamentary impeachment, had covered them with applause, and brought them forward in the face of all the world as the objects of perpetual admiration. Not less unquestionably just than highly virtuous was the assertion of the Commons of Great Britain, that there were acts which no political necessity could warrant, and that amidst flagrancies of such an inexplicable description, was the treatment of Cheit Sing. To use the well-founded and emphatic language of a right honourable gentleman (Mr. Pitt), the committee had discovered in the administration of Mr. Hastings, proceedings of strong injustice, of grinding oppression, and unprovoked severity. In this decision the committee had also vindicated the character of his right honourable friend, Mr. Burke, from the slanderous tongue of ignorance and perversion. They had, by their vote on that question, declared that the man who brought the charges was no false accuser; that he was not moved by envy, by malice, nor by any unworthy motives, to blacken a spotless name; but that he was the indefatigable, persevering, and, at length, successful champion of oppressed multitudes against a tyrannical oppressor. With sound justice, with manly firmness, with unshaken integrity, had his right honourable friend, on all occasions, resisted the timid policy of mere remedial acts: even the high opinion of Mr. Hastings' successor, even the admired worth of Lord Cornwallis's character, had been deemed by his honourable friend an inadequate atonement to India for the injuries so heavily inflicted on that devoted country. Animated with the same zeal, the committee had, by that memorable vote, given a solemn pledge of their further intentions. They had audibly said to India—You shall no longer be seduced into temporary acquiescence by sending out a titled Governor, or a set of vapouring resolutions. It is not with stars and ribands, and all the badges of regal favour, that we atone to you for past delinquencies. No! you shall have the solid consolation of seeing an end to your grievances, by an example of punishment for those that have already taken place. The House has set up a beacon, which, while it served to guide their own way, would also make their motions more conspicuous to the world which surrounded and beheld them. He had no doubt but in their manly determination to go through the whole of the business, with the same steadiness which gave such sterling brilliancy of character to their outset, they might challenge the world to observe and judge of them by the result. Impossible was it for such men to become improperly influenced by a paper bearing the signature of Warren Hastings, and put not many minutes before into their hands, as well as his own, on their entrance into the House. This insidious paper he felt himself at liberty to consider as a second defence, and a second answer to the charge he was about to bring forward; a charge replete with proof of criminality of the blackest dye, of tyranny the most vile and premeditated, of corruption the most open and shameless, of oppression the most severe and grinding, of cruelty the most hard and unparalleled. But he was far from meaning to rest the charge on assertion, or on any warm expressions which the impulse of wounded feelings might produce. He would establish every part of the charge, by the most unanswerable proof, and the most unquestionable evidence; and the witness whom he would bring forth to support every fact he should state, should be, for the most part, one whom no man would venture to contradict— Warren Hastings himself. Yet this character had friends, nor were they blameable. They might believe him guiltless, because he asserted his integrity. Even the partial warmth of friendship, and the emotions of a good, admiring, and unsuspecting heart, might not only carry them to such lengths, but incite them to rise with an intrepid confidence in his vindication. Again, Mr. Sheridan added, he would repeat that the vote of last session, wherein the conduct of this pillar of India, this corner-stone of our strength in the East, this talisman of the British territories in Asia, was censured, did the greatest honour to this House, as it must be the forerunner of speedy justice on that character which was said to be above censure, and whose conduct, we were given to understand, was not within the reach even of suspicion; but whose deeds indeed were such as no difficulties, no necessity could justify; for where is the situation, however elevated, and in that elevation however embarrassed, that can authorize the wilful commission of oppression and rapacity? If at any period a point arose on which inquiry had been full, deliberate, and dispassionate, it was the present. There were questions in which party conviction was supposed to be a matter of easy acquisition; and if this inquiry were to be considered merely as a matter of party, he should regard it as very trifling indeed; but he professed to God, that he felt in his own bosom the strongest personal conviction, and he was sensible that many other gentlemen did the same. It was on that conviction that he believed the conduct of Mr. Hastings, in regard to the Nabob of Oude and the Begums, comprehended every species of human offence. He had proved himself guilty of rapacity, at once violent and insatiable — of treachery, cool and premeditated — of oppression, useless and unprovoked—of breach of faith, unwarrantable and base—of cruelty, unmanly and unmerciful. These were the crimes of which, in his soul and conscience, he arraigned Warren Hastings, and of which he had the confidence to say he should convict him. As there were gentlemen ready to stand up his advocates, he challenged them to watch him—to watch if he advanced one inch of assertion for which he had not solid ground: for he trusted nothing to declamation. He desired credit for no fact which he did not prove, and which he did not indeed demonstrate beyond the possibility of refutation. He should not desert the clear and invincible ground of truth throughout any one particle of his allegations against Mr. Hastings, who uniformly aimed to govern India by his own arbitrary power, covering with misery upon misery a wretched people whom Providence had subjected to the dominion of this country; while, in defence of Mr. Hastings, not one single circumstance grounded upon truth was stated. He would repeat the words, and gentlemen might take them down. The attempt at vindication was false throughout.

Mr. Sheridan now pursuing the examination of Mr. Hastings' defence, observed, that there could not exist a single plea for maintaining that that defence against the particular charge now before the committee was hasty; Mr. Hastings had had sufficient time to make it up; and the committee saw that he had thought fit to go back as far as the year 1775 for pretended ground of justification from the charge of violence and rapacity.

[Mr. Sheridan here read a variety of extracts from the defence, which stated the various steps taken by Mr. Bristow in the years 1775 and 1776, to procure from the Begums aid to the Nabob.]

Not one of these facts, as stated by Mr. Hastings, was true. Groundless, nugatory, and insulting were the affirmations of Mr. Hastings, that the seizure of treasure from the Begums and the exposition of their pilfered goods to public auction (unparalleled acts of open injustice, oppression, and inhumanity) were in any degree to be defended by those encroachments on their property which had taken place previously to his administration, or by those sales which they themselves had solicited as a favourable mode of supplying a part of their aid to the Nabob. The relation of a series of plain, indisputable facts would irrecoverably overthrow a subterfuge so pitiful—a distinction so ridiculous! It must be remembered that, at that period, the Begums did not merely desire, but they most expressly stipulated, that of the thirty lacs promised, eleven should be paid in sundry articles of manufacture. Was it not obvious, therefore, that the sale of goods in the first case, far from partaking of the nature of an act of plunder, became an extension of relief, of indulgence, and of accommodation? But, however, he would not be content, like Mr. Hastings, with barely making assertions, or, when made against his statement, with barely denying them; on the contrary, whenever he objected to a single statement, he would bring his refutation, and almost in every instance Mr. Hastings himself should be his witness. By the passages which he should beg leave to read, Mr. Hastings wished to insinuate that a claim was set up in the year 1775 to the treasure of the Begums, as belonging of right to the Nabob.

[Here Mr. Sheridan, from a variety of documents, chiefly from the minutes of the Supreme Council, of which Mr. Hastings had been the president, explained the true state of that question.]

Treasure, which was the source of all the cruelties, was the original pretence which Mr. Hastings had made to the Company for this proceeding, and through the whole of his conduct he had alleged the principles of Mahomedanism in mitigation of the severities he had sanctioned; as if he meant to insinuate that there was something in Mahomedanism which rendered it impious for a son not to plunder his mother. But to show how the case precisely stood, when Mr. Hastings began the attacks, Mr. Sheridan read the minutes of General Clavering, Colonel Tonson, and Mr. Francis, who severally spoke of a claim which had been made by the Nabob on Bhow Begum in the year 1775, amounting to two and one-half lacs: the opinion contained in these minutes was, that women were, on the death of their husbands, entitled by the Mahomedan law only to the property within the Zenana where they lived. This opinion was decisive. Mr. Bristow used no threats; no military execution or rigour was even menaced; the Begums complied with the requisition then made, and the disputed property then claimed was given up. After this, the further treasure—namely, that which was within the Zenana—was confessedly her own. No fresh right was set up; no pretence was made of any kind to the residue. Nay, a treaty was signed by the Nabob and ratified by the resident, Mr. Bristow, that on her paying thirty lacs, she should be freed from all further application, and the Company were bound by Mr. Bristow to guarantee this treaty. Here, then, was the issue. After this treaty, thus ratified, could there be an argument as to the right of the treasure of the Begums? And if the Mahomedan law had ever given a right, was not that right then concluded? To prove, however, the reliance which the Princesses of Oude had entertained, even in the year 1775, of receiving protection and support from the British Government—an expectation so fatally disappointed in later times—Mr. Sheridan read an extract of a letter from the Begum, the mother of the Nabob, to Mr. Hastings, received at Calcutta, December the 22nd, 1775, where she says, "If it is your pleasure that the mother of the late Nabob, myself, and his other women and infant children, should be reduced to a state of dishonour and distress, we must submit; but if, on the contrary, you call to mind the friendship of the late blessed Nabob, you will exert yourself effectually in favour of us, who are helpless." And again: "If you do not approve of my remaining at Feyzabad, send a person here in your name to remove the mother of the late Nabob, myself, and about 2,000 other women and children, that we may reside with honour and reputation in some other place." Mr. Sheridan, in a regular progression of evidence, proceeded to state the successive periods, and finally to bring down the immediate subject in question to the day in which Mr. Hastings embraced the project of plundering the Begums; and to justify which he had exhibited in his defence four charges against them, as the grounds and motives of his own conduct.

1st, That they had given disturbance at all times to the Government of the Nabob, and that they had long manifested a spirit hostile to his and the English Government.

2ndly, That they excited the Zemindars to revolt at the time of the insurrection at Benares, and of the resumption of the Jaghires.

3rdly, That they resisted, by armed force, the resumption of their own Jaghires. And

4thly, That they excited, and were accessory to, the insurrection at Benares.

To each of these charges Mr. Sheridan gave distinct and separate answers. First, on the subject of the imputed disturbances, which they were falsely said to have occasioned, he could produce a variety of extracts, many of them written by Mr. Hastings himself, to prove that, on the contrary, they had particularly distinguished themselves by their friendship for the English, and the various good offices which they had rendered the Government. Mr. Hastings, Mr. Sheridan observed, left Calcutta in 1781, and proceeded to Lucknow, as he said himself, with two great objects in his mind—namely, Benares and Oude. What was the nature of these boasted resources? That he should plunder one or both; the equitable alternative of a highwayman, who, in going forth in the evening, hesitates which of his resources to prefer—Bagshot or Hounslow. In such a state of generous irresolution did Mr. Hastings proceed to Benares and Oude. At Benares he failed in his pecuniary object. Then, and not till then—not on account of any ancient enmities shown by the Begums—not in resentment for any old disturbances, but because he had failed in one place, and that he had but two in his prospect—did he conceive the base expedient of plundering these aged women. He had no pretence—he had no excuse—he had nothing but the arrogant and obstinate determination to govern India by his own corrupt will, to plead for his conduct. Inflamed by disappointment in his first project, he hastened to the fortress of Chunar, to meditate the more atrocious design of instigating a son against his mother—of sacrificing female dignity and distress to parricide and plunder. At Chunar was that infamous treaty concerted with the Nabob Vizier, to despoil the Princesses of Oude of their hereditary possessions. There it was that Mr. Hastings had stipulated with one, whom he called an independent Prince, "that, as great distress had arisen to the Nabob's Government from the military power and dominion assumed by the Jaghiredars, he be permitted to resume such as he may find necessary; with a reserve, that all such, for the amount of whose Jaghires the Company are guarantees,

shall, in case of the resumptions of their lands, be paid the amount of their net collections, through the resident, in ready money; and that no English resident be appointed to Furruckabad."

No sooner was this foundation of iniquity thus instantly established, in violation of the pledged faith and solemn guarantee of the British Government; no sooner had Mr. Hastings determined to invade the substance of justice, than he resolved to avail himself of her judicial forms, and accordingly dispatched a messenger for the Chief Justice of India to assist him in perpetrating the violations he had projected. Sir Elijah being arrived, Mr. Hastings, with much art, proposed a question of opinion, involving an unsubstantiated fact, in order to obtain even a surreptitious approbation of the measure he had predetermined to adopt. "The Begums being in actual rebellion, might not the Nabob confiscate their property?" "Most undoubtedly," was the ready answer of the friendly judge. Not a syllable of inquiry intervened as to the existence of the imputed rebellion, nor a moment's pause as to the ill purposes to which the decision of a Chief Justice might be perverted. It was not the office of a friend to mix the grave caution and cold circumspection of a judge with an opinion taken in such circumstances; and Sir Elijah had previously declared that he gave his advice not as a judge, but as a friend—a character he equally preferred in the strange office which he undertook of collecting defensive affidavits on the subject of Benares.

Mr. Sheridan said it was curious to reflect on the whole of Sir Elijah's circuit at that perilous time. Sir Elijah had stated his desire of relaxing from the fatigues of office, and unbending his mind in a party of health and pleasure; yet wisely apprehending that very sudden relaxation might defeat its object, he had contrived to mix some objects of business to be interspersed with his amusements. He had, therefore, in his little airing of nine hundred miles, great part of which he went post, escorted by an army, selected those very situations where insurrection subsisted and rebellion was threatened; and had not only delivered his deep and curious researches into the laws and rights of nations, and of treaties, in the capacity of the Oriential Grotius, whom Warren Hastings was to study, but likewise in the humbler and more practical situation of a collector of *ex parte* evidence. In the former quality his opinion was the premature sanction for plundering the Begums. In the latter character, he became the posthumous supporter of the expulsion and pillage of the Rajah Cheit Sing. Acting on an unproved fact, on a position as ideal as a datum of the Duke of Richmond's fabrication, he had not hesitated, in the first instance, to lend his authority as a licence for unlimited persecution. In the latter, he did not disdain to scud about India, like an itinerant informer, with a pedlar's pack of garbled evidence and surreptitious affidavits. What pure friendship! what a voucher of unequivocal attachment from a British judge to such a character as Warren Hastings! With a generous oblivion of duty and of honour; with a proud sense of having authorized all future rapacity, and sanctioned all past oppression, this friendly judge proceeded on a circuit of health and ease; and while the Governor-General, sanctioned by this solemn opinion, issued his orders to plunder the Begums of their treasure, Sir Elijah pursued his progress, and, passing through a wide region of distress and misery, explored a country that presented a speaking picture of hunger and of nakedness, in quest of objects best suited to his feelings—in anxious search of calamities most kindred to his invalid imagination.

Thus, while the executive power in India was perverted to the most disgraceful inhumanities, the judicial authority also became its close and confidential associate; at the same moment that the sword of government was turned to an assassin's dagger, the pure ermine of justice was stained and soiled with the basest and meanest contamination. Under such circumstances did Mr. Hastings complete the treaty of Chunar—a treaty which might challenge all the treaties that ever subsisted, for containing in the smallest compass the most extensive treachery. Mr. Hastings did not conclude that treaty till he had received from the Nabob a present, or rather a bribe, of £100,000. The circumstances of this present were as extraordinary as the thing itself. Four months afterwards, and not till then, Mr. Hastings communicated the matter to the Company. Unfortunately for himself, however, this tardy disclosure was conveyed in words which betray his original meaning; for, with no common incaution, he admits the present "was of a magnitude not to be concealed." Mr. Sheridan stated all the circumstances of this bribe, and averred that the whole had its rise in a principle of rank corruption. For what was the consideration for this extraordinary bribe? No less than the withdrawing from Oude not only all the English gentlemen in official situations, but the whole also of the English army; and that, too, at the very moment when he himself had stated the whole country of Oude to be in open revolt and rebellion. Other very strange articles were contained in the same treaty, which nothing but this infamous bribe could have occasioned, together with the reserve which he had in his own mind of treachery to the Nabob; for the only part of the treaty which he ever attempted to carry into execution was to withdraw the English gentlemen from Oude. The Nabob, indeed, considered this as essential to his deliverance; and his observation on the circumstance was curious; for "though Major Palmer," said he, "has not yet asked anything, I observe it is the custom of the English gentlemen constantly to ask for something from me before they go." This imputation on the English, Mr. Hastings was most ready, most rejoiced, to countenance, as a screen and shelter from his own abandoned profligacy; and therefore, at the very moment when he pocketed the extorted spoils of the Nabob, with his usual grave hypocrisy and cant, "Go," he said to the English gentlemen, "go, you oppressive rascals; go from this worthy, unhappy man whom you have plundered, and leave him to my protection. You have robbed him; you have plundered him; you have taken advantage of his accumulated distresses; but, please God, he shall in future be at rest, for I have promised him he shall never see the face of an Englishman again." This, however, was the only part of the treaty which he even affected to fulfil; and in all its other parts, we learn from himself that, at the very moment he made it, he intended to deceive the Nabob; and accordingly he advised general instead of partial resumption, for the express purpose of defeating the first views of the Nabob; and instead of giving instant and unqualified assent to all the articles of the treaty, he perpetually qualified, explained, and varied them with new diminutions and reservations. Mr. Sheridan called upon gentlemen to say if there was any theory in Machiavel, any treachery upon record, if they had ever heard of any cold Italian fraud which could in any degree be put in comparison with the disgusting hypocrisy and unequalled baseness which Mr. Hastings had shown on that occasion.

After having stated this complicated infamy in terms of the severest reprehension, Mr. Sheridan proceeded to observe, that he recollected to have heard it advanced by some of those admirers of Mr. Hastings, who were not so implicit as to give unqualified applause to his crimes, that they found an apology for the atrocity of them in the greatness of his mind. To estimate the solidity of such a defence, it would be sufficient merely to consider in what consisted this prepossessing distinction, this captivating characteristic of greatness of mind. Is it not solely to be traced in great actions, directed to great ends? In them, and them alone, we are to search for true estimable magnanimity: to them only can we justly affix the splendid title and honours of real greatness. There was, indeed, another species of greatness, which displayed itself in boldly conceiving a bad measure, and undauntedly pursuing it to its accomplishment. But had Mr. Hastings the merit of exhibiting either of these descriptions of greatness; even of the latter? He saw nothing great, nothing magnanimous, nothing open, nothing direct in his measures or in his mind. On the contrary, he had too often pursued the worst objects by the worst means. His course was an eternal deviation from rectitude. He either tyrannized or deceived, and was by turns a Dionysius and a Scapin. As well might the writhing obliquity of the serpent be compared to the swift directness of the arrow, as the duplicity of Mr. Hastings' ambition to the simple steadiness of genuine magnanimity. In *his* mind all was shuffling, ambiguous, dark, insidious, and little; nothing simple, nothing unmixed, all affected plainness and actual dissimulation. A heterogeneous mass of contradictory qualities, with nothing great but his crimes, and even those contrasted by the littleness of his motive, which at once denoted both his baseness and his meanness, and marked him for a traitor and a trickster; nay in his style and writing there was the same mixture of vicious contrarieties. The most grovelling ideas he conveyed in the most inflated language, giving mock consequence to low cavils, and uttering quibbles in heroics; so that his compositions disgusted the mind's taste as much as his actions excited the soul's abhorrence. Indeed, this mixture of character seemed, by some unaccountable but inherent quality, to be appropriated, though in inferior degrees, to everything that concerned his employers. He remembered to have heard an honourable and learned gentleman (Mr. Dundas) remark, that there was something in the first frame and constitution of the Company which extended the sordid principles of their origin over all their successive operations, connecting with their civil policy, and even with their boldest achievements, the meanness of a pedlar and the profligacy of pirates. Alike in the political and the military line could be observed auctioneering ambassadors and trading generals. And thus we saw a revolution brought about by affidavits; an army employed in executing an arrest; a town besieged on a note of hand; a prince dethroned for the balance of an account. Thus it was they exhibited a government which united the mock majesty of a bloody sceptre and the little traffic of a merchant's counting-house; wielding a truncheon with one hand, and picking a pocket with the other.

[Mr. Sheridan now went into a long statement to show the various irrefragable proofs exhibited in the minutes of the Bengal Council, of the falsity of the charge; viz., that the Begums were the ancient disturbers of the government. And equally to prove that the second charge also (namely, that the Begums had incited the Jaghiredars to resist the Nabob) was no less untrue, it being substantiated in evidence that not one of the Jaghiredars did resist.]

NO. XXXIV.

Mr. Sheridan maintained that it was incontrovertible that the Begums were not concerned either in the rebellion of Butbudder, or in the insurrection at Benares, nor did Mr. Hastings ever once seriously believe them to be guilty. Their treasures were their treasons, and Asophut Dowlah thought like an unwise prince when he blamed his father for leaving him so little wealth. His father, Shujah-ul-Dowlah, acted wisely in leaving his son with no temptation about him to invite acts of violence from the rapacious. He clothed him with poverty as with a shield, and armed him with necessity as with a sword.

The third charge was equally false. Did they resist the resumption of their own Jaghiredars? Though if they had resisted, he contended that there would have been no crime; for those Jaghires were by solemn treaty confirmed to them; but, on the contrary, there was not one syllable of charge against them. The Nabob himself, with all the load of obloquy which he incurred, never imputed to them the crime of stirring up an opposition to his authority.

To prove the falsehood of the whole of this charge, and to show that Mr. Hastings originally projected the plunder—that he threw the odium in the first instance on the Nabob—that he imputed the crimes to them before he had received one of the rumours which he afterwards manufactured into affidavits—Mr. Sheridan recommended a particular attention to dates; and he deduced from the papers these facts,—that the first idea was started by Mr. Hastings on the 15th of November, 1781; that Mr. Middleton communicated it to the Nabob, and procured from him a formal proposition, on the 2nd of December; that on the 1st of December Mr. Hastings wrote a letter to Mr. Middleton, confirming the first suggestion made through Sir Elijah, which letter came into the hands of Mr. Middleton on the 6th of December. He stated all the circumstances of the pains taken by Mr. Middleton to bring the Nabob at length to issue the Perwannas, and coupled this with the extraordinary minute written by Mr. Hastings on his return to Calcutta, where he stated the resistance of the Begums to the execution of the resumption on the 7th of January, 1782, as the cause of the measure in November, 1781. Mr. Sheridan then proceeded to prove that the Begums were, by their condition, their age, and their infirmities, almost the only two souls in India who could not have a thought of distressing that government, by which alone they could hope to be protected; and that to charge them with a design to depose their nearest and dearest relation was equally absurd. He did not endeavour to do this from any idea that, because there was no motive for the offences imputed to these women, it was therefore a necessary

s 2

consequence that such imputations were false. He was not to learn that there was such a crime as wanton, unprovoked wickedness. Those who entertained doubts on this point need only give themselves the trouble of reading the administration of Mr. Hastings. But, as to the immediate case, the documents on the table would bear incontrovertible testimony that insurrections had constantly taken place in Oude. To ascribe it to the Begums was wandering even beyond the improbabilities of fiction. It were not less absurd to affirm, that famine would not have pinched, nor thirst have parched, nor extermination have depopulated, but for the interference of these old women. To use a strong expression of Mr. Hastings on another occasion, "The good which those women did was certain, the ill precarious." But Mr. Hastings had found it more suitable to his purpose to reverse the proposition; yet, wanting a motive for his rapacity, he could find it only in fiction. The simple fact was, "their treasure was their treason." But, "They complained of the injustice." God of Heaven! had they not a right to complain? After a solemn treaty violated, plundered of all their property, and on the eve of the last extremity of wretchedness, were they to be deprived of the last resource of impotent wretchedness — complaint and lamentation? Was it a crime that they should crowd together in fluttering trepidation, like a flock of resistless birds on seeing the felon kite, who, having darted at one devoted bird and missed his aim, singled out a new object, and was springing on his prey with redoubled vigour in his wing, and keener vengeance in his eye? The fact with Mr. Hastings was precisely this: — Having failed in the case of Cheit Sing, he saw his fate; he felt the necessity of procuring a sum of money somewhere, for he knew that to be the never-failing recipe to make his peace with the Directors at home. Such, Mr. Sheridan added, were the true substantial motives of the horrid excesses perpetrated against the Begums —excesses, in every part of the description of which he felt himself accompanied by the vigorous support of most unanswerable evidence; and upon this test would he place his whole cause. Let gentlemen lay their hands upon their hearts, and with truth issuing in all its purity from their lips, solemnly declare whether they were or were not convinced that the real spring of the conduct of Mr. Hastings, far from being a desire to crush a rebellion (an ideal, fabulous rebellion!), was a malignantly rapacious determination to seize, with lawless hands, upon the treasures of devoted, miserable, yet unoffending victims?

Mr. Sheridan now adverted to the affidavit made by Mr. Middleton; and after stating how futile were the grounds upon which he had, to the satisfaction of his conscience, proceeded to the utmost extremity of violence against the Begums, he exclaimed: The God of Justice forbid that any man in this House should make up his mind to accuse Mr. Hastings on the ground which Mr. Middleton took for condemning the Begums; or to pass a verdict of guilty for the most trivial misdemeanor against the poorest wretch that ever had existed! He then revised and animadverted on the affidavits of Colonel Hannay, Colonel Gordon, Major MacDonald, Major Williams, and others. Major Williams, among the strange reports that chiefly filled these affidavits, stated one that he had heard—namely, that fifty British troops, watching two hundred prisoners, had been surrounded by six thousand of the enemy, and relieved by the approach of nine men. And of such extraordinary hearsay evidence were most of the depositions composed. Considering therefore the character given by Mr. Hastings to the British army in Oude, "that they manifested a rage for rapacity and peculation," it was extraordinary that there were no instances of stouter swearing. But as for Colonel Gordon, he afforded a flagrantly conspicuous proof of the grateful spirit and temper of affidavits designed to plunge these wretched women in irretrievable ruin. Colonel Gordon was, just before, not merely released from danger, but preserved from imminent death by the very person whose accuser he thought fit to become; and yet, incredible as it may appear, even at the expiration of two little days from his deliverance, he deposes against the distressed and unfortunate woman who had become his saviour, and only upon hearsay evidence accuses her of crimes and rebellion. Great God of Justice! (exclaimed Mr Sheridan) canst Thou from Thy eternal throne look down upon such premeditated turpitude of heart, and not fix some mark of dreadful vengeance upon the perpetrators? Of Mr. MacDonald he said, that he liked not the memory which remembered things better at the end of five years than at the time, unless there might be something so relaxing in the climate of India, and so affecting the memory as well as the nerves—"the soft figures melting away," and the images of immediate action instantaneously dissolving, men must return to their native air of England to brace up the mind as well as the body, and have their memories, like their sinews, re-strung.

Having painted the loose quality of the affidavits, he said that he must pause a moment, and particularly address himself to one description of gentlemen—those of the learned profession—within those walls. They saw that that House was the path to fortune in their profession; that they might soon expect that some of them were to be called to a dignified situation, where the great and important trust would be reposed in them of protecting the lives and fortunes of their fellow-subjects. One right honourable and learned gentleman in particular (Sir Lloyd Kenyon), if rumour spoke right, might suddenly be called to succeed that great and venerable character, who long had shone the brightest luminary of his profession, whose pure and steady light was clear, even to its latest moment, but whose last beam must now be too soon extinguished. And he would ask the supposed successor of Lord Mansfield to calmly reflect on these extraordinary depositions, and solemnly to declare whether the mass of affidavits taken at Lucknow would be received by him as evidence to convict the lowest object in this country. If he said it would, he declared to God he would sit down, and not add a syllable more to the too long trespass which he had made on the patience of the committee.

Mr. Sheridan went further into the exposure of the evidence, into the comparison of dates, and the subsequent circumstances, in order to prove that all the enormous consequences which followed from the resumption, in the rapacity of the women, and the imprisonment and cruelties practised on their people, were solely to be ascribed and to be imputed to Mr. Hastings. After stating the miseries which the women suffered, he said that Mr. Hastings had once remarked, that a mind touched with superstition might have contemplated the fate of the Rohillas with peculiar impressions. But if, indeed, the mind of Mr. Hastings could yield to superstitious imagination—if his fancy could suffer any disturbance, and, even in vision, image the proud spirit of Shujah Dowlah looking down upon the ruin and devastation of his family, and beholding that palace which Mr. Hastings had first wrested from his hand, and afterwards restored, plundered by that very army with which he himself had vanquished the Mahrattas; seizing on the very plunder which he had ravaged from the Rohillas; that Middleton, who had been engaged in managing the previous violations, most busy to perpetrate the last; that very Hastings whom, on his death-bed, he had left the guardian of his wife, and mother, and family, turning all those dear relations, the objects of his solemn trust, forth to the merciless seasons and to a more merciless soldiery. A mind touched with superstition must, indeed, have cherished such a contemplation with peculiar impressions. That Mr. Hastings was regularly acquainted with all these enormities committed on the Begums, there was the clearest proof. It was true that Middleton was rebuked for not being more exact; he did not, perhaps, descend to the detail; he did not give him an account of the number of groans which were heaved—of the quantity of tears which were shed—of the weight of the fetters—or of the depth of the dungeons; but he communicated every step which he took to accomplish the base and unwarrantable end

He told him that to save appearances they must use the name of the Nabob, and that they need go no farther than was absolutely necessary. This he might venture to say, without being suspected by Mr. Hastings of too severe a morality.

The Governor General also endeavoured to throw a share of the guilt on the Council, although Mr. Wheeler had never taken any share, and Mr. Macpherson had not arrived in India when the scene began.

After contending that he had shrunk from the inquiry ordered by the Court of Directors, under a new and pompous doctrine, that the majesty of justice was to be approached with supplication, and was not to degrade itself by hunting for crimes, forgetting the infamous employment to which he had appointed an English Chief Justice—to hunt for criminal charges against innocent, defenceless women—Mr. Sheridan said he trusted that that House would vindicate the insulted character of justice; that they would demonstrate its true quality, essence, and purposes; they would demonstrate it to be, in the case of Mr. Hastings, active, inquisitive, and avenging.

Mr. Sheridan remarked that he heard of factions and parties in that House, and knew they existed. There was scarcely a subject upon which they were not broken and divided into sects. The prerogative of the Crown found its advocates among the representatives of the people. The privileges of the people found opponents even in the House of Commons itself. Habits, connexions, parties, all led to diversity of opinion. But when inhumanity presented itself to their observation, it found no division among them: they attacked it as their common enemy; and, as if the character of this land was involved in their zeal for its ruin, they left it not till it was completely overthrown. It was not given to that House to behold the objects of their compassion and benevolence in the present extensive consideration, as it was to the officers it relieved, and who so feelingly describe the ecstatic emotions of gratitude in the instant of deliverance. They could not behold the workings of the heart, the quivering lips, the trickling tears, the loud and yet tremulous joys of the millions whom their vote of this night would for ever save from the cruelty of corrupted power. But though they could not directly see the effect, was not the true enjoyment of their benevolence increased by the blessing being conferred unseen? Would not the omnipotence of Britain be demonstrated to the wonder of nations by stretching its mighty arm across the deep, and saving by its fiat distant millions from destruction? And would the blessings of the people thus saved dissipate in empty air? No! If I may dare to use the figure, we shall constitute heaven itself our proxy, to receive for us the blessings of their pious gratitude, and the prayers of their thanksgiving. It is with confidence therefore, Sir, that I move you on this charge, "That Warren Hastings be impeached."

RESPECT TO BE PAID BY SOLDIERS TO THE RELIGIOUS CEREMONIES OF OTHER NATIONS.

I HAVE served in my profession in several countries and amongst foreigners, some of whom professed various forms of the Christian religion, while others did not profess it at all. I never was in one in which it was not the bounden duty of the soldier to pay proper deference and respect to whatever happened to be the religious institutions or ceremonies of the places where they might be. We soldiers do not go into these places to become parties to the religious differences of the people, or to trouble ourselves with their notions upon matters of faith; we go to perform a very different kind of duty—one which is purely military, and has no reference to the people's religion. I confess I never heard, however, that it was our custom to take any part in these religious rites; nor do I believe we do—except, perhaps, at Malta, where it is a long-sanctioned custom of the garrison, that a few artillery officers should cause small guns to be fired as some procession passes the platform; and I know that certain officers, on one occasion, disobeyed the usual order of their commandant, and—not on military, but on religious grounds—refused to comply with this ancient usage, and thought proper not to fire as this procession passed. What was the consequence? Why, they were brought to court-martial and cashiered—not because they would not form a part of any religious procession to which they were hostile—not because they would not conform to the rights of the natives, and worship any relic that was honoured by them, but for this plain and intelligible reason—that they had taken upon themselves to refuse obedience to the orders of their commander-in-chief on the spot, who according to a long prevailing custom, directed the usual salute to be made at the appointed time.—*The Duke of Wellington.*

A FREE CONSTITUTION THE PARENT OF ENGLAND'S PROSPERITY.

IT is to the liberty which we enjoy that the industry and exertion which happily distinguish England from many of the continental powers is to be ascribed; and to these advantages, which a free people only can possess, we owe all our superiority, which will not be affected by the largeness or smallness of our peace establishments.—*Palmerston.*

THE EARL OF DERBY.

Born 1799. *Living.*

[In a former part of this volume (see p. 110) a specimen of the later style of Lord Derby's oratory has been given. The extracts which now follow form the chief part of a speech delivered by him in the House of Commons, whilst he was still "the Rupert of debate" in that assembly, and the dreaded antagonist of O'Connell and his party. Lord Derby, then Mr. Stanley, was at the time of making this speech Chief Secretary for Ireland; and such was then the lawless condition of that country, that extraordinary powers were deemed necessary by the Executive, and accordingly a "Coercion Bill," as the measure conveying those powers was called, passed the House of Lords unopposed, and in the Commons contested only by O'Connell and his "tail," as the thirty or forty members under his influence were then called. It was during the debate on this bill, and on the evening of the 27th February, 1833, that this speech was delivered. A considerable portion of it was devoted to an accumulation of evidence relating to the gross crimes and outrages which then disgraced the history of Ireland. This, however, has been omitted in our present reprint, and, except as a justification for the measure which it supported, is not necessary for the proper appreciation of the speech.]

SPEECH ON THE DISTURBANCES (IRELAND) BILL, 27TH FEBRUARY, 1833.

SIR,—Although I never presented myself to the House with deeper feelings of regret and anxiety upon my mind, I must fairly say that I never presented myself to its attention with a more confident expectation and belief, that if there be any who yet doubt the necessity of the application of some strong and arbitrary measure for the peace of Ireland, for the repression of violence and disturbance, whether prædial or political, for the protection of life and property, for the maintenance of order and any established Government;—if, I say, there be any who still doubt the existence of this necessity, I entertain the most confident hope that I shall be able to show to the House sufficient grounds why not merely a bill, but why this bill—arbitrary and violent in its character as I confess it to be—is not only demanded by the strictest justice, but called for by the most imperious and pressing necessity. Sir, whatever the honourable gentleman who has just sat down may think of the characters and dispositions of the men who sit on this side of the House, as being adverse to rational and sober liberty, I may appeal with confidence to longer and to better known political lives than my own—the political lives of those with whom I have the honour to act—whether they have been, on former occasions, or whether they are likely to be on this, the men who, on light and trivial grounds, would interfere with the liberty and freedom of the subject. I appeal not only to our conduct in earlier days, but to the conduct we have pursued since we have been in office. I appeal not now to those extensions of popular rights which it has been our unceasing and arduous task to accomplish; but I appeal to the whole course of our conduct in Ireland, and I ask whether, night after night, and week after week, and month after month, we have not resisted importunities, and taunts, and pressings upon us, to go beyond the powers of the law to repress disturbances by means stronger than those of the ordinary course of justice. I ask if in the case of Clare,—I ask if in the case of Galway,—I ask if in the case of Queen's County, we manifested any desire to go beyond the ordinary powers of the law? In Clare we succeeded; in Galway we succeeded. I give every credit to the gentlemen of Clare and the gentlemen of Galway for the manner in which they came forward and assisted in repressing those disturbances. I give them credit for the courage and determination with which they took their proper station at the head of the population, for the manner in which they met threats and intimidation, likely to have deterred men in a humbler station and with poorer means of defence. I give them every credit for leaving their station as grand jurors of their respective counties, and taking upon themselves the invidious task of serving upon petty juries, by which they ensured the administration of justice, at a time when other classes of the population and the lower order of jurors shrunk as they did from administering the law with impartiality and firmness. I cast no imputation on the gentlemen of Queen's County. They have also come forward; many of them have served on petty juries; many of them served on petty juries at the special commission, when, had they not done so, and had they left the law to the ordinary mass of jurors, the law could not have been vindicated in Queen's County, and we should not have obtained even the partial success which has attended the special commissions. In the county of Kilkenny—I say this without any fear of offending any man, or set of men—for in a case of this kind I must discharge my duty openly and honestly—I say, in the county of Kilkenny, the gentlemen have shrunk from their duty. I say they have not placed themselves in the front of the battle as they might have done; they have not evinced the energy and firmness they might have displayed, and I am not casting an unjust imputation upon them when I say that if they had, in the first instance, taken a more prominent station, there might have been a better chance of putting an end to these disturbances.

Mr. O'CONNELL.—Hear, hear!

Mr. STANLEY.— When I make this admission, which the honourable and learned gentleman cheers, it is no reason why, when disturbances have arrived at their present height, and when the ordinary operation of the law, even were it wielded with the most earnest and most anxious desire to give it effect, and the most unflinching courage on the part of the gentlemen of the county, would no longer be able to cope with the spirit of outrage—I say in such a case it is no reason why we should not stop in and say, that whatever may be the mischief of establishing the injurious precedent of going beyond the law, it is our paramount duty, by any means, and by all means, to endeavour to restore the authority of the law, and the advantages of peace to this distracted country. But I say again, there is not at this moment that necessary degree of courage in Kilkenny. I have reason to believe that the gentry would not, at this moment, come forward; and I shall certainly have some occasion to show, in the course of my observations, that if there be intimidation and alarm, it is not altogether without foundation. I am very far from saying that the picture which it has been the duty of my noble friend to draw, or the picture which it will be my duty to draw, of the state of crime in Ireland, is uniformly applicable to the state of the country at large. On the contrary, I confine the whole of the statements I am about to make, with very few and trifling exceptions, to the extent of the province of Leinster. I do not say that there are not partial disturbances in other provinces; but I do say that I am content to rest our case, for the extraordinary powers we ask, on the circumstances and the present state of the province of Leinster. As portions of Ireland are more affected than others, we do not wish to apply the extraordinary powers of this bill indiscriminately to the whole of Ireland. We ask for powers undoubtedly without limitation, but we ask for those powers because, in the application of them, we act upon our own responsibility; because, if honourable gentlemen please, we act upon our responsibility to a reformed Parliament—upon our responsibility to a Parliament where the sense of the three countries is fully, fairly, and freely taken, and because it is impossible for me to say in the present state of the country, while marauding parties are going from county to county, carrying outrage and disturbance with them (for in many cases, I believe in most, outrages have arisen from bands of armed strangers patrolling the place in which they were committed)—I say it is impossible for me to say "here is the limit beyond which crime cannot pass; here is the limit to which alone it is necessary to give the Lord Lieutenant the power of applying the stringent provisions of this bill." I fear it will be necessary for me to trespass on the attention of the House, by reading to it several extracts from correspondents from various parts of the country, detailing individual acts of guilt which appear to me to cast a peculiar shade of atrocity and violence over the state of crime in Ireland. Honourable gentlemen, I should think, will not expect that, in reading portions of these letters, I can do more than state the districts from which they are written. The opinions expressed in these documents must be considered as the views entertained by nameless individuals; every gentleman must see that it would be impossible for me to lay before the House the names of the persons from whom this information is derived.

[Here Mr. Stanley read several letters describing the condition of the country, and the reign of terror which prevailed in various districts of Ireland.]

I have other letters to the same effect as those I have already read, from other parts of Kildare, Louth, Westmeath, Queen's County, and Kilkenny; but as the honourable gentleman who has just sat down has been pleased to attribute the greater part of the outrages which have been committed to the measures taken for enforcing the payment of tithes, I will only trouble the House further by reading to them a short extract of a letter from the Attorney-General for Ireland, which will show how far the honourable member is justified in his assertion. The Attorney-General says:—"I am just now condemned to my periodical duty of reading the informations preparatory to the circuits; those of the Home Circuit alone are equal to what the whole country produced two years ago; and yet they are only a partial exhibition of the quantity of actual crime. Shocking as the number is, it is only when we come to examine the facts of each case that any adequate idea can be formed of the utter demoralization of the country. I do not find, in 150 cases which I have gone through, a single one connected with tithe, nor an instance in which the person or property of a gentleman was the object of aggression; but the weak and destitute labourers, poor farmers, widows, and, in a word, the most defenceless classes of society, are the victims of this tyranny—all the operations of which are carried on in a state of cruelty that makes the blood run cold." If this, sir, be the liberty for which honourable gentlemen contend—if this be the liberty which we are charged with infringing—if it be the liberty, not of doing whatever may be harmless to others, but liberty to injure and wrong those who are most defenceless and unprotected—the liberty of the assassin—of the midnight burglar—of the determined conspirator against all the laws of the land; if, I say, this be the liberty with the infringement of which we are charged by the introduction of this bill, then, indeed, do I admit that we are most guilty. But if to protect the well-disposed and peaceable subject—if to guard the poor man's hearth and thatched cabin—if to maintain the public peace be the duty of a Government—call this a coercive, despotic, unconstitutional and arbitrary bill, if you will; but I contend that it is a bill which, so far from being intended to injure or destroy liberty, goes directly to preserve and perpetuate liberty in its truest character. We are told of this being as bad as the Insurrection Act! Why, the Insurrection Act is now actually in force against the well-disposed, in so far as it prohibits them from leaving their houses at night. But how is it in force? It is in force under an irresponsible authority—not that of the Government, but of the Whitefeet; and a double aggravation of the grievance is, that not only can no man leave his house by night without risk of exposing his property and family to rapine and outrage, but that no man can rest in his bed without being disturbed by the apprehension, and exposed to the danger, of these nocturnal legislators paying him a domiciliary visit for the purpose of putting in force their Insurrection Act.

My noble friend has stated details of outrages sufficient to justify Ministers in the course they have adopted, but he stated them in the plainest and simplest manner; and if I find anything to complain of in the speech of my noble friend, it is, that he has rather understated the case, and has not dwelt on all the horrible details of those atrocious offences with sufficient fulness and accuracy.

[Again the speaker entered with great minuteness into evidence and statistics to show the prevalence of the worst forms of crime throughout the length and breadth of the country. He then proceeded to assert the necessity of some extraordinary measure for its coercion, and continued as we here represent to the close of his speech.]

Sir, I have hitherto confined myself in what I have addressed to the House to making out a case, as I think I have done, of a system of combined outrage and insubordination existing in Ireland, which requires the intervention of some extraordinary authority, and with which the law in its present state is unable to cope. I shall now proceed to examine, although not in detail, for I am not aware that I am called upon to enter into detail on this occasion, the principal provisions of this bill, as they may be found applicable to such a state of affairs as I have described, and as is generally admitted to exist. I do not, sir, complain of the unusual discussion to which this bill has been subjected in its present stage, because I am ready to admit that though the ordinary practice of the House might have been to have postponed a discussion, even upon the principle of the bill, until a later stage of the measure, still I am ready to admit that the importance and the extraordinary character of the measure itself afford a sufficient justification for deviating in this instance from the ordinary course of parliamentary proceedings. Sir, I have already stated that the committee of last year recommended that the Insurrection Act should be so far put in force as to prohibit persons being out of their houses at night, and that they admit also, to the fullest extent, the necessity of domiciliary visits, subject, however, no doubt, to certain auxiliary controls; and let me state, at the outset, that to no checks upon the abuses which undoubtedly were practised under the former Act—to no control which shall not impair the efficiency of the measure, will I, or will the Government, offer any opposition in the progress of this bill. The system, however, of domiciliary visits I hold to be absolutely essential for the purpose of effecting the object which we have in view. But the tribunal proposed to be appointed by this bill is made a matter of objection, and, undoubtedly, we have not adopted the tribunal which was recommended by the committee of last year. Now, what was the tribunal which was recommended by that committee? It was to be a tribunal consisting of the magistrates of the neighbourhood, sitting at the quarter sessions, by adjournment from time to time, trying offences as they might arise. Now, if I know any one species of tribunal against which objections would be more fairly urged than another, it is precisely the tribunal recommended by that committee. If I know any objection which was more strongly urged than another against the former Insurrection Act; if I know any abuse which was more loudly complained of, or any part of the system which in its ultimate operation led to more permanently injurious consequences than another, it was the very fact that the trial of these offences, superseding the necessity of a jury, was entrusted to the resident local magistrates of the county. I know that it was asserted over and over again—I do not say it was asserted with truth—that the execution of this law, which they entrusted to the local magistracy, was perverted by them to their own purposes of revenge or of malice, to their own objects, and to private feelings or pecuniary motives. I do not say that these charges were well founded —I do not believe them to have been well founded—but I do say that it is a matter of perfect indifference, whether they be well founded or not, if they leave upon the minds of the peasantry and the feelings of those who have been subject to the operation of the law, an impression that the law has been so perverted by those very persons who, after having sentenced and transported their relations, are still living amongst them in the relative situations of landlords to tenants, and of local magistrates exercising the ordinary powers of the law, after having been entrusted with the execution of the arbitrary provisions of an extraordinary statute. We propose, therefore, undoubtedly to depart from the recommendation of the committee of last year, as tending to establish a tribunal much more objectionable on many grounds, and much more doubtful in its verdicts than a military tribunal.

I do not think it is necessary for me now to repel the charges, or rather to reply to the allegations which have been made without any ground stated, or without any foundation on which they can rest, by the honourable member for the City of London (Mr. Grote), who has characterized a military tribunal as one which would be likely to exercise the functions entrusted to it in an arbitrary and vindictive spirit, and which would give a verdict of conviction unjustified by the evidence that might be brought before it. Sir, such an assertion not only rests upon no solid foundation, but is contradicted by the experience of all those who are best acquainted with the proceedings of these tribunals.

The honourable member for the City of London thinks that it would be much more satisfactory, if powers beyond the ordinary law are to be given, that they should be confided to a tribunal possessed of a civil jurisdiction. Now, sir, in the first place, the honourable member is quite mistaken if he supposes that these military tribunals would not have the confidence of the people of Ireland. So far from this being the case, any gentleman who has attended to the debates in this House must know that, over and over again, when there has been any wish or intention to cry down the police, it has been the constant practice to set up in comparison with them the uniformly patient, friendly, and gentle conduct which has been evinced towards the people of the country by the military, with whom they may have happened to have come in contact. The peasantry in Ireland, we are told, regard the soldiers as their friends; they look to the officers for justice; and I will undertake to say, that when from the necessity of the case we have been compelled, as we often have, to give the commission of the peace to military officers stationed in particular districts, those military officers have generally been the magistrates to whom the people have been most ready and most willing to submit their complaints and differences. It is not either necessary for me to reply to the observations of the honourable member for the City of London, with reference to the members of such a tribunal being opposed by feeling to the liberty of the subject, and being inclined to found convictions on slight or insufficient evidence. But the honourable member says this tribunal is an unconstitutional one. Sir, I admit it; I state it to be unconstitutional—I state the whole of our measure to be unconstitutional. We have put it forward as an infringement of the Constitution; we have put it forward as such infringement solely on the ground of the stern and arbitrary necessity of the case— a necessity which leaves us no alternative but to resort to the employment of powers beyond the law, and to seek the means of permanent protection for the Constitution itself, by stepping for a time beyond the limits of that Constitution.

These, sir, being the grounds on which this measure has been brought forward, I confess, however paradoxical it may appear, that it is a peculiar recommendation to my mind on this part of the question, that this bill is so clearly, so obviously, so markedly a deviation from the ordinary course of the law, that it cannot, by possibility, be drawn into a precedent to be resorted to on occasions of less urgent necessity. But, sir, if we are not to appeal to a military tribunal, to what tribunal is it we are to have recourse? I wish to say nothing derogatory to the bar of Ireland; but I confess that, with regard to the judges, I should contemplate with the greatest jealousy, alarm, and repugnance, the employment of those whose characters ought to be beyond, not merely a stain, but even the imputation of a stain—of men who should strictly confine themselves to the letter as well as the spirit of the law—I say I should contemplate with the greatest jealousy the employment of such men in carrying into effect the powers proposed to be given by this bill, and exercising anything like an extraordinary judicial power. Admitting, then, that the judges are not the tribunal to which we should go, I should think there would be infinite danger in entrusting the powers established under this bill to a tribunal composed of barristers. However well disposed they might be to do their duty, they would be open to the suspicion of seeking to please the Government in their decisions; and they would be more especially exposed to this popular suspicion from the fact, that a great majority of the Irish bar entertain a political bias—I do not blame them or complain of them for so doing—opposed to the extension of popular rights. I feel confident, sir, that these honourable and high-minded men would not be swayed by such a bias in the performance of their duty; but of this I am equally sure, that their verdicts and their decisions would be open to such imputations, that they would not give the same general satisfaction, and would not excite the same confidence in their impartiality, as would be felt and entertained towards a tribunal constituted of persons who had no connexion with the country, and no dependence upon the local government of Ireland. But, sir, I repeat, that if we are to go beyond the law, and beyond the ordinary terms of the Constitution, let that departure be so broad and so marked, that we cannot lightly have recourse to it, as a precedent to be followed up and acted upon hereafter. Beware, sir, of sliding out of trial by jury. Do not make a gradual transition from the constitutional law to a tribunal which, under the semblance of being constitutional, may still maintain the appearance of a civil tribunal, and may reconcile men's minds the more easily to doing away, upon light and trifling grounds, with the inestimable advantage of trial by jury. I repeat, then, that the more this measure is at variance with the ordinary course of the law, the more, in my judgment, under the peculiar circumstances under which it is brought forward, does it come recommended as one that should be adopted by the House. I have hitherto confined myself, sir, altogether to prædial agitation. I am willing to admit the statement of the honourable member for the City of London, that this bill is divisible into two separate and distinct parts, one relating to prædial agitation, and the other to political disturbance. The honourable member for the City of London states that, however willing he might be to support that part of the bill which would go to give stronger powers to the Government for the purpose of putting down prædial agitation, nothing could induce him to support that part of it which is calculated to control the political liberty of the subject. Before we come to a consideration of this part of the subject, let us see whether the political liberty of the subject does at this time exist in Ireland.

Well, then, sir, with every disposition to promote rather than control the political liberty of the subject, I ask, is Ireland at this moment in a state in which the subject has a free exercise of political liberty? If it be not; if the honest free expression of political opinion be not uncontrolled and secure; if men can be subject to the loss of life or property, or to violence of any description, on account of the sentiments they may entertain that liberty does not exist, nor can it under the tyranny of societies which monopolize the name of public opinion—which control public opinion—which seek to "wield at their will the fierce democracy" of Ireland—which seek to usurp the power, the constituted authority, and offices of Government—which form but another mode, not of effecting the liberty, but of riveting the slavery—the political slavery—of Ireland. The honourable and learned gentleman sees no connexion between the outrages which have been committed in that country, or—to use the gentle term by which he designates them—between prædial agitation and that political agitation which he thinks so salutary to the Constitution of his country. Sir, I am not going to state that that learned gentleman, or those who act with him, have directly recommended those deeds of outrage any more than they recommended a run upon the Bank for gold. On the contrary, let me do justice to the honourable and learned gentleman; let me read a portion of a letter which he, the other day, addressed to the editor of a newspaper. "Let me implore of you," says the honourable gentleman, "not to injure commercial credit by calling for a run on the Bank for gold—let me entreat you to keep the people from running for gold." But why keep the people from running for gold? Because there was gold? Because there was no occasion for it; for "when this atrocious Algerine Act shall have passed, the run will take place of itself to the last banknote." That is not advice to run for gold; it is only a hint that such a run might embarrass the Government—might ruin the credit of the country—might cause great distress; but the hint is carefully kept out of sight that it would be the ruin of hundreds of his poorer countrymen. But the honourable gentleman does not recommend a run for gold—he does not recommend the Whitefeet offences; no—he always deprecates them—he addresses his exhortations to their perpetrators—he sends down pacificators, his ministers of tranquillity and of order. Sir, I should have been inclined to read to the House the last speech of one of these pacificators, but I am told that I must not, although it has appeared in all the newspapers.

SEVERAL HONOURABLE MEMBERS.—Read! read!

MR. STANLEY.—If I were to read this—

SEVERAL HONOURABLE MEMBERS.—Read! read!

MR. STANLEY.—Well, then, before I proceed to the last speech of the pacificator, let me be permitted to introduce him to the House. The gentleman, at a meeting of the volunteers of Ireland, of whom I shall have to say a word by-and-by, thus makes a declaration of his political allegiance to the honourable and learned member for Dublin:—"Honoured as I am by the confidence reposed in me by the father of his country, and by the people of Ireland, I stand in a position so high as to enable me to look down upon the malicious attempts of the enemies of Ireland to injure me with the contempt which they deserve. I said I was ready to go out upon the orders of O'Connell. I said deliberately the 'orders' of O'Connell, and repeat the word; for to O'Connell I pay a moral and a voluntary allegiance, because he has proved himself well worthy of it. I have acted under the orders of O'Connell, and am ready to do so again. If I got an order from O'Connell to stand upon a mine that was about to spring, I would obey that order without hesitation. I am now speaking calmly and deliberately upon, to me, one of the most important occasions I recollect in my life. I have been invested with a mission of deep and of grave importance. I am going among a peasantry irritated and infuriated by a system of the most tyrannical oppression." Well, now, what on another occasion was the language of this devoted vassal—this subject ready to obey all the orders of his master, no matter how despotic? "I told the men of Clare," says he, "that if such a crisis were to arrive, in consequence of any atrocious act of the Government, as that of Camden and Castlereagh in 1798, as that O'Connell should command us to have recourse to arms, and blood and convulsion, instead of our usual constitutional warfare by which we had achieved such resplendent and inevitable triumphs; in that case I would not order the Clare men to go into Cratloe wood to cut down trees for pike-handles, but that I would first send them to cut down the trees in my own domain of Lough O'Connell, and that I would, of course, myself not be idle, nor a mere looker on in the conflict." Observe, that this devoted vassal of the honourable and learned gentleman, who would put himself on a mine even if he knew it were about to be sprung (perhaps he may have done so already) were he so ordered by that gentleman; this is the individual who was sent down with that language in his mouth in the character of a pacificator. This is the man who is to show us that the prædial outrages have nothing to do with political agitation, and to tell us that he entreated the Whitefeet, perpetrators of those deeds of violence, as they valued the love of their chief, not to continue in them, lest, perchance, an awkward bill might be passed against them by this House, which might deprive them of the merit of voluntarily abandoning them. Now, hear the harangue of this minister of peace. In speaking of the Government, he says that "Lord Grey was an atrocious tyrant, but Brougham was the most tyrannical of the whole set. People formerly thought a good deal of kings; but times are changed; that's not the case now. He thought no more of William IV. than of a man in a tripe-shop!" This is, I must say, a low simile, coming from a gentleman, too, who stands in so high a situation as to be able to look down with contempt upon all the enemies of Ireland; but it is not the less mischievous for being low. He continues:—"If the same system were pursued by the Whigs as was carried on under the Governments of Lords Camden and Castlereagh, they (the people) might walk into his woods, and cut them down; and he hoped they would know how to make good use of the timber! I was here yesterday," he continued, "sitting on the rock of Carrickshock, speaking to the brave fellows who would not suffer themselves to be shot at; they were as much against the rascally Whitefeet as I am, and they are assisting me in putting them down. I asked them, if O'Connell found it necessary to order them out (though it would be the last thing he would resort to, and would lament it above all things), would they take him (Steele) for their leader? They all shouted out that they would follow me through the gates of hell."

Sir, a similar address was subsequently made at another place, which I will not, however,

NO. XXXV.

trouble the House with: the author of them is now about to abide the legal consequences of the language he has thought fit to hold. Well, then, sir, we are told that political agitation has nothing to do with prædial agitation—that the political agitators all hate the Whitefeet—that they want to put them down (though they set about it in an odd way); but is that the impression of the people? Is it the impression which the lower classes have? Do they not combine the system of outrage with cries for justice? Is that not the pretext on which they base their prædial agitation? Do they not think they are serving their cause by that course? Do not they think that in their violation of the law they are acting according to the orders of the honourable and learned member for Dublin—if not according to his orders, at least in consonance with his implied wishes? Trifling things will sometimes show the feelings of the multitude. I have before me a part of a ballad—a specimen of exceedingly bad poetry, but immoderately violent withal—which will illustrate what I just observed. I have also a manuscript copy of the same performance; but as the various readings are not material, I will take the printed version as circulated in the country. It was written and sung about the streets of Kilkenny, after the murder at Carrickshock, and while the prisoners in that affair were yet on their trial. I read it, not to exposeits violence and brutality, but to show that in the minds of the people there are political objects combined with these prædial outrages:—

THE DOWNFALL OF THE TITHES.

You banished sons of this distressed nation,
  Lend an ear to my joyful song,
Granua's sons they are liberated,
  They broke the chains they bore so long.
The wisp is kindled thro' this injured nation,
  Recall her heirs to revenge her wrong:
Not to pay those cursed demons;
  Tithes not legal on Slievenaman.
The wind a long time has been contrary,
  Which caused Erin's sons to be very sad,
But now quite suddenly it has turned fairly,
  A breezing gale through the nation ran,
Which filled poor Catholics with admiration
  To fly next day to Slievenaman.
May Heaven prosper you sweet Knocktopher,
  No less than Homer could your praises chaunt;
You loyal subjects that fought victorious,
  Fire and smoke could not your courage daunt.
They led the rabble (Police) along before them,
  Like wolves opposing the shepherd's flock,
Till in death's cold agonies they left them
  Groaning in the borheen of Carrickshock!
Who could desire to see better sport.
To see them groping among the rocks;
Their skulls all fractured, and eye-balls broken,
  Their fine long noses and ears cut off.
But Sergeant Wiley, that Orange rogue,
  He may thank his soles that so nimbly ran;
Yet all that's past is but a token
  To what we'll show them on Slievenaman.
We heard the text of the Divine says
  That when the date of the year is gone,
That one true Catholic without a weapon
  Would banish legions from Slievenaman.

Now, sir, I beg the reflection of the House to what follows, because here the poet has borrowed not his ideas only, but his very words, from the honourable and learned member:—

  The day of ransom, thank God, is dated,
    These cursed demons must quit the land;
  It's now those foreign and proud invaders,
    Shall feel the weight of each Irish hand.

The foreign and proud invaders! Why, sir, can anyone fail to trace here the fiery denunciations of the honourable and learned gentleman against the foreign Parliament—the Sassenach tyrants—the slavery under a foreign yoke? Who is it that furnishes to the ignorant people these topics of declamation, and then condemns the outrages which have been caused by the spirit of hatred and discontent which he has himself excited?—

  No vestry cess nor tithes we'll pay them,
    We'll banish preachers from our land.
  When persecution is terminated,
    And all those traitors are dead and gone,
  Poor Irish captives are liberated,
    All by the means of our noble Dan.
  The tree of liberty we'll plant so stainless,
    It shan't fade during the age of man,
  To show that Catholic Emancipation
    Was truly gained on sweet Slievenaman.

Sir, I read this, paltry and absurd as it is, not from a wish to connect it with the feelings and recommendations of the honourable and learned member—for I disclaim all intention to connect him with anything so base and atrocious—but I read it to show that, in the minds of the ignorant and deluded people, those denunciations and that advice which he has so liberally given have been perverted to a purpose which, in my conscience, I acquit him of having ever contemplated. I will not go any further—I will say no more as to the natural connection which every man, I think, must see between the acts of outrage which have been perpetrated in Ireland, and the injunctions of those who are daily holding up to public odium, as was observed the other day by an honourable gentleman on the other side of the House—the Lord Lieutenant, the judges, the grand jury, the clergy, the magistrates, the police—in short, all the constituted authorities of that country. Can any man hold up to public odium, to public hatred, and public contempt, all that is held sacred in the administration of the laws of his country, and then put his hand to his heart and say that he has no connection with the outrages which arise from resistance to the execution of those laws? But, sir, without connecting the political agitation of the country with the prædial outrages which distract it, I say, that the societies which are now spreading throughout Ireland, and more especially that which has been lately organized under the title of the Volunteers of Ireland, are inconsistent, not only with the freedom, but the very political existence of that country. There can be no law, no security, no government, if all is to rest upon an irresponsible and self-constituted body of volunteers, arming themselves to effect their purpose, and carrying it by violence and insubordination—answerable themselves to no laws, and teaching the people to despise and habitually to resist all law. I will read a portion of a speech delivered by the honourable and learned gentleman when he first formed his Society of Volunteers:—" The first object is, to put the volunteers in a state of action—to begin and put them in a state of activity. We are, as we ought to be, unarmed. The only difference between us and the volunteers of 1782 is, that we are unarmed, and that we wear no uniform; but I trust there is one species of uniform we will wear, and that is native manufacture. The best revolutions have been effected, and effected in decidedly the best manner, by unarmed bodies. It is the triumph of moral over physical force; and where opposite means are had recourse to, it generates a worse despotism than that which it is its object to subvert. But the armed force of 1782 had for its object merely to make an exhibition of their power, and the revolution they were instrumental in effecting was unstained by one drop of blood. The great revolution in which we had a part was effected by the same moral force of determined men, which rendered it impossible for the Government to resist them. I have often said, and I repeat it with pride and pleasure, that the revolution of 1829 was a scarless, stainless, and bloodless revolution. That was effected by these peaceable means, and with the same means the volunteers begin their glorious career to effect the regeneration of Ireland, by procuring a domestic Legislature, by giving a solution of the question, ' Shall Ireland be a nation or a province?' I say ' Ireland not a province, but a nation.' That is our charter. Let that be our first toast upon any of those festive occasions when we may meet to forward any of the great questions connected with the interests of Ireland,—' Ireland not a province but a nation.'" Now, that is a very pretty sentence, but it so happens that it is not new; for, looking over some records of transactions previous to the Union, in the years 1797 and 1798, I find that the object of some of the associations of that day was, that Ireland should be "a nation, and not a province," and this before that withering and desolating Union, which has, we are told, reduced her from a nation to a province. The watchword of the discontented was then, " Ireland not a province, but a nation;" it is now that of the volunteers, as they style themselves. They are not yet armed; but, to use the words of their chief, " Let no man tell me that the period will not shortly arrive when we shall not be unarmed, and that we shall not be permitted by law to carry arms. Let no man tell me that the day will not shortly arrive when the Peelers shall be dismissed, and their business entrusted to our management; for it is only a bad Government that requires such assistance as they can give. We shall take the place of the national guard of other countries, and do all the police duty of the country. There is no liberty if every man is not allowed to carry his own arms—every householder should have his own arms. I hope that every village in Ireland will have eighteen or twenty, ay, fifty volunteers—that they will meet and keep the peace at all markets and fairs, and who will permit no infraction of the law without bringing the perpetrators of it to justice." What powers are to be confided to this irresponsible band of volunteers, who take upon themselves the government of their country, under the pretence of doing justice to her people? Justice! why, it is the very pretext of the Whitefeet, who are rejected of all parties. They carry on their system under the name of justice! It is because the poor man is oppressed by his rich neighbour; it is because too much rent is exacted by the unfeeling landlord from the starving tenant; it is this that rouses the virtuous indignation of the Whitefeet, and calls forth their justice (rather of a summary kind), in opposition to that which is established by the Constitution of the country.

Sir, there is another speech of the honourable gentleman, in which he describes what he desires the volunteers should do:—" I am anxious that every man who pays a shilling a year should be enrolled among the volunteers of his parish, and that some one individual will accept the office of ' pacificator,' and that regulators will be also appointed." Regulators! Why, the honourable and learned gentleman borrows his very terms from the Whitefeet—the Whitefeet " regulators." Whitefeet have their regulators too. It was the " gentlemen regulators of the grievances of their oppressed country " who ordered the honourable member for Waterford to dismiss his Scotch steward. The honourable and learned gentleman thinks that this association will form a very effective means of preserving the peace. No doubt it will; the peace will be admirably preserved in favour of those who take part with its guardians. Again: the honourable gentleman declares as a consequence of their establishment, that " no man would dare to enter into a conspiracy against the people." Now, how does the honourable gentleman define the meaning of a conspiracy against the people? As a lawyer, how would he frame such an indictment in a court of justice? But the volunteers, among their other prerogatives, are to be entrusted with the power of judging, and acting on their judgment, as to what is a conspiracy against the people; the conspirators are to be tried by the gentlemen regulators, and punished by being "held up to the odium of their countrymen." We know what that phrase means. Again: the honourable gentleman says "It may be asked, do I intend to have the volunteers armed again? I answer, that I do. I love the institution of a national guard, and I contemplate the arming of the volunteers when the law authorizes it, but not sooner. They would thus become a national guard; and should not, I ask, every man of character and responsibility be armed. The state in which he lives is not free if he is not armed. As long as the law does not permit their arming, the volunteers will remain unarmed, but no longer. And I hope soon to see them reviewed in the Phœnix Park; and how then will my friend Tom Steele strut at their head." Further:—"Ireland will never be tranquillized until the volunteers spread through the country extensively. When once organized, petty sessions work will be greatly diminished. I wish the people to have recourse to arbitration. The Catholic clergy will assist the volunteers, and, instead of going before justices of the peace, and incurring expense, let the people have courts of arbitration of their own."

This, sir, is very right, being consistent! The honourable and learned gentleman objects to courts-martial, but he has no objection to courts of gentlemen regulators. Why, these are the honourable gentleman's courts-martial. They are armed, too! They are courts-martial in every respect, with this difference only—that instead of being subject to the laws of the Constitution, and amenable to the authority and prerogative of the Crown, they are to be subject to the laws—the tyranny—the unconstitutional and self-assumed prerogative of the honourable and learned gentleman himself. This system is already in operation. I have seen, not many days since, a letter desiring persons in a particular district to conform to the instructions it contained. The Catholic priests, it was said, would hold such sessions and such days of arbitration, and would select those days upon which the magistrates held the petty sessions, and meet, too, at the same place. They would not swear the people—oh, no! But a book would be lying before them, so that they might still consider themselves under the sanction of an oath if they thought fit; and an intimation was added, that the parties whose cases had been disposed of by this tribunal were afterwards at full liberty to go before a magistrate, but that there were modes of bringing them to their senses if they should adopt such a course. This, sir, is the natural, the necessary, the infallible consequence of such a system of unconstitutional authority as, under the sanction of the name of liberty, the honourable and learned member now desires to establish in the propagation of those societies over which he is to reign. This is the system of liberty with which Ireland is to be blessed—this is the system which is to abrogate all established and legitimate authority. Sentences are to be passed and executed by unpaid, irresponsible ministers, who want, say they, to preserve the peace of their country, and who would do it by stifling and impeding every expression of opinion—who would legitimatize and give sanction to what the honourable and learned gentleman calls the servile war—the war of poverty against property—the war carried on by the humbler classes against all that is established in the frame of civil society. This is the system which the honourable and learned gentleman is endeavouring to organize in his country—this is the tyranny against which I call upon this House to guard Ireland, by the interposition of a remedy which, if not constitutional, will at least be administered by those who are responsible to the Constitution, and the legal authorities of their country. Sir, the honourable and learned gentleman says that the system we are proposing to introduce is a system to be spread over all Ireland. Sir, this is not the fact; but, on the other hand, it is the fact with the system of pacificators to be introduced by the learned gentleman. Let a county be as peaceable as it will, it is still to be subjected to the control of these armed pacificators. Our measures are to extend but to those parts in which it is shown that a system of oppression exists beyond the control of the law. Again, to what classes of offences is our law to extend? Do we intend to supersede juries—to prevent all meeting of the ordinary tribunals? By no means. We take out of the calendar to be presented to our military courts, some of the heaviest offences among those which are to be subject to the cognizance of the honourable and learned member's tribunal. The honourable member's judges are to pass sentence in every case, civil as well as criminal. From their jurisdiction no class is to be exempt; we limit ours to certain specified cases of offences aimed by violence against the security of life and property.

Sir, I should be unwilling that an expression which fell from my noble friend should be interpreted beyond the sense in which he intended that the House should understand it. A question was put to my noble friend, or rather a hint was thrown out, that it was the intention of the Government to introduce this Act for the purpose of enforcing the payment of tithes. I distinctly and unequivocally say that we were influenced by no such intention, and that we should be wholly unjustifiable in introducing this Act in any district where no actual outrages of a Whiteboy character existed; but I say, also, that his Majesty's Ministers would be equally without justification, if, after having introduced it into any district where such outrages did prevail they did not extend its protection to every description of property within that district. And let me give this further qualification to that assertion which I think no honest man can object to, that by protection of every species of property, I do not mean any interference for the purpose of supporting and enforcing civil claims. I say that the clergyman ought to be as secure against violence, against outrage, against combination, and against intimidation, as any other man in the community; and that if he be subjected to violence, or outrage, or combination, or intimidation, he has a claim to, and he will receive from his Majesty's Government, the full protection of the law as it may exist in the district where he resides. I have been diverted, however, from one point to which I intended to allude, and with which I will conclude the observations which I have had the honour of offering to the House.

Sir, I have hitherto considered the unconstitutional, tyrannical, and arbitrary proceedings, organized systematically by the honourable and learned gentleman,—I have considered them as to the effect they will have upon the free expression of the opinions of the people of Ireland. But I doubt not, sir, they have a higher aim yet; and unless the honourable and learned gentleman utterly disclaims expressions which have been attributed to him in print, he aims, I say, at a power—a stretch of authority—more unconstitutional and tyrannical still: his aim is to trammel and control the freedom of debate and speech within these walls. Sir, I do not advert to expressions said to have been used by the honourable and learned gentleman, at a meeting of the humbler classes in this metropolis; I do not advert to expressions which I will not believe, till I hear them avowed, could have proceeded from the lips of—shall I say, any member of this assembly? No,—but from the lips of a man who had any pretensions, the very remotest pretensions, to the name and character of a gentleman. I do not, therefore, stop to comment upon expressions which speak of a system of individual robbery, legalized by its being carried on by those—no man, sir, could mistake the meaning of that which followed—not know that it was an allusion to the members of this House. But the honourable gentleman, I see, is ready to disclaim the use of the expression, and I will not disgust the House by mentioning it.

Mr. O'CONNELL.—I am quite ready to state what I said.

Several HONOURABLE MEMBERS. — State! State!!

Mr. STANLEY.—If I might be permitted to entreat the House to bear with me for a few moments longer, the honourable and learned gentleman would then have an opportunity of stating, as fully and fairly as he pleases, what were the words he used. I now deal, however, with that which I consider to be an attack upon the constitutional rights of this House, and one which, in my place as a member of this House, I should not have felt justified if I had not called the attention of the House to, in the presence of the honourable and learned member, when he may have an opportunity of disclaiming, denying, or qualifying what he is reported to have said.

Sir, when we go before the Sovereign at the meeting of Parliament, we do not ask—we demand of him the free exercise, for this Commons' House of Parliament, of liberty of speech and of unquestioned discussion. No constitutional Sovereign can deny that proud boast of this House; and it is assuming too much, for a subject to do that which is denied to the utmost extension of the prerogative of the Crown. Sir, it is too much, that any member of this House—addressing an organized body of volunteers unconnected with it by any tie—should presume to call their attention—should presume to ask their opinion, and to demand their influence in consequence of any speech or vote which any member has thought it his duty to give. I quote a letter attributed to the honourable and learned gentleman—I hope erroneously—and addressed to the Irish volunteers. It is dated the 10th of February, 1833; and after various advices as to what the volunteers were to do, says that the present advice of the writer was, "To banish every thought but that of making a good fight to prevent the evils that menace us. To be a good fight it must be strictly peaceable, legal, and constitutional. Get every parish in Ireland, if you can, to meet to petition Parliament against the menaced Algerine Acts. Let the meetings not be simultaneous —that is, let every parish meet quite independent of each other, and advise that none but parishioners should take part in each parish, except, indeed, when a few persons, not of the particular parish, but familiar with the practice of petitioning, may attend. Let the petitions be in the strongest terms consistent with decorum. In fact, we should, in the abstract, prefer death to slavery; but nothing could possibly injure us more than any threat of using violence. You will see in the papers the list of those who fought for Ireland." Why "fought" for Ireland?

Mr. O'CONNELL.—Oh! oh!

Mr. STANLEY.—Does the honourable gentleman mean to say that he alone is Ireland—that two opinions may not exist—that a man may not excuse his judgment by voting on one side of an Irish question as on another? Or does he think that he is already installed as dictator of Ireland? "You will, I am sure, be glad to see the member for Dundalk in the number. Young Talbot, of Athlone, voted in both majorities! Learn at once what the honest men of Athlone think of this desertion of his country. The two members for the county of Limerick voted also in the majorities against Ireland. Is there no honest spirit remaining in that county to call upon the gallant colonels to retrace their steps? Let there be an immediate demand made upon every popular Irish representative who still lingers in Ireland to attend at his post here without further delay."

Sir, does the honourable and learned gentleman admit that interference with the powers of Parliament?

MR. O'CONNELL.—Certainly.

MR. STANLEY.—Then I put it to this House, whether, in the abused and prostituted name of liberty, any frothy declaimer for popular rights ever put forward so flimsy a veil over a most unconstitutional and tyrannical interference with the privileges of the Legislature, by a self-constituted and arbitrary tribunal, by this outrageous appeal—not to the people, to whom alone the honourable gentleman is responsible for his conduct in Parliament, but to the Volunteer Society, which is to spread its mighty arms throughout Ireland until it brings everything within its grasp, and subjects everything to its uncontrolled and uncontrollable dominion?

I have now, sir, stated everything which I intended to advert to, at length—not more so, I trust, than the case demanded, or than was justifiable to the House; and having distinctly admitted the separation of the prædial from the political agitation—the outrages against life and property from those against constitutional liberty, which are a necessary consequence of the system which exists there—I now call upon you, in the name of liberty, as you wish to see constitutional freedom—the rights of property—life itself, protected against the effect of this system of violence and prædial outrage; I call upon you, as you respect constitutional rights, to guard their exercise from those who put on the mask of liberty the more safely to attack them—who use these associations to check every germ of public opinion. I call upon you to sanction, by your vote this night, the doctrine that you would rather infringe, for a time, the laws of the Constitution, than suffer those laws, together with all constitutional rights, to be absorbed—as they must be unless Parliament interferes—in one undistinguishable ruin and tyranny.

DANIEL O'CONNELL.

Born 1775. Died 1847.

[In fulfilment of the promise made in an earlier part of this volume, we here offer another specimen of O'Connell's eloquence. We have elsewhere had occasion to remark on the general characteristics of his style (see page 112), but perhaps the following estimate from an acute observer, not too favourably disposed, as will be seen, to the great agitator, may be interesting as a contemporary comment on his manner in the House of Commons:—"Anybody," writes the author from whom we quote, "who has heard him twice would see the same topics constantly recurring, the same strange alternations of the denunciative and the abusive with the pathetic and the descriptive; the same queer mingling of the serious and the ridiculous, of the sarcastic and the eulogistic; and what rendered him, notwithstanding, one of the most striking speakers existing? This: that the inexhaustible liveliness and vigour of his delivery kept pace with the singular variety of his topics. He was, in short, an astonishing actor; one moment he was storming with rage, the next his tones were soothingly pathetic, or affectingly descriptive; then in an instant came a funny Irish story, and ere the laughter was over a bitter stroke of sarcasm, oftener of abuse; while occasionally the vulgarity of his tone and the coarseness of allusion, contracted by familiarity with mobs, were disgusting, even to those of the liberal party who most applauded him." The above is extracted, with a few slight alterations, from a little work published several years ago, entitled, "The Critic in Parliament and Public," and containing some very graphic descriptions of the great parliamentary contests from 1835 to 1841. The speech of O'Connell's which we here print, was delivered on the 23rd February, 1814, on the occasion of a great meeting being held to decide what course should be pursued to recover Catholic rights. It is also interesting as representing, at so early a date, O'Connell's strong views on the Corn Laws, which became so fertile a subject of debate many years after.]

SPEECH DELIVERED 23RD FEBRUARY, 1814.

MR. O'CONNELL, in commencing his speech, said that he wished to submit to the meeting a resolution, calling on the different counties and cities in Ireland to petition for unqualified emancipation. It was a resolution which had been already and frequently adopted; when we had persevered in our petitions, even at periods when we despaired of success; and it became a pleasing duty to present them, now that the symptoms of the times seemed so powerfully to promise an approaching relief.

Indeed, as long as truth or justice could be supposed to influence man; as long as man was admitted to be under the control of reason; so long must it be prudent and wise to procure discussions on the sufferings and the rights of the people of Ireland. Truth proclaimed the treacherous iniquity which had deprived us of our chartered liberty; truth destroyed the flimsy pretext under which this iniquity is continued; truth exposed our merits and our sufferings; whilst reason and justice combined to demonstrate our right—the right of every human being to freedom of conscience—a right without which every honest man must feel that to him, individually, the protection of government is a mockery, and the restriction of penal law a sacrilege.

He then proceeded. Truth, reason, and justice are our advocates; and even in England, let me tell you, that those powerful advocates have some authority. They are, it is true, more frequently resisted there than in most other countries; but yet they have some sway among the English at all times. Passion may confound, and prejudice darken the English understanding; and interested passion and hired prejudice have been successfully employed against us at former periods; but the present season appears singularly well calculated to aid the progress of our cause, and to advance the attainment of our important objects.

I do not make the assertion lightly. I speak after deliberate investigation, and from solemn conviction, my clear opinion, that we shall, during the present session of parliament, obtain a portion, at least, if not the entire, of our emancipation. We cannot fail, unless we are disturbed in our course by those who graciously style themselves our friends, or are betrayed by the treacherous machinations of part of our own body.

Yes, everything, except false friendship and domestic treachery, forebodes success. The cause of man is in its great advance. Humanity has been rescued from much of its thraldom. In the states of Europe, where the iron despotism of the feudal system so long classed men into two species—the hereditary masters and the perpetual slaves; when rank supplied the place of merit, and to be humbly born operated as a perpetual exclusion; in many parts of Europe man is reassuming his natural station, and artificial distinctions have vanished before the force of truth and the necessities of governors.

France has a representative government; and as the unjust privileges of the clergy and nobility are abolished; as she is blessed with a most wise, clear, and simple code of laws; as she is almost free from debt, and emancipated from odious prejudices, she is likely to prove an example and a light to the world.

In Germany the sovereigns who formerly ruled at their free will and caprice, are actually bribing the people to the support of their thrones, by giving them the blessings of liberty. It is a wise and a glorious policy. The Prince Regent has emancipated his Catholic subjects of Hanover, and traced for them the grand outlines of a free constitution. The other states of Germany are rapidly following the example. The people, no longer destined to bear the burdens only of society, are called upon to take their share in the management of their own concerns, and in the sustentation of the public dignity and happiness. In short, representative government, the only rational or just government, is proclaimed by princes as a boon to their people, and Germany is about to afford many an example of the advantages of rational liberty. Anxious as some kings appear to be in the great work of plunder and robbery, others of them are now the first heralds of freedom.

It is a moment of glorious triumph to humanity; and even one instance of liberality freely conceded makes compensation for a thousand repetitions of the ordinary crimes of military monarchs. The crime is followed by its own punishment; but the great principle of the rights of man establishes itself now on the broadest basis, and France and Germany now set forth an example for England to imitate.

Italy, too, is in the paroxysms of the fever of independence. Oh, may she have strength to go through the disease, and may she rise like a giant refreshed with wine! One thing is certain, that the human mind is set afloat in Italy. The flame of freedom burns; it may be smothered for a season; but all the whiskered Croats and the fierce Pandours of Austria will not be able to extinguish the sacred fire. Spain, to be sure, chills the heart, and disgusts the understanding. The combined Inquisition and the court press upon the mind, whilst they bind the body in fetters of adamant. But this despotism is, thank God, as unrelentingly absurd as it is cruel, and there arises a darling hope out of the very excess of the evil. The Spaniards must be walking corpses—they must be living ghosts, and not human beings, unless a sublime reaction be in rapid preparation. But let us turn to our own prospects.

The cause of liberty has made, and is making, great progress in states heretofore despotic. In all the countries in Europe in which any portion of freedom prevails, the liberty of conscience is complete. England alone, of all the states pretending to be free, leaves shackles upon the human mind; England alone, amongst free states, exhibits the absurd claim of regulating belief by law, and forcing opinion by statute. Is it possible to conceive that this gross, this glaring, this iniquitous absurdity can continue? Is it possible, too, to conceive that it can continue to operate, not against a small and powerless sect, but against the millions, comprising the best strength, the most affluent energy of the empire?—a strength and an energy daily increasing, and hourly appreciating their own importance. The present system, disavowed by liberalized Europe, disclaimed by sound reason, abhorred by genuine religion, must soon and for ever be abolished.

Let it not be said that the princes of the Continent were forced by necessity to give privileges to their subjects, and that England has escaped from a similar fate. I admit that the necessity of procuring the support of the people was the mainspring of royal patriotism on the

Continent; but I totally deny that the ministers of England can dispense with a similar support. The burdens of the war are permanent; the distresses occasioned by the peace are pressing; the financial system tottering, and to be supported in profound peace only by a war taxation. In the meantime, the resources of corruption are mightily diminished. Ministerial influence is necessarily diminished by one-half of the effective force of indirect bribery; full two-thirds must be disbanded. Peculation and corruption must be put upon half-pay, and no allowances. The ministry lose not only all those active partizans; those outrageous loyalists, who fattened on the public plunder during the seasons of immense expenditure; but those very men will themselves swell the ranks of the malcontents, and probably be the most violent in their opposition. They have no sweet consciousness to reward them in their present privations; and therefore they are likely to exhaust the bitterness of their souls on their late employers. Every cause conspires to render this the period in which the ministry should have least inclination, least interest, least power to oppose the restoration of our rights and liberties.

I speak not from mere theory. There exist at this moment practical illustrations of the truth of my assertions. Instances have occurred which demonstrate, as well the inability of the ministry to resist the popular voice, as the utility of re-echoing that voice, until it is heard and understood in all its strength and force. The ministers had determined to continue the property-tax; they announced that determination to their partizans at Liverpool and in Bristol. Well, the people of England met; they petitioned; they repeated — they reiterated their petitions, until the ministry felt they could no longer resist; and they ungraciously, but totally, abandoned their determination; and the property-tax now expires.

Another instance is also now before us. It relates to the corn-laws. The success of the repetition of petitions in that instance is the more remarkable, because such success has been obtained in defence of the first principles of political economy, and in violation of the plainest rules of political justice.

This is not the place to discuss the merits of the corn-laws; but I cannot avoid, as the subject lies in my way, to put upon public record my conviction of the inutility as well as the impropriety of the proposed measure respecting those laws. I expect that it will be believed in Ireland that I would not volunteer thus an opposition of sentiment to any measure, if I was not most disinterestedly, and in my conscience, convinced that such measure would not be of any substantial or permanent utility to Ireland.

As far as I am personally concerned, my interest plainly is to keep up the price of lands; but I am quite convinced that the measure in question will have an effect permanently and fatally injurious to Ireland. The clamour respecting the corn-laws has been fomented by parsons, who were afraid that they would not get money enough for their tithes, and absentee landlords, who apprehended a diminution of their rack rents; and if you observe the names of those who have taken an active part in favour of the measure, you will find amongst them many, if not all, the persons who have most distinguished themselves against the liberty and religion of the people. There have been, I know, many good men misled, and many clever men deceived, on this subject; but the great majority are of the class of oppressors.

There was formed, some time ago, an association of a singular nature in Dublin and the adjacent counties. Mr. Luke White was, as I remember, at the head of it. It contained some of our stoutest and most stubborn seceders; it published the causes of its institution; it recited that, whereas butcher's meat was dearer in Cork, and in Limerick, and in Belfast, than in Dublin, it was therefore expedient to associate, in order that the people of Dublin should not eat meat too cheap. Large sums were subscribed to carry the patriotic design into effect, but public indignation broke up the ostensible confederacy; it was too plain and too glaring to bear public inspection. The indignant sense of the people of Dublin forced them to dissolve their open association; and if the present enormous increase of the price of meat in Dublin beyond the rest of Ireland be the result of secret combination of any individuals, there is at least this comfort, that they do not presume to beard the public with the open avowal of their design to increase the difficulties of the poor in procuring food.

Such a scheme as that, with respect to meat in Dublin—such a scheme, precisely, is the sought-for corn-law. The only difference consists in the extent of the operation of both plans. The corn plan is only more extensive, not more unjust in principle, but it is more unreasonable in its operation, because its necessary tendency must be to destroy that very market of which it seeks the exclusive possession. The corn-law men want, they say, to have the exclusive feeding of the manufacturers; but at present our manufacturers, loaded as they are with taxation, are scarcely able to meet the goods of foreigners in the markets of the world. The English are already undersold in foreign markets; but if to this dearness produced by taxation there shall be added the dearness produced by dear food, is it not plain that it will be impossible to enter into a competition with foreign manufacturers, who have no taxes and cheap bread? Thus the corn-laws will destroy our manufactures, and compel our manufacturers to emigrate, in spite of penalties; and the corn-law supporters will have injured themselves and destroyed others.

I beg pardon for dwelling on this subject. If I were at liberty to pursue it here, I would not leave it until I had satisfied every dispassionate man, that the proposed measure is both useless and unjust; but this is not the place for doing so, and I only beg to record at least the honest dictates of my judgment on this interesting topic. My argument, of the efficacy of petitioning, is strengthened by the impolicy of the measure in question; because, if petitions, by their number and perseverance, succeed in establishing a proposition impolitic in principle, and oppressive to thousands in operation; what encouragement does it not afford to us to repeat our petitions for that which has justice for its basis, and policy as its support!

The great advantages of discussion being thus apparent, the efficacy of repeating, and repeating, and repeating again our petitions being thus demonstrated by notorious facts, the Catholics of Ireland must be sunk in criminal apathy, if they neglect the use of an instrument so efficacious for their emancipation.

There is further encouragement at this particular crisis. Dissension has ceased in the Catholic body. Those who paralysed our efforts, and gave our conduct the appearance and reality of weakness, and wavering, and inconsistency, have all retired. Those who were ready to place the entire of the Catholic feelings and dignity, and some of the Catholic religion too, under the feet of every man who pleased to call himself our friend, and to prove himself our friend, by praising on every occasion, and upon no occasion, the oppressors of the Catholics, and by abusing the Catholics themselves; the men who would link the Catholic cause to this patron and to that, and sacrifice it at one time to the minister, and at another to the opposition, and make it this day the tool of one party, and the next the instrument of another party; the men, in fine, who hoped to traffic upon our country and our religion—who would buy honours, and titles, and places, and pensions, at the price of the purity, and dignity, and safety of the Catholic Church in Ireland; all those men have, thank God, quitted us, I hope for ever. They have returned into silence and secession, or have frankly or covertly gone over to our enemies. I regret deeply and bitterly that they have carried with them some few, who, like my Lord Fingal, entertain no other motives than those of purity and integrity, and who, like that noble lord, are merely mistaken.

But I rejoice at this separation—I rejoice that they have left the single-hearted, and the disinterested, and the indefatigable, and the independent, and the numerous, and the sincere Catholics, to work out their emancipation unclogged, unshackled, and undismayed. They have bestowed on us another bounty also—they have proclaimed the causes of their secession—they have placed out of doubt the cause of the divisions. It is not intemperance, for that we abandoned; it is not the introduction of extraneous topics, for those we disclaimed; it is simply and purely, veto or no veto—restriction or no restriction—no other words; it is religion and principle that have divided us; thanks, many thanks to the tardy and remote candour of the seceders, that has at length written in large letters the cause of their secession—it is the Catholic Church of Ireland—it is whether that Church shall continue independent of a Protestant ministry or not. We are for its independence; the seceders are for its dependence.

Whatever shall be the fate of our emancipation question, thank God we are divided for ever from those who would wish that our Church should crouch to the partizans of the Orange system. Thank God, secession has displayed its cloven foot, and avowed itself to be synonymous with vetoism.

Those are our present prospects of success. First, man is elevated from slavery almost everywhere, and human nature has become more dignified, and, I may say, more valuable. Secondly, England wants our cordial support, and knows that she has only to concede to us justice in order to obtain our affectionate assistance. Thirdly, this is the season of successful petition, and the very fashion of the times entitles our petition to succeed. Fourthly, the Catholic cause is disencumbered of hollow friends, and interested speculators. Add to all these the native and inherent strength of the principle of religious freedom, and the inert and accumulating weight of our wealth, our religion, and our numbers, and where is the sluggard that shall dare to doubt our approaching success?

Besides, even our enemies must concede to us, that we act from principle, and from principle only. We prove our sincerity when we refuse to make our emancipation a subject of traffic and barter, and ask for relief only upon those grounds which, if once established, would give to every other sect the right to the same political immunity. All we ask is "a clear stage and no favour." We think the Catholic religion the most rationally consistent with the divine scheme of Christianity, and therefore, all we ask is, that everybody should be left to his unbiassed reason and judgment. If Protestants are equally sincere, why do they call the law, and the bribe, and the place, and the pension, in support of their doctrines? Why do they fortify themselves behind pains, and penalties, and exclusions, and forfeitures? Ought not our opponents to feel that they degrade the sanctity of their religion, when they call in the profane aid of temporal rewards and punishments, and that they proclaim the superiority of our creed, when they thus admit themselves unable to contend against it upon terms of equality, and by the weapons of reason and argument, and persevere in refusing us all we ask—" a clear stage and no favour?"

Yes, Mr. Chairman, our enemies, in words and by actions, admit and proclaim our superiority. It remains to our friends alone, and to that misguided and ill-advised portion of the Catholics who have shrunk into secession—it remains for those friends and seceders alone to undervalue our exertions, and underrate our conscientious opinions.

Great and good God, in what a cruel situation are the Catholics of Ireland placed! If they have the manliness to talk of their oppressors as the paltry bigots deserve—if they have the honesty to express, even in measured language, a small portion of the sentiments of abhorrence which peculating bigotry ought naturally to inspire—if they condemn the principle which established the inquisition in Spain, and Orange lodges in Ireland, they are assailed by the combined clamour of those parliamentary friends, and title-seeking, place-hunting seceders. The war-whoop of "intemperance" is sounded, and a persecution is instituted by our advocates and our seceders—against the Catholic who dares to be honest, and fearless, and independent!

But I tell you what they easily forgive—nay, what our friends, sweet souls, would vindicate to-morrow in Parliament, if the subject arose there. Here it is—here is *The Dublin Journal* of the 21st of February, printed just two days ago. In the administration of Lord Whitworth, and the secretaryship of Mr. Peel, there is a government newspaper—a paper supported solely by the money of the people; for its circulation is little, and its private advertisements less. Here is a paper continued in existence like a wounded reptile, only whilst in the rays of the sun, by the heat and warmth communicated to it by the Irish administration. Let me read two passages for you. The first calls " Popery the deadly enemy of pure religion and rational liberty." Such is the temperate description the writer gives of the Catholic faith. With respect to purity of religion I shall not quarrel with him. I only differ with him in point of taste; but I should be glad to know what this creature calls rational liberty. I suppose such as existed at Lacedæmon—the dominion of Spartans over Helots—the despotism of masters over slaves, that is his rational liberty. We will readily pass so much by. But attend to this—

"I will," says this moderate and temperate gentleman, "lay before the reader such specimens of the Popish superstition as will convince him that the treasonable combinations cemented by oaths, and the nocturnal robbery and assassination which have prevailed for many years past in Ireland, and still exist in many parts of it, are produced as a necessary consequence by its intolerant and sanguinary principles."

Let our seceders—let our gentle friends who are shocked at our intemperance, and are alive to the mild and conciliating virtues of Mr. Peel, read this passage, sanctioned, I may almost say, certainly countenanced, by those who do the work of governing Ireland. Would to God we had but one genuine, unsophisticated friend, one real advocate in the House of Commons! How such a man would pour down indignation on the clerks of the Castle, who pay for this base and vile defamation of our religion—of the religion of nine-tenths of the population of Ireland!

But perhaps I accuse falsely; perhaps the administration of Ireland are guiltless of patronizing these calumnies; look at the paper and determine; it contains nearly five columns of advertisements—only one from a private person—and even that is a notice of an anti-Popery pamphlet, by a Mr. Cousins, a curate of the Established Church. Dean Swift has somewhere observed, that the poorest of all possible rats was a curate; and if this rat be so, if he have as usual a large family, a great appetite, and little to eat, I sincerely hope that he may get what he wants—a fat living. Indeed, for the sake of consistency, and to keep up the succession of bad pamphlets, he ought to get a living.

Well, what think you are the rest of the advertisements? First, there are three from the worthy Commissioners of Wide Streets; one dated 6th August, 1813, announcing that they would, the ensuing Wednesday, receive certain proposals. Secondly, the Barony of Middlethird is proclaimed, as of the 6th of September last, for fear the inhabitants of that barony should not as yet know they were proclaimed. Thirdly, the proclamation against the Catholic Board, dated only the 3rd day of June last, is printed lest any person should forget the history of last year. Fourthly, there is a proclamation stating that gunpowder was not to be carried coastwise for six months, and this is dated the 5th of October last. But why should I detain you with the details of state proclamations, printed for no other purpose than as an excuse for putting so much of the public money into the pocket of a calumniator of the Catholics? The abstract of the rest is that there is one other proclamation, stating that Liverpool is a port fit for importation from the

East Indies; another forbidding British subjects from serving in the American forces during the present, that is, the past war; and another stating, that although we had made peace with France, we are still at war with America, and that, therefore, no marine is to desert; and to finish the climax, there is a column and a half of extracts from several statutes; all this printed at the expense of government, that is, at the expense of the people.

Look now at the species of services for which so enormous a sum of our money is thus wantonly lavished! It consists simply of calumnies against the Catholic religion—calumnies so virulently atrocious, as, in despite of the intention of the authors, to render themselves ridiculous. This hireling accuses our religion of being an enemy to liberty, of being an encourager of treason, of instigating to robbery, and producing a system of assassination. Here are libels for which no prosecution is instituted. Here are libels which are considered worthy of encouragement, and which are rewarded by the Irish treasury. And is it for this—is it to supply this waste, this abuse of public money —is it to pay for those false and foul calumnies that we are in a season of universal peace to be borne down with a war taxation? Are we to have two or three additional millions of taxes imposed upon us in peace, in order that this intestine war of atrocious calumny may be carried on against the religion of the people of Ireland, with all the vigour of full pay and great plunder? Let us, agitators, be now taunted by jobbers in Parliament with our violence, our intemperance. Why, if we were not rendered patient by the aid of a dignified contempt, is there not matter enough to disgust and to irritate almost beyond endurance?

Thus are we treated by our friends, and our enemies, and our seceders; the first abandon, the second oppress, the third betray us, and they all join in calumniating us; in the last they are all combined. See how naturally they associate;—this libeller in *The Dublin Journal*, who calls the Catholic religion a system-of assassination, actually praises in the same paper some individual Catholics; he praises, by name, Quarantotti, and my Lord Fingal, and the respectable party (those are his words) who join with that noble lord.

Of Lord Fingal I shall always speak with respect, because I entertain the opinion that his motives are pure and honourable; but can anything, or at least ought anything, place his secession in so strong a point of view to the noble lord himself, as to find that he and his party are praised by the very man who, in the next breath, treats his religion as a system of assassination? Let that party have all the enjoyment which such praises can confer; but if a spark of love for their religion or their country remains with them, let them recollect that they could have earned those praises only by having, in the opinion of this writer, betrayed the one and degraded the other.

This writer, too, attempts to traduce Lord Donoughmore. He attacks his Lordship in bad English, and worse Latin, for having, as he says, cried peccavi to Popish thraldom. But the ignorant trader in virulence knew not how to spell that single Latin word, because they do not teach Latin at the charter schools.

I close with conjuring the Catholics to persevere in their present course.

Let us never tolerate the slightest inroad on the discipline of our ancient, our holy Church. Let us never consent that she should be made the hireling of the ministry. Our forefathers would have died, nay, they perished in hopeless slavery, rather than consent to such degradation.

Let us rest upon the barrier where they expired, or go back into slavery, rather than forward into irreligion and disgrace! Let us also advocate our cause on the two great principles—first, that of an eternal separation in spirituals between our Church and the state; secondly, that of the eternal right to freedom of conscience—a right which, I repeat it, with pride and pleasure, would exterminate the Inquisition in Spain, and bury in oblivion the bloody Orange flag of dissension in Ireland!

Mr. O'Connell and Agitation.

The great agitator, the prime mover of the whole machinery, escaped the execution of the sentence of the law, in consequence of the expiration of the Act of Parliament to which I have referred. Well, my lord, what has since taken place? This very person, the great agitator, whom the Government had prosecuted to conviction, was considered to be a person worthy of the honours which the Crown could bestow, and he received the highest favour which any gentleman of the bar ever received from the hands of the noble earl and his Government. He received a patent of precedence, which placed him next the Attorney-General, and above a gentleman who was once Attorney-General, but was still a member of the same bar. If this was not a premium given to that gentleman to continue his course of disturbing the country, I do not know what else could be so considered. I feel that no more effectual mode could be found to encourage agitation than to reward the promoter of it.— *The Duke of Wellington.*

SIR JOHN ST. AUBIN.

Time of George II.

[The two speeches which follow this note were both delivered in the House of Commons in the year 1733, on the occasion of a motion being introduced for the repeal of the Septennial Act, and the substitution of a three years' Parliament, in place of the old arrangement established in 1715. That by Sir John St. Aubin, in favour ot the motion, is a good specimen of the oratorical style of its time; and, indeed, is in the opinion of Mr. Hazlitt one of the most elegant and able compositions to be found in the records of the House of Commons. We may add that Sir John St. Aubin, its author, was at the time of its delivery member for Cornwall. The other speech, in defence of the Septennial Act, has an interest almost independent of its subject, as representing the manner in debate of Sir Robert Walpole, to whose hands the political fortunes of England were for so many years intrusted. Walpole, though an experienced debater, was not a great orator; but if the reader should desire to be better acquainted with his style, we may refer him to an elaborate comparison of the eloquence of Walpole and Pitt, contained in a note to this speech by Mr. Hazlitt, whom we have already quoted, in his "Eloquence of the British Senate," p. 333. The same author adds, that as good an idea of the talents of this celebrated man may be formed from his speech on the Triennial Act as from any that he has left behind him.]

SPEECH ON THE TRIENNIAL BILL.

MR. SPEAKER.—The honourable gentleman who made you this motion has supported the necessity of it by so many strong and forcible arguments, that there is hardly anything new to be offered. I am very sensible, therefore, of the disadvantages I must lie under in attempting to speak after him, and I should content myself with barely seconding him, if the subject matter of this debate was not of so great importance, that I should be ashamed to return to my electors, without endeavouring, in the best manner I am able, to declare publicly the reasons which induce me to give my most ready assent to this question.

It is evident, from what has been said, that the people have an unquestionable right to frequent new Parliaments by ancient usage, and that this usage has been confirmed by several laws, which have been progressively made by our ancestors, as often as they found it necessary to insist on this essential privilege.

Parliaments were generally annual, but never continued longer than three years, till the remarkable reign of Henry VIII. He was a prince of unruly appetites, and of an arbitrary will; he was impatient of every restraint; the laws of God and man fell equally a sacrifice as they stood in the way of his avarice, or disappointed his ambition. He therefore introduced long Parliaments, because he very well knew that they would become the proper instruments of both, and what a slavish obedience they paid to all his measures is sufficiently known.

If we come to the reign of King Charles I. we must acknowledge him to be a prince of a contrary temper; he had certainly an innate love for religion and virtue; and, of consequence, for the liberty of his country. But here lay the misfortune. He was led from his natural disposition by the insinuations of sycophants and flatterers; they advised him to neglect the calling of frequent Parliaments, and therefore, by not taking the constant sense of his people in what he did, he was worked up into so high a notion of prerogative, that the Commons, in order to restrain it, obtained that independent fatal power, which at last most unhappily brought him to his most tragical end, and at the same time subverted the whole constitution. And I hope we shall learn this lesson from it—never to compliment the Crown with any new or extravagant powers, nor to deny the people those rights which by ancient usage they are entitled to; but to preserve that just and equal balance from which they will derive mutual security, and which, if duly observed, will render our constitution the envy and admiration of the world.

King Charles II. naturally took a surfeit of Parliaments in his father's time, and was therefore extremely desirous to lay them aside. But this was a scheme impracticable. However, in effect he did so, for he obtained a Parliament, which by its long duration, like an army of veterans, became so exactly disciplined to his own measures, that they knew no other command but from that person who gave them their pay. This was a safe and most ingenious way of enslaving a nation; it was very well known that arbitrary power, if it was open and avowed, would never prevail here. The people were therefore amused with the specious form of their ancient constitution: it existed indeed in their fancy, but, like a mere phantom, had no substance or reality in it; for the power, the authority, the dignity of Parliaments were wholly lost. This was that remarkable Parliament which so justly obtained the opprobrious name of the Pension Parliament, and was the model from which, I believe, some later Parliaments have been exactly copied.

At the time of the revolution, the people made a fresh claim of their ancient privileges; and as they had lately experienced the misfortune of long and servile Parliaments, it was then declared, that they should be held frequently. But it seems their full meaning was not understood by this declaration; and therefore, as in every new settlement, the intention of all parties should be specifically manifested; the Parliament never ceased struggling with the Crown till the triennial law was obtained; the preamble of it, which the honourable gentleman has recited, is extremely full and strong; and in the body of the bill you will find the word "declared" before "enacted," by which I apprehend, that though this law did not immediately take place at the time of the revolution, it was certainly intended as declaratory of the first meaning; and therefore stands as part of that original contract under which the constitution was then settled. His Majesty's title to the crown is primarily derived from that contract; and if, upon a review, there shall appear to be any deviations from it, we ought to treat them as so many injuries done to that title. And I dare say that this House, which has gone through so long a series of services to his Majesty, will at last be willing to revert to those original stated measures of government, to renew and strengthen that title.

But I think the manner in which the septennial law was first introduced is a very strong reason why it should be repealed. People in their fears have very often recourse to desperate expedients, which, if not cancelled in season, will themselves prove fatal to that constitution which they were meant to secure. Such is the nature of the septennial law; it was intended only as a preservative against a temporary inconvenience. The inconvenience is removed, but the mischievous effects still continue; for it not only altered the constitution of Parliament, but it extended that same Parliament beyond its natural duration, and therefore carries this most unjust implication with it, that you may, at any time, usurp the most indubitable, the most essential privilege of the people, I mean that of choosing their own representatives; a precedent of such a dangerous consequence, of so fatal a tendency, that I think it would be a reproach to our statute-book if that law was any longer to subsist, which might record it to posterity. This is a season of virtue and public spirit. Let us take advantage of it to repeal those laws which infringe on our liberties, and introduce such as may restore the vigour of our ancient constitution. Human nature is so very corrupt, that all obligations lose their force unless they are frequently renewed. Long Parliaments become, therefore, independent of the people; and when they do so there always happens a most dangerous dependence elsewhere.

It has of late been denied that the people have a right of remonstrating to us. It has been called an unjustifiable control upon the freedom of our proceedings. But then, let them have more frequent opportunities of varying the choice of their representatives, that they may dismiss such as have unfaithfully withdrawn their attention from them.

The influence of the Crown is daily increasing; and it is highly requisite that Parliaments should be frequently responsible to their constituents; that they should be kept under the constant awe of acting contrary to their interests. Modern history, I believe, will inform us that some very dangerous attempts upon our liberties have been disappointed, not so much from the virtue of many in this House, as from the apprehensions they may have had of an approaching election.

It is true there is a provision against such whose places vacate their seats here; but this is no guard against secret pensioners and placeholders. Give me leave to say, that the laws with respect to them are very insufficient; and as we were not allowed to make them effectual, the people have no other remedy but a new election. I think that long Parliaments are a great hardship upon those who may be excluded out of this House, and ought reasonably to take their turn; but seven years is the purchase of a man's life. It is equally hard upon such whose private fortunes will not admit them to engage in so long and painful a service: it must be so to those who mean no private view nor advantage by it.

I think, too, nothing can be of greater use to his Majesty than frequent new Parliaments; that he may often take the fresh sense of the nation, and not be partially advised; for his measures will always have a greater weight, both at home and abroad, the more generally he refers himself to the opinion of his people.

A farther mischief of long Parliaments is, that a minister has time and opportunities of getting acquaintance with members, of practising his several arts to win them into his schemes; but this must be the work of time: corruption is of so base a nature that at first sight it is extremely shocking. Hardly anyone has submitted to it all at once; his disposition must be previously understood; the particular bait must be found out with which he is to be allured; and, after all, it is not without many struggles that he surrenders his virtue. Indeed there are some who will at once plunge themselves over head and ears into any base action; but the generality of mankind are of a more cautious nature, and will proceed only by leisurely degrees. One or two, perhaps, have deserted their colours the first campaign; some have done it a second; but a great many, who have not that eager disposition to vice, will wait till a third. For this reason, short Parliaments have been less corrupt than long ones; they are observed, like streams of water, always to grow more impure the greater distance they run from the fountain head.

I am aware it may be said that frequent new Parliaments will produce frequent new expenses; but I think quite the contrary. I am really of opinion that it will be a proper remedy against the evil of bribery at elections; especially as you have provided so wholesome a law to co-operate upon those occasions.

As to bribery at elections, whence did it arise? Not from country gentlemen, for they are sure of being chosen without it. It was the invention of wicked and corrupt ministers, who have from time to time led weak princes into such destructive measures, that they did not dare to rely upon the natural representation of the people. Long Parliaments first introduced bribery, because they were worth purchasing at any rate. Country gentlemen, who have only their private fortunes to rely upon, and have no mercenary ends to serve, are unable to oppose it, especially if at any time the public treasure shall be unfaithfully squandered away to corrupt their boroughs. Country gentlemen, indeed, may make some weak efforts, but as they generally prove unsuccessful, and the time of a fresh struggle is at so great a distance, they at last grow faint in the dispute, give up their country for lost, and retiro in despair. Despair naturally produces indolence, and that is the proper disposition for slavery. Ministers of state understand this very well, and are therefore unwilling to awaken the nation out of its lethargy by frequent elections. They know that the spirit of liberty, like every other virtue of the mind, is to be kept alive only by constant action; that it is impossible to enslave this nation whilst it is perpetually upon its guard. Let country gentlemen, then, by having frequent opportunities of exerting themselves, be kept warm and active in their contention for the public good. This will raise that zeal and indignation which will at last get the better of that undue influence by which the officers of the Crown, though unknown to the several boroughs, have been able to supplant country gentlemen of great characters and fortune who live in their neighbourhood. I don't say this upon idle speculation only; I live in a country where it is too well known; and I will appeal to many gentlemen in the House, to more out of it (and who are so for this very reason), for the truth of my assertion. It is a sore which has been long eating into the most vital part of our constitution, and I hope the time will come when you will probe it to the bottom. For if a minister should ever gain a corrupt familiarity with our boroughs; if he should keep a register of them in his closet, and by sending down his treasury mandates should procure a spurious representation of the people, the offspring of his corruption, who will be at all times ready to reconcile and justify the most contradictory measures of his administration, and even to vote every crude indigested dream of their patron into a law; if the maintenance of his power should become the sole object of their attention, and they should be guilty of the most violent breach of parliamentary trust, by giving the King a discretionary liberty of taxing the people without limitation or control, the last fatal compliment they can pay to the Crown; if this should ever be the unhappy circumstance of this nation, the people indeed may complain, but the doors of that place where their complaints should be heard will for ever be shut against them.

The power of the Crown is very justly apprehended to be growing to a monstrous, I should have said, too great a size, and several methods have been unsuccessfully proposed for restraining it within its proper bounds.

But our disease, I fear, is of a complicated nature, and I think that this motion is wisely intended to remove the first and principal disorder. Give the people their ancient right of frequent new elections, that will restore the decayed authority of Parliaments, and will put our constitution into a natural condition of working out her own cure. Upon the whole I am of opinion that I cannot express a greater zeal for his Majesty, for the liberties of the people, or the honour and dignity of this House, than by seconding the motion which the honourable gentleman has made you.

SIR ROBERT WALPOLE.
Born 1676. Died 1745.

SPEECH ON THE SAME OCCASION.

SIR,—Though the question has been already so fully and so handsomely opposed by my worthy friend under the gallery, by the learned gentleman near me, and by several others, that there is no great occasion to say anything farther against it; yet as some new matter has been started by some of the gentlemen who have since that time spoken upon the other side of the question, I hope the House will indulge me the liberty of giving some of those reasons which induce me to be against the motion. In general, I must take notice that the nature of our constitution seems to be very much mistaken by the gentlemen who have spoken in favour of this motion. It is certain that ours is a mixed government, and the perfection of our constitution consists in this,—that the monarchical, aristocratical, and democratical forms of government are mixed and interwoven in ours, so as to give us all the advantages of each, without subjecting us to the dangers and inconveniences of either. The democratical form of government, which is the only one I have now occasion to take notice of, is liable to these inconveniences—that they are generally too tedious in coming to any resolution, and seldom brisk and expeditious enough in carrying their resolutions into execution; that they are always wavering in their resolutions, and never steady in any of the measures they resolve to pursue, and that they are often involved in factions, seditions, and insurrections, which expose them to be made the tools, if not the prey of their neighbours. Therefore, in all the regulations we make in respect to our constitution, we are to guard against running too much into that form of government which is properly called democratical. This was in my opinion the effect of the triennial law, and will again be the effect, if ever it should be restored.

That triennial elections would make our Government too tedious in all their resolves is evident, because in such case, no prudent administration would ever resolve upon any measure of consequence till they had felt not only the pulse of the Parliament, but the pulse of the people; and the Ministers of State would always labour under this disadvantage, that as secrets of state must not be immediately divulged, their enemies (and enemies they will always have,) would have a handle for exposing their measures, and rendering them disagreeable to the people, and thereby carrying, perhaps, a new election against them before they could have an opportunity of justifying their measures by divulging those facts and circumstances from whence the justice and the wisdom of their measures would clearly appear.

Then, sir, it is by experience well known, that what is called the populace of every country are apt to be too much elated with success, and too much dejected with every misfortune; this makes them wavering in their opinions about affairs of state, and never long of the same mind; and as this House is chosen by the free and unbiassed voice of the people in general, if this choice were so often renewed, we might expect that this House would be as wavering and as unsteady as the people usually are; and it being impossible to carry on the public affairs of the nation without the concurrence of this House, the Ministers would always be obliged to comply, and, consequently, would be obliged to change their measures as often as the people changed their minds.

With septennial Parliaments, sir, we are not exposed to either of these misfortunes, because, if the Ministers after having felt the pulse of the Parliament, which they can always soon do, resolve upon any measures, they have generally time enough before the new election comes on to give the people a proper information, in order to show them the justice and the wisdom of the measures they have pursued; and if the people should at any time be too much elated, or too much dejected, or should, without a cause, change their minds, those at the helm of affairs have time to set them right before a new election comes on.

As to faction and sedition, sir, I will grant that in monarchical and aristocratical governments it generally arises from violence and oppression; but in democratical governments it always arises from the people's having too great a share in the government; for in all countries and in all governments there always will be many factious and unquiet spirits, who can never be at rest either in power or out of power. When in power, they are never easy unless every man submits entirely to their direction; and when out of power, they are always working and intriguing against those that are in, without any regard to justice or to the interest of their country. In popular governments, such men have too much game; they have too many opportunities for working upon and corrupting the minds of the people, in order to give them a bad impression of, and to raise discontents against those that have the management of the public affairs for the time; and these discontents then break out into seditions and insurrections. This, sir, would, in my opinion, be our misfortune if our Parliaments were either annual or triennial. By such frequent elections there would be so much power thrown into the hands of the people as would destroy that equal mixture which is the beauty of our constitution. In short, our Government would really become a democratical government, and might from thence very probably diverge into a tyrannical. Therefore, in order to preserve our constitution —in order to prevent our falling under tyranny and arbitrary power, we ought to preserve that law which I really think has brought our constitution to a more equal mixture, and consequently greater perfection than it was ever in before that law took place.

As to bribery and corruption, sir, if it were possible to influence, by such base means, the majority of the electors of Great Britain to choose such men as would probably give up their liberties; if it were possible to influence, by such means, a majority of the members of this House to consent to the establishment of arbitrary power, I would readily allow that the calculations made by the gentlemen on the other side were just, and their inference true; but I am persuaded that neither of these is possible.

As the members of this House generally are, and must always be, gentlemen of fortune and figure in their country, is it possible to suppose that any of them could, by a pension or a post, be influenced to consent to the overthrow of our constitution, by which the enjoyment not only of what he got, but of what he before had, would be rendered altogether precarious? I will allow, sir, that with respect to bribery, the price must be higher or lower generally in proportion to the virtue of the man who is to be bribed; but it must likewise be granted, that the humour he happens to be in at the time—the spirit he happens to be endowed with—adds a great deal to his virtue. When no encroachments are made upon the rights of the people, when the people do not think themselves in any danger, there may be many of the electors who by a bribe of ten guineas might be induced to vote for one candidate rather than another; but if the Court were making any encroachments upon the rights of the people, a proper spirit would without doubt arise in the nation, and in such a case I am persuaded that none, or very few even of such electors could be induced to vote for a Court candidate; no, not for ten times the sum.

There may, sir, be some bribery and corruption in the nation—I am afraid there will always be some; but it is no proof of it that strangers are sometimes chosen; for a gentleman may have so much natural influence over a borough in his neighbourhood, as to be able to prevail with them to choose any person he pleases to recommend; and if upon such recommendation they choose one or two of his friends, who are, perhaps, strangers to them, it is not from thence to be inferred that the two strangers were chosen their representatives by the means of bribery and corruption.

To insinuate, sir, that money may be issued from the public treasure for bribing elections, is really something very extraordinary, especially in those gentlemen who know how many checks there are upon every shilling that can be issued from thence, and how regularly the money granted in one year for the public service of the nation must always be accounted for the very next session in this House, and likewise to the other, if they have a mind to call for any such account. And as to the gentlemen in offices, if they have any advantage over country gentlemen in having something else to depend on besides their own private fortunes, they have likewise many disadvantages. They are obliged to live here in London with their families, by which they are put to a much greater expense than gentlemen of equal fortunes who live in the country. This lays them under a very great disadvantage, with respect to the supporting their interest in the country. The country gentleman, by living among the electors, and purchasing the necessaries for his family from them, keeps up an acquaintance and correspondence with them, without putting himself to any extraordinary charge; whereas a gentleman who lives in London has no other way of keeping up an acquaintance or correspondence among his friends in the country, but by going down once or twice a year at a very extraordinary charge, and often without any other business; so that we may conclude that a gentleman in office cannot, even in seven years, save much for distributing in ready money at the time of an election; and I really believe, if the fact were narrowly inquired into, it would appear that the gentlemen in office are as little guilty of bribing the electors with ready money, as any other set of gentlemen in the kingdom.

That there are ferments often raised among the people without any just cause, is what I am surprised to hear controverted, since very late experience may convince us of the contrary. Do not we know what a ferment was raised in the nation towards the latter end of the late queen's reign? and it is well known what a fatal change in the affairs of this nation was introduced, or at least confirmed, by an election coming on while the nation was in that ferment. Do not we know what a ferment was raised in the nation soon after his late Majesty's accession? And if an election had then been allowed to come on while the nation was in that ferment it might, perhaps, have had as fatal effects as the former; but, thank God, this was wisely provided against by the very law which is now wanted to be repealed.

It has indeed, sir, been said, that the chief motive for enacting that law now no longer exists. I cannot admit that the motive they mean was the chief motive, but even that motive is very far from having entirely ceased. Can gentlemen imagine, that in the spirit raised in the nation but about a twelvemonth since, Jacobitism and disaffection to the present Government had no share? Perhaps some who might wish well to the present establishment did co-operate; nay, I do not know but they were the first movers of that spirit; but it cannot be supposed that the spirit then raised should have grown up to such a ferment, merely from a proposition which was honestly and fairly laid before a Parliament, and left entirely to their determination. No, sir, the spirit was perhaps begun by those who are truly friends to the illustrious family we have now upon the throne; but it was raised to a much greater height than, I believe, ever they designed, by Jacobites, and such as are enemies to our present establishment, who thought they never had a fairer opportunity of bringing about what they have so long and so unsuccessfully wished for, than that which had been furnished them by those who first raised that spirit. I hope the people have now in a great measure come to themselves, and therefore I doubt not but the next elections will show that when they are left to judge coolly, they can distinguish between the real and the pretended friends to the Government. But I must say, if the ferment then raised in the nation had not greatly subsided, I should have thought a new election a very dangerous experiment; and as such ferments may hereafter often happen, I must think that frequent elections will always be dangerous: for which reason, in so far as I can see at present, I shall, I believe, at all times think it a very dangerous experiment to repeal the septennial bill.

THE END.

www.ingramcontent.com/pod-product-compliance
Lightning Source LLC
Chambersburg PA
CBHW032056220426
43664CB00008B/1026